A HISTORY
of
BIBLICAL INTERPRETATION

VOLUME 2

The Medieval through the Reformation Periods

© 2009 Wm. B. Eerdmans Publishing Co.

Published 2009 by
Wm. B. Eerdmans Publishing Co.
2140 Oak Industrial Drive N.E., Grand Rapids, Michigan 49505 /
P.O. Box 163, Cambridge CB3 9PU U.K.

Printed in the United States of America

15 14 13 12 11 10 09   7 6 5 4 3 2 1

Library of Congress Cataloging-in-Publication Data

A history of biblical interpretation / edited by
Alan J. Hauser & Duane F. Watson
p.   cm.
Includes bibliographical references.
Contents: v. 2. The Medieval through the Reformation Periods.
ISBN 978-0-8028-4274-9 (hardcover: alk. paper)
1. Bible — Criticism, interpretation, etc. — History.
I. Hauser, Alan J. II. Watson, Duane Frederick.
BS500.H575   2003
220.6′09 — dc21
2002035406

www.eerdmans.com

A HISTORY
of
BIBLICAL INTERPRETATION

VOLUME 2

The Medieval through the Reformation Periods

Edited by

Alan J. Hauser

&

Duane F. Watson

Associate Editor

Schuyler Kaufman

WILLIAM B. EERDMANS PUBLISHING COMPANY
GRAND RAPIDS, MICHIGAN / CAMBRIDGE, U.K.

Contents

Preface

In the preface to volume 1 we detailed the numerous reasons for the incredible variety of biblical interpretation throughout the past several millennia. These reasons, briefly stated, include the great variety of communities and individuals who have interpreted the biblical text, the open-ended and multilayered richness of the biblical text itself, the inclination of later biblical texts to interpret and build on earlier biblical texts, and the multitude of methodologies which have been used to interpret the biblical texts. These factors led to a great diversity in interpretation during the Middle Ages and the Renaissance and Reformation eras, continuing the heritage of interpretive diversity described in volume 1 for the Ancient Period.

Since this volume covers approximately 1000 years of interpretation of the Bible as a collection of sacred books, it is the most chronologically comprehensive of any of the volumes in this set. While it might be tempting to assume that this means that there was not a great deal of variety in interpretation during this period, such an assumption would be mistaken, even if one were to limit that assessment to the years prior to the Renaissance. One need only look, for example, at the variety of interpretive developments within Judaism during this period, including the gains made in Hebrew grammar and lexicography or the monumental work of Rashi and his followers, to see that this was hardly a stagnant era. Or one could look to the achievements of the Carolingian era and the later scholastic developments within the universities, beginning in the twelfth century. The Renaissance and Reformation eras, much as they often claimed to be going back to the learning of the ancient period, firmly based their interpretive analyses on the achievements of Jewish and Christian interpretation of the Middle Ages.

While individual groups or particular eras often viewed their interpretation of a particular biblical text as definitive, the passage of time inevitably led to new circumstances and new challenges, which engendered new interpretations and new methodologies. The prolific Renaissance and Reformation eras especially witnessed a burgeoning diversity of interpretive perspectives. New approaches to biblical interpretation are typically birthed in the complex matrix of social, political, intellectual, artistic, and religious factors that arise in each new age. Whether it is recognized or not, this contextually-bound response of the reader to the biblical text, firmly rooted in the reader's own age, can be just as important in understanding a particular interpretation as are the parameters of the biblical text itself.

At numerous points throughout the text of each chapter, references have been provided to particular works listed in the writer's bibliography. These are given so that the reader may pursue in more detail particular topics of interest raised in the course of the writer's argument.

Several persons deserve thanks for their assistance in the production of this volume. Thomas P. Benza, Jr., and Crystal Primeau did excellent work in the initial review of the manuscripts. Richard Spencer provided invaluable assistance, especially in the resolution of matters of language. Most especially, Schuyler Kaufman is to be recognized, both for her preparation of the subject index of this volume and for her excellent work helping to edit the manuscripts and ensure that they are in good form. For this reason, the title page lists her as Associate Editor. Without her, the volume could not have come into shape.

ALAN J. HAUSER, *Editor*
DUANE F. WATSON, *Editor*

Abbreviations

ABD	*Anchor Bible Dictionary*, ed. D. N. Freedman (New York: Doubleday, 1992)
ACW	Ancient Christian Writers
AJSR	*Association for Jewish Studies Review*
AnBib	Analecta Biblica
ANF	*Ante-Nicene Fathers*
ANTF	Arbeiten zur neutestamentlichen Textforschung
ARG	*Archiv für Reformationsgeschichte*
ASD	*Opera omnia Desiderii Erasmi Roterodami*. Amsterdam, 1969-.
ATR	*Anglican Theological Review*
b.	Babylonian Talmud
BETL	Bibliotheca ephemeridum theologicarum lovaniensium
BHS	*Biblia Hebraica Stuttgartensia*, ed. K. Elliger and W. Rudolph (Stuttgart: Deutsche Bibelstiftung, 1983)
BJRL	*Bulletin of the John Rylands University Library of Manchester*
BSHPF	Bulletin de la Société d'Histoire du Protestantisme
BZAW	Beihefte zu Zeitschrift für die Alttestamentliche Wissenschaft
CBQ	*Catholic Biblical Quartterly*
CCCM	Corpus christianorum: continuatio medievalis
CCSG	Corpus christianorum: series graeca
CCSL	Corpus christianorum: series latina
CCEL	http://www.ccel.org/
CCELP	http://www.ccel.org/p/pearse/morefathers/home.html

CH	*Church History*
CR	Corpus reformatorum
CSEL	Corpus scriptorum ecclesiasticorum latinorum
CTJ	*Calvin Theological Journal*
CWE	Collected Works of Erasmus
CWS	Classics of Western Spirituality
EncJud	*Encyclopedia judaica* (Jerusalem: Keter, 1972)
ET	English translation
ETL	*Ephemerides theologicae lovanienses*
ETR	*Études théologiques et réligieuses*
FLEWRH	Folger Library Edition of the Works of Richard Hooker
frag.	fragment
GCS	Die griechische christliche Schriftsteller der ersten (drei) Jahrhunderte
GNO	*Gregorii Nysseni Opera*
HBI[1]	*History of Biblical Interpretation* 1: *The Ancient Period,* ed. A. J. Hauser and D. F. Watson (Grand Rapids: Eerdmans, 2003)
HTR	*Harvard Theological Review*
HUCA	*Hebrew Union College Annual*
Int	*Interpretation*
ISTA	http://www.sacred-texts.com/
JAAR	*Journal of the American Academy of Religion*
JETS	*Journal of the Evangelical Theological Society*
JJS	*Journal of Jewish Studies*
JQR	*Jewish Quarterly Review*
JR	*Journal of Religion*
JSOTSup	*Journal for the Study of the Old Testament* Supplement Series
JTS	*Journal of Theological Studies*
KJV	King James Version
LB	*Des. Erasmi Roterodami opera omnia,* ed. J. Leclerc (Leiden, 1703-06).
LCC	Library of Christian Classics
LJb	*Literaturwissenschäftliches Jahrbuch*
LW	*Luther's Works,* ed. J. Pelikan and H. T. Lehmann (55 vols., St. Louis: Concordia; Philadelphia: Fortress, 1955-86)
LXX	Septuagint
MBW	*Melanchthons Briefwechsel. Kritische und kommentierte Gesamtausgabe. Regesten,* ed. H. Scheible (10+ vols., Stuttgart-Bad Cannstatt: Frommann-Holzboog, 1977-)
MQR	*Mennonite Quarterly Review*

ms(s).	manuscript(s)
MSA	*Melanchthons Werke in Auswahl (Studienausgabe)*, ed. R. Stupperich (7 vols., Gütersloh: Mohn, 1951-75)
MT	Masoretic Text
NewAdv	http://www.newadvent.org/
NGTT	*Nederduitse gereformeerde teologiese tydskrif*
NJPS	Jewish Publication Society Tanach Translation (1999)
NovTSup	*Novum Testamentum* Supplements
NPNF[1]	*Nicene and Post-Nicene Fathers*, Series 1
NPNF[2]	*Nicene and Post-Nicene Fathers*, Series 2
NT	New Testament
NTS	*New Testament Studies*
PG	*Patrologia Cursus Completus: Series Graeca* (Paris: Migne)
PL	*Patrologia Cursus Completus: Series Latina* (Paris: Migne)
OT	Old Testament
RHPR	*Revue d'histoire et de philosophie religieuses*
RSPT	*Revue de sciences philosophiques et théologiques*
RTAM	*Recherches de théologie ancienne et médiévale*
SC	Sources chrétiennes
SCJ	*Sixteenth Century Journal*
SJT	*Scottish Journal of Theology*
SM	*Supplementa Melanchthoniana*, ed. C. G. Bretschneider, et al. (4 vols., Leipzig: Haupt, 1910-26)
SNTSMS	Society for New Testament Studies Monograph Series
StPatr	Studia patristica
SVTQ	*St. Vladimir's Theological Quarterly*
ThH	*Théologie Historique*
TLL	http://www.thelatinlibrary.com/
TRHS	*Transactions of the Royal Historical Society*
TS	*Theological Studies*
TZ	*Theologische Zeitschrift*
VTSup	*Vetus Testamentum* Supplements
WA	*D. Martin Luthers Werke. Kritische Gesamtausgabe (Weimar Ausgabe)*, ed. J. K. F. Knaake and G. Kawerau (127 vols., Weimar: Böhlau, 1883)
WADB	the German Bible and its prefaces
WABr	letters
WATr	table talk
WTJ	*Westminster Theological Journal*
y.	Jerusalem Talmud
ZKG	*Zeitschrift für Kirchengeschichte*
ZTK	*Zeitschrift für Theologie und Kirche*

CHAPTER 1

Introduction and Overview

Alan J. Hauser and Duane F. Watson

THE SOPHISTICATION OF MEDIEVAL
BIBLICAL INTERPRETATION

The end of the ancient period of Western Civilization and the transition to the Middle Ages was dramatic and, in numerous ways, traumatic. As powerful changes occurred in the political sphere, they rippled through most other aspects of life. Yet we should not assume, as popular thinking would have it, that learning languished for centuries due to the splintering of the Roman Empire into a multitude of small political units. While the opportunity for learning was more restricted than it had been and often came to be focused especially in religious settings such as monastic communities, cathedral schools, and rabbinic academies, the years from approximately 500 to 1500 were almost never truly "dark" in the intellectual sense. Indeed, the learning of the ancients was not only passed on but was also used creatively to develop new ways to focus human knowledge.

This is especially true when one looks at the history and methods of biblical interpretation during the Middle Ages. Both the Jewish and the Christian communities used the wisdom of the late ancient period as a base on which to build systems of interpretation that addressed the important issues confronting the synagogue or the church in their various locales and during the various time periods in which Jews and Christians lived. Thus, the teachings of the ancient rabbis and church fathers, while respected within each heritage, were hardly followed slavishly; rather, they were studied care-

1

fully, filtered, and employed as needed to address the new and diverse challenges facing the changing communities.

There are many examples of outstanding biblical scholarship from this period, but here we only have space to cite a few specific examples. In Christian circles, we have Gregory the Great, who flourished in the closing decades of the sixth century (c. 540-604). Gregory was thoroughly familiar with the teachings of the ancient Greek and Latin fathers, but hardly felt bound by them, as may be seen, for example, in his disagreements with interpretive points made by Jerome (345-420). Gregory composed commentaries on Job, Ezekiel, Song of Songs, and 1 Kings. He was the first interpreter to connect Mary Magdalene with the "sinful woman" discussed in the Synoptic Gospels, even though he also identified her as the "Apostle of the Apostles" (see Mayeski, p. 96 below). His scholarship significantly influenced subsequent interpretation during the Middle Ages, especially through his discussion of the multiple levels of meaning contained in the biblical text, treated in more detail below. His insistence on close attention to the historical/literal meaning of the text, which could then provide a base for the more mysterious (and slippery) spiritual interpretations, was unfortunately not followed by all who came after him. Isidore of Seville (560-636), for instance, moves quickly to discussions of the spiritual meanings of a text. Gregory's work as an exegete had to compete for his time with numerous other tasks, such as his years in the papacy (590-604), his work on the civil administration and military defense of Italy, his zealous advocacy of monasticism (he founded seven monasteries and lived in one of them), and his work on medieval plainsong (often called "Gregorian Chant"). The links between plainsong, the *lectio divina* of the Cistercians (see below), and hymnody and liturgical lyrics in Eastern Orthodoxy (also treated below) provide an interesting opportunity for studying a unique, fascinating, and too often overlooked component of medieval exegesis.

The Venerable Bede (c. 673-735) was sent as a young boy to the twin monasteries of St. Peter and St. Paul in Northumbria. He became the premier scholar of Anglo-Saxon England, perhaps best known for his *Historia Ecclesiastica (History of the Church),* for which he is often called the "Father of English History." He also wrote treatises on Latin words and verse, the motion of the planets, the principles behind the calculation of the date for Easter, and other mathematical matters. His method of interpretation in biblical studies was tied closely to the ancient fathers, and he drew heavily from Augustine, Jerome, Ambrose, and Gregory the Great. He wrote commentaries on portions of Genesis and Exodus, Samuel, Kings, Tobit, Song of Songs, Ezra and Nehemiah, Mark, Luke, Acts, and the Catholic Epistles. These commentaries and homilies were composed in two parts: first, Bede treats the historical meaning of the text; he follows this with an analysis of the mystical meaning, which he saw to be pointing to the great mysteries of God, and God's plan for salvation (p. 97 below). Bede used Josephus and Eusebius extensively; he was especially knowledgeable in ancient Israelite law; he wrote textbooks on grammar and rhetoric — all this despite spending his life at the geographical fringes of the civilized world. An example of his sensitivity to his cultural environment may be seen when, in discussing Jerome's analysis of the story of the Syro-Phoenician woman in Mark's Gospel, Bede "omits Jerome's negative description of pagan peoples (lest it reflect badly on his own)" (pp. 97-98). Given Bede's accomplishments, it is hardly surprising that he received the title "venerable" and has been frequently cited in biblical exegesis even past the time of the Reformation.

One last example of the quality and variety of Christian biblical scholarship during the Middle Ages is the Cistercian School. As Mayeski notes (p. 105), this school "represents a full flowering of the ancient monastic tradition of *lectio divina,* the contemplative, careful reading of the biblical text." Key figures of this school, such as Bernard of Clairvaux (1090-1153) and William of St. Thierry (1075/80-1148), benefited from the new learning of the schools (see below) and hence profited from "the new scholastic advances in grammar and dialectic and . . . a new comprehension of Neoplatonic philosophy" (p. 105). Thus, a close study of the text was, for the Cistercians, the basis for "their originality in expounding the spiritual sense, the application of the text to the personal relationship with God and the human journey of life" (p. 105). The monastic community provided a useful environment in which to study the depth and variety of human behavior and, as Mayeski notes (p. 105), the Cistercians' "spiritual exegesis shows an almost modern psychological insight." The biblical-liturgical themes of creation and exodus become the tool for understanding the various stages of human life, as does the deuteronomic historian's understanding of history as a cycle of sin, repentance, and divine intervention. This exegesis is strongly christocentric and, within the monastic community, with its regular daily round of liturgical services, Scripture readings, chanting of hymns and psalms, and cycle of feasts, these monks were totally surrounded by "the thought world and images of the Bible" (p. 105). Here, "the method of *lectio divina,* used with scholarly care, produced biblical interpretations that are at once personal and ecclesial, traditional and contemporary" (p. 106).

In Jewish circles, we also see considerable variety in the approach to interpretation, as well as a steady enhancement in the quality of Jewish biblical scholarship. On the one hand, we observe the use of midrash by many generations of rabbis as a way of linking the practice of law (Torah) in each successive generation to specific passages in the Tanak (the Jewish Scriptures). Midrash is a creative, expansive treatment of the biblical text through a wide variety of interpretive means, all of which are designed to uncover the wealth of wisdom which the Jewish community believed was contained within the text of the Tanak. It thus provides a complement to the traditions found in the Mishnah and the Talmud, neither of which are particularly concerned to link rabbinic teachings about law to Jewish Scriptures. The numerous midrashim which have come down to us (such as *Genesis Rabbah, Leviticus Rabbah,* and the *Mekhilta*) are typically not the work of one writer but the accumulation of many generations of midrashic interpretation by numerous rabbis. This not only makes each midrash difficult to "date" but also means that contained within a single midrash one is likely to find a variety of opinions and interpretations of a given text, often with no attempt to reconcile them. As will be discussed in more detail below, the engine driving midrash is the need to find justification in the biblical text for later rabbinic teachings and practices.

Running parallel to midrash, complementing it (for some scholars), and competing with it (for others), is an interpretive approach described by the Hebrew term *peshat* (Harris, p. 141 below). In midrash the focus of exegesis is the detailed, specific, halakhic (legally oriented) issues of the contemporary Jewish community. Thus, in each age, the immediate concerns of the community are in the forefront. In *peshat,* however, the concerns of the Jewish scholars are focused on interpreting a biblical text according to its own context, not according to the needs of later generations. These two methods cannot be completely separated from each other, since elements of the methodology of one are necessarily bound up in the methodology of the other. Many later Jewish interpreters practiced, and often intermixed, these two approaches, although others strongly preferred *peshat.*

In its interpretive approach, *peshat* relies heavily on the advances in lexicography already begun in the Gaonic academies of Babylon in the early Islamic period, but then was advanced by scholars such as the Spaniard Menahem ibn Saruk (c. 910–c. 970), who wrote a dictionary of biblical Hebrew *in* Hebrew (rather than Arabic); the eleventh-century Spaniard Jonah ibn Janah, whose Hebrew lexicon was written in Arabic; and Rabbi David Kimhi ("Radak," 1160-1235) of Provence, whose work relied on that of ibn Janah but also surpassed it. These advances in lexicography were crucial to the understanding of biblical passages in their contexts. Likewise significant were developments in Hebrew grammar. Again we need to mention the Gaonic academies of Babylonia, which fostered the study of grammar, beginning with the work of Saadia Gaon (Saadia ben Joseph, 882-942). This was followed by the grammatical work of ibn Saruk, the comprehensive grammar of ibn Janah, and the grammar of David Kimhi. Both grammar and lexicography contributed substantially to the work of Jewish scholars in comparative linguistics, and all three were clearly essential to understanding biblical passages in their contexts. Intriguingly, this focus on *peshat* was in part fueled by the need to respond effectively to the polemics of Christianity against Judaism, most notably in northern France. Yet it was precisely this often polemical dialogue that enhanced the passing on to the Christian community of the advances that the Jewish community had made in grammar, lexicography, and linguistic studies. The dissemination of this Jewish work was vital to the work done in Christian interpretive circles in the later years of the Middle Ages and beyond.

Clearly, biblical interpretation during the Middle Ages, in both Christian and Jewish circles, was remarkably sophisticated and covered a broad methodological spectrum. It also was tied closely to the life and needs of each age and community. Although a number of generalizations for this period of biblical interpretation could certainly be made, caution must be exercised lest the richness and variety of interpretation be concealed by these generalizations.

We now turn to a more detailed discussion of the interpretation of Scripture in Western Christian circles, in Jewish circles, and in Eastern Orthodoxy. In these discussions, we will build on what has already been mentioned briefly concerning the variety and quality of Christian and Jewish interpretation in the Middle Ages.

WESTERN CHRISTIAN BIBLICAL INTERPRETATION

As Mayeski notes at the beginning of her chapter on early medieval Christian exegesis, interpretation during this period is pre-scientific, lacking not only the extensive modern scientific methods for contextualizing and analyzing a text but also "the scientific worldview that privileges empirical evidence and seeks to determine human and natural causalities" (p. 86). This lack of scientific methods and presuppositions does not, however, mean that medieval exegesis was uncritical. It had its own assumptions, standards, and methods for analyzing the text closely.

One key assumption was that the Bible is not an inanimate collection of texts to be probed and scrutinized like an artifact but "a living word, a sacred force or energy that enlivens the church" (p. 87). Therefore it was properly and fully understood only when it engaged the life of individual believers, energized the liturgy of the church, and inspired the life of the entire Christian community. There was a symbiotic relationship here: the Bible empowered the ritual of the liturgy and the life of the church, and these in turn empowered the interpretive skills and devotion of those who studied the Bible. One did not learn about the Bible by dissecting and studying it from an objective vantage point; rather, one learned how to understand the Bible by living it, by orienting one's entire being around it.

A second assumption was that the salvation history begun in the OT and fulfilled in the NT continued in the life of the church and pointed to the end of the age, by which time all nations would have received the message of the gospel. Thus, for a scholar such as Bede, the conversion of his own (previously pagan) people was a sign that the process of salvation history was moving forward.

Allied with this is a third assumption: the Bible is really one book, whose ultimate purpose is the salvation of the nations. Nevertheless, under that umbrella biblical interpreters were often sensitive to differences in character and genre among the various biblical books. Ultimately, however, each book contributed to the unity and purpose of the whole means of its own distinctives.

An important fourth assumption was that "sacred Scripture is a sophisticated literary text, requiring complex readings" (p. 89). The classical methods of literary criticism were studied and employed, as were biblical grammar and the various literary genres and rhetorical figures used by the biblical writers. Bede wrote his own textbooks on grammar and rhetoric to assist the literary study of Scripture. Subsequently, scholars such as Andrew of St. Victor took a sustained interest in consulting the Hebrew of the OT while studying the works of various rabbis to learn their understandings of the details of particular biblical texts.

The "learning of the fathers" accumulated with the passage of time. Subsequent writers such as Gregory, Bede, Alcuin, and Rabanus Maurus added to this existing body of knowledge. The task of the exegete was to weigh the various interpretations of the fathers, choose those perceived to be most insightful and accurate, and then apply them to the life and needs of his own community. The liturgy of the church was often a powerful context within which such exegesis was carried out, with passages interpreted in relation to other passages used in the worship service for the same day. For example, on Easter Sunday the story of the paschal lamb in the book of Exodus was interpreted in conjunction with the empty tomb stories in the Gospels. Psalms were often read or sung during the liturgy and were interpreted within the context of the Christian history of salvation (e.g., Psalms 2, 22, and 110). Biblical typology also crossed over into the life of the church, as when Bede sees the flood story of Genesis 6–8 prefiguring not only the triumph of Christ over evil but also the salvation of those gathered in the church for baptism (p. 91). In the monastic communities, *Lectio divina,* "the slow, vocalized reading of a biblical text, often repeated until memorized and meditated on until it culminates in prayer . . . taught the monk to read the Scriptures in the light of his own life and his life in the light of the Scriptures" (p. 91).

As previously noted in the discussion of Gregory, medieval exegetes believed that each scriptural text contained a multilayered configuration of meanings. The first level, the historical/literal meaning of the text, tells what actually happened, and forms the base for the other interpretations. At this level, grammar and etymology play a substantial role in the analysis of the text, especially in the schools, whose interpretive methodologies began to develop around 1100. Early in the Middle Ages, when the Vulgate was the dominant biblical text, the foundational task of the exegete was the learning of Latin grammar, using tools such as the grammars of Donatus and Priscian. Late in the Middle Ages, interest in the Hebrew and Greek texts and study of those languages came to play a larger role in the understanding of the historical/literal meaning of the text. The second level of meaning, the tropological, focuses on morality, addressing the individual's relationship to God. Allegorical interpretation discerns "the theological meaning (specifically, how the text reveals Christ and the church)." And the anagogical meaning "illuminates the ultimate end of history and the full reality of the end time" (p. 92).

While individual medieval scholars might find as few as two or as many as ten meanings within a particular text, the four levels of meaning just described were outlined by Latin fathers such as Augustine (354-430) and Cassiodorus (485–c. 580) and passed on by Gregory to subsequent medieval interpreters. However many levels of meaning medieval exegetes expounded, they were as a group consistent in their conviction that the extended sense (or senses) was superior to the historical/literal sense. The exegete's ability to uncover the extended senses was the ultimate measure of his skills. In all exegesis, the *trivium* of grammar, dialectic (the study of the logical development of thought and argumentation), and rhetoric (the study of language and its effect) was considered foundational tools for perceiving the meaning of the text (p. 94).

We conclude this survey of medieval Christian exegesis (up to the early twelfth century) with three final topics: the Carolingian period, the Victorines, and the formation of the schools in the eleventh and twelfth centuries.

Alcuin (c. 735-804) received his education at the cathedral school in York, England, and became its master in 766. Coming to the court of Charlemagne in 781, he had a talent for teaching and a strong commitment to the liberal arts, which is reflected in his assertion that "it is through Scripture that we grasp the underlying nature of knowledge, not the other way around," as Augustine had argued (p. 98). The interpretation of Scripture was, therefore, the most important means for gaining a liberal education. In his exegesis "Alcuin stressed the importance of grammar in interpreting the historical/literal sense" (p. 98). In his comments on the biblical text, Alcuin depended heavily on the church fathers, adding little of his own that was new. His skill was rather in his ability to select carefully and arrange into a coherent whole the excerpts from the fathers. This work of Alcuin and his contemporaries laid the groundwork for the later work of the schools, especially in their practice of glossing a text, as will be discussed below. Alcuin also undertook revision of the Latin biblical text, which by his time had suffered from several centuries of textual corruption.

Rabanus Maurus (c. 780-856 CE), a student of Alcuin, typifies the accomplishments of Carolingian biblical scholarship. He wrote commentaries on most of the books of the Bible aimed at educating church leaders. Like Alcuin, he possessed a detailed knowledge of patristic sources, which he frequently cited in his works, applying the wisdom of the fathers to his own age. Typical of medieval exegetes, Maurus preferred the extended senses of Scripture, but he also devoted considerable attention to discussion of the historical/literal interpretation of particular texts, as, for example, in his discussion of the books of Kings, which built on Bede's work. He also studied contemporary Jewish interpretation of the Torah. His commentary on Matthew's Gospel is, as Mayeski (pp. 99-100) quotes G. Brown, "sensibly arranged, all carefully integrated into a credible and coherent whole." Maurus's discussion of Paul's list of charismatic ministries "leads Maurus to some penetrating insights into the historical Pauline churches" (p. 100). In Mayeski's assessment of Carolingian exegesis she notes that these scholars depended heavily on those before them, such as the fathers and Gregory. They also set the stage for the major elements of later medieval exegesis: "an assumption that the historical/literal meaning of the text was only a foundation to its more important spiritual meaning, an emphasis on grammar and dialectic as the tools used to unlock all levels of scriptural meaning, the critical use of the patristic sources vis-à-vis the contemporary questions, and consultation with Jewish scholars" (p. 100).

The work of the Victorines revolves around three figures: Hugh (1096-1141), Richard (c. 1123-73), and Andrew (d. 1175). Hugh of St. Victor proposed three steps for biblical exposition, which were designed to rein in the "often exuberant use of the extended or 'higher' sense of the text." The interpreter should first "deal accurately with the actual words, through grammatical construction and syntax," second "determine what the divine writer means, his own 'sense,'" and third "grasp the full meaning of the text by reference to the coherent structure of Christian faith" (Mayeski, p. 103). Hugh emphasized that the intended meaning of the biblical writer must be the exegete's primary guide, even when looking at and sorting through the comments of the fathers on the text. This substantially parallels the perspective of the Jewish interpreters who advocated *peshat*, the contextual interpretation of a text, over the more homiletical and free-wheeling midrash, as will be discussed below. Hugh consulted Jewish scholars in Paris and carefully compared a literal Latin translation of the Hebrew Bible to the Vulgate. His work reflects that of Rashi and other Jewish scholars, whom he cites with appreciation for the quality of their scholarship (Mayeski, p. 104).

Richard of St. Victor was more interested in pursuing the spiritual sense of Scripture. Two of his best-known mystical treatises are *Benjamin Minor (The Twelve Patriarchs)* and *Benjamin Major (The Mystical Ark)*, "in which his commentary on the family of Jacob and on the Tabernacle structure his understanding of contemplation" (Mayeski, p. 104). *Benjamin Minor* describes the six-step process in the mystical ascent to heaven. Richard also wrote mystical commentaries on the Song of Songs and on Daniel 2 (Nebuchadnezzar's dream) and used allegory in his interpretation of biblical narrative. Yet, despite Richard's interest in contemplation and in the spiritual sense of Scripture, his own "commentary on the biblical text is carefully and completely literal" (p. 104). He wrote literal commentaries on the Apocalypse and on Ezekiel, which is remarkable, considering the tendency of his time to treat these books spiritually. His studies on Solomon's Temple, the Tabernacle, and Ezekiel's temple vision pay careful attention to measurement and detail and provide diagrams and sketches. Here his concern was, perhaps, focused more on aesthetics than on the literal understanding of these subjects. While he also explored and used the work of contemporary Jewish scholars, he viewed with concern the use of Jewish scholars by his colleague Andrew, which he regarded as too uncritical (p. 104), for example, Andrew's acceptance of the Jewish interpretation of Isa. 7:14 ("a young woman" rather than "a virgin").

Andrew of St. Victor chose to focus almost exclusively on the historical/literal sense of Scripture. This is why he regularly consulted the learning of the Jewish rabbis and checked the text of the Vulgate against the Hebrew text of the OT. He commented on all the books of the OT except Job, Psalms, Song of Songs, and Ruth and critically assessed the various Jewish and Christian sources available to him. Since "historical facts . . . did not have the authoritative status of the doctrines of faith" (p. 104), Andrew felt free to weigh various opinions about the historical meaning of a text, settling on those that reason told him would provide a sound base for pursuing the higher meanings of the text. In this regard he, like Hugh, paralleled Jewish contextual analysis, which will be discussed below. For historical analysis Andrew held Josephus in especially high regard. Andrew is often cited in the textual glosses compiled in the late Middle Ages. His strong concentration on the historical/literal sense of the text and his extensive use of Jewish as well as Christian sources exemplifies the considerable variety and the quality and comprehensiveness of scholarship that was sometimes present in medieval Christian biblical interpretation.

The schools will be treated in more detail later in this introductory chapter, but a brief treatment is appropriate here. It is in the schools that the gloss was developed, beginning especially in the late eleventh century. It is "a manuscript of the original text, in this case of a biblical book, with lecturer's notes written in the margins (widened for this purpose) or between the lines of the original text" (Mayeski, p. 100). The gloss grew out of the style of learning in the medieval classroom: in working through a particular biblical text, the master would comment on specific words or phrases, often focusing on questions of grammar, rhetoric, or logic. The patristic sources were referenced extensively, and students would take notes on all this in the margins. Some of these students eventually became teachers, and no doubt used their own class notes in lecturing. As time passed and individual scholars added both new references from the fathers and their own observations, the body of material in the glosses grew substantially. Eventually, *quaestiones*, brief theological discussions that had come to be inserted into the commentaries, were greatly expanded and were ultimately extracted from the commentaries and assembled separately, arranged according to topics rather than according to the biblical texts. An example is Peter Lombard's *Book of Sentences*, which soon became the primary text for theological study in the late Middle Ages. Thus, as grammatical and stylistic analysis of the text led to consideration of more systemic issues, the seeds were sown for the rise of Scholasticism, which will be discussed in detail below.

JEWISH BIBLICAL INTERPRETATION

As we turn to medieval Jewish biblical interpretation, we need to review several points made by Gary Porton in his article on Rabbinic Midrash in *HBI*[1]. The first concerns how the rabbinic community viewed the revelation of God to Moses on Mount Sinai. This revelation comprised both the written Torah, which could be studied by use of the normal tools of interpretation employed in the ancient world, and the oral Torah, which was passed down orally to the rabbis "in a continual chain of tradition that originated on Mount Sinai with Moses" (Porton, p. 202). Together, the written Torah and the oral Torah formed the complete and definitive revelation of God's will for both Israel and the rest of the world.

The rabbis defined their task as continual study of this comprehensive revelation from God, both written and oral, applying the wisdom it contains to their own age. This study was done in two different yet related ways. The first attended to the sayings and rulings of the fathers, which contained the application *in the spirit of Torah* of the revelation from God to the circumstances of each successive generation, but in most cases without direct links to particular passages of the Tanak (the Hebrew Bible, Torah, Prophets, and Writings). The accumulation of these sayings and teachings of many generations of rabbis led to the compilation of the Mishnah in 200 CE and of the Babylonian Talmud in 500 CE. Each of these written collections contains the wisdom of many rabbis organized according to topic areas, such as the Passover, gleanings, the Sabbath, bills of divorce, animal offerings, cleanliness, marks of leprosy, oaths, sisters-in-law, idolatry, the menstruant, etc. While it was assumed that all these teachings were derived from God's revelation on Mount Sinai, little attempt was made to tie them to specific biblical texts. The focus was on the real-life issues faced by each generation of rabbis, which could hardly have been anticipated in the texts of the Tanak. Thus the details of the practice of Jewish life throughout the centuries were not typically derived directly from exegesis of the text of the Tanak.

The second form of study linked specific rabbinic teachings to particular texts in the Tanak and is contained in the midrashim, which present extensive, often expansive, discussions of particular biblical texts. In some cases a midrash will explicate the entire text of a biblical book, as is the case of *Sifra,* which comments, at times in meticulous detail (even word-for-word), on the text of Leviticus. *Mekhilta* comments on approximately one-third of the text of Exodus. *Genesis Rabbah* at times comments on the details of the text of Genesis, but sometimes presents expositions only very loosely connected to Genesis. *Leviticus Rabbah* contains thirty-seven homilies on particular themes, not always following the order of the biblical text. *Pesiqta de Rab Kahana* also contains homiletical midrash, focusing on the biblical readings from the festivals and special Sabbaths. In all these midrashim, one finds discussions linking contemporary Jewish practice with particular biblical texts. As Porton notes, this is so because the lack of a direct link between rabbinic teachings and the Tanak apparently worried some rabbis (p. 206), though they were, as Porton also notes, convinced of the status of oral Torah as a legitimate independent entity and did not see it merely as a commentary on the written Torah.

The various midrashim are not the works of individual authors; rather, they bring together the work of many generations of rabbis. These rabbis interpret specific biblical passages in ways that allow them to justify current rabbinic teachings and practices in their own generation. Thus, the midrashim are collections of numerous units and pieces brought together by later editors, having been updated and revised in successive generations. As Bakhos notes (p. 117 below), this often makes it difficult to date a particular midrash or a saying or teaching contained within it. It is not unusual for interpretations to be given anonymously and for several interpretations to be given in sequence with no indication of the authority to be accorded to each interpretation. Since the rabbis presumed that the written and oral Torah contained all of God's revelation, it is not surprising that the midrashim often focus on minute details of the biblical texts, individual words or letters, repetitions, unusual spellings, word order, minor differences between parallel passages, and even the shapes of letters. All these can lead to rabbinic conclusions about the meaning and interpretation of a particular text (see Porton, pp. 210-12). Given the imagination and creativity of many rabbinic interpreters, such close study of detail provided the means, in each age, of relating contemporary Jewish practice to the revelation from God to Moses. Thus, midrash provided the link to the Tanak that was often absent in the rabbinic discussions contained in the Mishnah and Talmud. The reader is referred to the examples of midrash provided by Porton (pp. 209-19). The example from *Genesis Rabbah* about *aleph, bet,* and the creation of the world (pp. 215-16) is especially intriguing and illustrates midrashic imagination and creativity.

As Bakhos notes (p. 118 below), this interplay between the text of the Torah and the dynamic, changing practice of Jewish life in the late ancient period and in the Middle Ages provided the vitality of medieval Jewish midrashic interpretation. "Biblical figures populated the world of the rabbis, and biblical stories and events engaged their thoughts and fancy. . . . Subtlety, brevity of speech, and metaphoric discourse characterize the exegetical ways in which the rabbis grappled with the burning issues of their day" (p. 118). Bakhos also notes that "in developing a process of 'creative exegesis' the rabbis were able to make Scripture relevant to contemporary needs" (p. 119). She warns, however, against attempts to read the midrashim as "historical documents that lucidly reflect rabbinic culture" (p. 120). This problem is complicated by the numerous layers of collation and editing that have gone into the various collections of midrashim as we now have them, which makes it very difficult to tie a particular midrashic teaching to a specific historical context.

Bakhos lists themes that are frequently found in rabbinic midrash: belief in one God, the chosenness of Israel, and the centrality of Torah. While such an overview of themes is valuable, she cautions that this approach can skew our understanding of the midrashic texts, since "the rabbis did not systematically consider such topics in isolation," but rather mentioned them in the context of other ongoing exegetical discussions (p. 124). In this summary, we will briefly discuss her second theme, the chosenness of Israel, which has several interesting twists. It clearly reflects the concept of the otherness of non-Israelites. For example, in *Sifre Deuteronomy Piska* 312, which treats Deut. 32:9, the midrash asks why Moses spoke to "the congregation of Israel" (Deut. 31:30) rather than the congregation of Abraham or Isaac. The midrash notes that Abraham had something unfit coming from him, namely, Ishmael, and Isaac had something unfit coming from him, namely, Esau. Jacob, whose other name is Israel, did not have anything unfit coming from his loins, and hence the people bear his name "Israel." Thus, even though Abraham is portrayed as most righteous, as in the *Aqedah* (his near-sacrifice of Isaac, Genesis 22), it is Jacob's progeny that is deemed most worthy, because none of his offspring were unfit (p. 126). The rabbis used Gen. 25:27, "Jacob was a mild man who stayed in camp," to demonstrate "a variety of impeccable behavior they attribute to Jacob. Jacob, for example, was born circumcised, performed all the commandments, was righteous, innocent of unseemly conduct, and studied Torah" (p. 126).

As we turn to Harris's article, we encounter a trend in medieval Jewish biblical interpretation that is quite different from midrash. The Hebrew term *peshat,* introduced earlier, refers to interpretation of a biblical text according to *its* context rather than the needs of the Jewish community at a particular moment in history. As Harris notes, this new direction in Jewish exegesis is triggered to a large degree by "advances in Hebrew linguistics, lexicography, and philology achieved by Jewish scholars working in the Islamic world in the ninth to eleventh centuries" (Harris, p. 141 below). While some Jewish interpreters combined *peshat* and midrash in their interpretations, it would be safe to say that *peshat* gained favor as the years passed. The full implications of *peshat* will become clear as we discuss some of the schools, especially the Northern French School, and some of the individuals who played a major role in medieval Jewish interpretation. The seeds for this focus on *peshat* were already sown, however, in the early years of the renowned Jewish communities in Islamic lands.

We begin with the great Gaonic academies of Babylonia in the ninth and tenth centuries. Saadia Gaon (Saadia ben Joseph, 882-942) is the most significant figure here. He translated the Tanak into Arabic in two different

formats: one contained commentary on the text and was intended for scholars; the other, called the *Tafsir* (commentary), is more of a free translation or
paraphrase intended for the Jewish public. It remained popular among
Arabic-speaking Jews for many centuries. He also composed numerous biblical commentaries and grammatical works, including a study of biblical *hapax
legomena* (words occurring only once in the Tanak). His methodological
principles are outlined in his commentaries on Genesis and Job. According to
Saadia, the text should be understood "according to the well-known and
widespread meanings the words convey to the readers" (Harris, p. 142). The
meaning so derived can be tempered only by the factors of human reason and
tradition. Quoting Deut. 10:16, "You shall circumcise the foreskin of your
heart," Saadia notes that a literal interpretation would yield a meaning that
runs counter to common sense (reason), and therefore the passage must be
understood metaphorically. Exod. 23:19, "You shall not boil a kid in its
mother's milk," is a case where rabbinic tradition must override the simple
meaning of the words, since this text supports the Jewish dietary laws, which
separate meat and dairy products. One can see here not only an emphasis on
interpretive factors defined by *peshat,* with its focus on linguistic features
present in the text, but also an accommodation to Jewish tradition and its
need to tie rabbinic teachings to the Tanak.

Spain was the second great center of medieval Jewish biblical exegesis,
and by the tenth century it had surpassed Babylon as the center of Jewish
learning. Most of this scholarship took place in Arabic, with a strong emphasis on grammar and lexicography. The *Mahberet* is an early dictionary of biblical Hebrew, in Hebrew, by the grammarian Menahem ibn Saruk (c. 910–
c. 970). While superseded by subsequent dictionaries of biblical Hebrew in
Arabic, Menahem's dictionary, since it was written in Hebrew, was used extensively in Jewish communities in Christian Europe that did not know
Arabic. Judah ibn Hayyuj (tenth century) discovered the triliteral structure of
Hebrew verbs and many Hebrew nouns. In the early eleventh century, Jonah
ibn Janah composed a dictionary and a comprehensive grammar of Hebrew,
the latter using ibn Hayyuj's work on three consonantal roots as a base for a
comprehensive survey of biblical Hebrew. A number of scholars wrote commentaries in Arabic, but Rabbi Abraham ibn Ezra (1089-1164) chose to write
in Hebrew and thereby became the means by which much of the work of the
Judeo-Spanish linguists was conveyed to subsequent Jewish scholarship. He
will be discussed in more detail below.

The third center of medieval Jewish biblical exegesis was the Northern
French School of the eleventh and twelfth centuries. As Harris notes, the rabbis of the Northern French School "came to eschew the traditional rabbinic

Bible study based on the homiletical and legal midrashim and replaced it with the methodology they called *peshat*" (p. 144). The particular historical and cultural circumstances of these schools (see pp. 144ff.) encouraged the maturation of *peshat* with a strength and vitality that "came to influence all subsequent developments in medieval Jewish biblical exegesis" (p. 144). But the necessary groundwork had already been laid, as noted above, by the work in grammar, linguistics, and lexicography done in the Babylonian academies and by Jewish scholars in Islamic Spain.

Rabbi Solomon ben Isaac (Rashi, 1040-1105) is the early and leading figure of the French school. As Harris notes, "Rashi was a pioneer in what is probably the most important aspect of the development of *peshat* exegesis, namely, the abandonment of the authoritative midrash of the ancient rabbis in favor of newly understood contextual exegesis. Whereas midrash allows for a fanciful reading, encouraging embellishing details and often stressing a moral or legal teaching, *peshat* came to connote a reading that fit the 'actual' meaning of a text, as understood by a particular commentator" (p. 144). In his widely popular commentaries, which treat virtually every book of the Tanak, Rashi consistently employs a "more contextual, less midrashically-driven exegesis" (p. 146), though he does at times include midrashic interpretation. In his later years especially, Rashi appears to have had "an increased awareness of the importance of engaging in the interpretive process without turning to the [midrashic] traditions of the sages" (p. 146). Rashi's influence on Christian interpretation, especially through Nicholas of Lyra (1270-1349), was considerable.

While Rashi's works are by far the best preserved of the Northern French School, we also have manuscripts from other scholars. Rabbi Joseph Kara, one of Rashi's disciples, did view midrash as a source of religious wisdom but nevertheless explicitly rejects it as a reading methodology. Harris quotes (p. 147) from Kara's comments on 1 Sam. 1:17-18:

> anyone who does not know the contextual understanding of Scripture *(peshuto shel miqra)*, and prefers the midrash on some matter, is like one whom the current of a river has washed away and whom the depths of water have inundated, and who grasps at anything he can to save himself. Whereas if he had set his heart on the words of the Lord, he would have searched after the meaning of the matter and its contextual explanation — and in doing so would have fulfilled that which is taught by Scripture.

What is significant here is Kara's assertion that contextual exegesis does not reject religious values but rather fulfills the biblical injunction to study Scripture carefully.

Rashi's grandson, Rabbi Samuel ben Meir (Rashbam, c. 1080–c. 1170), was strongly devoted to *peshat,* even when it required that he interpret the Torah in a manner that went against rabbinic interpretation of legal matters. For example, the Jewish practice of wearing *tefillen* (phylacteries) during prayer and at other times during the day was based on passages such as Deut. 6:8 and Exod. 13:9, which reads, "And it shall be a sign for you on your hand, and as a memorial, between your eyes." While Rashi followed rabbinic tradition and took it as self-evident that these words referred to *tefillen,* Rashbam saw these words to be metaphorical: " *'And it shall be a sign for you on your hand'* — according to the depths of its contextual meaning *(peshuto),* it should be for you as a continuous memorial, *as if* it were written on your hand" (Rashbam, quoted in Harris, p. 149). Rashbam's commitment to *peshat* even when it led to interpretations that appeared to contradict Jewish law is remarkable. His disciple Rabbi Eliezer of Beaugency was also strongly devoted to *peshat* and articulated a view of the composition of the biblical books in which a redactor of each biblical book gathered the necessary materials, edited them, added to them, "and indeed, composed the books that constitute the Hebrew Bible" (p. 149). Thus, while Rabbi Eliezer's approach saw the biblical text to be divine in origin, it also clearly recognized the human element that played a major role in the formation of the biblical books. This view is also remarkable for its time.

Rabbi Joseph Bekhor Shor was another student of Rashbam. With his interest in the literary aspects of biblical literature, Bekhor Shor focused especially on Hebrew poetic parallelism. He uses it as an aid in clarifying the meanings of ambiguous or obscure Hebrew words. For example, Num. 24:17 reads "I see it, but not now, I behold it, but not soon; There goes forth a star from Jacob, there arises a meteor in Israel." Bekhor Shor comments (Harris, p. 151),

> *There arises a meteor:* One generally interprets (the word "meteor") as referring to a staff or a strap or (an organ of) government. However, since it is in parallel structure with regard to *there goes forth a star,* one must interpret it as referring to the language of "celestial bodies" (literally "a star").

Significantly, it is Bekhor Shor's reliance on his understanding of parallelism in Hebrew poetry "that leads him to interpret differently from what would otherwise have been his sense of the contextual understanding of the verse" (p. 151).

Harris mentions a number of factors that led to the development of *peshat* by these French Jewish scholars, but certainly a main factor was a "dissatisfaction with the type of reading engaged in by the talmudic masters. In the movement away from midrash and toward *peshat,* these medieval exegetes essentially expressed their autonomy in ascertaining the meaning of Scripture and their unwillingness to defer always to the authority of the ancients in interpreting the Bible (p. 157). It should be noted that similar movements were underway in Christian circles, where scholars like Andrew of St. Victor were beginning to turn away from heavy reliance on the accumulated tradition gathered from centuries of interpretation and exposition.

We now return to Abraham ibn Ezra, the Jewish interpreter from Islamic Spain mentioned earlier. While his roots lie in Spain, he wrote most of his commentaries later in life while he was living in Christian Europe. He wrote them in Hebrew because the Ashkenazic Jews did not know Arabic. Ibn Ezra served as a key conduit for the grammatical and lexicographical knowledge of Spanish Jewry to Jews living in Christian Europe. He was committed to philological, grammatically-oriented *peshat,* focusing on context and reason. "I will search out diligently the grammatical meaning of every word to the best of my ability, and according to this will I interpret" (quoted p. 152 below). As Harris notes, "He incorporated the scholarship of both Saadia and the great Spanish philologists and even referred to Karaitic exegesis, otherwise heretical in his estimation, when he found it to be grammatically and contextually sound" (p. 153).

Ibn Ezra criticized midrashic exegesis, especially in its homiletical form. For example, the ancient rabbis tended to be highly suspicious of Esau and therefore interpreted Gen. 33:4, "Esau . . . embraced him, fell on his neck, and kissed him," to mean that Esau had intended to bite Jacob to death. Ibn Ezra dismisses this midrash as "good only for those who are still nursing(!)" (quoted, p. 153). With regard to halakhic midrash (midrash relating to law), however, Ibn Ezra deferred to midrashic rabbinic interpretation. As Harris notes (p. 154), "Ibn Ezra has adopted Saadia's three principles of exegesis, namely, that Scripture should be interpreted according to the regularly, grammatically understood meaning of the Hebrew, conditioned both by one's sense of the rational and by devotion to the rabbinic interpretation (in matters of Jewish law)." Ibn Ezra also addressed the problem of anachronisms in the Bible "and either suggested and/or hinted at the possibility of post-Mosaic authorship, or raised the issue and rejected it." He also accepted the suggestion of Moses ibn Chiquitilla that Isaiah 40–66 may have been written by a sixth-century exilic poet rather than by the eighth-century Isaiah of Jerusalem. Harris notes in summary (p. 154), "Through his incorporation of Babylonian and Spanish linguistic scholarship, Abraham ibn Ezra created a type of *peshat,* or contextual exegesis, that was more philologically based than the more purely 'literary' contextual *peshat* developed by the northern French rabbinic exegetes." In matters of *halakhah,* Ibn Ezra was more inclined to defer to the teachings of the rabbis than were some of the northern French scholars mentioned earlier.

Rabbi David Kimhi (Radak, 1160-1235) of Provence synthesized the exegesis of the Spanish school and the French school. Early in his career he wrote a grammar *(Sefer Mikhlol)* and a dictionary of biblical Hebrew *(Sefer Hashorashim).* Because they were written in Hebrew and because of the quality of his work, they eclipsed previous works and became standard reference tools among both Jews and Christians. His grammar was used in Christian circles until Christian Hebraists of the Renaissance produced their own Hebrew grammars in Latin. During the post-Reformation period, his commentaries had substantial influence on the translations produced in areas where the Reformed churches were influential. He had a well-articulated knowledge of Christian theology, developed through his frequent treatment of polemical issues directed against Jews. His commentary on Psalms often addresses polemical matters and "functions as a sort of handbook aiding his Jewish readership to resist the ongoing Christian pressure to convert" (Harris, p. 156). For example, he produced an extensive refutation of christological interpretations of Psalm 2. In summarizing Radak's work, Harris notes (p. 156), "Particularly the way in which he represented a midrashist's sensitivity to the literary nature of Scripture without indulging in fanciful interpretations that were far from the contextual meaning has endeared his commentaries to generations of readers."

Rabbi Moses ben Nahman (Ramban, Nahmanides, 1194-1270) displays an interesting fusion of *peshat* with midrash and mysticism. An early *kabbalist,* he applied the mystical traditions of kabbalah to biblical exegesis, including *gematria,* which clearly goes beyond the strict contextual focus of *peshat,* deriving meaning from the numerical value of letters and words within a text, and interpretations based on the shapes of letters, thereby obtaining secret, mystical doctrines. Yet, at other times he diligently pursues the plain or contextual meaning of a text, even where other *peshat* commentators decline to do so. For example, in commenting on Gen. 12:10, Ramban alone among medieval Jewish commentators criticizes Abraham for placing Sarah in jeopardy with Pharaoh: "know, then, that Abraham our father sinned a terrible sin, albeit inadvertently, when he caused his innocent wife to be entrapped in iniquity, out of his fear that he would be killed" (quoted, p. 159 below). Ramban's younger contemporary R. Bahya ben Asher of Saragossa was the first Jewish interpreter to invoke explicitly the system of fourfold exegesis used in medieval Christian interpretation. It came to be known as *pardes* ("orchard," from a Persian loanword), an acronym for *peshat,* exegesis based on context; *remez,* philosophical or typological exegesis; *derash,* rabbinic homiletical and legal midrashim; and *sod,* mystical interpretation. While this is not identical to the fourfold system found in Christian interpretation (literal, allegorical, tropological, and anagogical), the parallels are clear.

Rabbi Levi ben Gershom (Ralbag, or Gersonides, 1288-1344) wrote commentaries on many biblical books, using a three-part approach to a passage. First, he explains difficult words or phrases. Then, he presents a contextual commentary on the entire passage. He concludes with philosophical, moral, and legal insights derived from the passage. Preferring the contextual or plain sense in most cases, he notes, in commenting on the Cain and Abel narrative in Genesis 4, "One should not interpret the Torah figuratively except in places where it is necessary" (quoted, p. 161). His commentaries on the Torah are contextual in orientation, while his commentaries on books such as Job and the Song of Solomon tend to provide extended philosophical interpretations.

Rabbi Isaac ben Judah Abarbanel (1437-1508), who straddled the end of the Middle Ages and the beginning of the modern period, was influenced by the Italian Renaissance. His commentaries contain extensive, often voluminous treatments of the biblical text. Harris's comment, assessing a treatment by Abarbanel of Genesis 18–19, aptly summarizes all of Abarbanel's work: "His questions are generally insightful and often brilliant; the exegesis itself is virtually encyclopedic in scope" (p. 163). Abarbanel begins his commentary on this text by raising thirty questions, followed by almost twenty densely packed pages of prose. Harris's example of Abarbanel's interpretation of Genesis 18:1, a verse often viewed as problematic in its context, reveals the strength of Abarbanel's skills as an interpreter. It is noteworthy that Abrabanel follows neither the customary rabbinic divisions of the text (*parashiyot,* "portions") nor the Christian chapter divisions. Rather, he divides the text "into literary units according to his own intuition" (p. 162), and then precedes his discussion of the unit with a series of questions that address the key exegetical issues in the text.

It will be helpful to make a few comments about the Karaites ("scripturalists"), who saw themselves as operating outside the realm of rabbinic interpretation. The Karaite movement was founded in the eighth century by Anan ben David, who separated from the rabbinic tradition in approximately 760 CE. The Karaites denied the authority of the rabbinic tradition, as contained in the oral Torah and recorded in the Mishnah, the Talmud, and various other rabbinic writings. They viewed the written Torah as the only valid authority for adjudicating religious law and the practices derived from it. They were scattered throughout the Jewish world — in Jerusalem, Spain, the Crimea,

Cyprus, the Balkan lands, Poland, and Lithuania. During the tenth century, the Karaites wrote commentaries on the Torah, lexicons, and treatises on religious law. David ben Abraham Alfasi was a famous Karaite lexicographer. Japheth ben Ali commented on the entire Torah and translated it into Arabic. In the thirteenth century, Aaron ben Joseph ha-Rofé (c. 1250-1320) produced a number of major biblical commentaries. Karaite interpretation of the Torah tended to be rigorous rather than lenient in, for example, matters related to purity and the celebration of the Sabbath. While, like many Protestants, they insisted on making Scripture alone the basis of their religion, they found, as did the Protestants, that this could be a difficult task without any recourse to human reason or community consensus.

EASTERN ORTHODOX BIBLICAL INTERPRETATION

As we turn to Eastern Orthodox interpretation, we enter, in many ways, a very different world. As Blowers notes, "Western periodizations [such as Medieval and Reformation] are virtually meaningless in the context of Eastern Christian self-understanding. The formative 'patristic' age of the Orthodox tradition, broadly speaking, extends well into the 'early medieval' era of Western historiography" (p. 172 below). It would be difficult to overestimate the influence of this formative patristic age in the Orthodox heritage. "Contemporary Eastern Orthodox biblical interpretation, in all its forms, unashamedly binds itself to this body of collective insight, rooted in the creative work of the Greek theologian-exegetes of the third through fifth centuries" (p. 172).

Orthodox interpretation is infused with the belief in "the mystical *presence* of the divine Logos within the text that conditions the whole dynamic of interpretation" (p. 172). Or, citing Maximus the Confessor, "all of Scripture [is] rendered transparent to the light of the incarnate Logos" (p. 173). Yet, "the Logos incarnate in Scripture forfeits none of his divine glory while accommodating himself to the constraints of human language" (p. 176). This means that any language, including that used in Scripture, does not have the capacity to convey fully the mysteries of God. While there must therefore be an unbridgeable gap between the words of Scripture and divine reality, there is also a need to search continually for the inexhaustible richness of meaning in Scripture, that is to say, the divine Logos disguised within it. For example, Gregory of Nyssa (c. 330–c. 395) argues in his *Homilies on the Song of Songs* that "the Song is 'literally' an allegory of the elusiveness of the Logos-Bridegroom hunted by the yearning soul (the interpreter). The erotic and anthropomorphic words and images of the text are an embodiment, an accommodation to passion-laden human beings, which, through exegetical inversion, affords a transforming, albeit relative and limited, semantic encounter with the Word" (p. 176). The text is thus the medium through which unspeakable truths are conveyed.

John Chrysostom (c. 347-407) speaks of God's philanthropic condescension, which is present in even the tiniest detail of the scriptural text. We also find the idea that the multiple levels of meaning in Scripture are designed to address, in at least some form, the spiritual capacity of every reader. Such an idea naturally follows from the notion of God's condescension through the incarnation to speak at a level and in a way that each human can understand.

Unlike interpreters in the Western tradition, with their notion of the four senses of Scripture, "Byzantine interpreters, without forfeiting terminological precision, tended to settle on the simpler distinction of 'literal' and 'spiritual' senses and to enhance the principle of *theōria,* or 'contemplative insight,' the church's sanctified intuition of the meaning of texts in relation to the christocentric totality of the Bible" (p. 178). The term *skopos* is used to refer to the encompassing spiritual purpose or objective of the individual biblical books or of Scripture as a whole, thereby raising the issue of the intended meaning of the text (what Western interpreters might call the "literal" sense). In the Eastern heritage, however, "this intentionality properly belongs not to the original scriptural authors . . . but to God, the true author of Scripture, who is guiding the audience of his Word *teleologically* toward the grand fulfillment of all scriptural 'prophecy' in the mystery of Jesus Christ" (p. 178).

The church's notion of *theōria* did not preclude finding new insights in the text, but new insights could not go against the previous judgments of the church councils and the fathers, whose judgments on Scripture were valued very highly. We can see this principle at work during some of the major christological controversies, as in the interpretations of Athanasius (c. 296-373), Gregory of Nyssa, Basil of Caesarea (330-79), and Maximus the Confessor (c. 580-662).

Crucial to Eastern Orthodox interpretation is the symbiotic relationship between study of Scripture, as in scholarly commentaries and homilies, and the coming to life of the revealed Word in the context of the worshiping community. Blowers, quoting Rousseau, notes that Scripture was "handed down not just as a text but within the framework of the liturgy, and of its associated homilies. . . . Access to truth, to put it simply, could occur only in the context of worship, which orchestrated the human response to revelation" (pp. 181-82). As Blowers also notes (p. 182), "The Liturgy provided the constellation of readings, prayers, hymns, ritual symbols, and sacramental actions

through which the larger Christian faithful achieved their own contemplation *(theōria),* their own appropriation of the scriptural revelation and its
spiritual and ascetical exigencies." The development of a carefully structured
set of readings for the liturgical year, closely paralleling the types presented in
the OT with their NT fulfillments and coordinated with the major events of
the church year, guaranteed that the story of salvation was regularly and continually dramatized in the liturgical ritual for all members of the Christian
community.

Blowers next turns to a discussion of the hermeneutical achievements
of the Byzantine fathers, noting that the most prolific period of Greek patristic biblical commentaries had already ended in the fifth century with
Theodoret of Cyrrhus (c. 393–c. 460), the last major Antiochene exegete, and
with Cyril of Alexandria (d. 444), whose influence on subsequent interpretation was immense. Already in the sixth century, catena ("chain") commentaries such as those of Procopius of Gaza (c. 475–c. 538) began to appear. These
commentaries primarily accumulated the comments of previous patristic authorities. Yet, as Blowers notes (p. 183), "the theological and spiritual interpretation of the Bible continued to thrive in other formats: in monastic literature, in liturgical hymns, in homilies, and in theological treatises and *scholia*
('notes'), if less and less in actual line-by-line commentaries."

As already noted, Cyril of Alexandria is a crucial figure in Eastern Orthodox interpretation. His understanding of christology, which drives his exegesis, is quite different from that of Origen (c. 185–c. 254), the famous exegete, also from Alexandria, who lived more than 200 years before Cyril. "If
Origen's exegesis focused on the pedagogy of the transcendent Logos who, by
his incarnation both in flesh and in Scripture, leads diligent souls beyond that
incarnate presence toward a share in his transcendence, Cyril's exegesis exalted the *incarnational* mystery itself, the 'one enfleshed nature of the Word,'
the one hypostasis of God *as man . . . ,* through whom salvation and deification are granted" (p. 183). In his exegesis of the OT, Cyril explores a wide spectrum of passages, showing how they point to Christ. For example, not only
does he see the death of innocent Abel to be pointing to Christ's innocent
death; he also sees the birth of another son, Seth, to Adam and Eve as prefiguring a renewed line of Adam in the humanity of Christ. Paul's Adam-Christ
typology is one of Cyril's favorites, and he uses it to interpret a great deal of
the OT and the NT. For example, Cyril sees in the baptism of Jesus (treated in
Cyril's *Commentary on John*) the coming of the new humanity which Jesus
brings. "The text's indication that the Spirit descended and 'remained on him'
(John 1:32) signals the fact that, in response to the degeneration of the image
of God and loss of the Holy Spirit among sinful humanity, God sent the Sec-

ond Adam to renew the Spirit's presence and thereby graciously restore the race" (p. 185). Cyril uses the image of Christ as the Second Adam in support of themes such as "re-creation, renewal, transformation, restoration, and recapitulation within the incarnational mystery of Christ" (p. 185). Blowers concludes by noting, "What Cyril has called here 'a mystical significance' is nonetheless an excellent specimen of the 'theologically literal' sense" (p. 185). Cyril left behind an elaborate configuration of christological images in the Bible. He possessed "the exegetical artistry to turn even the most latent images into windows on the economy of salvation" (p. 186).

Given the heavy emphasis within Eastern Orthodoxy on the liturgy as the proper place for fully comprehending the meaning of Scripture, it is not surprising that one of the figures Blowers discusses in detail is Romanos the Melodist (c. 485–c. 560). The greatest hymn-writer of the Byzantine tradition, Romanos showed his genius in the creation of *kontakia*, sermonic hymns containing a prelude and a refrain interspersed between stanzas. "Romanos glories in the pattern of cross-evocation, the ability of biblical images to suggest one another and thus to be collapsed together in a 'thick' but subtle narrative form" (p. 186). For example (as translated by E. Lash, quoted p. 186 below):

> Bethlehem has opened Eden, come let us see,
> we have found delight in the secret, come, let us receive the joys
>   of Paradise within the cave.
> There the unwatered root (cf. Isa. 11:1) whose blossom
>   is forgiveness has appeared.
> There has been found the undug well from which David once
>   longed to drink.
> (cf. 2 Sam. 23:13-17)

> There a virgin has borne a babe
> And has quenched at once Adam's and David's thirst.
> For this, let us hasten to this place where there has been born
>   *A little child, God before the ages.*

"Those who sing the *kontakia* in the present moment of the liturgy are drawn into the narratives, compelled to identify with the *dramatis personae* and to respond with their own praise and devotion" (p. 189). Like an icon, a *kontakion* does not simply tell a story: it draws one into worship, into the movement of God's love for us. There are substantial parallels to the *lectio divina* in the Western monastic heritage, in which the text is contemplated in depth in the context of the canonical hours.

Maximus the Confessor presents the entire interpretive enterprise as a grand passage from the letter to the spirit of the biblical revelation. The letter cannot be diminished or eliminated, since the *historia,* the literal meaning of the text, is empowered by, but also empowers, the spiritual meaning. His exegetical methods, like Origen's, focus on typology, tropology, allegory, and "the extracting of spiritual insights from grammatical and syntactical details of the biblical text" (p. 190), all enabling the reader to penetrate into and participate in the divine self-disclosure *(oikonomia).* One recalls here the rabbinic study of the tiniest details of the biblical text in the conviction that such study will bring to light a portion of the total revelation given to Moses on Mount Sinai.

Following Pseudo-Dionysius the Areopagite, Maximus sees revelation to come via two means: the created cosmos and the Bible. The Logos incarnates himself in both, and both together provide access through contemplation to the higher mysteries. Like Cyril, Maximus sees "the incarnational mystery of Christ as concealed in all of Scripture." "Maximus glories in the polyvalence of the biblical text" (p. 191). While he can agree with Origen's notion that the various levels of meaning are designed to accommodate the level of the individual's spiritual maturity, Maximus sees unity permeating this diversity. In his commentary on Jonah, the prophet is seen at various times as "a *typos* of fallen Adam (human nature), Christ, the Gentile church, and the unbelieving Jews. . . . The upshot is a veritable kaleidoscope of insights, all assumed valid, into the fullness of the economy of salvation" (p. 192).

Monastic biblical interpretation in Eastern Orthodoxy "was marked by a strongly *eschatological* and *existential* orientation, a longing for transformation in the 'last days'" (p. 192). Discussions between novices and their monastic elders, reflecting the anchoritic *oral* culture of the desert, often reflect the rich young man's question to Jesus, "Abba, what must I do to be saved?" (Luke 18:18). These discussions contain numerous inquiries by the novice about the meaning of Scripture, while "the sages' aphoristic responses discourage theological inquisitiveness (even reading itself) and invite practical response to the quickening and judging Word" (p. 192). The Byzantine monastic fathers found, in even the most obscure details of the narratives in the Bible, much light on the struggles they experienced in their ascetic lives. In the stories about the Bible's heroic figures such as Abraham, Moses, Elijah, Elisha, Job, John the Baptist, and Paul, they found details that could serve paradigmatically for the monastic virtues they espoused. The image of "the city," quite often Jerusalem in the military narratives of the OT, "could be allegorically internalized as a figure of the soul assailed by the passions" (p. 193).

These ascetic fathers "are concerned overall less with methods of interpretation than with the conditions under which Scripture's various meanings are rendered accessible to the Christian in the context of ascetic progress. . . . The reading of the Scriptures means one thing for those who have but recently embraced the life of holiness, another for those who have attained the middle state, and another for those who are moving rapidly toward perfection" (Blowers, in part quoting Stithatos, p. 193). Peter of Damascus (twelfth century), taking seriously Jesus' command to "search the Scriptures" (John 5:39), saw the Scriptures as possessing an inexhaustible wealth of meanings. As "the saint grows in knowledge, the interpreter must imitate the Word's own versatility by not settling absolutely on a given sense but being open to new insights, so long as they are 'in accordance with God's intention' and 'attested by the words of Scripture'" (p. 193). According to Peter, even secular knowledge could serve as an interpretive aid.

The rise of modern higher criticism has posed a substantial challenge to interpretation as practiced in the Eastern Orthodox tradition. Blowers notes that for Dumitru Staniloae, a twentieth-century Romanian theologian, interpretation is a process of "contemplative vision" of the many different revealed images of the Divine, such as one experiences when contemplating an icon. As Staniloae says (quoted p. 194), "The words of Scripture are the inevitable occasion for us to enter through the work of the Spirit into relation with the authentic person of Christ who transcends them." Interpretation is, therefore, "a thoroughly *ecclesial* process, since the church's tradition — in all its aspects — is the means by which divine revelation, communicated in words and images, is continuously embodied and *personalized*" (p. 194). The church, empowered by the work of the Spirit, is thus capable of absorbing the revelatory witness to Christ as received through many different venues. John Breck, an Orthodox exegete, argues not only for the value of patristic hermeneutics, but also for a revival of the ancient interpretive perspective of *theōria*, which, according to Breck, cannot be simply equated with the spiritual sense of the text or with any singular interpretive method, but rather "is a 'vision' of divine truth communicated by the Holy Spirit to the Church" (quoted, p. 194). This "presupposes both literal interpretation of the text in its native context — including the *theōria* of the biblical authors themselves — and discernment of the text's spiritual horizon for the church" (p. 194). Interpretation, as a function of the worshiping church, must include every form of scriptural exegesis "from rigorously scientific exegesis to liturgical hymnography" (Breck, quoted p. 194). Blowers concludes by noting that "Eastern Orthodox interpreters, fully aware of the challenges of postmodern hermeneutical culture, still find in their Greek patristic and Byzantine legacy the sufficient models by which to appropriate the continuing power of the Bible for and in the church. *Theōria* celebrates the revelation in all of its complexity, beauty, and capacity to speak an ever-contemporary word" (p. 195).

THE TEXT OF THE TANAK (OLD TESTAMENT)

Nothing is more fundamental to biblical interpretation than establishing the correct form of the text. This includes not only the actual words of the text but also the divisions within the text, the order of the books, the addition of vowels through the system of pointing developed by the Masoretes, changes made in the text due to scribal sensitivities or beliefs, and scribal comments on the text being copied. (Until the time of the Masoretes and their development of the system of pointing, the Hebrew text contained no vowels except in cases where the letters *waw* and *yodh* take on the character of vowels. This is similar to the usage of modern Hebrew in Israel.)

For early Christian interpreters the text of the Septuagint (the Greek translation of the Tanak) had a dominating influence on their interpretation of the OT that went virtually unchallenged, except for Jerome, who was viewed askance by his contemporaries (such as Augustine) for taking the Hebrew text seriously (see Leonard Greenspoon's article on the Septuagint in *HBI*[1]). Jerome of course used his knowledge of Hebrew when producing the Vulgate, but, once the Vulgate came to be widely used in the medieval church, it, and not the Hebrew text of the Tanak, was given unrivaled preference in Christian interpretation of the OT. Eventually, there was some interaction of Christian scholars with the Hebrew text of the Tanak, beginning in the twelfth century, as we will see below. As the Middle Ages drew to a close, the Hebrew text of the OT came to rival the OT of the Vulgate in various scholarly circles. Luther, for example, based his German translation of the OT on the Hebrew Tanak text published in 1495 by the Soncino brothers.

In order to treat the subject of the text of the OT in one article, we have had to move beyond the chronological bounds of this volume, beginning in the ancient period and ending in the contemporary age of electronic media. In his article "The Text of the Tanak," Fuller divides the development of the Hebrew text into four time periods: the transmission of the text up to the emergence of the proto-Masoretic Text (pMT); the pre-Masoretic period, which includes the emergence of a single text type (pMT) and relatively fixed features of the consonantal text; the Masoretic period; and the transmission of the Masoretic Text (MT) through the time of the first printed editions up to today's electronic forms of the text. The text of the Tanak thus has a transmission history lasting approximately 3000 years. Parts of the Tanak were certainly passed down in written form prior to the exile (e.g., Jeremiah 26; 2 Kgs. 22:10-13), and the process of written transmission accelerated after the exile. But it is only after the formation of the completed canon of the Tanak that we can envision copying and transmission of it as a single entity. Before that, "the various collections of text were transmitted separately or as smaller groups of collections" (p. 202).

The codex or "book" format was not used in the ancient Jewish communities. Rather, scrolls made of skins of goats or gazelles were used. Due to their bulk, the amount of text that could be included in a single scroll was limited. While the Torah was written on a single scroll, as were books like Isaiah and Jeremiah, a cluster of smaller books such as the minor prophets would be grouped together onto a single scroll. Although biblical manuscripts were usually prepared with great care, "there do not seem to have been established standards applied in the copying of each manuscript until perhaps the end of the first century CE" (p. 202). The scribal standards then adopted are preserved in the Babylonian Talmud and in the treatises *Masseket Sefer Torah* and *Masseket Soferim*.

As the biblical documents from Qumran demonstrate, "until the time of the destruction of the second Temple in 70 CE there was a great variety of texts in use, some related to each other and thus forming groups" (p. 203). The phrase "proto-Masoretic Text" (pMT) "refers to the form of the consonantal text of the canonical Jewish Scriptures that [eventually] became the dominant form of the text" (p. 202) no later than the time of the Bar Kochba revolt (132-35 CE). The manuscripts found at Qumran attest to the existence of the pMT group as early as the third century BCE. While some scholars relate the pMT to the Pharisees, Fuller indicates that this is only speculative. The many Essene biblical documents do not reflect a preference for any specific early form of the text.

What led to a single form of the text winning out over all others? Fuller lists several probable factors. The first is the war with Rome in 66-70 CE, which devastated Jewish Palestine, Jerusalem, and the Temple and led to the collection and preservation of Judaism's written traditions, vital to survival now that the Temple was gone. Other factors include the recognized diversity of the various textual families and the problems which that diversity posed, an awareness of differences between the Septuagint and the Hebrew forms of the text, the use of the Septuagint by Greek-speaking Christians (which also encouraged the development of new Greek translations that were closer to the Hebrew text), and "the development of interpretive methods dependent on specific features of the text, such as orthography and letter forms/shapes"

(p. 204). "The narrowing of text types and the creation of new Greek translations might well have been the work of decades; but certainly no later than 200 CE the pMT emerged as the single Hebrew text type. Variations among mss. existed, but by then they were relatively minor disagreements in orthography and . . . paratextual features" (p. 205).

The Masoretes began their work near the end of the talmudic period (c. 300-500 CE). Prior to this, according to Fuller, certain factors were beginning to solidify, such as the order for the canonical books. In *Baba Batra* 14b the order of the prophetic books is given as: Joshua, Judges, Samuel, Kings, Jeremiah, Ezekiel, Isaiah, and the twelve. The order of the writings is: Ruth, Psalms, Job, Proverbs, Ecclesiastes, Song of Songs, Lamentations, Daniel, Esther, Ezra, and Chronicles. It is interesting that, well before use of the codex form some five hundred years later, with the books still on a number of different scrolls, there is a presumed set order for the books. This order certainly has a significant impact on interpretation, as Sanders notes in his article "The Stabilization of the Tanak" in *HBI*[1], pp. 245-49.

The division of the text into sense units *(pisqot)* took place no later than the third century CE. Some of the texts found at Qumran and in the Judean desert divide the text into sense units, but there is apparently no well-developed system such as there is later in the Talmud and in the *Masorah.* As Fuller notes, paragraphs are typically indicated by spaces in the text. Sometimes the Hebrew letters *peh and samekh* are used to mark section divisions. Division of the text into verses apparently began during the talmudic period, when it became customary to mark the conclusion of a verse with *soph pasuq* (:). However, dividing the text into numbered chapters came much later and was apparently the work of Stephen Langdon, Archbishop of Canterbury, who added such numbers to the text of the Vulgate, perhaps to facilitate his disputes with the Cathars. The *Complutensian Polyglot,* produced by Cardinal Ximénes between 1514 and 1517, may have led to the incorporation of chapter and verse numbers into the Hebrew text. Ximenes' text presents the Vulgate in the central column in numbered chapters and verses, with the Septuagint on the left and the Hebrew text on the right, both numbered so that they correspond to the Latin text. It is unclear, however, when Hebrew texts published by Jews began to include chapter and verse numbers. Significantly, as Fuller notes, "These various ways of dividing up the text, which originate at different times, and in the case of chapters, from the text in another language, represent different traditions of exegesis that do not always agree with each other" (p. 208). The *pisqot* will not always mesh with the chapter divisions derived from the Christian Vulgate text, and there are also variations regarding verse divisions among the Hebrew texts. The ending of the first literary unit in Genesis at 2:4a is an example of how difficulties can arise regarding these divisions and numbering systems.

Fuller also deals with other textual markings originating from the pre-Masoretic period, such as dots above fifteen words in the MT and the decoration of certain letters in some synagogue scrolls with slim strokes at their tops. The functions of these rare markings are no longer known, but they continue to be included in the text. The functions of other markings are clear, such as the large *waw* in the word "Gihon" in Lev. 11:42, which marks the middle letter of the Torah.

Before turning to the work of the Masoretes, Fuller discusses the reading traditions of the text, some of which may have begun in the talmudic period, others in the early Masoretic period. *Ketib,* in Aramaic, means "[what is] written," and refers to a word presented in the consonantal text. *Qere,* also in Aramaic, means "[what is] read," referring to a word that is to be read in place of the word written in the consonantal text. The *qere* is typically denoted in the margin of the manuscript, where its consonants are written. The vowel points of the *qere* are usually given with the consonants of the *ketib* in the body of the text. The *ketib-qere* readings are not contained in scrolls used in synagogues.

The *ketib-qere* listings vary considerably from one manuscript to another, as do the types of readings designated as *ketib-qere.* The number of such readings can vary from a low of 800 to a high of 1500 (Fuller, p. 211). The Talmud mentions some types of such readings, such as euphemisms, and the consistent presentation of a *qere* reading for certain words in the text. Since they are mentioned in the Talmud, these *qere* readings must be quite old. Others, found only in later Masoretic manuscripts, or those based on the vocalization system, must be more recent. One example of a *ketib-qere* reading concerns the divine name YHWH. Since the divine name was regarded as too holy to be pronounced, *'adonai* came to be substituted for it in reading. YHWH is, therefore, vocalized with the vowels of *'adonai,* which is pronounced instead of the divine name as the text is read. Certain words in the text were viewed as harsh or vulgar and were replaced with euphemisms. Fuller (p. 211) provides an example from Isa. 13:16, in which the *qere* substitutes a verb meaning "to be lain with" for a verb meaning "to be raped." A third category of *ketib-qere* readings is those in which either a word contained in the text is not to be read, or in which a word not in the text is to be read (examples on p. 212).

An interesting parallel to the *ketib-qere* system is the *sebirin* ("suggested") notes. "The *sebirin* notes usually address a word that is unusual or difficult in its context and suggest another reading" (pp. 212-13). Since, unlike the *ketib-qere*, the *sebirin* are not part of the reading system, the *sebirin* are not binding. "The *sebirin* are intended to 'protect' the reading of the text, even though there seems to be a more likely reading" (p. 213, with examples). *Tiqqune sopherim* are readings where the scribes have corrected the text. Often, the correction involves only one consonant. "Typically, the concern of the *tiqqune sopherim* is to indicate corrections of texts which were understood to be somehow disrespectful of God" (p. 213). For example, in Gen. 18:22 the scribes corrected the original text, which read "Yahweh stood before Abraham" (implying subservience of Yahweh to Abraham), to "Abraham stood before Yahweh."

The term *masorah* (from which we derive "Masoretic") "refers to the traditional three-part apparatus of the biblical text: the vowels and the accents. within the text and the Masoretic commentary on the text in the margins" (Fuller, p. 214). The latter are found in the margins between the columns *(masorah parva, Mp)*, in the upper and lower margins *(masorah magna, Mm)*, and in the spaces at the end of books *(masorah finalis)*. "The vowels and accents provide direction for the proper reading of the text. The marginal notes provide information to ensure the proper copying of the text" (Fuller, p. 215). The *Mp* focus primarily on orthography and the frequency of forms, and also include notes such as the *ketib-qere* readings. The *Mm* supplement the *Mp*, often providing more specific information, such as places where an unusual spelling occurs. "Since biblical citations in the *masorah* predate the use of numbered chapters and verses, texts are referred to using key words or phrases from the context where the form occurs" (Fuller, p. 215). These notes are often very compact, making extensive use of abbreviations.

The date of the beginning of Masoretic activity is difficult to determine. Comments scattered throughout the Talmud allude to interests in the text and activities later evident in the *masorah*. Some of the notes regarding the text were no doubt transmitted orally before they came to be written down. It is also difficult to determine whether the vowels or the accents developed first. "The Masoretic period is usually considered to have begun in the sixth century [CE] and ended in the tenth." The culmination of this work is the production of the great Masoretic codices (Fuller, p. 214).

Although copies of the text used in the synagogue were on scrolls and contained only the consonantal text, scrolls no longer fit for synagogue use could be annotated with the various notes described above, and vocalized. Some of the older biblical scrolls found in the Cairo Geniza (repository for worn biblical scrolls or other material containing the name of God or biblical citations) contain vowels, accents, and Masoretic notes. As Fuller notes, "the recovery of these early scrolls with such notations indicates that the *masorah* began to be committed to writing prior to the eighth century" (Fuller, p. 216).

The Masoretic traditions developed, beginning in the sixth and seventh centuries, in three major Jewish communities: the Palestinian; the Babylonian; and the Tiberian. The first two appear to be older, while the later Tiberian system is far more developed. Each of the three systems used different symbols to represent the vowels. The Tiberian system came to be the most widely used, and appears in most surviving manuscripts. Near the end of the development of the Tiberian system, two families dominated the development of the Masoretic traditions: the family of ben Naphtali, and the family of ben Asher. The ben Asher tradition eventually won out, no doubt helped by the approval of Maimonides (1135-1204), and is reflected in the Leningrad Codex (from 1009 CE, commonly used today in scholarly circles as the base text of *Biblia Hebraica* (Fuller, p. 217).

"The main function of the vowels and the accents was to preserve the proper reading and recitation of the text. The accents . . . guide the recitation of the text during the service, . . . indicate word stress, and . . . indicate the syntactical relation between the words as either conjunctive or disjunctive" (Fuller, p. 216). The disjunctive accents indicated pauses in the text, which clearly can affect how one understands the meaning of the text. As Fuller noted, "the accents . . . present a specific understanding of the relation of the words to one another, thus excluding some meanings and emphasizing others" (Fuller, p. 219, referencing Tov).

In probably the seventh century, the codex (book form) "began to be utilized for copies of the Tanak intended for study purposes" (Fuller, p. 218). While, as noted above, copies for synagogue use could only contain the consonantal text, the study codices could contain the Masoretic notes, as well as a vocalized and accented text. The codex enabled the entire Tanak to be contained in one unit, and made it easier to quickly refer to readings from other books in the Tanak.

As time passed, the Masoretic notes themselves became the object of study, and they were sometimes copied in separate books, along with studies on various aspects of the *masorah*, Masoretic handbooks, etc. The growing body of material in the *masorah* provided an important resource for the beginning of grammatical analysis of biblical Hebrew. As noted above, Saadia Gaon (882-942) produced the first in a long line of grammatical studies of the Tanak by Jewish scholars. As Fuller says in summation, "The work of the Jewish grammarians is dependent on and grows out of the work of the Masoretes" (p. 220).

The Soncino brothers produced the first complete printed Hebrew Bible in 1488, followed by the Naples Bible in 1491-93, and a small octavo format edition in 1495, which was used by Luther for his translation of the OT into German. In Spain in 1514-1517, Cardinal Ximénes was the patron for the Complutensian Polyglot Bible, which contained the Vulgate, Septuagint, and Hebrew texts of the OT. At about the same time, Daniel Bomberg, a Christian from Venice, hired Felix Pratensis to produce the first Rabbinic Bible (1516-1517), which, in four volumes, contained the *targumim* and commentaries, but omitted the *Masorah*. The second Great Rabbinic Bible (1524-1525) was also sponsored by Bomberg, and edited by Jacob ben Hayyim. It became, for almost four hundred years, the standard printed Hebrew Bible. It also came out in four volumes, and, as Fuller notes, "included the Targumim and the commentaries of Rashi, Ibn Ezra, David and Moses Kimhi, and Levi ben Gershom. The *masorah* was gathered from different manuscripts for this edition. The Second Rabbinic Bible "became the standard text of printed forms of the Hebrew Bible for nearly four hundred years" (pp. 220-21).

The 1524-1525 edition sponsored by Bomberg was the basis of the first two editions of Kittel's *Biblia Hebraica* (first edition 1905-1906). For the third edition (1937), the Leningrad (L) manuscript (Firkowitch I. B19a) was used as the base, because it was the oldest complete ben Asher manuscript then known. In 1967, the next edition (Stuttgartensia) of *Biblia Hebraica* appeared. A new edition, *Biblia Hebraica Quinta*, is being sponsored by the United Bible Societies.

Another work in process is the *Hebrew University Bible*, which uses the Aleppo Codex (ca. 925), where it is still extant, as its base. It, like *Biblia Hebraica Quinta*, is being done as a diplomatic critical edition, which employs the text of a single manuscript, providing notes on variants from other manuscripts. This is different from an eclectic edition, which reconstructs the text on the basis of many manuscripts, providing critical notes on variants. The books of Isaiah and Jeremiah have appeared in the *Hebrew University Bible*, and Ezekiel is nearing completion. "Both the *Hebrew University Bible* and the *Biblia Hebraica Quinta* . . . include apparatuses in which much information is presented concerning the text beyond that gathered in the *masorah*. Both present readings from early Hebrew manuscripts, citations from rabbinic literature, and readings from ancient translations of the Hebrew Bible such as the Septuagint" (Fuller, p. 221).

The *Oxford Hebrew Bible* will be an eclectic critical edition. "It will use the Leningrad Codex as a copy text, but will present an emended version of L, one that attempts to remove errors in the text" (Fuller, p. 222).

In recent years, electronic forms of the text have become available. The

Michigan-Claremont text, which encodes the Leningrad Codex, provides the base for most electronic versions of the Hebrew text, whether online, or available in stand-alone computer software. Accordance is in an Apple format, while Bibleworks and Logos are in a format for Windows-based PCs.

THE TEXT OF THE NEW TESTAMENT

During the medieval period, the text of the New Testament was mainly found in manuscripts in Greek, Latin, Syriac, and Coptic. In the Greek-speaking church, the manuscripts used were predominantly of the Byzantine text-type, originating in the Greek-speaking church centered in Constantinople. In the western, Latin-speaking church, the main text was Jerome's Latin translation of the New Testament, contained in the Vulgate, which was completed around the turn of the fifth century CE.

Churches throughout Christendom had access to single copies of *portions* of the biblical text in Greek or Latin, usually in smaller divisions like the Gospels or Psalms. The texts of these partial and complete manuscripts varied from one another, due to changes introduced in the process of copying manuscripts. These changes, or variants, could be either unintentional or intentional. Unintentional variants include miscopying letters, duplicating letters or words (dittography), skipping over letters or words (haplography), skipping from the beginning of a word to another with the same beginning (homoioarchton), or skipping from the ending of a word to another with the same ending (homoeoteleuton). Intentional variants include modernizing the Greek and Latin texts to conform to usage at the time of the copying, harmonizing the text with similar readings in other portions of Scripture (especially true of the texts of the Synoptic Gospels), and theological changes motivated by current theological controversy.

These complete or partial manuscripts in Greek or Latin were, for the Christian parishes where they were kept, *the* canonical versions of those portion(s) of Scripture. Thus, they were the portion(s) of Scripture known and used and held as authoritative in their regions. These manuscripts were, of course, only some of many versions of each portion of Scripture that existed in Christendom. However, this trust in familiar, local manuscripts was shaken by new events, especially in the West. With the dawn of the Renaissance, copies of the Greek manuscripts began circulating from the East, especially after the fall of Constantinople in 1453. This major event brought scholars of Greek and their Greek manuscripts to the West, especially to Italy, allowing scholars to compare the Latin and Greek texts of the Bible. A serious critique of the

Vulgate ensued. For example, when Cardinal Bessarion (1403-72), who had been the Metropolitan of Nicaea, came to the West, he provided a scholarly critique of the Vulgate based on the Greek text (Elliott, pp. 229-30).

Such comparison and critique were facilitated by the invention of the printing press in the mid-fifteenth century. The first book printed, a copy of the Vulgate, was the Mazarin Bible, also known as the Gutenberg Bible (1453-55). Vernacular translations based on the Vulgate were printed in German, French, Italian and Dutch. Soon, Greek manuscripts were printed and circulated as well. The printing and distribution of the Vulgate, the vernacular translations, and the Greek New Testament soon made clear the inadequacies of the Vulgate as a translation. As Jerome's Vulgate was compared with the Greek New Testament, scholars recognized its deficiencies and, in conjunction with the rediscovery of primary texts, concluded that the Greek, rather than the Latin, should be the basis of translation and study. Eventually, the Greek text became the standard for biblical and theological study, as well as the basis for vernacular translations in the Reformation of the sixteenth century. This brings us to the *Complutensian Polyglot,* an early and important printed Greek New Testament commissioned by Cardinal Francisco Ximénes de Cisneros (1436-1517), Archbishop of Toledo. A polyglot version with the New Testament portion in Latin and Greek, it was printed in 1514, but not published until 1522, when the entire 6 volumes appeared together as a set. The *Complutensian Polyglot* was based on the Byzantine text-type, that is, medieval manuscripts previously transported from Byzantium, dating from the tenth century and later, probably borrowed from the Vatican Library. The *Complutensian Polyglot* and others like it in Latin, Hebrew, and Greek were published throughout Europe, stimulating scholarship (Elliott, pp. 230-32).

The first Greek New Testament to be published, and the most influential, was that of Erasmus of Rotterdam (1466/69-1536). His bilingual, three-column polyglot edition of the New Testament first appeared in 1516. It contained the Vulgate text, a new translation into Latin, and the Greek text. As he states in his introduction, Erasmus intended his Latin translation to correct the Vulgate with reference to the Greek text, not to present a Greek text *per se.* However, he placed the first published Greek New Testament before the public.

Erasmus's Greek New Testament had enormous influence upon translations into the vernacular (especially early English translations and the KJV), and on the events of the Protestant Reformation. His Greek text was used for Luther's German translation of the New Testament (1522), and for Tyndale's English translation (1526), as well as the translations of several other Reformers. The Greek New Testament gave the Reformers a means to critique Roman Catholic doctrine based on the Vulgate, and to support their own theological agenda. The Roman Catholic Church responded by reaffirming the authority of the Vulgate at the Council of Trent, in its fourth session of 1546 (Elliott, p. 237).

Although Erasmus's Greek New Testament also had enormous influence on subsequent editions of the Greek New Testament itself, his text was not without its flaws. There are places where he "corrected" the Greek text using the Latin. If a section of text was missing from his Greek manuscripts, he back-translated, that is, he used the Latin of the Vulgate to give a plausible reconstruction of the Greek. One notable example is the text of Rev. 22:16-21, missing from his Greek manuscripts, which he reconstructed from the Vulgate. Subsequent editions of Erasmus's Polyglot corrected both his Latin translation and his Greek text. The fourth edition used the *Complutensian Polyglot* to make some of these corrections (Elliott, pp. 234-35).

While virtually all the printed editions of the Greek New Testament up to 1881 were based on Erasmus's text, there were many other important editions. One was created by Robert Estienne (1503-59), whose Latinized name is Stephanus. He produced four editions, three in Paris (1546, 1549, 1550) and one in Geneva (1551). These editions were based on the Greek texts of Erasmus, and on the *Complutensian Polyglot*. The third edition from Paris contained the first printed critical apparatus, providing variant readings. The sole edition from Geneva is important because it was the first printed New Testament to be divided into verses, as arranged by Stephanus himself. Chapter divisions had been introduced in the early thirteenth century (probably by Stephen Langton), but Stephanus introduced the versification that we know today. Another version of the Greek New Testament was published by Theodore Beza (1519-1605) in Geneva in nine editions (1565-1604). This was a revised version of Stephanus's text, accompanied by a new Latin translation. The texts of Stephanus and Beza were used in the translation of the King James Version of 1611 (Elliott, pp. 239-40).

The Elzevirs, a publishing family in Leiden, published seven editions of the Greek New Testament (1624-78). The first edition (1624) reproduced the text of Stephanus, with revisions from the text of Beza. The second, revised edition (1633) contained a preface that used the phrase *textus receptus* ("received text"), which became the technical phrase designating the Greek text of Erasmus, Stephanus, and Beza, as well as the uncritical editions of Greek and Latin classical authors (Elliott, p. 241).

The text of Erasmus and those that followed — the *textus receptus* — is a Byzantine text type with origins that can be traced to the fourth and fifth centuries. It is the text of the majority of medieval manuscripts. These manuscripts originated in the Greek-speaking church centered in Constantinople.

In some measure this is unfortunate, because of the broad and enduring influence of Erasmus's edition of the Greek text on later editions. In subsequent centuries, manuscripts of the Alexandrian text type gradually were recognized as holding more authentic readings of the Greek New Testament, and thus as being more useful in reconstructing the original text. One such manuscript is Codex Vaticanus from the fourth century, which became central to the reconstruction of the original of the Septuagint and the New Testament. Vaticanus is unusual in that it is a complete Bible, including both the Old and New Testaments. Most other manuscripts of the New Testament are partial, containing the Gospels, Acts and the Catholic Epistles, the Pauline Epistles, or Revelation. Although Vaticanus was housed in the Vatican Library when Erasmus composed his edition, he did not have the opportunity to consult it, but depended on the librarians there to supply him with lists of variant readings. Vaticanus contains readings that are at odds with those of the Byzantine text type, and this probably kept its use to a minimum during Erasmus's work, and the work of those who followed him (Elliott, pp. 244-46).

Other important manuscripts of the Greek New Testament include Codex Bezae Cantabrigiensis, a bilingual Greek-Latin manuscript of the fifth century that contains the Gospels, Acts, and part of 3 John. It is of the Western text type. At one time it belonged to Beza, and was consulted by him and Stephanus in their editions of the Greek New Testament. Codex Claromontanus of the sixth century contains the Pauline Epistles, and was also once owned by Beza, and used in his third edition.

Codex Alexandrinus is a fifth-century manuscript of the entire New Testament and much of the Old Testament. It has a Byzantine text-type in the Gospels, and an Alexandrian text-type in the rest of the New Testament. It was known at the time of the early editions of the Greek New Testament, but did not arrive in the West until 1627, after the King James Version was translated. This discovery led Brian Walton to include variant readings from Codex Alexandrinus in notes at the bottom of the page of the Greek text in his Polyglot Bible (1655-57) (Elliott, p. 248).

Walton's work was a precursor to the major work of John Mill. Some call Mill's work the beginning of text criticism of the New Testament. Mill published an edition of the Greek New Testament in 1707, which included a critical apparatus listing over 30,000 variant readings among the Greek manuscripts when compared to the text of Stephanus (1550). However, public reaction was strong against making so explicit the variant readings among the manuscripts of the *textus receptus*. Text criticism of the New Testament would not fully bloom until the middle of the nineteenth century (Elliott, pp. 241-42).

Other ancient versions of the New Testament existed in manuscript form, and eventually were printed during this period. These include the oriental versions of the Syriac, Coptic, Georgian, and Armenian texts. These versions were often based on early Greek texts, and were consulted to find earlier readings, especially with the advent of rigorous text criticism in the nineteenth century.

SCHOLASTIC INTERPRETATION OF THE BIBLE

Scholasticism was an intellectual and cultural movement that emerged in the fourteenth and fifteenth centuries, and was defined and maintained by the universities of Europe. The movement was found widely in other schools as well. It espoused a rational, logical, and systematic approach to fields of knowledge, particularly those comprising the liberal arts (e.g., grammar, rhetoric, logic, arithmetic, geometry, astronomy, and music), and was used by the faculties in theology, law, and medicine.

The method of teaching in medieval scholasticism consisted of commentary on texts by both masters and students, and formal topical debate. Two texts were central to commentary and debate: the Bible, and the *Four Books of Sentences* by Peter Lombard, master of the cathedral school of Notre Dame in the mid-twelfth century. The *Sentences* provided opinions *(sententiae)* or analysis on a wide variety of theological and philosophical issues (Ocker, pp. 254-56).

By the end of the sixteenth century, new methods in philology and literary studies of the humanists had been combined with the logical methods of the medieval schools to create a more modern scholasticism. It was difficult to distinguish scholasticism from humanism in the writings of scholars and post-Reformation theologians, many of whom adapted the methods of the humanists for their own studies. The addition of philological and literary methods to scholasticism, coupled with the centrality of the Bible to analysis, led to the development of textual criticism of the Bible, comparative Semitic philology, and the study of the history of the ancient Near East. This development began the transformation of biblical studies. While the sixteenth century saw Lombard's *Sentences* no longer in use, the Bible continued to have a central place in scholastic education (Ocker, pp. 256-59).

Within medieval schools, the most important commentary used in the disputations was the *Glossa ordinaria,* the *Ordinary Gloss.* Glosses are explanatory notes added to a text, in this case, the Bible. Glosses are of two types: interlinear glosses — short notes added between the lines; and marginal glosses

— larger portions of texts added in the margins. In the case of the Bible, glosses were often drawn from the church fathers to help explain a text. Adding glosses to texts began in the eighth and ninth centuries in Northumbria and Ireland. It steadily increased in popularity and use, until, by the beginning of the eleventh century, glossing was widespread.

Glosses began as additions of a master's interpretation to individual biblical passages. In time, they became comprehensive, covering entire biblical books, and eventually, the entire Bible. Collections of these glosses offering interpretation of the entire Bible began to appear in Paris about 1220, and shortly thereafter were found in Germany and England. Anselm of Laon (d. 1117) was especially influential in creating the glossed Bible as a compendium of patristic interpretation. The most important glossed Bible was the *Ordinary Gloss,* nine volumes of interpretation of the Bible. Some glosses were a compilation from many interpreters, while others were derived from a single source. The *Ordinary Gloss* wielded vast influence in scholasticism, helped by the citations of it in Lombard's *Four Books of Sentences* (Ocker, pp. 259-60).

By the twelfth century, comprehensive, discursive commentaries emerged. The most influential discursive commentary, the *Historia scholastica* by Peter Comestor, chancellor of the school of Notre Dame, appeared in 1175. This comprehensive exposition of the Bible became widely used in the later Middle Ages. The most influential type of comprehensive commentary, the *postilla,* was developed in the Dominican school at the University of Paris in the early thirteenth century, under the influence of Hugh of Saint-Cher (d. 1263). The *postilla,* a running commentary composed originally as classroom lectures, became the typical Bible commentary of scholasticism. The *postilla* was intended to supplement the *Ordinary Gloss* with newer interpretations and theological outlooks. These supplements were often digressions on theological subjects suggested by the passage being interpreted, and focused essentially on the literal sense of the passage. The best discursive commentaries of the Reformation were *postillae,* especially those of Martin Luther, Martin Bucer, and John Calvin (Ocker, pp. 260-61).

While scholastic interpretation relied on the *Glossa ordinaria* and the *Historia scholastica,* scholastic interpreters also created some new tools for biblical study. A new edition of the Bible was published in Paris, with chapter and paragraph divisions. Stephen Langdon (d. 1228), Parisian master and future archbishop of Canterbury, created the chapter divisions by 1203. Shortly thereafter, Thomas Gallus (d. 1246) created paragraph divisions. The Dominicans in Paris created a concordance of Latin terms of the Bible between 1230 and 1235, a project now made possible by the establishment of chapter and paragraph divisions of the Bible. Concordances to canon law were also created, in order that authoritative opinions could guide exegesis.

Thus, the *Glossa ordinaria,* the *Historia scholastica, postillae,* concordances, and the chapter and paragraph divisions within the Bible were the main tools and fruits of the scholastic biblical interpretation. There was some adaptation of the literal, historical, and philological methods of biblical interpretation, but not in any great amount until the sixteenth century.

In the twelfth century, scholars began to use reason and dialogue on subjects independent of the Bible and sacred literature. In opposition, many theologians argued that the Bible must undergird all rational reflection, due to the nature of language and the world. Thomas Aquinas distinguished two kinds of biblical signification: verbal and natural. Verbal signification understands words to convey meaning directly to the mind, rather than from words to things to the mind. Natural signification is the moving of the mind from words to things to the mind to find meaning (Ocker, p. 266).

Natural signification underlies Victorine and early scholastic interpretation. Richard of St. Victor (d. 1173) argued that words were representational, but so were the things — physical and factual objects represented by a word. That is, both the words, and the objects they signify, are representational and have meaning. Hugh of St. Victor (d. 1142) argued that this additional meaning of things is present in objects and their properties, people's actions and experiences, numbers, places, times, and events. These additional meanings, denoted by the things to which words refer, are closer to the spiritual truth than the literal/historical sense of words themselves. These additional meanings are the spiritual senses. The Victorines relied upon a fourfold division of meaning in the Bible: literal, allegorical, tropological, and anagogical. In the work of the Victorines, an example of the combination of word, thing, and things signified would be the word "Jerusalem" in a biblical text, interpreted as referring to a city as a thing, but allegorically referring to the church, tropologically to the human soul, and anagogically to the heavenly city of God (Ocker, pp. 263-64).

As specifically developed by Hugh of St. Victor, there are three kinds of literature or sources of knowledge, two secular and one sacred. Secular literature includes philosophy and poetry. Philosophical works include those of the liberal arts. Poetic works include tragedies, comedies, satires, heroic verse and lyric, iambics, didactic poems, fables, histories, and prose. The sacred literature, the Bible, is greater than all forms of secular literature, and is the highest source of knowledge. The Bible is superior to both philosophy and poetry, because not only do its words signify things, but those things signify other things beyond the literal meaning of the biblical text. The Bible makes the connection between the visible and the invisible realities more accurately than secular literature. To understand the things in the Bible is to move from the literal to an understanding of spiritual things. Thus, the Bible is the source for the knowledge of God (Ocker, pp. 263-64).

For the Victorines, the historical/literal meaning of the text provides the basis for the spiritual meaning. Thus, the literal meaning received much attention. Anselm of Laon (d. 1117) adapted the *trivium* from the liberal arts (grammar, rhetoric, and dialectic) to help determine the literal meaning of biblical texts. This emphasis upon the literal and historical sense of the Bible resulted in more sophisticated exegesis, and became the basis of theological debate. Such emphasis eventually contributed to the diminution of interest in the several spiritual senses. This strong distinction between the literal and spiritual meanings in texts was maintained by Roman Catholic as well as Protestant scholars (Ocker, pp. 264-65).

The Victorines and early scholasticism relied upon natural signification of words, which understands that the mind moves from words to things to find meaning. Late medieval scholasticism relied upon verbal signification, arguing that the mind has the ability to find meaning directly from words, rather than things, by signifying a thing metaphorically. This new reliance on verbal significance helped spur a growing emphasis on the literal sense of the biblical text as the seat of revelation and the source of theology. Allowances were made, however, for genuine figurative speech in Scripture, which was not intended to be understood literally (Ocker, pp. 263-64).

Late medieval scholastic interpreters had confidence that the literal reading of texts could provide theological and philosophical knowledge. Denys van Leeuwen, the great fifteenth-century compiler of medieval scholastic thought, argued that the literal meaning was the meaning that the author intended. The spiritual meaning of the text *was* the literal meaning. The Victorines were wrong in arguing that the literal meaning of words pointed to the things they signified, which were the source of the spiritual meaning. There was now an alternative to the early Christian adaptation of allegorical interpretation from the Greeks and Philo, and to the work on the figurative language that had found its best formulation in the work of the Victorines (Ocker, pp. 266-68).

RENAISSANCE HUMANISTS

Biblical studies during the Renaissance were heavily influenced by humanism, which recovered the works of classical antiquity, and gave them priority over the works of the Middle Ages. The rallying cry of the humanists was *ad fontes,* "back to the sources." The rhetoric and philology of antiquity replaced the Aristotelian logic of the Middle Ages as the core of education. In biblical studies, this meant recovering the Hebrew and Greek texts of the Bible, rather than relying on the Latin of the Vulgate. It also brought renewed interest in the works of the Greek and Latin fathers, rather than relying on the works of medieval commentators.

The cause of the humanists was greatly facilitated by the invention of the printing press. As classical texts were discovered, they could be printed and disseminated quickly. The humanists aided the printers by being their translators, editors, and proofreaders. In biblical studies, translations of the Bible and editions of patristic works were readily produced on the new presses.

The humanist use of philology to analyze the Bible, and the production of critical editions, created controversy. The humanists closely studied the history and transmission of the biblical text. Theologians saw this critical work as a challenge to inspiration by those less qualified to deal with Scripture. Also, in the mind of the Roman Catholic Church, the humanists' close attention to the biblical text and the critical editions they produced aligned them with the Reformers, who were stressing *sola scriptura.* It was especially noted that some of the corrections of the biblical text proposed by humanists supported the positions of the Reformers. Eventually, however, both the Roman Catholic Church and the Reformers adopted the philological tools of the humanists in the service of biblical interpretation (Rummel, pp. 280-81).

During the fifteenth century, a person could learn Hebrew or Greek only by hiring an individual with that language skill. By the sixteenth century, however, biblical languages could be studied formally in educational institutions. Hebrew was studied, but with ambivalence by some. Scholars considered Hebrew inferior to Greek, which was, after all, the language of philosophy and other major disciplines of antiquity. Even so, by the beginning of the sixteenth century, Christian humanist scholars were producing important works on Hebrew, including several grammars.

Giannozzo Manetti (1396-1459) was a counselor in the court of King Alfonso of Naples. Manetti studied Hebrew, and read the Old Testament and medieval Hebrew commentaries under the tutelage of Jewish scholars. When he published a new Latin translation of the Psalter, it was considered disrespectful, because the "divinely inspired" Vulgate translation of the Septuagint had been commissioned by Pope Damasus, and translated by Jerome. To tamper with the Vulgate was to challenge the authority of the Pope, of the Church, and of inspiration itself. Manetti wrote an *Apologeticus,* published with his translation of the Psalter, in which he argued that Jerome himself distinguished authors of Scripture, who wrote under divine inspiration, from translators, who had no such inspiration. Manetti also pointed out that the manuscripts of the Vulgate extant at his time had many textual variants, which necessitated textual criticism and modification of the Vulgate translation (Rummel, pp. 282-83).

Christian scholars could build upon the rich resources produced by Jewish scholars. Key among Jewish resources was the Soncino Bible, the first complete published Hebrew Bible. It was published by Israel Nathan b. Samuel and Abraham b. Hayyim (1488). Another edition of the Hebrew Bible was in the *Complutensian Polyglot*, which contained the Old Testament in Hebrew, Greek, and Latin. It was published in Spain in 1522 by Cardinal Francisco Ximénes de Cisneros and a team of humanist scholars. The Hebrew text was produced from collating several Hebrew manuscripts, and represents an early attempt at text criticism (Rummel, pp. 283-85).

One of the most learned of the editors of the *Complutensian Polyglot* was Elio Antonio de Nebrija of the University of Alcalá (c. 1444-1522). He published the *Tertia Quinquagena*, summarizing some of the key assumptions of humanist scholars in the sixteenth century: that the biblical text should be studied in the original languages; the best text of the Bible is derived through collating manuscripts; and textual and literary criticism of the Bible is best done through philology rather than theology. In 1514, Nebrija withdrew from the editorial team of the *Complutensian Polyglot*, objecting that the collation of biblical manuscripts was confined to manuscripts of the *same* language. He argued for changing the Hebrew, Greek, or Latin manuscripts in light of readings found in manuscripts of the other languages (Rummel, p. 285).

Careful examination of the *Complutensian Polyglot* reveals that some collation based on manuscripts in different languages did occur. However, when it did, the Hebrew and Greek were changed to conform to the Latin, and not vice-versa. This was true especially when a change required by the original languages might challenge a position of the church that was based on the Latin reading. This characteristic of the *Complutensian Polyglot* shows that textual criticism was not fully developed among the humanists, and that they were reluctant to directly challenge the teaching authority of the church with the implications of their work (Rummel, pp. 285-86).

Hebrew studies were greatly advanced by the Italian Dominican Sanctes Pagninus (1470-1536). When he produced a Latin translation of the Old and New Testaments (1527/28), the Old Testament translation was based on a careful study of the Hebrew text. This translation was the basis for many editions of the Bible published in the latter half of the sixteenth century. Pagninus also produced Hebrew grammars and dictionaries (Rummel, p. 286).

Another major humanist scholar interested in the Hebrew Bible was Jacques Lefèvre d'Etaples (c. 1460-1536) of the Collège du Cardinal Lemoine in Paris. He published the *Quincuplex Psalterium* (1509), which set the Old Latin, Gallican, Roman, and Hebrew Psalters in parallel columns. Sebastian Münster, professor of Hebrew at the Universities of Heidelberg and Basel, produced a Hebrew dictionary and a Hebrew grammar in collaboration with Eliah Levita (1469-1549), the leading Jewish philologist at that time. Münster also produced a Hebrew Bible with Latin translation, and notes from rabbinical sources (1535) (Rummel, p. 286).

The fall of Constantinople in 1453 created a flood of scholar refugees who fled to the West, especially Rome, with knowledge of Greek, and with their Greek manuscripts. This immigration renewed scholarly interest in the study of the Greek language, and in documents originally written in Greek, like the Septuagint, the New Testament, and the Greek fathers.

Another early humanist who studied the Greek texts was Aurelio Brandolini (c. 1454-97), who taught rhetoric at Pisa and Florence. He also produced a summary of the historical books of the Old Testament in a polished style, to make them more accessible to the general public. He was strongly criticized for essentially creating a new Bible, especially since he was not a theologian. Brandolini wrote an apology that served as a preface for the work. Like many humanist scholars after him, he argued that there is no rigid distinction between scholars of language and scholastic theologians. Both needed language skills, and both discussed God (Rummel, pp. 288-89).

One of the most influential humanist scholars of the fifteenth century was Lorenzo Valla (1405-57), who had an appointment in the papal court in Rome. He was a very early, gifted text critic, who understood the need to collate the readings of extant manuscripts as a means of determining the original reading of biblical texts. He collated Greek and Latin manuscripts of the Gospels, annotating the differences that he found. His work was eventually published by Erasmus as *Adnotationes in Novum Testament* (1505) (Rummel, pp. 289-90).

Erasmus (c. 1466-1536) was the founder of Christian humanism — that is, the combination of the new learning of the humanists with Christian devotion. He lived in Basel, and was the key figure of the humanists. Like Valla before him, he collated Greek and Latin manuscripts, and published important translations and editions of patristic works. He is more noted, however, for publishing the New Testament with a revised Latin translation and a Greek text (first edition 1516). His edition of the New Testament became the standard for subsequent translations.

Erasmus's Latin translation diverged from the Vulgate in ways that affected interpretation and theology. The edition came with annotations that explained his modifications of the Latin text in light of classical philology. In subsequent editions, the notes were supplemented by engagement with the theological controversies that his translation had evoked.

Overall, the emphasis upon philology, historical contexts, and textual criticism profoundly influenced biblical interpretation. These new studies led to critical texts of the patristic works, and of Scripture. Their emphasis on primary sources over later interpretation seriously undermined the medieval method of interpreting texts using the allegorical, tropological, and anagogical methods. It also demonstrated that interpretation of texts had never been uniform in the church (Rummel, pp. 293-94).

MARTIN LUTHER

As we turn to a discussion of biblical interpretation during the Reformation and subsequent years, we enter in some ways into a very different world. During the Middle Ages, the Roman Catholic Church in the West placed great importance in the study of the Bible, as seen in the discussions above. Yet, the interpretation of the Bible was always, ultimately, under the authority of the Church. The Church was the arbiter when disputes arose concerning the meaning of Scripture, a tradition of hierarchical authority that goes back deep into the early history of the church. The Eastern Orthodox Church also assumed the interpretation of the Scriptures within the church and by the church, looking especially to the Greek fathers of the first several centuries for guidance in the interpretation of Scripture. Judaism, which paid considerable attention to the interpretation of its Tanak, nevertheless looked to the Mishnah and Talmud for guidance in the everyday affairs of life. Rabbinic decisions were typically not made primarily on the basis of an analysis of scriptural passages, and the rabbis often gave several opinions on one particular issue. When, however, we turn to Reformation figures such as Luther, Melanchthon, and Calvin, we encounter a very different perspective, with Scripture now becoming the ultimate arbiter of all matters of faith and practice. These reformers used what they saw to be the clear light of Scripture to cut through what they regarded as the many years of misleading and, indeed, damning teachings of the church. While they regarded this as a very liberating perspective, freeing people to learn for themselves the truth of Scripture, the central truths of Scripture were not at all as obvious or unambiguous to everyone as these reformers imagined they would be. Perhaps the most significant forces unleashed by their work were considerable diversity of opinion, and fragmentation within Christendom. In essence, each interpreter was set loose to advocate a particular interpretive opinion, and these opinions proliferated and came to be held with tenacity by the various groups. This diversity has had both positive and negative consequences for many aspects of life, and, as we will see, it has profoundly impacted the last 500 years of biblical interpretation.

Born into a family of modest means, Luther (1483-1546) studied philosophy and had his sights set on a career in law. A vow to become a monk, made during a thunderstorm, changed all that. Experiencing in his early monastic years the very *Anfechtung* (spiritual struggle) about which he would later write so eloquently, Luther was overpowered by his feeling that he could never satisfy the demands of an angry God, before whose expectations he, a sinner, always fell woefully short. Luther's commitment to Scripture as the ultimate authority in matters of faith and life no doubt is closely tied to his finding in his study of Scripture the answer to his own profound spiritual dilemma.

As Thompson notes (p. 299), Luther, for all his impact on the history of the church, was not primarily a theologian or a church official; rather, he was "first and foremost a biblical scholar and a preacher." The exegetical material he produced is massive. During his career, Luther lectured on Psalms, Romans, Galatians, Hebrews, Deuteronomy, the Minor Prophets, Isaiah, 1 John, Titus, Philemon, 1 Timothy, and Genesis (some of these on more than one occasion). We have Luther's own manuscripts on these lectures, and often the notes of his students. He also has left behind a number of works commenting on the task of biblical interpretation, such as *On Translating: An Open Letter, How Christians Should Regard Moses*, and *A Brief Instruction on What to Look for and Expect in the Gospels*. The sheer volume of material Luther has left behind, as evidenced in the 55 volumes of the American Edition of his works, has no doubt contributed substantially to the variety of opinions and perspectives attributed to him. Scholars advocating substantially different perspectives have been able to find something in his many works which appears to support their position. As Thompson notes, "The evidence of the nineteenth and twentieth centuries alone would suggest that interpreters have found it quite difficult to allow Luther to speak on his own terms" (p. 299).

Luther's growing conviction that Scripture must be the final arbiter in all matters of faith and life led him eventually to rebel against the authority of the papacy and the Roman Church, and to insist that the teachings of the Roman Church must submit to the authority of Scripture. While no doubt both Luther and the Roman Church came early to realize the considerable implications of Luther's challenge, it is doubtful that either could foresee the sweeping changes that would result from the stance that Luther took, changes for the Roman Church and Western Civilization, and for the future of biblical interpretation. We now turn to a discussion of Luther's understanding of Scripture, and its interpretation.

Thompson views as crucial "Luther's identification of Scripture as the word of God." It is this word of God that reveals Christ, the Word of God, to the student of Scripture. Luther recognized clearly that "God himself is the object of our worship, not the biblical text. But this did not prevent Luther from referring to Scripture in an unqualified fashion as the Word of God, and precisely for that reason according it a peculiar respect, and demanding that it be handled with care." Luther's "identification of the text [of Scripture] as the God's Word . . . explains Luther's tenacity when it comes to the actual wording of controversial passages" (p. 300). The exact words, and the order in which they appear, must be taken seriously, in order to avoid fanciful interpretations. Luther's position in this regard becomes especially clear in his disputations with Zwingli and others on the interpretation of the words of institution for the Lord's Supper. Luther, who argued for the "real presence" of Christ in the Lord's Supper, railed against Zwingli for trying to water down the meaning of the words "This is my body" by suggesting that they meant "this represents my body." Thompson quotes Luther: "For if they believed that these were God's words, they would not call them 'poor, miserable words,' but would prize a single tittle and letter more highly than the whole world, and would fear and tremble before them as before God himself. For he who despises a single word of God certainly prizes none at all" (p. 302).

Luther's commitment to the importance of studying the Scriptures in their original languages (for those capable of doing so) also reflects his strong sense of the authority of the biblical text. This respect for the Bible's authority is further reflected in his translation of Scripture into German, the vernacular of his people. Few Germans could read the Bible in its original languages, and Luther felt it to be vital that all people be able to study the word of God for themselves, with its true meaning reflected as accurately as possible in German. Luther did not, however, insist on a literal, word-for-word correspondence between words in the biblical languages and words in German. Thompson discusses Luther's famous translation of Rom. 3:28, in which he added the word "alone," arguing that it was necessary to do so in order to convey effectively the meaning of the Greek. According to Thompson, "The Greek words and the order of those words were the divinely appointed means of conveying a particular meaning in the original setting; the responsibility of the translator was to convey that same meaning as faithfully and clearly as possible in the receptor language" (p. 302). Clearly, Luther's understanding of a text involved presenting as clearly and articulately as possible the sense of the passage, rather than simply presenting the literal meaning of the accumulated words. Conveying the sense of the passage is crucial, because the Scriptures, as the word of God, are the final authority in all matters of faith and life.

Luther believed that Scripture, if studied fairly and with an open heart, conveyed its meaning with resounding clarity, and interpreted itself, with one passage shedding light on another. He consistently asserted this position throughout his career. Without his commitment to this clarity of Scripture, Luther's position on the authority of Scripture would have been meaningless. Regarding Scripture as being its own interpreter, Thompson notes, "Luther reacted against the medieval practice of explaining Scripture in terms of the comments made on each passage by the exegetes and theologians of the past. This 'glossing of the glosses,' rather than direct engagement with the biblical text, robbed Christian people of the enlightening treasure of God's word" (p. 304). Rather than depending on the comments of the fathers, Luther encouraged his students to focus on the context in which a biblical passage appears, and to rely on other, clearer passages that deal with the same issue as is found in a difficult passage.

Luther emphatically asserted the "Christ principle," arguing that the entire Bible gives testimony to Jesus Christ. Thompson says, quoting Luther, "Every prophecy and every prophet must be understood as referring to Christ the Lord, except where it is clear from plain words that someone else is spoken of." Luther presents a very picturesque image "of the Scriptures (in particular the Old Testament) as the swaddling cloths in which Christ is to be found." "Luther's point is that a knowledge of the words, grammatical constructions, and other features of the text is penultimate. The goal of studying the Scriptures is the knowledge of Christ and the response of faith" (Thompson, p. 305). Thus, the primary function of Scripture is to point people to Christ. "To expound the Scriptures . . . without reference to Christ is to distort their message" (p. 306). In assessing Luther's contributions to the history of biblical interpretation, Thompson stresses the importance of Luther's strong sense of the unity of Scripture, and Luther's emphasis on the ability of Scripture to give a clear testimony to Christ and the salvation he brings.

Thompson notes that Luther, when learning his skills as an exegete, would have studied the *Quadriga,* a scholastic tradition for identifying a literal sense and three spiritual senses in a text. Nicholas of Lyra (1270-1349) had subdivided the literal sense "into the literal-historical sense and the literal-prophetic sense. This gave a higher profile to the original historical situation of OT texts while it preserved a prophetic reference to Christ" (p. 307). Luther was negative about the literal-historical sense, viewing it as the "letter that kills." Instead, Luther chose to focus on Lyra's literal-prophetic sense which, according to Luther, conveyed the life-giving spirit. This had major implications for Luther's interpretation of Scripture. For example, in interpreting Psalm 4, Luther asserts, "the present psalm is understood first of all concerning Christ, who calls and is heard; then allegorically, concerning the church . . . ; and finally, in a tropological sense, concerning any holy soul" (Thompson, p. 308, quoting Luther). Crucial here is Luther's argument that the reference to Christ is the literal sense of the passage. Luther was not interested in tying the psalms to their historical situation as words from God to Israel prior to the coming of Christ. As Thompson notes, "Even as late as his treatment of Psalm 119 he could insist that the prophetic sense is the literal sense." Luther noted that "Our first concern will be for the grammatical meaning, for this is the true theological meaning." According to Thompson, Luther "sought to do justice both to the literal meaning of the text in its Old Testament context and its focus on Christ, which he remained convinced was the intention of the Holy Spirit" (Thompson, p. 308).

While medieval interpretation often talked about a letter/spirit antithesis, with the more edifying (and important) spiritual sense hidden within the literal sense or letter, Luther gradually moved away from this understanding. Although he never completely abandoned allegory and the spiritual senses of Scripture, he became more concerned that the pursuit of spiritual meanings could lead away from the clear message of Scripture, and so Luther moved to a different understanding of the dynamic of Scripture, one which maintains its clear christological focus. Luther's growing focus on the distinction between law and gospel is perhaps his most significant contribution to the history of biblical interpretation. "Instead of looking behind the law for its deeper meaning, Luther repeatedly encouraged his readers to look forward to its fulfillment and resolution in the gospel of Jesus Christ. The law reveals human sinfulness and so drives us to Christ; the gospel is the answer to that sinfulness and offers us the forgiveness and life that can only be found in Christ (Thompson, p. 309). Luther's understanding of law and gospel pervades both the Old and the New Testaments, and Luther certainly would not have been content with calling the Old Testament "law" and the New Testament "gospel." "There is no book in the Bible which does not contain both. Everywhere God has placed law and promise side by side. Through the law he teaches us what must be done; through the promise, how we can do it" (Thompson, p. 310, quoting Luther). As Luther sees it, the law convinces the sinner of his guilt, while the gospel conveys the good news of God's salvation offered through Christ. Since after salvation the righteous person continues to be a sinner, the person must continually be confronted and accused by the law, and receive forgiveness through the gospel of Christ. The study of Scripture, therefore, is a process of continually being confronted by the law, which accuses, and by the gospel, which delivers, and this process must permeate a person's life and study of Scripture. As Thompson notes, "Only then will believers genuinely despair of their good works and flee from god to God. Rightly dividing law and gospel is thus a hermeneutical necessity with immense pastoral implications" (p. 310).

As Luther's position on law and gospel clearly shows, the study of Scripture is not, for Luther, primarily an academic activity; rather it is a religious activity, and ongoing experience of the life of faith. This *Anfechtung*, or spiritual struggle, comes when one is confronted with God's revelation of himself. As Thompson notes, it "is not simply a matter of precision in handling the text, but of recognizing your position before the God who addressees you by means of this text" (p. 311). Thus, interpretation involves not so much human ingenuity, but rather a profound spiritual dimension. Thompson quotes Luther: "It is absolutely certain that one cannot enter into the Scripture by study or innate intelligence. Therefore your first task is to begin with prayer. . . . You must . . . completely despair of your own diligence and intelligence and rely solely on the infusion of the Spirit" (p. 311). The roots of Luther's conviction are not simply a "theology of humility," such as espoused by Bernard of Clairvaux, but lie deeper "in a long tradition of *lectio divina*, 'sacred reading,' which has been shown to have been joined to the academic study of Scripture by the scholars of the Abbey of St. Victor in Paris." As Thompson notes, "The interpreter of Scripture is first and foremost a forgiven sinner standing in the presence of his Creator, Redeemer, and Judge" (p. 312). Here, in his commitment to personal spiritual struggle as a key to understanding the text, as seen also in the *lectio divina* of many medieval communities, is one of Luther's strongest ties to the heritage of interpretation in the medieval church.

As Thompson notes, an aspect of Luther's approach to interpretation that is often overlooked is his emphasis on the spoken word. "There is a peculiarly aural nature to the Scriptures which is connected to the very nature of the relationship between the living God and his people. This is especially and essentially the case with the New Testament, which Luther held was not in the first instance a document, but rather a sermon" (Thompson, p. 312). In Luther's opinion, hearing is better than reading, because "the live voice teaches, exhorts, defends, and resists the spirit of error" (Thompson, p. 312, quoting Luther). Since God has not allowed himself to be seen by us directly, but rather reveals himself to us by means of words, as the *Deus absconditus* (hidden God), words, rather than images, are best able to confront the Christian disciple with the promises of God. In Luther's view, the Scriptures are not ancient documents describing what God has done in the past. Rather, they are immediate and contemporary, speaking directly to the hearer with words that address the hearer's need. Thus, interpretation is not primarily a matter of perceiving what the word of God is; rather, it is important to determine what the word of God says to you, how it applies to your own life.

Thompson warns "of the danger of undue systematization when it comes to Luther's principles of biblical interpretation" (p. 315). He was driven more by the text than he was by the need to systematize, a task he left to others, such as Melanchthon. Without question, Luther's influence on the subsequent history of biblical interpretation "has been immense. He played a major role in the eclipse of medieval exegetical methods. The search for spiritual meanings in biblical passages was replaced by an investigation of the theological import of the simple grammatical sense and the contexts of biblical passages" (p. 315). Luther's focusing on the law-gospel dynamic required a christological approach to all of Scripture, and stressed the impact of the teachings of Scripture on the life of the Christian believer. His emphasis on Scripture as the word of God, which he saw as the unchallengeable authority on matters of faith and life, set a new course not only for biblical interpretation, but also for the political and social life of the western world in the Post-Reformation era.

PHILIP MELANCHTHON

The skill and influence of Philip Melanchthon (1497-1560) as a biblical interpreter have often been overlooked, due to his close association with his more senior and highly famous colleague Martin Luther, and because Melanchthon has been primarily remembered as a systematic thinker and writer, as, for example, in his composition of the *Augsburg Confession* (1530). Like Luther, he had fairly humble beginnings, and advanced by virtue of his skill and hard work. Philip Schwartzerdt was orphaned at age nine by the death of his father, and raised in the household of the humanist and Hebraist Johannes Reuchlin, who directed his education, and gave him the hellenized form of his name, Melanchthon (black earth). While teaching Greek at the University of Wittenberg, Melanchthon began his theological studies under Luther, forging the close bond that would endure as long as both men lived. While Melanchthon's work in biblical interpretation shared a good deal with Luther's work, as in the stress of both men on the law-gospel hermeneutic for interpreting Scripture, Melanchthon made major contributions of his own through the commentaries he produced, through his carrying forward important principles of medieval and patristic biblical interpretation, through his use of "certain humanist techniques to develop a new rhetorical approach to the Bible, especially the Pauline corpus" (Wengert, p. 319), and through his blending dialectics with the Lutheran law-gospel hermeneutic.

Wengert indicates that scholars disagree about Melanchthon's humanistic background. Some, such as Maurer, see Melanchthon as a humanistic philosopher who was committed to the humanistic agenda "that champions the human being and its powers and is tied to certain anthropological and theological presuppositions from classical antiquity" (Wengert, p. 321, describing Maurer's position). Wengert disagrees, preferring instead to see Melanchthon not as a scholar championing humanism and its philosophical perspective, but rather as a humanist committed to "a common methodology and approach to texts marked by a concern for the sources *(ad fontes),* for history, and for poetics, and by a proper use of the classical languages (Latin and, later, Greek and even Hebrew) and their literatures" (Wengert, p. 321). Wengert argues that Melanchthon used the methods he had learned as a humanist to present his Lutheran convictions about the biblical texts he interpreted.

As Wengert notes, Melanchthon's volume of annotations on Romans and 1-2 Corinthians, which was published in 1522, "marked something of a revolution in the interpretation of Paul, and especially of Romans. Melanchthon was the first Christian exegete to organize and analyze Romans thoroughly on the basis of standard rules of rhetoric" (Wengert, p. 321). While ancient writers had occasionally observed Paul's use of rhetoric in his writings, medieval commentaries by and large bypassed such interests. However, "the rise of humanism in the fifteenth century brought a renewed interest in proper speaking and the use of Cicero and Quintilian for constructing good speeches and analyzing ancient ones" (Wengert, p. 322). In 1519, Melanchthon published a rhetorical handbook, *De rhetorica libri tres,* one of a number published during this period. Melanchthon's lectures on Romans in the early 1520s "laid out in meticulous detail the rhetorical contours of Paul's letter" (Wengert, p. 322). Furthermore, Melanchthon was interested in the *dispositio* (shape) of the text, which included the *epigraphē* (address), *exordium* (main body of arguments and responses to objections), and a conclusion. Melanchthon was also interested in the rhetorical turns of phrase and figures of speech that Paul uses. Melanchthon also focused on locating the central ar-

gument *(status)* of an author in any composition, and for him the *status* of
Romans "is that we are justified by faith" (Wengert, p. 322, quoting Melanchthon). Throughout his career, Melanchthon used rhetorical categories as
tools to interpret biblical texts. His lectures on John analyze some of Jesus'
speeches as orations, and his analysis of Old Testament books, especially
Psalms, uses rhetorical categories, as do his work on Colossians and his later
treatment of Romans. Melanchthon challenged Erasmus' interpretation of
Colossians, arguing that Erasmus ignored the *status* of the epistle.

A second cornerstone of Melanchthon's interpretive method was his
use of dialectical categories. He published his first book on dialectics in 1520,
and published in 1521 his lectures on rhetoric, in which he listed four genres
of speeches: demonstrative, deliberative, judicial, and didactic, having himself added this last, teaching category to the three classical genres of speech.
The basic rules of didactics come not from rhetoric, but from dialectics,
commonly used in the classrooms of Melanchthon's day. Dialectics involved
weighing and reconciling contradictory or associated arguments for the purpose of arriving at an answer which would resolve the conflict. Melanchthon's methodological interest in using a combination of rhetoric and dialectics had a powerful impact on his biblical interpretation. "Melanchthon
viewed Romans 5:12–8:39 as a *methodus,* or dialectical arguments on the
theological topics *(loci)* of sin, law, and grace" (Wengert, p. 323). This enabled Melanchthon to overcome the concerns of those who argued that Paul
was inconsistent in following the rules of good letter writing. "In the middle
of a good piece of rhetoric, Melanchthon argued, Paul had inserted specific,
dialectical arguments proving with certainty that human beings are justified
by faith" (Wengert, pp. 323-24). Furthermore, Melanchthon's interest in dialectics led him to focus on *loci communes,* or commonplaces. As Wengert
notes, citing Wiedenhofer, *loci communes* "denote the principles and essence
of a particular intellectual subject" (p. 324). Melanchthon used *loci communes* "in his biblical interpretation . . . as axioms derived from the central
principles and essence of theology. In Romans, Paul himself had . . . laid out
these *loci communes,* and developed a series of dialectical arguments concerning them" (Wengert, p. 325). This discussion concerning Paul's use of
loci communes in Romans led Melanchthon to conclude that Romans itself is
the key to understanding the primary themes of all of Scripture. "The Epistle
of Romans is didactic, teaching what the gospel is and, indeed, the source of
justification, and it is truly like a *methodus* of the entire Scripture and the
whole letter consists in one *locus:* the source of justification" (Wengert,
p. 325, quoting Melanchthon). Luther, likely under the influence of
Melanchthon's work, asserts in his 1522 preface to Romans, "This epistle is

really the chief part of the New Testament, and is truly the purest gospel" (Wengert, p. 325, quoting Luther). Here we have what many have called the Lutheran "canon within a canon."

Melanchthon used the *loci communes* he found in Paul as the basis for *Commonplaces of Theological Matters,* or *Theological Standards,* which he published in 1521. As Wengert notes, this was Protestantism's first systematic theology. Convinced that he had now found in Paul, and especially in the epistle to the Romans, the basic topics of Scripture, Melanchthon could organize all of Scripture within these encompassing categories. Likewise, when interpreting a particular biblical passage, he "could interrupt his interpretation of a specific passage to handle the general *locus communis* to which it was connected" (Wengert, p. 326).

As Wengert notes, Melanchthon considered the two most important dialectical questions to concern: what a thing is *("Quid sit?"),* and what its effects are *("Quid effectus").* Thus, "for Melanchthon, "the exegete must not simply inquire after the definition of a thing (intimately related to its *locus communis*), but also after its effect or impact on the hearer. . . . In fact, the deep concern for a thing's effect or purpose, especially as it 'moved the heart,' marked much of Renaissance humanism" (Wengert, p. 326). This interfaced nicely with the Lutheran hermeneutic concerning law and gospel, which not only analyzed a text as law or gospel, but also analyzed the effect of the text, as word of God, upon the hearer. Rather than trying to escape the literal sense of the text to uncover the more edifying and useful spiritual sense, as was often done in medieval interpretation, the exegete's purpose now was to see how "the text itself, as God's destroying and creating word, effected death and life (or terror and comfort) in the hearer" (Wengert, p. 327). This stress on meaning and effect was characteristic of Lutheran interpretation, and certainly dominated Melanchthon's interpretation. Like Luther, Melanchthon emphasized that law and gospel are found throughout the various books of Scripture, and he did not equate law with the Old Testament and gospel with the New Testament. This hermeneutical distinction between law and gospel was, for Melanchthon, key to understanding the Christian doctrine of justification. Where this distinction is extinguished, the doctrine of justification can be badly misunderstood, as in the case of the "Papists," who, according to Melanchthon, view people to be righteous and to merit forgiveness of their sins by their own works.

While the distinction between law and gospel was crucial to Lutheran biblical hermeneutics, it became necessary to distinguish between the various uses of the law. In 1522 Luther, "building on a suggestion by Nicholas of Lyra for uses of the law in Israel, . . . expanded it to God's two uses of the law among all people: a first, or civil, use to keep order in the world and restrain the wicked; a second, or theological, use that puts to death, or terrifies, the conscience by revealing its sin" (Wengert, p. 328). In 1534, in his commentary on Colossians, Melanchthon discusses a third use, which later Lutheran theologians called the "didactic." According to Melanchthon, in this third use, Christians studied the law to discern God's will so they could try to structure their lives according to it. The *Formula of Concord* (1580) saw this third use of the law as a guide to life, showing the works God desires. Calvin followed Melanchthon in defining three uses of the law in his *Institutes of the Christian Religion* (1536).

Melanchthon's work in biblical interpretation and associated areas was both productive and influential. His respect for patristic studies and for medieval biblical interpretation was emulated by many Protestant interpreters. He published a Greek grammar in 1518. As already noted, he also published books on rhetoric and dialectics. He also produced textbooks on theology which, as one can gather from previous discussions, Melanchthon was convinced "guided the reader in constructing appropriate theological commonplaces for biblical texts" (Wengert, p. 329). All Scripture was infused with the basic themes of Christian theology. The theological curriculum of Wittenberg, delineated by Melanchthon, required regular lecturing on Romans, John, the Psalms, Genesis, and Isaiah, in addition to Augustine's treatment of Pauline theology, *On the Spirit and the Letter*. Melanchthon was also interested in the geography of the Holy Land, publishing an edition of a work by Eusebius (which, in turn, was based on work by Jerome) treating Hebrew place names, as well as a new map of Palestine and Melanchthon's explanations of some place names. He also was working on a history of the world, having gotten to Charlemagne by the time of his death in 1560. In this work, he paid great attention to the reconstruction of biblical history. In addition, he was involved in a Wittenberg project to translate the Bible into German and Latin, contributing his own translations of 1 and 2 Maccabees. He also wrote numerous discussions of biblical themes.

While not as prolific as Luther in commenting on Old Testament books, Melanchthon did treat them extensively. He published works treating portions of Genesis and Exodus, and published works on Psalms on several occasions. He wrote introductions to Isaiah, Jeremiah, Lamentations, Haggai, Zechariah, and Malachi. He published several commentaries on Proverbs, in which he focused on the theological orientation of Proverbs, and, in his last commentary on Proverbs, he "stressed the difference between Solomon's proverbs and pagan writers" (Wengert, p. 331). He also published a commentary on Ecclesiastes. Melanchthon had a strong interest in the book of Daniel.

Sharing Luther's interest in the end of the world, Melanchthon interpreted Daniel's visions (chs. 7–12) "as predictions of history from the prophet's time to 1542, where the last, savage monarchy is the Turks" (Wengert, p. 331). This apocalyptic expectation evidenced by Luther and Melanchthon was fairly common among sixteenth-century Lutherans.

Melanchthon wrote two *postils,* commentaries on the Gospel texts that were read during the church year. Two works on Matthew appeared, neither apparently published with Melanchthon's consent, one based upon his 1519-1520 lectures on Matthew, the other consisting of sermon helps on difficult Matthean passages. His most significant work on the Gospels focused on John. His first commentary, published by Luther in 1523, was the first Protestant commentary on John. In it, "Melanchthon interpreted the entire Fourth Gospel as not simply as opposing christological heresies, as medieval and patristic exegetes had done, but as aimed at the problem of salvation and faith, as reflected in John 1:12. . . . By refocusing interpretation of John on faith and salvation, Melanchthon introduced an entirely new set of interpretive questions for Johannine exegesis and refocused many old ones" (Wengert, p. 332).

As already noted, Melanchthon's interpretation of Romans played a decisive role in the development of Protestant biblical exegesis. While Luther's lectures on Romans in 1515-1516 were not available in print until recent times, Melanchthon's comments were available beginning in 1522, and he continued to lecture and publish on Romans throughout his life. He also published works on 1 and 2 Corinthians. His commentary on Colossians went through several editions. In the 1528 edition, he took issue with Erasmus. "Whereas Erasmus viewed the early chapters of Colossians (especially ch. 2) in light of Paul's fight against Judaizers and thus regarded them as having very little practical application, Melanchthon viewed them as a summary of the entire gospel and, among other things, a refutation of justification by works or merit" (Wengert, pp. 333-34). As noted above, Melanchthon presented for the first time, in the 1534 edition, the concept of the third use of the law. Melanchthon also commented on 1 and 2 Timothy.

Melanchthon's influence upon his contemporaries and upon subsequent generations of interpreters was considerable. "He combined the latest literary techniques of Renaissance humanism with developments in Reformation theology to produce some of the most important commentaries of his age. His unique approach, especially in Paul's epistle to the Romans, combined rhetorical analysis of letters with a dialectical understanding of the main themes of Christian theology" (Wengert, p. 336). Melanchthon's commentary on Romans clearly influenced Calvin's interpretation of Romans. In addition to his commentaries on Romans, Melanchthon's commentaries on Colossians, Proverbs, and Daniel exerted substantial influence on Protestant commentators for generations.

JOHN CALVIN

John Calvin (1509-64), the French Protestant reformer from Geneva, was one of the central figures in the interpretation of the Bible during the Reformation. His pivotal role is partly explained by the volume of his written works and their wide distribution during his lifetime. He wrote commentaries on most of the books of the Bible. Scribes preserved his numerous extemporaneous sermons. Along with many of his contemporaries, Calvin insisted that Scripture alone was the ultimate authority in matters of faith and practice, and that the core teachings of the Bible are clear. He united the learning of the humanists with an increased emphasis upon the authority of Scripture. As a humanist, he was trained in Greek, Hebrew, history, and philosophy. However, he considered the Spirit of God to be the source of ultimate truth as the Spirit makes the Scripture the Word of God for believers (Pitkin, pp. 341-42).

Until recently, Calvin's interpretation has been considered highly distinctive, even unique. Two developments in scholarship have changed that perspective. First, new and important studies of medieval exegesis demonstrate that a wide variety of interpretive methods were already in place. This variety was augmented by the development of new methods of interpretation. There was also a wide range of attitudes concerning scriptural authority. Thus, recent scholarship facilitates and demands a more nuanced comparison of Calvin's biblical interpretation with that of his predecessors and contemporaries (Pitkin, pp. 342-44).

Second, previous scholarship on Calvin focused on his doctrine of Scripture, issues of biblical authority, or his understanding of the methods and goals of interpretation. Recent study has shifted to interpretation within the context of his commentaries and sermons. Examination of his actual works demonstrates that Calvin's exegesis stands on past exegetical tradition, as well as more contemporary developments in biblical scholarship. His work exhibits attitudes toward scriptural authority that can be found in the preceding medieval era, but grew to fruition in the sixteenth century (Pitkin, pp. 342-45).

The contemporary scholarly quest explores both the continuity and the discontinuity between Calvin's interpretation and the interpretation of the church fathers and other Reformers, thereby placing Calvin's hermeneutic within the broader history of interpretation, as well as developments in his own time. These efforts are accompanied by a study of the specific sources that Calvin used in his sermons, lectures, and commentaries, and how he used them. Calvin seems to have had access to a limited number of works by the church fathers; furthermore, he tended to cite sources from memory, and not identify these sources unless he wanted to disagree with them (Pitkin, pp. 345-46).

Calvin's biblical interpretation shares several emphases with previous exegetical traditions. Like those who preceded him, Calvin tried to reconcile the letter of Scripture with its spiritual meaning, respected and incorporated the exegesis of the church fathers, and paid careful attention to grammar and philology. Thus, Calvin's emphasis on the literal sense of Scripture and repudiation of allegory, his respect for and incorporation of the exegesis of the church fathers (especially Chrysostom and Augustine), and use of biblical languages and classical rhetoric are not unique to Calvin, but continue various strands of medieval interpretation (Pitkin, p. 346).

Calvin shared with his contemporaries a strong focus on the literal sense of Scripture. This concern to find a *single* literal sense was something new. Whereas previous interpreters understood the Scripture to have one literal and three spiritual senses (allegory, tropology, and anagogy), Calvin and his contemporaries found the spiritual sense *within* the literal interpretation, not beyond it. They not only consulted directly the tradition of interpretation of the past, but were conditioned by such interpretation to make certain assumptions and ask certain questions of the text, and to expect a certain range of answers. Calvin and his contemporaries also shared with medieval exegetes a concern for the grammar and philology of the biblical text. Thus, the increased skill in biblical languages was not a new development in exegesis; rather, it was a shift from Latin to Greek and Hebrew (Pitkin, pp. 346-49).

Another way to understand Calvin's interpretation is to look at the relationship between his theological works and his exegetical works. Such comparison allows us to see which passages were the norms of his theology and his exegesis, and how his theology shaped his exegesis and his exegesis shaped his theology. This relationship between theology and exegesis can be seen in Calvin's extensive program of teaching the Bible, especially at Geneva. He taught the Bible in academic lectures in Latin for students, sermons in French for the general population, commentaries in Latin and French for educated laity and clergy, and Bible study in French for laity and clergy (Pitkin, pp. 349-50).

A chief characteristic of Calvin's extensive teaching was that he interpreted the Bible verse-by-verse and book-by-book, rather than by themes.

Typically, Calvin's pattern of interpretation was to read the biblical text to be interpreted, make some philological, historical, and theological comments to explain the text, and then apply the text to the situation of his audience. He would tailor this pattern to each audience, giving students and clergy more philological, historical, and theological comments, but giving the general population more application to their situation. He used more philological, historical, and theological interpretation in written commentaries and lectures, while using less in sermons. This was an outgrowth of his rhetorical training, which emphasized the need to accommodate the message to the audience (Pitkin, pp. 350-52).

There are several prominent features of Calvin's interpretation of the Bible. One is "lucid brevity" *(perspicua brevitas)*. Calvin would begin by exploring the philological, rhetorical, historical, and theological aspects of the text being interpreted, and the history of its interpretation. Then, he would minimize all of these in favor of a concise and clear exposition of the text, modeling the fundamental clarity of Scripture itself. This approach applied to all forms of Calvin's exposition — sermon, lecture, and commentary — although there would be more technical detail in the lectures and commentary. Thus, lucid brevity was tailored to the situation and nature of the audience.

Another feature of Calvin's interpretation is his determination to find the mind of the author *(mens scriptoris)*, that is, to find the author's intention in writing. Whereas ancient and medieval interpreters looked for multiple meanings that God, the author of Scripture, intended, Calvin looked for what the human biblical author, under the guidance of the Holy Spirit, intended. He found the mind of the biblical author from the literal-historical sense of the text — the meaning conveyed by the words. This literal-historical sense included both the events that the author was describing, and the spiritual teachings he was trying to convey. These spiritual teachings were applicable both to the original audience and to later generations of Christians. Once the mind of the author was discovered, Calvin drew analogies between the situation addressed by the author and the situation(s) of his audience, and then applied moral and doctrinal lessons for the edification of members of his audience (Pitkin, pp. 352-55).

It is this combination of traditional elements of interpretation in a comprehensive program that makes Calvin so remarkable: verse-by-verse exposition, the literal sense understood as the home of spiritual significance, emphasis on being clear and brief, emphasis on the mind of the human author of Scripture, and application of Scripture to the situation of his audience (Pitkin, p. 355).

What is truly unique about Calvin's interpretation is an emphasis on the integrity and unity of the biblical past, the role of Paul in interpretation, and harsh criticism of biblical personages. Calvin saw a continuity from the history of Israel, through the early church, to his own time. The lesson that the biblical author expressed through the history he narrated was applicable to his own audience and to future audiences of Scripture. This continuity is also apparent in Calvin's interpretation of prophecy and the use of the Old Testament in the New Testament (Pitkin, pp. 355-57). Calvin's biblical theology and hermeneutic were shaped by Pauline theology as it came to him in the broad stream of tradition. This tradition did not provide him with authorities to quote in the medieval sense, but with shared questions and concerns. Calvin was very severe in his assessment of biblical figures, especially those in leadership, such as the patriarchs. He did not resort to traditional exegesis that attempted to minimize the sins of biblical figures. This is due both to his low estimate of human nature, both fallen and regenerate, and to his pastoral desire to use biblical figures as models for behavior. He did not want the misconduct of biblical figures to be imitated by the faithful for whose benefit he interpreted the texts. Calvin's exegetical principles and practices in his written works were very influential in the development of biblical studies in the period following the Reformation. This is especially true of his insistence on discovering the intention of the author through careful linguistic study, as well as investigation into the literary and historical context of the biblical books.

THE ENGLISH REFORMATION

As we turn to the English Reformation and its perspective on biblical interpretation, it would be tempting to focus on the fact that the English Reformation had its immediate cause in the political needs of King Henry VIII to have a male heir, more than in a more theologically-driven parting of the ways with the Roman Church, as in the case of Luther, Zwingli, and Calvin. That would, however, gloss over the different nature and character of the English Reformation and of biblical interpretation in England, whose roots go back deep into the Middle Ages. For that reason, Gibbs begins his discussion with medieval figures such as Bede, Alcuin, the Victorines, and Wycliffe. Gibbs also cautions that the Protestant Reformers, including certainly those in England, have "more in continuity with trajectories of medieval biblical interpretation than with tendencies in modern so-called 'critical' exegesis" (Gibbs, p. 373).

Gibbs notes that the Latin Bible played a key role in English Christianity from its beginning. "In no part of the western world was this version of Scripture studied more diligently and copied more carefully than in Great Britain and Ireland. One of the most reliable extant mss. of the Vulgate was made in England . . . and presented to Pope Gregory II in 716" (Gibbs, p. 374). Another key factor in early English Christianity was the authority accorded to the church fathers, as evidenced in the Venerable Bede (672-735), whom some consider as the last of the church fathers.

Although primarily remembered today for his *Ecclesiastical History of the English People,* Bede regarded himself first and foremost as a biblical interpreter. Bede analyzed rhetorical figures and tropes in both the Old Testament and the New Testament in *De schematibus et tropis.* He also studied Greek and a little Hebrew, but his exegetical efforts focused on the Vulgate and the Latin tradition surrounding it. His commentaries are basically lengthy series of notes on various biblical texts, drawn from established church fathers such as Ambrose, Augustine, Jerome, and Gregory. Bede did, however, also exhibit considerable independence in his own interpretation of particular texts. Since there were few educated laity in western Europe at this time, his commentaries were intended predominantly for the clergy. Bede's work was intended "to enhance private devotional study and the reading of Scripture in church and monastic services, but also to train English clergy to better carry out their missionary activity of making converts among the unlettered pagans" (Gibbs, p. 375). Bede continued the tradition of using allegory, seeing it to be useful especially for the purpose of spiritual edification.

Alcuin of York (c. 735-804), an English student of Bede's who became a key figure in the court of Charlemagne, set out in his commentaries to gather as much material from patristic sources as possible. He was very careful to avoid writing anything that was contrary to the interpretations of the fathers. "Bible study meant study of the sacred text together with the fathers; the two kinds of authority were inseparable" (Gibbs, p. 376). The Norman monk Lanfranc (d. 1089) went even further, relying heavily on the patristic writings, and regarded any new interpretations of scriptural passages as arrogant. John Scotus Eriugena (c. 810-877), an Irishman who also went to the Carolingian court "possessed a sufficient knowledge of Greek to enable him to consult works written in that language, [and] . . . to notice a number of discrepancies between what the Greek fathers had taught and what was generally accepted in his day" (Gibbs, p. 376). Consequently, he often questioned these accepted authorities, and noted that, at times, they even contradicted each other. Thus, the works of the fathers had to have a lower status than Scripture which, because it is inspired, could not be self-contradictory. In his *Commentary on the Gospel of John,* he noted that the fathers, as human authorities, had a lesser authority than the divine authority of Scripture.

Eriugena strove for a sound intellectual understanding of the text, and was disinclined to agree with the sharp distinction often made between the word and its spiritual meaning. Since the language of the text itself contains everything needed, he worked diligently to discern the best possible text, studying the textual variants himself.

Gibbs notes the two major paths taken in later medieval biblical exegesis, both of which were important venues for the treatment of biblical interpretation during the English Reformation. The first approach, as noted previously, focused on the fourfold interpretation of Scripture, with the literal sense leading to the three spiritual senses: the allegorical, the tropological or moral, and the anagogical. The basics of this system can be traced back to Origen. Gibbs notes that these three spiritual senses have "been regarded by most modern scholars of the 'critical' persuasion to be subjective, fanciful, and irrelevant. . . . But new literary and reader-oriented approaches in recent biblical interpretation make accessible not only a new appreciation of past exegesis, but also offer the possibility for contemporary readers to seek and find meaning and relevance in the medieval expositions of the spiritual senses of Scripture" (Gibbs, p. 378). The reader is referred to Gibbs's discussion of Leclercq, de Lubac, and Smalley on this subject (Gibbs, pp. 378-79).

The second approach, which pursued a more literal and historical form of exegesis, is exemplified in the school of St. Victor in France, discussed above. Several of its leading figures, Hugh, Richard, Andrew, Herbert of Bosham, and Stephen Langton, were English. While Hugh (1096-1141) encouraged both symbolic interpretation and the serious study of the literal meaning among his students, one of them, Andrew (d. 1175), strongly pursued the second option. Andrew "had a strong preference for the literal sense of Scripture . . . [and] believed that the meaning of a text had to be sought in the text itself, and not in external authorities, however venerable they might be." His consultation of Jewish scholars, noted above, was unusual for a Christian scholar of his age, and from these Jewish scholars he learned the subtleties of the Hebrew text. The fifteen manuscripts of his commentaries which have been discovered "reveal an awareness of Hebrew almost unique in the Middle Ages" up to that time. Andrew's pupil Herbert of Bosham (c. 1162-1194) went further than Andrew, and undertook the study of Hebrew. Like his teacher Andrew, Herbert "was ready to acknowledge that OT passages quoted in the NT as messianic may not have been so intended by the original authors" (Gibbs, p. 380), examples being Ps. 68:18 and Isaiah 53. Richard (c. 1123-1173) was more interested in pursuing the spiritual sense of Scripture, as in his commentaries on Song of Songs and on Daniel 2. Yet, he wrote literal commentaries on the Apocalypse and Ezekiel, which is remarkable at that time, when most scholars wanted to treat these books spiritually. His study of the Old Testament text typically pays close attention to the literal meaning. Stephen Langton (d. 1228), later Archbishop of Canterbury, moved from England to teach theology at the University of Paris. He worked to spread the ideas of the Victorines, "and as a result of his efforts, the literal interpretation of Scripture gained ground in France and England as the proper foundation for the spiritual exposition of the text" (Gibbs, p. 381). Langdon, who wrote a number of commentaries on Scripture, followed Andrew and Herbert in consulting Jews regarding the literal or historical meaning of the text of the Old Testament. A great deal of biblical interpretation during the English Reformation focuses around the translation of the Bible. John Wycliffe (c. 1324-1384) was the leading figure in the production of the first Bible in English in 1380. This translation, which included the books of the Apocrypha, was a very literal translation of the Latin (Vulgate) text current at that time. A second edition was produced in 1384, and was the only Bible available in English until the sixteenth century.

By approximately 1450, the Renaissance spirit of learning and culture called for a return "to the sources," which included a return to studying the original languages of the Bible. There were widely recognized problems with the text of the Vulgate. Roger Bacon (c. 1214-1292) had previously recognized these problems. He had suggested that an older manuscript was to be preferred to a newer one, that the reading suggested by a majority of manuscripts was to be preferred, and that persistent problems should be solved by consulting the Hebrew and Greek. As Gibbs notes, "The Hebrew and Greek studies of Erasmus and other Christian humanists, along with their attacks on corruptions of Latin texts, laid the foundation for a more philological interpretation that tended to give a new prominence to the literal and historical sense" (p. 382). The goal of many humanists was to be acquainted with Hebrew, Greek, and Latin. When Richard Foxe (c. 1448-1528), Bishop of Winchester, established Corpus Christi College at Oxford, he did so as a trilingual college, even though it was initially difficult to find competent teachers in Greek and Hebrew. Thus, the exclusive hold of the Latin version declined, aided by the publication of the first Hebrew Bible in 1488 and of Erasmus' Greek New Testament in 1516, and by the emphasis of scholars such as Erasmus and Luther on the right of all people to read the Bible in their own language.

John Colet (1466-1519) was a renowned English humanist who, in his biblical interpretation, broke away from the methods practiced by the scholastics, instead explaining the plain meaning of the text as seen in its historical context. In his lectures on the book of Romans, Colet treated the book as a whole, with little reference to the fathers or the Schoolmen (Scholastics).

Avoiding allegorizing, Colet focused on the meaning the writer intended to convey to the congregation being addressed. He did the same in his exposition of 1 Corinthians. As Gibbs notes, Colet "expressed admiration for the wisdom of Paul's method of first praising that part of the Corinthians' conduct which he could praise, before proceeding to criticize them" (p. 384).

Colet brought Erasmus of Rotterdam (1466-1536), a good friend of his, to Oxford in 1499. "Erasmus owed to Colet much of his insight into a different method of biblical interpretation — one that contrasted with the disputational scholastic way. . . . Erasmus offered a sharp contrast to Scholastic interpretation of Scripture, stating that his purpose was to help the reader arrive at the original and genuine meaning of the text" (Gibbs, p. 384). During his third visit to England in 1511, Erasmus worked extensively on his Greek New Testament, which first appeared in 1516. Erasmus's "desire for Christian reform was based on the Scriptures as the primary source [and] as the basis for purifying the corruptions of the church" (Gibbs, p. 385). He encouraged scholars to learn Greek and Hebrew to enable them to better understand Scripture. While viewing Scripture as the primary source, Erasmus also studied Greek and Roman classics, and the fathers of the Church.

Once Henry VIII broke with Rome, the early apologists for the Church of England disputed primarily with those who rejected Henry's supremacy over the Church of England. In contrast, toward the end of the sixteenth century, apologists often addressed "the opinions of more extreme proponents of the Reformation, as voiced by the nascent Puritans" (Gibbs, p. 386).

Thomas Cranmer (1489-1555), who became Henry's archbishop in 1532, had strong Protestant sympathies, but had to tone them down during the lifetime of Henry, who saw his split with Rome as primarily political, and was striving to establish a National Catholicism. For Cranmer, the Word of God is primary over traditions derived from the apostles and over church councils, and the church does not "have any capacity to make new articles of faith besides the Scripture, or contrary to the Scriptures" (Gibbs, p. 386). He was, however, willing to grant a secondary role to the church in bearing witness to the Word of God in the Scriptures, even as he renounced teachings of the church such as transubstantiation and prayers for the dead, which he felt do not have support in the Bible.

While there were not many commentaries written in England in the sixteenth century, translations of the Bible into English flourished. The first since Wycliffe was that of William Tyndale (1494-1536), who in 1522 proposed an English translation to the Bishop of London. Attracted to the ideas of Luther, and a bit too early for the English Reformation, Tyndale was rebuffed, and fled to Hamburg in 1525. Tyndale did his translation directly from Hebrew and Greek. For the New Testament, he relied heavily on Erasmus's Greek New Testament, supplemented by the Latin text, and on Luther's German New Testament. His New Testament was published in 1526, with revisions in 1534 and 1535. The 1526 edition was accompanied by *A Pathway to Scripture*, an introduction which has been called "the oldest hermeneutical study in English" (Gibbs, p. 388, quoting Bray). Unlike Luther and Melanchthon, "Tyndale argued that the OT is the law and the NT is the gospel" (Gibbs, p. 388). Tyndale regarded both the Old Testament and the New Testament as guidebooks for the Christian life, and the great men of both were models to be emulated. Tyndale's knowledge of Hebrew was sufficient for him to undertake the translation of the Old Testament, a task he was unable to complete before being burned at the stake in 1536. He worked with the Hebrew text, the Septuagint, the Vulgate, and Luther's German translation. He did the Pentateuch, Jonah, and had worked his way through Chronicles by the time of his death. He was condemned to death due to his Lutheran leanings, his negative comments about popes and bishops, and his substitution in his translation of words such as "elder," "repentance," and "congregation," for approved church terms such as "priest," "penance," and "church."

Miles Coverdale (1488-1569) brought Tyndale's work to completion. His is the first English Bible to be published. Coverdale used Tyndale's New Testament translation and his translation of the Pentateuch, and for the rest of the Old Testament he translated from the Latin and German. He used the Vulgate order, rather than the Hebrew, for the Old Testament, and included the Apocrypha. The entire Bible was published in 1535. Coverdale subsequently also worked on the Great Bible and on the Geneva Bible.

The first English "authorized" Bible, referred to commonly as the Great Bible (due to its size) or as Cranmer's Bible (due to his preface to the second edition), first came out in 1539. Translators used the Vulgate, Erasmus's Latin New Testament translation, and the *Complutensian Polyglot* of Cardinal Ximénes, a Hebrew, Greek, and Latin edition of the Bible. Coverdale's translation of the Psalms, revised by him for the 1539 Great Bible, still appears in the English *Book of Common Prayer*.

The government placed restrictions upon the reading of the Bible in 1543. "The authorized Great Bible alone was allowed, and its reading was limited to the upper classes" (Gibbs, p. 389). The restrictions were lifted toward the end of the reign of Edward VI (1547-1553), but reimposed under Mary Tudor (1553-1558). Some of those who fled to the continent during Mary's reign settled in Geneva.

A number of these refugees in Geneva, including Coverdale, helped produce the Geneva Bible in 1560 (New Testament alone in 1557). Its notes leaned pointedly toward Calvinism, thus offending readers who objected to Calvinist teachings. Tyndale's 1534 edition formed the primary basis for the New Testament. The Old Testament was a revision of the Great Bible, done with careful attention to the Hebrew and Latin editions. "The Geneva Bible was the most scholarly and accurate translation so far produced in England, and immediately received widespread reception and usage. For half a century, the people of England and Scotland read the Geneva Bible in preference to any other version and learned much of their biblical exegesis from the notes" (Gibbs, p. 390).

While the Geneva Bible was acceptable in Presbyterian Scotland, leaders in the English church did not like the strong Calvinism of its annotations. They therefore urged the production of what came to be called "The Bishops' Bible," since many of the revisors were bishops. Its first edition came out in 1568. It is clearly influenced by both the Great Bible and the Geneva Bible. Many of the marginal notes are adopted from the latter. The Bishops' Bible became the second "authorized" English version, being endorsed by a gathering of bishops in 1571. It did not, however, displace the Geneva Bible in popular usage.

Some Roman Catholic refugees fled from England to France, and settled in Douai and Rheims. There was no Roman Catholic translation of the Bible into English, which made it difficult for Roman Catholics to defend themselves against what they saw to be Protestant distortions in the available texts. Although the translation was completed by 1582, initially only the New Testament portion of the "Douai-Rheims Bible" or "Rheims-Douai Bible" was published. The Old Testament came out later, in 1609. The title page announced that the translation was made from the "authorized Latin," that is, the Vulgate, showing the status which this version still carried in the Roman Catholic Church. Significantly, "Approval of lay reading of the Bible was definitely not intended." "Annotations by [William Cardinal] Allen in the form of marginalia and notes at the ends of chapters rival the Geneva Bible in profuseness and match it in polemical nature" (Gibbs, p. 391). Interestingly, this first Roman Catholic translation into English exerted an influence on the King James Bible's revision of earlier translations.

John Jewel (1522-71), Bishop of Salisbury, argued against the English Catholics in his *Apology of the Church of England*. Affirming the primacy of Scripture above all other authorities, he argued that Scripture must be understood through the guidance of the Spirit, who had led the fathers of the early church to understand the true meaning of Scripture. "Jewel claimed that the Church of England had, as closely as possible, restored the ancient purity of apostolic times and the pattern of the primitive church" (Gibbs, p. 391). The authority of the early fathers was not, however, equal to that of Scripture.

Subsequent to the Council of Trent (1545-63), the English Recusant Thomas Harding (1516-72) challenged Jewel. In his work *A confutation of a booke intituled An apologie of the Church of England,* "Harding argued against Jewel that, although Scripture should be acknowledged as the supreme source of faith and morals, its meaning is not always clear, as is demonstrated by the fact that heretics as well as orthodox teachers allege it" (Gibbs, p. 392). Since the Holy Spirit guides the Church in such cases, the true meaning of Scripture cannot be grasped apart from the Church.

Almost everyone else in England strongly "reaffirmed the magisterial Reformers' doctrine of the unique authority and sufficiency of the Scriptures" (Gibbs, p. 392). Those of a more radical bent rejected any practice, custom, or tradition that was not specifically required in Scripture, and hence disapproved of a good deal of what the Church of England preserved from its Roman Catholic heritage.

Richard Hooker (1554-1600) emerged as the most skilled defender of the Church of England, articulating its position as being neither Calvinist nor Roman Catholic. He strongly defended the Church of England's "middle way." While affirming the Protestant principle of *sola scriptura,* he restricted "the perfection and sufficiency of the Scriptures *to the purpose for which they were given,* namely, the eternal salvation of human beings" (Gibbs, p. 393). He also went on to argue the need for reason and the authority of the church in understanding and interpreting the teachings of Scripture. He therefore rejected the Puritan claim that all aspects of worship and church polity had to be explicitly delineated in Scripture. Most church polity derived, appropriately, from human law and consensus. In addressing the Roman Catholics, Hooker challenged them "whenever they appealed to sources outside the Scriptures as necessary for salvation." This included church councils and ancient traditions. Preferring the literal sense, Hooker nevertheless "always subordinated his preference for the more literal to an overarching christocentric principle." Hooker followed Luther in affirming a central, Christ-centered core, and "it is only within this essential sphere that literal interpretation and strict obedience are in order" (Gibbs, p. 393).

When James VI of Scotland became King James I of England, he brought with him strong Protestant convictions and a personal interest in Bible study and translation. The Bishop's Bible had hardly thrived, and the Puritans were unhappy with the "authorized versions." When the king ordered work on a new translation to begin, he restricted the marginal notes to items necessary to explain the Hebrew or Greek of the text. This was due to the king's unhappiness with the marginalia of the Geneva Bible, which at times appeared to be seditious. While officially a revision of the Bishops' Bible, the new translation was basically built upon the Tyndale-Coverdale text. The Geneva Bible also had considerable influence, with additional influence from the Reims-Douai New Testament, Luther's German Bible, and some Latin translations. We do not know of any official authorization of the text, even though the title page in many editions reads "Appointed to be Read in Churches." There were weaknesses in the new version. The texts used were not always satisfactory, as no standard edition existed for the Hebrew Masoretic text of the Old Testament, and Erasmus's New Testament text was problematic. The translators' knowledge of Hebrew was not the best. Less problematic difficulties, such as archaisms and misspellings, were corrected in subsequent editions. Despite these flaws, the King James Bible dominated the English-speaking world for well over two centuries, exerting a powerful influence not only in religious circles, but also in literature, and, more broadly, in English culture.

THE ANABAPTIST REFORMATION

The "Anabaptist Reformation" took place within the context of the broader radicalism that coincided with the Reformation in Europe during the sixteenth century. This radicalism developed within an environment that included monastic reform movements, spiritualism, humanism, mysticism, anticlericalism, and peasant unrest. The Anabaptist movement could be found in territories now comprising Switzerland, Austria, the Czech Republic, Germany, Alsace, and the Netherlands. It had four main forms: Swiss Brethren, South German/Austrian Anabaptists, Dutch Mennonites, and communitarian Hutterites. While each form of Anabaptism had its unique hermeneutical emphases, as well as hermeneutics held in common with other Anabaptist groups, Anabaptism can be generally characterized as christocentric, with a stress on new birth, discipleship, the role of the Holy Spirit in the life of the believer and in the broader faith community, the independence of the church from state control, and the sharing of goods in community (Murray, pp. 403-4).

Significant developments in hermeneutics can be demonstrated within Anabaptist circles. These developments, which were in great flux at the beginning of the sixteenth century, due to regional religious and political influences, gained some standardization by the middle of that century. Even so, Anabaptist hermeneutics are difficult to construct, because there is no definitive Anabaptist work on hermeneutics from that period. As a group, Anabaptists were concerned with pragmatics, rather than systematic commentary or theology. Confessions focused on ecclesiological and ethical, rather than theological, matters (Murray, pp. 404-6).

This is not to say that an Anabaptist hermeneutic did not exist or cannot be constructed. Their leaders, especially those of the second generation, left works with methodology described and illustrated. A notable example is Pilgram Marpeck (c. 1495-1556), an Anabaptist leader in Switzerland, Austria, and southern Germany, who wrote the *Testamentserleutterung*, which discusses the relationship between the Old and New Testaments with hermeneutics clearly in mind. Anabaptist hermeneutics was also formulated in debate with opposition groups, which included Roman Catholics, Protestant Reformers, and Spiritualists. These debates determined which topics and issues received the most discussion. This also explains some variation in hermeneutical approach, as the Anabaptists tailored their response to the opponent being addressed (Murray, pp. 406-7).

Murray identifies six key focal points as the foundation of Anabaptist hermeneutics. One is that Scripture is sufficiently clear for anyone to interpret it and obey it without the help of scholarly learning. Private interpretation was possible, and a right of each Christian. Who has the right to interpret Scripture was a major point of contention between the Anabaptists and the Reformers. Anabaptists affirmed that Scripture was clear — even to the uneducated. They feared that scholarship obscured Scripture, that it could be used by scholars to justify evading the claims of Scripture upon the ethical life, and that it hardened the scholar against receiving new revelation (Murray, pp. 408-9).

The Reformers countered that there are textual difficulties in Scripture that cannot be resolved without scholarly work, which requires knowledge of ancient cultures, history, and linguistics. It could even be the case that the "plain meaning" of a text, derived from simply reading Scripture, looked little like the "plain meaning" derived after scholarly interpretation had determined the meaning of the text in its original context. While the Reformers affirmed the right of private interpretation, there was a continuing reliance upon reason, doctrinal considerations, traditional interpretation, and a growing restriction of interpretation to the learned clergy (Murray, pp. 409-10).

A second characteristic of Anabaptist hermeneutics is christocentrism. Anabaptists affirmed that Scripture, especially the words and deeds of Jesus, is clear to all readers. In fact, they affirmed that the words and deeds of Jesus clarify all other portions of Scripture. One implication of this hermeneutic in practice is that the New Testament has greater authority than the Old Testament, and the gospels have greater authority than any other portion of Scripture. The life and teachings of Jesus in the gospels are central to God's revelation. The Old Testament points forward to Jesus as the fulfillment of all God's promises, and the New Testament points back to Jesus as the founder, head, and power of the church. Of course, there were exceptions to this christocentricism. Anabaptists with an apocalyptic emphasis concentrated on the prophetic and apocalyptic portions of Scripture, in which Christ is not always so obviously central (Murray, pp. 410-11).

As a hermeneutic, christocentrism could be a literal and legal application of Jesus' teachings and deeds. For some Anabaptists for whom Jesus was a new lawgiver, it was just that. This was how some Reformers perceived the Anabaptist hermeneutic — as akin to works-righteousness. However, for most Anabaptists, a spiritual relationship with Jesus, which heeded the intention and spirit of his teachings and example, was essential to hermeneutics, and prevented legalism. Jesus' example in Scripture was crucial for developing a discipleship lived in communion with the risen Christ (Murray, p. 411).

The Reformers were christological or soteriological, rather than christocentric. They understood Jesus as the supreme revelation of God, and they understood the Christ event as the central act of God in history, which brings salvation to believers. For the Reformers, what God did through Jesus to enable salvation and justification by faith received more emphasis than did Jesus himself. For the Anabaptists, Jesus' sayings and deeds were emphasized, in order to plot a course for discipleship (Murray, pp. 411-12).

A third emphasis of Anabaptist hermeneutics is the relationship between the Old and New Testaments. This was a subject of great debate among the Reformers as well, and neither the Anabaptists nor the Reformers created a satisfactory hermeneutic on this subject. The Anabaptists saw a much greater discontinuity between the Testaments than did the Reformers. Anabaptists did not deny the authority of the Old Testament. However, the authority of the New Testament was primary, and the authority of the Old Testament was limited to where Christ affirmed it, and wherever it agreed with the New Testament. Of course, those Anabaptists with a more eschatological emphasis used prophetic and apocalyptic passages from the Old Testament without raising questions about their authority. Anabaptists also did not consider the Old Testament as a place to seek ethical and ecclesiological guidance. Overall, the Anabaptists were criticized for not affirming the unity of Scripture, depreciating the Old Testament, and not using the Old Testament as a framework for interpreting the New Testament (Murray, pp. 412-14).

A fourth emphasis of Anabaptist hermeneutics is the role of the Holy

Spirit in biblical interpretation. Like the Reformers, the Anabaptists had to find the balance between the written Word and the guidance of the Holy Spirit. They had to maintain the normative authority of Scripture, while allowing for the teaching function of the Holy Spirit. Their movement was diverse regarding the placement of emphasis. Some stressed obedience to the written Word and were more literal, while others stressed the revelatory role of the Spirit and were more spiritualistic. Some even stressed both as complementary (Murray, pp. 414-15).

In general, the role of the Spirit in interpretation was stressed more in Anabaptist circles than among the Reformers. Emphasis on the role of the Spirit was fueled in part by anticlericalism, and the desire to end the monopolizing of interpretation by clerics using reason, education, and tradition. It was also fueled by a desire to give to the less educated the right to interpret the Scriptures. The revelatory role of the Spirit enfranchised the uneducated — a role that also moved interpreters to incorporate the Scriptures into their lives. To prevent abuses of interpretation by the Spirit, the Anabaptists cautioned their constituents not to disguise personal desires as the voice of the Spirit, to use reason to test interpretations, and to test interpretations among the larger body of believers (Murray, pp. 415-16).

A fifth feature of Anabaptist interpretation is its focus on the congregation. This congregational hermeneutic went hand in hand with Anabaptist anticlericalism, egalitarian ecclesiology, and emphasis on the role of the Spirit. Such a hermeneutic set Anabaptists apart from the Roman Catholic Church, which restricted interpretation to the educated clergy, from the Spiritualists, with their emphasis on the individual's role in interpretation, and from the Reformers, who increasingly restricted the interpretation of the Bible to the clergy. In a congregational hermeneutic, the congregation needed to be composed of faithful believers with a heart for obedience, and open to the leading of the Spirit. The congregational hermeneutic was practiced to some degree in all Anabaptist circles, but some leaned more toward placing interpretation in the hands of the individual, and others leaned more toward placing interpretation in the hands of the clergy.

Leadership was still very important in Anabaptist interpretation. The leader was to guide and facilitate the discussion. The leader was to be sure that Scripture was being read, understood, and applied. The leader was to supply information on translation and interpretation of difficult passages, as well as tools for the laity to use in their own interpretation. These tools included topical concordances — collections of biblical quotations by topic. The leader presented these tools, along with interpretation to guide the laity to proper theology and ethics to apply in their own discipleship; however, the leader was not to dominate and obscure the contributions of the laity. As the sixteenth century progressed, this system was gradually replaced by a greater reliance upon educated clergy and interpretive traditions (Murray, pp. 416-19).

There were some criticisms of the congregational hermeneutic. First, local congregations had considerable autonomy to determine interpretation. Interpretation varied from congregation to congregation, depending upon factors like educational level and history, and there was no central authority to arbitrate the differences in interpretation. This diversity led to some bitter disputes. However, Anabaptists were, overall, biblically literate, and their emphasis on working toward consensus helped them sort out poor interpretation, and affirm more useful interpretation. A second criticism of the congregational hermeneutic is that the heavy reliance placed upon the teaching of the Spirit most often excluded the interpretation of the past as embodied in Christian tradition. This was exacerbated by the desire in Anabaptism to be free of the binding traditions of the Roman Catholic Church. In part, this led to an impoverished interpretation (Murray, pp. 418-19).

A sixth core conviction of Anabaptist hermeneutics is that biblical interpretation requires ethical application. The study of Scripture had to be put into practice. Anabaptists developed their interpretation within the context of active ministry. As an outgrowth of communal hermeneutics, interpretation needed to work within the discipleship, worship, and life of the community. The questions and emphases in interpretation derived from the concerns of the community. The focus upon the practical was a test of interpretation. If an interpretation worked in practice, then it was considered a good interpretation, and vice versa. While recognizing some difficulties in the interpretation of Scripture, Anabaptists stressed the clarity of Scripture, in order to quell hesitation to implement its precepts. Obedience to Christ and his Scriptures took precedence over education and theological study (Murray, pp. 419-21).

In addition, the state of obedience in the life of the interpreter was proportional to his or her ability to interpret adequately. Only those whose lives demonstrated active and faithful discipleship could be trusted with interpretation. Sin hindered the interpreter from actively seeking the truth in Scripture. Thus, faithfulness was a prerequisite for hermeneutics. Also, connections to ecclesiastical and secular powers diverted the interpreter from faithful interpretation, due to the desire to appease powers and preserve vested interests (Murray, pp. 421-23).

The Anabaptists had no structured hermeneutical system. However, the core hermeneutical assumptions just outlined were operative in the sixteenth century in various times and places. The weaknesses of this hermeneutic include marginalizing scholarship, subjugating the Old Testament to the New Testament, and a tendency toward literalism and legalism. As time progressed, the apocalyptic and spiritualist groups of Anabaptism disappeared, along with their individualist hermeneutics. Within the larger movement, the balance between Word and Spirit moved from Spirit to Word, and the balance between communal hermeneutics and the authority of leaders shifted toward the leaders. However, the stresses on the role of the Spirit in interpretation and on the individual's right to interpret, were lasting and positive influences (Murray, pp. 423-25).

BIBLICAL INTERPRETATION OF THE ROMAN CATHOLIC REFORMATION

The term "Counter-Reformation" refers to the reaction of the Roman Catholic Church to the theological, ecclesiological, political, and cultural repercussions of the Protestant Reformation. It covers the period from approximately 1520-40 to the end of the seventeenth century. It is focused particularly on the Council of Trent (1545-63), and the reform that it inspired. However, there were older reform movements within Roman Catholic religious orders and among the laity, accompanied by the use of Greek and Hebrew manuscripts of the Bible. It may be more accurate to refer to this period as the Roman Catholic Reformation; however, with regard to biblical interpretation, the impetus for reform was a reaction to Protestant interpretation — a reaction for which the title "Counter-Reformation" is still appropriate.

In terms of works produced, the Roman Catholic Reformation is roughly framed at the beginning by the *Bibliotheca Sancta* of Sixtus of Sienna (1566), who introduced the distinction between protocanonical and deuterocanonical literature. While acknowledging the later acceptance of the inspiration of the Old Testament Apocrypha, Sixtus, against Protestant objections, affirmed its canonicity. The Roman Catholic Reformation is framed at the end by the *Histoire critique de Vieux Testament* (Critical History of the Old Testament) of 1678 and the *L'Histoire critique des principaux commentateurs du Nouveau Testament* (Critical History of the Principal Commentators of the New Testament) of 1693 — both written by the French scholar Richard Simon. His work marks the beginning of critical exegesis in the Roman Catholic Church (Bedouelle, p. 429).

The main bases for biblical interpretation in the Roman Catholic Reformation were laid down by the Council of Trent in 1546. One major issue was to define the foundation of revelation. Protestant Reformers affirmed *sola scriptura,* "scripture alone" as the foundation of revelation. The Roman Catholic Church reaffirmed both oral and written traditions as the foundation of revelation: (1) the oral teaching of Christ himself, down through the apostles and their successors, who were led by the Holy Spirit; and, (2) the written Bible. Revelation comes from apostolic tradition *and* the Bible. This revelation is supplemented by ecclesiastical tradition and church teaching. All of these traditions represent the consensus of the Roman Catholic Church, which is the source of authentic interpretation (Bedouelle, pp. 430-32).

The stance that the Roman Catholic Church is the source of authentic interpretation is based partly on the recognition that the biblical canon was determined *by* the church. The corollary is that the church should thus supervise its interpretation. In practicality, this occurred in the preaching within the worship service, which translated texts pronounced in Latin, and then provided commentary in the vernacular languages, as well as instruction in the form of the catechism (Bedouelle, p. 432).

The Council of Trent reaffirmed that the Bible utilized in the Roman Catholic Church was to remain the Vulgate, and was to continue to include the Apocrypha (as affirmed by the Council of Florence in 1442), even though Roman Catholic exegetes treated these books as deuterocanonical. The Vulgate was declared the authentic version, faithful in matters of doctrine, and suitable for teaching and preaching. There was also a call for a revised Vulgate, corrected according to better Latin manuscripts; this resulted in the Sixto-Clementine edition of 1592 (Bedouelle, pp. 432-36).

Biblical interpretation in the Roman Catholic Reformation was guided by the premise that the Bible gives us reliable knowledge of history and the world. Moses gave the world true knowledge of theology, cosmology, natural history, world history, the Law, and poetry. Solomon provided true knowledge of science, and universal wisdom; thus, the Bible is the means for and the evidence of the unity of the cosmos. This concept spilled over into political debate of the Reformation and post-Reformation eras, which argued for the independence of government from the church, and for the divine right of kings. Roman Catholic interpreters argued from Scripture that the state is instituted by the providence of God as an instrument for the good of the Church and Christianity. All political authority is instituted by God; thus, the Papacy should be the final arbiter in matters of government in Christian society (Bedouelle, pp. 436-38).

Biblical interpretation in the Roman Catholic Reformation was also guided by the understanding that the true meaning of Scripture, which leads to salvation, comes from the Church, which is guided by the Holy Spirit. This position was articulated in *De constitutione theologia* by Juan Maldonado

(Maldonatus, 1533-83), a Jesuit biblical scholar who taught at the Collège de Clermont in Paris. He wrote exemplary commentaries on the Prophets and all four Gospels, which provided guidance on the interpretation of Scripture. Another major exegete was Cornelius van den Steen (1567-1637), a Jesuit professor at Louvain and the Roman College at Rome, who wrote commentaries on the entire Bible, except for the books of Job and the Psalms. He focused mainly on the historical sense of Scripture, but also attended to the other senses, the tropological and anagogical, while excluding allegory, which he compared to fantasy. The capstone work of interpretation in this period was that of the French Benedictine, Augustin Calmet (1672-1757), who published his 23-volume *Commentaire litteral sur tous les livres de l'Ancient et du Nouveau Testament* between 1707 and 1716. It was a master commentary on the entire Bible, including interpretations from both Jewish and Christian communities (Bedouelle, pp. 438-40).

Among the Roman Catholic mystics of the convents and monasteries, biblical interpretation had its own flavor. Such mysticism flourished in sixteenth-century Spain, in the Carmelite school, and in seventeenth-century France. Male mystics tended to have more formal biblical knowledge than female mystics. On the whole, men had more education; and, when combined with the restriction against reading the Bible in the vernacular, these factors placed women at a disadvantage. Still, Carmelite women had biblical knowledge, primarily through the liturgy, and from hearing preaching that discussed biblical texts (Bedouelle, pp. 440-41).

Images derived from the Bible, rather than Scripture itself, form the direct basis for mystical prayer. Verses and their images are given new meanings through the experience of the Holy Spirit. Central to the new meanings is the theology of the Cross of Christ, which guides interpretation. The mystics do not propose a particular interpretation of verses, but accept a plurality of meanings. Verses can be given a personal understanding that does not require direct connection with the biblical text.

Biblical interpretation among the French mystics was erudite. This is particularly true of Francis de Sales (1567-1622), whose works, such as *The Introduction to the Devout Life,* are among the finest interpretation of the period. He utilized all three medieval forms of the spiritual sense — the allegorical, tropological, and anagogical (Bedouelle, pp. 441-42).

Biblical interpretation also had to contend with the discovery of the New World. This discovery called into question the biblical account of the formation of the peoples of the earth from Noah's descendants (Gen. 10:32), for this listing does not include the peoples of the New World. Many ingenious solutions, based on the mysterious names in the Old Testament, were created to account for these peoples. Furthermore, missionary work in the New World and in the East — China, India, and Japan — did not rely heavily upon the Bible, since the encounter with different cultures made direct use of the Bible difficult. Nevertheless, Scripture was included in summaries of Christian doctrine and in catechisms (Bedouelle, pp. 442-44).

Scholarship also posed a challenge to biblical interpretation. Copernicus (sixteenth century) proposed his theory of heliocentrism, and Galileo (seventeenth century) supported it with his observations. The proposal that the earth revolved around the sun, rather than the earth being a fixed center of the universe, seemed to contradict certain passages of Scripture (Pss. 19:4a-6; 104:19; Joshua 10:12-13). Galileo offered a hermeneutic that took his observations into account. He affirmed the teaching of the Council of Trent that the Bible was the source of all salvation and truth and moral law. However, on matters of natural law, the Bible conformed to the understanding of the time in which it was written. Thus, the Bible was definitive on matters of religion, but not science. However, his hermeneutic failed to win the day, and the Roman Catholic Church continued to reaffirm the unity of religious and scientific truth (Bedouelle, pp. 444-45).

SCRIPTURES IN THE VERNACULAR UP TO 1800

Prior to the Reformation, biblical interpretation was considered the domain of scholars and theologians. The Bible, originally written in Hebrew and Greek, had been translated into Latin. This limited biblical interpretation to the scholars and clergy. Biblical interpretation came to the laity through sermons and church teaching, as mediated through these educated persons. Thus, in the Roman Catholic Church, the Latin Vulgate of Jerome functioned as the source text for interpretation and theology for a millennium.

During the Reformation, published copies of Hebrew and Greek texts of the Bible became readily available primarily through the efforts of Erasmus, Stephanus, and others. This allowed scholars to translate the biblical text into the vernacular. This availability of the Hebrew and Greek texts of the Bible, and the ensuing movement to translate Scriptures into the vernacular, helped democratize biblical interpretation. People no longer had to rely upon the Latin Vulgate or scholars for their interpretation and theology.

The availability of both texts and translations posed a threat to the Roman Catholic Church's authority, and to orthodoxy itself. The translation of any manuscript, including the Bible, requires interpretation, because an understanding of the source text is integral to the process. A translation also provides a source for further interpretation within the community that receives it. This interpretation may or may not agree with established interpretation. In the case of the interpretation of the Reformation, it often did not (Long, pp. 450-52)!

The earliest vernacular translations were interlinear glosses in Latin manuscripts of the Vulgate that basically supported church tradition. In this form, the glosses did not pose a threat to church authority and orthodoxy. However, that was not the case with independent, literal translations divorced from the Latin texts. Translations in the vernacular that utilized Greek texts highlighted problems in Roman Catholic theology, where interpretation was based too closely upon the Latin text, which was often at variance with the Greek text. Since words in any language have nuances, the Latin words chosen to translate the Greek words had different nuances, allowing for different interpretations. Vernacular translations highlighted these interpretive issues, and threatened to diminish the authority of the church. The church stood to lose credibility as a source for the interpretation of the Bible (Long, pp. 452-54).

More than just the credibility of the church was at stake, however. The vernacular translations also left the Bible open to interpretation by the laity — an interpretation divorced from the original source texts. The translation of the Bible opened up the opportunity for the laity and Reformers to interpret the Bible on their own, without control and guidance by the church, and this opened the door for "heresy." In fact, vernacular translations were typically associated with sedition and heresy. Put more pointedly, the church stood to lose control of the entire process of biblical interpretation when people could read Scripture for themselves.

This connection between heresy and vernacular translations was reinforced by the fact that many who challenged the church grounded their interpretations upon vernacular translations. One of the earliest translations of the entire Bible in English came from John Wycliffe (c. 1330-84). Wycliffe was an Oxford theologian and philosopher. The extent of his involvement with the actual translation is unclear, but the translation made under his leadership became known as the Wycliffe Bible, and was a literal translation of the Vulgate text. True to the belief of the time, it was literal so as to preserve the sacred character of the Bible. However, its literalness diminished its usefulness as a readable English translation. Wycliffe challenged the church on matters of doctrine, relying upon vernacular translation for support. His followers, the Lollards, produced an English translation to facilitate the challenges posed by Wycliffe (1380s and 1390s). This translation, limited by its sole reliance upon the Latin source, actually did not contain anything untoward (Long, pp. 454-57).

Although it was not his intention, Desiderius Erasmus (1466/69-1536) greatly facilitated vernacular translation. As mentioned above, in 1516 he published a revised Latin translation with a Greek original side by side, to justify his revisions of Jerome's Vulgate, hoping that his revisions of the Vulgate would contribute to reform in the Roman Catholic Church. However, the inclusion of a Greek text for comparison also gave translators into the vernacular a Greek source text to consult in their work, and thereby facilitated their challenge to the Roman Catholic Church (Long, pp. 457-58).

Martin Luther (1483-1546) was the first to use this newly available Greek text to create his own vernacular version, thereby supporting his reforming ideas, and making the Bible into a German text. He published his translation of the New Testament in 1522, and of the entire Bible in 1534/35. The Bible was now accessible to all literate Germans, independent of official interpreters of the church. Luther was able to change doctrine through translation, and then disseminate those changes through the distribution of his translation. Throughout Europe, Luther's translation of the Bible into German wielded great power in challenging the Roman Catholic Church, thereby freeing governments from the influence and control of the Church (Long, 458-59).

Olaus Petersson (1493-1552) and Lars Petersson (1499-1573) produced a Swedish translation of the Bible in 1541. Michael Agricola, a Finnish reformer who studied with Luther, produced a translation of the New Testament in Finnish in the early 1540s. Jacques Lefèvre d'Étaples produced a complete French translation of the Bible in 1528, using the Vulgate, the Greek, and the emended Latin text of Erasmus. Although Lefèvre's version was put on the index of forbidden books by the Roman Catholic Church, the need for an official French translation was strong. To meet that need, the Theology Faculty at Louvain University produced a French translation in 1550 (Long, pp. 463-65).

As mentioned above, Cardinal Ximénes de Cisneros commissioned the *Complutensian Polyglot* from the University of Alcalá, in Spain. Printed in 1514, but not published until 1522, it greatly facilitated translation into Spanish. This polyglot Bible contained the text of the Bible in Latin, Greek, Hebrew, and Aramaic. The first Spanish translation, the work of reformist monk Casiodoro de Reina, appeared in 1569. Reina used the *Complutensian Polyglot* and Erasmus's Polyglot. Vernacular Bibles in Italian are few, owing in part to the strong presence of the Roman Catholic Church there; however, a complete Italian version by Niccolò Malermi (or Malerbi) appeared in 1490 (Long, p. 465).

In England, William Tyndale produced his own English translation of the New Testament in 1524. He relied upon Latin and Greek source texts, as well as Luther's New Testament translation, and some of Luther's prologues and notes. He followed this with a translation of the Pentateuch (1530) and Jonah (1531). Tyndale had competency in Hebrew and Greek, as well as in translation, and his version is very readable (Long, pp. 459-61).

Tyndale's translation became a basis for the many English translations that followed. Most notable was the version of Miles Coverdale, who produced the first complete printed English translation of the Bible in 1535. In addition to Tyndale's translation of the New Testament, the Pentateuch, and Jonah, Coverdale used Luther's German translation to translate the remainder of the Hebrew Bible. This was necessary because Tyndale had not translated most of the Old Testament, and Coverdale did not have facility in Hebrew (Long, pp. 461-63).

English Protestant scholars left England during the reign of Mary Tudor (1553-58), who persecuted the Protestant reformers. They settled in Geneva, a hub of learning. From there, they continued their study and translation of the Bible. In 1560, one of these religious exiles, William Whittingham, produced the Geneva Bible, based on two previous translations. The Great Bible, published in 1539, was the basis for the Old Testament, and Tyndale's New Testament was the basis for the Geneva Bible's New Testament. The Geneva Bible was suspect in England for its association with Calvin, as was Tyndale's translation for its association with Luther. However, it was a success, because it was easy to read, and was based on good scholarship by a team of scholars working from the Greek and Hebrew (Long, pp. 465-67).

In response to Protestant English versions in the vernacular, the Roman Catholic college in Douai published the Douai-Rheims version of the New Testament in 1582, and the Old Testament in 1609. Gregory Martin, a Roman Catholic priest and one of the original scholars of St. John's College in Oxford, was the translator. He used the Vulgate as the basis of the translation, as ruled by the Council of Trent in 1546. However, the Greek was consulted for clarification. Unfortunately, the translation was too literal and was not useful for public reading or for private devotion (Long, pp. 467-68).

The King James Version of 1611 represented a shift in vernacular translations. It was an attempt to produce an English translation not associated with any particular religious group, in contrast to the Geneva Bible, Bishops' Bible, and Douay-Rheims version, which were all associated with specific religious groups. Even so, the wording of the Bishops' Bible formed the basis for the King James Version, while the Tyndale and Geneva versions were used where they were better translations of the source texts. The use of the Bishops' Bible as a basis lent familiarity and authority to the new version (Long, pp. 468-71). Each vernacular translation has to be evaluated in its individual context, according to its function, the texts the translators had to use, and the strategy of translation they followed. Subsequent translations were based on their predecessors, new manuscripts, and a growing facility with the primary languages.

CONCLUSION

By the end of the Reformation era, many of the primary factors were already in place which would lay the groundwork for the rise of modern biblical interpretation, which will be the focus of volume 3 of *A History of Biblical Interpretation*. The Jewish community had made major gains in the study of Hebrew grammar and lexicography. Within Christianity, the rapid renewal of interest during the Renaissance in ancient languages and literatures revived the study of the biblical text in Hebrew and Greek, as well as the study of the ancient church fathers. These new interests diminished and bypassed the dependence of many Christian scholars on the Latin of the Vulgate, and on the Church's interpretation of the Vulgate. The proliferation of translations of the Bible into vernacular languages profoundly affected biblical interpretation, opening the realm of interpretation to the common person, and enabling each reader to call into question the interpretation of authority figures in the churches, whose word had previously been accepted with little if any challenge.

The loosening of the Roman Catholic Church's firm grasp on the proper interpretation of the Bible unlocked doors that, once opened, could not be closed. Luther, Calvin, and Cranmer, for example, along with the Anabaptist reformers, articulately defined alternative interpretations of particular texts, and of the Bible as a whole, thereby revealing both the rich and diverse creativity contained within the biblical texts, and the frustrating inability of biblical scholars to agree on the interpretation of particularly important texts, or on the message of the Bible as a whole. As may be seen in the discussions in volume 1 of *A History of Biblical Interpretation*, this diversity of interpretation was already in evidence in the earliest centuries of the church. However, during the Middle Ages, church councils, and the authority of the Roman Church in the west, had considerably narrowed the options available to biblical interpreters. All that changed during the Renaissance and Reformation eras. When we add the rationality and empiricism that came to be nurtured during the closing centuries of the era treated in this volume, we have in place most of the factors necessary to prepare for the rise of modern biblical criticism.

Chronology

All dates are CE. Many birthdays are approximate

Josephus (37-100)
War of Jews with Rome: destruction of last Jewish temple (66-70)
Bar Kochba Revolt (132-35)
Proto-Masoretic text becomes dominant (early second century)
Irenaeus of Lyon (130-200)
Origen of Alexandria (185-c. 254)
Compilation of the Mishnah (200)
Division of the Hebrew text of the Tanak into sense units (*pisqot,* third
    century)
Eusebius (260-340)
Athanasius of Alexandria (296-373)
Gregory Nazianzen (Gregory of Nazianzus, 329-89)
Gregory of Nyssa (330-after 394)
Ambrose of Milan (339-97)
Jerome (345-420)
Evagrius of Pontus (346-99)
John Chrysostom (347-407)
Vulgate version (fifth century)
Augustine of Hippo (354-430)
Cyril of Alexandria (376/78-c. 444)
Theodoret of Cyrrhus (393-c. 457)
Pseudo-Dionysius the Areopagite (late fifth-early sixth century)
Romanos the Melodist (485-c. 560)
Cassiodorus (485-c. 580)
Masoretic period (c. sixth-c. tenth century)
Babylonian Talmud (500)
Division of Hebrew text of Tanak into verses (early talmudic period)
Gregory the Great (540-604, pope 590-604)
Isidore of Seville (560-636)
Maximus the Confessor (580-662)
Venerable Bede (673-735)
John of Damascus (675-c. 749)
Anan ben David (Karaite, fl. mid-eighth century)
Charlemagne (742-814)
Alcuin (735-804, to Charlemagne's court, 781)
Carolingian schools (785-850)
Rabanus Maurus (780-856)
John Scotus Eriugena (810-77)

School of Auxerre (c. 835-93)

Saadia Gaon (ben Joseph, 882-942)

Menahem ibn Saruk (910-c. 970)

Judah ibn Hayyuj (945-1000)

David ben Abraham al-Fasi, Karaite lexicographer (second half of tenth century)

Japheth ben Ali (Karaite, late tenth century)

Leningrad Codex (1009)

Symeon the New Theologian (949-1022)

Jonah ibn Janah (990-1050)

Berengar of Tours (1010-88)

Lanfranc of Bec (1010-89)

Bruno of Cologne or Bruno the Carthusian (1030-1101)

Rabbi Solomon ben Isaac (Rashi, 1040-1105)

Rabbi Joseph Kara (disciple of Rashi, 1070-1140)

Rabbi Samuel ben Meir (Rashbam, grandson of Rashi, 1080-c. 1170)

Rabbi Eliezer of Beaugency (disciple of Rashbam, twelfth century)

Rabbi Joseph Bekhor Shor (disciple of Rashbam, twelfth century)

Rabbi Abraham ibn Ezra (1089-1164)

Anselm of Laon (d. 1117)

Cistercian school (twelfth century)

Peter of Damascus (twelfth century)

William of St. Thierry (1075-1148)

Bernard of Clairvaux (1090-1153)

Hugh of St. Victor (1096-1141)

Peter Lombard (1095/1100-1160)

Glossa Ordinaria (begins late eleventh century)

Liber Sententiarum by Peter Lombard (1157/58)

Richard of St. Victor (1123-73)

Andrew of St. Victor (d. 1175)

Peter Comestor (d. c. 1179)

Herbert of Bosham (1120-94)

Rabbi David Kimhi (Radak, 1160-1235)

Rabbi Moses ben Nahman (Ramban, Nachmanides, 1194-1270)

Hugh of Saint-Cher (1200-1263)

Bonaventure, Giovanni de Fidanza (1217-74)

Thomas Aquinas (1225-74)

Stephen Langdon (divided biblical text into numbered chapters; 1150/55-1228)

Rabbi Bayha ben Asher of Saragossa (follower of Ramban, d. 1340)

Aaron ben Joseph ha-Rofé (Karaite, 1250-1320)

Nicholas of Lyra (1270-1340/49)

Rabbi Levi ben Gershom (Ralbag, Gersonides, 1288-1344)

Gregory Palamas (1296-1359)

John Wycliffe (1330-84; Wycliffite translation 1380-84)

Cardinal Bessarion (1403-72)

Lorenzo Valla (1407-57)

Gianozzo Manetti (1423-97)

Cardinal Francisco (né Gonzalo) Ximénes de Cisneros (1436-1517)

Rabbi Isaac ben Juda Abarbanel (1437-1508)

Elio Antonio de Nebrija (1444-1522)

Council of Florence (1442)

Aurelio Brandolini (1454-97)

Gutenberg Bible (1454/55)

Jacques Lefèvre d'Étaples (1460-1536; French Bible version 1528)

John Colet (1466-1519)

Erasmus (1466/69-1536)

Sanctus (Sanctes) Pagninus (1470-1536/41)

Karlstadt (Andreas Bodenstein, 1480-1541)

Martin Luther (1483-1546)

Ulrich Zwingli (1484-1531)

Miles Coverdale (1488-1569)

Soncino brothers publish first printed Hebrew text of the Tanak (1488)

Malermi/bi translation into Italian (1490)

Thomas Müntzer (1489-1525)

Thomas Cranmer (1489-1555)

William Tyndale (1494-1536)

Pilgram Marpeck (1495-1556)

Menno Simons (1496-1561)

Philip Melanchthon (1497-1560)

Stephanus (Robert Estienne, 1503-59)

Pierre Robert Olivétan (c. 1506-38; French Bible version 1535)

John Calvin (1509-64)

Thomas Harding (1516-72)

Erasmus's edition of the Greek New Testament (1516)

First Rabbinic Bible (1516-17)

Luther's 95 Theses launches the Protestant Reformation (1517)

Theodore Beza (1519-1605)

Sixtus Senensis (1520-69)

Casiodoro de Reina (1520-94)

Diet of Worms (1521)

Complutensian Polyglot (1522); chapters and verses numbered

Second Great Rabbinic Bible (1524-25)

Tyndale NT (1526)

Various diverse Anabaptist groups develop in different locales (sixteenth
century)

Schleitheim Confession (1527)

Juan Maldonado (Maldonatus, 1533-83)

Luther's translation of the Bible into German (1534/35, NT in 1522)

Tyndale Coverdale translation (1535)

Calvin's *Institutes of the Christian Religion* (1536, first edition)

Great Bible or Cranmer's Bible (1539)

Petersson translation into Swedish (NT 1526, Bible 1541)

Robert Bellarmine (1542-1621)

Agricola translation into Finnish (early 1540s)

Council of Trent (1546-63)

Richard Hooker (1554-1600)

Geneva Bible (1560)

De Reina translation into Spanish (OT 1567, NT 1569)

Francis de Sales (1567-1622)

Bishop's Bible (1568)

Royal Polyglot (Antwerp 1569-72)

Rheims-Douai Version (NT 1582, OT 1610)

Sixtine edition of the Vulgate (1590)

Authorized Version (KJV, 1611)

Francis Turretin (1623-87)

Augustin Calmet (1672-1757)

Internet Resources

Many of the texts discussed in this volume and the preceding volume (*HBI*[1]) have become available for downloading or reading online. The websites listed here either have these texts or have links to other sites that have the texts or discussions of them. This list should be used with these cautions:

- The Internet's coverage of ancient and medieval authors is far from even. The works of some authors appear on many websites, while those of others are apparently not available.
- Our knowledge of the web is not complete. A search may well turn up resources not mentioned here.
- The Internet is volatile. Sites come and go and change their contents. (And the advice given here will of course be little more than quaint within a few decades after the publication of this volume.)
- Translations of ancient and medieval authors that have become available online are often in the public domain. They will therefore often be not the latest and therefore not the most reliable, most readable, or most often cited translations.

First, wikipedia (http://www.wikipedia.org) has established itself as the site to visit for introductory articles on nearly every topic of human inquiry and for guides to resources on the same. It includes articles on nearly all the interpreters and interpretive movements named in *HBI*[1-2].

Other important websites for the works discussed in *HBI*[1-2] are:

New Advent
    http://www.newadvent.org/
Crosswire
    http://www.crosswire.org/study
Halsall
    http://www.fordham.edu/halsall/sbook.html
CCEL
    http://www.ccel.org/
Bible Gateway
    http://www.biblegateway.com
ICLNET
    http://www.iclnet.org
Perseus: Greco-Roman Materials
    http://www.perseus.org/cache/perscoll_Greco-Roman.html
Torrey
    http://torreys.org/bible/

Other sites that link to writings of authors of many times and places, including those discussed in *HBI*[1-2] are:

Project Gutenberg
    http://www.gutenberg.org/wiki/Main_Page
The Great Books Index
    http://books.mirror.org/gb.home.html
The Internet Sacred Text Archive
    http://www.sacred-texts.com/index.htm

The Bible itself appears in numerous versions on countless websites. The Apocrypha/Deuterocanonical books are often not included. Good starting points for the Bible in a number of modern languages are Bible Gateway and Crosswire. The latter has the Leningrad Codex, the Aleppo Codex, the Rahlfs LXX, the Peshitta, and several older editions of the NT in Greek. See also http://www.ntgateway.com/bible.htm. Links to original/ancient language resources are also found on Torrey's "page one."

Torrey's "page one" also links to scholarly resources for most of the topics and interpreters discussed in *HBI*[1], and Torrey has a separate links page dedicated to Philo. The texts of both talmuds are available at http://www.mechon-mamre.org (under "sources of the Oral Law"). An alternative portal is at http://www.shechem.org/etorahsr.html. There are original/ancient-language texts of the OT Pseudepigrapha and extensive notes at http://ocp.acadiau.ca. The nineteenth-century translation of the church fathers into English, comprising *ANF* and *NPNF,* is online at CCEL, NewAdvent and other sites. CCEL also has a number of additional patristic texts (see "More Fathers"). See also ICLNET and Torrey's "page one." The first edition of Migne's *Patrologia Latina* is at http://pld.chadwyck.co.uk. For Augustine, see also http://ccat.sas.upenn.edu/jod/augustine.html. For NT Apocrypha see Torrey's "page one" under "Gnostica"; for texts in English see http://www.webcom.com/~gnosis/library.html and http://www.comparative-religion.com/christianity/apocrypha/.

English translations of selections from some of the midrashic compilations have been published in unannotated form (tr. Samuel Rapaport, 1907) and are available at http://www.sacred-texts.com/jud/mhl/index.htm and http://www.sacred-texts.com/jud/tmm/index.htm. For NT textual criticism, see Torrey's "page one" and http://www.ntgateway.com/resource/textcrit.htm. Calvin and Luther are well represented at CCEL. Some of the volumes of Luther's Works (LW) are available online at www.archive.org. For other online resources see the article on "Martin Luther (Resources)" at wikipedia.org, www.iclnet.org/pub/resources/text/wittenberg/wittenberg-luther.html, www.iclnet.org.

CHAPTER 2

Early Medieval Exegesis:
Gregory I to the Twelfth Century

Mary A. Mayeski

The biblical interpretation that emerges from the long period between Gregory the Great and the twelfth-century schools belongs to what is currently considered "pre-critical" exegesis. It is certainly pre-scientific. What it lacks is not only scientific methods of contextualizing and analyzing the text but also, most importantly, the scientific worldview that privileges empirical evidence and seeks to determine human and natural causalities. But it is not uncritical, as I hope the following essay will demonstrate. It relied on methods and assumptions that required critical judgment and pursued a meaning that could stand the test of logical reasoning and literary analysis.

The first part of this chapter describes the distinguishing characteristics of early medieval exegesis, first according to the assumptions and intentions of the exegetes and then according to the contexts in which exegesis was done, the tools on which it depended, and the fourfold levels of meaning believed to be normative. This part will represent largely my own synthesis and perspective. The second part is a historical survey of the major exegetes and schools from Gregory the Great to the Victorines and Cistercians of the mid-twelfth century. It depends on work done by intellectual historians and medievalists throughout the twentieth century.

CHARACTER AND METHODS OF MEDIEVAL EXEGESIS

Assumptions

To understand the body of exegesis that was done between, roughly, 600 and 1100 CE, one must appreciate the assumptions of the exegetes who flourished during that period. To a large extent, they inherited these assumptions from the classical Christian exegetes of the first five centuries, though they modified them in various important ways. Like the church fathers, medieval exegetes believed, first of all, that the Bible was not only, nor even primarily, a text, or an inert artifact to be studied by whatever methods were to hand. Rather, it was first and foremost a living word, a sacred force or energy that enlivens the church. As the resurrected Christ lived on in the community, present in the word proclaimed and enacted in ritual and in the living community itself, so too did the scriptural word live on. This means that, although early medieval exegetes understood the meaning of the written words to be a determined meaning — theirs was not a postmodernist perspective — it was only fully realized and understood as enacted by the believing community, ritually in the liturgy, personally in the lives of believers, and corporately in the historical reality of community en route to the final consummation. In consequence, they assumed that interpretation of Scripture was an experiential process, an understanding achieved only by those who were practicing the realities they studied. We see this clearly in Augustine's *De doctrina christiana*, the foundational document for all medieval academic activity (Augustine 1973: 539).

A second important assumption is that all of sacred Scripture tells an extended and ongoing story, the story of salvation. Begun in creation, that story continued and encompasses the full history of God's chosen people as narrated in the Old Testament and as it came to its temporal fulfillment in the New Testament. But for medieval exegetes salvation history continued beyond the New Testament, with a future completion only in the end time. The life of the church, narrated in the Pauline Letters and the Acts of Apostles, continued into their own national story, insofar as it was the story of the evangelization of each specific *gens* (nation). Thus did medieval exegetes interpret Christ's final injunction to the apostles at the end of Matthew's Gospel: the biblical narrative would be completed only when the gospel was preached to the ends of the earth. Therefore, for early medieval exegetes, the story of salvation in Scripture was illuminated and clarified by the concrete history of their own peoples, insofar as it was a "history of salvation."

Obviously, this assumption about the Bible as the vehicle for the story

Early Medieval Interpreters of the Bible

Gregory the Great
Sermons: Forty on the Gospels are recognized as authentic *(Homiliarum in Evangelia Libri II)*. There are also twenty-two on Ezekiel *(Homiliarum in Ezechielem Prophetam Libri II)*, and two on the Song of Songs.
Dialogues: Four books, including the life of Benedict.
Magna Moralia (Moralium Libri XXXV), a commentary on Job.
Liber Regulae Pastoralis
Some 850 letters *(Epistolarum Libri XIV)*.
Quaestiones in Vetus Testamentum

In English:
NPNF[2] 12 and 13 contain the letters and the *Liber Regulae Pastoralis*. Online at CCEL and NewAdv.
Liber Regulae Pastoralis, in ACW 11 (Westminster: Newman).
A 1911 translation of the Dialogues is online at CCELP.
The Commentary on Job appeared in the four-volume Library of the Fathers (Oxford: Oxford University Press, 1844).

Bede *(see also chapter 13)*
Historia ecclesiastica gentis Anglorum in 5 books. The *Historia* has been translated into English several times (see the bibliography). It is available online in Latin at TLL. English excerpts are available online at http://www.fordham.edu/halsall/basis/bede-book1.html
On the Reckoning of Time. The *Greater Chronicle (Chronica maiora)* is ch. 66 of *On the Reckoning of Time.*
Bede wrote commentaries on many biblical books including the Pentateuch, 1-2 Kings, Esdras, Tobias, Song of Songs, Mark, Luke, Acts, some of the Epistles, and Revelation. Some of the commentaries are available in CCSL 119 and 120.

Other interpreters discussed in this chapter
(see the bibliography for sources):
The Carolingian Schools: Alcuin, Haimo, Heiric, Remigius, and Rabanus Maurus.
The glosses and Scholasticism: Berengar of Tours, Drogo of Paris, Lanfranc of Bec, Anselm of Canterbury, Bruno of Chartreux, Master Manegold, Anselm and Ralph of Laon, Peter Lombard, and Gilbert of Poitiers.
The Victorines: Hugh, Richard, and Andrew.
The Cistercian School: Bernard of Clairvaux, Aelred of Rievaulx, Isaac of Stella, William of St. Thierry,
John Scotus Eriugena (see also chapter 13).

of salvation means that medieval exegetes worked under a third assumption, namely, that the many books of Scripture constituted, in reality, one book. This did not mean, however, that they ignored the differences among its authors. In his "Letter to Marcellinus," Athanasius of Alexandria had described the Bible, in its variety of books, in the following way: "Each sacred book supplies and announces its own promise" (Athanasius 1980: 101). He then gives a thumbnail sketch of the particular character of each of the biblical books. Athanasius was attentive both to the differences among genres and books and at the same time to their essential and integral unity. Bede (c. 673-735; see below), also, while he continually treated the various biblical books as fully understood only in relationship to one another, had a strong sense of the uniqueness of Lukan theology, for example, as he indicated in his introduction to the story of the penitent woman in Luke 7 (1960a: III, 4-15).

A fourth assumption of the early medieval exegetes is that sacred Scripture is a sophisticated literary text, requiring complex readings. Following in the tradition of the fathers, medieval scholars believed that the methods of literary criticism inherited from secular classical authors were both necessary and appropriate to the interpretation of Scripture. They recognized the literary differences among biblical genres and the rhetorical figures and strategies used by biblical authors. They were aware of the ancient controversy over the benefits and dangers of using "pagan" models and methods in the interpretation of the sacred texts, but they did not abandon the tools of classical literary criticism. Though some scholars, like Bede, wrote their own handbooks, based on biblical rather than pagan models, Priscian's work on grammar remained a much-copied, much-utilized text (see Miller, Frosser, Benson 1973; Kendall 1975).

Intentions

Like all scholars, medieval exegetes can be judged only in terms of what they attempted to achieve. Their primary intention was to preserve the continuous tradition of biblical interpretation that had begun within the texts of Scripture themselves — the interpretation of Hebrew texts by the New Testament authors — and had been laid down most completely by the patristic authors. In their understanding, fidelity to the tradition was the guarantee that the exegete would discern the true meaning of the text, that is, its divinely intended meaning. The position of Irenaeus (fl. 180) in *Against the Heresies* (3.2-3) had long since passed into the received wisdom of the church. Since God, in Christ, had revealed the divine plan to the apostles, their successors (the bishops of the apostolic churches) were the sources of the biblical truth and hence the authentic interpreters of it (1979: 415-16). This meant that for early medieval exegetes, the work of the church fathers served as both resource and norm. In the fourth to eighth centuries, the problem was one of access to the patristic tradition, obtaining copies of the texts and learning to read them. By the tenth and eleventh centuries, the task grew more critical: discerning among the fathers' multiple interpretations those that were more accurate to the original text. Such discernment depended on the exegete's skill in interpreting the original text and hence on his skill in reading the Latin of the Vulgate translation.

Early medieval exegetes were also committed to their own pastoral obligations to a specific community of faith. Whether bishop, teacher, or monk, each exegete was vividly aware of his own Christian community and the concrete questions and problems that arose within it. Each came to the text with questions about whether or not infant baptism was appropriate (as Bede asked when interpreting the story of the Syro-Phoenican woman in Mark 7, 1960b: 523-25), or how the knightly class ought to comport itself (Dhuoda's concern in *Liber Manualis*, 1975). The medieval exegete's task was to negotiate the relationship between the questions of his people and the received wisdom of the ancient tradition. He did this with greater or lesser insight and originality according to his own skills and the resources at his disposal.

Biblical Methods

Three specific aspects of medieval biblical method require attention. The first is context, the specific context within which various important medieval exegetes worked. The second is method (properly so-called), in this case the method that drew several levels of meaning out of the single text — what scholars call the "allegorical method." The third is tools, a term that encompasses both the strategies of literary criticism and the various literary resources that exegetes had at their disposal, focused primarily around the classical liberal arts.

Contexts Early medieval exegetes generally worked within three specific social contexts, all of which helped to shape their interpretation: the context of liturgical action, the monastic context, and the context of the schools. The liturgical context is overarching, and we see its influence in a number of ways. Much of the exegetical work of the early Middle Ages, like that of its patristic antecedents, is found in homilies. That means that individual texts or pericopes are interpreted neither in themselves nor only in relationship to the

specific book in which they are found, but in relationship to the other biblical
selections chosen for the day's liturgy. Often a day's readings are typologically
related, especially on the important feast days or events of the church. From
the earliest days, for instance, the celebration of Easter was marked by the
proclamation of the story of the paschal lamb in the book of Exodus in conjunction with the Gospel empty tomb stories. The custom of singing or proclaiming a psalm in response to one or the other of the readings brought a
third text into the interpretative dynamic. This process of interpreting passages in relation to one another was founded on, and continued to promote,
the assumption that all the Scriptures were essentially one.

But the liturgical context also meant that the typology by which Old
Testament and New Testament texts were related to each other had a third
term in the ritual action of the worshiping community assembled before the
homilist. The flood (Genesis 6–8), for instance, not only prefigured the triumph of Christ over the forces of evil, but also the salvation of those assembled for baptism (Bede 1991: 122). Furthermore, a homily required that interpretation of Scripture take cognizance of the moral and spiritual needs of the
community assembled for worship. Justin Martyr (c. 150), in his *Apology I,*
explained that after the Scriptures were read, "the presider exhorts us to imitate these things" (1953: 287). That obligation continued to shape the interpretation of Scripture and gave the specific and changing needs of Christians an
influential role in medieval interpretation. The earliest exegetes were bishops
of large urban churches; bishops and monastic leaders continued to create
the bulk of early medieval exegesis. The lives, especially the ritual lives, of
their communities consistently shaped the exegetes' biblical understanding.

In the social world of the monastery, liturgy was the central and con-
trolling activity, with the Divine Office, a daily round of psalms, scriptural
readings, hymns, and prayers, added to the celebration of Eucharist. Monastic
exegesis was thus subject to strong liturgical influences, with an emphasis on
typological readings. But the monastic Rule (Fry 1982: 38-48) also imposed
the practice of *lectio divina,* which taught the monk to read the Scriptures in
the light of his own life and his life in the light of the Scriptures. *Lectio divina*
or "sacred reading" is the slow, vocalized reading of a biblical text, often repeated until memorized and meditated on until it culminates in prayer
(Leclercq 1960: 89-90). This practice reinforced the medieval habit of understanding salvation history as continuing into one's own time, place, and people. But in the monastery, the individual struggle for spiritual growth in a
community setting raised its own questions concerning the biblical text. To
answer these, exegetes began to give an increasingly strong emphasis to the
moral level of interpretation and to apply the text to the spirituality expected

of the monk. We see this most clearly in Gregory the Great, and after him it became a major theme of all medieval exegesis.

Finally, as the period we are considering progressed, the work of exegesis began to be done more and more in schools. Connected as they were to either monasteries or urban cathedral communities, the schools continued to be influenced by liturgical practice and by the search for the spiritual meaning of the text through *lectio divina*. But the academic context ultimately had its way, and school exegetes grew more and more interested in sharpening the traditional tools of exegesis (the arts of the *trivium*) and in providing new ones.

Fourfold Interpretation   Among the most important ways in which medieval exegetes depended on the fathers is their use of the multileveled interpretation of the Scripture, the so-called allegorical method. Scholars (e.g., Spicq 1944: 267-88; Daniélou 1961; Froehlich 1984; Riche and Lobrichon 1984; Mayeski 2001) frequently use the term "allegorical exegesis" to designate the process of assigning different levels of meaning to the same text, especially when they distinguish between pre-modern exegesis and the historical-critical method. Earlier exegetes often used the term generically as well, but when they sought to distinguish among the various levels of meaning, they named one of these levels the "allegorical meaning." The full and complex story of medieval usage by individual scholars has been told in Henri de Lubac's monumental four-volume work, *Exégèse Mediéval* (1959-62). He demonstrates how individual scholars might explore anywhere from two to ten levels of meaning within the text and how their emphasis on one or another of them varied greatly. For our purposes, a brief summary of the general method will suffice, with some more specific remarks reserved to the historical survey.

The medieval exegete found both explanation of and justification for the four levels of meaning in the fundamental Latin fathers. Cassiodorus (485–c. 580), in the prefaces to his commentary on the Psalms, itemized them (1990: 35-36). Augustine gave brief definitions of each in *De utilitate credendi* (1947: chs. 5-6) and *De Genesi ad litteram* (1982: 19). For our purposes, it is sufficient to recognize that the historical/literal meaning tells what actually happened, the allegorical meaning indicates the theological meaning (specifically, how the text reveals Christ and the church), the tropological meaning teaches the truth about the soul's relationship to God, and the anagogical meaning illuminates the ultimate end of history and full reality of the end time.

Though medieval scholars tended to use "historical" and "literal" interchangeably in describing the first level of meaning, in practice there were significant differences. The historical meaning focuses on the events narrated. In dealing with the historical sense, the scholar attributes a particular significance to all the concrete details of a story, taking information from natural history, historical records, and ordinary experience to clarify the meaning. In exploring the literal meaning, the exegete attends carefully to the etymological and grammatical structure of the text as a source of meaning. This was increasingly true in the context of the schools. It is important to remember that, for the medieval scholar, history is not scientific history as we now understand it. He did have a sense of historical change and development, and many scholars (like Bede) understood the value of primary documentation in illuminating the past. But for medieval exegetes, history is always salvation history, divinely initiated and providentially guided with an eternal *telos* (ultimate purpose) in heaven. So when the medieval historian works, he is not reconstructing a possible past from discrete artifacts; he is discerning the divine economy of salvation planned from all eternity. That providential plan includes his own people and his own time, and therefore the historical meaning of the text can include the way in which the story of his own community is mirrored in the text. Thus does Bede speak of the newly converted English as referred to in the story of the Canaanite woman: they are the "dogs" who, once converted, gather the bread of truth from the table of Holy Scripture (Bede 1960a: 525).

The extended meaning of the text develops this latter insight. It allows the exegete to apply the text to the creed his community proclaimed in becoming Christian (the allegorical meaning), the practice of Christian life expected of the community's members (the tropological), and the hope for the future fullness of life by which they were motivated to fidelity (the anagogical). Following Augustine, medieval exegetes were unanimous in their conviction that the extended sense (however they may have subdivided it) was the superior meaning, and determining it was the exegete's primary task. Through the use of the allegorical method, Scripture would become the basis of all the theological work and moral treatises of the Middle Ages and beyond.

Tools of Biblical Method   Given the intention of medieval exegetes to reappropriate and update the patristic legacy of biblical interpretation, the question of what was actually available to them is critical to our appraisal of their accomplishment. First was the fathers. Scholars had Jerome's work for most of the Old Testament books and for the Gospel of Matthew. In spite of his later condemnation of Origen, Jerome had depended heavily upon Origen's work in constructing his own commentaries; so later exegetes reading Jerome were in fact absorbing much of Origen (Gribomont 1992). Augustine contributed the standard interpretations of Genesis, Psalms, John's Gospel, and 1 John as well as work on Romans and Galatians (Oates 1948). For Luke there was the commentary of Ambrose (1956-58), and Bede's commentaries on Mark and Acts were the standard references for those books (Bede 1960b). Gregory the Great's *Moralia in Iob* was a kind of compendium of his predecessors; he had culled Greek and Latin sources widely, and his interpretations reached far beyond the text of Job (Gregory the Great 1844). The Antiochene thread of interpretation survived in the work of Ambrosiaster (Ambrosiaster 1908), an anonymous contemporary of Ambrose, and Latin translations of John Chrysostom (Chrysostom 1979; see also Clark 1982) and Theodore of Mopsuestia (Swete 1880-82; Devresse 1939) were extant as well. Finally, around 850 CE, a scholar from the Lyon region mined the excellent collection of Augustine to which he had access to construct a great *Collectaneum* of passages on Pauline texts. This would become the major source for later interpretations of Paul (Gibson 1971).

The primary tools of medieval exegetes were the liberal arts, the traditional academic disciplines that had been developed in the classical world. The full story of their medieval use and development is too vast and complex to be told here; some of that story will be unfolded in the section on biblical interpretation in the medieval schools below. Augustine had legitimated the use of the liberal arts in his *De doctrina christiana* (Augustine 1973: 543-55). Cassiodorus had laid out the application of the *trivium* — grammar, dialectic, and rhetoric — to biblical exegesis in his *Institutiones* (Cassiodorus 1937). Thereafter, the *trivium* would be the fundamental tools for biblical exegesis while arithmetic, music, astronomy, and geometry would be collateral sources of meaning.

For all medieval exegetes, the first task in biblical interpretation was to learn Latin, specifically the Latin of the Vulgate; grammar was, therefore, the first tool to be mastered. The grammars of Donatus and Priscian were available to students from the beginning (see Robins 1998), but the Vulgate Bible itself was the primary text; as the scholar advanced, he would progressively come to write and think within its thought world. When reading medieval exegesis, it is helpful to understand that an accomplished medieval Latinist spoke and wrote, not just Latin, but "Bible." His sentence structure, vocabulary, and stylistic devices were rooted in the Vulgate texts.

Dialectic, the study of the logical development of thought and argumentation, came second. In the early Middle Ages it was based on the "old logic" of Aristotle, which came to the medieval world through Cassiodorus (see Mair 1975) and Martianus Capella, but especially through Boethius in *De topicis differentiis* (Boethius 1978).

Rhetoric, the study of language and its effect, was a wide umbrella, covering many aspects of the structure of Latin. During the early Middle Ages, it was not as concerned with the composition of persuasive argument as in classical practice, but was part of the pedagogy of literacy. Augustine had alerted medieval scholars to the dangers of ignoring the complexities of figurative language in the *De doctrina christiana* (Augustine 1973). The study of rhetoric (based primarily on Cicero's *De inventione* [Cicero 1969] and the *Rhetorica ad Herennium,* also attributed to Cicero [1954]) enabled biblical exegetes to avoid these dangers by dealing competently with the literary character of the biblical texts.

HISTORICAL SURVEY:
THE DEVELOPMENT OF EARLY MEDIEVAL EXEGESIS

We turn now to specific authors and a brief historical survey of their work, the development of biblical exegesis from Gregory the Great to the schools of the eleventh and early twelfth centuries. Smalley laid out the definitive roadmap for this exercise in her *Study of the Bible in the Middle Ages* (1952). Her work, which also includes preliminary studies of the major thinkers, has not yet been fully superseded, nor have her critical judgments been invalidated. Her influence will be particularly visible in the section on the twelfth-century schools below.

Gregory the Great

Gregory the Great (540-604) — monk, diplomat, and bishop of Rome, as well as scholar — is the first of the early medieval exegetes and, indeed, a kind of fountainhead of all subsequent exegesis. He was the son of a Roman senator and was educated in the classical manner; he became *praefectus urbi* before abandoning civic life for the monastery. He founded monasteries and settled happily in one of them before the long arm of the Roman church reached him. He was first made one of the seven deacons of Rome, then papal *apocrisiarius,* in which office he served about seven years in Constantinople. It was during this time that Gregory began his monumental *Expositio in Librum Iob, sive Moralium Libri* (Gregory the Great 1844) in response to the requests made of him by monks in Constantinople. Soon after returning to his Roman monastery, he was elected bishop of Rome over his strongest objections, but continued his exegetical work. He wrote the *Expositio in Ezechial, XXV Homiliae in Evangelium* (Gregory the Great 1971; ET Gray 1990), and possibly a commentary on the Song of Songs (Gregory the Great 1963), as well as the *Cura Pastoralis* (Gregory the Great 1950), which was to become the medieval charter for governmental organization and virtues, with far-ranging secular and ecclesiastical influence.

Gregory consistently explained the process of exegesis, its purposes and methods, even as he modeled that process. He inherited from the patristic world the theory of the multiple senses of the scriptural text; he himself generally recognized three spiritual senses (allegory, anagogy, and tropology). He insisted that the historical sense was foundational and essential and that to ignore it was to risk serious misinterpretation. He also showed, however, a marked preference for the spiritual senses, not from unwillingness or inability to discover the historical meaning, but from a conviction that the many levels of meaning in the Scripture reflect the essential unknowability of the divine mystery (Dagens 1977: 7-13). Before such mystery, only learned ignorance is appropriate, a humble ascent from the simpler historical sense to the more obscure spiritual senses. Gregory's reputation as an exegete has suffered in some circles because his followers often imitated his preference for the extended meanings and ignored his insistence on the historical/literal meaning. Isidore of Seville, for instance, hurries on intentionally to the spiritual, as he tells us explicitly in his preface to the *Quaestiones in Vetus Testamentum* (PL 83, 208B, C; see Wasselynch 1965).

Since he himself read widely in both the Greek and Latin fathers, Gregory's commentaries and homilies continue the traditional lines of interpretation as the classical authors set them up. But he was also an independent thinker. He cites Jerome, for instance, in order to correct him, and he does not cite him often (Evans 1986: 88). He also developed independent interpretations that would become *topoi* of the tradition. He was the first to conflate the stories of Mary Magdalene with those of an anonymous sinful woman in the Synoptic tradition, and forever made her name synonymous with "the fallen woman," but also called her "the Apostle of the Apostles" (Gregory the Great 1990). In terms of exegesis, Gregory the Great is one of the bridges between patristic theology and the Middle Ages — an aqueduct, rather, that carried the living waters of biblical understanding from the world of classical Christian faith to the Germanic world. From there, it was diverted into many streams and nourished new forms of Christian life, which were new responses to radically new challenges.

The Venerable Bede

Bede (673-735), known as the Venerable, was a monk at the twin monasteries of Jarrow and Wearmouth in Northumbria in Britain, a location that would have been, in the early eighth century, close to the farthest reaches of the known world. Its isolation and geography ought to have consigned Bede to oblivion; instead, he was probably the best educated man in his day and was extensively cited in all biblical exegesis up to the Reformation and beyond. Better known today for his *History of the English Church and Peoples* (Bede 1955), Bede and his contemporaries valued his exegetical work more highly. In almost every way, Bede's exegesis is more like that of the fathers who preceded him than that of the exegetes who would follow him. He wrote commentaries on the Gospels of Mark and Luke, two volumes of homilies on the Sunday and feast day readings of the church year, as well as commentaries on Revelation, Acts, the Catholic Epistles, and various Old Testament books and sections (see Bede 1962, 1967, 1969a, b, and c; 1972, 1983a and b). He also wrote textbooks on grammar and rhetoric (see Bede 1975) and scientific treatises on the calculation of time (used for dating the yearly Easter feast; see Bede 1977) and on the nature of things — a cosmography that drew on the work of Isidore, Pliny, and Suetonius (Bede 1980). Bede was committed to the Augustinian ideal of solid learning in support of biblical understanding and faith.

Bede's method of exegesis was entirely patristic and owed much to the theory and practice of Gregory the Great. Typically, he divides his commentaries and homilies into two parts, discussing first the historical meaning of the text and then the "mystical" (by which Bede designates all higher meanings: theological, moral, and eschatological). We must remember the Greek root of the word "mystical" here. In Bede's usage, it indicates all the meanings that point to the great *mystērion* of God and God's plan for salvation. He pays more attention than Gregory to the historical/literal meaning of the text. He had at his disposal the historical works of Josephus and Eusebius, which he used at length, and he had read the historical books of the Old Testament with such careful attention that he had mastered a usable understanding of ancient Hebrew law and practice. In his commentary on Luke 1:5, for instance, he establishes the complex line of Jewish priestly structures and considers the historical possibility whereby someone of the line of Abijah might marry Elizabeth of the tribe of Aaron (1960a: 21-22). He freely explores the scientific and medical knowledge of his own day, limited as it was, to illuminate, for instance, the doctrinal affirmations of Mary's virginity and divine maternity.

Bede cites patristic authorities at length, but always with discrimination. He pays careful attention to how the fathers may clarify the situation of his own times and people and treats the fathers with originality and critical judgment. In his commentary on the story of the Syro-Phoenician woman in Mark's Gospel (1960b: 523-25), for instance, he takes a long passage from Jerome but omits Jerome's negative description of pagan peoples (lest it reflect badly on his own). He highlights the antithesis between the bread and the crumbs, rather than that between the children and the dogs, and turns it into a parabolic exhortation to biblical study (Mayeski 1995). His pastoral purpose is evident here and throughout. In the same piece of commentary as it appears in one of the homilies, he uses the woman's intercession for the healing of her daughter as an opportunity to discuss the validity of infant baptism.

The Carolingian Schools

Though the Carolingian period (the period during which Charlemagne and his descendents ruled a united Francia, c. 785-850) did not produce an abundance of memorable exegesis such as we find in Gregory and Bede, its intellectual activity in interpreting the Bible is foundational and formative for all subsequent biblical interpretation. With the publication of the *Admonitio Generalis* in 789 (see Bettenson and Maunder 1999: 106), Charlemagne sought to establish schools throughout the empire and to initiate a far-reaching literacy project, laying the groundwork for significant intellectual advances. By the end of the Carolingian period, schools at monastic and cathedral sites were teaching the liberal arts. The Vulgate text had undergone significant corrections. The number of manuscripts available for study had increased exponentially, and biblical exegesis was widely pursued (McKitterick 1994: 319).

Alcuin   A Northumbrian scholar formed in the tradition of Bede, Alcuin (fl. 785) provided the structure of the curriculum for the Carolingian schools. In his *De vere philosophia* (PL 100-101), he provides a program of the liberal arts that is not just a reflection of educational practice in late antiquity but a result of his own Neoplatonic speculation about the nature of knowledge. He transforms Augustine, insisting that it is through Scripture that we grasp the underlying nature of knowledge, not the other way around (Marenbon 1994: 172-73). Biblical exegesis became, then, the hermeneutical key by which all knowledge was accurately situated and understood, not just the appropriate teleology for a liberal education.

Alcuin stressed the importance of grammar in interpreting the historical/literal sense. Alcuin's influence in promoting the historical meaning may account for the increase of interest in Cassiodorus's *Ecclesiastical History* (PL 101.69-70); it was increasingly copied in Carolingian *scriptoria* and was regularly used after that time (see Laistner 1948). Alcuin also influenced the development of dialectic in relation to the study of Scripture. He wrote a *De dialectica* (PL 101.949A-74C), promoted Boethius's *Opuscula Sacra* (2000), and translated Aristotle's *De decem categoriis* (Aristotle 1980). The *Opuscula*, an odd assortment of small works dealing with both theological (i.e., philosophical) and logical topics, supported the medieval conviction that these two disciplines were intellectually connected. Alcuin's preface to a presentation copy of *De decem categoriis* explains how the whole created sensate world could be reduced to order through proper signification and the application of the rules of logic (Gibson 1982: 53).

By the later Carolingian period, scholars had mastered this "old logic" and understood its usefulness in resolving intellectual conflicts. In the school of Auxerre (the collection of exegetical and philosophical work done by the scholars of the monastery at Auxerre c. 835-893), logical studies of the Bible bore abundant fruit. Between 840 and c. 900, three generations of scholars, principally Haimo (Contreni 1976), Heiric (Jeauneau 1991), and Remigius (Leonardi 1975) standardized the theological curriculum, wrote commentaries on the philosophical works of Martianus Capella and Boethius, and began to speculate on how the universe was put together (Boethius 1978). Theological education and the ability to expound upon the biblical text had come far.

Rabanus Maurus   Though it would be misleading to try to separate the achievements of the Carolingian schools from those of monastery and cathedral schools, the academic developments of a place like Auxerre is not representative of Carolingian exegesis as a whole. More typical of the Carolingian exegete is Rabanus Maurus (c. 780-856), called the "Preceptor of Germany." As Archbishop of Mainz, he undertook a massive project of evangelization to deepen and spread the faith in his diocese through biblical education. He wrote commentaries on almost all the books of the Bible for the education of church leadership, both clerical and lay (Rabanus Maurus 1878). In these commentaries, he intended essentially to transmit the patristic tradition and to bring its wisdom to bear on his own time and place. He cites much, but carefully, with marginal sigla to indicate his sources. These sources range widely through the Alexandrian and Antiochene fathers such as Origen, Augustine, Jerome, and Ambrosiaster. Like all his contemporaries, Maurus had a marked preference for the extended senses of Scripture; yet he made his own contribution to the development of historical/literal interpretation as well. He developed Bede's work on the spiritual exposition of 1-2 Kings (Bede 1972) by finding the literal meanings of the text in scattered patristic references and in the works of Josephus. He also used some contemporary Jewish material on the interpretation of the law (Smalley 1952: 43). Even today underrated as an exegete, Maurus was more original than he probably intended to be. Nearly half of his Matthew commentary, for example, is original, "sensibly arranged, all carefully integrated into a credible and coherent whole" (Brown 1994: 41). Furthermore, his very selection of sources reveals a discriminating and critical mind, and his pastoral applications demonstrate originality of insight. His attempt, for instance, to find the structures of his own church in the list of charismatic ministries listed in the Pauline epistles leads Maurus to some penetrating insights into the historical Pauline churches (Rabanus Maurus 1878: PL 112, 116A, B).

Taken together, Maurus's accomplishments and those of the exegetes in the schools demonstrate the full achievement of the period. Carolingian scholars laid down the major lines along which medieval exegesis would further develop: an assumption that the historical/literal meaning of the text was only a foundation to its more important spiritual meaning, an emphasis on grammar and dialectic as the tools used to unlock all levels of scriptural meaning, the critical use of the patristic sources vis-à-vis the contemporary questions, and consultation with Jewish scholars.

School Glosses and Scholasticism

Grammatical and logical skills developed slowly from the middle of the ninth through the tenth century, as did critical appropriation of the patristic legacy. By the middle of the eleventh century two trends emerged in the work of the schools, both related to biblical exegesis: the reclamation and critical use of the fathers had begun to flower into that instrument known as the *Glossa ordinaria,* and philosophical reflection grounded in grammar and dialectic began to shape exegesis in the direction of theology. A kind of school textbook, the gloss was a manuscript of the original text, in this case of a biblical book, with lecturer's notes written in the margins (widened for this purpose) or between the lines of the original text. The notes were almost entirely taken from the patristic sources. The glossators cite not only the major Latin fathers, Bede, and certain Greek fathers, notably Origen (in translation), but also Carolingian authors like Rabanus Maurus and John the Scot (810-877; John the Scot 1972). Individual anonymous masters occasionally added comments of their own. Evans has described the creation of the gloss: the master would "go over the existing commentaries, to select and prune and to draw everything together into a relatively uniform whole, covering all the necessary points briefly, clearly and authoritatively" (1984: 38).

The beginnings of the gloss lie in obscurity; manuscripts were passed around, with later masters editing and adding to the work of their predecessors. Smalley tracked the early development of biblical glosses and judged the earliest pieces to devolve from Berengar of Tours (d. 1088), his friend Drogo of Paris, and Lanfranc of Bec (d. 1089). Bruno of Chartreux at Rheims and Master Manegold in Paris played early roles, but the most important contributions seem to have come from the lectures of Anselm of Laon (d. 1117) and his brother Ralph (d. 1133) at the school of Laon (see Smalley 1952, 1969, 1978). This brings the story into the early twelfth century. By mid-century, Peter Lombard (1100-1160) and Gilbert of Poitiers (1076-1154), a pupil of Anselm, were continuing the work at Paris and helping to effect the transition to a new kind of biblical reflection and theology that would become Scholasticism.

The gloss was a school text and represents a method of exegesis dictated by the pedagogical process of the medieval schoolroom. Typically, the master read a passage from the original biblical text, pausing to comment on words, phrases, or sentences from the perspective of grammar or logic. Periodically he would interrupt the flow of reading and commentary to address a specific question — his own, his students', or one raised by earlier authors. It is in the nature of these questions and the way they are answered that the content of biblical exegesis begins to change. The change was the result of increased sophistication in the disciplines of grammar and rhetoric, a sharpening of the time-honored tools of medieval exegesis that had begun in the Carolingian schools, largely in the work of Alcuin.

Increased grammatical competence had revealed that the biblical text did not always conform to the standard rules of syntax or the conventional uses of words. And yet medieval scholars required that "Every word had to be accounted for, in its context. Specific explanations had to be found for every oddity of expression or grammatical superfluity" (Evans 1984: 7). Grammatical inquiry thus gave rise to epistemological considerations and ultimately raised the profound question of the inadequacy of human language for discourse about divine revelation. This stimulated a renewed interest in ancient theological doctrines and a new desire to see the elements of the Christian creed in their complex unity. By the mid-eleventh century, exegetes had also developed their understanding of Boethian dialectic (what was called the "old logic") into a significant tool for biblical and theological discourse. With it, they began to speculate about and classify the natural world, in search of the "knowable order," even as they looked for coherence and completeness in the ancient doctrines. They began to see two different "worlds" behind the appearances of the natural order: the spiritual realities of which phenomena were but a symbol, and the substance, genera, and species that connected the phenomena in a logical order (Southern 1948: 34). Scriptural exegesis could illuminate the first of these two worlds, while the second required theological speculation. The marriage of these two lines of thought brought forth progeny in the form of new classroom questions and ultimately the new discipline of theology.

Scholars have seen the evidence for these new developments in grammar and dialectic primarily in the work of Lanfranc of Bec (d. 1009) and Anselm of Canterbury (c. 1033-1109). Gibson has noted Lanfranc's contributions (1978). She demonstrates that in studying the Pauline Epistles Lanfranc had for the first time begun to read Paul with a concern for the dialectical structure of his thought, searching for its logical consistency, and imagining Paul as engaged in a debate with intellectual opponents. Additionally, dialectic moved, in some instances, from being a tool of scriptural analysis to one of constructive theology, as theologians began to isolate the theological questions and build a coherent and comprehensive theological structure upon the foundation of the scriptural text.

Anselm of Canterbury, who moved from the schoolroom at Bec to the bishopric of Canterbury, demonstrates the earliest movement of this sort. Evans offers a penetrating analysis of his contribution. She notes that Anselm neither wrote commentaries nor explicitly cited the fathers. Rather he strove to lead students to think inside the biblical language, understanding how it functions. In the *De veritate, De Libertate Arbitrii,* and *De casu Diaboli* (see Davies and Evans 1998), he explores critical issues of interpretation through the principles of grammar and dialectic, using individual texts only occasionally but subject to such intense scrutiny that the method is apparent (Evans 1984: 18-20). The shift in emphasis is obvious. So too is the new academic atmosphere of intellectual curiosity and audacity of experimentation.

Together, then, the advancements in grammar and dialectic combined to pose new questions to the scholar engaged in the careful, critical reading of the biblical text. These changes were soon reflected in the kind of writings that emerged from the schoolrooms. The *quaestio,* originally a brief theological interruption in the commentary, began to grow at the expense of the commentary itself, a development well represented by Abelard's commentary on Romans. Soon the *quaestiones,* with their extended explanations, were extracted from the commentary and circulated as texts in themselves. Finally, they were rearranged into compilations that seemed to the author to represent a more coherent organization than that of their original scriptural context. Thus was born Peter Lombard's (1100-1160) *Book of the Sentences* (see Brady 1971-81), which became, in less than fifty years, the primary text for theological study, replacing the combined tool of text and commentary and receiving its own set of glosses and commentaries. In the beginning, the separation of the theological questions from the biblical text was probably not much noticed. By the time scholars reached this level of theological study, they had so mastered the original text and standard commentaries that they knew well the original location of the theological questions. But over time the separation would have critical consequences for both exegesis and theology. The stage was set for the developments known as Scholasticism.

The Victorines

But Scholasticism was by no means the only exegetical method of the twelfth century. At the Abbey of St. Victor, founded in 1110 by William of Champeaux, several generations of scholars restructured the academic curriculum and took exegesis in a different direction, seeking to return it to the roots and spirit of monastic *lectio divina*.

Hugh of St. Victor   The first of these notable scholars, Hugh of St. Victor (1096-1141), valued the sophisticated use of dialectic but deplored the growing separation between theological *quaestiones* and the biblical text. He wanted to return to the Augustinian ideal of the *De doctrina christiana* while maintaining the higher level of critical thought that had developed. He organized the liberal arts curriculum as sequential stages parallel to the threefold exposition of Scripture (published in the *Didascalicon;* see Taylor 1961). In the first stage, the student learned the traditional arts and sciences, which were necessary for the historical reading of the text. After this, the student would study Christian doctrine in order to read, on an allegorical level, the New Testament books rich in doctrine (the Gospels and Epistles) and the Old Testament books that contain the clearest foreshadowings of the Christ (e.g., Isaiah and the Psalms). According to Hugh, the third stage of learning, the tropological, involves a synthesis of learning and virtue. Here what is wanted is contemplation, not only of the biblical text taken as a whole, but also of the works of God in nature. Hugh writes very little about this stage.

Hugh's understanding of biblical exposition tamed the often exuberant use of the extended or "higher" sense of the text. He proposed three steps: to deal accurately with the actual words, through grammatical construction and syntax; then to determine what the divine writer means, his own "sense"; finally, to grasp the full meaning of the text by reference to the coherent structure of Christian faith. In arriving at this "full meaning," Hugh unequivocally states that the intended meaning of the author must guide the exegete, even in selecting from among patristic commentaries (Smalley 1952: 94-95). By making the historical sense the first object of three equal stages of study, Hugh gave it a new importance. For his own historical commentary he consulted the Jewish scholars in Paris. He obtained a literal Latin translation of the Hebrew Bible (with which he compared the Vulgate text), attempted to learn Hebrew himself, and made comments in his *Notulae* ("a collection of short notes"; see Smalley 1952: 97-98) that duplicate opinions of Rashi, a Jewish rationalist exegete of Northern France. He cites Jewish scholars with learned appreciation (Stiegman 2001: 129-55). Subsequent scholars at Saint Victor's would build on this new emphasis on the literal/historical sense.

Richard of St. Victor In contrast with Hugh, Richard of St. Victor (d. 1173) was most original and interesting when he was expounding the spiritual sense of Scripture. He is best known for his *Benjamin Minor* and *Benjamin Major* (Zinn 1979), in which his commentary on the family of Jacob and on the Tabernacle structure his understanding of contemplation. In spite of this purpose, Richard's commentary on the biblical text is carefully and completely literal. He has great interest in the important buildings of the Jewish Scripture — Solomon's temple, the Tabernacle, the Temple in which Ezekiel had the vision of living creatures. In the commentaries on all these texts, he attends to every detail of measurement and often gives diagrams and sketches to illustrate his verbal commentary. He also consulted Jewish masters and folded their information into his own opinions. But he looked with a severely critical eye at the Jewish consultations done by his colleague and brother monk Andrew, not because Andrew sought out Jewish interpretations but because Richard believed that he used them too uncritically, a judgment not always shared by others.

Andrew of St. Victor Andrew of St. Victor (d. 1175) is a true anomaly in medieval exegesis. He shows virtually no interest in the doctrinal or spiritual meanings of the biblical text and instead gives the most thorough historical exegesis of the whole period. Following Hugh's spirit and example, Andrew extensively consulted the Jewish rabbis and regularly checked the Vulgate text against the Hebrew. He follows the traditional procedure of consulting patristic authors, but limits himself almost exclusively to Jerome and Josephus with some occasional use of Augustine and Bede (Signer 1991). He comments entirely upon the books of the Old Testament, and even here he writes neither commentary nor gloss but a series of *notulae* (notes), *compositiones* (an orderly arrangement), and *expositiones historicae* (historical interpretations), selecting Old Testament passages of particular interest and/or difficulty, to which he gave detailed critical attention. Perhaps because he is concentrating so single-mindedly upon the historical/literal sense, Andrew has no difficulty in the critical use of his sources. Historical facts, even in the Middle Ages, did not have the authoritative status of the doctrines of faith, and Andrew, in expounding the historical sense, rejects or approves various traditional and Jewish opinions as reason and study guide him. He had a modest appreciation of his own work; he accepted the medieval axiom that the historical sense was only the necessary foundation for the higher meanings of the text, and he believed himself merely an artisan refining the groundwork. Extant manuscripts and library catalogues, however, indicate the scope of his post-humous reputation. He seems to have been read in Cistercian as well as English monastic circles and, a hundred years later, Roger Bacon (1214-1292) credits him with redirecting appropriate scholarly attention to the original sources (Smalley 1952). He was quoted by later scholars such as Peter Chanter, Peter Comestor, and Stephen Langton (Smalley 1952), *inter alios*. The Victorines had stimulated a new, critical interest in the literal sense of Scripture that would not be lost.

The Cistercian School

In addition to the academic schools and the school of St. Victor, there is also the Cistercian school of biblical exegesis, which represents a full flowering of the ancient monastic tradition of *lectio divina*, the contemplative, careful reading of the biblical text. The Cistercians were not removed from the academic accomplishments and interests of their time; most of those who distinguished themselves in exegesis — Bernard of Clairvaux (1090-1153), Aelred of Rievaulx (1109-67), Isaac of Stella (1100-78), William of St. Thierry (c. 1075/80-1148) — had been educated in the schools before committing themselves to Cistercian life. Their biblical interpretation was marked by the new scholastic advances in grammar and dialectic and by a new comprehension of Neoplatonic philosophy gleaned for the most part from Cicero. What most characterizes their biblical interpretation is the new life they breathe into the earlier tradition of monastic exegesis. They show their originality in expounding the spiritual sense, the application of the text to the personal relationship with God and the human journey of life. Here they are enriched by their close observation of human behavior in the monastic community; their spiritual exegesis shows an almost modern psychological insight. Their exegesis is entirely christocentric; they see the redemptive work of God enacted in human history as a coherent, programmatic, and progressive whole. The great liturgical themes of creation and exodus become the hermeneutical key for understanding the stages of human life. They appropriate the deuteronomic historian's view of history as a cycle of sin, repentance, and divine intervention in order to interpret the lives of their monastic communities and of individual monks. Living within the round of liturgical services and the cycle of feasts, chanting and reading the Scriptures daily, they think entirely within the thought world and images of the Bible. Their commentaries and treatises read almost like a concordance of memory (Leclercq 1961: 95-96), in which words and phrases from one text are expanded and illuminated by their echoes in other books. For the Cistercian exegetes (see Bernard of Clairvaux 1971-1980; Aelred of Rievaulx 2001; William of St. Thierry 1978), the method of *lectio divina,* used with scholarly care, produced biblical interpretations that are at once personal and ecclesial, traditional and contemporary. The monastic line of biblical exegesis had reached its apogee.

CONCLUSION

The range of biblical interpretation by the middle of the twelfth century was wide and diverse. Scholastic interpretation was moving steadily in the direction of philosophical synthesis. The Victorines built a solid basis for pursuing the historical meaning of the text and kept alive an earlier tradition of consultation with Jewish authorities. The monastic line, with its emphasis on moral and liturgical interpretation, flowered with the reforming energy of the century. However, a profound unity grounded all the diversity: a respectful, critical attention to the tradition and a conviction that the biblical text was the foundation of all Christian life and thought.

BIBLIOGRAPHY

Aelred of Rievaulx

2001   *The Liturgical Sermons.* Trans. T. Berkeley and M. B. Pennington. Kalamazoo: Cistercian.

Ambrose

1956-58 *Expositio Evangelii secundum Lucam.* Ed. G. Tissot. SC 44, 52; Paris: Cerf.

Ambrosiaster

1908   *Quaestiones Veteris et Novi Testamenti.* Ed. A. Souter. CSEL 50; Vienna: Geroldi.
1966-69 *Commentaria in XIII Epistulas Paulinas.* 3 vols. Ed. H. J. Vogels. CSEL 81; Vienna: Geroldi.

Aristotle

1980   *Categories and Propositions (De interpretatione).* Trans. H. G. Apostle. Grinnell: Peripatetic.

Athanasius

1980   *The Life of Antony and the Letter to Marcellinus.* Trans. R. C. Gregg. Mahwah: Paulist.

Augustine

1947   *De utilitate credendi.* In *The Fathers of the Church, Writings of St. Augustine,* vol. 4. Trans. L. Meagher. New York: Cima.

1973   *De Doctrina Christiana.* Ed. P. Schaff. Trans. J. F. Shaw. *NPNF*[1], 2, 515-97. Grand Rapids: Eerdmans.

1982   *De Genesi ad litteram.* Trans. J. H. Taylor. ACW 41; New York: Newman.

Bede (the Venerable)

1955   *A History of the English Church and People.* Trans. L. Sherley-Price. New York: Penguin.

1960a   *In Lucam.* CCSL 120; Turnhout: Brepols.

1960b   *In Marci Evangelium Expositio.* CCSL 120; Turnhout: Brepols.

1962   *In primam partem Samuhelis.* CCSL 119; Turnhout: Brepols.

1967   *In principium Genesim.* Ed. C. W. Jones. CCSL 118A; Turnhout: Brepols.

1969a   *De tabernaculo.* CCSL 119A; Turnhout: Brepols.

1969b   *De Templo.* CCSL 119A; Turnhout: Brepols.

1969c   *In Esram et Neemiam.* CCSL 119A; Turnhout: Brepols.

1972   *In Regum Librum XXX quaestiones.* CCSL 119; Turnhout: Brepols.

1975   *De Schematibus et Tropis.* Ed. C. B. Kendall, 142-71. CCSG 123A; Turnhout: Brepols.

1977   *De tempore ratione.* Ed. C. W. Jones and T. Mommsen. CCSL 123B; Turnhout: Brepols.

1980   *De temporibus.* Ed. C. W. Jones and T. Mommsen. CCSL 123C; Turnhout: Brepols.

1983a   *In Cantica Canticorum.* CCSL 119B; Turnhout: Brepols.

1983b   *In Habacuc.* Ed. J. E. Hudson. CCSL 119B; Turnhout: Brepols.

1990   *Ecclesiastical History of the English People.* Rev., ed., and trans. L. Sherley-Price. New York: Penguin.

1991   "Homily 12," in *Bede the Venerable, Homilies on the Gospels I.* Trans. L. T. Martin and D. Hurst. CCSL 122; Kalamazoo: Cistercian.

Bernard of Clairvaux

1971-80   *Sermon on the Song of Songs,* vols. I-IV. Trans. K. Walsh and I. Edmonds. Kalamazoo: Cistercian.

Bettenson, H., and C. Maunder

1999   *Documents of the Christian Church.* Oxford: Oxford University Press.

Boethius

1973   *The Theological Tractates.* Ed. H. F. Stewart and E. K. Rand. 3rd ed. Loeb Classical Library 248; Cambridge: Harvard University Press.

1978   *De topicis differentiis.* Trans. E. Stump. Ithaca: Cornell University Press.

2000   *Opuscula Sacra* and *De consolatione Philosophiae.* Ed. C. Moreschini. Munich: Saur.

Brady, I. C. (ed.)

1971-81   *Sententiae in IV libris distinctae,* 2 vols. Grottaferrata: Editiones Collegium S. Bonaventurae ad Claras Aquas.

Brown, G.

1994 "Introduction: The Carolingian Renaissance," in McKitterick (ed.) 1994: 1-51.

Cassiodorus

1937 *Institutiones.* Ed. R. A. B. Mynors. Oxford: Clarendon.

1990 *Explanation of the Psalms.* Ed. W. J. Burghardt and T. Comerford, trans. P. G. Walsh. ACW 51; New York: Paulist.

Catry, P.

1972a *Epreuves du juste et mystère de Dieu. Le commentaire littéral du livre de Job par saint Grégoire le Grand.* Paris: Institut d'Études augustiniennes.

1972b "Lire l'écriture selon saint Grégoire le Grand," *Collectanea Cisterciensia* 34: 177-201.

Cavadini, J. D. (ed.)

1995 *Gregory the Great: A Symposium.* Notre Dame Studies in Theology; South Bend: Notre Dame University Press.

Chrysostom, J.

1979 *Saint John Chrysostom: Discourses against Judaizing Christians.* Trans. P. W. Harkins. The Fathers of the Church, 68; Washington: Catholic University of America Press.

Cicero, Marcus Tullius

1954 *Rhetorica ad Herennium.* Ed. H. Caplan. Loeb Classical Library 403; Cambridge: Harvard University Press.

1969 *De inventione, De Optimo, Genera Oratorum, Topica.* Ed. H. M. Hubbell. Loeb Classical Library 386; Cambridge: Harvard University Press.

Clark, E. A.

1982 *Jerome, Chrysostom, and Friends: Essays and Translations,* 2nd ed. (New York: Edwin Mellen).

Contreni, J. J.

1976 "The Biblical Glosses of Haimo of Auxerre and John Scottus Eriugena." *Speculum* 51: 411-34.

Dagens, C. S.

1977 *Grégoire le Grand. Culture et expérience chrétienne.* Paris: Études Augustiniennes.

Daniélou, J.

1961 *From Shadows to Reality: Studies in the Biblical Typology of the Fathers.* Westminster: Newman.

Davies, B., and G. R. Evans (eds.)

1998 *Anselm of Canterbury: The Major Works.* Oxford: Oxford University Press.

Devresse, R.

1939 *Le Commentaire de Theodore de Mopsueste sur les Psaumes.* Vatican City: Biblioteca Apostolica Vaticana.

Dhuoda

1975   *Liber Manualis.* Ed. P. Riché. SC 225; Paris: Cerf.

Evans, G. R.

1984   *The Language and Logic of the Bible: The Earlier Middle Ages.* Cambridge: Cambridge University Press.

1986   *The Thought of Gregory the Great.* Cambridge: Cambridge University Press.

Froehlich, K. (ed.)

1984   *Biblical Interpretation in the Early Church.* Philadelphia: Fortress.

Fry, T. (ed.)

1982   *The Rule of St. Benedict in English.* Collegeville: Liturgical.

Gibson, M.

1971   "Lanfranc's 'Commentary on the Pauline Epistles.'" *JTS* 22: 86-112.

1975   "The Continuity of Learning Circa 850–Circa 1050," *Viator* 6: 1-13.

1978   *Lanfranc de Bec.* Oxford: Clarendon.

1982   "Boethius in the Carolingian Schools." *TRHS* 32: 43-56.

1993   "The *artes* in the 11th Century," in *'Artes' and Bible in the Medieval West.* Ed. M. Gibson, 121-26. Aldershot: Variorum.

Gregory the Great

1844   *Magna Moralia, "Library of the Fathers."* 4 vols. Oxford: Oxford University Press.

1862   *Quaestiones in Vetus Testamentum. PL* 83.

1950   *Pastoral Rule.* ACW 11; Westminster: Newman.

1963   *Canticum Canticorum.* Ed. P. Verbraken. CCSL 144; Turnhout: Brepols.

1971a   *Expositio in Ezechial, XXV Homiliae in Evangelium.* Trans. T. Gray. Etna: Center of Traditionalist Orthodox Studies.

1971b   *Homiliae in Hiezechihelem.* Ed. M. Adriaen. CCSL 142; Turnholt: Brepols.

1990   "Homily 25," in *Forty Gospel Homilies,* trans. D. Hurst, 187-99. Kalamazoo: Cistercian.

Gribomont, J.

1992   "Jerome," in *Encyclopedia of the Early Church I,* 430-31. New York: Oxford University Press.

Irenaeus

1979   *Against the heresies. ANF,* vol. 1, ed. and trans. A. Roberts and J. Donaldson, 315-567. Grand Rapids: Eerdmans.

Isidore of Seville

1844-64 Preface to *Quaestiones in Vetus Testamentum* (*PL* 83, 208B, C).

Jeauneau, E.

1991   "Heiric d'Auxerre Disciple de Jean Scot," in *L'Ecole carolingienne d'Auxerre, de Muretha à Remi, 830-908.* Ed. D. Iogna-Prat, C. Jeudy and G. Lobrichon, 353-70. Paris: Beauchesne.

John the Scot (Scotus)

1972   *Commentarius in Evangelium Johannis.* Ed. and trans. E. Jeauneau. SC 180; Paris: Cerf.

Justin Martyr

1953   *Apology I.* In LCC 1: *Early Christian Fathers.* Ed. and trans. C. C. Richardson, 242-89. Philadelphia: Westminster.

Kendall, C. B. (ed.)

1975   "Bede, Venerabilis, *De Arte Metrica et De Schematibus et Tropis.*" In C. B. Kendall, M. H. King, and F. Lipp, eds., *Bede Venerabilis Opera, Pars 1, Opera Didascalia.* 59-171. CCSL 123A. Turnhout: Brepols.

Laistner, M. L. W.

1948   "The Value and Influence of Cassiodorus' Ecclesiastical History," *HTR* 41: 51-67.

Leclercq, J.

1960   *The Love of Learning and the Desire for God.* Trans. C. Misrahi. New York: Fordham University Press.

Leonardi, C.

1975   "Reigio di Auxerre e l'eredita della scuola carolingia." In *I classici nei medioevo e nell'humanesimo.* Genoa: Universita di Genova.

Lubac, H. de

1959-62 *Exégèse Médiéval.* 4 vols. Paris: Montaigne.

Mair, J. R. S.

1975   "A Note on Cassiodorus and the Seven Liberal Arts." *JTS* 26: 419-21.

Marenbon, J.

1981   *From the Circle of Alcuin to the School of Auxerre: Logic, Theology, and Philosophy in the Early Middle Ages.* Cambridge: Cambridge University Press.

1994   "Carolingian Thought," in McKitterick (ed.) 1994: 171-92.

Matter, E. A.

1984   "Exegesis and Christian Education: The Carolingian Model," in *Schools of Thought in the Christian Tradition,* ed. P. Henry, 90-105. Philadelphia: Fortress.

Mayeski, M. A.

1995   *Dhuoda: Ninth Century Mother and Theologian,* 80-85. Scranton: University of Scranton Press.

1997   "'Let Women Not Despair': Rabanus Maurus on Women as Prophets," in *TS* 58: 237-53.

2001   "Catholic Theology and the History of Exegesis," in *TS* 62: 140-53.

McKitterick, R.

1994   "The Legacy of the Carolingians," in McKitterick (ed.) 1994: 317-23.

McKitterick, R. (ed.)

1994   *Carolingian Culture: Emulation and Innovation.* Cambridge: Cambridge University Press.

Miller, J. M., M. H. Frosser, and T. W. Benson (eds., trans.)

1973   "On Schemes and Tropes," in *Readings in Medieval Rhetoric,* 96-122. Bloomington: Indiana University Press.

Oates, W. J. (ed.)

1948   *Basic Writings of St. Augustine.* 2 vols. New York: Random House.

Rabanus Maurus

1878   *Opera Exegetica. PL* 112.

Riche, P., and G. Lobrichon

1984   *Le Moyen age et la Bible.* In *Bible de tous les temps,* vol. 4. Paris: Beauchesne.

Robins, R. H.

1998   Review of *The Sankt Gall Priscian Commentary.* 2 vols. Studien und Texte zur Keltologie, 1; Münster: Nodus; and *Zur Zuverlässigkeit der bedeutendsten lateinischen Grammatik. Die "Ars" des Aelius Donatus.* Mainz and Stuttgart: Steiner. *Classical Review,* new series, 48:2 366-68.

Signer, M. A. (ed.)

1991   *Andrew of St. Victor, Expositionem in Ezechielem.* CCCM 53E; Turnhout: Brepols.

Smalley, B.

1938   "Andrew of St. Victor." *RTAM* 10: 358-73.

1952   *The Study of the Bible in the Middle Ages.* Oxford: Oxford University Press, first published in 1941.

1969   "An Early Twelfth Century Commentary on the Literal Sense of Leviticus." *RTAM* 36: 78-99.

1978   "Some Gospel Commentaries of the Early Twelfth Century." *RTAM* 45: 84-129.

Southern, R. W.

1948   "Lanfranc of Bec and Berengar of Tours," in *Studies in Medieval History,* ed. R. W. Hunt, 27-48. Oxford: Clarendon.

1970   "Aspects of the European Tradition of Historical Writing 2: Hugh of St. Victor," *TRHS* 21: 159-79.

Spicq, C.

1941-42 "Pourquoi le Moyen âge n'a't'il pas d'avantage pratiqué l'exégèse littérale," *RSPT* 30: 169-79.

1944   *Esquisse d'une histoire de l'éxegèse Latine au moyen age.* Bibliothèque Thomiste 26. Paris: Librairie philosophique J. Vrin.

Stiegman, E.

2001   "Bernard of Clairvaux, William of St. Thierry and the Victorines." In G. R. Evans, ed., *The Medieval Theologians,* 129-55. Oxford: Blackwell.

Stump, E.

1978   *Boethius's De Topicis Differentiis.* Ithaca: Cornell University Press.

Swete, H. B.

1880-82   *Theodori episcopi Mopsuesteni in epistulas B. Pauli commentarii,* 2 vols. Cambridge: Cambridge University Press.

Taylor, J. (trans.)

1961   *Didascalicon: A Medieval Guide to the Arts.* New York: Columbia University Press.

Wasselynch, P.

1965   "L'influence de l'exégèse de S. Grégoire le Grand sur les commentaires bibliques médiévaux." *RTAM* 32: 157-204.

William of St. Thierry

1978   *Exposition on the Epistle to the Romans.* Trans. John Baptist Hasbrouk. Spencer: Cistercian.

Zinn, G. A.

1993   "Texts within Texts: The Song of Songs in the Exegesis of Gregory the Great and Hugh of St. Victor." In A. E. Livingstone, ed., *Biblica et Apocrypha, Orientalia, Ascetica.* StPatr 25; Leuven: Peeters.

Zinn, G. A. (ed., trans.)

1979   *Benjamin Major and Benjamin Minor.* New York: Paulist.

CHAPTER 3

Jewish Midrashic Interpretation in Late Antiquity and the Early Middle Ages

Carol Bakhos

Rabbinic biblical interpretation, midrash (pl. midrashim), of the late antique and early medieval period is preserved in a series of exegetical and homiletic collections that are considered classical rabbinic texts, such as *Mekhilta, Sifra, Sifre Deut., Gen. Rab., Lev. Rab.,* and *PRK* (see pp. 115-16 for abbreviations). As we move into the medieval period, approximately 640-1000 CE, in addition to compilations similar to those of the classical period we notice the emergence of an innovative form of interpretation in which biblical narratives are used didactically to impart religious lessons on such themes as the chosenness of Israel, the Sabbath, the centrality of Torah study and the observance of mitzvoth (commandments). *PRE,* for example, also discusses the calendar and astronomy, and is replete with stories and legends also found in earlier non-rabbinic texts such as *Jubilees.* It thus integrates the structure of classical midrash within the framework of retelling biblical history. Even later midrashic works of the fourteenth and fifteenth centuries such as *Yalkut Shimoni* and *MHG* (see Fisch 1940), not only anthologize earlier midrashim, but also supplement traditional material. So, while the period approximately between the sixth and fifteenth centuries reflects, *inter alia,* an attempt to compile scriptural interpretation of earlier generations, the later compilations supplement the classical texts of the fifth and sixth centuries. This should not be surprising given the nature of rabbinic interpretation and the very process of textual transmission of rabbinic texts, both of which accommodate emendation while attempting to preserve both text and tradition.

In *HBI*[1] Porton discusses the meaning of the word "midrash," places rabbinic interpretation within the context of Hellenism and late antiquity,

and explores topics such as the role of midrash in the synagogue and the rabbinic schoolhouse. With this rich background in mind, we will address here
the role that study of textual transmission plays in our use of midrashic texts
for historical purposes; midrash as history, literature, and commentary; and
rabbinic themes in and basic features of the midrashic collections.

From the outset, it is important to note that the interpretations found in
these collections have an oral history prior to the early medieval period that
perhaps reaches as far back as several hundred years earlier than their putative
dates of redaction. Exegetical concerns, as manifest in the activities of Jewish interpreters, take on new forms in the redacted compilations of the later period.
In other words, the very formation of these compilations sheds light on rabbinic exegesis of the early medieval period. One can only speculate as to what
prompted the interest in collating sage sayings, rabbinic homilies, and in general rabbinic scriptural interpretation. The decline of Palestine as the center of

The period of the Tannaim	first and second centuries
The period of the Amoraim	third-fifth centuries
The period of the Geonim	seventh-thirteenth centuries in Babylon
The period of the Rishonim	eleventh-sixteenth centuries
The period of the Acharonim	sixteenth century to the present

intellectual activity in the mid-fourth century may have given rise to the need
and interest in compiling such works. Christian claims to the biblical heritage
may also have factored into the need to preserve rabbinic discourse in writing,
but again, such statements are only suggestive since the rabbis made no effort to
state explicitly their priorities, concerns, and desiderata. We therefore have no
way of knowing why they collected midrashim, discrete units of rabbinic musings, and teachings on legal and non-legal matters into massive volumes. We
can, however, safely say that the compilations reflect an ordering based on
Scripture, that scriptural verses serve as proof-texts, and, even though we must
shy away from depicting "the rabbis" as a monolithic group, that the compilations give, certainly on a *prima facie* level, the impression of concordance, despite the multiple and varying voices found within rabbinic literature.

TEXTUAL TRANSMISSION

Studies of the process of transmission, far more complex than previously regarded, coupled with the influence of postmodern literary criticism on the

study of rabbinic literature, have given rise to a reexamination of the role of textual criticism in such study and have called into question the very meaning of "text." What role do transmitters of texts play in our understanding of a compilation? How, for example, does a later insertion of a heading affect our reading of the original? To what extent do later copyists shift the meaning of the original work? Are later copyists transmitters or authors of additional text? For some, given the very fact that medieval copyists emend and thus reconstruct texts, Hebrew manuscripts are therefore unreliable historical artifacts (see, for example, the exchange between Schäfer [1986] and Milikowsky [1988] and Schäfer's response [1989]). Despite the corruption of texts by "the free critical editing of learned copyists and the whimsical copying errors of preoccupied poor scribes" (Beit-Arie 1993: 50), since they are our only sources, we should treat them circumspectly and "above all refrain from establishing authentic texts, or even critical editions, and rather resort to the safe synoptic presentation of the transmitted texts, while proposing our critical analysis and reconstruction in the form of notes" (p. 51).

But have recent forays into manuscript transmission decidedly put an end to classical textual criticism? If it is futile to search for the *Urtext,* must we therefore abandon all attempts to discover the textual history of rabbinic works? Other scholars take a more optimistic view of the situation, arguing that even though we have yet to find the *Urtext* of a given work, this does not mean it is inconceivable that we will. Indeed, stemmatic analysis is necessary and can lead to the reconstruction of the *Urtext.* As Milikowsky contends, "The very fact that the manuscript traditions of these rabbinic texts allow for stemmatic analysis indicates that we are dealing with clearly distinguishable texts, to which we can apply the accepted canons of textual criticism" (1988: 205). Since scribes were not compelled to copy what was before them and therefore took it upon themselves to tailor the text to suit their purposes, we cannot afford to ignore the transmission history of a given text. While in many cases it is indeed notoriously difficult to reconstruct that history, we must use our philological tools and redactional methods to trace the history of transmission.

Aware that the medieval transmission of rabbinic texts is a complex process that calls into question endeavors to establish authentic texts and create critical editions, scholars are therefore confronted with the nettlesome and arguably insoluble problem of dating rabbinic sources. Indeed, scholarly wrangling over how to define a rabbinic text as "early" or "late" and discussion of how textual transmission calls into question the very value of rabbinic texts as historical sources are far from over. In the sense that rabbinic writings were transmitted gradually in a cumulative manner, they are resistant to fixed

Important Midrashic Compilations

title(s)	abbreviation	date of compilation CE*
Tannaitic Midrashim		
Sifra	Sifra	Tannaitic-early Amoraic
Sifre Deuteronomy	Sifre Deut.	Tannaitic-early Amoraic
Sifre Numbers	Sifre Num.	Tannaitic-early Amoraic
Mekhilta de Rabbi Ishmael	Mekhilta	Tannaitic-early Amoraic
Midrash Rabbah (Mid. Rab.) Aggadic midrashim on the Pentateuch and the Megillot (Song of Songs),		
Genesis Rabbah	Gen. Rab.	5th century
Exodus Rabbah (Shemot Rabbah)	Exod. Rab.	9th-11th centuries
Leviticus Rabbah	Lev. Rab.	5th century
Numbers Rabbah	Num. Rab.	12th century
Deuteronomy Rabbah	Deut. Rab.	9th-10th centuries, possibly earlier
Ruth Rabbah	Ruth Rab.	5th century
Esther Rabbah	Esth. Rab.	4th-5th centuries, completed eleventh century
Ecclesiastes Rabbah	Eccl. Rab.	6th-8th centuries
Shir Ha-shirim Rabbah (Song of Songs Rabbah)	Song Rab.	6th-7th centuries
Lamentations Rabbah	Lam. Rab.	5th century
Later compilations		
Midrash Ha-Gadol	MHG	13th-14th centuries
Midrash Psalms (Midrash Tehilim, Shocher Tov)	Mid. Pss.	Possibly 9th-11th centuries
Pesikta de Rav Kahana	PRK	6th-7th centuries
Pirke de Rabbi Eliezer	PRE	8th-early 9th centuries
Psalms Rabbah	Ps. Rab.	
Tanhuma Yelammedenu	Tanhuma	9th century
Tanna de-be Eliyahu, Seder Eliyahu	SE	Variously dated 3rd-10th centuries
Yalkut ha-Makhiri	Yal. Mak.	14th century
Yalkut Shimoni	Yalkut	12th-13th centuries

publication	description
Neusner 1988	Tannaitic midrash on all of Leviticus with close readings of small portions; mainly halakhic, with some aggadic material
Neusner 1987b	Tannaitic midrash on Deuteronomy
Neusner 1986	Tannaitic midrash on Numbers
Lauterbach 1933	Halakhic and aggadic midrash focusing on Exod. 12:1-23:19 and chs. 31-35
Ruth, Lamentations, Ecclesiastes, and Esther)	
Freedman 1983	Verse-by-verse collection of aggadic midrashim compiled into an exegetical commentary
Braude and Kapstein 1981	Aggadic midrash
Israelstam and Slotki 1983	Aggadic homiletical midrash
Friedlander 1981	Exegetical commentary on chs. 1-7, homiletic commentary on the rest
Lehrmann 1974	Midrashic homilies, each beginning with a halakhah
Neusner 1989	Complete commentary on Ruth
Neusner 1989	Incomplete aggadic material on Esther
Cohen 1961 (1971)	Encyclopedic, almost verse-by-verse
Braude and Kapstein 1975; Neusner 1989-90	Aggadic midrash on the Song of Songs
Neusner 1989b	Verse-by-verse collection of aggadic midrashim compiled into an exegetical commentary
Marguiles, Steinsalz, Rabinowitz, Fisch 1975	Yemenite midrashic compilation on the Pentateuch
Buber 1891	Homiletical midrashim
Braude and Kapstein 1975	A cycle of Palestinian homiletical midrashim on selected Sabbath and festival passages
Friedlander 1981	Pseudepigraphic narrative midrash attributed to the tanna Eliezer ben Hyrkanos
Berman 1996, Townsend 2003	Literary homilies based on the triennial cycle of weekly biblical lections
Braude and Kapstein 1981	Interpretation of legal provisions with focus on study of Torah and proper moral conduct
Ha-Darshan 1968	A compilation of midrashim that focuses primarily on the Prophets, Job, Psalms, and Proverbs
Ha-Darshan 1968, Friedlander 1981	Midrashic thesaurus to the Bible, halakhic and aggadic passages of the Talmud, and midrashic works, arranged in biblical order

dating. Be that as it may, wide acceptance of a basic chronology based on comparative philological and literary analyses makes it nonetheless possible to use these rabbinic works for historical purposes. As S. Stern rightly notes (1994: xxiii):

> [I]t is fair to assume that at some point, redacted works began to emerge and to be treated, if only by name, as single identifiable entities. Thus the Talmud itself treats the Mishna, if not as a finished product, at least as an identifiable work around which its argumentation can revolve. In this respect it may be possible to assign approximate dates to these redacted works, even if the continuous process of multilayer redaction did not entirely cease thereafter, and even if we find that variations between different manuscript traditions and early printed editions can be quite considerable.

And, as Herr notes (1972a: 1509, emphasis added), even though we cannot establish "with even approximate certainty the period when a Midrash or aggadic work was compiled," we can nevertheless determine the relationships among the various corpora, that is, whether one work makes use of another:

> Thus, for instance, where Midrash A and Midrash B contain parallels, it is possible to determine whether A drew on B, or B on A, or whether both drew on a third common source, extant or not. After one arrives by use of this method, though *with great caution,* at a determination of precedence, it becomes clear that other additional indications exist (literary forms, language, style, etc.).

To be sure, recent studies in manuscript transmission point to the need for caution when considering rabbinic texts as historical documents, yet at the same time such studies do not make it impossible to appreciate the treasure trove of rabbinic works as literary artifacts that can offer insight into rabbinic cultural and intellectual history.

MIDRASH AS LITERATURE, HISTORY, AND COMMENTARY

Biblical figures populated the world of the rabbis, and biblical stories and events engaged their thoughts and fancy; yet theirs was not a world unto itself. Subtlety, brevity of speech, and metaphoric discourse characterize the exegetical ways in which the rabbis grappled with the burning issues of their day. We must, however, consider the degree to which midrashic texts illustrate rabbinic attitudes regarding extra-textual issues. Can midrash, in other words, tell us something about rabbis' social and political concerns? Are midrashic texts literary expressions of rabbinic views about non-Jews, Christianity, chosenness, and the rise of Islam, or are they merely texts whose primary focus is biblical interpretation? Many rabbinic scholars treat rabbinic literature *qua* literature. Kugel (1986), for example, has worked mainly on exploring the rabbis' exegetical and hermeneutical presuppositions. His work analyzes the midrashic process as a text-oriented, philological phenomenon that is less about extra-textual factors and more about the scriptural verses. Fraenkel, an Israeli midrash scholar, also concerns himself with the literary aspects of midrash. His *Darkhei ha-ʿaggada vehamidrash* (1991) is a systematic and exhaustive attempt to analyze the literary aspects of midrash, especially that of rabbinic storytelling. Meir (1974, 1999) is a New Criticism scholar of midrash, and Hasan-Rokem's numerous studies on the folkloristic aspects of rabbinic literature (e.g., 2000, 2003) contribute greatly to our appreciation for and knowledge of rabbinic narratives. Moreover, the work of Goldberg, focusing on the synchronicity of rabbinic texts (1985), examines the basic forms and function of literary units.

The dual nature of rabbinic interpretation is not lost on these scholars, but while they concern themselves with the literariness of midrash, others are interested in midrash's relevance for understanding the rabbinic worldview. Heinemann, who emphasizes the cultural and ideological aspects of midrash, is of this latter ilk. The rabbis, he writes, "looked back into Scripture to uncover the full latent meaning of the Bible and its wording; at the same time, they looked forward into the present and the future. They sought to give direction to their own generation, to resolve their own religious problems, to answer their theological questions" (1974: 49). In stressing the dual aspect of folkloric midrashim *(aggadot),* Heinemann calls our attention to two levels of meaning, "one overt, the other covert": "The first deals openly with the explication of the biblical text and the clarification of the biblical narrative, while the second deals much more subtly with contemporary problems that engaged the attention of the homilists and their audience." For Heinemann, the second level is of greater import. "The aggadists do not mean so much to clarify difficult passages in the biblical text as to take a stand on the burning questions of the day, to guide the people and to strengthen their faith" (1974: 49). Indeed, in developing a process of "creative exegesis," the rabbis were able to make Scripture relevant to contemporary needs. They could cull the verses in order to contend with contemporary concerns.

To be sure, all midrashim are characterized by this second (covert) level of meaning, but reading midrashim (whether smaller units of interpretation

or extensive compilations) as historical documents that lucidly reflect rabbinic culture is a hazardous enterprise. Depending on how one uses
midrashic sources, one can gain insight into rabbinic Judaism. Yet, although
consideration of the then-contemporary situation can contribute to understanding the hermeneutical reasons that give rise to a particular midrash, one
ought to avoid reading those reasons too readily into the text.

How and whether to provide historical contexts for midrash has been
discussed in the past, most explicitly by Fraade (1991: 14-15), who examines
the "inextricable interconnection" between the hermeneutics and historicity
of scriptural interpretation:

> These two tendencies, even as they face, and view commentary as facing
> opposite directions, are really two sides of the same coin. That is the coin
> that presumes that the hermeneutics and historicity of scriptural com
> mentary can conveniently and neatly be detached from one another, in
> the first case by viewing the hermeneutics of commentary's interpreta
> tions apart from the socio-historical grounding of its performance and in
> the second by viewing the historicity of commentary's representations
> apart from the hermeneutical grounding of its performance. . . . I wish to
> deny neither of these facings or groundings, but to assert their inextrica
> ble interconnection.

Whether or not one aspect of these two tendencies overshadows the
other in certain cases, we must remember that they are intrinsically interrelated. The issue, therefore, is not whether extra-textual factors are part of exegesis but *how* and *when* we can use such texts as historical sources. We are
therefore concerned with two integrated issues, which are often dealt with
separately by scholars: the utility of midrashic texts as historical sources and
the use of history as a hermeneutical tool to explain difficulties and surprising patterns or shifts in rabbinic texts. To illustrate this point, let us look at
some related sample texts. *PRE* 31 narrates the last of Abraham's ten trials, the
Aqedah, the binding of Isaac (all extracts are my own translations):

> On the third day they reached Zophim and when they reached Zophim,
> Abraham saw the glory of the Shekhinah standing on the top of the
> mountain, as it is said, "On the third day Abraham lifted up his eyes, and
> saw the place from a distance" (Gen. 22:4). What did he see? He saw a pil
> lar of fire standing from the earth to the heavens. He said to Isaac his son,
> "My son, do you see anything on one of these mountains?" He said to
> him, "Yes, I see a pillar of fire standing from the earth to the heavens." He

said to Ishmael and Eliezer, "Do you see anything on one of these moun-
tains?" They said to him, "No." He considered them asses and said to
them, "Remain here with the ass" (v. 5). He said to them, "Just as the ass
does not see anything, so too you do not see anything," as it is said, "And
Abraham said to the youths, 'Remain here with the ass'" (v. 5), a people
resembling an ass.

According to Heinemann, the motif of a people resembling a donkey began as
an anti-Christian polemic (1974, 122-29). His assertion is based on an examination of the earliest sources of this midrash, *Gen. Rab.* 56.2 and parallel
sources such as *Tanhuma, Wayyera* 46 (see Berman 1996) and *Lev. Rab.* 20.2.
Gen. Rab. 56.2 reads as follows:

> Abraham said to Isaac, "My Son, do you see what I see?" Isaac answered,
> "Yes." Abraham then turned to his *two servants* and said, "Do you see
> what I see?" "No," they replied. Since you do not see it, "Stay here with the
> ass" (Gen. 22:5), for you are like the ass. . . . R. Isaac said, "Everything hap-
> pened as a reward for worshiping. Abraham returned from Mount
> Moriah only as a reward for worshiping: 'And the people believed . . . then
> they bowed their heads and worshiped' (Exod. 4:31). The Torah was given
> only as a reward for worshiping: '. . . And worship from afar' (Exod 24:1)."

There is no mention of "a nation resembling a donkey," a phrase included in
Lev. Rab. 20.2 and *Tanhuma, Wayyera* 46 which is a play on "ʿim [with] the
ass," and "ʿam [people or nation] of asses." The rabbis, Heinemann maintains
(1974: 121), were not concerned only with biblical exegesis or with explaining
the *Aqedah*, but also with God's revelation to Israel and not to the other nations of the world. The midrash in *Gen. Rab.* 56.2 was retailored, thus giving
rise to other midrashim which address Israel's chosenness, such as *PRE* 31 and
Tanhuma, Wayyera 46. The ability to "see," better yet to "understand," is exclusively reserved for Israel and is not for the nations of the world.
(Heinemann [1974: 123] refers to Philo of Alexandria, who writes, "Israel —
one who sees God" [see Ginzberg 1909: 5.307, n. 253]. Heinemann also discusses the notion of "seeing" as it is found in the story of Joseph and
Potiphar's wife [124-25].) The anti-Christian polemic here, Heinemann contends, is thus a later development not found in *Gen. Rab.* 56.2.

Eccl. Rab. 9.6 and later compilations such as *PRE* include the names of
the servants, Eliezer and Ishmael, and also refer to "a people." *PRK* does not
refer to Eliezer and Ishmael, but does mention "a people resembling an ass,"
thus calling Heinemann's thesis into question. And, according to Milikowsky

(forthcoming), most mss. of *Lev. Rab.* 20.2 include their names, but the Munich and Oxford 51 mss. (before emendation) do not. Instead, ʿavadav, "his servants," is found. It is therefore unclear whether to attribute the insertion of the names to the editor of *Lev. Rab.*, since the change may have occurred during the transmission of the text.

Furthermore, it is noteworthy that the rest of *Gen. Rab.* 56.2, while not seemingly polemically charged, makes an exclusivist claim to Torah, which Israel received as a reward for worshiping God. Is it therefore anti-Christian? Rather than assuming that the change in *Tanhuma* and *Lev. Rab.* is indicative of anti-Christian polemic, we might consider it merely a play on "with" and "people" that the later texts preserve. In this instance, it is exceedingly difficult to argue that the change evinces an anti-Christian polemical reading.

Heinemann does not explicitly discuss how this midrash plays itself out in *PRE*, but, given his conception of the development of midrashim, one could construct his position as follows: in *PRE* the polemic is not only anti-Christian, but also anti-Islamic. Both nations, Christianity (the servant Eliezer) and Islam (the servant Ishmael), cannot "see." Whereas in *Lev. Rab.* "nations resembling a donkey" is anti-Christian polemic, in *PRE* the phrase is used against both competing monotheisms. Therefore, to categorize the midrash as polemical seems to miss the point that even in the earlier compilations the midrash maintains the *sui generis* status of the Jewish inheritors of the Torah. Moreover, in detecting a development indicative of a rabbinic response to Christianity and then to Islam, in this instance we must not lose sight of the clever ways in which the rabbis pun and delight in double entendres. In *PRE* we may very well have before us an example of how both textual and extra-textual factors come into play, but iterations of the midrash in later compilations are not always necessarily indicative of a polemical agenda. Again, this is not to say that we cannot locate occurrences of rabbinic attempts to contend with competing theological claims of Christianity or Islam, for example, *Song Rab.* 7.3.3.

It remains unproven that the rabbis' emphasis on the chosenness of Israel is a direct response to Christian claims of being the "true" Israel, particularly in the Hasan-Rokem period (200-500 CE), when the rabbinic sages (the amoraim) were engaged in the study of Mishnah and the tannaitic traditions. Yet, the following midrash in *Song. Rab.*, dated to the middle of the sixth century (Strack, et al., 1992: 342), is compelling evidence of the rabbis' awareness of Christian claims:

> A *mashal:* The wheat, the chaff and the stubble were arguing with one another. This chaff said, "For my sake the ground had been sown." The stub-

ble said, "For my sake the ground had been sown." The wheat said to them, "Wait until the threshing time comes and we will see for whom the ground had been sown." When the threshing time arrived and they were all brought to the floor, the farmer went out to winnow it. The chaff was scattered to the winds; he took the straw and threw it on the ground; he cast the stubble into the fire. He took the wheat and piled it in a heap and when all the passers-by saw it they kissed it. . . . So, of the nations some say, "We are Israel and for our sake the world was created," and others say, "We are Israel, and for our sake the world was created." Israel says to them, "Wait for the day of the Holy One, Blessed be He, and we will know for whom the world was created," as it is written, "For the day will come and burn like a furnace" (Mal. 3:19). And it is written, "You shall fan them, and the wind will carry them away," but of Israel it is said, "And you shall rejoice in the LORD; you shall glory in the Holy One of Israel" (Isa. 41:16).

At first glance, one cannot help but make an association between this midrash and Christianity, but the midrash may be referring to other groups, such as the Samaritans and Gnostics, in addition to Christians. Furthermore, at a time when Christianity was propounding supersessionist claims, one would expect to find midrashim expressing a similar sentiment to that found in this extract. This, however, is not the case, for in Hasan-Rokem literature we find only a few examples — approximately twenty — where the marginalization of Israel's kin, that is, the "illegitimate" children of Abraham, is emphasized. Regarding their content, they are very similar to tannaitic midrashim: mainly concerned with issues of halakhah. Even though there are relatively more midrashim of this type in Hasan-Rokem corpora, this is insufficient evidence to support the hypothesis that competing Christian attestations had an appreciable bearing on the development of these midrashim.

Zunz (1892) and Lachs (1965) argue for a later dating of *Song Rab.* (Strack, et al., 1992: 342), claiming that it was originally composed in the mid-seventh to eighth centuries and that its final version was produced in the second half of the eighth century. This could imply that the midrash is a polemic against both Christianity and Islam, represented by the chaff and stubble, respectively.

Although the midrash is apocalyptic, we could nonetheless read it in light of real events and not just in terms of rabbinic affirmation of Israel's chosenness. The midrash before us is oriented toward future events. Apocalyptic midrashim, which share affinities with the exegetical works from Qumran called the *pesharim*, deal with the actual present in the guise of prophesying the future. We also find this phenomenon in post–seventh-century CE rabbinic sources that portray the Ishmaelites in apocalyptic terms.

Thus, what we have here is a good example of how the rabbis utilized biblical interpretation to contend with their concerns vis-à-vis competing theological claims. The very structure of a *mashal,* a parabolic literary form employing certain poetic and rhetorical techniques, lends itself to ulterior readings. The purpose of the *mashal* is to convey abstract concepts and entities such as God, the people of Israel, and covenant by means of personification, reference, symbol, or allegory. The chaff and stubble represent other groups, quite possibly Christianity and Islam, who claim to be Israel, but in the end days, Judaism will be vindicated, and will declare the glory of God. The midrash in *Song Rab.* is therefore a good example of the interconnectedness of the hermeneutics and historicity of midrash.

THEMES IN RABBINIC INTERPRETATION

Rabbinic biblical interpretation deals with wide-ranging topics. Since we are unable to explore in any great detail many of the topics raised in midrashic texts, we will limit our discussion to a few major interwoven, recurring themes: the oneness of God, the chosenness of Israel, and the centrality of Torah. It should be noted at the outset, however, that the rabbis did not systematically consider such topics in isolation, and therefore this approach to rabbinic literature skews our understanding of the very nature of texts that, consciously or not, eschew thematic organization. And, while we must pay careful attention to how different rabbinic corpora deal with a theme (noting possible variances among the earlier and later compilations), we need not forego our endeavor entirely. Despite changes, significant or otherwise, there are fundamental themes that resound throughout rabbinic literature in particular and the Jewish tradition in general.

The belief in one God is the central tenet of the Jewish faith, proclaimed twice a day by religious Jews in the recitation of the *Shema* ("Hear, O Israel, the Lord our God, the Lord is One . . ."). Anyone who negates God is called a *kofer ba-ʿiqqar,* "one who denies the 'root' or primary principle of faith." This denial can take on many forms, from outright rejection of Torah and the commandments to performing deeds that ignore the presence of the omnipotent, omniscient, and omnipresent God. Thus, for example, we read in *Gen. Rab.* 24.1 (*cf. Midrash Psalms* 24:2):

> It is written, "Woe unto them who seek deep to hide their counsel from the Lord . . ." (Isa. 29:15). R. Levi said: To what can the matter be compared? This may be compared to a master builder who built a city with se-

cret chambers, canals, and caves. Eventually he became a ruler and the inhabitants of the country hid from him in those chambers and caves. He said to them, "Fool, are you seeking to hide from me? It is I, after all, who built all these chambers and caves; to what purpose then is your hiding?" Similarly, "Woe unto them that seek deep! . . . And their works are in the darkness, etc. . . . O your perversity! Shall the potter be esteemed as the clay?" (v. 16). You liken the created object to its creator, the plant to its planter! So, too, the Holy One, blessed be he, said to the wicked, "Fools! Why do you hide the wickedness in your hearts? It is I who built the human, and I know all the chambers and secret recesses within."

According to the midrash, we must be mindful of God's active and ever present role in our lives, for to do otherwise is a rejection of God.

Rabbinic texts often highlight the chosenness of Israel vis-à-vis "others," such as the unrighteous offspring of Abraham and Isaac. In reviewing texts that pit the descendants of Abraham through Isaac against Ishmael and the children of Keturah, a discernible pattern based on theoretical formulations of group identity emerges. In other words, midrashim that distinguish Ishmael and other marginalized figures from Israel do not symbolize specific religious and ethnic groups, but rather use an imagined "other" to represent non-Jews in general. The extent to which we can utilize these texts as descriptions of rabbinic attitudes toward the non-Jews whom they encountered in daily life is exceedingly limited, if it is at all possible. And yet, they tell us something about the ways in which the rabbis maintained fundamental notions of Israel.

Let us look at two examples of how the rabbis used biblical figures as fabricated antipodes to chosen Israel. In *Sifre Deut. Piska* 312 on Deut. 32:9 we read:

"For the LORD's portion is his people, [Jacob is the lot of his inheritance]" (Deut. 32:9). It may be compared to a king who had a field and gave it to tenants. The tenants began to rob him [They took from the produce of the field what they owed the king], so he took it from them and gave it to their children and they became wickeder than the previous. A son was born to him and he said to them, "Get out of what is mine. I do not want you in it. Give me my portion so I will recognize it." So when Abraham our father came into the world something unfit came from him, Ishmael and all the children of Keturah. Isaac came into the world and something unfit came from him, Esau and all the chieftains of Edom. They became wickeder than the previous ones. When Jacob came into the world nothing unfit came from him, rather all his children were proper when they were born, as it is said, "And Jacob was a perfect man dwelling in tents" (Gen 25:27). When will the LORD recognize his share? From Jacob, as it is said, "For the LORD's portion is his people, Jacob his own allotment."

The midrash asks why Scripture says, "Speak to the children of Israel," and not the children of Abraham or Isaac. Only Jacob's children deserve unprecedented recognition; they merit God's direct commandments because of their own merits and because of their father: "Jacob was fearful all his days and said, 'Woe is me, perhaps something unfit will come out from me as it came out from my fathers. . . . From Abraham came Ishmael. From Isaac came Esau, but from me nothing unfit will come forth as came forth from my fathers,' and thus it is said, 'And Jacob vowed a vow, saying . . .'" (see Freedman 1983). This notion that both Abraham and Isaac produced blemished offspring is fairly common in rabbinic literature of the Amoraic period. The rabbis would create an imagined "other" in order to reflect the special status of chosen Israel. Thus, Esau and Ishmael do not necessarily represent other real communities such as the Samaritans or Christians — at least not in these midrashim.

These texts reflect an unconscious introspective analysis on the part of the rabbis who, in the process, formulate images of self vis-à-vis other. In his reading of the Dinah story, Geller (1996) draws our attention to a similar phenomenon. "In that story, and in biblical religion as a whole, the Canaanites are, in effect, a literary device, a use of imagery and typology to clarify the difficult idea of divine transcendence. Historical Canaanites are irrelevant . . ." (p. 154). To be sure, the "other-ing" of foreigners, and people outside the group, is a phenomenon found in the religious and secular literature of societies and cultures throughout the world, so it is no surprise that rabbinic texts reflect this literary phenomenon.

Significantly, in the aforementioned midrash and other related midrashim, even Abraham fathers unfit descendants. The rabbis go out of their way to make sure Abraham is portrayed as most righteous (e.g., *Gen. Rab.* 30.10; Freedman 1983), but it is Jacob whose progeny are deemed "fit." As in the case of Abraham's near-sacrifice of Isaac (the *Aqedah*), Isaac is depicted as a willing victim, so too Jacob is favorably portrayed. Thus, the rabbis use Gen. 25:27, "But Jacob was a mild man who stayed in camp," as a prooftext for a variety of impeccable behavior they attribute to Jacob. Jacob, for example, was born circumcised, performed all the commandments, was righteous, innocent of unseemly conduct, and studied Torah (Mihaly 1964: 105; for primary texts see Freedman 1983).

Despite all its nuances and permutations over the span of centuries, another major theme underlying much of rabbinic thought is the centrality of

Torah. "The spectrum of relationships between God and the individual Jew or the Jewish people," writes Urbach, "as it emerges from the Bible, is closely linked to the theme of the precept. . . . God reveals Himself to man as the *commanding* God" (1975: 315). But did God choose Israel or did Israel choose God? Did Israel have a choice? If God had given the Torah to the nations of the world, would they have accepted it? The rabbis address such queries and advance varied responses in several tannaitic and amoraic midrashim on the giving of Torah and the observance of commandments.

Hirshman (1999) detects a strain of universalism peculiar to the school of Rabbi Ishmael. For example, he observes that legal discussions in the corpus attributed to R. Ishmael (as opposed to that of Rabbi Aqiba; see Rodkinson 1903) do not explicitly use the Noahide commandments *(mitzvoth shel bene noah)*. In his article (2000), Hirshman examines several tannaitic texts that attest to a form of universalism in rabbinic Judaism and thus demonstrates that rabbinic attitudes toward non-Jews and God's giving of the Torah to Israel are not uniform throughout rabbinic literature.

Why God gave the Torah to Israel and not to the nations of the world is a question the rabbis contend with in *Sifre Deut.* 343 on Deut. 33:2, "The LORD came from Sinai":

> When the Holy One, blessed be he, is about to exact punishment from Seir, he will shake the entire world with its inhabitants just as he shook it with the giving of the Torah. . . . The matter may be compared to a king who wanted to give a gift to one of his children but the king was afraid on account of his brothers, his friends and his relatives. What did the son do? He stood and dolled himself up and cut his hair. The king said to him, "To you, I am giving you a gift." Thus, when Abraham our father came into the world, something unfit came from him, Ishmael and the sons of Keturah. They became more evil than the previous ones. And when Isaac came, something unfit came from him, Esau and all the chieftains of Edom. They became more evil than the previous ones. When Jacob came, nothing unfit came from him, but rather all the children born to him were perfect, as it is said, "And Jacob was a perfect man dwelling in tents" (Gen 25:26). The Holy One, blessed be he, said to him, "I am giving the Torah to you," as it is said, "The LORD came from Sinai; he rose upon them from Seir."

Here again, Israel is set apart from all the unfit progeny of Abraham and Isaac. The king wanted to give something special to one son, but did not until the son set himself apart. So, too, God gave the Torah to Israel when it set itself apart. As seen above, in *Gen. Rab.* 56.2 Torah is given as a reward for wor-

ship, but this is not the only reason, for it is also understood that God gave Israel the Torah with the foreknowledge that Israel would accept it (see *Gen.
Rab.* 1.4).

Mekhilta Bahodesh 5 (see Lauterbach 1933) makes it clear why God offered the Torah to the other nations first: "The nations of the world were
asked to receive the Torah in order not to give them a reason to say before the
Shekinah, 'Had we been asked to receive the Torah, we would have accepted it
upon us.'" The midrash, however, is slightly different in *Lam. Rab.* 3.1 (see
Neusner 1989). Beginning with an exchange between the people of Israel and
God, it reads:

> The congregation of Israel said before the Holy One, blessed be he, "Thus
> it was said to me, that no other nation has accepted the Torah but me."
> The Holy One, blessed be he, said, "No, I made all the other nations unfit
> for your sake." It said to him, "No, they did not accept it. Why did you go
> to Mount Seir? Was it not to give the Torah to the children of Esau?"

An exceedingly difficult question that rabbinic scholars must ask is
whether these midrashim attest to anti-Christian polemics. Did the rabbis re-
act to their surroundings to the extent that all biblical interpretation is a by-
product of and response to stimuli outside the purview of what they deemed
"Jewish"? In other words, must we see the rabbinic notions of chosenness as a
response to Christianity or other groups that are competing for the same theological heritage? The rabbis clearly did not live in a vacuum, nor were they im-
pervious to Christian and Samaritan claims, but we have to be careful not to
view midrashic texts through the lens of Christian polemic. We can safely say
that the community of Israel and its covenantal relationship with God were
significant ideological notions that informed biblical interpretation, whether
or not other groups challenged those notions. At the same time, this does not
preclude the possibility that Christianity factored into the ways in which the
rabbis expressed their theological beliefs and ideological suppositions.

The authority of Scripture and the freedom of interpretation, despite
ideological restraints, provided the rabbis with the opportunity not only to
reflect on Scripture, but also to ponder the daily affairs of the world. Midrash,
the inextricable interplay of written text and daily life, is the point at which
the world of Scripture and the world of the rabbis intersect. Early medieval
Jewish biblical interpretation yielded no major theological treatises, no philosophical disquisitions, but rather, it built a rich storehouse of exegesis marked
by playful and profound musings, mundane and fanciful imagery, and by an
awareness of the sacred in the ordinary activities of daily life.

MIDRASHIC COMPILATIONS

Each of the rabbinic compilations from the third through sixth centuries follow one of two methods of arrangement. Verse-by-verse compilations, such as *Gen. Rab.* and *Lam. Rab.*, are categorized as "exegetical midrashim." Others, such as *Lev. Rab.* and *PRK*, are arranged as chapters of homilies clustered around particular topics and are known as "homiletical midrashim."

Tannaitic Compilations

The earliest midrashic collections are often referred to as "halakhic midrashim," since they deal primarily with issues of halakhah (rabbinic law). They are also exegetical by nature, and thus often provide word-by-word explications of verses in Exodus, Leviticus, Numbers, and Deuteronomy. These compilations — the *Sifre to Deuteronomy* and *Sifre to Numbers,* the *Sifra* (on Leviticus), and the *Mekhilta de Rabbi Ishmael* on Exodus — are also known as "tannaitic midrashim," because the language of the halakhic texts is mishnaic Hebrew and the sages mentioned are both *tannaim* (rabbis of the period from the turn of the era to the third century) and first-generation *Amoraim* (rabbis of the third and fourth centuries CE). Divided into nine tractates, *Mekhilta de Rabbi Ishmael* is a verse-by-verse exposition of Exod. 12:1–23:19, and it often expounds every word of a verse. The collection also includes interpretation of Exod. 31:12-17 and 35:1-3. Although the *Mekhilta* concentrates on the halakhic portions of Exodus, it does contain extensive narrative sections. *Sifra,* a running exegetical commentary on Leviticus in its entirety, is a collection of midrashim that discusses halakhic matters almost exclusively. Like the *Mekhilta,* the language of the *Sifra* is mishnaic Hebrew, but it also contains several Greek words.

The broad references to compilations as either halakhic or aggadic at times belie the ways in which characteristics of one genre are found in the other. Thus *Mekhilta* shares features of aggadic texts (folkloric midrashim), even though it is a halakhic expository work. Let us look, for example, at an interpretation in the *Mekhilta,* tractate *Nezikin* (Damages) 13 on Exod. 22:1-3 (see Lauterbach 1933):

> If a thief is found breaking in and is smitten and dies, there shall be no bloodguilt for him. If the sun rises on him, there shall be bloodguilt for him — shall make restitution; if he has nothing, then he shall be sold for his theft. If the theft be found in his hand alive, whether it be ox, or ass, or sheep, he shall pay double.

Regarding what it means that the thief shall pay double, the midrash expounds:

> You find that you must say: There are seven kinds of thieves. First, there are those who steal the hearts of people: he who urges his neighbor to be his guest when in his heart he does not mean to invite him, he who frequently offers gifts to his neighbor knowing well that they will not be accepted, and he who makes his guest believe that he is opening a barrel of wine especially for him when in reality it has been sold to the retailer. Also one who cheats in measuring and swindles in weighing, one who mixes seed of St. John's bread among seeds of fenugreek or sand among beans or puts vinegar into oil. For this reason it is used for anointing kings. And furthermore he is accounted as one who, if he could, would deceive the Most High.

Given the nature of halakhic discourse, we would expect to find an in-depth discussion of the meaning of "the theft found in his hand alive," or what it means that the thief must pay double. Is the list of animals, "ox, or ass, or sheep," inclusive or exclusive, and what happens if the stolen creature is found dead? The midrash proceeds to discuss cursorily these issues but first lists seven arguable forms of thievery. Although it is fitting to include this list in a discussion of thievery, it is curious, given that the *Mekhilta* is a tannaitic compilation that deals with the halakhic verses of Exodus. As Strack, Stemberger, et al. (1992) note, "[It is] a basic difference whether a midrash expounds the biblical text verse by verse and often word by word, or whether it merely gives a devotional commentary on individual verses or on the main theme of the weekly reading from the Torah or the Prophets" (p. 26). So, while there are fundamental differences between the halakhic and aggadic compilations, we should keep in mind that these are broad terms that ought not limit our perception of the works as, first and foremost, compilations of interpretation that use Scripture as a springboard for theological, social, and cultural musings.

Midrash Rabbah

The *Midrash Rabbah* (*Mid. Rab.* = "The Large Midrash"), a major compilation of rabbinic interpretations of the books of Torah and the five *megillot* (scrolls) — Lamentations, Esther, Ruth, Song of Songs, and Ecclesiastes — is a collection of *aggadic* (folkloric or non-halakhic) literature, composed for the most part in Palestine over a period of several hundred years. Based on internal evidence, the earliest part, *Gen. Rab.*, dates from the fifth century CE, while the latest, *Num. Rab.*, dates from the twelfth century.

Gen. Rab. is a good example of an aggadic exegetical compilation. Here we find both simple and elaborate explanations of words and phrases of the verse at hand. All of the *parashiyot* ("chapters," singular *parasha*) except for 13, 15, 17, 18, 25, 35, and 37 contain one or more proems, *petihtot* (singular *petihta*). A proem is a verse, usually from the Writings (especially from Psalms or the Wisdom Literature), sometimes from the Prophets, but rarely from the Torah, that is seemingly extraneous, but through a chain of interpretations is connected to the verse at the beginning of the section. For example, regarding the second half of Gen. 7:1 ("And the lord said to Noah: 'Come, you and your entire household unto the ark; for you I have seen righteous before Me in this generation'"), *Gen. Rab.* 32.2 opens by quoting Ps. 11:7: "For the Lord is righteous, He loves righteousness; the upright shall behold his face." And how is Ps. 11:7 related to Gen. 7:1? The midrash continues:

> R. Tanhuma in R. Judah's name and R. Menaham in R. Eleazar's name said: No man loves his fellow-craftsman, but a sage loves his companion. R. Hiyya loves his fellow-craftsmen and R. Hoshaya loves his. The Holy One, blessed be He, also loves His [in the sense that God is righteous and loves those who are also righteous, and in that respect they are God's fellow craftsmen]. Therefore, "For the Lord is righteous, He loves righteousness; the upright shall behold his face" (Ps. 11:7) applies to Noah, as it is written, ". . . for you I have seen righteous before Me in this generation."

The proem from Psalms is quoted to explicate Gen. 7:1 by showing that God actually loves to see the righteous who, being righteous like him, are in a sense God's companions.

Homiletic Midrashim

The collections of homilies share a structural arrangement: a series of proems (*petihtot*), the body (*gufa*) of the homily, and an eschatological ending or peroration. The *petihta's* structure exemplifies a fundamental aspect of midrash, namely, the desire to unite the diverse parts of the tripartite canon — Torah, Prophets, and Writings — into a seamless whole that reflects the oneness of God's Word. D. Stern writes (1986: 108):

[E]ach and every verse is simultaneous with every other, temporally and semantically; as a result, every verse, no matter how remote, can be seen as a possible source for illuminating the meaning of any other verse. While this tendency is manifest throughout midrash — every place two otherwise unconnected verses are joined in order to reveal new nexuses of meaning — the petihta is undoubtedly its most sophisticated literary expression.

In his general discussion of the midrashic proem, Jaffee locates its *Sitz im Leben* in the rabbinic house of study, for its sophisticated literariness is "hardly suited for oral presentation" (1983: 167). According to Heinemann, given the formal structure of the homilies of *Lev. Rab.*, the homilies were composed of various parts of sermons delivered in the synagogue which were welded together to create what he terms the "literary homily" (Heinemann 1971b: 143). Thus, while homilies were delivered publicly, they nonetheless bear the earmarks of well-crafted works of literature.

In addition to *Lev. Rab.*, *Deut. Rab.*, and *Num. Rab.*, several compilations employ the framework of the homiletical midrashim. *Pesikta de Rab Kahana* (*PRK;* see Braude and Kapstein 1975), dating from 500-700 CE, is arranged according to selected passages or sections read on special Sabbaths or festal days. Each *piska*, "section," has a unified theme that is appropriate to the scriptural reading of the day, arranged according to the Palestinian reading cycle. *Leviticus Rabbah* and *PRK* have five chapters in common (see Strack, Stemberger, et al. 1992: 315), which provides scholars with ample fodder to discuss the literary relationship between the two.

Comprising various sermons on diverse themes, *PRK* nonetheless maintains an underlying thread throughout the *pesiktoth*, namely, the chosenness of Israel as God's people, to whom God bestowed the gift of Torah. Moreover, *PRK* deals with biblical narratives, and espouses fundamental rabbinic articles of faith; yet, at the same time, it retells anecdotes about notable rabbis such as R. Akiba (second century CE), R. Simeon bar Yohai (second century CE) and R. Abbahu (third century CE), and their legendary ways. The bulk of these stories (often seen as sources of purportedly biographical data) illustrates virtuous, exemplary conduct, most especially in these rabbis' dedication to Torah. For example, in *Piska* 4.4 (see Braude and Kapstein 1975), we discover that, on his return from a trip to Caesarea, R. Abbahu's face was shining because he had learned something new related to Torah. Rabbinic protocol is also related in many of the *piska'ot*. *Piska* 26.7 illustrates the principle that a student shall not render a legal decision unless he is at least twelve miles away from his master. Thus, when the late-third-century rabbi Tanhum bar R. Jeremiah was told that his master lived only three miles away, he ceased from rendering legal decisions.

Later compilations, which are more difficult to date, include *Midrash Psalms* (*Tehillim;* see Buber 1891), *Exodus Rabbah* (see Herr 1972b) and the *Tanhuma-Yelamdenu* literature (see Berman 1996). Since it incorporates earlier material, it is difficult to pinpoint the date of redaction of *Mid. Pss.* from the opening words of 11.27. Zunz, for example (1892), locates its redaction in the last centuries of the Geonic period (eighth-eleventh centuries), but Buber (1891) proposes an earlier date for the portion on Psalms 1–118 and contends that only later editions give the impression of a later date. Albeck, like Zunz, subscribes to the later date (1947: 55-57). As Strack, Stemberger, et al., note (1992: 351), we must assume an extended period of development from the talmudic period (third-sixth centuries CE) to the thirteenth century. *Exodus Rabbah* (see Shinan 1984), like *Pss. Rab.,* is composed of two parts, the first an exegetical midrash on Exodus 1–10, the second a homiletic midrash on Exodus 12–40. Zunz (1892) dates the entire work to the eleventh or twelfth century, whereas Herr (1972b: 1261-63) considers the first part later than the second, thus dating it no earlier than the tenth century. Shinan (1984: 19) contends that the first part is from the tenth century (see also Strack, Stemberger, et al. 1992: 335-37).

The *Tanhuma* literature, "a group of homiletic midrashim on the Pentateuch which are transmitted in many versions" (Strack, Stemberger, et al. 1992: 331), includes not only the two editions of *Tanhuma,* the *Ordinary Edition* and the Buber edition (see Berman 1996), but also various handwritten recensions. This literature also comprises the second parts of *Exod. Rab.* and *Num. Rab., Deut. Rab.,* parts of *Pesiqta Rabbati* and other midrashim (Strack, Stemberger, et al. 1992: 331). The commonly held date for the *Tanhuma* literature is the early ninth century.

Given the complex textual transmission of *Deut. Rab.,* it is difficult to date it with even a modicum of certainty. Based on its language and reference to Palestinian rabbis and locations, it more likely than not originated prior to the Babylonian Talmud, but its textual history makes it impossible to date it as early as the fifth century. Zunz (1892) dates it to the tenth century, although Lieberman (1974) disagrees with this late dating.

Traditionally ascribed to a first-century *tanna* (sage) mentioned in the *Mishnah,* Rabbi Eliezer ben Hyrkanos, *PRE* is an eighth–early-ninth-century work that draws on the classical rabbinic texts, while expanding and developing its sources' motifs and narratives. Its author's retelling of biblical stories incorporates mystical language and imagery, along with fairly detailed discussions of astronomy and the calendar, making it unlike earlier rabbinic works.

The intention of *Tanna de-be Eliyahu,* also known as *Seder Eliyahu* (see Braude and Kapstein 1981), is expressed at the outset: to urge right moral conduct *(derekh eretz),* and to glorify the study of Torah, the Law. It contains interpretations of legal issues by means of parables and stories derived from the author's adventurous peregrinations. While there is no scholarly consensus as to its final redaction, it seems likely that the work was composed after the Babylonian Talmud and before the ninth century, even though it is often considered a tenth-century work (Strack, Stemberger, et al., 1992: 369-71).

As this brief survey of some of the well-known compilations attests, further work in the field of dating rabbinic texts is sorely needed.

MIDRASHIC ANTHOLOGIES

Thesaurus-like collections characterize the post-classical and mid to late medieval period of rabbinic literature. Noteworthy are *Yalkut Shimoni* (known as the *Yalkut;* see Ha-Darshan 1968), *Yalkut ha-Makhiri* (see Buber 1891), and the *Midrash Ha-Gadol* (see Fisch 1940). The *Yalkut Shimoni,* compiled from more than fifty works and covering the entire span of the Hebrew Bible, is one of the most well-known and comprehensive anthologies. The compiler, Shim'on ha-Darshan, availed himself of the wealth of rabbinic literature and amassed rabbinic sayings into an exhaustive collection ordered according to the verses of the Bible. The work is dated to the thirteenth century, but at the end of the fifteenth century, it circulated widely and received popular attention.

Compiled by Makhir ben Abba Mari in Spain, *Yalkut ha-Makhiri* (preserved in manuscript at Leiden University library), unlike the *Yalkut Shimoni,* deliberately excludes writings treated in the *Midrash Rabbah* and focuses primarily on the Prophets, Job, Psalms, and Proverbs. A late-thirteenth or fourteenth-century work, the *Yalkut ha-Makhiri* uses early as well as late sources, such as *Tanhuma, Midrash Job, Seder Eliyahu Rabbah,* and *Midrash Mishle* (Proverbs). Makhir ben Abba Mari also preserves work not found in his sources, thus making this collection a valuable resource.

The largest collection of midrash, the Yemenite anthology on the Pentateuch known as *Midrash Ha-Gadol* (see Fisch 1940), is almost universally attributed to David ben Amram of Aden. Dated to the fourteenth century, *MHG* is divided according to the annual reading cycle. Its sources are extensive, including not only the classical and later midrashic works, but also the Babylonian and Palestinian Talmuds, geonic writings, writings of Alfasi (see Cohen 1928-29), and especially of Maimonides (see Twersky 1982; Strack, Stemberger, et al. 1992: 387). In this case, the compiler may be regarded as the author, for he "frequently inserts his own explanatory glosses." "Thus there results a mosaic-like composition, an entirely new work with its own style, whose sources can often no longer be reconstructed" (Strack, Stemberger, et al. 1992: 387).

There are several other collections of midrashic works of this period that blend collation and commentary. In the early medieval period, we also notice a rise in Bible commentaries, but this does not preclude an interest in midrash. The biblical interpretations of the rabbis as we find them in compilations of the early medieval period were often mentioned or alluded to in Bible commentaries, and even today as part of the very bedrock of the Jewish tradition, they find their way into contemporary sermons.

CONCLUSION

The midrashic compilations briefly discussed here reflect the richness of rabbinic biblical interpretation, spanning well over a thousand years. In their attempt to make Scripture relevant and real to their contemporary situation, the rabbis employed a variety of exegetical methods, such as the use of prooftexts, word-play, and *mashals* (parables). Examples of these methods are found in *Gen. Rab.* 24.1, which we examined above. The midrash begins with a verse from Isa. 29:15, "Woe unto them who seek deep to hide their counsel from the Lord," and ends with Gen. 5:1, "This is the book of the generations of Adam," the verse that requires explication. By means of word association, the rabbis draw on these seemingly disparate verses to shed light on the meaning of Gen. 5:1. In this instance, the appearance of "book" in Isa. 29:18 and in Gen. 5:1 is the philological lynchpin which launches the rabbis' exegesis. Thus, in order to demonstrate God's omniscience, the rabbis compare God to a master builder who builds a city with secret chambers, canals, and caves, an architect who is all too familiar with the minutiae of his work. Multiple interpretations of any given verse are one of the most striking features of rabbinic exegesis. Indeed, underlying the rabbinic approach to Scripture is the notion that God's word cannot be constricted to a particular interpretation but rather has multiple meanings that are beyond human comprehension. In a sense, the exegete is both humbled before the word of God, knowing that one's understanding of its meaning is never fully comprehensible, and at the same time free to derive as much meaning from it as possible.

The rabbis engaged in biblical exegesis not only for the purpose of understanding the Bible, but more importantly to make its meaning relevant to their world. In a sense, the world of the Bible mirrors their world, and their world, or perhaps worlds, is made manifest in their biblical interpretation.

Themes such as the chosenness of Israel are pervasive because to varying degrees the self-understanding of Judaism as set apart is of paramount importance to the rabbis.

Any discussion of midrashic compilations must take into account the role of textual transmission, and the degree to which these multi-layered works are useful to historians. To be sure, recent studies in manuscript transmission caution us to use rabbinic texts ever so carefully for historical inquiry, but we must nevertheless view these documents as literary artifacts that, even if modestly, provide an understanding of the rabbinic ethos.

BIBLIOGRAPHY

Albeck, H.
1947   The Sermons of Israel. Jerusalem: Mosad Bialik.

Bakhos, C.
2006   Ishmael on the Border: Rabbinic Portrayals of the First Arab. Albany: State University of New York Press.

Beit-Arie, M.
1993   "Transmission of Texts by Scribes and Copyists: Unconscious and Critical Influences." BJRL 75: 33-51.

Berman, S. A. (ed.)
1996   Midrash Tanhuma-Yelammedenu: An English Translation of Genesis and Exodus from the Printed Version of Tanhuma-Yelammedenu, with an Introduction, Notes, and Indexes. New York: Ktav.

Braude, W. G., and I. J. Kapstein
1975   Pesikta de-Rab Kahana: R. Kahana's Compilation of Discourses for Sabbaths and Festal Days. Philadelphia: Jewish Publication Society.
1981   The Lore of the School of Elijah: Tanna debe Eliyahu. Philadelphia: Jewish Publication Society.

Bregman, M.
1981   "The Triennial Haftarot and the Perorations of the Midrashic Homilies." JJS 32: 74-84.

Buber, S.
1891   Midrasch Tehillim: Edited for the first time with introduction by Solomon Buber. Wilna. Repr. Hildesheim: Olms, 1966.

Calvin, J.
2001   The Institutes of the Christian Religion. Ed. J. T. McNeill; trans. F. L. Battles. LCC. 2 vols. Westminster: John Knox.

Cohen, A.

1961   "Ecclesiastes Rabbah VII, 12, 1." Trans. in *Ecclesiastes Rabbah 195*. London: Soncino.

Cohen, B.

1928-29 "Three Arabic Halakic Discussions of Alfasi," *JQR* n.s. 19: 355-410.

Cohen, N.

1981   "Structure and Editing in the Homiletic Midrashim," *AJSR* 6: 1-20.

Dan, J.

1974   *The Hebrew Story in the Middle Ages* (Hebrew). Jerusalem: Keter.

Finkelstein, E. A.

1993   *Sifre al Sefer Devarim* (Hebrew). New York: Jewish Theological Seminary.

Fisch, S.

1940   *Midrash Hagadol on the Pentateuch. Edited for the First Time from Various Yemeni Manuscripts, with a Commentary and Introduction.* Manchester: Manchester University Press.

Fraade, S.

1991   *From Text to Commentary: Torah and Its Interpretation in the Midrash Sifre to Deuteronomy.* Albany: State University of New York.

Fraenkel, J.

1991   *Darkhel ha-ʿaggada vehamidrash.* (Hebrew). Masada: Yad Letalmud.

Freedman, H. (trans.)

1983   *Rabbah: Genesis.* London: Soncino.

Friedlander, G. (trans.)

1981   *Pirke de Rabbi Eliezer.* New York: Sepher-Hermon.

Geller, S.

1996   *Sacred Enigma: Literary Religion in the Hebrew Bible.* London: Routledge.

Ginzberg, L.

1909   *Legends of the Jews.* 7 vols. New York: Simon and Schuster.

Goldberg, A.

1985   "Form-Analysis of Midrashic Literature as a Method of Description," trans. R. B. K. Ulmer. *JJS* 36: 159-74. Repr. in *Rabbinische Texte als Gegenstand der Auslegung. Gesammelte Studien.* 80-95. Vol. 2. Texte und Studien zum Antiken Judentum, 73. Tübingen: Mohr, 1999.

1986   "The Semikah." Trans. R. B. K. Ulmer. *Proceedings of the Ninth World Congress of Jewish Studies, Division C.* Jerusalem: The World Union of Jewish Studies. 1-6.

1987   "Quotation of Scripture in Hekhalot Literature." Trans. R. B. K. Ulmer. First Congress of Mysticism in Hekhalot and Merkavah Literature. *Jerusalem Studies in Jewish Thought* 6: 37-52.

Ha-Darshan, Rabbi S. A.

1968   *Yalkut Shimoni al ha-Torah, Compiled by Rabbi Shimon Ashkenazi HaDarshan of Frankfurt (circa 1260)* (Hebrew). Facsimile edition; 5 vols. Jerusalem: Vagshal.

Hartman, G. H., and S. Budick (eds.)

1986   *Midrash and Literature.* New Haven: Yale University Press.

Hasan-Rokem, G.

2000   *Web of Life: Folklore and Midrash in Rabbinic Literature.* Trans. B. Stein. Stanford: Stanford University Press.

2003   *Tales of the Neighborhood: Jewish Narrative Dialogues in Late Antiquity.* Berkeley: University of California Press.

Heinemann, J.

1968   "The Triennial Lectionary Cycle." *JJS* 19: 41-48.

1971a   "'Omanut ha-qompozisyah be-Midrash Va-Yiqra Rabbah." *Hasifrut* 2: 808-34.

1971b   "Profile of a Midrash: The Art of Composition in Leviticus Rabbah." *JAAR* 39: 141-50.

1974   *Aggadot Ve-Toldotehen.* (Hebrew). Jerusalem: Keter.

1986   "The Nature of Aggadah," in Hartman and Budick (eds.) 1986: 41-55.

Herr, M. D.

1972a   "Midrash," *EncJud* 11:1507-23.

1972b   "Exodus Rabbah," *EncJud* 11:1261-63.

Hirshman, M.

1999   *Torah lekhol ba'e ha-'olam* [Torah for the Entire World]. Tel Aviv: Hakibbutz Hameuchad.

2000   "Rabbinic Universalism in the 2nd and 3rd Centuries." *HTR* 93: 101-15.

Israelstam, J., and J. J. Slotki (trans.)

1983   *Leviticus Rabbah.* London: Soncino.

Jaffee, M. S.

1983   "'The Midrashic' Proem: Towards the Description of Rabbinic Exegesis," in W. S. Green, ed., *Approaches to Ancient Judaism,* Vol. 4: *Studies in Liturgy, Exegesis and Talmudic Narrative,* 95-112. Chico: Scholars.

Kugel, J.

1986   "Two Introductions to Midrash." In Hartman and Budick (eds.) 1986: 77-104.

1990   *In Potiphar's House: The Interpretive Life of Biblical Texts.* Cambridge: Harvard University Press.

Lachs, S. T.

1965   "Canticles Rabbah." *JQR* 55: 235-55.

Lauterbach, J. Z. (trans.)

1933   *Mekhilta de Rabbi Ishmael.* Philadelphia: Jewish Publication Society.

Lehrmann, S. M.

1974   *Midrash Debarim Rabbah: Edited for the First Time from the Oxford Ms. No. 147 with an Introduction and Notes.* 3rd edition; Jerusalem.

Lieberman, S.

1974   *Midrash Debarim Rabbah.* 3rd ed. Jerusalem: Wahrmann.

Marguiles, M., A. Steinsalz, Z. M. Rabinowitz, and S. Fisch (eds.)

1975   *Midrash ha-Gadol. Midrash Haggadol on the Pentateuch.* 5 vols. Jerusalem: Mossad Harav Kook.

Meir, O.

1974   "'The Wedding in Kings' Parables (in the Aggada)," in I. Ben-Ami and D. Noy, eds., *Studies in Marriage Customs,* 167-90. Folklore Researches Center Studies, 4. Jerusalem: Hebrew University of Jerusalem Institute of Jewish Studies.

1999   "Proverbs Uttered by Characters in the Stories of the Talmud and the Midrash," *De Proverbio* 5 (9) = http://www.deproverbio.com/DPjournal/DP,5,2,99/OFRA/TALMUD.htm

Mihaly, E.

1964   "A Rabbinic Defense of the Election of Israel." *HUCA* 35: 103-35.

Milikowsky, C.

1988   "The *Status Quaestionis* of Research in Rabbinic Literature," *JJS* 39: 201-11.

2009   *Seder Olam, Critical Edition with Introduction and Commentary. Part I: Critical Edition* (Hebrew). Jerusalem: Israel Academy of Sciences.

Neusner, J.

1985   *Genesis Rabbah: The Judaic Commentary on Genesis, A New American Translation.* Brown Judaic Studies; Atlanta: Scholars.

1986   *Sifré to Numbers: An American Translation* I: *1-58.* Brown Judaic Studies; Atlanta: Scholars.

1987a   *From Tradition and Imitation: The Plan and Program of Pesiqta Rabbati and Pesiqta de Rab Kahana.* Atlanta: Scholars.

1987b   *Sifre to Deuteronomy: An Analytical Translation.* 2 vols. Atlanta: Scholars.

1988   *Sifra: An Analytical Translation.* Atlanta: Scholars.

1989a   *Esther Rabbah 1: An Analytical Translation.* Brown Judaic Studies; Atlanta: Scholars.

1989b   *Lamentations Rabbah: An Analytical Translation.* Atlanta: Scholars.

1989c   *Ruth Rabbah: An Analytical Translation.* Brown Judaic Studies; Atlanta: Scholars.

1989-90   *Song of Songs Rabbah: An Analytical Translation.* Atlanta: Scholars.

Porton, G.

2003   "Rabbinic Midrash." *HBI*[1], 198-224.

Rodkinson, M. L. (ed.)

1903   *New Edition of the Babylonian Talmud. Original Text Edited, Corrected, Formulated, and Translated into English. First Edition Revised and Corrected by I. M. Wise.* Vol. I: *Tract Sabbath.* Boston: Boston New Talmud.

Sarason, R.

1982   "The Petihot in Leviticus Rabba: 'Oral Homilies' or Redactional Constructions."
        JJS 38: 557-68.

Schäfer, P.

1986   "Research into Rabbinic Literature: An Attempt to Define the Status Quaestionis."
        JJS 37: 139-52.

1989   "Once Again the *status quaestionis* of Research in Rabbinic Literature: An Answer
        to Chaim Milikowsky." *JJS* 40: 89-94.

Shinan, A. (ed.)

1984   *Midrash Shemot Rabbah, Chapters I–XIV: A Critical Edition Based on a Jerusalem
        Manuscript, with Variants, Commentary, and Introduction* (Hebrew). Tel Aviv: Dvir.

Stein, E.

1931-32 "Die homiletische Peroratio im Midrasch." *HUCA* 2: 353-71.

Stern, D.

1986   "Midrash and the Language of Exegesis: A Study of Vayikra Rabbah, Chapter I." In
        Hartman and Budick (eds.) 1986: 105-24.

Stern, S.

1994   *Jewish Identity in Early Rabbinic Writings.* Leiden: Brill.

Strack, H. L., G. Stemberger (eds.), J. Neusner, and M. Bockmuehl (trans.)

1992   *Introduction to the Talmud and Midrash.* Minneapolis: Fortress.

Townsend, J. T.

2003   *Midrash Tanhuma: Translated into English with Indices and Brief Notes: Exodus and
        Leviticus.* New York: KTAV.

Twersky, I.

1982   *The Code of Maimonides (Mishneh Torah): Introduction.* Yale Judaica Series. New
        Haven: Yale University Press.

Urbach, E.

1975   *The Sages: Their Concepts and Beliefs.* Jerusalem: Magnes.

Zunz, L.

1892   *Die göttesdienstlichen Vorträge der Juden historisch entwickelt.* 2nd ed. Frankfurt am
        Main: Kauffman; repr. Hildesheim: Olms, 1966.

CHAPTER 4

Medieval Jewish Biblical Exegesis

Robert A. Harris

This chapter surveys important trends and personalities in the history of medieval Jewish biblical exegesis. It begins with an examination of the advances in Hebrew linguistics, lexicography, and philology achieved by Jewish scholars working in the Islamic world in the ninth to eleventh centuries. It was these achievements that to a great extent determined the subsequent course of Jewish biblical interpretation. The chapter then moves to the exegesis of Rashi and the northern French "school" he essentially founded in the eleventh and twelfth centuries. Next to be considered is the twelfth-century polymath Abraham ibn Ezra, who assimilated the Judeo-Arabic scholarship of the great Hebrew grammarians while in his native Spain and then disseminated this scholarship during his later peregrinations throughout Christian Europe. These twin pillars of Jewish exegesis, the European and Islamic worlds, were synthesized in different ways by each of the remaining scholars treated here, David Kimhi, Nahmanides, Gersonides, and Abarbanel, from the twelfth through fifteenth centuries.

JEWISH EXEGESIS IN THE ISLAMIC WORLD

Babylonia

It may be said that medieval Jewish biblical exegesis begins with the Gaonic academies of Babylonia in the early Islamic age. While this chapter will not focus in detail on the accomplishments of scholars associated with those schools in the fields of grammar, comparative linguistics, and lexicography, no introduction to the subject of Jewish Bible study would be complete without at least a brief appraisal of the work of Saadia Gaon. Saadia ben Joseph (882-942), born in Egypt and later head *(gaon,* pl. *geonim)* of the prestigious academy of Sura, was active in virtually all areas of Jewish scholarship and communal leadership during his prodigious career. He produced authoritative works in many fields, encompassing liturgy and Hebrew language and philosophy, in addition to his work in biblical exegesis. His biblical studies yielded significant results in two complementary areas, translation and commentary. Saadia authored a translation of the Bible into Arabic and composed a commentary as well; the Arabic word *tafsir* ("explication") is used of both of these activities (Brody 2000). This work was continued by several of the *geonim* who followed him. While much of their scholarship has been published, a significant portion remains in manuscript (Zucker 1984; Kafih 1973; Goodman 1988).

Several of Saadia's commentaries (e.g., Genesis, Job) contain extensive methodological introductions. In these, Saadia addresses, among other subjects, what he considers to be the three fundamental principles upon which his biblical scholarship is based: (1) Biblical texts should be understood, first and foremost, according to the well-known and widespread meanings the words convey to the readers. This meaning ought to be tempered by only two other factors, (2) human reason and (3) tradition. If the literal meaning of a verse would yield an illogical interpretation, then the metaphorical understanding should be preferred. Thus, "You shall circumcise the foreskin of your heart" (Deut. 10:16) should not be understood according to the widespread meaning of its words, since that would yield an interpretation counter to common sense. Similarly, texts such as Exod. 23:19, "You shall not boil a kid in its mother's milk," should be construed not simply according to the meaning of its words, but according to the rabbinic tradition that mandates a complete separation of meat and dairy products in the Jewish cuisine (Brody 2000).

A variety of historical factors provided the context for Saadia and the Geonim who followed him to pursue their biblical exegesis. Among these was the rise of Islam, with its emphasis on the purity of the Arabic language and the excellence of God's revelation in the Koran. Jewish scholars such as Saadia needed to provide a concomitant demonstration with regard to the Hebrew language and the Hebrew Bible. Additionally, more explicit polemics against rabbinic midrash, both from within the Jewish community by the Karaites — schismatic Jewish rivals of the rabbinic community, who themselves produced a prodigious amount of serious Hebrew linguistic scholarship and biblical exegesis (see Polliack 2003) — and externally by Christians and Muslims, spurred the geonim to create a new type of exegesis that would answer the needs both of literalists and linguists, on the one hand, and Jewish traditionalists, on the other. Saadia's *tafsir* provided just such a response.

Spain

The second great phase of medieval Jewish biblical exegesis occurred in Spain, whose Jewish community had, by the middle of the tenth century, succeeded Babylonia as the most prominent center of Jewish learning. As in the earlier period, the vast majority of this scholarship took place in the Arabic language; likewise, most was not purely exegetical in character, but rather featured a variety of grammatical and lexicographical works with exegetical import. One of the first important compositions was the *Mahberet* (see Saenz-Badillos 1986; Filipowski 1854), a dictionary of biblical Hebrew written in the Hebrew language by the grammarian and poet Menahem ibn Saruk in the tenth century. While this work was in time superseded by more sophisticated dictionaries composed in Arabic, the *Mahberet* achieved prominence in Jewish communities in Christian Europe, where Arabic was not read or understood. Menahem's dictionary engendered scholarly debate, chiefly embodied in the *Teshuvot* ("Responses") of Dunash ibn Labrat (tenth century), and the writings of their respective disciples and advocates. As most of this scholarship was also composed in Hebrew, it, too, was accessible to the Jews of Europe (Saenz-Badillos 2000).

However, the great advances made among Spanish Jews in both Hebrew language and biblical exegesis were achieved in works composed in Arabic. In particular, in the late tenth century, Judah ibn Hayyuj's discovery of the triliteral nature of Hebrew verbs (and most nouns) had profound implications for subsequent biblical and Hebrew studies. The most important of these were the comprehensive grammar *(Sefer Hariqmah)* and dictionary *(Sefer Hashorashim)* written by Jonah ibn Janah in the early eleventh century. Ibn Janah synthesized the linguistic system outlined by Hayyuj and fully described biblical Hebrew for the first time. Although ibn Janah did not produce formal exegetical works, his grammar and dictionary include many explanations of verses and even broader biblical contexts (in addition to virtually all the individual words), and so essentially provided a philological gateway to the Bible for any interested student (Maman 2000). Among the scholars who assimilated the information embodied in works of ibn Janah and ibn Hayyuj were two late-eleventh-century exegetes, Moses ibn Chiquitilla and Judah ibn Balam. Like most of the Spanish Jewish grammarians and linguists before them, ibn Chiquitilla and ibn Balam wrote their commentaries in Arabic. Much of their exegetical output either is not extant or remains in manuscript. However, all of these were followed by a twelfth-century exegete who did write in Hebrew and who cited all of the previously-mentioned scholars extensively: Rabbi Abraham ibn Ezra (1089-1164). It is through his work that the scholarship of the great Judeo-Spanish linguists was mediated to later generations. But before assessing the significance of ibn Ezra, we need to backtrack and consider the development of biblical exegesis among the Jews of Christian Europe.

THE NORTHERN FRENCH SCHOOL

The eleventh and twelfth centuries saw the rise of a revolution in biblical studies among northern French rabbinic scholars. These included such illustrious figures as Rabbi Solomon ben Isaac, or Rashi (1040-1105), and lesser-known masters such as Rabbi Joseph Kara (1050-1130); Rashi's grandson, Rabbi Samuel ben Meir, or Rashbam (1080-1160); Rashbam's student, Rabbi Eliezer of Beaugency (mid-twelfth century); and Rabbi Joseph ben Isaac Bekhor Shor (mid to late twelfth century), a disciple of Rashbam and Rashbam's younger brother, Rabbi Jacob Tam. These rabbis came to eschew the traditional rabbinic Bible study based on homiletic and legal midrashim and replaced it with the methodology they called *peshat,* or the interpretation of biblical texts according to context. Although this methodology had its antecedents and analogies in the Judeo-Islamic world (Sarna 1971), the northern French approach arose out of its own particular circumstances (see below). Especially as exemplified by Rashi, it came to influence all subsequent developments in medieval Jewish biblical exegesis.

Rashi

Rashi was a pioneer in what is probably the most important aspect of the development of *peshat* exegesis, namely, the abandonment of the authoritative midrash of the ancient rabbis in favor of newly understood contextual exegesis. Whereas midrash allows for a fanciful reading, encouraging embellishment of details and often stressing a moral or legal teaching, *peshat* came to connote a reading that fit the "actual" meaning of a text, as understood by a particular commentator. While Rashi never fully abandoned midrash in his

Torah commentary (in fact, fully three-quarters of his comments in that work relate in some way to a midrashic reading of rabbinic origin), he did articulate a vision of what an individually-derived, contextual reading should look like. This is most famously seen in his commentary on Gen. 3:8:

> There are many homiletic midrashim [on these verses], and the rabbis have long ago arranged them in their proper place in Genesis Rabba and the other midrashim. Whereas I have only come to explain Scripture according to its contextual [*peshuto*] understanding, and according to the *aggadah* that reconciles the words of Scripture, each word understood according to its character.

Thus, Rashi expressed awareness of both midrashic and contextual interpretations and claimed a preference for the latter.

A case in point would be his comment on Gen. 1:1-3 (see Berliner 1905). The scriptural text may be variously construed, as can be seen by contrasting various modern translations. The NJPS translation renders: "When God began to create heaven and earth — the earth being unformed and void, with darkness over the surface of the deep and a wind from God sweeping over the water — God said, 'Let there be light'; and there was light." More famously, the KJV translates: "In the beginning God created the heaven and the earth. And the earth was without form, and void; and darkness was upon the face of the deep. And the Spirit of God moved upon the face of the waters. And God said, Let there be light: and there was light." The question of whether to treat the first verse as an independent sentence (KJV) or as a subordinate clause, with the primary clause not to be found until v. 3 (NJPS), centers around how to understand the initial Hebrew words *bereshit bara' 'Elohim.* Literally taken, the verse appears to mean "At the beginning of . . . God created." Sensitive to the difficulty of such a literal rendering, Rashi initially offers two midrashic interpretations of the verse. Following an ancient midrashic rule of word substitution, he turns to two biblical verses in which the word *reshit* ("the beginning of") is found. The first of these is Prov. 8:22:

> "The LORD created me at the beginning of His course
> As the first of His works of old."

Since the beginning of that chapter features "Wisdom" calling out, and since for the rabbis there is no "wisdom" other than Torah (*Gen. Rab.* 1.6), Rashi feels free to substitute the midrashically-derived word "Torah" for the biblical *reshit,* and render: "On behalf of Torah *(be-reshit)* did God create heavens and

earth." Thus, he neatly repairs the difficulty in the ambiguous opening word
— and gives a spiritually uplifting message to the oppressed members of the
Jewish community. Similarly, since the word *reshit* also appears in Jer. 2:3 ("Israel was holy to the LORD, the first fruits [*reshit*] of his harvest"), Rashi per-
forms an equivalent substitution and comments, "on behalf of Israel *(be-
reshit)* did God create heavens and earth" (see *Lev. Rab.* 36.4). This comment
likewise solves the dilemma of the difficult literal meaning of the Hebrew
words of Gen. 1:1 and offers an additional homiletical message.

However, Rashi is aware that neither of these interpretations satisfies
the contextual meaning of the Hebrew text. So, he turns to his readers and
says, "But if you desire to interpret the verse contextually *(peshuto)*, this is
how you should do it . . ." (see Berliner 1905; Cohen 1997-99). He proceeds to
suggest that one would do well to read the second Hebrew word of the verse,
the finite verb *bara'* ("[God] created") as though it were a gerund (*bero'*, "creating"). This involves a modest revocalization and does not affect the consonantal text. Thus, Rashi's third, contextual, interpretation is indeed the one
underlying the NJPS rendering, and more particularly that of the recent
Schocken Bible: "At the beginning of God's creating of the heavens and the
earth . . . God said: Let there be light." This interpretation yields no particular
spiritual lesson similar to Rashi's midrashic interpretations and merely —
contextually! — indicates how the Bible's initial verses ought to be read. It is
important to clarify that Rashi is not correcting or rejecting the midrash.
Rather, he provides both a midrashic *and* a contextual reading to offer his
readership the fullest possible accounting of biblical language he can
(Greenstein 1993). While one should not oversimplify the problems associated with Rashi's "dual readings," it is best to understand his exegetical efforts
as an early stage in the developing *peshat* methodology (Kamin 1980; Gelles
1981: 28-33).

Rashi wrote commentaries on virtually every book of the Bible (Gruber
2004: 52-75). In general, his commentaries on the Prophets and Writings are
characterized by a more contextual, less midrashically-driven exegesis. While
this is due partly to the relative lack of ancient midrash on the later books of
the Bible (e.g., there is no "midrash Isaiah"), it is also due to Rashi's increased
awareness of the importance of engaging in the interpretive process without
turning to the traditions of the sages (see Rashi on Isa. 26:11; Rashbam's commentary on Gen. 37:2, where he cites Rashi's regret over not having enough
time to redo his commentaries in light of "the newer contextual interpretations being innovated daily"; Rosin 1881; ET Lockshin 1989). Thus, it is quite
likely that Rashi wrote his commentaries on the Prophets and the Writings
later in his lifetime, and so those exegetical works more faithfully reflect his

recently developed inclinations to write comments more purely contextual (Gruber 2004: 57).

Other Exegetes of the Northern French School

The ravages of the Middle Ages were not kind to much of the scholarly achievements of the great northern French biblical exegetes. Crusades, disputations, book-burnings, and whole-scale expulsions of the Jewish communities of northern Europe all contributed to the near-total destruction of Jewish biblical scholarship from the period. Other than Rashi, whose commentaries have been preserved in hundreds of manuscripts and printed editions and have received the greatest amount of scholarly attention over the generations, the exegetical works of the other outstanding representatives of the northern French school survive in a precious few manuscripts, which were hardly consulted until modern times. Nonetheless, these exegetes — each of whom probably composed commentaries on most of the Bible — are now experiencing a renaissance in modern studies of the history of medieval biblical interpretation, and a survey of some of their achievements is apropos (Harris 2004).

Rabbi Joseph Kara was one of Rashi's chief disciples. Although only a few of his comments on the Torah have been identified (and indeed, he may not have composed an independent Torah commentary of his own), he was one of the scholars chiefly responsible for the production and transmission of Rashi's commentaries. He did, however, compose commentaries on the Prophets (Cohen 1992-2005). While Kara on occasion expresses an appreciation for the value of midrash as a source of religious wisdom, he explicitly rejects it as *reading* methodology (Cohen 1992-2005):

> anyone who does not know the contextual understanding of Scripture [*peshuto shel miqra*], and prefers the midrash on some matter, is like one whom the current of a river has washed away and whom the depths of water have inundated, and who grasps at anything he can to save himself. Whereas if he had set his heart on the word of the Lord, he would have searched after the meaning of the matter and its contextual explanation — and in doing so would have fulfilled that which is taught by Scripture (from his comment on 1 Sam. 1:17-18).

Kara's claim that the search for contextual exegesis does not represent a rejection of religious values — but is, indeed, a response to a biblical commandment — is a point not to be overlooked. It has long been assumed, but never proved, that the *peshat* commentaries offered little to attract their study by Jewish communities who needed more spiritually-inclined commentaries. And there is no doubt that the practitioners themselves, the rabbinic exegetes whose works we are surveying, did not feel that they were violating any kind of religious principle (see Grossman 2000: 371; Shereshevsky 1982). Rather, they averred that contextual exegesis was long sanctioned by the talmudic authorities, even if the latter did not regularly engage in that type of study.

Rashi's grandson, Rabbi Samuel ben Meir ("Rashbam"), was the most prominent rabbi to give voice to these sentiments. The absolute devotion to *peshat* is characteristic of all of Rashbam's extant biblical commentaries (Torah [Rosin 1881; Lockshin 1989], Job [Japhet 2000], Song of Songs [Thompson 1988; Jellinek 1855], Koheleth [Japhet and Salters 1985]). Whether treating the Torah's narratives or, more significantly, the Torah's laws, Rashbam goes out of his way to announce his absolute adherence to *peshat* as a reading strategy. His introduction to Exodus 21 is a pithy case in point (Rosin 1881; emendations Rosin's, translation mine):

> Let knowers of wisdom know and understand that I have not come to explain rabbinic law *(halakhot),* even though this is the essence of Torah, as I have explained in my Genesis commentary (e.g., at Gen. 1:1; 37:2). For it is from the apparent superfluousness of scriptural language that rabbinic homilies *(aggadot)* and law are derived. Some of these rabbinic interpretations can be found in the commentary of our Rabbi Solomon, my mother's father, may the memory of the righteous be for a blessing. But I have come to explain the contextual meaning of Scripture. And I will explain the statutes and laws according to common sense (literally "the way of the world"). And I will do this even though the rabbinic understanding of the laws is the essence, as the rabbis taught: "law uproots Scripture" (*b. Sota* 16a).

This audacious statement, presented at precisely the point where the Torah moves from being essentially narrative to essentially legal, is all the more significant when it is understood that the author had himself composed an important Talmud commentary and was one of the leading rabbinic figures of his generation.

Let us consider one example in which Rashbam's willingness to expound Torah against the ancient rabbinic interpretation, even when touching on matters of law and Jewish observance, may be seen. Rabbinic Judaism had long enjoined the donning of *tefillen* (the so-called "phylacteries") during prayer and at other times during the day. This practice, ostensibly derived from such biblical passages as Exod. 13:9 and Deut. 6:8, involves preparing leather boxes containing parchment scrolls of verses from the Torah and wearing them on the arm and forehead. It is one of the central features of Jewish prayer and is a much-cherished ritual in rabbinic Judaism (see *b. Menahot* 32a-44a). But its biblical antecedents are only suggestive. That Exod. 13:9 refers to *tefillin* was self-evident to Rashi, who commented: "*And it shall be a sign for you* — the Exodus from Egypt shall be a sign for you — *on your hand and as a memorial between your eyes* — i.e., you should write these paragraphs, and fasten them on your head and arm" (see Berliner 1905; Katzenelenbogen 1986-93). What Rashi and the rabbis of antiquity had seen as the Torah's first reference to *tefillin* Rashbam, on the other hand, interpreted as simply metaphoric language: "*And it shall be a sign for you on your hand* — according to the depths of its contextual meaning *(peshuto)*, it should be for you as a continuous memorial, *as if* it were written on your hand. This usage is similar to *place me as a seal upon your heart* (Song 8:6)" (see Rosin 1881; Katzenelenbogen 1986-93). That Rashbam himself practiced the rabbinic ritual is beyond question. However, his willingness to read the biblical injunction according to its own context, even when the result of this reading appeared to contradict Jewish law, is an indication of just how dedicated he was to his exegetical principles (Lockshin [ed.] 1989).

Rashbam's principal disciple was Rabbi Eliezer of Beaugency. Although Eliezer's Torah commentary has not survived, his commentaries on Isaiah, Ezekiel, and the Twelve Minor Prophets are extant (see Nutt 1879; Poznanski 1913; Harris 1997). Eliezer's devotion to the *peshat* and almost complete neglect of rabbinic midrash are as complete as that of his master. His commentaries are replete with observations on the literary nature of biblical composition, and he regularly paraphrases difficult and allusive prophetic language (see Harris 1997: 130-55). Although Eliezer of course approaches the biblical text as divine in origin, he does evince awareness that the books of the Bible underwent a process of redaction before achieving their final status in the canon of Jewish Scriptures. Like several of the other northern French exegetes, he articulates an understanding of the role of the human, non-prophetic redactor who did more than simply serve as the receptacle of divine writ (see also, e.g., Rashbam's commentary on Koheleth 1:2; Japhet and Salters 1985). Rather, the redactor of each biblical book gathered up the words and speeches of the various prophets and edited, indeed composed, the books that constitute the Hebrew Bible.

A case in point is Eliezer's commentary on Ezek. 1:1-4. He specifically refers to the responsibility of a redactor for the composition of the present biblical text (Poznanski 1913, translation mine):

And I saw visions of God. . . . I looked, and lo, a stormy wind . . . : Ezekiel's words did not continue from the beginning, and even his name he did not make explicit, since the context of the book will make it clear below, as in *and Ezekiel shall become a portent for you* (Ezek. 24:24). And, relying on this, he allowed himself to abbreviate, as I have told you with regard to *(in the) thirtieth year,* that (there) the content of the book provides the proof for its (meaning, i.e., of the "thirtieth year"). But the redactor who wrote all of his words together added to what Ezekiel had left unclear and abbreviated, in these two verses.

This comment is significant on several grounds. First, whereas Rashi had assigned the third person narration in Ezek. 1:2-3 to the Holy Spirit, Eliezer attributes it to a redactor. Thus, the comment demonstrates Eliezer's exegetical independence in contradicting Rashi's authority (Greenstein 1984: 249). More importantly, the comment clarifies how Eliezer has related to the redactor's role in composing the biblical text. He has depicted a redactor taking prophetic material in some sort of prior stage, adding to it, and compiling a finished literary product. For Eliezer, as for his teacher Rashbam, the redactor is not identical with the prophet whose speeches are included in the book that bears his name.

Rabbi Joseph Bekhor Shor is the final northern French commentator whose work we will consider. Although traces of commentaries he wrote on various biblical books have been found, only his Torah commentary is available to us today (Gad 1983; Nevo 1994). He was a student both of Rashbam and of Rashbam's younger brother Rabbi Jacob Tam. Like the other exegetes of the northern French school, Joseph often comments with an eye to the literary quality of biblical composition. Among the features to which he is sensitive is the structure of poetic parallelism. Employing language that he apparently learned from Rashbam, Bekhor Shor regularly calls attention to parallel structures; more significantly, he relies on his recognition of the structure to clarify the meaning of difficult or ambiguous words.

For instance, Bekhor Shor uses his understanding of synonymous parallelism as an aid in clarifying the meaning of a word in the poetic oracles of Balaam. Following Balak's three failed attempts to arrange for Balaam to curse Israel, the prophet offers one final vision before departing. He declares to the king: "I see it, but not now, I behold it, but not soon; there goes forth a star from Jacob, there arises a meteor from Israel . . ." (Num. 24:17). Early in his comment, Bekhor Shor notes the parallelism between "see" and "behold." More compelling is what he says about "star" and "meteor," the second of which may be variously construed, depending on the context (Gad 1983; translation mine):

> *There arises a meteor:* One generally interprets (the word "meteor") as referring to a staff or a strap or (an organ of) government. However, since it is in parallel structure with regard to *there goes forth a star,* one must interpret it as referring to the language of "celestial bodies" (literally "a star").

What is significant about this comment is that it is *precisely* Bekhor Shor's comprehension of parallelism ("since it is in parallel structure . . .") that leads him to interpret the word differently from what would otherwise have been his sense of the contextual understanding of the verse.

The origins of northern French contextual exegesis *(peshat)* are to be found in a number of different factors, namely, the influence of Spanish Judaism and of the Islamic world and in the same complex historical processes that led to the twelfth-century renaissance in Christian Europe (Grossman 2000: 326-30). Additionally, northern French *peshat* developed in the context of the often polemical relationship between Judaism and Christianity. Faced with an ever more compelling Christian environment, in the sense of its being both culturally enriching and theologically challenging, the northern French rabbinic exegetes developed an approach to reading that would meet the needs of the Jewish community. Jewish readership needed commentaries that would take advantage of the advances achieved in the Judeo-Islamic world of Spain, would enable them to take part in the ongoing twelfth-century renaissance, and would provide them a basis on which to refute Christian polemics — not only according to Jewish religious teachings, but also on the basis of the "common sense meaning" of Hebrew Scriptures that *peshat* commentaries provided. At least in part, the adoption of *peshat* by the rabbis (and of *ad litteram,* or "literal," exegesis by contemporary church scholars) afforded both Jew and Christian a kind of common ground on which to engage in interfaith polemics.

However, in addition to these factors, the *peshat* methodology espoused by the northern French commentators was at least in part born out of dissatisfaction with the type of reading engaged in by the talmudic masters. In the movement away from midrash and toward *peshat,* these medieval exegetes essentially expressed their autonomy in ascertaining the meaning of Scripture and their unwillingness to defer always to the authority of the ancients when it came to interpreting the Bible.

RABBI ABRAHAM IBN EZRA

Abraham ibn Ezra hailed from Spain and thoroughly assimilated all the grammatical and lexicographical knowledge of the luminaries of the Spanish school such as Ibn Hayyuj, Ibn Janah, and Ibn Gikatilla (see Sarna 1971; 1993; Simon 2000). While he achieved renown as a liturgical and secular poet, philosopher, philologist, and more, our concern here is with ibn Ezra's achievements in biblical exegesis. Forced to leave Spain in c. 1140 under circumstances that are not entirely clear, ibn Ezra moved first to Italy, and later to France and England. It was while he lived in Christian Europe that he wrote his many biblical commentaries. Because of European Jewry's lack of knowledge of Arabic, he wrote all his exegetical works in Hebrew. Apparently, he wrote commentaries on the Torah, Isaiah, the Twelve Minor Prophets, Psalms, the Five Scrolls, and Daniel (Friedlander 1963-64, 1964; Simon 1989, 2000). After he moved from Italy to France he prepared additional versions of his commentaries on several books, resulting in the Italian and French recensions still extant (the so-called "long" and "short" versions; Simon 2000).

Ibn Ezra practiced a particularly philological, grammatically-oriented *peshat,* governed by context and reason, as well as by philosophical and natural "truths" he was able to ascertain. He articulates his exegetical program in the introduction to his commentary on the Torah. He denounces at length Geonic, Karaitic, and Christian exegesis. Geonic exegesis is characterized by extremely long and detailed commentaries of very brief passages of Scripture, so long and discursive as not really to function well as "commentary." Karaitic exegesis was threatening to Ibn Ezra not so much on the basis of its status as grammatically sensitive commentary, but because Karaism as a sect had entirely rejected both the rabbis as religious leaders of Judaism and the literary products of rabbinic Judaism (Talmud, Midrash, and Halakha/rabbinic law) as authoritative in any way. Ibn Ezra rejected rabbinic midrash as commentary (although not as a legitimate religious source) because it was not grammatical and contextual in orientation. He accepted it only when it came to determining Halakha.

Ibn Ezra characterized his own methodology (Cohen 1992-2005; see also Strickman and Silver 1988; translation mine):

> The foundation of my commentary, upon which I will rely, for it is the most straightforward, in my eyes and in the presence of God: . . . I will search out diligently the grammatical meaning of every word, to the best of my ability, and according to this will I interpret. . . .

In fact, the vast preponderance of his comments keep to this method quite consistently. He incorporated the scholarship of both Saadia and the great Spanish philologists and even referred to Karaitic exegesis, otherwise heretical in his estimation, when he found it to be grammatically and contextually sound.

Generally, he disparaged midrashic exegesis. A case in point would be his comment on Gen. 33:4, the moment of reunion between Jacob and Esau. The ancient rabbis, suspicious of Esau as they tended to be in all matters, noted the ancient scribal markings on "kissed" and took it to mean that Esau had intended to bite Jacob to death. Ibn Ezra dismisses this midrash as "good only for those who are still nursing (!)" and notes that context dictates the conclusion that "Esau intended no harm to his brother." His critical attitude is particularly pronounced with regard to homiletic midrashim; he qualifies the critique in matters of halakhic midrash, the ancient rabbinic interpretations that were regarded as the foundation of Jewish law.

As in his introduction to his commentary on the Torah, he articulates his preference for *peshat* over midrash even as he defers to the rabbis in all matters of halakhah:

> In favor of midrash, the way of *peshat* does not turn aside, even though the Torah has infinite (literally "seventy") levels of interpretation. Except in matters of law, if we find two interpretations of verses, and one of these accords with rabbinic interpretation . . . we will rely on their truth without doubt, emphatically (literally "with strong hands").

An illustration of this may be found in Ibn Ezra's commentary on Exod. 13:9. Above we have already seen how his northern French contemporary Rashbam interpreted this verse as metaphoric language. Ibn Ezra expresses awareness of this possibility, but prefers the rabbinic interpretation (Katzenelenbogen 1986-1993):

> *And it shall be a sign for you* . . . : There are those who dispute what our holy fathers taught [i.e., that this verse refers to *tefillin*] and instead teach that *for a sign and a memorial* [Exod. 13:9] should be understood along the lines of *for they shall be a chaplet of grace on your head and necklaces around your neck* [Prov. 1:9]. Also (they explain) *you should bind them for a sign upon your hand* [Deut. 6:8] as similar in meaning to *bind them [the commandments] continually upon your heart; tie them around your neck* [Prov. 6:21]. Similarly, [they understand] *and write them upon the doorposts of your house* [Deut. 6:9] along the lines of *write them on the*

tablet of your heart [Prov. 3:3]. So [here, according to their logic], how should we understand *as a sign and a memorial?* As "it should be well-versed in your mouth, that with a strong hand did the LORD bring you out of Egypt." But this is not the proper way! For at the beginning of that book [Proverbs] it is written "the proverbs [Heb. *mishlei*] of Solomon." And moreover all that Solomon mentions is according to the way of allegory [*mashal*]. But in the Torah it is not written that it is allegory — God forbid! Rather we should understand it only according to its own sense! Therefore, let us never remove meaning from its context [*peshat*], as long as its sense does not contradict common sense, like *you should circumcise the foreskin of your heart* [Deut. 10:16]; there we have to understand it according to reason.

It is evident that ibn Ezra has adopted Saadia's three principles of exegesis, namely, that Scripture should be interpreted according to the regularly, grammatically understood meaning of the Hebrew, conditioned both by one's sense of the rational and by devotion to the rabbinic interpretation (in matters of Jewish law; Brody 2000). In this case, however, much as Exod. 13:9 might seem to ibn Ezra to be metaphorical (and he builds a good case!), he feels that the rabbinic interpretation must of necessity override any other explanation of the verse.

Ever since Spinoza wrote his "Political-Theological Treatise," ibn Ezra has been famous for his critical daring in assigning portions of the Torah to post-Mosaic authorship (Spinoza 1991: 161-72). At several points in the course of explicating the Torah (e.g., Gen. 12:6; 36:31; Deut. 1:2; 34:1) ibn Ezra addressed the problem of anachronisms and suggested or hinted at the possibility of post-Mosaic authorship, or raised the issue and rejected it. Additionally, he accepted the suggestion, apparently first made by Moses ibn Chiquitilla, that Isaiah 40–66 emanate from a sixth-century exilic prophet, not from the eighth-century Isaiah ben Amoz, whose name the book bears (Simon 1983).

Through his incorporation of Babylonian and Spanish linguistic scholarship, Abraham ibn Ezra created a type of *peshat*, or contextual exegesis, that was more philologically based than the more purely "literary" contextual *peshat* developed by the northern French rabbinic exegetes. While the two approaches might have come into conflict, especially in areas where ibn Ezra feared that the more "unbridled" *peshat* of the French might threaten halakhic observance (Simon 1965; Lockshin [ed.] 1989), their shared commonalities, particularly with regard to the exegesis of non-legal narrative and prophetic texts without recourse to the midrash of the sages, enable them to be seen as complementary methodologies, both intent on interpreting Scripture contextually.

RABBI DAVID KIMHI

Rabbi David Kimhi, or Radak (1160-1235), was a Provençal exegete who combined a variety of methodologies (see Cohen 2000; Talmage 1975). Having been educated by his father, Rabbi Joseph Kimhi, and by his brother, Rabbi Moses Kimhi, both of whom were prominent exegetes in their own right, Radak mediated their scholarship, citing them frequently in his own commentaries.

In general, Radak may be said to have synthesized the exegesis of the Spanish school, particularly as exemplified by Rabbi Abraham ibn Ezra, and the French school, particularly as exemplified by Rashi. Radak began his scholarly career by writing a grammar (*Sefer Mikhlol;* Rittenberg 1966) and a biblical Hebrew dictionary (*Sefer Hashorashim;* Biesenthal 1967). These books were essentially based on the scholarship of Jonah ibn Janah, but due both to their own excellence and to their being written in Hebrew, these books soon eclipsed earlier works and became standard tools of reference among Christians as well as Jews (Talmage 1975: 54-58).

Radak composed commentaries on Genesis (but not, apparently, on the remainder of the Torah), the Prophets, Psalms, Proverbs, and Chronicles (Talmage 1990). Although he does on occasion refer to rabbinic midrash, especially as transmitted by Rashi (see his comments on 1 Sam. 14:32 and 1 Kgs. 18:30), Radak's general methodology is oriented toward the *peshat*. Notable for the clarity of his Hebrew prose, his exegesis is especially characterized by paraphrases of difficult and allusive biblical language. While he understood the principle of parallelism and often employed the phrase *kefel ha-inyan be-millim shonot* ("Scripture repeats the matter in different words") to note its presence in biblical composition, he refrained from interpreting according to that principle in contexts where he could provide a literary, even midrashic-style, explanation (Cohen 2000).

An example of where Radak both displays a sound knowledge of Hebrew grammar and yet manages at the same time to offer his readership a comforting rabbinic message may be found in his comment on Gen. 25:23 ("and the elder shall serve the younger"). Radak points out that a single explanation for this clause is not obvious (Cohen 1992-2005):

> Scripture has not included the direct object indicator *('et)* for these words, and so their meaning is in doubt: the text has not made clear who shall serve whom, the elder serving the younger, or the younger serving the elder. However, there is some measure of explanation, for in the majority of cases the subject of the verb is the preceding noun, ex-

cept in cases in which there is no doubt [that the reverse is correct], such as: *Water wears away stone* [Job 14:19, literally "stones, does wear away, [does] water"] and *fire boils water* [Isa. 64:1, literally "water, boils, [does] fire"]. Whereas this case (Gen. 25:23) is one in which the matter is not clarified by the prophecy, for sometimes the elder shall serve the younger, as happened during David's time, and sometimes the younger shall serve the elder, as is the case today. The prophecy does contain a slight clarification in that in most days the elder shall serve the younger, therefore the subject of the verb came first, and so shall it be again after our exile is restored. . . .

Thus, the prophecy to Rebecca in Gen. 25:23 is ambiguous, allowing both an interpretation appropriate for biblical contexts and one that extends encouragement to Radak's own Jewish contemporaries.

Radak will often address polemical issues, displaying a distinct understanding of Christian theology. This tendency is found particularly in his Psalms commentary (see Cohen 1992-2005), which often functions as a sort of handbook aiding his Jewish readership to resist the ongoing Christian pressure to convert (e.g., see his comments on Pss. 45:18; 110:7).

Although Radak was dedicated to the methodology of *peshat,* he escaped both the controversy occasionally associated with Abraham ibn Ezra and the oblivion suffered by most of the rabbinic masters of the northern French school. His commentaries and linguistic works are extant in dozens of manuscript copies and have been widely published in many printed editions as well. Perhaps the most significant reason for this was the manner in which he both represented the Spanish *peshat,* lucidly addressing the grammatical and philological issues present in the biblical text, and paid respect to the homiletical insights of the rabbis. The way in which he represents a midrashist's sensitivity to the literary nature of Scripture without indulging in fanciful interpretations that are far from the contextual meaning has particularly endeared his commentaries to generations of readers.

RABBI MOSES BEN NAHMAN (RAMBAN, OR NAHMANIDES)

Rabbi Moses ben Nahman (1194-1270) was a Catalonian-born scholar whose erudition was prodigious both in breadth and depth. He was an accomplished talmudist, combining the Spanish legal traditions with the newer French "tosaphistic" methodology. The latter was a type of penetrating dialectic aimed at resolving apparent contradictions among talmudic texts from different treatises and pioneered by Rashi's grandson, Rabbenu Tam (Urbach 1986).

Ramban was steeped in the philosophical tradition and became involved in the Maimonidean controversy, which was a complex, multistage conflict lasting from the twelfth through the fourteenth centuries. While it had many causes and manifestations, the main dimension was the bitter reaction of rabbis who felt that Maimonides' synthesis of Greek philosophy and Jewish tradition was wrongheaded. While Nahmanides tried somewhat to steer a middle course between radical proponents and detractors and sincerely admired the vast erudition of Maimonides, he may be said to have sided ultimately with an anti-Maimonidean position (Silver 1965).

A sometime counselor to King James of Aragon, Ramban was chosen by the king to engage in a disputation with the Jewish apostate Pablo Christiani in Barcelona (Chazan 1992; Chavel 1978). Ramban "won" the debate and was forced to flee Spain as a result. Arriving in the land of Israel by 1267, he wrote his commentary on the Torah there (Chavel 1959; 1971-76) during the last few years of his life (Elman 2000).

Ramban's commentary may be seen as a fusion of the Spanish school of *peshat* with the more midrashically-inclined aspects of Rashi's exegesis; he refers to both frequently and particularly esteems Rashi. Indeed, in his introduction to his Torah commentary he articulates these two as prominent influences on his methodology (Cohen 1992-2005, translation mine):

> But what can I do, when my soul longs for the Torah . . . but to go forth, in the footsteps of the early ones . . . to write, like them, contextual explanations [*peshatim*] of scriptural passages as well as midrashim, both in legal and narrative contexts. . . . And I will place as a light before my face . . . the commentaries of our Rabbi Solomon [Rashi] . . . on Scripture, Mishnah and Gemara — his is the most honored place [literally "the birthright is his due," after Deut. 21:17]. . . . And with Rabbi Abraham ibn Ezra there shall be "open rebuke and hidden love" (see Prov. 27:5).

Additionally, Ramban was one of the most prominent early kabbalists, whose mystical tradition of learning he applied in his biblical exegesis. He calls this approach by a variety of names, most regularly referring to it as *sod* ("secret") and *'emet* ("truth"). He adapts mystically-oriented ancient midrashim and weaves them into an approach to Scripture utterly unlike anything we have seen thus far. The Torah, he writes in his introduction (Cohen 1992-2005),

. . . preceded the creation of the world [*b. Shabbat* 88b] . . . *and is written in black fire against a background of white fire* [*y. Shekalim* 13]. . . . Everything that was transmitted to Moses our rabbi in the Gates of Wisdom [*b. Rosh Hashana* 21b] — everything was written in the Torah either explicitly or through hints, in the words or their numerological value *(gematriyyot),* in the shape of the letters. . . . Indeed, these hints are not understandable except through mouth to mouth [i.e., through an oral tradition that began with] Moses our Rabbi. . . . Moreover, we have a mystical tradition *(kabbalah shel emet)* that the entire Torah is Names of the Holy One, Blessed be God [see Zohar Yitro 87.1], that words may be separated into (Divine) names (when dividing their letters) in another way. . . .

This is, to be sure, an approach to Scripture that is not strictly contextual in the least. For it is obvious to see that once a commentator has freedom to manipulate letters of words and allow them to permute into "hidden meanings," or when one interprets texts based upon the numerical value of their letters, then the derived explanation may be far from the "plain" meaning of the biblical text.

An example of this may be found in Ramban's commentary on Gen. 24:1 ("and the LORD had blessed Abraham in all things"). The question that had attracted Jewish interpreters during the ages was the meaning of "in all things." How exactly had God blessed Abraham? Ramban approaches this question through a variety of methodologies. After first summarizing the comment of ibn Ezra (without attribution) that God had given Abraham "wealth, possessions, honor, sons, and all sorts of things that a man craves," Ramban reviews a variety of midrashic opinions that center around whether the verse teaches that Abraham had been additionally blessed with a daughter (*b. Baba Batra* 16b). This extended discussion enables Ramban to claim that the verse alludes to "secret" mystical doctrines (Cohen 1992-2005):

These other rabbis [represented in the midrash that Ramban cites] have innovated in their interpretation of this verse a matter profoundly deep, and they have expounded about it a secret [*sod*] from the secrets of the Torah. They have said that the word *bakol* ["in all things"] alludes to a great matter, namely, that the Holy One, Blessed be God, has an attribute called "allness," for it is the foundation of everything (*kol,* "all," i.e., God's beyond-infinite self). Indeed, the prophet Isaiah referred obliquely to this when he said (44:24): *I am the* LORD, *the maker of everything (kol).* Likewise did Solomon refer to this attribute (Eccl. 5:8): *the greatness of all the land is in "all" (kol).* This is the eighth attribute of God's thirteen attributes, and another attribute called "daughter" emanates from it, and through that attribute God governs everything *(kol).* And this is God's "House of Judgment" that is hinted at whenever God's holy name YHWH is employed by the text. . . . This attribute (of justice) was like a daughter to Abraham. And the Torah alludes to a great matter in that God blessed him with this attribute that is itself embodied in (God's own attribute) of *kol.* . . .

One should not derive from this example that Ramban always avoids the contextual explanation; indeed, at times he rigorously pursues the plain sense of a text, even when other, more typically *peshat,* commentators shy away from it. For example, alone among the medieval exegetes herein reviewed, he boldly criticizes Abraham for endangering Sarah's life (in his comment on Gen. 12:10), and states that "know, then, that Abraham our father sinned a terrible sin, albeit inadvertently, when he caused his innocent wife to be entrapped in iniquity, out of his fear that he would be killed. . . ."

These examples by no means exhaust the range of concerns and principles which Ramban encompasses in his exegesis of the Torah. For example, throughout his commentary he addresses issues of structure and sequence (see, e.g., on Lev. 16:23) and disagrees with Rashi and ibn Ezra regarding the degree to which the Torah deviates from chronological order: unlike the earlier two rabbis' inclination to expand the ancient rabbinic rule *ain mukdam u-me'uhar ba-torah,* literally "there is no early or late in the Torah," Ramban wishes to severely limit its application (see his comments on Gen. 11:32 and Exod. 31:18; Elman 2000). He also subjects the Torah to typological exegesis *(remez),* indicating, for example, that events in the lives of the patriarchs presage circumstances in later Israelite history (see his comments on Gen. 12:6; 32:26; Exod. 1:1; Funkenstein 1993: 98-121).

The principle of the "fourfold exegesis," well-known from much earlier Christian sources, was not explicitly invoked in Jewish circles until the work of Ramban's younger contemporary, R. Bahya ben Asher of Saragossa (Chavel 1976). It came to be known as *pardes,* originally a Persian loanword in the Bible meaning "orchard" (e.g., Eccl. 2:5), but which already in the rabbinic period acquired mystical connotations (e.g., *b. Hagigah* 14b). In the thirteenth century it was turned into an acronym alluding to four methods of explicating Scripture: *peshat* (contextual exegesis), *remez* (philosophical or typological exegesis), *derash* (the homiletical and legal midrashim of the rabbis), and *sod* ("secret," or mystical interpretation). It is apparent that these four correspond in some measure at least to the four methods articulated in Christian sources: literal, allegorical, tropological, and anagogic exegesis (Smalley 1952:

1-36). Ramban may not have explicitly adopted the methodological "program" of *pardes,* but through his devotion to the full range of methodologies in his exegesis of the Torah he may be seen as the earliest prominent Jewish biblical exegete to functionally implement its principles.

RABBI LEVI BEN GERSHOM (RALBAG, OR GERSONIDES)

Truly a "Renaissance Man," Rabbi Levi ben Gershom (1288-1344) was a Provençal scholar who excelled in many fields (e.g., philosophy, law, mathematics, and astronomy) in addition to biblical exegesis. His major philosophic work was *Wars of the Lord,* which contains much philosophically-oriented commentary on the Bible. He wrote commentaries on the Torah, Former Prophets, Proverbs, Job, Song of Songs, Ruth, Koheleth, Esther, Daniel, Ezra-Nehemiah, and Chronicles (see Cohen 1992-2005; Brenner 1993). Apparently, he also wrote a commentary on Isaiah, though that work is no longer extant (Feldman 1984: 11-16).

Ralbag's commentaries, particularly on the Torah, are characterized by a three-part division. Typically, in the first part of each section of commentary, he offers an explanation of words and phrases that are, in his estimation, difficult to understand *(be'ur hamillot).* Following this, he presents a running contextual commentary on the entire passage *(be'ur divrei haparashah* or *be'ur hasipur).* Finally, in an extensive section entitled *to'aliyyot,* or "lessons," he derives mainly philosophical, but also moral and legal, insights from the pericope under consideration. While Ralbag does not treat each biblical text in this three-part approach — to be sure, he does not attempt to endow narrative texts in Joshua or Judges with many philosophical insights — he does so enough of the time for it to be thought of as expressing his overall approach to exegesis (Feldman 1987: 213-47).

We may see an example of this full approach by excerpting Ralbag's lengthy commentary on Gen. 22:1, the verse beginning the narrative of Isaac's near sacrifice by his father. Ralbag first attempts to determine the specific nature of the "test" (Cohen 1992-2005):

> In my estimation, the matter of this test is that the prophecy came to Abraham in doubtful language. God had said to Abraham, of Isaac: *ve-ha'alehu sham le'olah,* and this phrase may be understood [idiomatically] that Abraham should "sacrifice" Isaac there as a burnt offering or [literally] that he should "bring him up" there to offer a burnt offering, so that Isaac could be educated in the worship of the Lord. . . .

Following his explanation of several difficult words and phrases, Ralbag turns his attention to the interpretation of the entire narrative. In turns paraphrasing and supplementing the language of the biblical text, he recasts vv. 5-8 (see Cohen 1992-2005), smoothing many difficulties along the way:

> As soon as Abraham saw the place [from afar], he separated from his servants and told them to wait there with the donkey while he and the boy [Isaac] go to that place and worship God, after which they would return to them. Now, Abraham did not want to inform his servants about the secret [prophecy from God to sacrifice his son], for he did not yet know how the matter would be resolved. So, Abraham took the wood for the sacrifice, and put it on his son Isaac, and he took in his hand the fire and the knife. Isaac then asked his father where the sheep was for sacrificing, for he had already seen that Abraham had brought with him the fire and the wood, and from this he had understood that Abraham wished to sacrifice a burnt offering there. This is an indication that Abraham was already accustomed to offering up burnt offerings and that Isaac had already learned this about him. [In response to Isaac's question] Abraham said to him, by way of prayer, "would that God will provide" [a sacrificial animal], and that God will clarify [literally "understand"] that which he said to me [in v. 2] as the sheep will be the offering. . . .

Following this, Ralbag provides eight "lessons" to be derived from the narrative. Here is his presentation of the third lesson (Cohen 1992-2005):

> The third lesson is in the category of "moral attributes" [*middot*]. It is that a person should hasten to perform the Lord's commandments, even when his performance of them causes him pain and sorrow. For do you not see that Abraham our Father hastened to perform this commandment, and arose early in the morning [v. 3] to fulfill with speed what was in his eyes both strange and troubling.

The "lesson" derived by Ralbag here is more in the realm of moral homily than philosophical exegesis. Moreover, at various points he professes a preference for a "plain sense" or contextual exegesis, as in a critical remark he directs toward exegetes who would allegorize narratives where he thought such interpretation was not warranted (in his commentary on the Cain and Abel narrative in Genesis 4): "one should not interpret the Torah figuratively except in places where it is necessary to read it so" (Feldman 1987: 213-47). Indeed, much of his Torah commentary is contextual in its exegetical orientation. However, in other commentaries, most notably on such books as Job or Song of Songs, he provides a consistent and extended philosophical interpretation (Kellner 1998). Nevertheless, it is important to remember that for Ralbag there was no essential conflict between the truth of the Bible and the truth of philosophy. Providing the interpretive connection between the two is perhaps the overarching theme of his exegetical program.

RABBI ISAAC ABARBANEL

The final exegete whose work we will survey is Rabbi Isaac ben Judah Abarbanel (1437-1508). His life neatly straddles what may be regarded as the transition, for Jewish exegesis, between the end of the Middle Ages and the dawn of modernity. Living during the midst of the Italian Renaissance, the influence of which is reflected in his writings, Abarbanel was born in Portugal and was active in the court of King Alfonso V of Portugal. After being accused of participation in a conspiracy against the crown, he left Portugal and settled in Spain. He spent approximately ten years there before the 1492 expulsion of Jews from Spain and lived out his remaining years in Italy. A famed financier and counselor to royalty, he was a prolific scholar, composing treatises in many different fields (e.g., philosophy, liturgy, *belles lettres*). He wrote voluminous commentaries on the Torah and the Former and Latter Prophets and a long messianic exegetical work on Daniel *(Ma'ayenei Ha-yeshu'a)*, among his other compositions. Although he lived most of his life in Portugal and Spain, he wrote most of his works in Italy (Lawee 2001: 9-25).

Abarbanel's commentaries are characterized not only by their length, but also by two distinctive features of organization. First, he divides Scripture into literary units according to his own intuition, paying heed neither to prior rabbinic *parashiyot* ("portions") nor to Christian chapter divisions. Second, he prefaces each unit with a series of questions that address a variety of exegetical issues in that section. In addition, characteristic of Abarbanel's exegesis are the introductions he wrote to his commentaries, particularly those on the Former Prophets. These introductions, in attempting to determine the identity of the biblical authors and in clarifying the circumstances in which they wrote their work, among other purposes, display all the hallmarks of the Aristotelian *accessus* formula (Lawee 2003). Developed into several fixed forms by the thirteenth century, these are introductions that may contain such observations as considerations of a biblical author's purpose in composing the work, his arrangement of the text, and the historical time period to which the book may be dated (Minnis 1984: 15-72).

To get an idea of the comprehensiveness, if not to say prolixity, of Abarbanel's writing, let us consider a sample of his writing. One of his pericopes corresponds to Genesis 18–19. He prefaces his commentary on this section by asking no fewer than thirty questions. The comments themselves consist of nearly twenty pages of dense prose in the standard editions, two columns per page (see Abarbanel 1964). That being said, his questions are generally insightful and often brilliant; the exegesis itself is virtually encyclopedic in scope.

His first question concerns the purpose of Gen. 18:1 and its connection with the preceding and the following narratives:

> What is the reason for this vision, in which God appeared to Abraham? For we have found with regard to it neither a speech nor any commandment at all! Whereas our rabbis have taught that "God came to visit the sick" [*b. Sota* 14a], but the division of the portion raises difficulty for their reasoning, for if this were the case, the Torah should have included this verse above [i.e., together with 17:23-27], in the narrative about the circumcision. And while Ramban wrote that one should not be concerned about the division between the portions, for the matter is juxtaposed [i.e., even despite the Masoretic separation of 18:1 from the preceding Torah portion], why should we not be concerned? Surely Ezra [who according to tradition was responsible for the Masoretic divisions] understood and was well-aware about the meaning of the division when he made the division! Moreover, it is still difficult why Scripture would not clarify that this vision came [for the purpose of describing God's] visit to Abraham and giving him honor, when it was for that very purpose.

It is clear from Abarbanel's formulation of this question that he is not satisfied with the midrashic solution of the ancient rabbis, which claimed that the verse showed God engaged in the commandment of visiting the sick, namely Abraham, who was healing from the circumcision operation performed at the end of ch. 17. For one thing, the verse is separated from the preceding narrative by a Masoretic division; for another, the narrative itself yields no evidence that God's "visiting the sick" was the purpose of the vision. In context, the verse seems to "dangle" between the circumcision narrative and the visit of the three angels in 18:2ff. Therefore, it may come as a surprise that Abarbanel begins his actual commentary on the narrative by announcing that he will read it first in conjunction with the midrashic interpretation, and only *then* according to its context (Abarbanel 1964):

I am going to explain the verses of this portion [Genesis 18–19] in a way
that will resolve all of the [thirty!] foregoing questions. First of all I will
interpret the vision [of 18:1] according to the way of midrash, and I will
resolve the difficulties that attend (the narrative) with it. Then I will interpret according to the context *(peshat),* as this seems to me. Moreover, I
will not occupy myself with the interpretation of the Teacher of the *Guide*
[*for the Perplexed,* i.e., Maimonides], nor will I respond to the difficulties
raised by Ramban, since that would not be fitting to do in the present
work. . . .

At this point, Abarbanel launches into a lengthy reading (almost two columns in length) that attempts to justify the rabbinic midrash, despite his
criticism of it earlier in the question. He follows this with a briefer, contextual interpretation:

The reason for this vision and its purpose according to the *peshat* is to inform Abraham of the wickedness of the Sodomites and their sin and the
destruction that had been decreed against them and against all of the cities of the plain [19:25]. This was done so that Abraham could plead their
defense [18:23-32], inasmuch as he, the father of the Gentiles [see 17:4-5],
could seek forgiveness and pardon for every person. And also the vision
was for Abraham to teach and caution his children and the people of his
covenant that they should keep the way of the Lord [18:19], so that (a
punishment) like the overturning of Sodom and Gomorrah [Deut. 29:22;
Isa. 13:19, etc.] would not happen to them. It is for this reason that the text
began "The Lord appeared to him by the terebinths of Mamre," that God
appeared to him to inform him of this. And the verse is connected to "the
outrage of Sodom and Gomorrah is so great" [Gen. 18:20], i.e., that God
appeared to him and told him this.

Thus, the contextual interpretation of the vision of God in Gen. 18:1, according to Abarbanel, is to connect it with God's speech to Abraham in 18:20. It is
a neat resolution of the difficulty inherent in a verse that describes an appearance of God that has no immediate and clear purpose, and although it is quite
similar to an interpretation of the verse offered earlier by Bekhor Shor, there
is no evidence that Abarbanel did not come to it on his own.

It is clear that great treasures await patient readers who make their way
through the immense amount of exegetical resources created by Abarbanel. Indeed, his questions alone are worth the effort for the way in which they highlight narrative and other types of compositional difficulties in the biblical text.

*   *   *

Jewish biblical exegesis had by no means run its course by the end of the fif-teenth century. Succeeding generations saw the publication of biblical com-mentaries that stressed a variety of competing methodologies and approaches. Even as Abarbanel's contemporary Isaac Arama had combined philosophic and homiletic concerns in his *Akedat Yitzhad,* so too the sixteenth century wit-nessed the publication of such overtly homiletic Torah commentaries as the Sabbath sermons of Moses b. Alshikh or the Kli Yakar of Epraim of Luntshitz. On the other hand, the work of Italian Rabbi Ovadia Seforno (1475-1550) dem-onstrated a blending of philosophical and contextual approaches that in many ways carried forward the work of the twelfth-century peshat commentators. Other areas of exegetical works include kabbalistic commentaries, pietistic works, collections of midrashic exegesis, and early precursors of modern historical-critical and literary scholarship. These were all supplemented by the many examples of the super-commentary genre, which took as their departure not the biblical text itself but the work of an earlier exegete, usually Rashi. However, it was during the medieval period under review that exegetes had laid the groundwork in all the major areas (contextual, midrashic, philo-sophic, and mystical) followed by later scholars.

BIBLIOGRAPHY

Abarbanel, I.

1964   *Commentary on Torah.* Jerusalem.

Berliner, A. (ed.)

1905   *Rashi: The Commentary of Solomon B. Isaac on the Torah* (Hebrew). 2nd ed. Frank-furt: Kauffmann.

Biesenthal, J. H. R., and F. Lebrecht (eds.)

1967   *Sefer Hashorashim of Rabbi David B. Joseph Kimchi* (Hebrew). Jerusalem; repr. Berlin: Bethge, 1847.

Braun, M., and F. Rosenthal

1900   *Gedenkbuch zur Erinnerung an David Kaufman.* Breslau: Schottländer.

Brenner, B., and E. Freiman (eds.)

1993   *The Pentateuch with the Commentary of Rabbenu Levi Ben Gershom* (Hebrew). Maaleh Adumim, Israel.

Brody, R.

1998   *The Geonim of Babylonia and the Shaping of Medieval Jewish Culture.* New Haven: Yale University Press.

2000   "The Geonim of Babylonia as Biblical Exegetes." In Saebø (ed.) 2000: 74-88.

Chavel, C.

1959   *The Commentary on the Torah by Rabbi Moshe Ben Nahman (Ramban)* (Hebrew). Jerusalem: Mossad Harav Kook.

1971-76 *Nahmanides: Commentary on the Torah.* New York: Shilo.

1976   *Rabbenu Bahya: Commentary on the Torah.* Jerusalem: Mossad Harav Kook.

1978   *Nahmanides: Writings and Discourses.* Vol. II. New York: Shilo.

Chazan, R.

1992   *Barcelona and Beyond: The Disputation of 1263 and Its Aftermath.* Berkeley: University of California Press.

Chomsky, W. (ed.)

1952   *David Kimhi's Hebrew Grammar (Mikhlol).* New York: Bloch.

Cohen, M.

2000   "The Qimhi Family." In Saebø (ed.) 2000: 1.388-415.

Cohen, M. (ed.)

1992-2005 *Mikra'ot Gedolot 'Haketer': A Revised and Augmented Scientific Edition of 'Mikra'ot Gedolot' Based on the Aleppo Codex and Early Medieval Manuscripts.* Ramat Gan: Bar Ilan University.

Elman, Y.

1993   "'It Is No Empty Thing': Nahmanides and the Search for Omnisignificance." *The Torah U-Madda Journal* 4: 1-83.

2000   "Moses Ben Nahman/Nahmanides (Ramban)." In Saebø (ed.) 2000: 416-32.

Feldman, S.

1984   *Levi Ben Gershom: The Wars of the Lord.* Vol. 1. Philadelphia: Jewish Publication Society of America.

1987   *Levi Ben Gershom: The Wars of the Lord.* Vol. 2. Philadelphia: Jewish Publication Society of America.

1999   *Levi Ben Gershom: The Wars of the Lord.* Vol. 3. Philadelphia: Jewish Publication Society of America.

Filipowski, H. (ed.)

1854   *Mahberet Menahem.* London: Hebrew Antiquarian Society.

Friedlander, M. (ed.)

1963-64 *Essays on the Writings of Abraham ibn Ezra.* 4 vols. London: Society of Hebrew Literature; repr. London, 1873-77.

1964   *The Commentary of Ibn Ezra on Isaiah.* New York: Feldheim (orig. Jerusalem: MYP, 1873).

Funkenstein, A.

1993　*Perceptions of Jewish History* (Hebrew and English). Berkeley: University of California Press.

Gad, H. (ed.)

1983　*Rabbi Yosef Bekhor Shor: Commentary on the Torah* (Hebrew). Jerusalem: Mossad Harav Kook.

Gelles, B.

1981　*Peshat and Derash in the Exegesis of Rashi.* Études sur le Judaisme Médiéval 9; Leiden: Brill.

Goodman, L. E. (ed.)

1988　*The Book of Theodicy: Translation and Commentary of the Book of Job by Saadiah Ben Joseph Al-Fayyumi.* Yale Judaica Series 25; New Haven: Yale University Press.

Greenstein, E. L.

1984　"Medieval Bible Commentaries." In B. Holtz, ed., *Back to the Sources,* 212-59. New York: Summit.

1993　"Sensitivity to Language in Rashi's Commentary on the Torah." In M. I. Gruber, ed., *The Solomon Goldman Lectures,* 51-71. Chicago: Spertus College of Judaica Press.

Grossman, A.

2000　"The School of Literal Exegesis in Northern France." In Saebø (ed.) 2000: 1.321-71.

Gruber, M. I. (ed.)

2004　*Rashi's Commentary on Psalms.* The Brill Reference Library of Judaism, 18. Leiden: Brill.

Harris, R. A.

1997　"The Literary Hermeneutic of Rabbi Eliezer of Beaugency." Ph.D. dissertation, Jewish Theological Seminary.

2004　"Medieval French Biblical Interpretation." In J. Neusner, A. J. Avery-Peck, and W. S. Green, eds., *Encyclopedia of Judaism, Supplement* 2. 5.2045-61. Leiden, Boston: Brill.

Herczeg, Y., et al. (eds.)

1995　*The Torah: With Rashi's Commentary Translated, Annotated, and Elucidated.* Brooklyn: Mesorah.

Japhet, S. (ed.)

2000　*The Commentary of Rabbi Samuel Ben Meir (Rashbam) on the Book of Job.* Publications of the Perry Foundation for Biblical Research in the Hebrew University of Jerusalem. Jerusalem: Magnes.

Japhet, S., and R. Salters (eds.)

1985　*The Commentary of R. Samuel Ben Meir (Rashbam) on Qoheleth* (Hebrew and English). Jerusalem: Magnes/Leiden: Brill.

Jellineck, A.

1855   *Commentar zu Kohelet und dem Hohen Liede von R. Samuel ben Meir.* Leipzig:
        Schnauss.

Kafih, Y. (ed.)

1973   *Job with the Translation and Commentary of Rabbenu Saadia Ben Yosef Fayyumi*
        (Arabic and Hebrew). Jerusalem: The Committee for the Publication of Saadia's
        Books, The American Academy for Jewish Research.

Kamin, S.

1980   "Rashi's Exegetical Categorization with Respect to the Distinction between
        Peshat and Derash." *Immanuel* 11: 16-32.

Kanarfogel, E.

1993-94 "On the Assessment of R. Moses ben Nahman (Nahmanides) and His Literary
        Oeuvre." In J. Kabakoffn, ed., *Jewish Book Annual,* 158-72. New York: Jewish Book
        Council.

Katzenelenbogen, M. L. (ed.)

1986-93 *Torat Hayyim* (Hebrew). 7 vols. Jerusalem: Mossad Harav Kook.

Kellner, M. (ed.)

1998   *Commentary on Song of Songs: Levi Ben Gershom (Gersonides).* Yale Judaica Se-
        ries. New Haven: Yale University Press.

Lawee, E.

2000   "Isaac Abarbanel's Intellectual Achievement and Literary Legacy in Modern
        Scholarship: A Retrospective and Opportunity." In I. Twersky and J. Harris (eds.)
        1993: 213-47.

2001   *Isaac Abarbanel's Stance toward Tradition: Defense, Dissent, and Dialogue.* Albany:
        State University of New York Press.

2003   "Introducing Scripture: The *Accessus ad Auctores* in Hebrew Exegetical Literature
        from the Thirteenth through the Fifteenth Centuries." In J. D. Mcauliffe, et al.,
        eds., *With Reverence for the Word: Medieval Scriptural Exegesis in Judaism, Chris-
        tianity and Islam,* 157-79. Oxford: Oxford University Press.

Leibowitz, N.

1995   *Torah Insights.* Trans. A. Smith; Jerusalem: Eliner Library: The Joint Authority for
        Jewish Zionist Education, Department for Torah and Culture in the Diaspora.

Leibowitz, N., and A. Newman (eds.)

1980-81 *Studies in the Weekly Sidra.* 6 vols. Jerusalem: World Zionist Organization Dept.
        for Torah Education and Culture in the Diaspora.

Lockshin, M. I.

1989   "Tradition or Context: Two Exegetes Struggle with Peshat." In J. Neusner, E. S.
        Frerichs and N. M. Sarna, eds., *From Ancient Israel to Modern Judaism: Intellect in
        Quest of Understanding,* 173-86. Atlanta: Scholars.

2003   "Rashbam as a 'Literary' Exegete." In J. D. Mcauliffe, et al., eds., *With Reverence for the Word: Medieval Scriptural Exegesis in Judaism, Christianity and Islam*. Oxford: Oxford University Press.

Lockshin, M. I. (ed.)
1989   *Rabbi Samuel Ben Meir's Commentary on Genesis: An Annotated Translation*, vol. 2. Lewiston: Mellen.

Maman, A.
2000   "The Linguistic School: Judah Hayyuj, Jonah Ibn Janah, Moses Ibn Chiquitilla and Judah Ibn Balam." In Saebø (ed.) 2000: 261-81.

Minnis, A. J.
1984   *Medieval Theory of Authorship: Scholastic Literary Attitudes in the Late Middle Ages*. Aldershot: Wildwood.

Munk, E.
1998   *Midrash Rabeinu Bachya, Torah Commentary*. Jerusalem: Lampda.

Nevo, Y. (ed.)
1994   *The Commentary of Rabbi Yosef Bekhor Shor on the Torah* (Hebrew). Jerusalem: Mossad Harav Kook.

Nutt, J. W. (ed.)
1879   *Commentaries on the Latter Prophets by R. Eliezer of Beaugency: Isaiah* (Hebrew). London: Baer.

Pearl, C.
1988   *Rashi*. London: Halban.

Polliack, M. (ed.)
2003   *Karaite Judaism: A Guide to Its History and Literary Sources*. Leiden: Brill.

Poznanski, S. (ed.)
1913   *Commentary on Ezekiel and the Twelve Minor Prophets by Eliezer of Beaugency* (Hebrew). Warsaw: Mikize Nirdamim.

Rittenberg, Y. (ed.)
1966   *Sefer Mikhlol of Rabbi David Kimhi* (Hebrew). Jerusalem: Lyck.

Rosenbaum, M., and A. M. Silberman (eds.)
1929   *Pentateuch and Rashi's Commentary*. Jerusalem: Silberman.

Rosin, D. R.
1880   *Samuel Ben Meir als Schrifterklärer*. Breslau: Koebner.

Rosin, D. R. (ed.)
1881   *The Torah Commentary of Rashbam* (Hebrew). Breslau: Shtatlander.

Saebø, M. (ed.)
2000   *Hebrew Bible/Old Testament: The History of Its Interpretation*. Vol. 1: *From the Be-*

ginnings to the Middle Ages (until 1300). Part 2: The Middle Ages. Göttingen: Vandenhoeck und Ruprecht.

Saenz-Badillos, A.

1986   Menahem ben Saruq: Mahberet (Hebrew and Spanish). Granada: Universidad de Granada, Universidad Pontificia de Salamanca.

2000   "Early Hebraists in Spain: Menahem ben Saruq and Dunash ben Labrat." In Saebø (ed.) 2000: 96-109.

Sarna, N.

1971   "Hebrew and Bible Studies in Medieval Spain." In R. D. Barnett, ed., The Sephardi Heritage, 323-66. New York: KTAV.

1993   "Abraham Ibn Ezra as an Exegete." In I. Twersky and J. M. Harris (eds.) 1993: 1-27.

Schachter, J. F.

1997   Ibn Ezra on Leviticus. Hoboken: KTAV.

2003   Ibn Ezra on Deuteronomy. Hoboken: KTAV.

Shereshevsky, E.

1982   Rashi: The Man and His World. New York: Sefer Hermon.

Silver, D. J.

1965   Maimonidean Criticism and the Maimonidean Controversy, 1180-1240. Leiden: Brill.

Simon, U.

1965   "The Exegetical Method of Abraham Ibn Ezra as Revealed in Three Interpretations of a Biblical Passage" (Hebrew). Bar Ilan 3: 92-138.

1983   "Ibn Ezra between Medievalism and Modernism: The Case of Isaiah XL–LXVI." VTSup 36: 257-71.

1989   Abraham Ibn Ezra's Two Commentaries on the Minor Prophets: An Annotated Critical Edition. Vol 1: Hosea, Joel, Amos (Hebrew). Ramat Gan: Bar Ilan University Press.

1991   Four Approaches to the Book of Psalms. Trans. L. J. Schramm. Albany: State University of New York Press.

2000   "Jewish Exegesis in Spain and Provence and in the East in the Twelfth and Thirteenth Centuries: Abraham Ibn Ezra." In Saebø (ed.) 2000: 377-87.

Smalley, B.

1952   The Study of the Bible in the Middle Ages. Oxford: Basil Blackwell.

Spinoza, B.

1991   Tractatus Theologico-Politicus. Trans. S. Shirley. Leiden: Brill.

Strickman, H. N., and A. M. Silver

1988   Ibn Ezra's Commentary on the Pentateuch: Genesis. New York: Menorah.

1996   Ibn Ezra's Commentary on the Pentateuch: Exodus. New York: Menorah.

1999   Ibn Ezra's Commentary on the Pentateuch: Numbers. New York: Menorah.

Talmage, F.

1975   *David Kimhi: The Man and His Commentaries.* Cambridge: Harvard University Press.

Talmage, F. (ed.)

1990   *The Commentaries on Proverbs of the Kimhi Family* (Hebrew). Jerusalem: Magnes.

Thompson, Y.

1988   "The Commentary of Samuel Ben Meir on the Song of Songs." D.H.L. dissertation, Jewish Theological Seminary.

Touitou, E.

2003   *Exegesis in Perpetual Motion: Studies in the Pentateuchal Commentary of Rabbi Samuel Ben Meir* (Hebrew). Ramat Gan: Bar Ilan University Press.

Twersky, I., and J. M. Harris (eds.)

1993   *Rabbi Abraham Ibn Ezra: Studies in the Writings of a Twelfth-Century Jewish Polymath.* Cambridge: Harvard University Press.

2000   *Studies in Medieval Jewish History and Literature.* Cambridge: Harvard University Center for Jewish Studies.

Urbach, E. E.

1986   *The Tosaphists: Their History, Writings, and Methods* (Hebrew). 5th ed. Jerusalem: Mossad Bialik.

Van der Heide, A.

1984   "Rashi's Biblical Exegesis." *Bibliotheca Orientalis* 41: 292-318.

Wolfson, E. R.

1989   "By Way of Truth: Aspects of Nahmanides' Kabbalistic Hermeneutic." *AJSR* 14.2: 103-78.

Zucker, M. (ed.)

1984   *Saadya's Commentary on Genesis* (Arabic and Hebrew). New York: The Jewish Theological Seminary of America.

CHAPTER 5

Eastern Orthodox Biblical Interpretation

Paul M. Blowers

Essaying Eastern Orthodox biblical interpretation in a volume on Medieval and Reformation hermeneutics demands qualification from the outset. These Western periodizations are virtually meaningless in the context of Eastern Christian self-understanding. The formative "patristic" age of the Orthodox tradition, broadly speaking, extends well into the "early medieval" era of Western historiography. As the late Russian theologian and ecumenist Georges Florovsky has argued, moreover, the "age of the fathers" lived on, authoritatively, in an "organic continuation" of insight represented in Maximus the Confessor (580-662, Blowers and Wilken 2003) and John of Damascus (c. 675–c. 749, Louth 2003) and even beyond them in Byzantine writers as late as Symeon the New Theologian (949-1022, de Catanzaro 1980), Gregory Palamas (1296-1359, Meyendorff 1983), and other fathers of the *Philokalia*, the spiritual handbook of the Orthodox heritage (Florovsky 1972: 109-13). Contemporary Eastern Orthodox biblical interpretation, in all its forms, unashamedly binds itself to this body of collective insight, rooted in the creative work of the Greek theologian-exegetes of the third through fifth centuries (see Breck 1986: 49-92; Stylianopoulos 1997: 101-22). "The Church is 'Apostolic' indeed," Florovsky writes. "But the Church is also 'Patristic.' . . . 'The mind of the Fathers' is an intrinsic reference in Orthodox theology, no less than the word of Holy Scripture, and indeed never separated from it" (1972: 107).

Sketching the formation of Orthodox hermeneutics must therefore begin with the appropriation of that patristic legacy before turning to the specific achievements of representative interpreters of the Byzantine age, and ultimately to the response of contemporary Orthodoxy to modern biblical criticism.

THE GREEK PATRISTIC HERMENEUTICAL LEGACY IN THE BYZANTINE/ORTHODOX TRADITION

The Logos in Scripture: Divine Transcendence and Accommodation

Byzantine Christianity inherited from the earlier Greek fathers, especially the Alexandrians, less a "theory" of divine inspiration of Scripture than a theology of the mystical *presence* of the divine Logos within the text that conditions the whole dynamic of interpretation. The Logos "incarnates" himself in the flesh of Scripture, while the Holy Spirit authors the text and models its every detail to salvific ends. For Origen, the Logos embodies himself such that the text becomes a filter of his divinity (*Comm. on Matt.* frag., in *PG* 17.89A-B; *Comm. on John* 1.19, Preuschen 1903: 23) and a means for drawing pious souls toward the sublime mystery of his identity as the exalted Son of God (see Gögler 1963: 260-70; Behr 2001: 169-78). The analogy is exploited in Origen's interpretation of the Transfiguration pericope (Matt. 17:1-8), on which Maximus the Confessor later picks up (*Chapters on Theology and Economy* 2.14, PG 90.1132A; *Ambigua* 10, PG 91.1128A-B). For Origen, Christ's radiant garments signify to the disciples the divine glory within the "sayings and letters of the Gospels" (*Comm. on Matt.* 12.38, Klostermann 1935: 154); Maximus agrees (*Chapters on Theology and Economy* 2.14, *PG* 90.1132A), but also speaks of the resplendent "garments" as symbolizing all of Scripture rendered transparent to the light of the incarnate Logos, just as his transfigured "face" evokes his inner-Trinitarian relation to the Father (*Ambigua* 10, *PG* 91.1128A-B).

This incarnational analogy bespeaks a broader revelatory schema, or economy *(oikonomia)*, wherein the Logos, indeed the whole Trinity, is working pedagogically through the created order, through Scripture, and supremely through Jesus of Nazareth himself, to restore and deify all rational beings. *Oikonomia* — often translated "salvation history" but perhaps better understood as the whole strategy of divine self-disclosure — takes precedence over "history" (at least in the modern historicist sense) as descriptive of the salvific and revelatory order of the Logos. For Greek patristic and Byzantine exegetes, *oikonomia* (and subsidiarily *historia* itself) implies a dimensionality that embraces both the *temporal* sequence of revelation, thus warranting the prophetic and "mimetic" reading of the Bible cherished by the Antiochene tradition, and

Some Principal Eastern Orthodox Theologians/Exegetes

All dates are CE; many birthdates are approximate

Origen	185-254	Commentary on Matthew		PG 17
		Commentary on John		PG 14
		On First Principles IV	c. 229	PG 9
Maximus the Confessor	580-662	Chapters on Theology and Economy		PG 90
		Ambigua		PG 91
		To Thalassius: On Diverse Difficulties from Holy Scripture	c. 625	PG 91
		Mystagogia		PG 91
		Opuscula		PG 91
Gregory of Nyssa	330–c. 395	Against Eunomius	380-383	PG 45
		To Ablabius		PG 45
		Homilies on the Song of Songs		PG 44
		On the Inscriptions of the Psalms	c. 379	PG 46
		Life of Moses		PG 91
Pseudo-Dionysius	fl. c. 500	Celestial Hierarchy		PG 3
		Ecclesiastical Hierarchy		PG 3
		Divine Names		PG 3
Athanasius of Alexandria	296-373	Orations against the Arians	337ff.	PG 26
Epiphanius	315-403	Panarion	c. 375	PG 42
Gregory of Nazianzus	329-390	Theological Orations	380	PG 37
Basil of Caesarea	330-79	Against Eunomius		PG 31

the *hierarchical* relation between material symbol and spiritual truth which, most notably for the Alexandrians and their later followers in the East, had privileged allegorical and anagogical interpretations (see Young 1997: 161-85). Incorporating the insights of both the Antiochene and the Alexandrian schools, Byzantine theologians, as we will see, focused on understanding more

Evagrius of Pontus (Ponticus)	346-99	*Scholia*		various editions
John Chrysostom	347-407	*Homilies*		PG 47-62
Cyril of Alexandria	375-444	*Commentary on John*	c. 425	PG 74
		Glaphyra on Genesis		PG 69
Theodoret of Cyrrhus	393-460	*Commentary on Psalms*		PG 80
Romanos the Melodist	fl. c. 540	*Kontakia*	c. 540	PG 155
Germanus of Constantinople	634-733	*De vitae termino*		
John of Damascus	675-749	*On the Divine Images*		PG 94
Symeon the New Theologian	949-1022	*Discourses*	c. 980ff.	
Nikitas Stithatos	1020-?	*Philokalia*		PG 120
Peter of Damascus	fl. c. 1150			
Gregory Palamas	1296-1359			

Compilations

title	representing traditions or writings from	compiled when	by
Apophthegmata Patrum ("Sayings of the Desert Fathers")		late fourth and fifth centuries	
The Philokalia	4th through the 11th centuries, including Symeon the New Theologian, Gregory Palamas	18th century	Nikodemos of the Holy Mountain (1749-1807) and Makarios of Corinth (1731-1805)

deeply how Jesus Christ, the Logos incarnate, is the intersection of the two axes of history and hierarchy, or to put it another way, how the *mystērion* of Christ is the rallying point for all the various senses of the biblical text.

Given this interconnection of christology and hermeneutics in the writings of the Greek fathers, the dialectic of divine transcendence and condescension (or *kenōsis*) central to incarnational doctrine had an analogue in biblical interpretation. The Logos incarnate in Scripture forfeits none of his divine glory while accommodating himself to the constraints of human language. For the influential fourth-century Cappadocian bishop Gregory of Nyssa, whose "apophatic" theology (i.e., his use of "negations" to predicate the infinite God), directed against Neo-Arian rationalism, imbues his whole approach to biblical exegesis, the Orthodox interpreter must therefore be acutely aware of the incapacity of scriptural language, or any human language, to comprehend or convey wholly theological mysteries like God's nature (see especially *Against Eunomius* 2; Jaeger 1960, part 1). As Gregory writes in his treatise *To Ablabius,*

> We . . . following the suggestions of Scripture, have learnt that that [divine] nature is unnameable and unspeakable, and we say that every term either invented by the custom of men, or handed down to us by the Scriptures, is indeed explanatory of our conceptions of the Divine Nature, but does not include the signification of that nature itself (ET Moore and Wilson, NPNF[2] 5.332).

Negatively, this implies an unbridgeable chasm *(diastēma)* between scriptural words and divine reality; positively, it prompts a never-ending search for the inexhaustible meaning of Scripture, or, more precisely, for the divine Logos ever disguised within it (see Mosshammer 1990: 103-11). Gregory's *Homilies on the Song of Songs* (PG 44) demonstrates this pursuit. The Song is "literally" an allegory of the elusiveness of the Logos-Bridegroom hunted by the yearning soul (the interpreter). The erotic and anthropomorphic words and images of the text are an embodiment, an accommodation to passion-laden human beings, which, through exegetical inversion, affords a transforming, albeit relative and limited, semantic encounter with the Word (e.g., *Homily* 1, *PG* 44.776A-777C, 780C-781C; see also Canévet 1983: 31-64, 299-347). The fragrant "spikenard" of the Bridegroom (Song 1:12), to recall but one example, symbolizes the Logos present to and in the virtuous soul, yet simultaneously "inaccessible, intangible, and incomprehensible" (*Homily* 3, *PG* 44.824A-B). The Song is not only "about" this mystery; its provocative text, like all of Scripture, is *ontologically* "the indispensable medium through which unspeakable truths are spoken" (Mosshammer 1990: 111; cf. Young 1997: 144-45).

Variations on the theme of divine accommodation through Scripture appear pervasively in Greek patristic and Byzantine biblical interpretation. John Chrysostom regularly expounds God's philanthropic condescension *(synkatabasis)* manifested in every minute detail of the scriptural text (see De Margerie 1994: 191-210), just as Maximus later speaks of its underlying salutary arrangement *(eutaxia)* by the Spirit (*To Thalassius* 10, Laga and Steel 1980: 83). The same principle informs the idea that the multiple senses of Scripture are scaled to the spiritual disposition or capacity of its readers, a point to be discussed later in this essay. With Gregory of Nyssa, however, the hermeneutical dialectic of divine transcendence and accommodation took on a new level of philosophical sophistication that further inspired Pseudo-Dionysius the Areopagite, the mysterious oriental author of the sixth century whose corpus of writings has had important legacies both East and West (Canévet 1983).

Though composing no commentaries or homilies on the Bible, Pseudo-Dionysius projects a grand vision of the "procession and return" of divine illumination through the descending celestial and ecclesiastical "hierarchies." The goal is the "uplifting" *(anagōgē)* of all creatures toward union with the Trinity, higher beings imaging the divine beauty for lower beings in a sublime conversion of the whole created order (*Celestial Hierarchy* 1.1-3, *PG* 3.164D-168B; *Ecclesiastical Hierarchy* 1.2-4, *PG* 3.372C-376C). For the Areopagite, this process of cosmic illumination is mirrored in the Bible itself, with its hierarchical arrangement of types and symbols. In the *Divine Names,* he copiously studies the broad and differentiated scriptural titles and attributes of God which enlighten the faithful as they are communicated in the reading of Scripture or in the "hierarchical traditions" of the liturgy (*Divine Names* 1.4, *PG* 3.589D-593A). Echoing Origen's notion of the *skandala* (Spirit-implanted "obstacles") in the biblical text, Pseudo-Dionysius expounds at length on the more unseemly images of God in Scripture ("ointment," "cornerstone," "lion," etc.) and, exercising the interpretive inversion familiar from Gregory of Nyssa, relishes in the "dissimilarity" that paradoxically evokes the ineffable and boundless glory of the Trinity (*Celestial Hierarchy* 2.1-5, *PG* 3.136D-145B; see also Rorem 1984: 84-96).

Though suspected of Monophysite ties by some subsequent Orthodox critics, Pseudo-Dionysius's hermeneutical influence in the East was secured by his revered devotees. Maximus the Confessor thoroughly exploits yet modifies the Areopagite's vision of cosmos and Scripture as corollary media of the revelation of the Logos, which will be discussed further on in this essay. John of Damascus refers to Pseudo-Dionysius's analysis of scriptural images in building his defense of the veneration of painted icons of Christ (*On the Divine Images* 3.21, *PG* 94.1341A), while Symeon the New Theologian, Gregory Palamas, and other writers in the *Philokalia* also profited from the Areopagite's teaching on divine illumination.

Theōria, the *Skopos* of Scripture, and Orthodox Doctrine

Christian interpreters of the Byzantine age also inherited from their patristic forerunners an entire constellation of definitions of the various senses of Scripture and hardly had to justify their willingness to defer to spiritual meanings beyond the literal, be they moral-spiritual, prophetic, doctrinal, or otherwise. Unlike the Western tradition, where the doctrine of the "four senses" took on a whole afterlife of its own (see De Lubac 1998; 2000), Byzantine interpreters, without forfeiting terminological precision, tended to settle on the simpler distinction of "literal" and "spiritual" senses and to enhance the principle of *theōria,* or "contemplative insight," the church's sanctified intuition of the meaning of texts in relation to the christocentric totality of the Bible. Already with fourth- and fifth-century exegetes, *theōria* begins to appear, sometimes as a general term for the process of contemplative interpretation (e.g. Theodoret, *Comm. on Ps.* 45:12, *PG* 80.1205C, using the verbal form *theōrein*), or for the intuited meaning itself, the living and transforming truth which, as Gregory of Nyssa says, is "always taking place" (*Life of Moses* 2; Ferguson and Malherbe 1978: 82) in the foreground of interpretation (see also Kerrigan 1952: 116-22). To be sure, there persist in Maximus and other Byzantine theologians, especially in the tradition of monastic exegesis, designations of "tropology," "allegory," "anagogy," and the like (see Blowers 1991: 185-203). But the deep conviction concerning the one "mind" *(dianoia)* of Scripture (Young 1997: 29-45) and the richly "figural" tapestry of *historia* connecting the OT and NT, coupled with the need to demonstrate the harmonious voice of Scripture in the ongoing debates with Jews and heretics, induced models of contemplative interpretation that would coordinate and integrate the various moral, prophetic, and doctrinal implications of texts.

As Young has shown, rigid distinctions among senses or methods of interpretation are not altogether helpful in understanding the latent rules of language and referentiality governing patristic exegesis (1997; 2003). The pervasive notion of the *skopos* (e.g. Origen, *On First Principles* 4.2.9, Crouzel and Simonetti 1980: 336), the overarching spiritual "objective" or purpose of individual biblical books and of the Bible as a whole, is more central in analyzing patristic and Byzantine exegesis. *Skopos* raises the issue of "intended" meaning, which moderns so often identify with the "literal" sense. For the fathers, however, this intentionality properly belongs not to the original scriptural authors (*pace* the concern of Antiochene exegetes for the authors' own perspectives) but to God, the true author of Scripture, who is guiding the audience of his Word *teleologically* toward the grand fulfillment of all scriptural "prophecy" in the mystery of Jesus Christ.

In his treatise *On the Inscriptions of the Psalms,* for example, Gregory of Nyssa shows how the aim *(skopos)* of the whole Psalter is to guide the faithful toward the goal *(telos)* of blessedness, or assimilation to God through the life of virtue (1, pref., McDonough 1962: 24-26; ET Heine 1995: 83-85), a purpose especially evidenced in the numerous Psalms entitled "To the end *(telos)*" in the Septuagint. In fact, argues Gregory, the Spirit intentionally set the Psalms in an order different from the sequence of the historical events they reflect because the Spirit's own sequence serves this ultimate *skopos* of spiritual formation (2.11, McDonough 1962: 115-24; ET Heine 1995: 163-70).

The principle of the *skopos* of Scripture could be invoked for purposes of edification, to be sure, but also — and perhaps most famously — was crucial to doctrinal demonstration and polemics against heretics who were also sophisticated interpreters. In the wake of the Council of Nicaea, Athanasius set an important precedent in his *Orations against the Arians* by countering an entire armada of Arian prooftexts. Against the Arian rendering of Phil. 2:9-10 ("Wherefore God has highly exalted him . . .") as evincing the created Son's promotion in reward for his moral progress, Athanasius argues (*Oration* 1.37-45, *PG* 26.88B-105B) that this text can only be understood in the full light of Phil. 2:6-11, with its intimation of the preexistence and incarnation of one who, in his divinity, became human to deify humanity (exalting the flesh rather than being exalted through it). It is not a "dark saying" but a "divine mystery" that, throughout Scripture, the already exalted God is still said to undergo "exaltation." But here in Philippians 2 the "exaltation" specifically refers to the Son's *humanity,* not his divinity.

A similar but more elaborate logic applies in Athanasius's long counter-exegesis of Prov. 8:22 (Wisdom's proclamation, "The Lord created me the beginning of his ways . . ."). The semantic analysis of "created" requires consideration of the oblique nature of proverbial language, appropriation of the saying to the *oikonomia* (the ministry of incarnation, not the divine essence), and deference to the description of the Son as "begotten," not created, elsewhere in Scripture (*Oration* 2.44-82, *PG* 26.240C-321A).

Gregory of Nyssa adds a slightly different tack in his explanation of Prov. 8:22 in *Against Eunomius* 3 (Jaeger 1960: 10-23). Recognizing, like Athanasius, that proverbs by nature communicate enigmatic rather than plain meanings, he notes that in the antecedent sequence of Prov. 8:12-21, Wisdom is credited with appointing and empowering kings. In a superficially literal sense, Wisdom would *ipso facto* have to take the blame for kings who rule wickedly — an absurdity. Syntax *(syntaxis)* already tells us, then, that the whole passage must be taken enigmatically. The enigma is partially resolved by looking elsewhere in Scripture, such as to John 1:3, affirming that the Word

(Wisdom) *by whom* everything was made cannot himself be created. But Prov. 8:22 itself still holds the key. Like Athanasius, Gregory notes Wisdom's specification that "God created me *the beginning of his works*," signaling the premeditated economy of the incarnation, the Son's assumption of *created* flesh for the salvation and deification of humankind. Basil of Caesarea similarly responds to Eunomius's assertion that Acts 2:36 ("God *made* him both Lord and Christ") proves a created Son: "[Luke] does not impart information to us in a theological manner, but deploys rather the language appropriate to the visible dispensation *(oikonomia)* of the created order" (*Against Eunomius* 2.3; ET Rousseau 1994: 114).

Young's comment on Athanasius's doctrinal exegesis could easily extend to Gregory of Nyssa, Cyril of Alexandria, and other Eastern interpreters: "His exegesis is neither literal, nor typological, nor allegorical. Rather it is deductive" (1997: 40). It is a richly textured complex of reading strategies designed to understand every passage of Scripture in the light of the divine *skopos* of the Bible intuited through the church's *theōria*. Indeed, since intentionality belongs to the divine Author himself, the upshot is a *theologically* "literal" sense (De Margerie 1994: 118-23, 216, 243; Kerrigan 1952: 61-87) that does not exclude allegory or any other useful method.

The salvific divine *skopos* of Scripture is unchanging, but the church's theological contexts are ever-changing. The church's *theōria* does not exclude *new* insight into texts, though no new insight could in principle contradict the antecedent judgment of the councils and the fathers who have sifted the great theological mysteries of Scripture. As John of Damascus writes,

> Where can you find in the Old Testament or in the Gospels explicit use of such terms as "Trinity" or "consubstantial" or "one nature of the Godhead" or "three persons," or anything about Christ being "one person with two natures"? But nevertheless, the meanings of all these things are found, expressed in other phrases which the Scriptures do contain, and the fathers have interpreted them for us. We accept them, and anathematize those who will not. (*On the Divine Images* 3.11; ET Anderson 1980: 71)

The prospect of new interpretive insight building on — but not contradicting — the fathers can be seen in the last phase of the christological controversies, the seventh-century Monothelite crisis on the issue of whether one or two wills were operative in Christ's person. Patriarch Sergius of Constantinople hoped to use Gregory Nazianzen's earlier exegesis of Jesus' sayings in John 6:38 ("For I have come down from heaven, not to do my own will, but the will of him who sent me") and Matt. 26:39 ("Father, if it be possible, let this cup pass from me; nevertheless, not my will but thine be done") to support the doctrine of a single will in Christ. Asserting that these statements could not come from an intrinsically resistant or contrary *human* will, Nazianzen had understood Matt. 26:39 in the light of John 6:38, attributing both sayings to the Son of God, who was denying having a separate will from the Father proper to his own divine person (*Oration* 30.12, Gallay 1978: 248-50). Sergius inferred from this, christologically, the absolute absence of a human will in the Savior. Quoting Nazianzen's text for himself, however, Maximus the Confessor challenged Sergius's inference, arguing that these sayings of Jesus, as proper to his *humanity,* definitely indicate an operative *human* will that is *different from* the divine will but *not contrary to* it (*Opusculum* 6, PG 91.65A-69A; cf. *Opusculum* 3, PG 91.48C-D). Clearly, for Maximus this was not a contradiction of the exegesis of Gregory "the Theologian." Nazianzen, after all, had interpreted these sayings of Jesus in a properly *trinitarian* context. In the new context of post-Chalcedonian *christology,* Gregory's dismissal of a "resistant" human will in Christ was no longer immediately relevant, now that the church had discerned the presence of a perfect (deified) human will in the composite hypostasis (substantive reality) of Christ which was the subject of these declarations of obedience in John 6:38 and Matt. 26:39.

The Ecclesial Setting of Biblical Interpretation

Crucial to understanding the historical development of biblical hermeneutics in the Byzantine and later Orthodox tradition is the fact that theological exegesis and the use of Scripture for proscribing heresy did not function in isolation from the larger communal life of the Church. Celebrated biblical expositors like the Cappadocian fathers, John Chrysostom, Cyril of Alexandria, and others were pastor-theologians challenged to model in their interpretations, whether in commentaries or homilies, the "transition from *theologia* to *oikonomia,* from theological reflection and argument to religious experience in the company of fellow believers" (Rousseau 1994: 127). Scripture itself was:

> handed down not just as a text but within the framework of the liturgy, and of its associated homilies. It was not just a question of thinking as you were taught to think. The very act of ministering the word to a community was like a saving gesture, built into the tradition itself; and fidelity to that tradition constantly called to mind, would automatically bring salvation to the present generation. . . . Access to truth, to put it simply,

could occur only in the context of worship, which orchestrated the human response to revelation. (p. 128)

Liturgy was (and is) a medium of "performative" interpretation of the Bible. The structure of the Divine Liturgy of St. John Chrysostom (see Hellenic College Faculty 1986), which did not achieve final form until the tenth century, ultimately constituted a spectacular re-presentation of the unfolding biblical drama of salvation and deification. The Liturgy provided the constellation of readings, prayers, hymns, ritual symbols, and sacramental actions through which the larger Christian faithful achieved their own contemplation (theōria), their own appropriation of the scriptural revelation and its spiritual and ascetical exigencies. As Maximus the Confessor writes in his Mystagogia, a commentary on the Divine Liturgy,

> [T]he divine readings from the sacred books reveal the divine and blessed desires and intentions of God most holy. Through them each one of us receives in proportion to the capacity which is in him the counsels by which he should act, and we learn the divine and blessed struggles in which by consistent fighting we will be judged worthy of the victorious crowns of Christ's kingdom. (PG 91.689B-C; ET Berthold 1985: 199)

In a similar commentary from the eighth century, Patriarch Germanus of Constantinople notes that "the antiphons of the liturgy are the prophecies of the prophets, foretelling the coming of the Son of God" and the mystery of his incarnation, while "the entrance of the Gospel signifies the coming of the Son and his entrance into the world" (ET Meyendorff 1984: 73). For Maximus the Little, entrance of the Gospel and closing of the doors behind the priest who reads the text indicate the advent of the "logos of spiritual contemplation (gnōstikē theōria)" descending from heaven like a High Priest to discipline "carnal" understanding and initiate the worthy in the holy mysteries (Mystagogia 13-15, PG 91.692A-693C). The Great Entrance into the Eucharistic liturgy thereupon signals the faithful's eschatological admission to "the new teaching which will take place in the heavens concerning the oikonomia of God for us and the revelation of the mystery of our salvation which is in the most secret recesses of the divine" (Mystagogia 16, PG 91.693C-D; ET Berthold 1985: 201).

The development of coordinated readings for the whole liturgical year — appearing at least as early as the fifth century in the influential Lectionary of Jerusalem (see Renoux 1997) — and rituals specific to the liturgical seasons provided further guidance to the ecclesial appropriation of Scripture.

Through the careful selection of readings set out within liturgical time, and particularly the paralleling of OT types with NT fulfillments, the economy of salvation was continuously dramatized for the Christian faithful such that the contemporary life of the church was itself to be experienced as the denouement of the sacred history.

THE HERMENEUTICAL ACHIEVEMENT
OF THE BYZANTINE FATHERS

The most prolific era of Greek patristic biblical commentaries ended in the fifth century with the work of Theodoret of Cyrrhus, the last of the great Antiochene exegetes, and with Cyril of Alexandria, whose influence on subsequent Byzantine (Chalcedonian) theology, as well as on the Oriental Orthodox (non-Chalcedonian) churches, was immense. The sixth century already saw the beginnings of florilegia ("excerpts") and catena ("chain") commentaries like those of Procopius of Gaza (*PG* 87.21-1220, 1545-1753, 1817-2717), which largely accumulated the comments of earlier patristic authorities. Yet, the theological and spiritual interpretation of the Bible continued to thrive in other formats: in monastic literature, in liturgical hymns, in homilies, in theological treatises and *scholia* ("notes"), if less and less in actual line-by-line commentaries.

Cyril of Alexandria and the Scriptural Mystery of Christ

Cyril of Alexandria is famed more for his fierce opposition to Nestorian christology in the era of the Council of Ephesus (431) than for his exegetical achievements. Yet he thoroughly exploited the legacy of his Alexandrian predecessors, pursuing tropological (moral) and allegorical meanings in the OT, whether in the Pentateuch, the Psalter, or the Prophets, in the name of the "spiritual" — *christocentric* — sense. What had changed dramatically, and in a way crucial to later Orthodox theology, was the christological context itself. If Origen's exegesis focused on the pedagogy of the transcendent Logos who, by his incarnation both in flesh and in Scripture, leads diligent souls beyond that incarnate presence toward a share in his transcendence, Cyril's exegesis exalted the *incarnational* mystery itself, the "one enfleshed nature of the Word," the one hypostasis of God *as man* (see McGuckin 1994: 207-16), through whom salvation and deification are granted. All of Scripture is tributary to this transforming reality. Its overall *skopos* is the mystery of Christ (*Glaphyra on Gen., PG* 69.308C).

Christ himself invited such investigation of this saving mystery. As Cyril
writes in the opening of his *Glaphyra* ("Polished Comments") *on Genesis*:

> "Search the Scriptures," Christ proclaimed to the Jewish people (John
> 5:39). He spoke in the clearest of terms, for no other reason than that
> some might be strong enough to attain to eternal life, lest they dig up the
> letter of the Law like a treasure and not diligently seek the pearl hidden
> therein, which is precisely Christ, "in whom all the treasures of wisdom
> and knowledge are hidden" as the blessed Paul says (Col. 2:3). . . . Hence,
> since the diligent quest to cherish the mystery of Christ clearly and obvi-
> ously brings about eternal life, and is the way of all contentment for us,
> come now, let us once again go before others in imposing profitable labor
> even on ourselves, and hasten to glean those things through which the
> mystery of Christ may be signified effectively to us, and simultaneously to
> explain how each of those things might be pregnant with meanings. . . .
> First, for what it is worth, we will explain what happened historically,
> such that, transposing *(metaplattontes)* the narrative through figure *(ty-
> pos)* and shadow *(skia)*, we will render a clear account, our explanation
> disposing us toward the mystery of Christ *(mystērion Christou)*, with
> Christ himself as the projected goal *(peras)*, since it is true that Christ
> himself is the end *(telos)* of the Law and Prophets (cf. Rom. 10:4). (*PG*
> 69.13A-16A)

Throughout his OT commentaries, Cyril holds true to form, digging beneath a broad spectrum of narratives and images to unearth the mystery of
Christ. The Bible, interpreted in terms of the gracious unity of OT and NT,
is one grand, "thick" narrative of the advent of the Second ("Last") Adam
and of the faithful's share in his progeny. Along the way, we are guided by
numerous typologies, such as that of Cain and Abel, Cain being both a
Satan-figure (cf. John 8:39-40) and a *typos* of the Jews who repudiated and
executed the Christ, and Abel, the shepherd and giver of firstfruits, being a
Christ-figure whose death indicts the sinful (*Glaphyra on Genesis, PG*
69.37C-44B). The typology is rich, for not only is Abel's innocent death a
prefiguration of Christ's, but the birth of another son to Adam and Eve signals the propagation of a renewed Adamic line — a figure of the new humanity in Christ:

> It would be appropriate to include what is further stated in the text. For
> after the death of Cain, it says, "Adam knew his wife Eve, and she con-
> ceived and gave birth to a son, and named him Seth, saying, 'For God

raised up for me another seed in place of Abel, whom Cain killed'" (Gen. 4:25). Then it continues, "Adam lived one hundred and thirty years, and begat a son in his own likeness and image, and named him Seth" (Gen. 5:3). Consider, then, that after Abel's death a son was again born, Seth, who most resembled him — Adam, that is — in the image and likeness of God. For, after the death of the carnal Emmanuel, another seed appeared straightaway to Adam, possessing in himself the supreme beauty of the divine image. . . . For those of us who believe in Christ through the Spirit, Christ himself confirms the fact that his death has become a root and a basis, as it were, of our race when he says, "Truly, truly I say to you, unless a grain of wheat falls into the earth and dies, it remains alone; but if it dies, it bears much fruit" (John 12:24). (*PG* 69.44B-C)

Cyril thus gives special prominence to the Pauline Adam-Christ typology (Rom. 5:12-19; 1 Cor. 15:22, 45) and uses it as an exegetical paradigm to interpret much non-Pauline material from the OT and NT alike (see Wilken 1971: 93-142, 181-209). In his *Commentary on John,* to cite but one example, Cyril interprets the baptism of Jesus in terms of the advent of the new humanity. The text's indication that the Spirit descended and "remained on him" (John 1:32) signals the fact that, in response to the degeneration of the image of God and loss of the Holy Spirit among sinful humanity, God sent the Second Adam to renew the Spirit's presence and thereby graciously restore the race (Pusey 1874: 134-47; see also Keating 1999).

Cyril develops the powerful image of Christ as the Second Adam consistently throughout his *Commentary on John* to support the themes of re-creation, renewal, transformation, restoration, and recapitulation within the incarnational mystery of Christ (Wilken 1971: 115-18). Often explicit (e.g., in the exegesis of Christ's "I am" sayings and in the passion and resurrection narratives), sometimes it is implicit. Treating Jesus' healing of the blind man with clay and spittle (John 9), for instance, Cyril finds a certain "mystical significance" in the narrative's details: the Lord's anointing the clay with his own spittle bespeaks his prerogative as Creator; his application of the mud to the blindness (of all Gentiles) indicates that the healing can come only by contact, by enabling the blind to share in his sanctified "Body of the True Light," the mystery of his enfleshment. Furthermore, the spittle and Jesus' command to wash in the pool of Siloam together evince the mystery of baptism, through which this participation is granted to all believers (Randell 1885: 19-20). What Cyril has called here a "mystical significance" is nonetheless an excellent specimen of the "theologically literal" sense discussed earlier.

The Interpretive Poetics of Romanos the Melodist

Cyril bequeathed to later generations of Eastern Orthodox biblical interpreters a grand mastery of christological images in the Bible, and the exegetical
artistry to turn even the most latent images into windows on the economy of
salvation. Celebrated as the greatest hymnographer of the Byzantine tradition, the Syrian-born Romanos the Melodist (c. 485-c. 560 CE) took this kind
of exegetical artistry to new creative heights in the liturgical form of *kontakia,*
sermonic hymns, each consisting of a prelude and stanzas interposed with a
recurring short refrain (see Trigg 2002).

Obviously, the hymn writer does not have the luxury of extended commentary, which makes Romanos's ability to enhance, intricately combine,
and dramatize exegetical themes in lyrical form all the more striking. Such
poetic virtuosity was not unprecedented; Romanos found inspiration in the
majestic hymns of the fourth-century Syriac writer Ephrem (see McVey 1989;
Brock 1990). Moreover, he was able to weave much traditional exegesis into
his verse, while still adding his own nuances. Romanos glories in the pattern
of cross-evocation, the ability of biblical images to suggest one another and
thus to be collapsed together in a "thick" but subtle narrative form. In his
kontakion On the Nativity, for example, the following reconfiguration appears
in stanza 1:

> Bethlehem has opened Eden, come let us see,
> we have found delight in the secret, come, let us receive the joys
>   of Paradise within the cave.
> There the unwatered root (cf. Isa. 11:1) whose blossom
>   is forgiveness has appeared.
> There has been found the undug well from which David once
>   longed to drink (cf. 2 Sam. 23:13-17).
> There a virgin has borne a babe
> And has quenched at once Adam's and David's thirst.
> For this, let us hasten to this place where there has been born
>   *A little child, God before the ages.*
>   (ET Lash 1995: 3)

Romanos is a master at exaggerating ironies and dramatic elements present in
the biblical stories to great liturgical effect. The betrayal of Jesus, for example,
becomes an irony of cosmic proportions in the Melodist's *kontakion On Judas*
(stanza 1):

Who, when they heard it, has not grown numb?
Who, when they saw it, has not trembled?
Jesus kissed by guile,
Christ sold by envy, God seized by design?
What sort of earth was it that bore this outrage?
What sort of sea endured to look on this unholy deed?
How did heaven submit, how did air permit, how did the
    world survive
when the Judge was being bargained for, then sold and betrayed?
    Be merciful, merciful, merciful to us,
    You who are patient with all, and wait for all.

                                       (ET Lash 1995: 115)

Elsewhere Romanos, learning from Ephrem, often creates dramatic dialogues among biblical characters to heighten suspense. His *kontakion On the Ascension* stages a conversation between the departing Christ and the apostles, who express to him their godly separation anxiety:

"High over you, my disciples,
as God and maker of the whole world
I stretch out my palms, which the lawless stretched out, bound
    and nailed.
And so, as you bow your heads beneath my hands,
Understand, know, my friends, what I command.
For, as though baptizing, I lay my hands upon you now,
And, having blessed you, send you out
Enlightened, and made wise.
Upon your heads, praise and majesty,
Upon your souls, illumination, as it is written,
For I shall pour upon you of my Spirit (Acts 2:17-18), and you will be
    accepted by me,
taught and chosen, faithful (cf. Rev. 17:14) and my own.
I am not parting from you.
    I am with you and there is no one against you."

In saying this, the Saviour caused
the apostles much great grief.
At once they wept and, groaning deeply, said to the teacher,
"Are you leaving us, O Compassionate? Parting from those
    who love you?

You spoke to us like someone going on a journey.
These words indicate a departure,
and this is why we are troubled,
since we long to be with you;
we seek your face (Ps. 23 [24]:6), for it delights our souls.
We have been wounded, bound by the most sweet sight of you.
There is no God but you (Isa. 45:5; Ps. 17[18]:31). Do not take yourself
        far away from those who love you.
Stay with us (cf. Luke 24:29) and say to us,
'I am not parting from you.
    I am with you and there is no one against you.'"
                                              (ET Lash 1995: 196-97)

In his *kontakion On the Lament of the Mother of God* (stanza 1), the
Theotokos is taken off her guard, as it were, by her son's journey to Golgotha:

As she saw her own lamb being dragged to slaughter (cf. Isa 53:7),
Mary the ewe-lamb, worn out with grief, followed with the
        other women, crying out,
"Where are you going, my child? For whose sake are you
        completing the course (cf. 2 Tim. 4:7) so fast?
Is there once again another wedding in Cana (cf. John 2:1-11)?
Are you hurrying there now to make wine for them from water?
Should I go with you, my child, or rather wait for you?
Give me a word, O Word. Do not pass me by in silence, you who
        kept me pure,
    my Son and my God."
                                              (ET Lash 1995: 143)

Later in the dialogue, the son responds to the Theotokos (stanza 12):

When he heard this, the One who knows all things before their birth
        answered Mary, "Courage, Mother,
Because you will see me first on my coming from the tombs.
I am coming to show you by how many toils I ransomed Adam,
And how much I sweated for his sake.
I shall show it to my friends by showing the marks
In my hands (John 20:20), and then you will see Eve, Mother,
Living as before, and you will cry out with joy:

'He has saved my forebears,
   my Son and my God.'

(ET Lash 1995: 148)

In these kinds of dramatic formats, Romanos carefully interweaves *theologia* and *oikonomia,* exhibiting how the Savior's incarnate works and the interactions of his ministry at once conceal and reveal his divine identity. Those who sing the *kontakia* in the present moment of the liturgy are drawn into the narratives, compelled to identify with the *dramatis personae* and to respond with their own praise and devotion. The *kontakion* thereby functions much like an icon: "it does not simply tell a story, but draws us into the movement of God's love for us, and to worship" (Louth 1995: xx). It is little surprise that, although this musical form fell from regular use in the Byzantine liturgy as early as the seventh century, vestiges of the *kontakia* have survived in the Orthodox office of Matins even to this day.

The Cosmos, the Bible, and the Mystery of Christ:
Maximus the Confessor

Maximus the Confessor, seventh-century Byzantine monk and theologian, has been credited with developing, on the basis of Chalcedonian christology, a mature synthesis of Greek patristic theology and spirituality that decisively shaped subsequent Orthodox thought. His achievement in biblical interpretation is less well known but significant for a number of reasons. First, Maximus merges the antecedent streams of magisterial and monastic exegesis. His preference for the literary form of "question-and-response" in his exegetical writings, most notably in his massive commentary *To Thalassius: Concerning Diverse Difficulties from Holy Scripture,* bears this out (Laga and Steel 1980, 1990; see also Blowers and Wilken 2003: 97-171). This genre, rooted both in academic tradition and in monastic catechesis, becomes for Maximus a prime means to fuse theological interpretation with moral-spiritual pedagogy (see Blowers 1991: 28-94). In *To Thalassius* he deals with numerous exegetical obscurities that he must not only "resolve" but turn into positive instruction for the spiritual life.

One question, for example, concerns the longstanding problem of post-baptismal sin. If, as John says, "he who is born of God does not sin, because his seed dwells in God, and he cannot sin" (1 John 3:9), and yet he who is born of water and Spirit is himself born of God (John 3:5-6), how are those thus born of God through baptism still able to sin? Maximus answers by distinguishing two "births" associated with baptism, one which through faith bestows the grace of adoption only *potentially,* and a second which, operating through the Christian's knowledge and experience, *actualizes* that grace in the perfect conversion of the will leading to deification. Clearly, whoever has not undergone the second baptism is still capable of sinning. "But were we to prepare our will with knowledge to receive the operation of these agents — water and Spirit — then the mystical water would, through our practical life, cleanse our conscience, and the life-giving Spirit would bring about unchanging perfection of the good in us through knowledge acquired in experience" (*To Thalassius* 6, Laga and Steel 1980: 69-71; ET Blowers and Wilken 2003: 104).

On the level of theoretical hermeneutics, Maximus depends heavily on Alexandrian "anagogy" in portraying the entire interpretive enterprise as a grand transition or passage *(diabasis)* from the letter to the spirit of the biblical revelation (see Blowers 1991: 95-117). Such cannot be an annihilation of the letter, for, as Maximus states, his goal is "the power of the literal meaning *(historia)* in the Spirit, which is constantly being realized and abounding into its fullness" (*To Thalassius* 17, Laga and Steel 1980: 111; ET Blowers and Wilken 2003: 105). Not surprisingly, his technical exegetical methods are thoroughly congenial with Origen's. Typology, tropology, allegory (in its various forms, including onomastics, number symbolism, etc.), and the extracting of spiritual insights from grammatical and syntactical details of the biblical text all enable the interpreter to penetrate, and participate in, the larger *oikonomia* wherein the Logos is leading all creatures toward salvation and deification (see Blowers 1995; 1991: 196-228).

> Just as the understanding of the Law and the Prophets as precursors of the coming of the Word in the flesh instructed souls about Christ, so has the same glorified Word of God incarnate become a precursor of his spiritual coming and he instructs souls by his words about the acceptance of his visible divine coming. This coming he always effects by changing those who are worthy from the flesh to the spirit of the virtues. And he will do this also at the end of time, clearly revealing to all what is still secret (cf. 1 Cor. 2:7). (*Chapters on Theology and Economy* 2.29, *PG* 90.1137C-D; ET Berthold 1985: 154)

A major achievement of Maximus, under the influence of Pseudo-Dionysius the Areopagite, is his reworking of the doctrine of the twin revelatory economies of the created cosmos and the Bible. The two are perfectly reciprocal, even interchangeable: Scripture is itself a "cosmos" of sorts, just as the cosmos is a "bible" (*Ambigua* 10, PG 91.1128D-1129A). Both, in their complexity yet integrity, are "inscribed" with the Logos; he incarnates himself in both; and both provide symbolic access to him. Hence the contemplation of created nature *(physikē theōria)* and the contemplation of Scripture *(graphikē theōria)* function confluently in the pursuit of higher mysteries (see Blowers 2002). Maximus bases this mutual relation of cosmic and scriptural revelation on his vision of the *logoi* — the causal "principles" of creatures, the spiritual "meanings" of Scripture — which in their diversity unfold the "intentions" of God for the world (*To Thalassius* 13, Laga and Steel 1980: 95; cf. Pseudo-Dionysius, *Divine Names* 5.8, *PG* 3.824C). Everything points to the Logos who "wills always to bring about the mystery of his embodiment in all things" (cf. 1 Cor. 15:28) (*Ambigua* 7, *PG* 91.1084C-D). All revelation anticipates the full eschatological epiphany of the Logos in the *logoi,* an epiphany that has already begun in the world and in the text.

The *logoi* therefore hold the key to the Bible's true *skopos.* Much like Cyril, Maximus envisions the incarnational mystery of Christ as concealed in all of Scripture. The title "Christ" in the NT actually signals the whole "Christic mystery," "the mystery hidden from the ages, having now been manifested" (Col. 1:26):

> This is the great and hidden mystery, at once the blessed end *(telos)* for which all things are ordained. It is the divine purpose *(skopos)* conceived before the beginning of created beings. In defining it we would say that this mystery is the preconceived goal for which everything exists, but which depends for its existence on nothing. With a clear view to this end, God created the essences of created beings, and such is, properly speaking, the terminus of his providence and of the things under his providential care. Inasmuch as it leads to God, it is the recapitulation of the things he has created. It is the mystery which circumscribes all the ages, and which reveals the grand plan of God (cf. Eph. 1:10-11), a super-infinite plan infinitely preexisting the ages. (*To Thalassius* 60, Laga and Steel 1990: 75)

In searching out this mystery in Scripture, Maximus glories in the polyvalence of the biblical text (see Blowers 1991: 185-92). While occasionally echoing Origen's principle of levels of meaning accommodated to the level of the believer's spiritual maturity, Maximus values unity in diversity. His commentary on Jonah in *To Thalassius* 64 is a salient example. Here, Maximus plays exegetically with a whole variety of onomastic renderings of "Jonah" and with five "situations" from the prophet's career. Depending on the interpretive angle, Jonah is a *typos* of, in turn, fallen Adam (human nature), Christ, the Gentile church, and the unbelieving Jews (Laga and Steel 1990: 187-241). The upshot is a veritable kaleidoscope of insights, all assumed valid, into the fullness of the economy of salvation. For Maximus, the highest spiritual or intellectual *(gnōstikos)* meaning is often simply that which provides the deepest access into the mystery of the incarnation.

Monastic Exegesis and the Fathers of the *Philokalia*

No portrait of the formation of Eastern Orthodox biblical interpretation would be complete without the heritage of monastic exegesis, with its deep roots in the deserts of Egypt, Palestine, and Syria. Early collections of the *Apophthegmata patrum* ("Sayings of the Desert Fathers") and the exegetical works of monastic theologians like Evagrius of Pontus (346-99) spawned a monastic wisdom tradition which, perpetuated by later Byzantine spiritual writers in the *Philokalia,* assumed a permanent place in the spiritual life of Orthodox Christianity. Monastic biblical interpretation was marked by a strongly *eschatological* and *existential* orientation, a longing for transformation in the "last days." Numerous "conferences" between novice monks and their elders — recorded in the *Apophthegmata* but reflecting the decidedly *oral* culture of the desert (see Burton-Christie 1993) — are styled after the rich young ruler's encounter with Jesus (Luke 18:18-30): "Abba, what must I do to be saved?" (cf. Ward 1975: 5, 26, 34, 104, 132, 133). Queries about the meaning of Scripture are relatively abundant, and typically the sages' aphoristic responses discourage theological inquisitiveness (even reading itself) and invite practical response to the quickening and judging Word (see Blowers 1997: 230-33).

Both from the *Apophthegmata* and from erudite authors like Evagrius, whose exegetical *scholia* on Psalms, Proverbs, and Ecclesiastes presuppose Alexandrian anagogical techniques, the Byzantine monastic fathers learned to treat the biblical text as a mirror on the ascetic and contemplative life. The Bible was teeming with heroic figures — Abraham, Moses, Elijah and Elisha, Job, John the Baptist, Paul, and others — who already modeled the monastic virtues (see Nilus of Ancyra, *Ascetic Discourse,* in Palmer, et al., 1979: 208-44). Its narratives, even of the most obscure events, could be "transposed" so as to illuminate the struggles of the ascetic life. Broaching the tension between life in the desert and life in the city, "[Abba Poemen] said, 'David wrote to Joab, "Continue the battle and you will take the city and sack it." Now the city is the enemy.' He also said, 'Joab said to the people, "Be courageous and let us play the man for our people, and for the cities of our God'" (1 Chron. 19:13). Now we ourselves are these men" (*Apophthegmata*: Poeman 193-94; ET Ward 1975: 194). The "city" (quite often Jerusalem in OT war stories) could also be allegorically internalized as a figure of the soul assailed by the passions (foreign armies and kings); such appears already in Origen and is used by later monastic exegetes (e.g., Maximus, *To Thalassius* 48-50, Laga and Steel 1980: 331-91).

These and other interpretive devices appear regularly in the *Philokalia* and contribute to the formation of an Eastern *lectio divina* akin to that of the Western monastic tradition (see Breck 2001: 67-86). But the fathers of the *Philokalia* are concerned overall less with methods of interpretation than with the conditions under which Scripture's various meanings are rendered accessible to the Christian in the context of ascetic progress. As Nikitas Stithatos, disciple and biographer of Symeon the New Theologian in the eleventh century, writes, "the reading of the Scriptures means one thing for those who have but recently embraced the life of holiness, another for those who have attained the middle state, and another for those who are moving rapidly toward perfection" (ET Palmer, et al., 1995: 133-34). Symeon himself warns that the Bible's spiritual treasures are hidden from the unworthy and graciously available to the believer only by "going through all God's commandments and taking the Paraclete with him" to illuminate its mysteries (*Discourse* 24; ET de Cantanzaro 1980: 261-66).

Peter of Damascus (twelfth century) takes Jesus' command to "search the Scriptures" (John 5:39) as a basis for unremitting inquiry, since the inexhaustibility of Scripture enables new meanings to appear as the saint grows in knowledge. The interpreter must imitate the Word's own versatility by not settling absolutely on a given sense but being open to new insights, so long as they are "in accordance with God's intention" and "attested by the words of Scripture." Peter even sanctions the cautious use of "secular knowledge" as an interpretive aid, provided it "acts as a vehicle for the higher wisdom of the Spirit" (ET Palmer, et al., 1984: 263-68).

POSTSCRIPT: ORTHODOX BIBLICAL INTERPRETATION IN THE WAKE OF HIGHER CRITICISM

Needless to say, the kind of "secular knowledge" informing higher-critical biblical studies in the past century and a half has presented the Eastern Orthodox churches — like their Roman Catholic and Protestant counterparts — with unprecedented challenges. Twentieth-century Orthodox thinkers like Georges Florovsky and the late Romanian theologian Dumitru Staniloae responded to the perceived demythologizing of the Bible in much historical-critical scholarship and aspired to a neo-patristic hermeneutical synthesis faithful to tradition but also capable of engaging modern sensibilities. Florovsky advocated theological interpretation informed by a view of history as the theater of divine action. He found inspiration in Irenaeus of Lyons's understanding of the incarnation of Christ as a *recapitulation* (cf. Eph. 1:10) of the history of all creation, an event which itself interprets the sacred history as a whole — a sacred history, moreover, which is presently unfinished and continuing to unfold in the prophetic reality of the church (Florovsky 1972: 21-23, 35-36; cf. Staniloae 1980: 121-29; 1994: 15-36). "All hermeneutical 'principles' and 'rules' should be re-thought and re-examined in this eschatological perspective," says Florovsky, for which reason both he and Staniloae promoted the retrieval and disciplined use of typology, rid of allegorizing tendencies (Florovksy 1972: 26-32; cf. Staniloae 1980: 111, 139-48).

Staniloae in particular conscientiously appropriated the legacies of patristic interpretation discussed earlier. Echoing the principle of the "incarnation" of Christ in Scripture, he writes: "The words of Scripture are the inevitable occasion for us to enter through the work of the Spirit into relation with the authentic person of Christ who transcends them . . ." (1994: 44). Interpretation is once again for him a process of *contemplative vision* or discernment of the multiplicity of revelatory images of the divine (supremely the "image" of Christ's own humanity), akin to the veneration of icons cherished in Orthodox devotion (1980: 130-51). Interpretation is also, Staniloae insists, a thoroughly *ecclesial* process, since the Church's tradition — in all its aspects — is the means by which divine revelation, communicated in words and images, is continuously embodied and *personalized* (1994: 37-78).

Eastern Orthodox biblical scholars have largely followed the theologians' lead in their appraisal of biblical higher criticism and favorable reception of the "neo-patristic synthesis" (see Stylianopoulos 1997: 67-77, 128-45, 155-85; Breck 1986: 25-47). John Breck represents many Orthodox exegetes in appealing not only for serious consideration of patristic hermeneutics (2001: 33-66; 1986: 49-92; cf. Stylianopoulos 1997: 101-22) but also for revitalization of the ancient model of *theōria*. *Theōria* cannot, Breck asserts, simply be equated with the "spiritual sense" or with a singular interpretive method; rather, it is a "'vision' of divine truth communicated by the Holy Spirit to the Church," which presupposes both literal interpretation of the text in its native context — including the *theōria* of the biblical authors themselves — and discernment of the text's spiritual horizon for the church. Thus it "embraces every aspect of biblical interpretation: from rigorously scientific exegesis to liturgical hymnography" (Breck 1986: 110-12).

Recovery of the contemplative aspect of *theōria* would do much to restore to exegesis its doxological quality. Interpretation of the Word of God is properly a function of the worshiping Church. It is closely united to sacramental grace and to spiritual warfare as it is to preaching of the Word. Like the sacraments and ascetic struggle, its sole purpose is to guide the Church into ever deeper union with her glorified Lord (pp. 112-13).

Stylianopoulos argues for a "multilevel hermeneutic" in contemporary Orthodoxy, one which respects properly *exegetical,* theologically *interpretive,* and ultimately *transformative* levels, all of which dynamically interrelate, have ecclesial anchoring, and incorporate the exercise both of critical reasoning and mystical intuition (1997: 187-238). Such recommendations indicate that Eastern Orthodox interpreters, fully aware of the challenges of postmodern hermeneutical culture, still find in their Greek patristic and Byzantine legacy the sufficient models by which to appropriate the continuing power of the Bible for and in the church. *Theōria* celebrates the revelation in all of its complexity, beauty, and capacity to speak an ever-contemporary word. The late Russian émigré theologian Sergius Bulgakov, who assured Orthodox Christians that historical-critical study of the Bible would actually enhance spiritual perception of the "ways of God," epitomizes Orthodoxy's confidence in the vitality of the revelation:

> The Bible is an entire universe, it is a mystical organism, and it is only partially that we attain to living in it. The Bible is inexhaustible for us because of its divine content and its composition, its many aspects; by reason, also, of our limited and changing mentality. The Bible is a heavenly constellation, shining above us eternally, while we move on the sea of human existence. We gaze at the constellation, and it remains fixed, but it is also constantly changing its place in relation to us. (1988: 17, 20-21)

BIBLIOGRAPHY

Anderson, D.
1980   *St. John of Damascus: On the Divine Images.* Crestwood: St. Vladimir's Seminary.

Aulen, C.
1951   *Christus Victor.* New York: Macmillan.

Behr, J.
2001   *The Way to Nicaea.* Formation of Christian Theology 1; Crestwood: St. Vladimir's Seminary.

Berthold, G. C. (ed., trans.)

1985   *Maximus Confessor: Selected Writings*. CWS; New York: Paulist.

Blowers, P. M.

1991   *Exegesis and Spiritual Pedagogy in Maximus the Confessor: An Investigation of the "Quaestiones ad Thalassium."* Christianity and Judaism in Antiquity 7; Notre Dame: University of Notre Dame Press.

1995   "The Anagogical Imagination: Maximus the Confessor and the Legacy of Origenian Hermeneutics." In G. Dorival and A. le Boulluec, eds., *Origeniana Sexta: Origène et la Bible / Origen and the Bible: Actes du Colloquium Origenianum Sextum, Chantilly, 30 août-3 septembre 1993*, 639-54. BETL 118; Leuven: Peeters.

1997   "The Bible and Spiritual Doctrine: Some Controversies within the Early Eastern Christian Ascetic Tradition." In Blowers (ed.) 1997: 229-55.

2002   "The World in the Mirror of Holy Scripture: Maximus the Confessor's Short Hermeneutical Treatise in *Ambiguum ad Joannem 37*." In Blowers et al. (eds.) 2002: 408-26.

Blowers, P. M. (ed., trans.)

1997   *The Bible in Greek Christian Antiquity*. The Bible Through the Ages 1; Notre Dame: University of Notre Dame Press.

Blowers, P. M., A. Christman, D. G. Hunter, and R. Young (eds.)

2002   *In Dominico Eloquio/ In Lordly Eloquence: Essays on Patristic Exegesis in Honor of Robert Louis Wilken*. Grand Rapids: Eerdmans.

Blowers, P. M., and R. L. Wilken (trans.)

2003   *St. Maximus the Confessor: On the Cosmic Mystery of Jesus Christ*. Popular Patristics Series; Crestwood: St. Vladimir's Seminary.

Breck, J.

1986   *The Power of the Word in the Worshiping Church*. Crestwood: St. Vladimir's Seminary.

2001   *Scripture in Tradition: The Bible and Its Interpretation in the Orthodox Church*. Crestwood: St. Vladimir's Seminary.

Brock, S.

1990   *St. Ephrem the Syrian: Hymns on Paradise*. Popular Patristics Series; Crestwood: St. Vladimir's Seminary.

Bulgakov, S.

1988   *The Orthodox Church*. Trans. L. Kesich. Crestwood: St. Vladimir's Seminary.

Burton-Christie, D.

1993   *The Word in the Desert*. New York: Oxford University Press.

Canévet, M.

1983   *Grégoire de Nysse et l'herméneutique biblique. Étude des rapports entre le langage et la connaissance de Dieu*. Paris: Études Augustiniennes.

Crouzel, H., and M. Simonetti (eds., trans.)

1980   *Traité des principes* Tome IV. SC 268; Paris: Cerf.

de Catanzaro, C. J. (ed., trans.)

1980   *Symeon the New Theologian: The Discourses.* CWS; New York: Paulist.

De Lubac, H.

1998   *Medieval Exegesis,* vol. 1. Trans. M. Sebanc. Grand Rapids: Eerdmans.

2000   *Medieval Exegesis,* vol. 2. Trans. M. Sebanc. Grand Rapids: Eerdmans.

De Margerie, B.

1994   *An Introduction to the History of Exegesis,* vol. 1: *The Greek Fathers.* Trans. I. de la Potterie. Petersham: St. Bede's.

Ferguson, E., and A. Malherbe (trans.)

1978   *Gregory of Nyssa: The Life of Moses.* CWS; New York: Paulist.

Florovsky, G.

1972   *Bible, Church, Tradition: An Eastern Orthodox View.* Collected Works of Georges Florovsky 1; Belmont: Nordland.

Gallay, P. (ed., trans.)

1978   *Grégoire de Nazianze: Discours 27-31 (Discours théologiques).* SC 250; Paris: Cerf.

Gögler, R.

1963   *Zur Theologie des biblischen Wortes bei Origenes.* Düsseldorf: Patmos.

Heine, R. (ed., trans.)

1995   *Gregory of Nyssa's Treatise on the Inscriptions of the Psalms.* Oxford: Oxford University Press.

Hellenic College Faculty (eds.)

1986   *The Divine Liturgy of St. John Chrysostom.* Brookline: Holy Cross Orthodox.

Jaeger, W. (ed.)

1960   *Gregorii Nysseni Contra Eunomium Libri,* parts 1-2. GNO 1-2; Leiden: Brill.

Keating, D.

1999   "The Baptism of Jesus in Cyril of Alexandria: The Re-creation of the Human Race." *Pro Ecclesia* 8: 201-22.

Kerrigan, A.

1952   *St. Cyril of Alexandria: Interpreter of the Old Testament.* AnBib 2; Rome: Pontifico Instituto Biblico.

Kesich, V.

1993   "The Orthodox Church and Biblical Interpretation." *SVTQ* 37: 343-51.

Klostermann, E. (ed.)

1935   *Origenes: Matthäuserklärung.* GCS Origenes Werke 10; Leipzig: Hinrichs.

Laga, C., and C. Steel (eds.)

1980   *Maximi Confessoris Quaestiones ad Thalassium.* Vol. 1. *Quaestiones I-LV una cum latine interpretatione Ioannis Scotti Eriugenae.* CCSG 7; Turnhout: Brepols.

1990   *Maximi Confessoris Quaestiones ad Thalassium.* Vol. 2. *Quaestiones LVI-LXV, una cum latine interpretatione Ioannis Scotti Eriugenae.* CCSG 22; Turnhout: Brepols.

Lash, E. (ed., trans.)

1995   *Kontakia on the Life of Christ: St. Romanos the Melodist.* San Francisco: Harper-Collins.

Louth, A.

1995   "An Invitation to the Christian Mystery." In E. Lash (ed.) 1995: xv-xxii.

Louth, A. (trans.)

2003   *St. John of Damascus: Three Treatises on the Divine Images.* Popular Patristics Series; Crestwood: St. Vladimir's Seminary.

Luibheid, C. (ed., trans.)

1987   *Pseudo-Dionysius: The Complete Works.* CWS; New York: Paulist.

McDonough, J. (ed.)

1962   *Gregorii Nysseni: In Inscriptiones Psalmorum.* GNO 5; Leiden: Brill.

McGuckin, J. A.

1994   *St. Cyril of Alexandria: The Christological Controversy. Its History, Theology, and Texts.* Supplements to *Vigiliae Christianae* 23; Leiden: Brill.

McVey, K. (trans.)

1989   *Ephrem the Syrian: Hymns.* CWS; New York: Paulist.

Meyendorff, J. (trans.)

1984   *Gregory Palamas: The Triads.* CWS; New York: Paulist.

Meyendorff, P. (ed., trans.)

1983   *St. Germanus of Constantinople: On the Divine Liturgy.* Crestwood: St. Vladimir's Seminary.

Moore, W., and H. A. Wilson (eds., trans.)

1979   *Select Writings and Letters of Gregory, Bishop of Nyssa.* NPNF[2] 5; Grand Rapids: Eerdmans.

Mosshammer, A.

1990   "Disclosing but Not Disclosed: Gregory of Nyssa as Deconstructionist." In H. R. Drobner and C. Klock, eds., *Studien zu Gregor von Nyssa und der christliche Antike,* 99-122. Supplements to *Vigiliae Christianae* 7; Leiden: Brill.

Palmer, G. E. H., P. Sherrard, and K. Ware (eds., trans.)

1979   *The Philokalia: The Complete Text Compiled by St. Nikodimos of the Holy Mountain and St. Makarios of Corinth,* vol. 1. London: Faber and Faber.

1984   *The Philokalia: The Complete Text Compiled by St. Nikodimos of the Holy Mountain and St. Makarios of Corinth,* vol. 3. London: Faber and Faber.

1995   *The Philokalia: The Complete Text Compiled by St. Nikodimos of the Holy Mountain and St. Makarios of Corinth,* vol. 4. London: Faber and Faber.

Preuschen, E. (ed.)

1903   *Origenes: Das Johanneskommentar.* GCS Origenes Werke 4; Leipzig: Hinrichs.

Pusey, P. E. (trans.)

1874   *Commentary on the Gospel of John by Saint Cyril, Archbishop of Alexandria,* vol. 1. Library of Fathers of the Holy Catholic Church 43; London: Smith.

Randell, T. (trans.)

1885   *Commentary on the Gospel of John by Saint Cyril, Archbishop of Alexandria,* vol. 2. Library of Fathers of the Holy Catholic Church 48; London: Smith.

Renoux, C.

1997   "The Reading of the Bible in the Ancient Liturgy of Jerusalem." In Blowers (ed.) 1997: 389-414.

Rorem, P.

1984   *Biblical and Liturgical Symbols within the Pseudo-Dionysian Synthesis.* Studies and Texts 71; Toronto: Pontifical Institute of Medieval Studies.

Rousseau, P.

1994   *Basil of Caesarea.* Transformation of the Classical Heritage 20; Berkeley: University of California Press.

Staniloae, D.

1980   *Theology and the Church.* Trans. R. Barringer. Crestwood: St. Vladimir's Seminary.

1994   *The Experience of God.* Trans. I. Ionita and R. Barringer. Orthodox Dogmatic Theology 1; Brookline: Holy Cross Orthodox.

Stylianopoulos, T.

1997   *The New Testament: An Orthodox Perspective.* Scripture, Tradition, Hermeneutics 1; Brookline: Holy Cross Orthodox.

Trigg, J. W.

2002   "Romanos's Biblical Interpretation: Drama, Imagery, and Attention to the Text." In Blowers, et al. (eds.) 2002: 380-94.

Ward, B. (ed., trans.)

1975   *The Sayings of the Desert Fathers: The Alphabetical Collection.* Cistercian Studies 59; Kalamazoo: Cistercian.

Wilken, R. L.

1971   *Judaism and the Early Christian Mind: A Study of Cyril of Alexandria's Exegesis and Theology.* New Haven: Yale University Press.

Young, F.

1997   *Biblical Exegesis and the Formation of Christian Culture.* Cambridge: Cambridge
        University Press.

2003   "Alexandrian and Antiochene Exegesis." In *HBI*[1], 334-54.

CHAPTER 6

The Text of the Tanak

Russell Fuller

"Tanak" is the transliterated acronym made up of the first letters of the Hebrew names for the three sections of the canonical Jewish Scriptures, *Torah*,
Nevi'im, and *Ketuvim*. This chapter treats the history, development, and preservation of the text of the Tanak from the emergence of the standard form of
the consonantal text through the production of the Masoretic Text (MT), the
standardization of the scriptural text, including accents, vowel pointing, and
marginal notes, to the first printed editions, down to the development of electronic forms of the text.

TEXT TRANSMISSION BEFORE THE EMERGENCE
OF A PROTO-MASORETIC TEXT

Transmission and interpretation go hand in hand with each other, inextrica-
bly linked in the transmission history of the text. The text, or form of the text,
chosen for copying is the text that is interpreted. The text interpreted by the
community is the text the community will preserve and transmit to the next
generation. The process of interpretation has the potential to change the
form of the text, even if only in small ways.

The text of the Tanak has a transmission history of approximately 3000
years, and counting. It is only from the first century CE, the time from which
we have a completed canon of Scripture, that we may speak of the text of the
Tanak as a single entity, copied and transmitted as a single whole. Before that,

the various collections of text were transmitted separately or as smaller groups of collections.

The texts of the Tanak were copied on scrolls usually made from the skins of animals such as goats or gazelles. A scroll is a strip of leather rolled from one end. The length of a biblical scroll is limited, so a number of scrolls were needed for the entire Tanak. The Torah was customarily written on a single scroll. Likewise, the longer prophetic compositions — Isaiah, Jeremiah, Ezekiel — would each be written on a single scroll.

Usually only one side of the scroll was smoothed and prepared to receive writing. If a composition was too long for a single piece of leather, then the copyist or scribe would sew pieces of leather together to make a scroll long enough for the composition. The scribe might also impress dry lines onto the leather to guide the writing of the composition and to delineate the edges of columns. Various scribal signs were sometimes used to indicate corrections or passages of special interest. The biblical mss. from Qumran give us excellent examples of these and other scribal practices from as early as 275 BCE. Biblical mss. were usually prepared carefully; however, there do not seem to have been established standards applied in the copying of each ms. until perhaps the end of the first century CE. Usually semiformal or formal scripts were used for biblical mss., although several from Qumran were copied in semi-cursive scripts. The biblical mss. from Qumran and elsewhere in the Judean Desert show that there was widespread variation in scribal practices in the last three centuries BCE. By the first century CE, scribal practice in the copying of biblical mss. became standardized. Those rules are preserved in the Babylonian Talmud and the treatises *Masseket Sefer Torah* and *Masseket Soferim,* the latter compiled in the ninth century CE.

THE EMERGENCE AND DOMINANCE
OF THE "PROTO-MASORETIC TEXT"

The expression "proto-Masoretic Text" (pMT) is based on the later history of the text. It refers to the form of the consonantal text of the canonical Jewish Scriptures that became the dominant form of the text. All other variant forms of the text, that is, any text that differed from the pMT, went out of use and were eventually replaced or superseded by the pMT. The pMT became the dominant form of the text between 70 and 132 CE. This time range is arrived at on the basis of the scarcity of ms. evidence for other text forms after this time, as well as the assumption that the interpretive practices of the rabbis by the time of the Bar Kochba revolt required a standardized form of the text.

Some scholars speculate that the pMT was the form of the consonantal text favored by the Pharisees, who are assumed to have been the dominant group in Judaism after the destruction of Jerusalem in 70 CE. The textual forms favored by other groups are assumed to have disappeared along with the groups. This scenario is possible, but speculative (Würthwein 1995: 14). The Essenes, an important group in this period, do not seem to have favored any single form of the consonantal text. It has also not been demonstrated that the Pharisees favored a single form of the text, let alone that this was the pMT. These are assumptions.

It is important to note that there was never a single text that was or could be labeled *the* "proto-Masoretic Text." Rather, the ms. evidence from the Judean desert demonstrates that until the time of the destruction of the Second Temple in 70 CE, there was a great variety of texts in use, some related to each other and thus forming groups. The biblical mss. from Qumran attest to this diversity of textual traditions as well as to the early existence of the proto-Masoretic group in the period ca. 275 BCE to 68 CE. We do not have enough evidence to determine when and where the proto-Masoretic group originated. This textual group or family was apparently in existence by the time of the earliest extant mss. If this is correct, then it would mean that the proto-Masoretic group is as old as the Greek translation of the Torah in the third century BCE. Texts recovered from Masada that date to the end of the first Jewish war against Rome (66-73 CE) seem to belong to this group. Likewise, texts dating to the period between the Jewish wars (73-132 CE), such as the biblical texts found in the Nahal Hever and the Wadi Murabba'at, also belong to the proto-Masoretic group. To this date, no texts belonging to another textual group have been recovered, which leads scholars to assume that none survived. The first Jewish War seems to have been the point after which textual diversity declined so rapidly that no physical evidence of other textual traditions survived.

Although the proto-Masoretic group was apparently the only surviving textual group, the tradition is not monolithic. Texts belonging to the proto-Masoretic group differ from each other in numerous small details. The Hebrew Minor Prophets scroll from the Wadi Murabba'at, dating approximately 50-100 CE, differs from the consonantal text of the MT fifty-four times. Usually, this involves orthographic differences, but four times the differences correspond to readings found in the *ketib-qere* (see pp. 211-12) lists of the *masorah* (the traditional three-part apparatus of the Hebrew text). This is the amount of variation we might expect among mss. of the same group. From this time on, differences among mss. of the proto-Masoretic family become less prevalent.

The assumption, which still seems quite common (see Cohen 1956; Neusner 1980), that the Pharisees immediately preceded the rabbis who assumed authoritative roles after 70 CE, may be a complicating factor in the assumption that the pMT was the text favored by the Pharisees and thus had authoritative status early on. First, the Pharisees were certainly not the only group during this period. Second, although the pMT is clearly the favorite text of the rabbis, at least based on references in the Talmud, it does not follow that we can assume that the pMT was the favorite text of the Pharisees. The pMT emerges as the only attested text type by the time of the Bar Kochba revolt (132-35 CE). It is also known among the biblical mss. found at Qumran — as one of many text types utilized by the Jewish community there.

The emergence of a single form of the text may have been the result of a number of factors. The war of 66-70 threatened the existence of Jews and Judaism in Palestine and may have inspired survivors to gather and collate existing traditional materials, including biblical mss. The collation of biblical manuscripts and recognition of the differences between Greek and Hebrew forms of the text made the diversity of Hebrew forms of the text apparent. The development of interpretive methods dependent on specific features of the text, such as orthography and letter forms/shapes, would have encouraged the standardization of the text. And it would have been a natural development at this point, between 70 and 138 CE, to choose a single form of the text that eventually would become the only surviving form as older copies went out of use and were discarded.

Christian appropriation of the LXX, along with the recognition that the Hebrew and Greek texts frequently did not agree with each other, contributed to the abandonment of the LXX in Jewish communities and the development of new Greek translations that agreed more closely with the contemporary Hebrew text of the Bible. The Greek Minor Prophets ms. (R) from Nahal Hever is a good example of such projects. The Hebrew text used to produce R was not yet identical with the pMT. The translations of Aquila, Theodotion, and Symmachus are examples of new translations, inspired perhaps by the diversity among Hebrew texts, the use of the LXX by Christians, and the development of new interpretive methods such as halakhic, or legal, midrash (see Strack and Stemberger 1992).

Johanan ben Zachai and his colleagues at Jabneh may have played a leading role in the standardization of the text (Strack and Stemberger 1992: 74-75). The narrowing of Hebrew text types may also be associated with Rabbi Akiba and his followers (see Nadich 1998). The translation of Aquila (see Greenspoon 2003: 100-102) has been attributed to Aquila of Pontus, one of Akiba's followers called "the Proselyte," a pagan who converted to Judaism, and then to Christianity (see also Barthélemy 1963). The narrowing of text types and the creation of new Greek translations might well have been the work of decades; but certainly no later than 200 CE the pMT emerged as the single Hebrew text type. Variations among mss. existed, but by then they were relatively minor disagreements in orthography and in the paratextual features discussed below.

THE STATE OF THE TEXT BEFORE THE BEGINNING OF THE ACTIVITY OF THE MASORETES

The Masoretes, scholars who specialized in the traditions governing the production and proper reading of the Hebrew biblical text, began their activity at the end of the talmudic period (*circa* 300-500 CE). The talmudic literature mentions several features of the consonantal text that might therefore be pre-Masoretic, though there is some variation in opinion concerning when these features developed. Tov (1992) lists them under the *masorah,* and Yeivin (1980) assumes that they are pre-Masoretic. In the ms. evidence from 200 BCE to 100 CE, most of these features described in the Talmud are not attested.

Apparently, most of the features discussed below developed between the time the proto-Masoretic Text (pMT) became the dominant text type (*ca.* 132 CE) and the beginning of the talmudic period (*ca.* 300 CE), but we have no textual evidence from this time. However, three features — the order of the books, the division of the text into sections, and the extraordinary points — are attested in mss. from the Second Temple period and are therefore the most ancient types of features that are also found later in the pMT and the MT.

Order of the Books

Before the introduction of the codex in the seventh century, the collection of the Jewish Scriptures was transmitted on scrolls. The entire collection would take numerous scrolls. The order of books within sub-collections such as the Torah that were written on single scrolls was fixed. Did questions of order arise at this stage? And what might order mean for a collection of scrolls? Although we have little evidence for the history of the text in this stage of its development, we do have some information preserved in the Talmuds and in related collections of legal material outside the Talmuds

known as *baraita*. A *baraita* preserved in Baba Batra 14b and dated by some
to no later than the end of the second century (Segal 1997) addresses the
question of the order of the biblical compositions: "Our Rabbis taught: the
order of the Prophets is Joshua, Judges, Samuel, Kings, Jeremiah, Ezekiel,
Isaiah, and the Twelve . . . ; The order of the Ketuvim is Ruth, the Book of
Psalms, Job, Proverbs, Ecclesiastes, the Song of Songs, Lamentations, Daniel, the scroll of Esther, Ezra, and Chronicles" (Sarna 1971-72: 827). This
baraita offers evidence that the order of the Major Prophets was not yet
what came to be normative in the age of the codex. This is important information, but what is most interesting is that, although the collection is
transmitted on scrolls, a set order is asserted for the entire collection. If the
baraita is older than the use of the codex, then it must refer to the organization of the collection of scrolls, possibly for storage in a library. It is also
possible that the *baraita* reflects the order of study of the collection in a
school curriculum (Sarna 1971-72: 827-28). However it is to be understood,
it anticipates by almost five hundred years questions of order in the collection that will become relevant with the adoption of the codex form and the
consequent fixed order of compositions in the collection.

Division of the Text into Sections

The division of the text into sense units called *pisqot* (somewhat like paragraphs) is an early feature of the consonantal text since *pisqot* are mentioned
as early as the third century CE in legal material (Yeivin 1980: 41-42). Some
mss. from the Judean Desert show a division into sense units that sometimes
correspond to the "open" and "closed" sections, *petuchot* and *setumot* respectively, known later in the Masoretic manuscripts. Although this "paragraph-
ing" practice is well attested in biblical mss. from Qumran and the Judean
Desert, there seems to have been no standardized system that corresponds to
the system of open and closed sections recognized in the Talmud and the
masorah (Oesch 1979).

Paragraphs are called *pisqot* or *parashiyyot* (paragraphs), and are
marked by spaces in the text. There are two types of *pisqot*. An "open" section,
a *petuchah* (pl. *petuchot*), is one in which the word beginning a new paragraph must be written at the beginning of the line. A "closed" section, a
setumah (pl. *setumot*), is one in which the word beginning a new paragraph is
written on the same line as the last word of the previous paragraph, or, if
there is not room, it is written after an indentation on the new line. These
possibilities may be graphically represented as follows (Yeivin 1980: 41):

	petuchah (open)	*setumah* (closed)
(a) if the paragraph ends at the be- ginning of a line	‖‖‖‖‖‖‖‖‖‖‖‖‖‖‖‖‖ ‖‖‖ ‖‖‖‖‖‖‖‖‖‖‖‖‖‖‖‖§	‖‖‖‖‖‖‖‖‖‖‖‖‖‖‖‖‖‖ ‖‖‖‖‖‖‖‖‖§ ‖‖ ‖‖‖‖‖‖‖‖‖‖‖‖‖‖‖‖‖‖
(b) if the paragraph ends at or near the end of a line	‖‖‖‖‖‖‖‖‖‖‖‖‖‖‖‖‖ ‖‖‖‖‖‖‖‖‖‖‖‖‖‖‖‖‖ ‖‖‖‖‖‖‖‖‖‖‖‖‖‖‖‖§	‖‖‖‖‖‖‖‖‖‖‖‖‖‖‖‖‖ ‖‖‖‖‖‖‖‖‖‖‖‖‖‖‖‖‖ ‖‖‖‖‖‖‖‖‖‖‖‖‖‖‖§

Some mss. and printed editions use the letters *peh* (פ) and *samekh* (ס) to mark open and closed sections, respectively. The division of the text into sense units indicates an exegesis based on the content of the text (Tov 1992: 51). The number and placement of the *pisqot* is later fixed by the *masorah.*

Graphic indication of the division of the text into verses apparently was introduced later than the division into paragraphs. In biblical mss. from Qumran, scribes simply left a single letter space blank between verses, as they also did between words within a verse *(pasuq).* The indication of the division into verses seems to have begun during the talmudic period, since there are legal rulings that mention this feature of the text (Yeivin 1980: 42). It became customary to indicate the end of a verse with *silluq* (:).

Division of biblical texts into numbered chapters is a very late feature, originating among Christians in the thirteenth century. Stephen Langton, arch- bishop of Canterbury, is credited (Würthwein 1995: 98) with this innovation in the Vulgate, the authoritative text on all matters of western Christian doctrine and interpretation at that time (see Brown 2003). Smalley (1970: 221-24) claims that the text was divided into units to allow teachers to refer to specific passages more easily. Another factor in the development of chapter and verse division and numbering in the Vulgate may have been the need for a shorthand way of referring to the text during theological disputes with heretical Christian groups such as the Cathars. Langton was certainly involved in such disputes.

How did numbered chapters and verses "migrate" (Smalley 1970: 221-24) from the Vulgate to Hebrew mss.? This process probably also began in the con- text of a Christian edition of the biblical text. The first of the great polyglot editions was the *Complutensian Polyglot* produced by Cardinal Ximénes de Cisneros between 1514 and 1517, but it was not published until 1522. It features the text of the Vulgate in the central column, divided into numbered chapters and verses. To the left of the Vulgate is the LXX, and to the right is the Hebrew text, both aligned with the Vulgate and likewise divided into numbered chap- ters and verses (Mulder 1990: 118; Würthwein 1995: 226-27). Interestingly, this practice did not spread immediately to Jewish editions of the MT. Neither the first Rabbinic Bible, published 1516-17, nor the famous second Rabbinic Bible, published 1524-25, adopted this division into numbered chapters and verses (Tov 1992: 405). Although modern printed editions of the Rabbinic Bible, also known as the *Miqra'ot Gedolot*, do include chapter and verse numbers, it is unclear when these were added to the text of these editions.

Since the division into chapters is late, originating in the Vulgate, it does not always correspond to the placement of expected chapter division based on the content. For example, the end of Genesis 1 does not correspond with the end of the first literary unit, which is in 2:4a. In Hebrew mss., both places are marked by *petuchah*.

It is evident from the Genesis example that these various ways of dividing up the text, which originate at different times, and in the case of chapters, from the text in another language, represent different traditions of exegesis that do not always agree with each other. Thus the *pisqot* will not always correspond with chapter divisions, and the verse divisions, although from the talmudic period, do not always correspond to the older *pisqot*. Thus, *pisqot* can occur in the middle of a verse (Yeivin 1980: 42-43; Tov 1992: 53-54).

Extraordinary Points

Fifteen words in the MT are written with dots above the word, and, in one case, below the word (Gen. 16:5; 18:9; 19:33; 33:4; 37:12; Num. 3:39; 9:10; 21:30; 29:15; Deut. 29:28; 2 Sam. 19:20; Isa. 44:9; Ezek. 41:20; 46:22; Ps. 27:13). These dots are part of the consonantal text and have no connection with the vowels or accents in either the Babylonian or the Tiberian traditions. Those in the Torah are written in Torah scrolls. Yeivin points out the possibility that by the rabbinic period the meaning of these points was already unknown (Yeivin 1980: 46). Dotted letters and words are also found in Hebrew mss. from the Dead Sea Scrolls, where they seem to indicate errors in the text. An example is 4QXII^e frag. 14, Zechariah (Zech. 5:9), which has dots above and below letters of the second line to indicate emendation of the text. Dotan notes ancient evidence for this feature of the consonantal text, suggesting a date as early as the second century BCE for this phenomenon (Dotan 1971-72: 1407).

Suspended Letters/*Litterae Suspensae*

There are four suspended letters in the Bible. In Judg. 18:30 the *nun* of Manasseh is suspended, probably indicating the addition of *nun* to the original reading ("Moses") in order to avoid linking Moses to an idolatrous cult. Each of the other three passages, Ps. 80:14 and Job 38:13, 15, has a raised *ʿayin* (**ע**). While in Ps 80:14 it may indicate the middle letter of the book of Psalms, in Job it is more likely to represent early corrections, adding an omitted letter, which may also be the case in Ps. 80:14. The practice of adding an omitted letter above the line is well attested in the texts from the Judean Desert. *ʿAyin*, *ʾaleph*, (**א**), *waw* (**ו**), and *yod* (**י**) were frequently omitted in those texts.

"Crowns"/*taggim*

Some letters in the Torah are given additional strokes of three or seven lines attached to the top of the letters. This practice varies from ms. to ms. These *taggim* are illustrated in Part Two of Birnbaum 1954-57 (Babylonian Manuscript #191, Sephardic Manuscript #245, Ashkenazic Manuscript #347). In some synagogue scrolls, certain letters may be decorated with slim strokes at the tops of letters, also known as *taggim*, or *ziyyunim*. The strokes are only added to the letters *gimel* (**ג**), *zayin* (**ז**), *tet* (**ט**), *nun*, (**נ**), *ayin* (**ע**), *tsade* (**צ**), and *shin* (**ש**) (see also Yeivin 1980: 38). The *taggim* are mentioned in *b. Menaḥot* 29b. *Taggim* are generally not added in codices. This is apparently an ancient practice the meaning of which is no longer known.

Large and Small Letters

There are several places where additional either large or small letters are written. Since this usage was never legally fixed, the number of such letters varies from ms. to ms. Older mss. generally have fewer. *Leningrad B19A*, the oldest complete codex of the Hebrew Bible in existence, dated to 1009 CE, has large letters in Num. 27:5 and Deut. 6:4 (2 large letters) and small letters in Isa. 44:14; Jer. 39:13; and Prov. 16:28. The editors of *BHS* add Lev. 11:42. The function of the large or small letters is not always clear. In Lev. 11:42, *waw* (**ו**) in the word "Gihon" is written larger because it is the middle letter of the Torah (see Mulder 1990: 94).

Inverted *nun*

This symbol has numerous names in rabbinic literature (Dotan 1971-72: 1408). In printed Bibles it takes the form of an inverted *nun*. The inverted *nun* occurs only twice in Num. 10:35, 36 and seven times in Ps. 107:23-28, 40. In Num. 10:35, 36 it may serve to set apart the text between the *nuns*. In *Leningrad B19A,* this text falls between *setumah* and *petuchah*. This does not explain the function of the inverted *nuns* in Psalm 107.

Oddly Shaped Letters

In some places "oddly shaped" letters are found. This usually refers to final form letters in the middle of a word or initial/medial form letters at the end of a word. The origin of this interchange is difficult to explain. It can only happen with *kap* (כ\ך), *mem* (מ\ם), *nun* (נ\ן), *peh* (פ\ף), and *tsadeh* (צ\ץ), since only these letters have final forms. An example of a final form in the middle of a word is found in Isa. 9:6 where the morpheme *lmrbh* (למרבה) shows final *mem* (ם) instead of the expected medial form (מ). This reading also appears in the *ketib-qere* lists. An example of an initial/medial form at the end of a word is in Num. 2:13.

Summary of Textual Features before the Period of the Masoretes

These textual features are a part of the transmission and interpretation of the text before the activity of the Masoretes began. Some of these features are known from Hebrew mss. of the Second Temple period (order of the books, division into sections, and extraordinary points), and thus may go back as far as the first century CE. Suspended letters, crowns *(taggim),* and the large or small letters seem to have developed later, during the talmudic period. All these features represent ways of interpreting the consonantal text. This is especially clear with the various ways of dividing the text into sense units. All are transmitted as an integral part of the consonantal text, demonstrating their antiquity.

READING TRADITIONS

Some of the reading traditions seen in the MT are mentioned in the Talmud and are thus presumably pre-Masoretic. Others may have originated with the early Masoretes.

Ketib-Qere

Ketib is an Aramaic participle meaning "(what is) written," in this case referring to a word written in the consonantal text. *Qere* is an Aramaic participle
meaning "(what is) read." The *qere*, therefore, is the word that should be read
in place of the word written in the consonantal text. Usually, the *qere* is indicated in the margin of a ms., for example, in *Leningrad B19A*, by the letter *qof*
with a dot over it (קּ), with the consonants of the *qere* written above the dot.
The vowels of the *qere* are written with the *ketib* in the body of the text. See
Gen. 8:19, for example, in *BHS*, which reproduces this system of presentation.
In many early mss., a symbol resembling a large final *nun* (ן) is placed in the
margin opposite the *ketib* to indicate the *qere*. This symbol continued in use
through the twelfth century (Yeivin 1980: 52-53). The *ketib-qere* readings are
not marked in synagogue scrolls since they are a part of the reading tradition
rather than a part of the consonantal text.

There is great diversity among mss. in the indication of *ketib-qere*, also a
great variety in the types of readings designated as *ketib-qere*. For these reasons, the number of *ketib-qere* may range from about 800 to about 1500
(Yeivin 1980: 55; Tov 1992: 58). Some types of *ketib-qere*, such as the perpetual
qere for some words (see below) and euphemisms, are mentioned in the Talmud and therefore must be quite old. Other types of *ketib-qere* are found only
later in Masoretic mss., and some are based on the vocalization system. These
readings are presumably no older than the eighth century CE (Yeivin 1980: 59).

Types of Ketib-Qere include:

Qere Perpetua/Constant Qere: The constant *qere* is not marked by a
marginal note. The vowels of the *qere* are simply written with the
ketib. The best known perpetual *qere* is that of the divine name
YHWH, which is vocalized either as its *qere*, *'adonai* or, if it happens
to stand next to that word in the text, as *'elohim*. Similarly, the name
Jerusalem (*yrwslm*, ירושלם) is vocalized as if written *yrwslym* (Yeivin
1980: 58-59).

Euphemisms: As Yeivin points out (1980: 56), the *qere* replaces the *ketib*
sixteen times with a euphemism softening the harshness or vulgarity
of the *ketib*. An example is Isa. 13:16, where the *ketib* is *tishagalnah*
("to be raped") and the *qere* has *tishakabnah* ("to be lain with").

Unusual forms: *ketib-qere* may involve unusual forms, especially forms
with spellings that depart from the norm in biblical usage. *Ketib-qere*
can also indicate scribal errors of various sorts, such as letters omitted or transposed (metathesis). For an example of the latter, see

2 Sam. 20:14, where the *ketib* is *wayyiqqalahu* and the *qere* is *wayyiqqahalu.*

Ketib we-la qere and *Qere we-la ketib:* Yeivin (1980: 57) includes in his discussion of the *ketib-qere* readings those labeled as *ketib wa-la qere* ("that which is written, but not read"), as in 2 Kgs. 5:18 and Jer. 51:3, and *qere we-la ketib* ("that which is read, but not written"), as in 2 Sam. 8:3; 16:23. In these cases, the reader is instructed to read a word not in any way indicated in the text, or to omit a word written in the text. Since twelve of these cases are mentioned in the Talmud, they seem to be part of the pre-Masoretic reading traditions.

As stated above, some types of *ketib-qere* are mentioned in the Talmud, and therefore predate the development of the vowel system. Other *ketib-qere* are based on the vowel system and therefore date from no earlier than the eighth century CE, indicating that this system of textual interpretation developed over a period of perhaps two or three hundred years.

This long period of development makes discerning the origin of the *ketib-qere* system and its purpose somewhat difficult and ambiguous. Several theories concerning its origin have been suggested. Morrow (1991) suggests that the *ketib* preserves the written traditions of the scribes while the *qere* preserves the reading traditions of the synagogue. The Masoretes preserved both traditions through the *ketib-qere* system. This theory seems to assume that scribes were somehow separate from the synagogue and that it took a third group, the Masoretes, to bring the two sets of traditions together. In addition, this theory does not seem to account adequately for the antiquity of some of the *ketib-qere* readings, but assigns to the Masoretes the major role in their creation.

Another theory (see Talmon 1964 for examples) conceives of the *qere* as a collection of variant readings from other sources. This theory makes good sense of the older readings found in the *ketib-qere* system. But this theory does not address the fact that only one variant has been preserved for each example.

Yet another theory (Yeivin 1980: 61; Dotan 1971-72: col. 1421a) suggests that the *qere* developed as corrections to the text. Later, optional variants were recorded in the same way, and eventually the optional variants (and corrections) became obligatory.

Sebirin

Similar to the readings preserved in the *ketib-qere* system are the *sebirin* notes. *Sebirin* means "suggested." The *sebirin* notes usually address a word that is unusual or difficult in its context and suggest another reading. There are two significant differences between the *sebirin* readings and the *ketib-qere* readings: the *sebirin* are not a part of the reading tradition as the *ketib-qere* are, and thus, are not binding, and the *sebirin* are intended to "protect" the reading of the text, even though there seems to be a more likely reading. For examples of *sebirin*, see Gen. 19:23; Exod. 21:30 (see also Yeivin 1980: 62-63). The text is correct as preserved.

Tiqqune Sopherim: Corrections of the Scribes

The *tiqqune sopherim* are readings where the scribes have corrected the text. The *tiqqune sopherim* comments, which are found in the *masorah magna,* give the original reading. The earliest lists give either eight or eleven places where the text was "corrected," but these early lists do not use the term *tiqqun,* "correction" or "emendation," but rather *kinah,* meaning "euphemism." The later lists, which give eighteen places where the text was changed by the scribes, introduce the term *tiqqun.* It is possible that the use of these two terms indicates a development in thinking. The *tiqqun* lists may originally have suggested euphemistic substitutions, which were later understood as corrections or emendations. A well-known *tiqqun* refers to the text of Gen. 18:22, "Abraham stood before Yahweh." While the original text read "Yahweh stood before Abraham," the corrected text removes the theologically inappropriate idea that God might have stood waiting before Abraham. Most of the *tiqqune sopherim* refer to small changes in the text, many times of only a single consonant. For example, Zech. 2:12 in the MT reads, "Whoever touches you touches the pupil of his own eye" ("his own eye" *'ynw*). The *tiqqun* informs us that this is a correction of the scribes: the original text read "my eye" (*'yny*) referring to the eye of God. Typically, the concern of the *tiqqune sopherim* is to indicate corrections of texts which were understood to be somehow disrespectful of God. Sometimes, as in Zech. 2:12, the original reading agrees with ancient variants known from Hebrew or Greek witnesses (Tov 1992: 64-67; Fuller 1990).

Itture Sopherim: Omissions of the Scribes

Like the *tiqqune sopherim,* the *itture sopherim* are attributed to the ancient scribes. Five times the scribes are said to have omitted a *waw.* These notes apparently indicate corrections that were made, like the *tiqqune sopherim,* as opposed to a reading tradition indicated in the margin, as with the *ketib-qere* system.

The *'al Tiqre* Notes

In rabbinic literature, there are comments from the rabbis phrased: "Do not read (*'al tiqre*) X (= *ketib*), but rather Y." That is, the interpolations seem to be suggested emendations of the *ketib*. But scholars now think that these statements are not suggested emendations but are rather exegetical or midrashic in nature (see Yeivin 1980: 61-62). Unlike some of the *qere* notes, the *'al tiqre* probably do not preserve ancient variant readings known to the rabbis (Tov 1992: 59).

THE MASORETIC PERIOD

The Development of the MT

The term *masorah* (*mswrh:* מסורה), as commonly used by biblical scholars, refers to the traditional three-part apparatus of the biblical text: the vowels and accents within the text and the Masoretic commentary on the text in the margins between the columns, in the upper and lower margins, and in the spaces at the ends of books. In addition, many mss. have additional Masoretic lists after the books at the end.

The date of the beginning point of Masoretic activity, especially the recording of notes, is difficult to determine. The sort of interest in the text evident later in the *masorah* is already apparent during the talmudic period (c. 300-500 CE), as indicated by comments found in various places in the Talmud. Notes later included in the *masorah* were certainly transmitted orally (Yeivin 1980: 135) and perhaps written on scrolls intended for private use.

It is also difficult to know if the vowels developed before the accents or vice versa. Scholarly opinions can be cited in support of either view (see Kelly, et al. 1998: 15 for a discussion of both views). Since the marginal comments are concerned primarily with orthography, some scholars think this indicates that they predate the vocalization system (see Dotan 1971-72: 1416-17). It is likely that all three features developed over some time. The Masoretic period is usually considered to have begun in the sixth century and ended in the tenth. The culmination of the Masoretic tradition in this period was the production of the great Masoretic codices.

The vowels and accents provide direction for the proper reading of the text. The marginal notes provide information to ensure the proper copying of the text. The *masorah* written between the columns of text is called the *masorah qetannah* or, in Latin, the *masorah parva*, abbreviated *Mp*. The *masorah* written in the upper and lower margins is called the *masorah gedolah* or *masorah magna*, abbreviated *Mm*. The *Mp* contains notes that focus mostly on the orthography and the frequency of forms. These notes may mention the specific spelling of a given form or its vocalization. The *Mp* also contains all the marginal notes discussed above, such as the *ketib-qere* readings. There may also be notes on a specific verse as a whole if its length is unusual or if it marks a special point in the composition such as the midpoint. The *Mm* could be viewed as a type of supplement to the *Mp*. For example, if the *Mp* contains a note that a word spelled in a certain way occurs three times, the *Mm* will list the places where the form occurs. The *Mm* also contains lists of noted forms. In addition to the *Mp* and the *Mm*, many manuscripts contain additional Masoretic lists and treatises at the end. This material came to be referred to as the *masorah finalis*. Since biblical citations in the *masorah* predate the use of numbered chapters and verses, texts are referred to using key words or phrases from the context where the form occurs.

Both the *Mp* and the *Mm* make extensive use of abbreviations, which can make them very difficult to use without extensive practice. In addition, the language of the Masoretic notes is Aramaic. The annotated glossary of Kelly, Mynatt, and Crawford (1998) is an exceptionally helpful tool in learning to read Masoretic notes. Yeivin gives an extensive discussion of Masoretic terms (Yeivin 1980: 80-122). *Biblia Hebraica Quinta* (see de Waard 1998) will contain both the *Mp* and the *Mm* translated with citations of biblical passages using chapter and verse numbers. This feature should be a great help in making the important information of the *masorah* more accessible.

As is well known, copies of the Hebrew text for use in the synagogue must be written on scrolls and may not contain anything beyond the consonantal text. However, scrolls which were no longer fit for use in the synagogue could be annotated. Extant scrolls of this type provide the earliest evidence for the recording of the *masorah*, the vowels, and the accents. Such scrolls come to us from the Cairo Geniza. The term "geniza" refers to a storage room for biblical scrolls and other material that might contain the name of God or biblical citations but had become too worn for continued use. The Cairo Geniza was the geniza of the Ben Ezra Synagogue of Old Cairo (Fustat), which had been forgotten and was rediscovered by the community in the late nineteenth century. Material from the geniza was sold to many institutions around the world in the last decades of the nineteenth century. This material had accumulated for several centuries, most from the tenth to thirteenth centuries. Some of the older biblical scrolls from this collection show Masoretic notes, vowels, and accents. These materials provide most of the manuscripts in the Babylonian and Palestinian Masoretic traditions. Next to the discovery of the Dead Sea Scrolls, the materials from the Cairo Geniza were the most important discovery of the modern period for the history of the study of the Hebrew Bible (Reif 1994). The recovery of these early scrolls with such notations indicates that the *masorah* began to be committed to writing prior to the eighth century.

The *masorah* and the vowel and accent systems did not develop in one single location. There were many vibrant Jewish communities during this period and we know of three major Masoretic traditions, Palestinian, Babylonian, Tiberian. The Palestinian and Babylonian systems are generally thought to be older than the Tiberian system, which is far more developed. The Tiberian system is named after the city of Tiberias, a center of Jewish learning in the eighth and ninth centuries. The Tiberian system became the most widely accepted system; most surviving manuscripts are Tiberian. These three major Masoretic systems begin to develop in the sixth to seventh centuries (Dotan 1971-72: 1416). Both the Palestinian and the Babylonian systems used symbols placed above the letters, while the Tiberian system primarily uses symbols below or to the side of the letters. All three systems used different symbols to represent the vowels. They differed from each other not only in the symbols, but also in the quality of the vowels represented by the symbols.

The main function of the vowels and the accents was to preserve the proper reading and recitation of the text. The accents *(te'amim)* in particular have three functions: to guide the recitation of the text during the service according to musical motifs or tropes, to indicate word stress, and to indicate the syntactical relation between the words as either conjunctive or disjunctive (Yeivin 1980: 157). In addition, three symbols do not have a strong relation to the tropes: *maqqef, paseq,* and *ga'ya.* These three symbols indicate, respectively, conjunction — two words chanted with a single stress as though they were one, separation of the pronunciation of two words, and word stress — using the technique of slowing down the articulation of a syllable or word (Tov 1992: 68). The accents are not musical notes; they do not indicate pitch or the duration of a given note (see Dotan 1971-72: 1460-61) The accents refer to the groups of notes or tropes to which the words are chanted, and guide the reader in fitting the words to the tropes properly.

In the Tiberian system, there are two sets of accents, one for the three poetic books Job, Proverbs, and Psalms and a second set for the twenty-one prose books. The system of accents for the poetic books differs considerably from the prose set and is more complex.

Within each set of accents are two types of accents, disjunctive ("rulers" or *domini*) and conjunctive ("servants" or *servi*). Ancient interpretation is often reflected in the indication of the type of relationship between words. The disjunctive accents in particular were used by the Masoretes to indicate pauses in the text that could strongly affect the meaning (Tov 1992: 69-71). *BHS* includes a useful table of accents for both the poetic and the prose books, categorized according to whether they are disjunctive or conjunctive. Yeivin (1980: 157-274) has an extensive discussion of the Tiberian accent system, with numerous examples.

The Vocalization System

The Tiberian vocalization system became dominant in Jewish communities throughout the world. There were probably numerous subsystems within Tiberian tradition. By the tenth century, these are reduced to only two or three. Two families from Tiberias came to dominate the tradition, the family of ben Naphtali and the family of ben Asher. Members of these families are sometimes mentioned in the *masorah* along with a few other figures from the last generations of the Masoretes. The eventual reception of the tradition of ben Asher seems to have been assured by the approval of Maimonides (1135-1204) and his use of a codex annotated by Aaron ben Moses ben Asher, the last member of the ben Asher family. This was probably the Aleppo Codex. The ben Asher tradition is the most highly respected within Judaism; most surviving mss. and all printed editions reproduce a ben Asher text. The most famous example of a manuscript that reproduces a form of the ben Asher text is the Leningrad Codex, dating from 1009 CE (see Freedman 1998).

Scholars have questioned the authenticity of the Tiberian vocalization system. That is to say, they have questioned the assumption that it reproduces an ancient reading tradition accurately. These questions developed during the study of the differences between the Tiberian vocalization and the transcriptions of Hebrew words found in Origen's Hexapla, the Greek versions, and in some of Jerome's commentaries (see Barr 1967). For example:

	MT	Transliteration
Jer. 32:7	dodeka	dodach
Ps. 36:1	le'ebed	laabd

These two examples illustrate the different treatment of the second person masculine singular suffix and the vocalization of segolate nouns. In the first example the Masoretes have vocalized the form as *dodeka* (your uncle) with the second person masculine singular possessive suffix pronounced "*-ka.*" The form as given in transliterated sources, however, is *dodach,* which seems to suggest that before the time of the Masoretes, the suffix was not pronounced "*-ka*" but perhaps as "*-ak.*"

In the second example the form is vocalized in the MT as *leʿebed* ("of the servant"), whereas in the transliteration it is *laabd.* The meaning is not changed, but the vowel pattern for this type of noun in Tiberian Masoretic Hebrew is *ʿebed* with "e" vowels (seghol [..]), one of which comes between the last two consonants of the word, "b" (beth [ב]) and "d" (daleth [ד]). Usually in Tiberian Masoretic Hebrew, two consonants at the end of a word will have a vowel between them. In the transliterated form, *laabd,* the form occurs without the vowel between the two final consonants. Scholars explain such differences as due to either changes in the Hebrew language between the time of the transliterations and the Masoretic forms or regional or dialectical variations in pronunciation. If the first explanation is correct, then the Masoretic vocalization represents a more recent pronunciation, further removed from that of the biblical period. If the second explanation is correct, then the Masoretic vocalization is simply a regional or dialectical variation in pronunciation.

Because of differences like these, some scholars have suggested that the Tiberian vocalization did not preserve an authentic memory of early pronunciation of the text but is rather an artificial reconstruction based on what the Masoretes thought the word should sound like (see Tov 1992: 48-49 for a discussion of this view). The dual quality of the ב-ג-ד-כ-פ-ת (b-g-d-k-p-t) letters is also part of this argument. More recent evidence, however, has led to a revision of this view. For example, some of the Qumran manuscripts contain an orthography that uses the same form of the second person masculine singular suffix as the Masoretes. It seems more likely that, instead of being artificial, the Tiberian vocalization may show late or possibly dialectical forms (see Holmstedt 2000).

The Impact of Format: Scroll vs. Codex

It was probably in the seventh century that the codex (book) form began to be utilized for copies of the Tanak intended for study purposes. Unlike scolls intended for liturgical use, these codices could contain a vocalized and accented text and Masoretic notes. The text of the entire Tanak could be contained in a single codex. The change in format not only allowed the copying of the entire

---

Manuscripts of the Hebrew Bible

Second Temple Period to the Earliest Masoretic Codices
Various manuscripts from the Judean desert (Reed 1994):
  Qumran (from c. 275 BCE to c. 68 CE)
  Masada (before 73 CE)
  Wadi Murabba'at (50-100 CE)
The Cairo Codex (C, 896 CE; see Yeivin 1980: 20-21)
The Aleppo Codex (A, c. 925 CE; Yeivin 1980: 16-18)
British Museum Manuscript *Or* 4445 (B, c. 925 CE; Yeivin 1980: 19-20)
The Leningrad Codex (L, 1009 CE; Yeivin 1980: 18-19)

---

collection onto a form that was easier to handle and to store, but it also forced the community to fix the order of compositions in the collection.

The oldest extant Masoretic codices are listed in the accompanying table. The Cairo Codex contains the Prophets. The Aleppo Codex originally contained the entire Tanak but was damaged in a fire during anti-Jewish riots in 1948, and approximately 86 pages were destroyed (Yeivin 1980: 16-18). It is used as the base text of the Hebrew University Bible. The Leningrad Codex contains the entire Tanak and has been used as the base text of the *Biblia Hebraica* since 1937.

SUMMARY OF THE WORK OF THE MASORETES

The work of the Masoretes resulted in the preservation of the text of the Tanak. Their vowel and accent systems preserved the proper reading of the text. The collection of notes and observations in the *Mp* and the *Mm* assured the proper copying of the text and eventually its proper printing. The vowel and accent systems also allowed the Masoretes to present a definite understanding of the meaning of the text. Especially the accents, which have as much to do with the syntax of the verses as the chanting, present a specific understanding of the relation of the words to one another, thus excluding some meanings and emphasizing others (Tov 1992: 69-71).

The Masoretic notes contained in the *Mp* and the *Mm* were supplemented by additional notes and observations gathered at the ends of individual books, the ends of sections, such as the Torah or the Nevi'im, as well as at the end of the codices. This material might include lists of open and closed sections or of the *sedarim* and other materials. The *masorah* itself became the object of study (see Yeivin 1980: 125-31) and has sometimes been published separately along with various studies on different aspects of it. From the tenth century to the present, there is an almost uninterrupted stream of Masoretic handbooks and individual studies (Yeivin 1980: 144-55). This begins with the work *Diqduqqe ha-Te'amim*, attributed to Aaron ben Moses ben Asher in the tenth century CE. Many of these important older works have been edited and published in critical editions (see Yeivin 1980: 150-52).

By the tenth century, much of the material gathered in the *masorah* pertained to more than the preservation of the text and the reading tradition. The material of the *masorah* is important as the beginning of a description of the language of the text, a grammatical analysis. The grammatical study of the language of the Tanak may be said to begin in the tenth century, with the work of Saadia ben Joseph, normally known as Saadia Gaon. The work of Saadia is the first in a long line of grammatical studies, long before the "rediscovery" of the Hebrew language among Christian scholars in western Europe in the twelfth century. The work of the Jewish grammarians is dependent on and grows out of the work of the Masoretes.

THE POST-MASORETIC PERIOD

The time span from the oldest known codices in the ninth century to the first printed Hebrew Bible is less than six hundred years. The first complete printed Hebrew Bible was produced by the Soncino brothers in 1488 (see Mulder 1990: 116-19 for a discussion of the following editions). This was followed in 1491-93 by the Naples Bible, also produced by Soncino. In 1495, Gershom Soncino, who had moved to Brescia, produced an improved version of the 1488 Bible in a small octavo format, a sort of pocket edition. The folio-sized volumes were too difficult to transport. The Soncino 1495 edition was used by Luther for his translation of the OT. In 1514-17, the first Polyglot Bible was printed at Alcalá de Henares (Latin Complutum) under the patronage of Cardinal Ximénes de Cisneros. This first printed Bible produced in Spain was not authorized by Pope Leo X until 1520, three years after the death of Cardinal Cisneros. A facsimile edition was issued beginning in 1983.

Slightly later than the printing of the Polyglot, in 1516-17, Daniel Bomberg, a Christian merchant who settled in Venice, hired Felix Pratensis to edit the first Rabbinic Bible. This was published in four volumes and included the Targumim and commentaries but not the *masorah*. In 1524-25, Bomberg produced the Second Great Rabbinic Bible, edited by Jacob ben Hayyim ibn

Adonijah, and it became the standard text of printed forms of the Hebrew Bible for nearly four hundred years. It, too, was issued in four volumes and included the Targumim and the commentaries of Rashi, Ibn Ezra, David and Moses Kimhi, and Levi ben Gershom. The *masorah* was gathered from different mss. for this edition. The first break from the Rabbinic Bible came in 1611, when Buxtorf produced a small-format edition which, unlike previous editions, was based partially on Sephardic manuscripts. This edition served as the basis of the first critical edition, prepared in 1720 by Michaelis, who used nineteen printed editions as well as five mss. from Erfurt.

Between 1905 and 1906, the first edition of Kittel's well-known *Biblia Hebraica* was produced (see Tov 1992: 374-76; Würthwein 1995: 42-43 for discussions of *Biblia Hebraica* editions). The basis of the first and second editions was the 1524-25 edition of Bomberg with certain variations and additions. In 1937, for the third edition, the Firkowitch I. B19a (also known as Leningrad [L]) ms. was used, because it represented the oldest complete Ben Asher Masoretic ms. known at that time (for a facsimile edition of Leningrad Codex, see Freedman 1998). Beginning in 1967, the next edition of *Biblia Hebraica (Stuttgartensia) (BHS)* began to appear. It includes the *Mp* in the margin in slightly revised form. There is currently another revision in process that has been labeled *Biblia Hebraica Quinta.* This revision is being carried through with the assistance of the United Bible Societies (see Weis 2002 for a discussion of this project; see de Waard 1998 for a discussion of the forthcoming edition).

The *Hebrew University Bible* uses the Aleppo Codex where it is extant and includes both the *Mp* and the *Mm* of the Aleppo Codex. Since 1975, Isaiah (Goshen-Gottstein 1995) and Jeremiah (Tov, Talmon, and Rabin 1997) have appeared. Currently, Ezekiel is in an advanced state of preparation.

Both the *Hebrew University Bible* and *Biblia Hebraica Quinta* continue the tradition of diplomatic critical editions. A diplomatic edition gives the text of a single ms. with critical notes on variants from other witnesses, as opposed to an eclectic edition, which gives a text reconstructed on the basis of many mss. along with critical notes and variants from other witnesses. Like the earlier editions, *Biblia Hebraica Quinta* will offer suggested emendations in the apparatus. Both editions also correct and in some places complete the *masorah* transmitted with the manuscript and include apparatuses in which much information is presented concerning the text beyond that gathered in the *masorah.* Both present readings from early Hebrew manuscripts, citations from rabbinic literature, and readings from the ancient translations of the Hebrew Bible such as the LXX.

Another type of edition of the Hebrew text will be that of the *Oxford*

Hebrew Bible (Hendel 1998: 109-15; Hendel, et al. forthcoming). It will use the Leningrad Codex as a copy text, but will present an emended version of L, one that attempts to remove errors in the text, thus an eclectic critical edition.

In addition to many fine printed editions of the MT, there are also electronic forms of the MT available for most computer platforms. Most of these versions, both those online and those used in stand-alone computer software, derive from the Michigan-Claremont text, first encoded by H. Van Dyke Parunak and R. Whitaker from the Leningrad Codex text and corrected by a team led by A. Groves and E. Tov.

CONCLUSION

In this chapter, we have discussed some of the important contributions to the transmission and interpretation of the text of the Hebrew Bible, especially the activities of those scholars called the Masoretes. From the time the text first achieved written from, an important goal has been the accurate transmission of the text with as few errors as possible. Alongside this goal has been the complementary goal of the accurate reading and interpretation of the text. The work of the Masoretes, the slow development of the material we call the *masorah* was and is an essential element in achieving these goals. The *masorah* preserves data fundamental to the development and preservation of reading traditions and of grammar.

Grammar especially is a natural outgrowth of the thousands of detailed observations in the *masorah.* Yet the *masorah,* which achieved a climax in its development in the eighth to ninth centuries CE, became disassociated from individual mss. not long thereafter and became more of a decoration than a commentary on the text that it accompanied. It was only with the rise of printing that the process of recovering the *masorah* began. Especially in the last century, much progress has been made in the study of this ancient collection of traditions that provide the information that allows us to read the text of the Hebrew Bible.

BIBLIOGRAPHY

Barr, J.
1967   "Vocalization and the Analysis of Hebrew Among the Ancient Translators." In
        B. Hartmann, ed., *Hebräische Wortforschung. Festschrift zum 80 Geburtstag von
        Walter Baumgartner.* VTSup 16, 1-11. Leiden: Brill.

Barthélemy, D.

1963   *Les devanciers d'Aquila.* VTSup 10; Leiden: Brill.

Birnbaum, S. A.

1954-57 *The Hebrew Scripts.* Two parts. London: Paleographia.

Brown, D.

2003   "Jerome and the Vulgate," in *HBI*[1], 355-79.

Cohen, G. D.

1956   "The Talmudic Age." In L. W. Schwartz, ed., *Great Ages and Ideas of the Jewish People,* 141-212. New York: Modern Library.

Dotan, A.

1971-72 "Masorah," in *EncJud* Supplement, 1402-82.

Dotan, A. (ed.)

2001   *Biblia Hebraica Leningradensia: Prepared According to the Vocalization, Accents, and Masora of Aaron ben Moses ben Asher in the Leningrad Codex.* Peabody: Hendrickson.

Elliger, K., and W. Rudolph (eds.)

1967-77 *Biblia Hebraica Stuttgartensia.* Stuttgart: Deutsche Bibelgesellschaft.

Freedman, D. N. (ed.)

1998   *The Leningrad Codex: A Facsimile Edition.* Grand Rapids: Eerdmans/Leiden: Brill.

Fuller, R.

1990   "Early Emendations of the Scribes: The *Tiqqune Sopherim* in Zechariah 2:12." In H. W. Attridge, J. J. Collins, and T. H. Tobin, eds., *Of Scribes and Scrolls: Studies on the Hebrew Bible, Intertestamental Judaism, and Christian Origins,* 21-28. Lanham: University Press of America.

Goshen-Gottstein, M. H.

1965   *The Book of Isaiah, Sample Edition with Introduction.* Jerusalem: Magnes.

Greenspoon, L.

2003   "Hebrew into Greek: Interpretation in, by, and of the Septuagint," in *HBI*[1], 80-113.

Hendel, R. S. (ed.)

1998   *The Text of Genesis 1–11: Textual Studies and Critical Edition.* Oxford: Oxford University Press.

Hendel, R. S., et al. (eds.)

forthcoming *The Oxford Hebrew Bible.* New York: Oxford University Press.

Holmstedt, R. D.

2000   "The Phonology of Classical Hebrew: A Linguistic Study of Long Vowels and Syllable Structure." *Zeitschrift für Althebräistik* 13: 145-56.

Kelly, P. H., D. S. Mynatt, and T. G. Crawford (eds.)
1998   *The Masorah of Biblia Hebraica Stuttgartensia: Introduction and Annotated Glossary.* Grand Rapids: Eerdmans.

McCarthy, C.
1981   *The Tiqqune Sopherim and Other Theological Corrections in the Masoretic Text of the Old Testament.* Göttingen: Vandenhoeck und Ruprecht.

Morrow, W. S.
1991   "Ketib and Qere," *ABD* 4.24-30.

Mulder, M. J.
1990   "The Transmission of the Biblical Text." In M. J. Mulder, ed., *Mikra: Text, Translation, Reading, and Interpretation of the Hebrew Bible in Ancient Judaism and Early Christianity,* 87-135. Philadelphia: Fortress.

Nadich, J.
1998   *Rabbi Akiba and His Contemporaries.* Northvale: Aronson.

Neusner, J.
1980   *Torah from Our Sages: Pirke Avot.* Chappaqua: Behrman.

Oesch, J. M.
1979   *Petucha und Setuma. Untersuchungen zu einer überlieferten Gliederung im hebräischen Text des AT.* Freiburg: Universitätsverlag; Göttingen: Vandenhoeck und Ruprecht.

Reed, S. A.
1994   *The Dead Sea Scrolls Catalogue: Documents, Photographs, and Museum Inventory Numbers.* Revised and edited by M. J. Lundberg and M. B. Phelps. Missoula: Scholars.

Reif, S. C.
1994   "The Cairo Genizah and Its Treasures, with Special Reference to Biblical Studies." In D. R. G. Beattie and M. J. McNamara, eds., *The Aramaic Bible: Targums in the Historical Context,* 30-50. JSOTSup 166; Sheffield: JSOT.

Revell, E. J.
1992a   "Masorah," *ABD* 4.592-93.
1992b   "Masoretes," *ABD* 4.593-94.
1992c   "Masoretic Accents," *ABD* 4.594-96.
1992d   "Masoretic Studies," *ABD* 4.596-97.
1992e   "Masoretic Text," *ABD* 4.597-99.
1992f   "Scribal Emendations," *ABD* 5.1011-12.

Rodkinson, M. L.
1918   *The History of the Talmud from the Time of Its Formation, about 200 B.C., up to the Present Time* 1: *Its Development and the Persecutions since Its Birth up to Date, Including All Religious Disputes and Brief Biographies of the Separated Sects.* Boston: Talmud Society.

Sarna, N.

1971-72 "Bible, The Canon, Text, and Editions," *EncJud* Supplement, 814-36.

Scott, W. R.

1995   *Simplified Guide to BHS: Critical Apparatus, Masora, Accents, Unusual Letters and Other Markings.* 3rd ed.; Dallas: Bibal.

Segal, E.

1997   "Anthological Dimensions of the Babylonian Talmud," *Prooftexts* 17: 33-61.

Smalley, B.

1970   *The Study of the Bible in the Middle Ages.* Notre Dame: University of Notre Dame Press.

Snaith, N. H.

1971-72 "Bible, Printed Editions (Hebrew)," *EncJud* Supplement, 836-41.

Stenring, K. (trans.), R. A. Gilbert, and A. E. Waite (eds.)

2004   *Book of Formation or Sepher Yetzirah: Attributed to Rabbi Akiba Ben Joseph.* Berwick: Nicolas-Hays.

Strack, H. L., and G. Stemberger (eds.); J. Neusner and M. Bockmuehl (trans.)

1992   *Introduction to the Talmud and Midrash.* Minneapolis: Fortress.

Talmon, S.

1964   "Aspects of the Textual Transmission of the Bible in the Light of the Qumran Manuscripts." *Textus* 4: 95-132.

Tene, D.

1971-72 "Hebrew Linguistic Literature [up to the Sixteenth Century]," *EncJud* 1352-90.

Tov, E.

1992   *Textual Criticism of the Hebrew Bible.* Minneapolis: Fortress; Assen/Maastricht: Van Gorcum.

Tov, E., S. Talmon, and H. Rabin (eds.)

1997   *Sefer Yirmeyahu.* Jerusalem: Magnes.

Waard, J. de

1998   *Biblia Hebraica Quinta fasciculus extra seriem Librum Ruth.* Stuttgart: Deutsche Bibelgesellschaft.

Waltke, B. K., and M. O'Connor (eds.)

1990   *Introduction to Biblical Hebrew Syntax.* Winona Lake: Eisenbrauns.

Weil, G. E.

1971   *Massorah Gedolah.* Rome: Pontifical Biblical Institute.

Weis, R. D.

2002   "Biblia Hebraica Quinta and the Making of Critical Editions of the Hebrew Bible."

A Journal of Biblical Textual Criticism 7 = http://rosetta.reltech.org/TC/vol07/
Weis2002.html.

Würthwein, E.
1995   *The Text of the Old Testament.* Trans. E. F. Rhodes. 2nd ed.; Grand Rapids: Eerdmans.

Yeivin, I.
1980   *Introduction to the Tiberian Masorah.* Trans. E. J. Revell. Missoula: Scholars.

CHAPTER 7

The Text of the New Testament

J. Keith Elliott

Although the NT was originally composed in Greek, it was soon translated into other languages, notably Latin, Syriac, Coptic, Gothic, Armenian, Georgian, and Slavonic. Inevitably, prior to the invention of the printing press, the dissemination of the text was dependent on handwritten copies made by scribes. Accidental errors and deliberate changes were introduced at each stage of copying. Modern textual critics are able to collect, collate, and then determine the significance of the differences among mss., those in Greek as well as the early translations, with a view to re-establishing what may have been the original text of the NT. The reestablishment of the original text of the translations shows us the word choices that ancient translators made and thus indicates how the Greek text read at the time of these translations.

As a consequence of recent scholarly endeavor, different types of text have been identified in surviving mss. Mss. sharing certain characteristics were sorted into "text types." These characteristics include common additions, omissions, and changes to the text that can be traced back to a particular ms. or groups of mss. Broader categories or text-types are also identified and given names (not always entirely appropriate) such as "Western" or "Neutral," "Alexandrian," and "Byzantine" or "Syrian." The Western text originated as early as the middle of the second century and is characterized by paraphrase. The Alexandrian text is characterized by careful philological work and a concern for literary style. The Neutral text, although not "neutral," has been considered the best representation of the original text of the NT, with less corruption. The category with the largest number of mss. is the so-called Byzantine text-type, a grouping that exhibits a certain fixity and standardization, and was the dominant text throughout the Middle Ages. It is traced to the fourth century, and is a mixed text with characteristics of the Western, Alexandrian, and Neutral text-types. More will be said about this text-type below. But, in general terms, this was (and is) the text commonly distributed and used in the Greek-speaking church, and was the basis for the *textus receptus,* the edition used for the translation of the KJV NT (Metzger and Ehrman 2005: 176-80).

The Latin versions of the NT had a similarly checkered tradition, until they too became standardized. The earliest Latin translations (the so-called "Old Latin" versions) were relatively free and varied considerably. In the Latin Vulgate, Jerome tried to bring some unity to the tradition (see Brown 2003), although the Vulgate itself, like all early literature, became subject to the vagaries of copying over time, and it, too, was corrupted (Metzger and Ehrman 2005: 100-109).

THE ENTRY OF GREEK INTO THE WEST

For centuries, the churches owned, used, and relied upon single ms. copies of the Scriptures. Most churches or monasteries and, in rare cases, individuals would have had access to only one copy of the Bible, typically in separated sections. For instance, they might have a fourfold Gospel book, the Torah, a Psalter, or the Pauline corpus. For them, the form of the text that happened to be in their mss. was the definitive, canonical version of those writings. Almost no one saw multiple copies of a particular text. This made it very unlikely that readers would be aware of textual differences, since they would not be able to compare one copy with another, and note any variant readings. Some rare scholars, like Jerome and Origen (see *HBI*[1], 48; Brown 2003: 357), did pursue comparative studies, and were concerned with such variation. It was not until the time of the Renaissance and Reformation, however, that anything comparable to textual criticism as a science was to emerge. As we enter the Renaissance period, we observe that the standardized form of the Latin text of the NT was increasingly compared with and challenged by Greek copies of the NT that circulated in the West, first as mss., and later in printed editions.

Printing created a revolutionary change in the way the biblical text could be transmitted. It was no longer necessary for texts to be reproduced as individual copies written by scribes, although mss. continued to be written for some time afterwards, especially in remote places. Multiple copies of the same text could be widely distributed, and this multiplication had the effect of democratizing literary culture, standardizing the text, and encouraging scholars to edit the texts, including the Bible, more scientifically.

The first printed Bible, named the Mazarin Bible after a copy in the library of Cardinal Jules Mazarin (1602-61), was the Vulgate version (see Brown 2003). This was Gutenberg's forty-two-line Bible, published in the 1450s. The first Hebrew Bible was printed in 1488 in Soncino. By 1500, the Bible had been printed in part or completely in several vernacular languages including German (Mentel Bibel: 1466), French, Italian, Catalan, Dutch (1470s), and Czech (before 1500) (Darlow and Moule 1903; see also chapters 15 and 16 below). These first printed translations of the Bible had all been based on the Vulgate.

Latin had been the language of the Christian Scriptures in the West for a millennium and was assumed by the Roman Catholic Church to be superior to the Greek (and Hebrew). The Renaissance changed that. A move against Latin began in Protestant circles, for whom the Latin was too closely associated with the church of Rome. From the sixteenth century on, scholars began to emphasize the importance of the Greek text as the repository of divine revelation and the ultimate standard by which the Vulgate and other translations of the NT should be judged. This attitude clearly influenced not only the way in which the Scriptures were read and interpreted, but also the choice of text on which those interpretations were based (see also chapters 9 and 14 below).

Even with this emphasis on the Greek text, the printing of the Bible in Greek came relatively late. Few in the West knew Greek, and even fewer needed a Bible in that language. The absence of proper Greek fonts may also have contributed to the delay in printing Greek texts. The *Magnificat* and *Benedictus* were printed in Greek, annexed to a printed Greek Psalter in Milan in 1481, and were later printed in Venice, in 1486. The Aldine Press in Venice republished the 1486 edition in 1496-97. John 1–6 in Greek was published in Venice in 1504, and John 1:1-14 in Tübingen in 1514 (Metzger and Ehrman 2005: 137-38); but the whole NT in Greek had to await Erasmus's 1516 edition (discussed below) and the *Complutensian Polyglot* (1522). Thus, no printed Greek NT was available prior to 1516. Luther's German NT (1522; see chapter 10 below), translated from Erasmus's Greek edition, was preceded by some eighteen separate German translations from Latin. Tyndale's English translation (1526) also used the Greek text of Erasmus (see chapter 16 below).

The Fall of Constantinople in 1453 was a key moment and had two differing consequences. On the one hand, the collapse of the center of the Greek-speaking church meant that the Greek-speaking Christians were unable to initiate (or were inhibited in developing) printing presses. On the other hand, the removal of Greek mss. from Constantinople to the West made them available to Western scholars, particularly in Italy. The arrival in the

West of Cardinal Bessarion (1403-72), Metropolitan of Nicaea, helped stimulate the learning of Greek. An eminent scholar, Bessarion drew attention to deficiencies in the Latin Vulgate by comparing it to the underlying Greek. As we shall see, scholarship such as Bessarion's set a precedent in biblical studies. After his death, Bessarion's library of Greek and Latin mss. was bequeathed to Venice, and formed the beginnings of the Biblioteca Marciana (Monfansani 1995). The Biblioteca della Badia at Grottaferrata also became a major depository of Greek texts in Italy, including many biblical mss., and became an important center for Greek learning during the Renaissance, largely due to Bessarion's influence.

The *Complutensian Polyglot*

Desiderius Erasmus of Rotterdam's *Novum Instrumentum* of 1516 (2001a) was the first edition of the Greek NT printed and published. The NT for the multi-volume *Complutensian Polyglot* was the first edition of the Greek NT actually printed. Cardinal Francisco (*né* Gonzalo) Ximénes de Cisneros (1436-1517), Archbishop of Toledo, had inaugurated an edition of the *Polyglot* that for the NT portion was to be in Latin and Greek. This NT was ready two years earlier than Erasmus's edition — the subscription to Revelation has the date January 10th, 1514 — but it was not published until it appeared as volume V of the complete six-volume Bible about 1522. It was printed in Spain in Alcalá de Henares, known in Latin as Complutum (Spottorno 2002; see also Bedouelle's article in this volume).

One explanation proffered by modern scholars for the publication delay from 1514 to 1522 is that the *Polyglot* could not be published until all the mss. loaned by the Vatican for the purpose of editing the Greek text had been returned by the editors. Perhaps a more plausible explanation of the delay is the legal disputes in Spain regarding the disposal of Ximénes' estate, to which the printed copies of the *Polyglot* belonged. Another cause for the delay may have been a reluctance to publish a Bible in any language other than Latin. Even when the work was published, the Latin OT was printed between the Hebrew (on the left) and the Septuagint (in the right-hand column). The explanation for that arrangement is offered in the prologue to volume I, namely, that it is like Christ on the cross between two criminals *(Mediam autem inter as latinam beati Hieronymi translationem velut inter synagogam et orientalem ecclesiam posuimus: tanquam duos hinc et inde latrones medium autem Iesum, hoc est Romanam sive Latinam ecclesiam collocantes . . . !)*. This shows that the Vulgate was being privileged even before the formulation of Trent in 1546, when the Vulgate was confirmed as the official translation of the Roman Catholic Church (see chapter 15 below).

In his dedication to Leo X, Ximénes states that the NT was finished first. In the preface to the NT the editors claim to have consulted ancient texts. However, "ancient" mss. were not actually used. The text-type of the Complutensian NT is typically medieval (see below on the Byzantine text-type).

In any case, given the actual dates printed on the published volumes (Volume V: NT, 1514; and Volumes I-IV: Old Testament, July 10th, 1517, shortly before Ximénes' death), there was a very long delay before the *Complutensian Polyglot* was actually published in 1522. The late publication of this *Polyglot* may be satisfactorily explained by the fact that Erasmus's *Novum Instrumentum* (1516) had an imperial privilege issued by "Maximilianus Caesar Augustus" (i.e., Maximilian I, d. 1519), and this was printed on its title page. This forbade the importing of another Greek NT for four years in the whole of the Holy Roman Empire. Thus, Ximénes and his staff knew they would have to wait until 1520 at least if they were to sell the *Polyglot* in Europe. Nevertheless, an Aldine edition in 1518 largely repeated Erasmus's text, but without acknowledgement (Metzger and Ehrman 2005: 137-49).

There were many errors in the *Complutensian Polyglot* edition of the NT: typographical slips, wrong augments and orthography, grammatical mistakes, and the occasional accidental inclusion of editorial matter into the text. As a result, the *Complutensian Polyglot* was reprinted, with some changes and additions, in Antwerp by Plantin in 1569-72. The Greek NT of this *Polyglot* was reprinted by the same printer in 1573, 1574, 1583, and 1584, and in Geneva by various printers in 1609, 1610, 1612, 1619, 1620, 1622, 1627, and 1628 (Bentley 1983: 70-111).

It is claimed that Cardinal Ximénes spent some 50,000 ducats buying mss., a sum said to represent one quarter of the Cardinal's annual income. It was obviously not the habit then to indicate which mss. were being followed, any more than it had been for scribes to identify their exemplars. Such information, normative in modern critical editions, was not revealed in those early years. One of the six or seven editors of the *Polyglot*, Stunica (Jacobus López de Stunica, also known as Diego López Zúñiga) refers to a Codex Rhodiensis, but it is not known what that ms. is, and it is probably no longer extant. Codex Vaticanus certainly was not consulted, although it was then in the Vatican Library (see below). Mainly, what were consulted were Byzantine mss. from the tenth century and later (Bentley 1983: 70-111).

No NT mss. seem to have been in Alcalá, where the *Complutensian Polyglot* was printed. An early catalogue lists the mss. likely to have been there at the beginning of the sixteenth century. Tregelles (1854: 15-18) reproduces this

catalogue, but there are no NT Greek mss. in it. Therefore, the tradition that
Vatican mss. were loaned is probably accurate. However, although there are
some 224 continuous-text mss. of the NT in the Vatican today (and approximately 120 lectionaries), none has been identified as having been consulted by
the editors of the *Complutensian Polyglot*.

The so-called *Comma Johanneum* (i.e., 1 John 5:7b-8a, see below) was
translated into Greek from the Latin in the *Polyglot*. Certain other verses
(Rom. 16:5; 2 Cor. 5:10; 6:15; Gal. 3:19) were likewise probably translated from
Latin. A key issue is the extent to which the Latin proved the dominant part-
ner. We shall see similar influences when we turn to Erasmus's edition below.
Of course, in many ways such a practice is not surprising, given the familiarity of the Latin wording to editors of that time. However, there are a thousand
textual differences between the Greek and the Latin columns, including the
omission in Greek of Acts 8:37 and 9:5. This would be expected, since the
Greek and Latin mss. each have their own history of transmission and textual
corruption (Metzger and Ehrman 2005: 250-71).

As a result of the increased learning of the age, several other polyglots
were published. The *Antwerp Polyglot* (1569-72), the *Paris Polyglot* (1629-45),
and Walton's *London Polyglot*, which also incorporated the Syriac text (1655-
57), were significant milestones. The printing of editions in more than one
language may reflect either a lack of confidence that any one of these was superior to the other or, on a more mundane level, that readers needed cribs. In
any case, the polyglots stimulated scholarship (Hall 1966). The readers of
polyglots were polymaths equally at home in Greek, Latin, and Hebrew. The
growing number of study editions (for surely the main purpose in such publications was to help the scholar in the study more than the devout in the
church) facilitated an academic rather than devotional reading. Now the text,
sacred though it might be deemed, could be examined not only by the pious,
oriented to the principle of *"sola scriptura"* as encouraged by Protestantism,
but also by humanists desiring to study the Bible alongside, and in a comparable way to, secular literature.

Erasmus (1466/69-1536)

Erasmus's 1516 edition, published by Johann Froben of Basle, has the honor of
being the first published NT in Greek. Whatever Erasmus's motives in producing this bilingual edition may have been (we offer a suggestion below), as
early as 1515 Froben himself seems to have been determined to be the first to
publish a Greek NT. Possibly, he had been alerted to the plans afoot in Alcalá

and solicited Erasmus's help to achieve his end. Erasmus obliged. It may be no coincidence that Luther posted his theses in 1517. As we shall see later, the appearance of a Greek NT was seized upon by Protestants and used by them against the reliability of the Latin text — despite the promotion of the Greek NT by the church in Rome. Pope Leo X thanked Erasmus for his edition in a letter of 1518, and this was printed in the second and later editions (Bentley 1983: 112-93).

Erasmus's bilingual edition was a Greek text with a new translation or revision of the Latin, not a reproduction of the Latin Vulgate. It has been plausibly argued by de Jonge (1984) that Erasmus's main intention in publishing this *Novum Instrumentum* was to establish his own new Latin version. The claim of the long Latin title of the *Novum Instrumentum* that this was to be a revised and improved version may give some clue to his purpose. Since no printed Greek NT existed at the time, his edition could not therefore claim to be a "revised" text of the Greek NT, and the claim that this edition was an improvement must therefore apply to the Latin. Thus, in publishing a revised Latin NT, Erasmus was providing a better edition of the Scriptures in the European language, Latin, thereby promoting the spiritual and moral uplifting of Europe.

Erasmus had been working on aspects of the Latin and Greek text since 1512, encouraged no doubt by the criticisms of the Vulgate by Lorenzo Valla, the Renaissance humanist (1407-57), written some fifty years earlier (Bentley 1983: 32-69). Erasmus had discovered Valla's *Annotationes* in a monastery near Leuven in 1504, and published them in the following year (de Jonge 1988a, 1988b). The 1516 publication of the bilingual text was mainly understood as a publication of a Latin text. Erasmus's contemporaries criticized him for producing a new translation — they were less concerned with his Greek column. For instance he was criticized for having *mysterium* ("mystery") instead of *sacramentum* ("that which binds or obligates") at Eph. 5:32, a change seen as an attack on the sacrament of marriage, since the emphasis shifts from a binding sacrament to merely the mysterious aspect of the relationship between Christ and the church (Bentley 1983: 194-219; Rummel 1986: 123-80).

The publication sought to justify a new translation into Latin and to prove that Erasmus's Latin was compatible with the Greek. Nevertheless, on occasion, the Greek was a back-translation from the Latin. In other words, Erasmus used the Vulgate where he thought the Greek mss. were deficient. For instance, Acts 9:5-6, not extant in Greek at this point, was introduced from the Latin. As we have seen, this is in contrast to the *Complutensian Polyglot* text. Erasmus's annotations at Acts 9:5-6 show that he was aware that his Greek mss. lacked the longer text found in Latin. Nevertheless, he prints the longer read-

ing in a Greek reconstruction and this reading infiltrated the KJV: "It is hard
for thee to kick against the pricks. And he trembling and astonished said,
'Lord, what wilt thou have me to do?'" (Metzger and Ehrman 2005: 142-45).

Another place where Erasmus was obliged to retrovert from Latin was
the very end of Revelation, and that was a cause for criticism of his editions.
His available Greek witness (1r, now renumbered 2814 in the official Münster
register of Greek NT mss.) is lacking the last six verses (Rev. 22:16-21). So
Erasmus supplied the deficiency by translating the Latin into Greek. He
thereby created some readings that have no support in any known Greek witness. For example, at Rev. 22:19 he has in Greek "book of life," but all pre-
sixteenth-century Greek mss. have "tree of life." The word "book" came from
Latin mss. that had misread *ligno* ("wood") as *libro* ("book")! This error also
survives in the KJV (Metzger and Ehrman 2005: 142-45). Even if de Jonge is
right in saying that Erasmus was more concerned with producing a Latin NT
that could be justified by reference to Greek, the procedure at the end of Revelation may still be explained by the fact that he also needed to produce a
continuous and complete Greek text (de Jonge 1984).

There was the added complication of disentangling the actual biblical
text of Revelation from the accompanying commentary used in ms. 2814. This
meant that elsewhere in Revelation Erasmus sometimes used the Vulgate and
translated its wording into Greek. Examples are found, among others, at Rev.
2:2, 17; 3:5, (12,) 15; 13:10; some of those were still being perpetuated in later
editions of testaments dependent on Erasmus's edition.

At Matt. 14:12; Mark 1:16; and elsewhere, Erasmus "corrected" the Greek
of his ms. 2, possibly from the Latin. A gloss at Acts 10:6 appears in Erasmus's
Greek text, translated by him from Latin mss. That reading, unsupported by
Greek mss. (with the exception of the fifteenth-century ms. 69, where it appears in the margin in a hand later than the time of Erasmus), even persists in
the KJV! Acts 8:37 is not in the Greek ms. principally used by Erasmus (now
numbered 2815), although it is to be found in the margin of 2816, another of
his mss. He included the verse because he considered it to have been accidentally omitted by scribes *(arbitror omissum librariorum incuria).* Again, this
contrasts with text of the *Complutensian Polyglot* (Bentley 1983: 137-73).

The 1516 edition, like the *Complutensian Polyglot,* was dedicated to the
Pope, Leo X. Unfortunately, it was very faulty. Scrivener says it was the faulti-
est book he knew! (1894: 2.185). In many ways the Greek in the *Polyglot* is superior to Erasmus's (especially in Revelation).

New, corrected editions of Erasmus's text were subsequently printed.
The second edition (1519), which became the *Novum Testamentum* not
Novum Instrumentum, includes corrigenda, but many errors still survive in

the Greek. Some changes in the Greek were due to Erasmus's now having had use of another ms. (ms. 3). But, again, it was the Latin that caused further controversy. At John 1:1, instead of using *verbum* (word), the traditional (Vulgate) word found in his first edition, Erasmus translated the Greek *logos* (word) as *sermo* (conversation, discourse). That was deemed to be almost heretical (Metzger and Ehrman 2005: 145-46). The 1519 edition, however, formed the main basis for Luther's *Das Neue Testament Deutzsch* (1522) and Tyndale's 1526 translation, as well as perhaps the Tuscan (1530) and Spanish (1543) translations. These latter two, however, are more likely to be based on the 1527 and 1539 editions (see chapter 16 below). According to Erasmus, 3,300 exemplars of the first two editions were printed.

The third edition (1522) adds the Johannine Comma (*Comma Johanneum:* 1 John 5:7b-8a) because a Greek ms. had been found or, rather, written to order (see below). The Comma was subsequently repeated, with grammatical corrigenda in subsequent editions. This 1522 printing became probably the most influential of Erasmus's editions (de Jonge 1980)

The fourth edition (1527) has Greek, the Latin Vulgate, and Erasmus's Latin. The inclusion of the Vulgate may be seen as another attempt to defend his own Latin, and demonstrate its superiority over Jerome's version. This may be yet another clue to Erasmus's main purpose in publishing these editions. (Only in this fourth edition, and in the posthumous edition of 1542, sometimes called the seventh edition, does the Vulgate appear.) The title page of the 1527 edition gives a more neutral explanation of the added column, namely to enable a reader to compare his Latin with the Vulgate and to mark agreements and disagreements between them. In the Book of Revelation changes were introduced, many of them on the basis of the *Complutensian Polyglot,* a copy of which Erasmus had obtained by then (Metzger and Ehrman 2005: 148). Some of the original retranslations from Latin into Greek in Revelation were nevertheless unwittingly preserved, and these remained to influence later editions of the NT in Greek, as well as vernacular versions that were ultimately dependent on Erasmus's edition.

The fifth edition (1535) contains the Greek and Erasmus's Latin translation, again with changes made as a result of the *Polyglot.* The recent publication of Erasmus's NT text in the *Opera Omnia* (Erasmus 2001, 2004) is based on the 1535 edition, and shows variants in all five editions if these differ from the printed text for both the Greek and for Erasmus's Latin.

Whatever Erasmus's motives, he did edit a Greek NT, and eventually Greek was declared superior to Latin for the text of the NT. His Greek text may be described as eclectic. Outside Revelation, it is evident that he followed more than one ms. His "Apologia" in the preface of his first edition indicates

Mss. known to have been used by Erasmus

1. Basle Univ. Lib. A.N.IV 2, 12th century, e a p. This Ms. 1 was generally avoided, but nevertheless seems to have influenced Erasmus's choice of readings at Matt. 22:28; 23:25, etc.
2. Basle Univ. Lib. A.N.IV 1, 12th century, e. A plate of one page of this Ms. 2 appears in the 2nd edition of Aland and Aland (1989), and shows Erasmus's additions and the compositor's marks (2 and 2815 and a transcript of 2814 went to Froben for use by the typesetter). Ms. 1 was also in the hands of the proofreaders, who used it to emend the text, contrary to Erasmus's wishes.

817. Basle Univ. Lib. A.N.III 15, 15th century, e, with Theophylact's Commentary.

2815. Basle Univ. Lib. A.N.IV 4, 12th century, a p. This ms. had been loaned to Erasmus by its then owners, the Amerbach family.

2816. Basle Univ. Lib. A.N.IV 5, 15th century, a p.

2817. Basle Univ. Lib. A.N.III 11, 11th century, p.

2814. Augsburg University Library Bibl. Cod. I 1.4.1, 12th century, r. This ms. was borrowed from Johannes Reuchlin (1354/55-1422), the German humanist whose bilingual edition of the Psalter (Hebrew and Latin) may have influenced Erasmus in his decision to prepare a printed NT.

Erasmus also seems to have notes based on 69 (the Leicester codex), or a closely related ms. (69 contains e a p r). These would have come from his time in England (1511-14).

2105. Oxford Bodleian Auct. E 1.6, 14th (12th?) century, p, with Theophylact's Commentary. Erasmus used it mainly for this commentary.

Possibly, he also had E 07 Basle Univ. Lib. A.N.III 12, 8th century, e, but this has been disputed.

For his 1519 edition, Erasmus also had ms. 3 (now in Vienna, but then with the Augustinian canons of Corsendonck), and other (now unidentifiable) mss.

Erasmus's 1519 and 1522 editions also made use of the 1518 Aldine edition, which had been based on Erasmus's first edition, and on some Venetian mss.

By 1527, Erasmus also had access to the *Complutensian Polyglot*.

that he had used four Greek mss., presumably in Cambridge, during the preparation of a first draft. These have not been identified. By contrast, the Greek mss. he had to hand in Basle are relatively well-known. The consensus is that he mainly used mss. that had been bequeathed in 1443 to the Dominican monastery in Basle by John Stojkovic of Ragusa.

These and others are listed here with the currently registered number given first, followed by the library classification mark and the contents (shown under the conventional letters: e = Gospels; a = Acts and Catholic Epistles; p = Pauline corpus; r = Revelation) (Brandt 1998; Tarelli 1943, 1947).

Ms. 1 (of the twelfth century but with an older text form) is not Byzantine in type; rather, it has leanings to the Alexandrian text-type. Erasmus distrusted it, because of its tendency to support the Latin Vulgate. Modern text critics, by contrast, value it as an important witness, together with its allied family grouping, of which it is the head (family 1). Excluding 1 and E (07), Erasmus in 1516 had two mss. for the Gospels (2, 817), four for Paul (2105, 2815, 2816, 2817), two for Acts and the Catholic Epistles (2815, 2816), and one for Revelation (2814). In addition, notes on the readings in 69 (or a ms. of the same family, family 13) would have been to hand. Most of these are Byzantine in text-type. However, we need to remember that Erasmus valued ancient testimony, such as that found in works of Jerome, as may be seen in his defense of his reading at Acts 13:33 as "first" (Psalm) in the Vulgate, rather than "second" (Psalm), common to Greek mss. (Tregelles 1854: 29).

Erasmus's notes ("annotations") to his text were augmented in 1516-35. Some refer to readings found elsewhere (e.g., his notes to Heb. 1:3), but the mss. from which those readings were taken have not been identified. Erasmus also refers to some new readings (e.g., at 2 Pet. 3:1; Rev. 2:18), but these are not found in our current stock of extant mss. (Rummel 1986).

The importance of Erasmus's bilingual editions was that the sacrosanct Latin text of Jerome could be, and was, increasingly criticized by reference to the Greek. On one level, Erasmus's Latin is more elegant than Jerome's, and the objections to it were based on principle. Stunica, one of the editors of the *Complutensian Polyglot,* accused Erasmus's Latin text of being an open condemnation of the official Catholic Vulgate. As we saw above, the *Polyglot* tried to avoid this problem at least in its OT. The Council of Trent, in 1545-63, occasioned by the spread of Protestantism, therefore reaffirmed its view of the official nature of the Vulgate at its fourth session of 1546, and an edition was issued under the authority of Sixtus V in 1590 (the so-called Sixtine edition). This edition was promoted as definitive, and its text was declared inviolate and unalterable. The publication of Erasmus's and subsequent editions of the NT in Greek, as well as his own Latin version, necessitated and acted as a catalyst for such a declaration and for the publication of this officially sanctioned Vulgate (see chapter 15 below). However, the faults in the Sixtine edition required a revision, and this was issued in 1592 under Clement VIII. This Clementine edition was also promoted as "authoritative." In the Clementine revision, there are 3,000 changes from the "inviolate and unalterable" Sixtine edition!

The Johannine Comma *(Comma Johanneum)*

The *Comma Johanneum* refers to the additional words after 1 John 5:7a ("for there are three who bear witness"): ". . . in heaven, the Father, the Word and the Holy Spirit and these three are one, and there are three who bear witness on earth. . . ." In Greek, these words (with variations) are found today in the following mss. ranging from the tenth to the eighteenth centuries.

> 61, sixteenth century,
>
> 88, fourteenth century (the Comma is added in a sixteenth-century hand),
>
> 221, tenth century (added as a variant in the nineteenth century),
>
> 429, fourteenth century (added as a variant in the sixteenth century),
>
> 629, fourteenth-fifteenth centuries,
>
> 636, fifteenth century (added by a later hand),
>
> 918, sixteenth century,
>
> 2318, eighteenth century (a copy of the *textus receptus*), and
>
> 2473, seventeenth century (also a copy of the *textus receptus*).

Modern scholars reject the words, denying that they were original to 1 John (Metzger and Ehrman 2005: 146-48). They were introduced, probably accidentally, from a marginal gloss that saw in the three witnesses a trinitarian reference. The words are absent from all ancient versions (Syriac, Coptic, Slavonic, Ethiopic, Armenian) and appear in only certain Latin mss. No Greek fathers cite the words, even though in some cases the addition could have been useful in trinitarian controversies. The words first appear in Greek only after 1215 in a Greek version of the Latin Acts of the fourth Lateran Council. They are represented in some Latin sources from the fourth century onward. Since they occur in the Clementine Vulgate of 1592, they were consequently deemed authoritative by the Roman church. The *Complutensian Polyglot* had earlier retranslated this portion of text into Greek, but this did not include verse 8c. No Greek witnesses used for that edition contained the words.

It is significant that Lorenzo Valla failed to provide a "note" on these disputed words, even though he should have seen that they were absent from the Greek mss. he had at his disposal (he did include a note on v. 8c). He was probably hesitant to cause a theological problem. The compilers of the *Polyglot* may have shared that hesitation and thus included the verses. Erasmus himself was more principled, but even he eventually bowed to popular pressure to include this section. Erasmus had excluded the words from his first edition, and that omission (or, as he preferred to say, the "non-inclusion") was one of several criticisms of his edition. Erasmus indicated that he would have included these words only if a Greek witness including them were produced. The discovery of the inclusion of the Comma in ms. 61 (sixteenth century) persuaded Erasmus to include the words in his third edition in order to silence his critics over what he regarded as a minor point. However, Erasmus rightly suspected that ms. 61 was recent (de Jonge 1980).

LATER EDITIONS OF THE GREEK NEW TESTAMENT

The influence of the *Complutension Polyglot* and especially of Erasmus's editions was profound. In effect, the text of Erasmus, with relatively few changes, dominated all subsequent editions of the printed Greek NT for over three hundred years (Reicke 1960). The main editions may be sketched briefly (Turner 1924). The Aldine *Graeca Biblia* (a complete Bible in Greek), published in Venice in 1518, was used subsequently by Erasmus as if it were an authority to the Greek independent of his own. Actually this Aldine edition was mainly based on Erasmus's edition. It even perpetuated many of the typographical and other errors of his first edition. At the beginning of the sixteenth century, Aldus had even contemplated publishing a trilingual polyglot (prompted by his having heard of Ximénes' project), but it was never accomplished.

The 1534 Greek NT of the publisher Simon de Colines (Colinaeus) is said to have been based on Erasmus, the *Complutensian Polyglot,* and unknown mss. It occasionally supports "neutral" readings instead of Byzantine readings, but these are due to the influence of the Vulgate. The *Comma Johanneum* is not included.

Stephanus

Stephanus, or Robert Estienne (1503-59), Colines's stepson, produced three editions of the NT in Paris and one in Geneva (see chapters 9, 15, and 16 below). The Paris editions are:

1. 1546. A text based on Erasmus and on the *Complutensian Polyglot.* A good deal of the original Greek, especially in Revelation, was restored.
2. 1549. This has a similar text. Both the first and second editions are small format.

3. 1550. This became very influential, and in effect was treated as the standard Greek NT until 1881. It was the first Greek text with a critical apparatus, and included the witness of mss. collated by his son, Henry
Stephanus. This rudimentary and often faulty apparatus began the process of critical collation of Greek NT mss. Known as the *editio regia*, it
was based on Erasmus's editions of 1527 and 1535.

After the publication of his third edition, Stephanus moved to Geneva
and became a Calvinist. He reprinted his 1550 Greek testament in 1551 alongside the Vulgate and Erasmus's Latin, but without the 1550 critical apparatus.
This 1551 edition is the first to introduce versification (the introduction of
modern chapters is credited to Stephen Langton in the early thirteenth century).

Theodore Beza (1519-1605)

In Geneva, Beza published revisions of Stephanus's text, together with his
own Latin translation in 1565. Once again, we see that Latin was considered
important enough to merit inclusion, and retranslation of the Latin was considered a valuable aid to understanding the Greek text. A separate edition of
Beza's Latin had appeared in 1556, that is, ten years before his bilingual
(Greek-Latin) text. Further editions of Beza's Latin testament were subsequently published (Metzger and Ehrman 2005: 151-52).

Folio editions of the Greek NT were published in 1565, 1582, 1588-89, and
1598. This last edition, together with the last two editions of Stephanus, was
used for the KJV. Octavo editions appeared in 1565, 1567, 1580, 1590, and 1604,
and one was published posthumously in 1611. Not only do we see here a proliferation of editions promoting basically the same Greek text, but also the
wide dissemination of a text favored by Protestantism (Metzger and Ehrman
2005: 151-52).

Beza, who knew mss. 05 and 06 (see below), published a text that differs
from Stephanus some one hundred and fifty times, according to Scrivener's
calculation (1894). This is not a highly significant difference, but there are important changes. In Luke 2:22, for example, Beza read "her" (purification), as
did the *Polyglot*, a reading lacking ms. authority, but which, notwithstanding,
appears in the KJV. Yet again, we see the shaky textual basis for a reading
found in this influential English version.

The Elzevirs

The Elzevir (or Elzevier) family of Leiden were printers, publishers, and booksellers. The founder of the firm was Louis (ca. 1540-1617), who had seven sons. Three main editions of the Greek NT were published under this family's imprint. Unlike several other editions (e.g., Erasmus, Stephanus, and Beza), it is the publishing house by which the editions are known. The names of their editor(s) were not promoted. After much research, with painstaking detail, and using incontrovertible evidence, de Jonge argued in 1971 that the prefaces to the second and third editions are by Daniel Heinsius. He also suggested that the editor was probably Heinsius. Subsequently (1978), de Jonge reached the conclusion that the editor was another Leiden professor, Jeremias Hoelzlin (1583-1644).

The Leiden Elzevir editions are as follows. The first (1624) was a reprint of Stephanus's third edition, with changes based on Beza. This small format edition was published by Louis's grandson Isaac Elzevir (1596-1651), apparently in collaboration with Isaac's brother Abraham (1592-1652) and his uncle Bonaventure (1583-1652). The second (1633) was a text with changes from the earlier edition, published by Abraham and Bonaventure. Details are given by de Jonge (1978, esp. pp. 120-21 and Appendix I). The edition has a Preface written by Daniel Heinsius (1580-1655) (according to the identification by de Jonge). This is the preface that includes the words: *Textum ergo habes, nunc ab omnibus receptum: in quo nihil immutatum aut corruptum damus . . .* ("thus, you now have the universally received text, in which we present nothing that has been changed or is corrupted"). This casual phrase, almost a publishers' blurb, gave rise to the term *"textus receptus,"* which came to be used not only of this particular edition published in 1633 but by extension of the Greek text found in all the editions by Erasmus, Stephanus, and Beza, and beyond as well. The term even came to be used as a common description of current uncritical standard editions of Greek and Latin classical authors. The third edition (1641) was a revised version of the second edition, also published by Abraham and Bonaventure. There are also four later Amsterdam Elzevir editions.

The *Textus Receptus*

After our period other editions were published. Among them, those by John Fell in 1675 and by John Mill(s) in 1707 are noteworthy. Mill(s), a fellow at Queen's College, Oxford, had been encouraged by Fell and demonstrated the growing attention to variation between mss. and the need to collate and compare witnesses. His edition of the NT, therefore, contained the first extensive apparatus. This showed some 30,000 variants; the exhibition of such deviations (many shown then for the first time to be present in older witnesses) caused enormous adverse criticism. Readers became alarmed that the reliability of Scripture might be undermined. This furor retarded scholarly attempts to depart from the security and familiarity of the *textus receptus* (Fox 1954: 43-88). For that reason, the increasing awareness of mss. (many of them ancient) whose texts differed from the *textus receptus* did not result in the toppling of this text from its pedestal until the mid-nineteenth century.

All editions of the *textus receptus*, as loosely defined, are worthy of study in their own right. Although they are based on and are dependent upon Erasmus (and to a lesser extent on the text of the *Complutensian Polyglot*), they sometimes contain material no longer available, especially readings from mss. no longer extant.

The *textus receptus* is close to the *koine* (common) text of the Byzantine church, which may be traced back to the fourth and fifth centuries. Differences exist between the printed editions, but these are not so great. This proliferation of a stereotypical text, which originated with Erasmus, was unstoppable. It influenced the NT text of Western Christianity for centuries. It is the text of the majority of mss. of the medieval period. Not only do the largest number of extant Greek NT mss. come from the later periods (as is only to be expected), but they come from the Greek-speaking church centered on Constantinople — a narrower geographical base than in the first two Christian centuries, when Greek was the *lingua franca* of the Mediterranean world. Many consider that the Byzantine text-type was an ecclesiastically inspired or carefully controlled revision. Others see this text-type evolving naturally through the normal processes of scribal emendations, errors, and changes without ever being officially sanctioned or produced.

Even though the text in the majority of these later mss. conforms to this so-called Byzantine text-type, with its alleged conflated readings, interpolations, and additions, not all medieval mss. are Byzantine. One notable exception is 579, a Gospel ms. of the thirteenth century, now in Paris. Its text-type represents the so-called Alexandrian text of the great uncials, like that in Codex Vaticanus from nine centuries earlier. Efforts are being undertaken to identify other exceptional mss. among the bulk of Byzantine witnesses.

Most of the Greek mss. extant today are housed in the world's great libraries in, among other places, London, Paris, Vatican City, Oxford, Grottaferrata, St. Petersburg, Athens, and on Mount Athos. The numbers of those surviving from the ninth to the sixteenth centuries are roughly as follows: ninth: 17; tenth: 132; eleventh: 460; twelfth 590; thirteenth: 570; fourteenth:

540; fifteenth: 249; sixteenth: 140. Inevitably, the largest numbers come prior to the impact of the invention of printing and of the fall of Constantinople. Most Greek NT mss. have become available to modern scholars comparatively recently, thanks to concerted efforts to scour ancient depositories, and as a result of archaeological digs, but, as will be shown below, some famous Greek mss. have been available in the West for centuries.

The dependency of almost all the early printed editions on Erasmus's or Stephanus's text implies that, in each case, that text was increasingly being treated as if it were as sacrosanct as the Latin Vulgate promulgated by the Council of Trent! The influence of the text that ultimately goes back to Erasmus was immense. Even today, the *textus receptus* has its adherents: there are Christians who promote the text-type of the majority of Byzantine mss. and, as a consequence, favor the KJV above other English versions, because the *textus receptus* was the textual basis of its NT. There is even a society that promotes the "Majority Text." These mss. may be the majority of those of the NT, but their late dates and all the accumulated textual corruption make their use as the basis for translation unacceptable. One currently available Greek text is *The Greek New Testament according to the Majority Text* (Hodges and Farstad 1985). The *textus receptus* itself remains in print. It may even be suggested that the anchoring of the *textus receptus* as the definitive NT text has had the effect of influencing Protestantism's obsession with promoting dubious theories about infallible autographs and even of the inerrancy of Scripture, which have had a deleterious and debilitating influence on the editing of the NT in both Greek and English (Letis 1997).

MANUSCRIPTS OF THE GREEK NEW TESTAMENT

As we have seen, the printed editions were based on ms. copies of the NT. In subsequent centuries, other mss., some betraying a differing textual complexion from the *textus receptus,* were gradually being recognized by scholars as more reliable witnesses to the original text of the NT than that found in the medieval mss. Since 1881, most printed editions of the Greek NT differ considerably from the text in the edition of Erasmus, Beza, or Stephanus. Many of these differences are due to the ms. base used by their editors. When editing a critical edition of the Greek NT, most modern scholars dismiss as secondary the distinctive readings characteristic of the Byzantine text-type. Significantly, some of the mss. now adopted as authoritative for reestablishing the authentic text of the Greek NT were known to scholars as early as the fifteenth or sixteenth century.

Codex Vaticanus

The most famous authoritative ms. is Vaticanus, Greek codex 1209 (Cod. gr. 1209), in the Vatican Library. Vaticanus is recorded in the Vatican catalogues of 1475: *"Biblia: Ex membr(anis) in rubeo";* and 1481: *"In primo banco bibliothecae graece. Biblia in tribus columnis ex membranis in rubeo."* This second entry (and probably the earlier one) refers to the ms. written in three columns, now designated Codex Vaticanus (given the letter B, and, for the NT, the numeral 03). Although a few scholars had gained access to readings in the ms., it was not consulted properly until the end of the nineteenth century, by which time it was back in the Vatican, after a sojourn in Paris, whither Napoleon had removed it. The Vatican seemed reluctant to allow the readings of a ms. whose text differs so much from the *textus receptus* to be freely available — even to (or especially to) scholars of the caliber of Constantine Tischendorf. Centuries earlier, J. G. de Sepulveda, the Vatican librarian, had sent a letter to Erasmus in 1533 noting the resemblances between B and the Vulgate (Rummel 1986: 40).

It is certain that Erasmus had been supplied with some of the distinctive readings of B. Sepulveda had a list of 365 variant readings in 1533. Which readings these were is not known. In his annotations of 1535 at Acts 27:16, Erasmus cites the name of the island as "Kauda" (Cauda). Only B is known to have had that reading in his day. This shows that even in Erasmus's time mss. were being compared and their differences noted. Such a practice of course goes back to Origen. However, it was only after Erasmus's time that such differences were recorded in the critical apparatus of printed editions. Only in very recent times have readers of a critical edition been encouraged to use the critical apparatus for exegesis and for assessing the editorial judgment about the text printed.

In any case, as appears in Erasmus's own correspondence as well as in his annotations to 1 John 5:7, Erasmus had asked Paulus Bombasius at the Vatican Library as early as 1521 to check the readings of B at 1 John 5:7-8 (and 4:3), and received a transcript of 1 John 4:1-3 and 5:7-11 (Rummel 1986: 40). The fourth-century date and distinctive character of the ms. were not known to Erasmus. It is unlikely, however, that he would have accepted any of the non-Byzantine readings of Vaticanus, since all he was concerned about then was to locate any Greek witness containing the *Comma Johanneum.* Of course, he would have accepted such a distinctive reading in any Greek ms. — as indeed he was to do in 1522 (Metzger and Ehrman 2005: 146-48; Rummel 1986: 132-33). In modern times, the text of Vaticanus has formed the cornerstone of most critical editions of the Septuagint and the NT.

Vaticanus is now known to have been written in the fourth century. Skeat has argued (1999), convincingly in my opinion, that the provenance of the ms. was Caesarea. Even though that proposal may not satisfy all text critics, it is clear that a complete Bible in Greek was produced, and that it was a handsome edition (Skeat 1999). Possibly, one of its functions was to demonstrate between one set of covers the extent of the canon of the Old Testament and NT, as recently defined and established in the fourth century. It was rare for mss. to be written that contain the entire NT in Greek. Complete Bibles in Greek are even rarer, despite the likelihood that fifty such Bibles had originally been written at one time, fulfilling Constantine's request for such a quantity (Skeat 1999). Only Codex Vaticanus and Codex Sinaiticus survive from that time. Vaticanus resides at the Vatican Library, while the bulk of Sinaiticus is at the British Museum, with leaves at St. Catherine's Monastery in the Sinai, the Leipzig University Library, and the Russian National Library in Saint Petersburg. Together with the later Codex Alexandrinus (further, see below) and Codex Ephraemi Rescriptus, Codex Vaticanus and Codex Sinaiticus were written to be complete Bibles in Greek. These complete Bibles did not, however, initiate a trend. Normally, what was copied was the four Gospels alone — the bulk of our mss. are Gospel mss. — or one other section, whether Acts and the Catholic Epistles, the Pauline corpus, or Revelation. Occasionally, we find mss. that contain more than one section, but only rarely are all four conventional divisions of the NT (Gospels, Acts and Catholic Epistles, the Pauline Corpus, Revelation) present. Only sixty or so out of the currently registered stock of 5,000 Greek NT mss. are complete NTs.

Any mss. that have survived down to our time have done so by sheer chance. The total number we have is perhaps only a tiny proportion of the many mss. produced in the ancient and medieval periods. Similarly, the ways in which Vaticanus and Sinaiticus survived were fortuitous. The story of the finding of Sinaiticus is well known, and need not detain us further (see Metzger and Ehrman 2005: 62-65), but the story of Vaticanus is worth retelling, because it is relevant to the way in which such a ms. was treated, and its text disregarded, in the late Middle Ages.

The original fourth-century codex had been used over several centuries, as may be detected from a perusal of the ms. itself or of one of several photographic reproductions, including the splendid new millennium facsimile edition (Bibliothecae Apostolicae Vaticanae 1999). There are later aids and markings added to the ms., such as *scholia* (marginal annotations) and comments in Greek for clarification of the text. These additions suggest that the ms. continued to be read in a Greek-speaking environment. It was even re-inked in the ninth and tenth centuries to facilitate its continuing legibility.

However, at some stage it seems to have fallen into disuse: folios of Psalms, the beginning of the Bible (Gen. 1–46:28), and the end (everything following Heb. 9:14) were lost, damaged, or soiled. What we have now is the fourth-century ms. written in a bold majuscule (uppercase letters) hand, supplemented by additions in a minuscule (cursive) hand of the fifteenth century. Thus, the missing chapters were made good, although the Pastoral Epistles are strangely absent.

The ms. had fallen into disuse because majuscule writing in *scriptio continua* (that is, without divisions between words) became unfashionable. Such script was difficult for medieval readers to decipher. Because scribes in the fifteenth century were incapable of writing in uncial (majuscule) script, the (partial) restoration of the missing pages was done in a cursive hand that is obviously incompatible with the rest of the ms. A motive suggested for this restoration is that the ms. was hastily patched up in the early fifteenth century and presented to the pope as a gift by the Greek delegates to the Reunion Council of Florence (1438-39) (Skeat 1984). Thereafter, it ended up in the Papal Library in Rome. The case of an early ms. like Codex Vaticanus surviving in use in the Middle Ages is rare: normally a fourth-century ms. would have long since been discarded or made a palimpsest. (Palimpsests are parchment mss. that have been erased and reused.)

Unfortunately, the writer of the fifteenth-century additions has not been identified by palaeographers. Such an identification could indicate the provenance of the ms. immediately prior to its arrival in Rome before 1475. Nevertheless, what the story about its arrival in the Vatican Library tells us is that the ms. was recognized as an old Greek biblical ms. because of its script, and as such was suitable as a gift. Scholars of that time were not interested in the distinctiveness or importance of the actual text in the ms. as a reliable or potential witness for the creation of a critical edition of the NT in Greek. We have to wait until the time of Johann Griesbach in the eighteenth century and then Karl Lachmann in the nineteenth century before scholars in general became convinced that a search for the oldest mss. of the Greek NT was relevant for a critically established edition — and even longer before seeing the beginnings of a concerted effort to publish an ancient form of the text with an apparatus of variant readings (Metzger and Ehrman 2005: 165-67, 170-71).

The reason Vaticanus was not utilized more was precisely because it was so different from the prevailing Byzantine text-type of the majority of medieval mss. and, of course, because it had been unavailable for so long. Even Bombasius claims to have located it only "with difficulty." Thus, Vaticanus would have been discounted as a maverick copy.

Codex Bezae Cantabrigiensis

An assessment of being maverick would have been even truer of Codex Bezae Cantabrigiensis (Cambridge University Library Nn 2.41), now registered as D or 05. It is a bilingual (Greek-Latin) ms. of the fifth century containing the Gospels, Acts and part of 3 John (now surviving only in Latin), and, as its name indicates, had once belonged to Beza. Beza himself was quite open about the problematic nature of "his" ms. When he presented it to the University of Cambridge in 1581 (where it is still housed), he hoped it would be used judiciously "lest it offend." Beza was dissatisfied with its often wildly different text. However, he frequently cited Codex Bezae in the annotations to the second, third, and fourth editions of his *Novum Testamentum* (1582-98).

Beza claims that he obtained the ms. from Lyons (at the monastery of St. Irenaeus) some time after 1562, the year when that city was sacked. Its earlier history and the original provenance of the ms. are unknown, although it may have been written in Berytus, modern Beirut (Parker 1992: 267-78). Even today, when compared to a stock of 5,000 Greek NT mss., the distinctiveness and uniqueness of many of the readings of Codex Bezae are apparent — although sometimes it is supported by certain Latin mss. This text-type is usually erroneously called "Western." A NT based on this so-called Western text would include many peculiar readings, especially in Acts. Many of the unusual readings of Codex Bezae can be explained by a scribal anti-Jewish bias, which affected the transcription of the text (Epp 1966).

Stephanus made use of Codex Bezae, stating that it had been collated by friends prior to 1550, in Italy. There is good reason for thinking that the ms. had been brought to Italy for consultation at the Council of Trent in 1546. However, Stephanus was not always accurate in his transcriptions. Walton in his 1657 *Polyglot* (Walton 1657) made use of full collations of the ms. prepared especially for him by James Ussher, Archbishop of Armagh (Knox 1967), a noted scholar and historian. Mill(s) and, later, Wettstein also collated Codex Bezae for their NTs. Mill(s)'s was published in 1707 (Mill[s] 1707) and Wettstein's was published in 1751-52 (Wettstein 1751-52).

Codex Claromontanus

Codex Claromontanus (D 06), of the sixth century, now in Paris, contains the Pauline Letters. It, too, had once belonged to Beza. He used it to a limited extent in his third edition of 1582. Its readings are also to be found in Walton's *Polyglot*.

Codex Alexandrinus

Another famous codex, the Codex Alexandrinus, a fifth-century ms. now in the British Library (Royal I.D VIII), contains the complete NT (plus much of the Old Testament in Greek). It had been promised in 1625 by Cyril Lucar, Patriarch of Constantinople, to King James I (VI), but it arrived in England later, during the reign of Charles I. It was used soon afterwards by Walton in his *Polyglot*. Modern scholarship brands its text predominantly Byzantine in the Gospels, but Alexandrian (the old "neutral" text-type) in the rest of the NT. Its early history is unknown.

Manuscript Formats

In addition to studying the texts themselves, scholars investigating the production of the NT should also examine the differing formats in which the Bible was made (Metzger and Ehrman 2005: 3-33). In the twelfth century, many Bibles came glossed with learned comments. In the heyday of monasticism, particularly in the twelfth and thirteenth centuries, several sumptuously illuminated and decorated Bibles were produced. Thomas Aquinas's *Catena Aurea* in the thirteenth century is a noteworthy collection of earlier comments and glosses (Aquinas 1999). Earlier, Sedulius Scottus, the ninth century Irish poet and biblical scholar, had also added glosses to biblical mss.

By the thirteenth century, small-format, portable Bibles were being produced, mainly in Paris. At about the same time, picture Bibles also told stories through art, especially stories from the Book of Revelation. Trinity College, Cambridge ms. R 16.2 is a splendid example of an illustrated Apocalypse. The NT text was being transmitted with more than words.

VERSIONS

The multifarious attempts to translate the Scriptures into Latin resulted in Jerome's effort to stabilize the tradition by producing the Vulgate. Many copies of that version themselves became corrupted and contaminated. As we saw above, later attempts (in 1590 and 1592) were made to establish the definitive version of Jerome's Vulgate as a counter to Protestantism's championing of the original scriptural languages.

The oriental versions — Syriac, Coptic, Georgian, and Armenian — continued to be copied by hand, and many mss. survive (Metzger and

Ehrman 2005: 94-134). The Ethiopic was printed in 1548-49 in Rome, and the fifth-century Peshitta Syriac was printed as early as 1555. These and other versions continue to be consulted by editors of the Greek text, since they can often reveal the underlying Greek text from which their NT was derived.

English versions originated early, often in the form of interlinear glosses. The famous seventh-century Latin Lindisfarne Gospels were supplied with an Anglo-Saxon gloss in the Northumbrian dialect in the tenth century; Mercian dialect glosses appear in the Rushworth Gospels. In the fourteenth century, the so-called Wycliffite English versions were translated from Latin (Metzger and Ehrman 2005: 108, 125-26). But by that time nascent Protestantism, in the form of Lollardy, made it appear as if any translation away from Latin was a criticism of the church of Rome and its adherence to the Scriptures in Latin. As a result, the Wycliffite versions were condemned. Nevertheless, some 180 ms. copies survive (see chapter 16 below).

It may have been thought that printed copies of the Greek NT could have had only a limited influence until classical learning had fully established itself. But early on, Protestants saw the advantages of translating Scripture into vernacular languages from Hebrew and Greek (rather than Latin). Greek mss. and printed editions thus became of paramount importance. As noted earlier, the first printed English NT was Tyndale's in 1526, a translation based on Erasmus's Greek text (second edition, 1519) of only seven years earlier. This version had a tremendous influence on all subsequent translations into English for centuries. The catalogue of later versions includes Coverdale (1535), Matthew (1537), Taverner (1539), the Great Bible (1539), the Geneva Bible (1560), the Bishops' Bible (1568) leading on to the Authorized Version (KJV) in 1611. All these used the Greek text for the translation of the NT. Only the Roman Catholic Rheims-Douai version of 1582-1610 continued the tradition of translation from the Vulgate.

During the Renaissance/Reformation period, the study of the NT was profoundly affected by a revolutionary change in the method by which literature was reproduced and disseminated, namely, the invention of the printing press. Also revolutionary was the supplanting of the Latin text of the Bible, which had been dominant in the West for over a thousand years, by new, vernacular versions throughout Christendom, typically based on Old Testament editions in Hebrew, and the NT editions in Greek. Scholars and churchmen now had in their possession the means to produce increasingly reliable translations of the Bible in multiple copies.

Even if Erasmus's intentions in printing a Greek NT had been to promote his own Latin translation, the momentum that his publication initiated became unstoppable. Soon, it became normative, in Protestantism initially, for new translations to be made from the Bible's original languages. Making such translations available to the general reader rapidly multiplied the ways in which the Scriptures were read and opened the door to new methods of interpreting the Bible.

BIBLIOGRAPHY

Aland, K.

1994   *Kurzegefaßte Liste der griechischen Handschriften 1.* Gesamtübersicht. 2nd ed.; ANTF 1; Berlin and New York: de Gruyter.

Aland, K., and B. Aland

1989   *The Text of the NT.* Trans. E. F. Rhodes. 2nd ed. Grand Rapids: Eerdmans; Leiden: Brill.

Amphoux, C.-B., and J. K. Elliott (eds.)

2003   *The New Testament Text in Early Christianity: Proceedings of the Lille Colloquium July 2000/Le texte du Nouveau Testament au début du christianisme. Actes du colloque de Lille Juillet 2000.* Histoire du texte biblique 6; Lausanne: Zèbre.

Aquinas, Thomas

1999   Catena Aurea: *A Commentary on the Four Gospels Collected Out of the Works of the Fathers.* Trans. J. H. Newman. London: Saint Austin.

Backus, I. D.

1980   *The Reformed Roots of the English New Testament: The Influence of Theodore Beza on the English New Testament.* Pittsburgh: Pickwick.

Bentley, J. H.

1983   *Humanists and Holy Writ: New Testament Scholarship in the Renaissance.* Princeton: Princeton University Press.

Beza, T.

1582-98 *Novum Testamentum, cum versione Latina veteri, et nova Theodori Bezæ.* Geneva.

Bibliothecae Apostolicae Vaticanae

1999   *Bibliorum Sacrorum Graecorum Codex Vaticanus B* (Facsimile). Rome: Istituto Poligrafico e Zecca dello Stato.

Birdsall, N.

1970   "The New Testament Text" in P. R. Ackroyd and C. F. Evans, eds., *The Cambridge History of the Bible* 1: *From the Beginnings to Jerome,* 308-77. Cambridge: Cambridge University Press.

Brandt, P.-Y.

1998   "Manuscrits grecs utilisés par Erasme pour son édition du Novum Instrumentum de 1516." *TZ* 54: 120-24.

Brown, D.

2003   "Jerome and the Vulgate." *HBI*[1], 355-79.

Darlow, T. H., and H. F. Moule

1903   *Historical Catalogue of the Printed Editions of Holy Scripture in the Library of the British and Foreign Bible Society.* 2 vols.; London: Bible House.

de Hamel, C.

2001   *The Book: A History of the Bible.* London: Phaidon.

de Jonge, H. J.

1971   *Daniel Heinsius and the Textus Receptus of the New Testament: A Study of His Contributions to the Editions of the Greek New Testament Printed by the Elzeviers at Leiden in 1624 and 1633.* Leiden: Brill.

1978   "Jeremias Hoelzlin: Editor of the '*Textus Receptus*' Printed by the Elzeviers, Leiden 1633." In T. Baarda, A. J. F. Klijn and W. C. van Unnik, eds., *Miscellanea Neotestamentica* I, 105-28. NovTSup 47; Leiden: Brill.

1980   "Erasmus and the *Comma Johanneum.*" *ETL* 56: 381-89.

1984   "Novum Testamentum a Nobis Versum: The Essence of Erasmus's Edition of the NT." *JTS* n.s. 35: 394-413.

1988a   "Wann ist Erasmus' Übersetzung des Neuen Testaments entstanden?" In J. Sperna Weiland and W. T. M. Frijhoff, eds., *Erasmus of Rotterdam: The Man and the Scholar,* 151-57. Leiden: Brill.

1988b   "The Date and Purpose of Erasmus' Castigatio Novi Testamenti: A Note on the Origins of the Novum Testamentum." In A. C. Dionisotti, A. Grafton, and J. Kraye, eds., *The Uses of Greek and Latin: Historical Essays,* 97-110. London: Warburg Institute.

Elliott, J. K., and I. Moir

1995   *Manuscripts and the Text of the New Testament.* Edinburgh: Clark.

Epp, E. J.

1966   *The Theological Tendency of Codex Bezae Cantabrigiensis in Acts.* SNTSMS 3; Cambridge: Cambridge University Press.

Erasmus, Desiderius

1516   *Novum Instrumentum omne, diligenter ab Erasmo Rot. Recognitum et Emendatum.* Basel: Froben.

2001   *Opera Omnia Desiderii Erasmi.* VI, 2. *Novum Testamentum ab Erasmo recognitum II: Evangelium secundum Iohannem et Acta Apostolorum.* Ed. A. J. Brown. Amsterdam: Elsevier.

2004   *Opera Omnia Desiderii Erasmi.* VI, 3. *Novum Testamentum ab Erasmo recognitum III: Epistulae Apostolicae (Prima Pars).* Ed. A. J. Brown. Amsterdam: Elsevier.

Fox, A.

1954   *John Mill and Richard Bentley: A Study of the Textual Criticism of the New Testament, 1675-1729.* Oxford: Oxford University Press.

Hall, B.

1966   *Great Polyglot Bibles.* San Francisco: Book Club.

Harris, J. R.

1901   *The Annotators of the Codex Bezae.* London: Clay.

Hodges, Z. C., and A. L. Farstad

1985   *The New Testament According to the Majority Text.* 2d ed. Nashville: Nelson.

Knox, R. B.

1967   *James Ussher, Archbishop of Armagh.* Cardiff: University of Wales Press.

Letis, T. P.

1997   *The Ecclesiastical Text.* Philadelphia: Institute for Renaissance and Reformed Biblical Study.

Mentel, J. (ed. and trans.)

1466   *Mentel Bibel.* Strassbourg: Mentel.

Metzger, B., and B. D. Ehrman

2005   *The Text of the New Testament.* 4th ed. Oxford: Oxford University Press.

Mill(s), J.

1707   *Hē Kainē Diathēkē: Novum Testamentum, cum lectionibus variantibus MSS. Exemplarium, Versionem, Editionum, SS. Patrum et Scriptorum Ecclesiasticorum, et in easdem notis.* Oxford: Studio et labore Joannis Millii.

Monfansani, J.

1995   *Byzantine Scholars in Renaissance Italy: Cardinal Bessarion and Other Emigrés: Selected Essays.* Collected Studies Series. Aldershot: Variorum.

Parker, D. C.

1977   "The Development of Textual Criticism since Streeter." *NTS* 24: 149-62.

1992   *Codex Bezae: An Early Christian Manuscript and Its Text.* Cambridge: Cambridge University Press.

2001   "The Making of the Bible II: Texts and Translations: The New Testament." In John Rogerson, ed., *The Oxford Illustrated History of the Bible,* 110-33. Oxford: Oxford University Press.

Reicke, B.

1960   "Erasmus und die neutestamentliche Textgeschichte." *TZ* 22: 254-65.

Rummel, E.

1986   *Erasmus' Annotations on the New Testament: From Philologist to Theologian.* Erasmus Studies. Toronto: University of Toronto Press.

Scrivener, F. H. A.

1894   *A Plain Introduction to the Criticism of the New Testament.* Ed. E. Miller. 4th ed. 2 vols. New York: Dell.

Skeat, T. C.

1984   "The Codex Vaticanus in the Fifteenth Century." *JTS* n.s. 35: 454-65.

1999   "The Codex Sinaiticus, the Codex Vaticanus, and Constantine." *JTS* n.s. 50: 583-625.

Spottorno, V.

2002   "The Textual Significance of Spanish *Polyglot* Bibles." *Sefarad* 62: 375-92.

Tarelli, C. C.

1943   "Erasmus' Manuscripts of the Gospels." *JTS* 44: 155-62.

1947   "Erasmus' Manuscripts of the Gospels." *JTS* 48: 207-208.

Tregelles, S. P.

1854   *An Account of the Printed Text of the Greek Testament.* London: Bagster.

Turner, C. H.

1924   *The Early Printed Editions of the Greek Testament.* Oxford: Oxford University Press.

Walton, B. (ed.)

1657   *Biblia sacra polyglotta, complectentia textus originales, Hebraicum, cum Pentateucho Samaritano, Chaldaicum, Graecum.* 6 vols. London: Roycroft.

Wettstein, J. J.

1751-52 *Novum Testamentum Graecum.* 2 vols. Amsterdam.

Wilson N. G.

1992   *From Byzantium to Italy: Greek Studies in the Italian Renaissance.* London: Duckworth.

CHAPTER 8

Scholastic Interpretation of the Bible

Christopher Ocker

SCHOLASTICISM

"Scholasticism" refers to the cultural movement associated with universities and other schools in medieval Europe. Schools spread through cities, monasteries, and cathedrals in France, Italy, and Germany in the eleventh and twelfth centuries. These became more sophisticated than schools established during the previous two hundred years in the Carolingian Empire and the Saxon kingdom, where cathedral schools had provided elementary education to clergy and nobility alike. By the end of the twelfth century, at places where several schools treated common subjects — law at Bologna; the liberal arts, theology, medicine, and law at Paris; the liberal arts, theology, and law at Oxford; medicine at Montpellier — the schools, led by their masters, had begun to work cooperatively. In the early thirteenth century, papal and royal charters formed the schools into corporate bodies with an organization of personnel and curricula that became increasingly regimented over the course of the next hundred years. These super-schools came to be called universities and proliferated throughout Europe in the fourteenth and fifteenth centuries. By 1500, at least 75 universities had been founded. Most, though not all, exist today (De Ridder-Symoens 1992: 35-107, 307-441).

A substantial number of other schools were associated with cathedrals and monasteries, many of which belonged to the new religious orders, especially the mendicant orders of the Dominicans, Franciscans, Carmelites, and Augustinian Hermits (De Ridder-Symoens 1992: 35-67; Mulchahey 1998; Roest 2000). Other schools were founded by cities for elementary training in

Latin grammar, elementary philosophy, and/or basic religious texts. Some students advanced from these schools to study at universities, but most would not stay long enough to take degrees. Teachers in these other schools often spent at least some time at a university. In other words, there was much regular traffic between universities and other schools. Thus, although Scholasticism was a cultural movement defined and maintained in the universities, it also encompassed the culture of many other widely dispersed schools (De Ridder-Symoens 1992: 144-94, 280-304).

Scholasticism advocated a rational and systematic approach to several fields of knowledge. Its rational approach was developed and promoted through a basic course of study in the seven liberal arts — grammar, rhetoric, logic, arithmetic, geometry, astronomy, and music. By the late thirteenth century, arts faculties concentrated on the first three, called the *trivium,* and within the *trivium,* they concentrated on logic. Scholasticism was perfected in the three "higher" faculties of theology, law, and medicine. The method of teaching consisted of two main elements: explanation of or commentary on key texts by advanced students and masters alike, and formal topical debate (De Ridder-Symoens 1992: 307-441; Courtenay 1987).

Scholasticism changed dramatically after the Reformation. The dominant position of universities as the foremost centers of intellectual activity, as the venue in which authoritative texts like the Bible received their most sophisticated interpretation, was undermined in the sixteenth century. Humanism, which originated in Italy outside universities, came to dominate Italian urban schools in the fifteenth century, posing an alternative to Scholasticism (Witt 2000; Kristellar 1955: 3-23). But the humanists' stress on ancient languages, classical literature, and classical rhetoric eventually affected university teachers, too, as humanism spread to northern Europe in the late fifteenth and early sixteenth centuries (Grafton and Jardin 1986; De Ridder-Symoens 1996). By the second half of the sixteenth century, old universities and new academies, Protestant and Catholic schools alike, combined the new philological and literary methods of the humanists with the logical methods of medieval schools in what we may call a new, early modern Scholasticism.

The Bible was one of the two standard textbooks commented upon in theology faculties. The other textbook, composed by Peter Lombard, a master of the school of the cathedral of Notre Dame at Paris in the middle of the twelfth century, was the *Four Books of Sentences* (1981). A collection of opinions or *sententiae* on the full gamut of theological subjects from the holy Trinity to the final judgment and the sufferings of hell, the *Four Books of Sentences* offered rudimentary analysis of theological and philosophical problems (Rosemann 2004). The course of study, for both first and advanced university degrees in theology, prescribed hearing and eventually performing lectures on the Bible and the *Sentences,* along with participation in topical debates called quodlibetal disputations and delivery of "sermons" (i.e., speeches on discrete theological and philosophical problems).

By the end of the thirteenth century, lectures on the *Sentences* (and commentaries, the published forms of the lectures), quodlibetal disputations, and sermons all seemed increasingly abstract and remote from biblical narrative. Reflecting the full benefit of the European rediscovery of Aristotle in the late twelfth and early thirteenth centuries, lectures and commentaries on the *Sentences* applied logic to theological and metaphysical problems with incredible sophistication. Throughout the late Middle Ages, scholars and churchmen routinely lamented this trend, criticizing theology for its exaggerated subtlety and contrasting it with the simplicity of biblical doctrine. It was a truism widely shared (Ocker 2002: 112-23). The claim that theological argumentation was unnecessarily complex and subtle and overpowered the simplicity of biblical doctrines was adapted by humanists and reformers in the early sixteenth century and contributed to the misleading but persistent belief that Scholasticism gave little place to Bible study.

In fact, from the thirteenth through the fifteenth centuries the Bible remained a firm part of the theological curriculum, not just in the universities but also in the far-flung schools of the mendicant orders, whose curriculum was modeled on that of the university theology faculties. Although the topic has hardly been studied, lectures on the Bible also took place sporadically during the late Middle Ages in city and cathedral schools, as, for example, Johann Müntzinger's lectures on Paul's letters at Ulm (Ocker 2002: 13, 65-68, 137-38) and Hermann Schildesche's lectures on the senses of Scripture at Würzburg (Ocker 2002: 94-106). When in the early sixteenth century John Colet, who had previously lectured on St. Paul's letters at Oxford, continued biblical lectures in St. Paul's Cathedral, London (Colet 1985; see also chapter 13 below), and Martin Luther lectured on the Psalms, Romans, Galatians, and Hebrews at the University of Wittenberg (Brecht 1985; see also chapter 10 below), their innovations lay in the content of their lectures, not in the fact that they commented on the Bible. Scholasticism's self-critical stance, its insistence on the dangers of speculation — in spite of its often highly speculative character — can be taken, at least in part, as a reflection of the ongoing importance of Bible study in late medieval schools (Ocker 2002: 112-23).

In the sixteenth and seventeenth centuries, an infusion of humanism's textual and philological methods into the schools gave birth to the textual criticism of the Bible, comparative Semitic philology, and, to some extent, study of ancient Near Eastern history, all of which transformed biblical scholarship (Shuger 1994). The early contributors to these developments, most notably Desiderius Erasmus (for this and the following, see Bedouelle and Roussel 1989; Rummel 1986; Laplanche 1986, 1994; Zac 1965; Shuger 1994; see also chapter 9 below), Santi Pagnini, Sebastian Münster, Paul Fagius, Olivétan, and Robert Estienne, among others, were independent scholars, not professors, and the same remained true of some of the most important Bible scholars of the next century, most notably Hugo Grotius, John Lightfoot, Brian Walton, and Baruch Spinoza (if we should call Spinoza a Bible scholar). They represent the international, early modern "republic of letters" (see Bots and Waquet 1997), much of it shaped and led by men holding church livings or otherwise patronized, among whom many of the historical and philological innovations of early modern exegesis were made (Laplanche 1994). Does this mark the end of the Scholastic interpretation of the Bible?

Through the course of the sixteenth century, Peter Lombard's *Sentences* ceased to be accepted as a standard textbook in Catholic as well as Protestant schools, but the Bible continued to occupy a consistent place in the theological curriculum. Many Bible scholars of the sixteenth and seventeenth centuries were, at least for a time, professors. For example, Tommaso de Vio Cajetan (d. 1534), after serving as professor in Padua, Paris, and Rome and after serving in a variety of high offices in his order and the church, produced Bible commentaries at Rome in 1527. These he continued while exiled from Rome to his episcopal see in Gaeta in 1528-29 and after returning to Rome from 1529 to 1534 (Congar 1934-35; see also Thomas de Vio Cajetan 2005). We might assume that his offices as bishop and cardinal granted him the repose to study and write, but it is equally possible and would have been far more typical had he prepared these many commentaries as lectures for the Dominican convent or the papal court (the matter has never been investigated). Sixtus Senensis (d. 1569), while a member of the Dominican convent of Genoa, likely composed his influential commentary on the entire Bible while teaching in the convent school. Frans Tittelmans, while professor in the Franciscan convent at Louvain, produced a long commentary on the Psalms (1531; see also Meier-Oeser 1997). This also very likely was composed in conjunction with his teaching. Louis Cappel, author of an exhaustive philological and historical commentary (1650; see also Shuger 1994: 11-16), was professor at the Calvinist academy of Saumur late in the century; and Isaac Casaubon, the classical scholar and translator of the NT (1587), was professor at the Calvinist academies of Geneva and Montpellier before enjoying royal pensions at Paris and Canterbury (1587; see also Laplanche 1994: 50-68; Shuger 1994: 13-17). Johannes Gerhard, Lutheran professor at Jena in the early seventeenth century and author of the imposing nine-volume, extremely influential *Loci theologici* (1657), completed a long commentary on the Gospels begun by Martin Chemnitz and continued by Polycarp Lyser (Chemnitz, Gerhard, and Lyser 1652). Several of these figures are easily identified as "Scholastic" thinkers by reason of their teaching profession in theology faculties and the expository and disputational style of their writing, as, for example, Cajetan, Tittelmans, and Gerhard. The close proximity of biblical exposition to Scholastic theology is also suggested by the example of Gisbert Voetius, professor at the Reformed Protestant University of Utrecht in the second and third quarters of the seventeenth century (Voetius 1965). He was famous for his criticism of Cartesian philosophy and taught Arabic, Syriac, logic, physics, and metaphysics, while also serving as the principal preacher in Utrecht.

It is among such people that we should seek the late history of Scholastic interpretation of the Bible. Yet, it would be impossible to summarize this history at the present time. We are hindered, in part, by the complex nature of early modern school culture. As previously indicated, there is by the late sixteenth century no clean line between Scholastic and humanist methods to be found in the work of many post-Reformation theologians, and the work of influential scholars, such as those just named, adapted the humanist arsenal to their various needs. Likewise, there was much contact and cross-fertilization, some, but not all, polemically charged, between arts professors, who taught languages and ancient literature, and theologians (one thinks of Casaubon and Voetius). Just as it would be premature to conclude that Scholastic Bible interpretation after the Reformation ceased, it would be difficult at this point to say what exactly made the interpretation of some people "scholastic" in the sixteenth and seventeenth centuries other than the fact that those people taught in schools. It is also clear that the environment of the schools no longer enjoyed a monopoly on intellectuals. To identify the characteristics of biblical interpretation in early modern Scholasticism would, therefore, require us to delimit narrowly its intellectual environment and the culture of it, by the careful study of theological curricula, lectures and disputations, as well as the work of teachers who interpreted the Bible in theology faculties or who supported that work in arts faculties, in particular places over the course of decades. Such study has not yet been undertaken. An important exception is Laplanche's examination of biblical interpretation and political thought in Calvinist academies of the seventeenth century (1986). Laplanche focuses on political ideas in the academies. Recent studies of early modern biblical interpretation in general have concentrated on thought rather than contexts. Consider, for example, Harrison (1988), Hill (1993), and Shuger (1994). Neither does there appear to be any study of the relationship of the interpretation of the Bible in post-Reformation schools to late medieval Bible scholarship. The importance of late medieval texts, topics, and problems in seventeenth-century theology and philosophy — Protestant, Catholic, and early Enlightenment alike — is, by contrast, well known (Muller 2003; Ashworth 1982). I will therefore focus on medieval schools.

THE LITERATURE OF BIBLE STUDY

The medieval schools produced an impressive body of exegetical literature, among which several texts proved especially influential and representative of medieval trends. The most important commentary was called the *Ordinary Gloss* (see chapter 2 above), the culmination of a long process of adding glosses to Bibles (Froehlich and Gibson 1992). The glosses included brief explanatory notes added between the lines (interlinear glosses) and longer explanations taken from patristic literature and placed in the margins (marginal glosses, a technique also found in Jewish commentaries on the Talmud; Riché and Lobrichon 1984: 98, 234-35). The earliest biblical glosses in the West were probably composed in Northumbria and Ireland by the turn of the eighth to ninth centuries (pp. 98-99), but glossing increased in the third quarter of the eleventh century in the monastic and cathedral schools that mark the beginnings of Scholasticism in the north of France (Landgraf 1948: 39-47). At first, glosses were added to a single book of the Bible as it was interpreted by a school's master. Glosses gradually assumed a more comprehensive design, especially under the influence of Anselm of Laon (d. 1117; Riché and Lobrichon 1984: 101, 103, 112-14; Froehlich and Gibson 1992: vii-xi; see also chapter 2 above), to the effect that a glossed Bible could seem to represent patristic opinion on all Scripture.

By the middle of the twelfth century, glossed Bibles began to circulate in France, England, and Germany, apparently from a center of production at Paris, whose famous schools attracted book-buying students and teachers from throughout western Christendom (Riché and Lobrichon 1984: 95-114). Around 1220, the first complete glossed Bibles were produced. At about the same time, what was by then a more or less standard text came to be called the *Glossa ordinaria,* or *Ordinary Gloss,* to Scripture. Its status was promoted, if not at first achieved, in connection with the theology faculty of the new University of Paris (Froehlich and Gibson 1992; Riché and Lobrichon 1984: 101, 103, 112-13). Some parts of the *Ordinary Gloss* (glosses to the Psalter, Song of Songs, Pauline Epistles, and the Apocalypse) were compiled from many authors. Some of it drew on single sources (Bede on Ezra to Nehemiah, Mark,

Acts, and the Catholic Epistles; Rabanus Maurus on the Pentateuch and 1 and 2 Maccabees; see Froehlich and Gibson 1992: ix). The *Ordinary Gloss* was reproduced in nine volumes following a format described in the sixth century by the Italian monk Cassiodorus (d. c. 580), an arrangement of the biblical text also followed in Romanesque display Bibles and texts for common use: (1) Genesis to Ruth, (2) six books of Kings, (3) the four Major and the twelve Minor Prophets, (4) the Psalter, (5) Wisdom literature, (6) lives from Job to Nehemiah, (7) the four Gospels, (8) Pauline and other Epistles, and (9) Acts and the Apocalypse (Froehlich and Gibson 1992: xi).

The *Ordinary Gloss* exercised a tremendous influence in Scholasticism. Peter Lombard's citations of it in his *Four Books of Sentences* and the widely-used commentary on it by Peter Comestor, chancellor of the University of Paris in the third quarter of the twelfth century (Smalley 1964: 178-79; Morey 1993: 10), did much to publicize its usefulness (more on Comestor below).

There soon emerged other more discursive forms of commentary in twelfth-century monastic schools, under a variety of names: "commentary," "exposition," "explanation," "reading" *(lectura), postilla* (a term of uncertain meaning, possibly *"post illam glossam";* Zier 1993: 15), "questions," "little notes" *(notule),* and "annotations" or "distinctions" on such-and-such book (Häring 1982: 173-75; Morey 1993). Twelfth-century scholars also collected topical opinions in books of *"Sentences"* (the school of Laon played an important role here; Smalley 1964: 49-51; Riché and Lobrichon 1984: 103-7), which they supplemented with books of "questions" (Landgraf 1948: 35-39, 40-42; De Ghellinck 1948: 133-48). Some of these opinions and questions were taken from the commentaries of famous masters like Anselm of Laon. Peter Lombard's *Four Books of Sentences* was one of the more abstract but comprehensive of these collections. Others, like the commentary on the Psalms by Bruno, founder of the Carthusian Order (d. 1101), added questions to their commentaries (Riché and Lobrichon, 172-75).

In connection with the school of Saint Victor in the second and third quarters of the twelfth century (see chapter 2 above), a variety of works on theology and on the OT clarified the distinctions between "historical" and "spiritual" meanings, according to principles adapted from Augustine's *On Christian Doctrine* (Augustine 1958; see also Norris 2003) and explained in Hugh of Saint Victor's *Didascalicon* (1961). Soon after, Peter Comestor, chancellor of the cathedral school of Notre Dame and a master at the University of Paris, acceded to the pleas of his friends and compiled, by the year 1175, a comprehensive exposition of the entire Bible. The result came to be known as the *Historia Scholastica,* the first comprehensive and — unlike the glosses — fairly coherent treatment of the Bible in Europe, and one of the most widely used exegetical works of the later Middle Ages (Smalley 1964: 179; Riché and Lobrichon 1984: 195; Morey 1993: 10).

In the early thirteenth century, in the Dominican school at the University of Paris under the leadership of Hugh of Saint-Cher (Mulchahey 1998: 485-526), scholars developed yet another type of comprehensive commentary called a *"postilla."* The name *"postilla"* and the format and approach associated with it became the most typical Bible commentary of Scholasticism. The thirteenth-century *postilla* was a running commentary, ordinarily composed as lectures, especially in the schools of the mendicant orders in the thirteenth century. Originally, it was supposed to complement the *Ordinary Gloss* by including interpretations from more recent scholars. Postillators sometimes used questions to digress from viewpoints they found in the *Ordinary Gloss* (Buc 1994: 150), or they added questions or topical "articles" to address key theological ideas believed to play an important role in a commentary. Good examples from the fourteenth century can be found in the Matthew commentary of Jacques Fournier (Ocker 2002: 56-57), the Acts commentary of Johannes Klenkok (Ocker 1993), and the commentaries of Nicolai Eimerich (Ocker 2002: 63-64). Digressions on theological subjects suggested by a passage could be found scattered throughout *postillae*. They usually had a bias toward the literal sense, although their understanding of what the literal sense was and how it represented knowledge was changing, as I will explain below.

The *postilla* form was used by the greatest Scholastic Bible commentators, such as Bonaventure and Aquinas in the mid-thirteenth century (for the following, see Smalley 1964: 264-81; Ocker 2002: 43-44; see also chapter 2 above), and the Dominican Nicholas de Gorran in the fourth quarter of that century, the Franciscan Nicholas of Lyra in the second quarter of the fourteenth century, John Wyclif in the third and fourth quarters of that century (see chapter 13 below), and Denys van Leeuwen (generally known as Dionysius the Carthusian) in the second and third quarters of the fifteenth century (see 1896-1935). The discursive running commentaries of the Reformation, such as those of Martin Luther (Brecht 1985; see also Norris 2003; see also chapter 10 below), Martin Bucer (Bucer 1988; see also chapter 11 below), and John Calvin (see chapter 12 below), followed the basic format of the *postillae*.

Scholastic interpreters relied heavily on twelfth-century products like the *Glossa ordinaria* and the *Historia Scholastica*. They also devised new tools of study. These included a new edition of the Bible. The Parisian master and future archbishop of Canterbury Stephen Langton (d. 1228) divided the Bible into chapters by 1203 (Riché and Lobrichon 1984: 202; see also chapter 13 below). Another scholar, Thomas Gallus (d. 1246), divided the chapters into

paragraphs (Froehlich 2000: 508). The Vulgate thus paragraphed soon became the standard edition of the Bible at Paris, and from there it moved to all
universities. At Paris, Dominicans made an alphabetical concordance of the
Vulgate (the new chapter divisions providing an efficient means of referencing), probably between 1230 and 1235. The concordance was succeeded by a
deluxe bookstore edition put together by the year 1275 (Riché and Lobrichon
1984: 115-22; for tools of study, see also Mulchahey 1998: 485-526). Interpreters
also used concordances to canon law as a source of authoritative opinions to
apply in their exegesis. Two concordances composed in the fourteenth century harmonized canon law and Scripture, one by the abbot Jean of Nivelles,
and another by the Bolognese law professor Johannes Calderinus (Ocker 1991:
137-43). The *Ordinary Gloss,* the *Historia Scholastica, postillae,* and concordances, together with a Bible divided into chapters, became the chief tools for
the Scholastic interpretation of the Bible.

　　This literature reveals a certain historical development of hermeneutics.
Scholastic interpretation adapted monastic reading practices to the new intellectual criteria of the schools. This adaptation gave birth to a renewed emphasis on literal, historical meaning, while scholars sought to maintain the
superior value of "mystical" comprehension. But the importance of
historical-literal interpretation should not be anachronistically overempha-
sized. The distinction between literal and spiritual was eroded by an increasingly logical approach to language and textual meaning in Scholasticism. Furthermore, Scholastic commentaries reveal very limited concern with
historical and philological approaches to the literal text of the Bible, at least
until the sixteenth century. The exceptions were Andrew of St. Victor and
Nicholas of Lyra (Berndt 1991; for Lyra's impact, see Ocker 2002: 179-83; Krey
and Smith 2000; Reinhardt 1987; see also chapter 2 above). Let us look at this
development more closely, beginning with the distinction of literal and spiritual meanings.

BIBLICAL HERMENEUTICS IN EARLY SCHOLASTICISM

In the twelfth century, scholars began to collect into separate books the questions and "sentences" that were earlier treated within commentaries. The new
books became increasingly dialectical, and this disciplined use of logic distinguished them from Bible commentaries. De Ghellinck (1948) and Landgraf
(1948), two modern historical theologians, argue that this trend marks the beginning of Scholasticism as an intellectual movement begun at least in part by
the rational consideration of ideas apart from biblical reading and compre-

hension. In the twelfth century, many monks thought this rationalism served as an excuse to abandon the traditional sources of religious knowledge — the Bible and other sacred literature — for a self-indulgent rationalism (Gibson 1995: 41, 45). But scholars of the monastery school of St. Victor countered that Bible reading undergirded rational theological reflection, and this function had to do with the nature of language and with the nature of the world, as we can see by briefly reviewing their theory of signification. (See chapter 2 above for further background on the Victorines.)

The Victorines argued from a theorem about the nature of language, which I quote from Richard of St. Victor (d. 1173), who took special interest in explaining spiritual meanings of texts: *non solum voces, sed et res significativae sunt,* "not only words, but things also are representational" — a "thing" here being the physical or factual object represented by a word (Richard of St. Victor 1958: 1.2.3; see also Matter 1990: 49-85). To give a traditional example often repeated from an ancient monk named Cassian (1958: 2.190-91), the word "Jerusalem" refers to a real, historical city, but the city may in turn refer to other things by a bolder transference of meaning. According to allegory, the city refers to the church. According to tropology, it refers to the human soul. According to anagogy, it refers to the heavenly city of God.

Moreover, the aphorism "not only words, but things also are representational" explained how the Bible, a literary product, was greater than all secular literature and hence a source of the highest form of knowledge. There are two kinds of secular literature, according to Hugh of St. Victor (d. 1142), one of the first masters of that monastic school: writings on the seven liberal arts that contain philosophy and writings dependent on the arts that are not philosophical — tragedies, comedies, satires, heroic verse and lyric, iambics, didactic poems, fables, histories, and prose. Let us call these two kinds of secular literature "philosophy" and "poetry." In both, words mediate knowledge of the subject matter of a piece of writing, but in poetry, words often mediate knowledge of a subject obscurely, under various images (Hugh of St. Victor 1961: 87-88). The Bible, Hugh argued, following an ancient Christian argument, formed a distinct third kind of literature (Ohly 1977). Like philosophy, it is utterly devoid of fiction; like poetry, it uses figurative language. However, its figures must work differently, insofar as their meanings are derived from truths, not fabrications. In poetry, figures of speech merely express human inventiveness. Not so in the Bible, according to most if not all Christian thinkers in the West since patristic times. The Victorines said that Scripture, unlike poetry, contains the "far more excellent" significance of things (Hugh of St. Victor 1961: 121-22); or, as Richard of St. Victor noted, "in divine literature not only do meanings signify things, those things signify other things" (1879b: 375). What in secular literature was obscure became in the Bible profound.

Scripture not only tells stories, but the minute elements of a story. Its "things," *res* (rocks, trees, virtually any objects), in turn function as signs that indicate meanings that may seem to have nothing to do with the biblical passage. Hugh of St. Victor named six "circumstances" under which "things" bear meaning, an adaptation of the doctrine of circumstances in medieval grammar: physical objects as such and their properties, persons who signify mysteries in their deeds and experiences, numbers in their various arrangements and computations (he names nine), places, times (such as seasons), and events (Hugh of St. Victor 1879: 20-24; Ocker 2002: 73-75). Those meanings were believed to be closer to spiritual truth, and were called the spiritual senses or allegory. In this manner, the Victorines formulated the difference between literal/historical and spiritual meaning.

The possibility of allegorical meaning was attributed to a layered quality of the meaningfulness of texts. There were surface and subsurface layers of meaning. Scholars found the same in nature (Ohly 1977: 48-86; Meier 1977). The physical qualities of gemstones, for example, or qualities associated with the characteristics and habits of animals, or even the materials used to render a picture of those animals — silver, gold, colors — could bear spiritual interpretations. Numbers could be allegorically interpreted (Meyer 1975); so, too, could events. This undermines a distinction often made between allegory and typology (see Ocker 2002: 16-19). These things could be so understood abstractly (knowledge at once philosophical and religious), because of the nature of the world. Creation was a divine work, and the qualities of created things, their "properties," betrayed the character of their maker. "All nature bespeaks God. All nature teaches human beings. All nature imparts reason, and there is nothing barren in the universe" (Hugh of St. Victor 1879: 805; cf. 1961: 145). The visible world was the necessary starting point of knowledge of God, and in the same way, so too was sacred literature. What distinguished the Bible from other literature was not magical language, but accurate representation of the real connection between visible and invisible reality, between particular objects and the universe. To achieve spiritual knowledge of a thing indicated by the text of the Scripture was to move from word to thing to the divine.

The progression from word to thing to the divine began with literal, historical meaning. Scholars who played a key role in the consolidation of gloss technique — Lanfranc, abbot of Bec (d. 1089), Berengar of Tours (d. 1088), Drogo of Paris (late eleventh century), and Bruno the Carthusian (d. 1101) — promoted the use of the *trivium*, the non-mathematical core of the medieval liberal arts (grammar, rhetoric, and dialectic) in literal interpretation (see chapter 2 above). The adaptation of the *trivium* to Bible study was especially evident in the work of the school of Laon at the turn of the eleventh to twelfth centuries and in the work of its most important teacher, Anselm of Laon (d. 1117; Riché and Lobrichon 1984: 105). The Victorines built on those foundations and demonstrated that this kind of literal interpretation was prerequisite to spiritual knowledge, using the theory of biblical signification we have just considered. The results were a new sophistication in literal exegesis and a new emphasis on the role of literal interpretation in theological argument, seen best in Andrew of St. Victor's Hebrew exegesis of the OT (Berndt 1991: 157-63, 201-13). Theologians in the next century would build on this development. With the establishment of universities, the faculties of theology required students to come with a Master of Arts degree, with the exception of members of religious orders, who were granted advanced standing for work done in monastic schools. This prerequisite reflects the ongoing Augustinian conviction that the liberal arts support Bible study, and it reflects a Scholastic goal: the reconciliation of textual, especially biblical, authority with rational analysis (see Evans 1984: 1.31-36).

The difference between literal and spiritual senses seemed clear. The fourfold division of meanings laid out by Cassian in the early fifth century now was taken to describe the standard possibilities. It was expressed in a rhyme that first appears in a Dominican textbook of the late thirteenth century and soon after, less obscurely, at the beginning of Nicholas of Lyra's *postilla*:

Littera gesta docet	The letter teaches events
quid credas allegoria	allegory what you should believe
quid agas tropologia	tropology what you should do
quo tendas anagogia.	anagogy where you should aim.

(Froehlich 2000: 512; see also chapter 2 above). The fourfold meaning of the Bible was maintained and presented most famously by Thomas Aquinas (*Summa theologiae* 1.1.a.10) and by many other Scholastic theologians, who also repeated the Victorine theorem on biblical signification (see Ocker 2002: 31-32 n. 2 for examples). In short, the Victorine theory of biblical signification and the distinction between literal and spiritual senses were carried over into Scholasticism. Throughout the late Middle Ages, scholars insisted that the Bible bears both literal and mystical meanings.

We expect to find this approach to biblical meaning among early modern Catholic writers. It was especially promoted in the commentaries of

Sixtus Senensis (1566). But by the middle of the seventeenth century, it can also be found adapted by Protestant Scholastic writers, for example, the Geneva professor Francis Turretin, who gave an ingenious account of mystical meaning while he sought, like many Protestant theologians, to combat what they considered the hyper-literalism of "Socinian" scholars who, like Faustus Socinus in the sixteenth century, abandoned the doctrine of the trinity because it lacked sufficient warrant in the literal sense of Scripture (Turretin 1696: 165-70; see also Muller 1999).

To summarize this very brief look at early Scholasticism, the study of the literal sense became more sophisticated, but it was generally subordinate to the mystical understanding of texts. Did this remain true in late medieval Scholasticism? No, for two reasons: the Victorine theory of biblical signification and the approach to textual knowledge implied by it became problematic, and the authority of surface meaning — the literal sense — grew.

BIBLICAL HERMENEUTICS
IN LATE MEDIEVAL SCHOLASTICISM

When Thomas Aquinas described biblical signification, he distinguished between two kinds (Delegue 1987: 20, 44). Natural signification corresponds to the Victorine view. Verbal signification works rather differently: words rather than things *(res)* convey meaning directly to the mind, even when that language is figurative, in which case words signify imagistically, not by moving the mind from words to the consideration of a transference of meaning in things, as in the Victorine view, but by simply signifying metaphorically (see Ocker 2002: 31-48). This verbal approach to signification helps account for the growing preoccupation of late medieval commentators with the literal sense, construed primarily as a repository of theological knowledge. In this case, revelation was associated primarily with the literal sense, not with contemplative insight into the meaning of creation, as was the case with the Victorines (Ocker 2002: 149-61). Accordingly, most late medieval theologians insisted that literal meaning held priority in theological argument; and, in any event, their commentaries were preoccupied with theological problems, not philological or historical problems. This can be readily observed in the theological digressions, questions, and addenda that late medieval scholars frequently added to their commentaries — for example, Jacques Fournier, Robert Holcot, John Baconthorpe, Johannes Klenkok, Nicolai Eimerich, Johann Müntzinger, John Wyclif, Wendelin Steinbach, and others (see Ocker 2002: 93-106).

The priority of literal meaning arose from a general conviction that Christian dogma was understood even by the writers of the OT because biblical language, as prophetic speech, presupposed a kind of holy conversation between God, ancient sacred writers, and inspired readers. At the same time, scholars developed techniques for handling figurative language within the parameters of the literal sense, as "parabolic" (Aquinas) or "figurated" (Hermann of Schildesche) senses, which lessened the burden previously borne by spiritual allegory to resolve problematic or inconvenient passages of the Bible (Ocker 2002: 93-106). They developed techniques for treating figurative speech within the parameters of the literal sense, many appealing to what Bonaventure and Thomas Aquinas described as the "parabolic" meaning of texts, or what the Augustinian friar and cathedral school professor Hermann of Schildesche in the middle of the fourteenth century called the non-historical, figurated senses of the Bible (Ocker 2002: 93-106). Others relied on what Lyra called the "double-literal" sense in the case of prophetic passages of both historical and future application (Ocker 2002: 142-49).

All this suggests growing confidence in the ability of the literal text as such, even at its most obscure and bizarre figurative moments, to convey religious and philosophical knowledge. It marks a dramatic departure from earlier approaches to figurative language that culminated in the work of the Victorines. In late antiquity, Christians followed the precedent of the allegorical interpretation of Homer and Hesiod done by Greek philosophers centuries earlier, and the precedent of Philo of Alexandria's allegorical interpretation of the LXX, using allegory to evade the apparent absurdity or obscenity of some biblical passages. The point was repeated by the Victorines: "The Divine Page, in its literal sense, contains many things which seem both to be opposed to each other and, sometimes, to impart something which smacks of the absurd or the impossible. But the spiritual meaning admits no opposition; in it, many things can be different from one another, but none can be opposed" (Hugh of St. Victor 1961: 140). The problem was, to theologians, psychological: some things in the Bible could excite the soul the wrong way, but the spiritual meaning of Scripture could only do the soul good.

By the late Middle Ages, this use of spiritual interpretation as a kind of interpretation of last resort had lost some of its force, so much so that in the early fifteenth century Dionysius Carthusianus could criticize theologians who say that "the literal meaning is that which is first signified by the literal words" while claiming that there are places in Scripture, "especially the Prophets," impossible to interpret literally. He offered an alternative directly opposite the Victorine theory of biblical signification, built on the idea of authorial intention. The literal sense is the meaning first intended by the author, therefore: "every passage of holy scripture has a literal meaning, which is not always what is first signified by the literal words, but is often what is designated through the thing that is signified by the literal words" (1896-1935: 4:362-63). What the Victorines called spiritual meaning, Dionysius called literal. Even Nicholas of Lyra, Dionysius alleged, was too allegorical, by occasionally appealing to a sense "rather mystical and spiritual than literal," for example, in his exegesis of Jacob's deathbed speech to his son (Gen. 48:21). Against Lyra, Dionysius said Jacob "speaks metaphorically . . . namely through similes of corporeal things. In such language, the literal sense is not what is immediately signified through terms, but what is signified through those things, according to their properties and the similarities to that which is principally designated." He rehearses examples: a lion is David, "or rather Christ"; a vine "literally designates the synagogue, Christ, and even the church" (1896-1935: 1:444).

Interpreters began to recognize that what was described in the twelfth century as a quality of thought *beyond* speech, was actually a quality *of* speech. This allowed Scholastic theologians, building on twelfth-century ideas, to see the Bible as a book of theology, albeit one with a peculiar organization. Hugh of St. Victor had said that the Bible is divided symmetrically in two parts, the OT and NT. Each of these is subdivided in three. The OT contains Law, Prophets, and hagiographers, and the NT contains Gospel and apostles and fathers of the church, whose "works are so limitless that they cannot be numbered" (Hugh of St. Victor 1961: 103-4). Within each Testament, the parts progress from past to present, from doctrine to practice, beginning with the core teachings of law and gospel, which through books about their dissemination (prophets and apostles) culminate in books about living (hagiographers and fathers). This arrangement of books in the Bible helped facilitate spiritual progress. The Bible is organized to be effective, just as the NT, it was believed, builds upon and improves the OT.

Even when the parts of the Bible were put in a linear, historical frame, as Bonaventure (Seybold 1971: 124.) did, it is important to remember this underlying interest in human progress (see Ocker 2002: 24-28). The point was made at length by the late-thirteenth-century Dominican Nicholas de Gorran (*Postilla super Genesim* f. 151, ff. 9vb-10va), who noted that the subdivisions of biblical parts reflect the symmetrical structure of the two main parts, OT and NT. Each subdivision and its subcategories present figures of Christ in ways unique to each particular genre. Prophecy, with Law and Psalms one of three principal parts of the OT, is divided into that which concerns the head of the church, that is, Christ, and that which concerns Christ's mystical body, the church itself, and he cites textual examples of each (Christ, as in the incarnation, passion, and ascension, on the examples of Isa. 7:14; 9:6; 11:1; 16:1; Jer. 11:19; Dan. 7:13; the church as the mystical body of Christ, on the example of Ezekiel 40, read with John 2:19; *Postilla super Genesim*, f. 10rb). The NT presents the same content without figures in two categories, knowledge about Christ himself (the Gospels) or about Christ's body the church (the rest of the NT). The material on the church receives a further subdivision into books dealing with the church's origin (Acts), its consummation (the Apocalypse), and its progress (the letters), which last subdivision is further divided into books that address particular groups: Latin (Romans), Greek (the Corinthian letters), Jewish converts (Hebrews), common subordinate clergy (1 Corinthians to 2 Thessalonians), and prelates (1 Timothy to Hebrews).

The concept of the Bible's organization around the two Testaments seems to have remained prevalent in the late Middle Ages. In the fourteenth century, John Baconthorpe and Nicholas of Lyra used the distinction of OT and NT to describe the organization of a single book of the Bible, the Gospel according to Matthew (Smalley 1981: 289; see also Smalley 1958). Nicholai Eimerich broke up the Gospels into particular aspects of Christ's identity and life: Matthew treated his humanity, John his divinity, Luke his passion, and Mark his resurrection (Eimerich 1973). The Gospels record Christ's history and doctrines, said Heinrich of Langenstein. In the early fifteenth century, Dionysius the Carthusian, who attributed the threefold division of the Bible to Jerome and his Jewish source, offered little more than a paraphrase of Hugh of St. Victor (see 1896-1935: 1.13).

The basic threefold division of the two Testaments was challenged by the Franciscan Pierre Aureol in the early fourteenth century. He gave a more strictly literary division of the Bible into eight parts, distinguished not by theological content per se but by distinct modes of writing: political and legal, chronical and historical, "hymnic" and quasi-poetical, prophetic and homiletical, dialectic and disputational, monastic or ethical and consultative, testimonial and affirmative, and epistolary and conditional. But even so, he preserved the conviction that biblical teaching taken as a whole had a single purpose and a single subject, in spite of the literary variety of its parts (1896; see also Henninger 1989: 150-73).

That point was commonly made by Scholastic theologians. The subject of the Bible is the essence of God effecting, through Christ, the work of human restoration, according to Alexander of Hales (Seybold 1971: 120-21; see also Marcolino 1970). It is theology, Bonaventure explained (1864: 1.15-16): a book that illumines the now unreadable book of creation, whose teachings have been obscured by sin (see also Mercker 1971: 16-37, 65-72). It is theological narrative in simple form, said Nicholas de Gorran (twelfth century). According to Lyra, the subject is God — or Christ, according to Johann Michael, Ugolino of Orvieto (Eckermann 1990: 49-65; Zumkeller 1990) and Jan Hus (1966: 14-15). Jacques Fournier noted that in the Gospels the subject is more specifically defined as Christ, divine and human (*Postilla* MS 550.10ra). "The book containing sacred Scripture, although divided into many partial books, comprises one book, which is called by the general name 'Bible' and is named 'the book of life,'" said Nicholas of Lyra (*Postilla super totam Bibliam* 1.1ra). The description of the Bible as a book of theology was reinforced in Scholasticism by a metaphysical definition of the book's "causes," which evolved out of a technique of commentary introduction adapted from twelfth-century grammar (see Minnis 1988: 9-159). An account of the Bible's "causes" allowed theologians to describe the Bible as both divine and human speech, meaningful by virtue of its historical and metaphysical origins as well as its effects. This was the point of medieval discussions of biblical inspiration (see Ocker 2002: 123-42, 149-61).

These convictions about the Bible's peculiar literary qualities — its thematic organization, the causal definition of the Bible, the inspiration of biblical writers and readers — can be seen in one very common feature of Scholastic commentaries, namely, their preoccupation with doctrine. Although it might surprise a sixteenth-century Protestant, it should not surprise us that the Bible was generally accepted in late medieval Scholasticism as the foremost theological authority (Schüssler 1977). Likewise, religious thought was assumed to be closely related to the intellectual content of biblical narrative. Scholastic Bible commentaries can therefore be taken as a methodical attempt to read biblical texts within a comprehensive body of knowledge, the same body of knowledge systematically and dialectically explored in lectures on Lombard's *Sentences*.

In late medieval Scholasticism, a particular view of biblical textuality evolved. It was believed to be physically manifest in the Bible's literary organization, which reflected the religious purpose of Scripture to document the history of salvation. Theories of verbal signification and of the divine inspiration of writers and readers reinforced this textuality, encouraging a decidedly theological orientation to the meaning of biblical literature, rather than a philological or historical focus (Nicholas of Lyra's *Postilla literalis*, with its brief comments and comparative use of Hebrew commentators, is hardly typical of late medieval Bible scholarship).

That history and philology should undergird religious doctrine must have always been presupposed, if only because divine truth was considered constant, no matter how much human circumstances change. But I speak against a certain received opinion. Medieval Bible interpretation is perhaps most famous for the fourfold sense, and Scholasticism has often been thought to bring this hermeneutic to maturity. Spontaneous, seemingly undisciplined appeals to mystical senses by some late medieval authors have been called a regression from separate and systematic treatments of historical and spiritual senses (de Lubac 1954-64: 2.2:369-91).

The regression presumably matched an alleged pre-Reformation Scholastic decline. Good Scholastic exegesis was supposed to cordon off the literal from the allegorical, allowing scholars the freedom to pursue their historical and philological investigations on the letter (Smalley 1964: 196-355; but cf. Feld 1977; see also Lerner's important observations, 1996: 181-88). A similar phenomenon can be observed in some precincts of the republic of letters in the sixteenth century, where history and philology helped reinforce the separation of religious truth from the ancient experiences narrated in the Bible, giving rise to the historicism that eventually produced modern critical exegesis (see Laplanche 1994: 50-68, emphasizing the role of the Reformed academy at Saumur; also Shuger 1994: 45-50, emphasizing this development's ethnographic quality). I have argued that in Scholasticism, divine revelation was increasingly associated with the Bible's literal sense, without really historicizing the literal sense. The ambition was to recognize the past in the present, and vice versa, while reading.

This was precisely opposite an endeavor to treat ancient Israel or the early church as a distant, alien, or fixed culture. All the more reason to study the specialized literature outlined above, under the heading "The Literature of Bible Study." Late medieval scholars could experience the Bible as what one might call "a multidimensional space," to borrow Barthes's famous characterization of texts after "the death of the author." "We know now that a text is not a line of words releasing a single 'theological' meaning (the 'message' of the Author-God) but a multi-dimensional space in which a variety of writings, none of them original, blend and clash" (1978: 146). The late medieval concept of divine speech helped coordinate coactors — readers, writers, and God — precisely because the language of the text, and presumably all speech, was so potentially ungovernable.

Such uncertainty over God's discourse, theologians believed, could not stand, as Henry de Langenstein once explained (*Commentaria;* see Ocker 2002: 149-61). It is true that Scholastic theologians insisted that biblical meaning is univocal, but they did not believe its one truth was mechanically made. Meaning was determined within a community of biblical writers, ancient theologians, and dialectically trained students, whose opinions and arguments were all liberally intermixed. The line of words did not release single meanings, nor did a hierarchical church simply pronounce upon the meanings. What was fixed was to occur supernaturally, or we could say, inter-subjectively, in a conversation between God, the reader, prophets, and saints.

CONCLUSION

The vast majority of late medieval commentaries on the Bible have never been edited and must be examined in manuscript. In many instances, we are simply reading from a scholar's notebook. The fact that most of these commentaries exist only in a living, abbreviated script, produced without the intervention of a machine, makes the medieval commentator's process, with its collusion of several pasts and the interpreter's present, strikingly manifest on the page. The collusion was effected by reading, writing, copying, and adapting commentary books, almost always in the curriculum of a late medieval school. There remains a great deal to be learned.

BIBLIOGRAPHY

Aquinas, Thomas
1969   *Summa Theologiae.* Vol. 1: *The Existence of God.* Garden City: Doubleday.

Armogathe, J-R. (ed.)
1989   *La Bible de tous les temps 6: Le Grand Siècle et la Bible.* Paris: Beauchesne.

Ashworth, E. J.
1982   "The Defeat, Neglect, and Revival of Scholasticism." In N. Kretzmann, A. Kenny, and J. Pinborg (eds.), *The Cambridge History of Later Medieval Philosophy,* 787-96. Cambridge: Cambridge University Press.

Augustine of Hippo
1958   *On Christian Doctrine.* Trans. D. W. Robertson. Indianapolis: Bobbs-Merrill.

Aureol, P. (= Pierre Aureolus, Peter Oriole)
1896   *Compendium sensus litteralis totius divinae Scripturae a clarissimo theologo fr. Petro Aureoli O.Min.* Ed. P. Seeboeck. Quaracchi.

Barthes, R.
1978   *Image-Music-Text.* Trans. S. Heath. London: Hill and Wang.

Bedouelle, G., and B. Roussel, eds.
1989   *La Bible de tous les Temps 5: Le temps des Réformes et la Bible.* Paris: Beauchesne.

Berndt, R.
1991   *André de Saint-Victor (1175). Exégète et théologien.* Paris: Brepols.
2000   "The School of St. Victor in Paris." In M. Saebø, ed., 2000: 1.2: 467-94.

Bonaventure

1864   *Opera omnia.* Ed. A. C. Peltier. Paris: Vives.

Bots, H., and F. Waquet

1997   *La République des Lettres.* Paris: Belin.

Brecht, M.

1985   *Martin Luther.* 3 vols. Philadelphia: Fortress.

Brinkmann, H.

1980   *Mittelalterliche Hermeneutik.* Tübingen: Niemeyer.

Buc, P.

1994   *L'Ambiguïté du livre. Prince, pouvoir, et peuple dans les commentaires de la Bible au Moyen Age.* ThH 95; Paris: Beauchesne.

Bucer, M.

1988   *Enarratio in Evangelion Iohannis.* Ed. I. Backus. Leiden: Brill.

Cajetan, Thomas de Vio

2005   *Opera omnia quotquot in Sacrae Scripturae expositionem reperiuntur.* 5 vols. Hildesheim: Olms. Repr. London: Prost, 1639.

Cappel, L.

1650   *Critica sacra.* 6 vols. Paris.

Casaubon, I.

1587   *Novum Testamentum.* Geneva.

Cassian, J.

1955-59 *Conférences.* Ed. E. Pichery. 3 vols. SC 42, 54, 64; Paris: Cerf.

Chemnitz, M., J. Gerhard, and P. Lyser

1652   *Harmonia evangelistarum a Martino Chemnitio primum inchoata, D. Polycarpo Lysero post continuata, atque D. Johanne Gerhardo tandem felicissime absoluta.* 2 vols. Frankfurt and Hamburg.

Chenu, M-D.

1957   *La théologie comme science au treizième siècle.* Paris: Vrin.

Colet, John

1985   *John Colet's Commentary on First Corinthians.* Ed., trans. and annotated by B. O'Kelley and C. A. L. Jarrot. Binghamton: Medieval and Renaissance Texts and Studies.

Comestor, P. (= Peter, Petrus)

1879   *Historia Scholastica.* PL 198. Ed. A. Hamman. Repr. Paris: Garnier, 1974.

Congar, M.-J.

1934-35 "Bio-Biographie de Cajétan." *Revue thomiste* 39: 3-49.

Courtenay, W. J.

1987   *Schools and Scholars in Fourteenth-Century England.* Princeton: Princeton University Press.

Delegue, Y.

1987   *Les machines du sens. Fragments d'une sémiologie médiévale.* Paris: Archives du Commentaire.

Dionysius Carthusienus (= Denys van Leeuwen)

1896-1935   *Opera omnia.* 42 vols. Cura et labore monachorum sacri ordinis Cartusiensis favente Pont. Max. Leone XIII. Tournai: Pratis.

1991   *Dionysii Cartusiensis Opera selecta.* Vol. 1 A and B: *Prolegomena. Bibliotheca manuscripta. Studia bibliographica.* Ed. K. Emory. Brepols: Turnhout.

Eckermann, W.

1990   "Zwei neuentdeckte theologische Principien Hugolins von Orvieto." In W. Eckermann, ed. *Schwerpunkte und Wirkungen des Sentenzenkommentars Hugolins von Orvieto O.E.S.A.,* 43-83. Würzburg: Augustinus.

Eimerich, N.

1973   *Le Manuel des inquisiteurs.* Transcribed and completed by F. Peña; introduction, translation from Latin, and notes by L. Sala-Molins. Bibliothèque de l'évolution de l'humanité; Paris: Mouton. Reprint Rome: Directorium inquisitorum, 1976.

Evans, G.

1984/85   *The Language and Logic of the Bible.* 2 vols. Cambridge: Cambridge University Press.

Farge, J. K.

1985   *Orthodoxy and Reform in Early Reformation France: The Faculty of Theology of Paris, 1500-1543.* Leiden: Brill.

Feld, H.

1977   *Die Anfänge der modernen biblischen Hermeneutik in der spätmittelalterlichen Theologie.* Vorträge des Instituts für Europäische Geschichte, 66. Wiesbaden: Steiner.

Fournier, J.

Postilla. Ms. in the Biblioteca Nacional de Catalunya, Barcelona: Ms. 550, f. 10ra.

Froehlich, K.

2000   "Christian Interpretation of the Old Testament in the High Middle Ages." In M. Saebø, ed., 2000: 1.2: 496-558.

Froehlich, K., and M. Gibson (eds.)

1992   *Biblia Latina cum glossa ordinaria: Facsimile Reprint of the Editio Princeps, Adolph Rusch of Strassburg 1480/81.* Brepols: Turnhout.

1996   *A History of the University in Europe* 2: *Universities in Early Modern Europe.* Cambridge: Cambridge University Press.

Gerhard, J.

1657   *Loci Theologici Cum pro adstruenda Veritate, tum pro destruenda quorumvis Contradicentium Falsitate, per theses nervose, solide & copiose explicati; Ab Autore Ipso Revisi et Locis Innumeris Aucti, Indicibusque, Materiarum, Locorum Scripturae, Autorum, Rerumque & Verborum exornati, & a mendis innumeris repurgati; In Novem Tomos et Exegesin Divisi Editio Novissima, ac quam plurimis hinc inde augmentis ditata, & illustrata Francofurti.* 9 vols. Hamburg: Hertelius.

Ghellinck, J. de

1948   *Le mouvement théologique du xiie siècle.* Bruges: Tempel.

Gibson, M.

1995   "The *De doctrina christiana* in the School of St. Victor." In E. D. English, ed., *Reading and Wisdom. The* De doctrina christiana *in the Middle Ages,* 41-47. Notre Dame: University of Notre Dame Press.

Gorran, Nicholas de

13th century   *Postilla super Genesim.* Ms. in Universitätsbibliothek, Würzburg: M. p. th. f. 151, f. 11rb.

Grafton, A., and L. Jardin

1986   *From Humanism to the Humanities: Education and the Liberal Arts in Fifteenth- and Sixteenth-Century Europe.* Cambridge: Harvard University Press.

Häring, N.

1982   "Commentary and Hermeneutics." In R. L. Benson, G. Constable, and C. D. Lanham, eds., *Renaissance and Renewal in the Twelfth Century,* 173-200. Cambridge: Harvard University Press.

Harrison, P.

1988   *The Bible, Protestantism, and the Rise of Natural Science.* Cambridge: Cambridge University Press.

Heinrich of Friemar

1477 or 1497   *Praeceptorium divinae legis.* Cologne: n.p. (falsely attributed to Nicholas of Lyra).

Henninger, M.

1989   *Relations: Medieval Theories, 1250-1325.* Oxford: Oxford University Press, 1989.

Hill, C.

1993   *The English Bible and the Seventeenth-Century Revolution.* London: Penguin.

Hugh of St. Victor

1879   *De scripturis et scriptoribus sacris praenotatiunculae, and Didascalicon. PL* 175. Ed. A. Hamman. Repr. Paris: Garnier, 1974.

1961   *Didascalicon: A Medieval Guide to the Arts.* Trans. J. Taylor. New York: Columbia University Press.

Hus, Jan

1966   *I Liber Sententiarum,* incepcio 1.2.14-15. In *Opera omnia* (repr. 1905). Osnabruck: Biblio.

Krey, P. D. W., and L. Smith

2000   *Nicholas of Lyra: The Senses of Scripture.* Leiden: Brill.

Kristellar, P. O.

1955   *Renaissance Thought: The Classic, Scholastic, and Humanist Strains.* Ed. M. Mooney. New York: Columbia University Press.

Landgraf, A. M.

1948   *Einführung in die Geschichte der theologischen Literatur der Frühscholastik.* Regensburg: Gregorius.

Langenstein, H. de (= Henricus de Hassia)

[14th C.]   *Commentaria in prologis Biblie et Genesin.* Stadtbibliothek Mainz, HS I 172, ff. 187rb-188rb.

Laplanche, F.

1986   *L'Écriture, le sacré et l'histoire. Érudits et politiques protestants devant la Bible en France au xviie siècle.* Amsterdam: Holland University Press.

1994   *La Bible en France entre mythe et critique xvi(e)-xix(e) siècles.* Paris: Michel.

Lerner, R. (ed.)

1996   *Neue Richtungen in der hoch- und spätmittelalterlichen Bibelexegese.* Munich: Oldenbourg.

Lombard, P. (= Petrus Lombardus)

1981   *Sententiae in IV. libris distinctae.* 2 vols. Rome: Grottaferrata.

Lubac, H. de

1954-64   *Exégèse médiévale. Les quatre sens de l'Écriture.* 2 vols., with 2 parts each. Paris: Aubier.

Marcolino, V.

1970   *Das Alte Testament in der Heilsgeschichte. Untersuchung zum dogmatischen Verständnis des Alten Testaments als heilsgeschichtliche Periode nach Alexander von Hales.* Münster: Aschendorff.

Matter, E. A.

1990   *Voice of My Beloved: The Song of Songs in Western Medieval Christianity.* Philadelphia: University of Pennsylvania Press.

Meier, C.

1977   *Gemma spiritualis. Methode und Gebrauch der Edelsteinallegorese vom frühen Christentum bis ins 18. Jahrhundert.* Munich: Fink.

Meier-Oeser, S.

1997   "Frans Tittelmans." *Biographisch-Bibliographisches Kirchenlexikon.* 12:190-92.

Mercker, H.

1971   *Schriftauslegung als Weltauslegung. Untersuchungen zur Stellung der Schrift in der Theologie Bonaventuras.* Munich: Schöningh.

Meyer, H.

1975   *Die Zahlenallegorese im Mittelalter. Methode und Gebrauch.* Munich: Fink.

Minnis, A.

1988   *Medieval Theory of Authorship: Scholastic Literary Attitudes in the Later Middle Ages.* 2nd ed. Aldershot: Scolar.

Morey, J. H.

1993   "Peter Comestor, Biblical Paraphrase, and the Medieval Popular Bible." *Speculum* 68:6-35.

Mulchahey, M. M.

1998   *"First the Bow Is Bent in Study." Dominican Education before 1350.* Toronto: Pontifical Institute of Medieval Studies.

Muller, R. A.

1999   *Ad Fontes Argumentorum: The Sources of Reformed Theology in the Seventeenth Century.* Utrechtse theologische reeks 40. Utrecht: Universiteit Utrecht.

2003   *After Calvin: Studies in the Development of a Theological Tradition.* Oxford: Oxford University Press.

Müntzinger, J.

14th C.   *Liber leccionum epistolarum sancti.* Basel: Universitätsbibliothek. A V 28, ff. 146r-226v.

Nicholas of Lyra

1492   *Postilla literalis super totam Bibliam,* 4 vols. Strasbourg: Mentelin. Facsimile ed. 1971. Franfurt a. M.: Minerva.

Norris, R. A., Jr.

2003   "Augustine and the Close of the Ancient Period." *HBI*[1] 380-408.

Ocker, C.

1991   "The Fusion of Exegesis and Papal Ideology in Fourteenth-Century Theology." In M. Burrows and P. Rorem, eds., *Biblical Hermeneutics in Historical Perspective,* 131-51. Grand Rapids: Eerdmans.

1993   *Johannes Klenkok: A Friar's Life, c. 1310-1374.* Transactions of the American Philosophical Society, 83.5. Philadelphia: American Philosophical Society.

2002   *Biblical Poetics before Humanism and Reformation.* Cambridge: Cambridge University Press.

Ohly, F.

1977   "Vom geistigen Sinn des Wortes im Mittelalter." In F. Ohly, ed., *Schriften zur mittelalterlichen Bedeutungsforschung.* 1-31. Darmstadt: Wissenschaftliche Buchgesellschaft.

Reinhardt, K.

1987   "Das Werk Nicolaus von Lyra im mittelalterlichen Spanien." *Traditio* 43: 321-58.

Reynolds, S.

1996   *Medieval Reading: Grammar, Rhetoric and the Classical Text.* Cambridge: Cambridge University Press.

Richard of St. Victor

1874   *Speculum ecclesiae. PL* 177: 335-80. Ed. A. Hamman. Repr. Paris: Garnier, 1974.

1958   *Liber exceptionum.* Ed. Jean Châtillon. Paris: Vrin.

Riché, P., and G. Lobrichon, eds.

1984   *La Bible de tous les temps* 4: *Le Moyen Age et la Bible.* Paris: Beauchesne.

Ridder-Symoens, H. de

1992   *A History of the University in Europe:* 1: *Universities in the Middle Ages.* Cambridge: Cambridge University Press.

1996   *A History of the University in Europe:* 2: *Universities in Early Modern Europe.* Cambridge: Cambridge University Press.

Roest, B.

2000   *A History of Franciscan Education (c. 1210-1517).* Leiden: Brill.

Rosemann, P. W.

2004   *Peter Lombard.* Oxford: Oxford University Press.

Rummel, E.

1986   *Erasmus' Annotations on the New Testament: From Philologist to Theologian.* Toronto: University of Toronto Press.

Saebø, M. (ed.)

2000   *Hebrew Bible/Old Testament: The History of Its Interpretation* 1: *From the Beginnings to the Middle Ages (until 1300).* Vol. 1, part 2. Göttingen: Vandenhoeck und Ruprecht.

Schüssler, H.

1977   *Der Primat der Heiligen Schrift als theologisches und kanonistisches Problem in Spätmittelalter.* Wiesbaden: Steiner.

Seybold, M.

1971   *Die Offenbarung. Von der Schrift bis zum Ausgang der Scholastik.* Freiburg: Herder.

Shuger, D.

1994   *The Renaissance Bible: Scholarship, Sacrifice, and Subjectivity.* Berkeley: University of California Press.

Sixtus Senensis

1566   *Bibliotheca Sancta.* Venice.

Smalley, B.

1958   "John Baconthorpe's Postille on St. Matthew," *Medieval and Renaissance Studies* 4: 91-145.

1964   *The Study of the Bible in the Middle Ages.* Notre Dame: University of Notre Dame Press.

1981   *Studies in Medieval Thought and Learning: Abelard to Wyclif.* London: Hambledon.

Steneck, N.

1976   *Science and Creation in the Middle Ages: Henry of Langenstein (d. 1397) on Genesis.* Notre Dame: University of Notre Dame Press.

Tittelmans, F.

1528   *Elucidatio in omnes epistolas apostolicas.* Antwerp.

1529   *Collationes quinque super epistolam ad Romanos Beati Pauli.* Antwerp.

1530   *Libri duo de authoritate Apocalypsis.* Antwerp.

1531   *Elucidatio in omnes Psalmos. Elucidatio canticorum ferialium. Adnotationes ex hebraeo atque Chaldaeo.* Antwerp.

1536   *Commentarii in Ecclesiasten Salomonis.* Antwerp.

1543   *Elucidatio in Evangelium secundum Joannem.* Antwerp.

1545a   *Elucidatio in Evangelium secundum Matthaeum.* Antwerp.

1545b   *Elucidatio in Evangelium secundum Matthaeum et Joannem.* Paris.

1547a   *Elucidatio paraphrastica in Librum Iob.* Antwerp.

1547b   *Commentarii in Cantica Canticorum.* Antwerp.

Turretin, F.

1696   *Institutio theologiae elencticae.* Leiden: Haring.

Voetius

1965   "*Disputationes Theologicae Selectae,* Extracts." In J. Beardslee, ed., *Reformed Dogmatics.* New York: Library of Protestant Theology.

Wicks, J.

2008   "Catholic Old Testament Interpretation in the Reformation and Early Confessional Eras." In M. Saebø, ed., *Hebrew Bible/Old Testament: The History of Its Interpretation,* Vol. 2. Göttingen: Vandenhoeck und Ruprecht.

Witt, R.

2000   *In the Footsteps of the Ancients: The Origins of Humanism from Levato to Bruni.* Studies in Medieval and Reformation Thought 74. Leiden: Brill.

Zac, S.

1965   *Spinoza et l'interprétation de l'Écriture.* Paris: Presses universitaires de France.

Zier, M.

1993   "The Manuscript Tradition of the Glossa Ordinaria for Daniel, and Hints at a Method for a Critical Edition." *Scriptorium* 47: 3-25.

Zumkeller, A.

1990   "Leben und Werke Hugolins von Orvieto." In W. Eckermann, ed., *Schwerpunkte und Wirkungen des Sentenzenkommentars Hugolins von Orvieto O.E.S.A.,* 3-42. Würzburg: Augustinus.

CHAPTER 9

The Renaissance Humanists

Erika Rummel

THE HISTORICAL CONTEXT

Two features of Renaissance Humanism had a direct bearing on the course of biblical studies in early modern Europe: the privileging of classical antiquity over the "dark" Middle Ages and a preference for rhetoric and language studies over the traditional academic core subject, Aristotelian logic. In their efforts to recover the legacy of Antiquity, humanists turned from historical interpretations to the sources themselves. *Ad fontes,* "back to the sources," became their watchword. In biblical studies, the search for authentic witnesses of the past meant reaching beyond the Vulgate version of the Bible to the original Hebrew and Greek texts, and beyond medieval commentators to the early Greek and Latin fathers (Bentley 1983: 3-31).

The proponents of the "New Learning," as the humanistic initiative was called, adopted classical models of style and made a concerted effort to purge Latin of medieval accretions. The progress of the New Learning was closely linked with the rise of print culture. Humanists were quick to take advantage of the new medium to further the revival and dissemination of *probi autores,* the "great authors" of classical Antiquity. They became avid manuscript collectors and served printers as editors, proofreaders, textual critics, and translators. Extending their expertise to biblical texts and commentaries, humanists collaborated with printers to produce a spate of critical editions and translations of scriptural texts and exegetical writings from the patristic age (Rummel 1985). The application of these pioneering philological skills to Scripture was, however, controversial. The history and transmission of the biblical text had never before been subject to such rigorous scholarly examination. Many people, therefore, reacted with indignation. They saw attempts to revise or correct the biblical text as tampering with the Word of God, or as a challenge to the principle of inspiration (Bentley 1983: 194-219; Rummel 1995a: 96-125).

The humanistic enterprise also met with strong resistance from professional theologians, who were determined to safeguard their exclusive right to deal with sacred texts. They branded biblical humanists as interlopers, dilettantes who were liable to theological error on account of their lack of professional training and their exposure to non-Christian thought (Bentley 1983: 194-219; Rummel 1995a). Erasmus dismissed such concerns as paranoia and professional jealousy. In the eyes of the Scholastic doctors, he said sarcastically, "it is heresy to speak Greek, and to speak like Cicero is heresy too" (CWE 23.32).

The Reformation movement superimposed a new element on the controversy between theologians and humanists. Catholic apologists connected the interest humanists had shown in the biblical text with the principle of *sola scriptura*, "Scripture alone," embraced by the Reformers. They took note, moreover, of the instances in which the revisions and emendations proposed by humanist editors supported the Reformers' doctrine and accused them of having inspired or certainly facilitated Reformation thought. A new wording introduced by Erasmus in his edition of the NT is a prime example (*Novum Instrumentum omne,* 1516). In Matt. 4:17, he changed the Vulgate translation *poenitentiam agite* ("do penance") to *resipiscite* ("repent"), shifting the emphasis from works to faith, a point elaborated by Luther in his *Ninety-Five Theses* (see chapter 10 below; Aland, 1967). The humanists themselves occasionally linked cultural with religious reform. In his inaugural lecture on Greek at Wittenberg (1518) the young Melanchthon exhorted his audience to abandon the "frigid glosses, concordances, and discordances" of the Scholastics (Keen 1988: 55; see chapters 8 and 11 in this volume). Only "when we turn our mind *to the sources* shall we begin to savour of Christ" (CR 11.23). Using the humanists' watchword, Melanchthon connected their quest to recover the golden age of Antiquity through elimination of the medieval tradition with the quest to return to the golden apostolic age through elimination of Scholastic theology. The Reformation debate, however, focused not merely on the recovery of source texts but more particularly on their interpretation (Rummel 1995a). Soon the confessional parties deployed humanistic philology in the service of exegesis, redirecting its original purpose and converting it from a scholarly to a partisan tool. This strategic use of philology, labelled "dogmatic humanism" by Shuger (1994: 22), was characteristic of the era of confessionalization in the later sixteenth century (Rummel 2000).

EDITIONS AND TRANSLATIONS OF SOURCE TEXTS

During the fifteenth century, a knowledge of Hebrew or Greek could be acquired only through private initiative, usually by engaging the services of a native speaker. By the beginning of the sixteenth century, the humanistic emphasis on language studies had resulted in the foundation of public lectureships and colleges dedicated to the teaching of biblical languages. They became part of the curriculum at the University of Alcalá (founded by Cardinal Cisneros in 1508), at Oxford (Corpus Christi College, founded by Bishop Foxe in 1518), at Louvain (Collegium Trilingue, a legacy of Jerome Busleyden, 1518), at the University of Wittenberg (where Frederick of Saxony instituted a Greek lectureship in 1518), and at Paris (the Collège des Lecteurs Royaux, under the patronage of Francis I in 1530) (Kittelson and Transue, 1984).

The Hebrew Text and Translations from the Hebrew

The attitude of Renaissance humanists toward Hebrew studies was not unequivocal (Rummel 1995a: 96-125). Leonardo Bruni (1370-1444), the Italian humanist and Greek scholar (Botley 2004: 5-62), expressed his reservations in these terms: "What comparison is there between the erudition of the Greeks and the crudeness of the Jews? For we learn the Greek tongue for the sake of philosophy and other disciplines. It confers perfection on Latin letters . . . but there can be no such attraction in learning Hebrew" (Trinkaus 1970: 2.817 n. 45). Bruni's younger contemporary Gianozzo Manetti (1423-97), the Italian politician and humanist scholar (Botley 2004: 63-114) used even stronger language. He argued that the Jews, "content with their own [culture] and seeking no other, have long lacked foreign languages . . . thence long conditioned by a crass and supine ignorance of all things, they lie moribund, like unclean swine in mud, and in this way they are buried alive in their own perfidy as in a sepulchre" (Trinkaus 1970: 2.593). Their ignorance of Greek and Latin, he said, had deprived them of an opportunity to study the NT. Their cultural isolation was responsible for their persistence in a "false" religion. When Manetti himself took up Hebrew studies, reading the OT and medieval Hebrew commentaries with the help of Jewish tutors, the desire to convert Jews to Christianity was uppermost in his mind. Among the fruits of his research was not only a translation of the Psalter, but also a book *Contra Judaeos et Gentes,* in which he showed up the "errors" of Jews and pagans (Botley 2004: 99-114). While Christian Hebraists such as Giovanni Pico della Mirandola, the Italian philosopher in fifteenth-century Italy, and Johann Reuchlin, the humanist in sixteenth-century Germany, stimulated interest in Hebrew studies, a certain ambivalence prevailed. Erasmus's attitude was characteristic. Criticizing the humanist and Strasbourg reformer Wolfgang Capito (1478-1541), who had authored a popular Hebrew grammar, he wrote: "I could wish you were more inclined to Greek than to that Hebrew of yours. . . ." In his view, Hebrew literature was "full of the most tedious fabrications" and "spread a kind of fog over everything" (CWE 5.347).

In spite of such misgivings, interest in Hebrew studies grew. Several Hebrew grammars were published by Christian scholars at the beginning of the sixteenth century, for example, by Conradus Pellicanus (1507), Johann Reuchlin (1509), and Sanctes Pagninus (Santi Pagnini), the Italian monk (1526). Humanists who turned to OT studies could build on and benefit from earlier research by Jewish scholars. The Psalms had been printed in 1477 together with the commentary of Kimhi (1160-1225), the Jewish rabbi, grammarian, Bible commentator, and philosopher. The Psalms were followed by the *editio princeps* of the Pentateuch with *Targum Onkelos* and Rashi's commentary (Bologna, 1482; Banitt 1985). The first complete Hebrew Bible (the "Soncino Bible") had been produced in 1488 by the printer Israel Nathan b. Samuel with the help of Abraham b. Hayyim, the scholar who had also been involved in the Bologna Pentateuch. The first Hebrew Bible to receive the papal imprimatur was published in 1516-17. It was the result of a collaboration between the Christian printer Daniel Bomberg of Amsterdam, who set up shop in Venice, and Felix Pratensis, a converted Jew. In 1524-25, a second edition of Bomberg's Great Rabbinic Bible was produced with the help of Jacob b. Hayyim (Mulder 1990: 116-19; see chapter 6 above).

Another edition of the Hebrew text went forward in Spain, prepared by a team of humanists under the direction of Cardinal Ximénes de Cisneros (for a complete discussion see Olin 1990). It was part of the multivolume *Complutensian Polyglot* (so called after the Latin name for Alcalá, the place of publication) (Bentley 1983: 70-111; see chapter 7 above). Work on the Polyglot may have begun as early as 1502, but it was only in 1510 that the printer of the edition, Arnao Guillén de Brócar, established his press in Alcalá. The first four volumes contained the OT in Hebrew, Greek, and Latin (as well as the Aramaic text of the Pentateuch). The fifth volume contained the Greek and Latin texts of the NT. The sixth volume provided lexicographical and grammatical aids. The printing was completed in 1516, but the papal imprimatur was not granted until 1520, and distribution did not begin until 1522 (see chapter 7 above).

The Polyglot text was based on the collation of a respectable number of mss. Biographers of Cisneros mention seven Hebrew mss. His prologue to the

Polyglot, addressed to Pope Leo X, states that Greek and Latin mss. were purchased or borrowed from the Vatican and from the library of the late Cardinal Bessarion in Venice (Olin 1990: 61-64). Textual criticism was a new skill, and Cisneros felt obliged to explain its purpose and advantages. He justifies the humanistic call *ad fontes* and the practice of collating mss. to arrive at the correct reading. No translation could recapture the full meaning of the original, he said. Moreover, there were discrepancies among the mss. And (Olin 1990: 62-63)

> wherever there is diversity in the Latin manuscripts or the suspicion of a corrupted reading (we know how frequently this occurs because of the ignorance and negligence of copyists), it is necessary to go back to the original source of Scripture, as St. Jerome and St. Augustine and other ecclesiastical writers advise us to do, to examine the authenticity of the books of the Old Testament in light of the original Hebrew text and of the New Testament in light of the Greek copies. And so that every student of Holy Scripture might have at hand the original texts themselves and be able to quench his thirst at the very fountainhead of the water that flows unto life everlasting and not have to content himself with rivulets alone, we ordered the original languages of Holy Scripture with their translations adjoined to be printed.

Some of the arguments that Cisneros presented had already made their appearance in the apologetic writings of fifteenth-century Italian humanists (Rummel 1995a: 96-125) and in Erasmus's prolegomena to his NT edition (see below). They in turn can be traced back to Jerome, whose work on the scriptural text exposed him to objections and hostilities remarkably similar to those encountered by Renaissance humanists. Not surprisingly, Jerome became a kind of patron saint for biblical humanists; they frequently invoked his example of learned piety to justify their own research (Rummel 1995a: 101-125).

For his project, Cisneros had assembled a group of distinguished humanists. The responsibility of individual scholars remains a matter of some discussion. It appears, however, that the preparation of the Hebrew text was entrusted to the *conversos* (converted Jews) Pablo Coronel and Alfonso de Zamora, that of the Greek text to Hernán Núñez de Guzmán and Demetrios Ducas, the latter a Cretan emigré and the only non-Spaniard on the editorial team. Juan de Vergara and Diego López de Zúñiga may have prepared the Vulgate text (Bentley 1983: 70-91). Cisneros also attempted to attract Erasmus, hoping to benefit from his experience in preparing his own NT edition, but the humanist declined the invitation. Later developments suggest that the envisioned collaboration would not have gone smoothly. In 1520, Erasmus clashed with López de Zúñiga over text-critical and exegetical questions. The result was a bitter and drawn-out controversy (Bentley 1983: 194-213). Erasmus's NT edition was also attacked by Elio Antonio de Nebrija, but de Nebrija did not publish his criticism.

Nebrija (c. 1444-1522), the most prestigious of the editors working on the *Complutensian Polyglot,* moved to the University of Alcalá in 1513 from Salamanca, where he had occupied the chair of grammar. One of the principal Spanish humanists, Nebrija had been exposed to the New Learning during his studies in Italy in the 1460s. On his return to Spain, he championed a revival of classical Latin. His application of philology to biblical studies, however, aroused the suspicion of the Inquisitor, who confiscated his manuscripts. In 1507, the scholarly Cisneros was appointed Inquisitor General. He returned the manuscripts to the author and gave him permission to publish his research under the title of *Tertia Quinquagena,* fifty annotations concerning biblical usage and the etymology of biblical names (Nebrija 1516b; Bentley 1983: 82-86). In an *Apologia* addressed to his new patron, Nebrija offered a defense of biblical humanism, which sums up the principal concerns and issues confronting humanists at the turn of the sixteenth century (Nebrija 1516a; Bentley 1983: 81-82). He argued that textual and literary criticism of the Bible required philological rather than theological training. He emphasized the importance of collating mss. to establish the correct text and studying the text in the original languages to establish the correct meaning.

Nebrija's approach, still novel at the time, did not have the full support of his more cautious colleagues on the Complutensian project. Under these circumstances, he withdrew from the team in 1514. In a letter of resignation addressed to Cardinal Cisneros he explained that he disagreed with the editorial policy adopted by the team. He objected, for example, to the practice of keeping language traditions separate, that is, of collating only same-language mss. It was an approach that relieved editors of controversial choices (Bentley 1983: 88-91). A detailed study of the text by Bentley (91-111) shows that the policy to which Nebrija objected was not in fact followed uniformly. Whenever the Polyglot editors did cross language lines, however, they altered the Greek to make it conform to the Vulgate, not vice versa. Such inconsistencies point to two features characteristic of early biblical humanism: the lack of a fully developed method of textual criticism and a reluctance to break with tradition in a way that might be interpreted as a challenge to the teaching authority of the church (Bentley 1983: 194-219). Thus, Erasmus candidly admitted in the preface to his second edition of the NT (1519) that he had shied away from the radical revision dictated by scholarly considerations to avoid scandal: "I introduced changes rather sparingly, fearing that certain people would not suffer such great novelty" (*Opera omnia* [ed. Leclerc] 6.3).

In the 1520s, the Italian Dominican Santes Pagninus (1470-1536) contributed substantially to the advance of Hebrew studies. The most influential of his many learned works was his Latin translation of both Testaments (Lyon, 1527/28, dedicated to Pope Clement VII), with the OT based on a careful study of the Hebrew text. His translation and study aids (Hebrew grammars and dictionaries) were consulted extensively by both Catholics and Reformers such as Agostino Steuco, Michael Servetus, and Jean Mercier. Moreover, his translation was used in editions of the Bible published during the latter half of the sixteenth century (Centi 1945).

One of the earliest scholars in northern Europe to take an interest in the Hebrew Bible was Jacques Lefèvre d'Étaples (c. 1460-1536), who taught at the Collège du Cardinal Lemoine in Paris and was distinguished for his work on Aristotle (Bedouelle 1976: 28-36). A journey to Italy in 1491-92 brought him into contact with the New Learning, and on his return to France he himself became the center of a humanistic circle. Retiring from his teaching post, he took up residence with his patron Guillaume Briçonnet, abbot of Saint-Germain-des-Près, and turned to Scripture studies. Although his knowledge of Hebrew was limited, he published the *Quincuplex Psalterium* (1509), containing in parallel columns the Old Latin, the Gallican, the Roman, and the Hebrew Psalters, to which he added a *Psalterium conciliatum* and a commentary (Bedouelle 1976: 173-80). In later years, Lefèvre turned to NT scholarship. Among the fruits of his labor were a revised Latin text of the Pauline Epistles and a French translation of the NT (Bedouelle 1976: 141-230).

It was only in the 1530s that other humanists in central and northern Europe began to take an active part in the publication of the Hebrew Bible. Sebastian Münster, who taught Hebrew at the Universities of Heidelberg and Basel, published study aids that were widely used in his time: several dictionaries, among them an adaptation of Kimhi's classic dictionary, and a Hebrew grammar in collaboration with the leading Jewish philologist Eliah Levita. In 1535 he published a Hebrew Bible with a Latin translation and annotations drawn from rabbinical sources (Friedman 1983). Evincing the characteristic humanist appreciation for language studies and the need to consult the original texts, he cautioned his readers (Bedouelle 1976: 223-24):

> Numerous passages in Scripture are so obscure and complex that one cannot well understand them without recourse to the Jewish tradition. . . . Do not allow yourselves to be prejudiced against the rabbinical text and commentaries, Christian Reader, as long as you have obtained a

good knowledge of Christ; rather, it will benefit you to see the agreements and disagreements among our traditions.

Münster was one of the few biblical humanists critical of Pagninus; he based his own text on the text edited by Felix Pratensis.

Pagninus's work found more appreciation in France and the Netherlands. His Hebrew grammar and thesaurus were incorporated in Robert Estienne's edition of the Hebrew OT (Paris, 1539-44; Metzger and Ehrman 2005: 149-52). Another prominent entry among the editions of the sixteenth century came from Plantin's press: the *Royal Polyglot* (Antwerp, 1569-72), edited by the Benedictine Arias Montanus under the patronage of Philip II. The edition offered, in four parallel columns, the Hebrew text, the Vulgate, a new Latin translation from the LXX, and the LXX itself, with the targums and their Latin translations printed at the foot of the page. The Latin translation of the Hebrew text by Sanctes Pagninus was given in a separate volume. Like the *Complutensian Polyglot,* the *Royal Polyglot* provided lexicographical and grammatical aids as well as indices, including a list of variant readings drawn up by theologians from Louvain.

The New Testament: The Greek Text and the Vulgate

Until the fifteenth century, knowledge of Greek was a rare accomplishment in western and central Europe. In the wake of the fall of Constantinople, however, Greek emigrants flooded into Italy, reviving Greek studies there and rekindling an interest in the LXX and the Greek fathers. Northern Europe lagged behind Italian initiatives by almost half a century. Study of Greek was only gradually introduced there at the beginning of the sixteenth century. Erasmus complained that in his youth "there was no supply of Greek books, and no less a shortage of teachers" (CWE 9.301).

Several editions and revisions of the LXX and Vulgate published in conjunction with the Hebrew text have already been mentioned. We now turn our attention more specifically to Greek studies and translations from the Greek. Giannozzo Manetti was the first Renaissance humanist to embark on a new Latin translation of the LXX. Political intrigues in his native Florence had forced him to move to Rome, where he became secretary to Pope Nicholas V. After two years, he departed for the court of King Alfonso of Naples, who made him a councillor (Botley 2004: 63-70). It was there that he began translating the Greek NT and the Hebrew Psalter. Manetti's work did not go unchallenged. He defended himself in the *Apologeticus,* published together with the translation of the Psalter. The main charge brought against him was disrespect for Jerome, to whom, in Manetti's time, the Vulgate was ascribed. In the common opinion, it had been formally commissioned by Pope Damasus and was composed under divine guidance. Any correction or revision was therefore regarded as a challenge to Jerome's erudition, the Pope's authority, and the principle of inspiration. This attitude would still prevail in the sixteenth century. In 1526, Pierre Cousturier, a graduate of the University of Paris, indignantly rejected the idea of revising the biblical text: "The Vulgate has been revised so thoroughly that no flaw can be found in it. Anyone who thinks differently is out of his mind. . . . It is beyond doubt that Jerome himself undertook the emendation, not only taking prudent counsel but also being guided in a mysterious way by the Holy Spirit" (*De Tralatione Bibliae,* 1525, 49 recto). Manetti argued in vain that Jerome himself had distinguished between inspired prophets and translators, who relied on human skills. He furthermore pointed out that the Vulgate mss. in circulation contained numerous textual variants introduced by careless or ignorant scribes. It was therefore necessary to emend the text (Botley 2004: 82-114).

Manetti salutes the humanistic principle *ad fontes,* but like other biblical scholars, shies away from a rigorous implementation of his theories when dealing with the sacred writings. He notes that a translation cannot always capture the nuances of the original; language studies allowing the reader to go to the source texts were therefore necessary. Enunciating his theory of translation, he distinguishes between versions of secular and sacred (or more generally, philosophical) texts. A literal translation was never satisfactory, he said, but special considerations applied to the biblical text. One must be careful not to diverge too far from the original, and one need not be overly anxious about stylistic niceties. Like many humanists, Manetti believed that the literary and rhetorical qualities of a text played an important role in enhancing the message, but he made a special case for the Bible (Botley 2004: 99-114). Biblical translators were governed by "certain narrower laws of translation, and constrained by certain limits" (Trinkaus 1970: 2.598).

We find similar arguments in the writings of Manetti's contemporary and compatriot Aurelio Brandolini (c. 1454-97). He, too, found it necessary to defend his approach to biblical studies. He moved to Rome in the 1480s, where he enjoyed papal patronage and associated with other humanists in Pomponio Leto's Roman Academy (c. 1460-1500) devoted to the promoting of classical studies. He taught humanities and pursued antiquarian and philosophical interests. In 1489, he left Rome for the court of the Hungarian king Matthias Corvinus. Returning to Italy after the king's death in 1490, he taught rhetoric at Pisa and Florence, where he became a member of the Order of Hermits of St.

Augustine. In the 1490s, he produced an epitome of the historical books of the OT (extant in manuscript only). It was an attempt to make the Bible more accessible to the general reader by rewriting it in a literary style. The apologetic preface preceding the text confirms the difficulties confronting biblical humanists in the fifteenth century. Brandolini reported that absurd charges had been brought against him, his critics claiming that he had written a "new Bible." They insisted that he had no right to engage in biblical studies, that this task was reserved for professional theologians. He was wrong, moreover, "to write about sacred matters, using a polished style and cultured speech." Brandolini challenged his critics, questioning the definition of "theologian": "What prohibits me from being both a man of letters and a theologian? For all disciplines are so intricately connected and related that whoever wishes to master one of them must somehow touch on and draw on all of them." An academic degree did not automatically or exclusively confer competence, Brandolini noted: "I speak about God in a way that is not without learning, and that is what makes a man a theologian" (Rummel 1995b: 86-90). Indeed, ignorant medieval scribes and commentators had vitiated the Bible — they, rather than he, had changed the old Bible and created a new one. Brandolini's arguments foreshadow the polemic between humanists and Scholastic theologians over competence and professional qualifications, which became endemic to northern universities at the beginning of the sixteenth century (Rummel 1995b).

Perhaps the best known and most influential biblical humanist of the fifteenth century was Lorenzo Valla (1405-57). Valla taught rhetoric in Pavia, entered the service of Alfonso I, king of Naples, in 1435 and obtained a position at the papal court in Rome in 1448. Already notorious for exposing the Donation of Constantine as a forgery, he embarked on a collation of Greek and Latin mss. of the NT. The circulation of his notes in manuscript was necessarily limited; they did not become widely accessible until 1505, when they were published by Erasmus under the title *Adnotationes in Novum Testamentum* (Chomarat 1978; Bentley 1983: 32-69; Rummel 1986: 85-88).

Explaining his reasons for collating mss., Valla borrowed arguments from Jerome. By the time his annotations were published, many of these arguments had become commonplaces of apologetic literature. Biblical humanists often compared the original text to a clear source and translations and corrupt transcriptions to polluted runnels; they distinguished between the inspired authors of the Bible and the scribes and translators, who were subject to error. Valla was among the first humanists to cast doubt on Jerome's authorship of the Vulgate. He argued that, even if Jerome was the author of the translation or revised the Vulgate versions in circulation in his day, the text had been corrupted in the intervening centuries and was once

again in need of revision and correction. Valla had an exceptionally clear understanding of the nature and historical development of a text. He challenged
his critics to tell him "What is Holy Writ? Does every translation of the Old or
New Testament qualify? But there is a multitude and variety of conflicting
translations!" (*Antidotum primum*, 1978: 112). In the absence of an autograph,
he said, the textual critic had to choose among diverse readings in the surviving ms. copies (Bentley 1983: 36-49).

Valla himself did not produce a new text or translation of the Vulgate
but merely a set of annotations on the Gospels, in which he commented on
the discrepancies in the mss. collated by him and pointed out errors, obscurities, and idiomatic lapses in the Vulgate translation. Although his observations were primarily philological, they clearly had exegetical implications. In
fact, Valla suggested that some longstanding theological disputes could be
settled, once theologians understood that their lack of philological training
had prevented them from understanding the literal meaning of the biblical
text. The need for language training remained, however, a controversial question. In 1516, Erasmus drew up a curriculum for theology students, in which
he insisted that language studies were fundamental to their training: "Our
first care must be to learn the three languages Latin, Greek, and Hebrew, for it
is plain that the mystery of all Scripture is revealed in them" (*Methodus*, Erasmus 1933: 151). Cousturier, whose polemical tract *De tralatione* has already
been mentioned, countered: "We do not need a knowledge of foreign languages for an understanding of Holy Writ. . . . It is completely insane and
smacks of heresy for anyone to affirm that one should sweat over foreign languages for this purpose" (*De tralatione*, 63 recto).

Erasmus (c. 1466-1536), whose work spanned literature, pedagogy, and
theology, was regarded by both admirers and critics of his time as the principal
representative of humanism. He was, moreover, a founding father of what is
now termed "Christian humanism," the fusion of the New Learning with the
Modern Devotion. A member of the Augustinian Order, he studied for some
years at Paris without, however, taking a degree. After travels in England and
Italy, he took up residence in Louvain, living as an independent scholar. He
had been made councillor to Prince Charles (later Charles V) and also received
income from church prebends conferred on him by high-ranking patrons. At
the end of 1521, he moved to Basel, where for many years he remained the central figure of the humanist circle at the Froben Press (Rummel 2004).

Following in the footsteps of Valla, whose annotations on the NT he had
brought to the public's attention, Erasmus collated Greek and Latin mss. for his
edition of the NT (*Novum Instrumentum omne*, 1516). It contained the Greek
text and a lightly revised Vulgate text on facing pages, followed by extensive

notes explaining textual problems and editorial decisions. Since his knowledge of Hebrew was slight, Erasmus relied on the help of the Basel humanist and later reformer Johannes Oecolampadius whenever the OT was quoted and Hebrew had a bearing on the text. In his prefatory letter to the reader, Erasmus stressed that he was acting in the capacity of a philologist and was solely concerned with textual criticism: "Let no one, like a selfish guest, demand supper in place of a light luncheon" (CWE 3: 198). This was a preemptive strike aimed at professional theologians who might question his qualifications. He had a doctorate in theology, conferred on him by the University of Turin *per saltum*, that is, without his having fulfilled the standard prerequisites. Graduate theologians therefore grouped him with the "theologizing humanists," as Noël Beda, the syndic of the faculty of theology at Paris, called them (Rummel 1995a: 83-84).

It was obvious, moreover, that textual and literary criticism could not be neatly separated from exegesis, as Erasmus would have his readers believe. Clearly, the verbal changes he introduced affected the interpretation of the passage in question. Luther's use of Erasmus's edition (Luther's copy, with marginal annotations, is extant) was noted by Catholic theologians. In subsequent revisions of the NT (1519, 1522, 1527, 1535) Erasmus responded to their criticisms, sometimes by modifying a translation that had given offense, but more often by adding explanations and prooftexts to his notes. In this process, the nature of his annotations changed significantly. In the first edition, the bulk of his commentary was concerned with philological questions, especially the meanings of words in light of classical usage. In later editions, references to patristic authors, as witnesses to the text and interpreters of its meaning, became preponderant (Rummel 1986, 1989; Botley 2004: 115-63).

Erasmus also continued his search for new mss. and incorporated new evidence in subsequent editions. Of the numerous mss. he used, some are unidentified, others have been destroyed, but several, dating from the twelfth and thirteenth centuries and used as printer's copy, are preserved in the Universitätsbibliothek in Basel. They came from the library of John of Ragusa (d. c. 1443), the Dominican theologian who had made an important collection of Greek mss. while in Constantinople and had left them to the Basel Dominicans on his death in 1443. Ironically, Erasmus was suspicious of the venerable Greek codex Vaticanus (B) and paid slight attention to the variants reported to him by a Roman contact, Paolo Bombasio (Bentley 1983: 34-35).

Erasmus's editorial decisions involved him in numerous polemics, which fill two of the ten folio volumes in the Leiden *Opera Omnia* (1701-03). To cite one notorious case, in his first edition Erasmus omitted the *"Comma Johanneum"* (1 John 5:7), which was missing from all the Greek mss. he had consulted and which he therefore regarded as spurious. Faced with stiff opposition and eventually with evidence from an English ms., he reluctantly restored the verse in the third edition. We now know that the English ms. was a modern forgery and that the evidence was expressly fabricated by Erasmus's opponents, who feared that omitting the verse would endanger the doctrine of the trinity (de Jonge, 1980). Erasmus again raised eyebrows when he retranslated Rev. 22:16-21 from the Latin Vulgate into Greek himself, because the only Greek ms. of Revelation at his disposal lacked those verses. He replaced the verses in the third edition, after he was able to consult the *Complutensian Polyglot*. Since publication of the Polyglot was delayed, Erasmus' Greek NT became the *editio princeps* (see chapter 7 above).

Although the NT edition was Erasmus's *magnum opus*, his numerous editions and translations of patristic writings were of equal importance for the advancement of biblical studies. He collaborated with Froben's printing house in producing editions of Jerome, Augustine, Tertullian, Basil, Cyprian, Arnobius, Hilary, Ambrose, Origen, and Chrysostom. The collation of manuscripts and the revision of the text involved a formidable amount of work. "Let me say just one thing, which is bold, but true," he said in his preface to the Jerome edition. "I believe that the writing of his books cost Jerome less effort than I spent in the restoring of them" (CWE 61.10).

It is clear that Erasmus regarded his patristic editions as a significant contribution to scholarship. He expressed disappointment, therefore, at the lack of recognition he received in theological circles. "Certain people set on me like barking dogs," he wrote, "because I do not write, as they would prefer, about indulgences" (CWE 9.298). He did, however, enter the Reformation debate, engaging in a polemic with Luther over the question of free will. The controversy has received a great deal of attention for its doctrinal implications, but it is also significant as a showcase of humanistic methodology and as such is relevant in the present context. In the *Diatribe on Free Will* (1524), Erasmus examined evidence on both sides of the question, citing biblical passages for and against the concept of free will. In light of the conflicting evidence he encountered, Erasmus the humanist suspended judgment; Erasmus the Catholic, however, supported the concept of free will. He explained that he had no fondness for assertions and preferred the Skeptic method of argumentation ending in *epochē*, suspension of judgment, but was constrained by the teaching authority of the church. In his response, *On the Bondage of the Will*, Luther rejected not only the principle of free will, but also Erasmus's skepticism, insisting on the need to defend articles of faith with "Stoic" assurance. Catholic theologians likewise rejected any form of skeptical inquiry as destabilizing (Rupp and Watson 1978). The increasing polarization of views in the age of religious strife resulted in an emphasis on clear-cut and authoritative definitions of articles of faith. Rigorous enforcement of orthodoxy by all confessional parties discouraged scholarly initiatives.

Both the Erasmian version and the *Complutensian Polyglot* were used by Simon de Colines for his edition of the Greek NT (Paris 1534). The Greek text in the *Royal Polyglot,* printed by Estienne, represented a new collation based on Paris mss. Finally, the edition of Theodore Beza (Geneva, 1565), based on additional ms. evidence, notably the so-called Codex Bezae, deserves mention here (Metzger and Ehrman 2005: 151-52).

Many humanists supported the translation of Scripture into the vernacular. This reflected larger historical developments, such as the rise of the middle class and the impact of print culture on reading habits. It was not necessarily an endorsement of Luther's "priesthood of all believers," as was sometimes alleged by Catholic controversialists. Giving the general reader access to the Bible was a goal that agreed with the humanists' call *ad fontes.* The Bible was, after all, the essential source of Christian teaching. Perhaps humanists also saw the laity as fellow victims of the "closed shop" mentality of Scholastic theologians. Thus, Erasmus proclaimed in his *Paraclesis* that Scripture was everyone's business. It should be recited by the farmer at his plow, the weaver at his loom, and the traveler on the road (*Ausgewählte Werke,* ed. Holborn and Holborn, 142). For further information regarding vernacular translations produced in the Renaissance, see chapter 16 below.

THE IMPACT OF HUMANISM ON BIBLICAL STUDIES

It remains to sum up the effects of the humanistic method on biblical studies in the Renaissance. Since the Renaissance humanists were pioneers of philology and textual criticism, their method was not fully developed, and its application therefore remained uneven. The prevailing cultural bias also limited the implementation of the humanistic method. This was an age that regarded theology as queen of sciences, and "all innovation dangerous" (to quote the *Faerie Queen*). Such habits of thought encouraged a self-deprecatory attitude. Erasmus's instructions to the Christian scholar are characteristic (*Ausgewählte Werke,* ed. Holborn and Holborn, 80):

> *Absit impia curiositas* [away with impious curiosity]. Distrust your own judgment, submit yourself to the Holy Spirit, our teacher, that He may shape and form your judgment. . . . If you read anything that appears to be at variance with Christ's teaching, take care not to misinterpret the text; rather, assume that you have not understood what you were reading.

The desire to avoid *impia curiositas* conditioned the approach of many biblical scholars.

Despite such constraints, humanistic ideas had a profound influence on the history of exegesis. The humanists' promotion of language studies and their emphasis on historical context became key factors in subsequent methodologies. Of equal importance was their principle of privileging sources over interpretations or, more generally, respect for the historical pedigree of a text.

The impact of these ideas can be seen in the acceptance, by the end of the sixteenth century, of language studies as a standard requirement for theology students. Similarly, the humanistic call for a return to the sources generated an interest in collecting and collating mss. and resulted in critical editions of the Bible as well as of patristic writings. By the middle of the sixteenth century, critical editions of the works of all major patristic authors, Greek and Latin, had appeared. The accessibility of these prooftexts played a major role in the Reformation debate. Under the influence of humanistic philology, sixteenth-century exegetes broke away from the medieval pattern of interpreting the text according to the four senses (historical, figurative, tropological, anagogical) and focused on the grammatical and historical sense. Luther's protest that the literal sense was suffocated by mystical expositions and Erasmus's milder criticism of allegorical interpretation as playful are characteristic of this development. Both the recovery of the patristic tradition and the comparative historical method championed by humanists demonstrated that Christian teachings and practices were neither static nor uniform.

These findings were not always welcomed, however, and humanists were denounced for spreading doubt and inducing skepticism where firm belief was required. To the protagonists in the confessional debate, scholarly detachment was no virtue. The confessionalists favored doctrinal certainty over latitudinarianism, an inclusive approach to doctrine. They co-opted rather than adopted the New Learning, reshaping it to suit the process of confessionalization, which came to dominate the late sixteenth century.

BIBLIOGRAPHY

Aland, K., ed.

1967   *Martin Luther's 95 Theses with the Pertinent Documents from the History of the Reformation.* Saint Louis: Concordia.

Backus, I.

1995   "Erasmus and the Spirituality of the Early Church." In H. M. Pabel, ed., *Erasmus' Vision of the Church*, 95-114. Kirksville: Sixteenth Century Journal Publishers.

Backus, I., and F. Higman (eds.)

1990   *Théorie et pratique de l'exégèse. Actes du troisième colloque international sur l'histoire de l'exégèse biblique au XVIe siècle.* Geneva: Droz.

Banitt, M.

1985   *Rashi: Interpreter of the Biblical Letter.* Tel Aviv: Chaim Rosenberg School of Jewish Studies, Tel Aviv University.

Bedouelle, G.

1976   *Lefèvre d'Étaples et l'intelligence des écritures.* Geneva: Droz.

1989   *Les Temps des Réformes et la Bible.* Paris: Beauchesne.

Bedouelle, G., and B. Roussel (eds.)

1989   *Bible de tous les temps* 5: *Le temps des Réformes et la Bible.* Paris: Beauchesne.

Bentley, J.

1983   *Humanists and Holy Writ: New Testament Scholarship in the Renaissance.* Princeton: Princeton University Press.

Botley, P.

2004   *Latin Translation in the Renaissance: The Theory and Practice of Leonardo Bruni, Giannozzo Manetti and Desiderius Erasmus.* Cambridge Classical Studies. Cambridge: Cambridge University Press.

Boyle, M. O.

1977   *Erasmus on Language and Method in Theology.* Toronto: University of Toronto Press.

Camporeale, S.

1972   *Lorenzo Valla. Umanesimo e teologia.* Florence: Nella sede dell'Istituto.

Centi, T. M.

1945   "L'attività letteraria di Santi Paginini nel campo delle scienze bibliche," *Archivum Fratrum Praedicatorum* 15: 5-51.

Chomarat, J.

1978   "Les Annotations de Valla, celles d'Erasme et la grammaire." In O. Fatio and P. Fraenkel, eds., *Histoire de l'exégèse au XVIe siècle Geneva,* 202-28. Geneva: Droz.

Cousturier, P.

1525   *De Tralatione Bibliae.* Paris: Vidoue.

D'Amico, J.

1988   "Humanism and Pre-Reformation Theology." In A. Rabil, ed., *Renaissance Humanism: Foundations, Forms, and Legacy,* 349-79. Philadelphia: University of Pennsylvania Press.

de Jonge, H. J.

1980   "Erasmus and the *Comma Johanneum.*" *ETL* 56: 381-89.

1984   "*Novum Testamentum a nobis versum:* The Essence of Erasmus' Edition of the New Testament," *JTS* 35: 394-413.

Erasmus, Desiderius

1516   *Novum Instrumentum omne, diligenter ab Erasmo Roterodamo recognitum et emendatum, &c.* Basel: Froben, 1516.

1933   *Desiderius Erasmus. Ausgewahlte Werke.* Ed. A. and H. Holborn. Munich: Beck.

Friedman, J.

1983   *The Most Ancient Testimony: Sixteenth-Century Christian Hebraica in the Age of Renaissance Nostalgia.* Athens: Ohio University Press.

Hamilton, A.

1996   "Humanists and the Bible." In J. Kraye, ed., *The Cambridge Companion to Renaissance Humanism,* 100-117. Cambridge: Cambridge University Press.

Hoffmann, M.

1994   *Rhetoric and Theology: The Hermeneutic of Erasmus.* Toronto: University of Toronto Press.

Holborn, A., and H. Holborn (eds.)

1933   *Desiderius Erasmus. Ausgewählte Werke.* Munich: Beck.

Holeczek, H.

1975   *Humanistische Bibelphilologie als Reformproblem bei Erasmus von Rotterdam, Thomas More und William Tyndale.* Leiden: Brill.

Junghans, H.

1970   "Der Einfluss des Humanismus auf Luthers Entwicklung." *Lutherjahrbuch* 37: 37-101.

Keen, R.

1988   *A Melanchthon Reader.* New York: Lang.

Kittelson, J., and P. Transue (eds.)

1984   *Rebirth, Reform and Resilience: Universities in Transition, 1300-1700.* Columbus: Ohio State University Press.

Matheson, P.

1990   "Humanism and Reform Movements." In A. Goodwin and A. MacKay, eds., *The Impact of Humanism on Western Europe,* 23-42. London: Longman.

Maurer, W.

1967   *Der junge Melanchthon zwischen Humanismus und Reformation.* 2 vols. Göttingen: Vandenhoeck & Ruprecht.

Metzger, B., and B. D. Ehrman

2005   *The Text of the New Testament.* 4th ed. Oxford: Oxford University Press.

Moeller, B.

1959   "Die deutschen Humanisten und die Anfänge der Reformation." *ZKG* 70: 46-61.

Mulder, M. J.

1990   "The Transmission of the Biblical Text." In M. J. Mulder, ed., *Mikra: Text, Translation, Reading, and Interpretation of the Hebrew Bible in Ancient Judaism and Early Christianity,* 87-135. Philadelphia: Fortress.

Nebrija, Elio Antonio de

1516a   *Apologia cum quibusdam sacrae scripturae locis non vulgariter expositis.* Alcalá.

1516b   *Tertia Quinquagena.* Alcalá.

Olin, J.

1978   "Erasmus and the Church Fathers." In J. Olin, ed., *Six Essays on Erasmus,* 33-48. New York: Fordham University Press.

1990   *Catholic Reform from Cardinal Ximenes to the Council of Trent, 1495-1563.* New York: Fordham University Press.

Rabil, A.

1972   *Erasmus and the New Testament: The Mind of a Christian Humanist.* San Antonio: Trinity University Press.

Rashkow, I.

1990   "Hebrew Bible Translation and the Fear of Judaization." *SCJ* 21: 217-34.

Rice, E.

1985   *Saint Jerome in the Renaissance.* Baltimore: Johns Hopkins University Press.

Rummel, E.

1985   *Erasmus as a Translator of the Classics.* Erasmus Studies 7. Toronto: University of Toronto Press.

1986   *Erasmus' Annotations on the New Testament: From Philologist to Theologian.* Toronto: University of Toronto Press.

1989   *Erasmus and His Catholic Critics* 1: *1515-1522.* Bibliotheca Humanistica and Reformatorica 45. Nieuwkoop: De Graaf.

1995a   *The Humanist-Scholastic Debate in the Renaissance and Reformation.* Cambridge: Harvard University Press.

1995b   "In Defense of 'Theologizing Humanists': Aurelio Brandolini's 'In sacram Ebreorum historiam . . . prefatio.'" *Humanistica Lovaniensia* 44: 90-106.

2000   *The Confessionalization of Humanism in Reformation Germany.* Oxford Studies in Historical Theology. New York: Oxford University Press.

2004   *Erasmus.* London: Continuum.

Rupp, E. G., and P. S. Watson

1978   *Luther and Erasmus: Free Will and Salvation.* Rev. ed. LCC. Philadelphia: Westminster.

Shuger, D.

1994   *The Renaissance Bible: Scholarship, Sacrifice, and Subjectivity.* Berkeley: University of California Press.

Steinmetz, D. (ed.)

1982   *The Bible in the Sixteenth Century.* Durham: Duke University Press.

Trinkaus, C.

1970   *In Our Image and Likeness: Humanity and Divinity in Italian Humanist Thought.*
2 vols. Chicago: University of Chicago Press.

Valla, Lorenzo

1978   *Antidotum primum.* Ed. A. Wesseling. Assen: Van Gorcum.

CHAPTER 10

Biblical Interpretation
in the Works of Martin Luther

Mark D. Thompson

Martin Luther's engagement with the Scriptures was undeniably the critical catalyst for the tumultuous Reformation in the European churches in the sixteenth century. The man at the center of this revolution in Christian thinking was himself first and foremost a biblical scholar and preacher, teaching the Scriptures in the University of Wittenberg and the nearby *Schloßkirche* (castle church) from 1513 until his death in 1546. He produced a wealth of exegetical material, much of which has survived (see list, p. 301). The amount of material goes a long way toward explaining the variety of conclusions drawn from it in the last century and a half. Any attempt at a synthesis of Luther's comments on the nature and use of Scripture, scattered as they are across his thirty-three years as a teacher, and recorded in a variety of different forms produced in a range of contexts, requires selection and evaluation — and in these, any attempt is open to the distorting influence of our own theological concerns and modern theological debates. The evidence of the nineteenth and twentieth centuries alone would suggest that interpreters have found it quite difficult to allow Luther to speak on his own terms.

LUTHER ON THE AUTHORITY OF SCRIPTURE

Luther's approach to biblical interpretation cannot be separated from his convictions about the nature of Scripture and its place in the life of the church and the individual Christian. His renowned protest against the doctrine and practice of the Roman church arose, as he himself insisted, from his own submission to the teaching of the Scriptures. Faced with instructions to recant all that he had written to that point, Luther told the emperor, the Imperial Diet, and the representatives of the Vatican assembled in Worms in April 1521 that he was bound to the text of Scripture, which he considered to be the word of God.

> Unless I am convinced by the testimony of the Scriptures or by evident reason — for I can believe neither pope nor councils alone, as it is clear that they have erred repeatedly and contradicted themselves — I consider myself conquered by the Scriptures adduced by me, and my conscience is captive to the word of God. (WA 7.838.4-7 = LW 32.112)

In the course of his early lectures and through fierce debates with men like Cajetan, Prierias, and Eck, Luther had come to recognize the text of Scripture as the final court of appeal in matters of Christian faith and life. Of course, accepting the authority of Scripture was unexceptional in medieval Christendom. Only those on the fringes of orthodoxy dared to challenge the teaching of the Bible openly. But Luther went further than his teachers and contemporaries by being prepared to acknowledge points of divergence between the Bible and the teaching tradition of the Roman church and insisting that at those points the teaching of the papacy must give way to a straightforward reading of the biblical text (e.g., WA 7.315.28-34 = LW 32.11; WA 8.484.24–485.27 = LW 36.136-37).

Critical at this point was Luther's identification of Scripture as the word of God. He recognized, of course, the primacy and unique character of Christ's claim to be the Word of God. As he told his students at table in 1540, only *verbum incarnatum,* "the incarnate Word," is *substantialiter Deus,* "in substance God" (WATr 4.695.16–696.2 = LW 54.395). God himself is the object of our worship, not the biblical text. But this did not prevent Luther from referring to Scripture in an unqualified fashion as the Word of God, and precisely for that reason according it a peculiar respect and demanding that it be handled with care. Although throughout the twentieth century a distinction between Scripture and the Word of God was anachronistically attributed to Luther by some (e.g., Barth 1938: 545; Watson 1947: 151-52; Ebeling 1951: 199-205; Reid 1957: 66-68; Ruokanen 1987: 9), this was ultimately a misreading, particularly of those texts in which Luther speaks about the testimony of the OT to Christ. More recent detailed investigation of Luther's work has made clear that it is Christ, not the Word of God, which Luther says is found wrapped in "the swaddling cloths of Scripture" (WADB 8.12.1-8 = LW 35.236). Further, contrary to Karl Barth's famous misreading of one of Luther's ser-

Luther's Lectures on the Bible			
Psalms (the *Dictata super Psalterium*)	1513-15	WA 55	LW 10, 11
Romans	1515-16	WA 56	LW 25
Galatians	1516-17 (revised for publication in 1519)	WA 56	LW 27
Hebrews	1517-18	WA 57/2	LW 29
Psalms (the *Operationes in Psalmos*)	1518-21	WA 5	
Deuteronomy	1523-24	WA 14	LW 9
Minor Prophets	1524-26	WA 13	LW 18-19
Isaiah	1527-30	WA 31/2	LW 16-17
1 John	1527	WA 20	LW 30
Titus	1527	WA 25	LW 29
Philemon	1527	WA 25	LW 29
1 Timothy	1527-28	WA 26	LW 28
Galatians	1531 (revised for publication in 1535)	WA 40/1	LW 26-27
Genesis	1535-45	WA 42-44	LW 1-8

In addition to the lectures we have access to many sermons of Luther, the prefaces he provided for each biblical book in the German Bible (1522-35), and a number of important comments on the task of biblical interpretation, including *A Brief Instruction on What to Look for and Expect in the Gospels* (1521), *How Christians Should Regard Moses* (1525), and *On Translating: An Open Letter* (1525). In a wide variety of other contexts, mostly polemical, Luther made direct comments about the place of Scripture in the Christian life and the way in which it ought to be read.

mons from 1522, it is *die Seele*, the soul, and not *die Heylige Schrifft*, Holy Scripture, which "holds fast God's word" (WA 10.75.1-10). Whatever other developments there might be in Luther's approach to Scripture, his conviction that Scripture is the Word of God remains constant throughout his career (Thompson 2003: 68-90).

It is this identification of the text as God's Word that explains Luther's

tenacity when it comes to the wording of controversial passages. The exact
words written and the order they were written in cannot be avoided. They
constrain the interpreter from fanciful interpretation. Luther made this point
repeatedly in his various pieces on the words of institution in Matthew 26 and
Luke 22. He explained why he did not consider the figurative interpretations
circulating among the congregations of Strasbourg in 1524 a live option: "I
am a captive and I cannot free myself. The text is too powerfully present, and
will not allow itself to be torn from its meaning by mere verbiage" (WA
15.394.19-20 = LW 40.68). He railed against Zwingli and others for attacking
his preoccupation with those "five poor, miserable words" (τοῦτό ἐστιν τὸ
σῶμά μου, "this is my body"), insisting:

> With such arguments, however, they reveal against their own intention
> what kind of spirit they have and how dearly they value God's words,
> since they abuse these precious words as "five poor, miserable words,"
> that is, they do not believe that they are God's words. For if they believed
> that these were God's words, they would not call them "poor, miserable
> words," but would prize a single tittle and letter more highly than the
> whole world, and would fear and tremble before them as before God
> himself. For he who despises a single word of God certainly prizes none at
> all. (WA 26.449.34–450.24 = LW 37.308)

Luther did of course recognize that fidelity to the actual words of Scripture raised special problems for those who translated the text from the original Hebrew and Greek. Incidentally, while he prized vernacular translations,
his insistence on the importance of the biblical languages was itself a further
reflection of his commitment to the authority of the text. However, he did not
consider that such commitment demanded a literal word-for-word correspondence in translation. He insisted that his own translation of Rom. 3:28 as
*so halten wyrs nu, das der mensch gerechtfertiget werde, on zu thun der werck
des gesetzs, alleyn durch den glawben,* "we hold that one is justified by faith
alone without doing works of the law" — famously adding the word *alleyn,*
"alone" — was in fact more faithful to the meaning and form of the Greek
original than that of his opponents. The Greek words and the order of those
words were the divinely appointed means of conveying a particular meaning
in the original setting; the responsibility of the translator was to convey that
same meaning as faithfully and clearly as possible in the receptor language
(WA 30.2.637-43 = LW 35.190-98).

LUTHER ON THE CLARITY OF SCRIPTURE

Of course, an appeal to an authoritative text would make little sense if that text was inaccessible or unintelligible. If that were indeed the case, then the interposition of the teaching authority of the church would be justified. It is not surprising, then, that from its earliest stages Luther's exegetical career was marked by a robust confidence in the clarity of the Scriptures when dealt with honestly and with faith. This element in Luther's theology has been the subject of much scholarly interest (e.g., Beisser 1966; Rothen 1990; Allison 1995: 1-48; Callahan 1996). However, it is Luther's own words that provide us with the classic statement of the basic idea. Amid his defense of those elements of his teaching condemned by Rome in 1520, he asked:

> Or tell me, if you can, who finally decides when two statements of the fathers contradict themselves? Scripture ought to provide this judgement, which cannot be delivered unless we give to Scripture the chief place in everything, that which was acknowledged by the fathers: that is, that it is in and of itself the most certain, the most accessible, the most clear thing of all, interpreting itself, approving, judging and illuminating all things. (WA 7.97.19-24)

It has been suggested that Luther could not sustain this perspective amid the fragmentation of the evangelical cause in the wake of the eucharistic debates (McGrath 1993: 151-55). However, the evidence of Luther's own writings suggests otherwise. He asserts the clarity of Scripture as part of the debate over indulgences (e.g., WA 8.99.14-23 = LW 32.217), in his debate with Erasmus in 1525 (e.g., WA 18.606.1–609.14 = LW 33.24-28), in the debate with the Swiss over the Supper in the late 1520s (e.g., WA 33.87.28-32 = LW 37.28-29; Thompson 1998), and even in his later exegetical work in the 1530s and 1540s (e.g., WA 44.720.3-27 = LW 8.192-93). The prominence of this idea in Luther's thinking throughout his teaching career is explained by the fact that without it his appeal to biblical authority would have been next to meaningless.

Luther, in fact, appealed to a twofold clarity of Scripture in his debate with Erasmus over the state of the human will and its role in salvation. He presented this idea in summary form near the beginning of his response to the great humanist scholar: "To put it briefly, the clarity of Scripture is twofold, just as its obscurity is twofold: one external and related to the ministry of the word, the other located in the understanding of the heart" (WA 18.609.4-5 = LW 33.28). According to Luther, neither of these dimensions is strictly natural, an inherent property of a set of words or of the human fac-

ulty of comprehension. Both are the work of the Spirit of God. Yet, external
clarity is necessarily entailed by God's gracious choice to express himself
within the normal and accessible conventions of human language. The words
of the biblical text are not infinitely pliable. As Luther would later argue, even
a heathen, a Jew, or a Turk could rightly explain what is being said at any particular point (WA 26.406.27-29 = LW 37.272). Internal clarity, it too a work of
the Spirit, is necessary, because the sin-darkened heart prevents understanding even if a person is able to recite everything in Scripture (WA 18.609.5-9 =
LW 33.28).

This affirmation of Scripture's clarity is the context in which we find the
hermeneutical principle that "Scripture is its own interpreter" (WA 7.97.24;
638.26–639.11 = LW 39.164; Mostert 1979). Luther reacted against the medieval
practice of explaining Scripture in terms of the comments made on each passage by the exegetes and theologians of the past. This "glossing of the glosses,"
rather than direct engagement with the biblical text, robbed Christian people
of the enlightening treasure of God's word. Instead of a preoccupation with
the *comments* of the fathers, Luther called for a commitment to their *method*,
namely, an engagement with the words of the passages themselves in the context of the entire Bible. Rather than using the comments of the fathers to explain difficult passages, Luther encouraged his students and others to use the
biblical context — comparing "what precedes with what follows" (WA
18.713.3-7 = LW 33.181; WA 40/2.36.25–37.8 = LW 27.29; WA 45.555.23-33 = LW
24.104) — and especially to use other clearer passages of Scripture that deal
with the same issue to explain the difficult passages. "One must know that
Scripture without any glosses is the sun and the whole light from which all
teachers receive their light, and not vice versa" (WA 7.639.1-2 = LW 39.164).
He insisted that even his own exegetical endeavors must be seen in this context: "I do not desire to be honored as one who is more learned than all, but
Scripture alone to rule: to be interpreted, neither by my spirit nor any human
spirit, but understood through itself and by its own spirit" (WA 7.98.40–99.2;
cf. WA 10/2.728.18-21 = LW 52.286).

THE CHRIST PRINCIPLE

Another constant and distinctive element in Luther's approach to biblical interpretation was his conviction that the focus of the entire Bible is its testimony to Jesus Christ. Of course, this too was unexceptional in the medieval
context. The "Christ principle" was the common property of the exegetical
tradition. Indeed, Faber Stapulensis, whose 1509 commentary (see Stapulen-

sis 1979) Luther is known to have consulted as he prepared his first series of lectures on the Psalms, had insisted on a christological focus in interpreting Scripture. But Luther was arguably more rigorous in his application of this principle than most before him (Ebeling 1942: 280). In his preface to his glosses on the Psalms, he declared "every prophecy and every prophet must be understood as referring to Christ the Lord, except where it is clear from plain words that someone else is spoken of" (WA 55/1.6.25–8.1 = LW 10.7). The appeal to John 5:39 that follows makes clear that Luther was convinced that such a perspective is actually mandated by Scripture itself. Further, Luther's second preface to these lectures rebuked those "who have a carnal understanding of the Psalms, like the Jews, who always apply the Psalms to ancient history apart from Christ" (WA 55/1.2.9-12 = LW 10.3).

This christological focus was not merely a preliminary stage in Luther's development as a biblical exegete. The evidence is clear that he never abandoned his conviction that the principal function of Scripture was to direct people to Christ. The *Kirchenpostille,* a collection of sermons Luther published in 1522, included the insistence that "all Scripture tends towards Christ" (WA 10/1/1.15.7 = LW 35.122). He asked Erasmus in 1525, "Take Christ out of the Scriptures and what will you find left in them?" (WA 18.606.29 = LW 33.26). At table in 1532 he told his students "Christ is the central point of the circle around which everything else in the Bible revolves" (WATr 2.439.25-26).

We have already mentioned Luther's graphic image of the Scriptures (in particular the OT) as the swaddling cloths in which Christ is to be found. He could even say "simple and lowly are these swaddling cloths, but dear is the treasure, Christ, who lies in them" (WADB 8.12.7-8 = LW 35.236). Luther's point is that a knowledge of the words, grammatical constructions, and other literary features of the text is penultimate. The goal of studying the Scriptures is the knowledge of Christ and the response of faith. Yet, Luther's boldness went even further. In the year before he died he published another collection of sermons, known as the *Fastenpostille,* and in it he allegorized about the nature of Scripture from the other end of the Gospel narrative:

> For Holy Scripture is the garment which our Lord Christ has put on and in which He lets Himself be seen and found. This garment is woven throughout and so wrought together into one that it cannot be cut or parted. But the soldiers, i.e., heretics and schismatics, take it from Christ crucified. It is their particular mischief to want to have the coat entire, persuading everyone that all Scripture agrees with them and is of their opinion. (WA 52.802.1-8)

It is in this light that we are to understand Luther's famous axiom that the primary purpose of Scripture is "to preach and inculcate Christ" (WADB 7.385.25-27). The task of the exegete then is to look for *was Christum treibet*, "that which drives home Christ." To expound the Scriptures (and at this point he had in mind particularly the OT) without reference to Christ is to distort their message. Infamously, Luther could apply this principle to the canon itself, asking hard questions of books such as the Epistle of James, which did not appear to exhibit the focus on Christ appropriate to genuine Scripture. This is what Kooiman meant when he spoke of Luther's "kerygmatic criticism" (1961: 225).

One of Luther's oft-cited comments in this regard is from a series of theses he prepared for a disputation in 1535:

> 49. Therefore, if the adversaries press the Scriptures against Christ, we urge Christ against the Scriptures. 50. We have the Lord, they the servants; we have the Head, they the feet or members, over which the Head necessarily dominates and takes precedence. (WA 39/1.47.19-22 = LW 34.112)

Luther's concern here, especially when viewed in context, is not to diminish the authority of the Scriptures. Rather, he is so thoroughly convinced that the entire Bible testifies to Christ and the salvation he has wrought that he simply refuses to countenance an interpretation of a biblical passage which suggested otherwise. Such an interpretation ignores both the nature and the intention of Scripture. Subsequent generations may not have been persuaded by such an insistence on preaching Christ from every part of the Bible, nor by his claims to consistency in the application of this principle. Nevertheless, no one seriously doubts that his sense of the unity of Scripture which gives a clear testimony to Christ and salvation in him remains a key part of Luther's contribution to the history of biblical interpretation.

LUTHER'S "HERMENEUTICAL SHIFT": FROM LETTER AND SPIRIT TO LAW AND GOSPEL

So far, we have examined those theological and hermeneutical convictions which remained constant throughout Luther's teaching ministry. From his earliest lectures right through to his death he insisted on the authority of Scripture, its God-given clarity when dealt with honestly and with faith, and its fundamental unity in its focus on Christ crucified. But early in his teaching Luther gained a new insight into precisely how the text — in particular the

OT text — testifies to Christ, and thus how it relates to the Christian believer. This "hermeneutical shift" has itself been a focus of detailed scholarly attention (Ebeling 1942; Preus 1967; Pilch 1970; Reinke 1973; McGrath 1985: 75-81), largely because it has been proposed as the real catalyst for the radically different soteriology with which he would challenge Rome. It is perhaps fair to suggest that the current consensus is that "Luther's hermeneutical and soteriological insights developed symbiotically, with each dimension to his thought reinforcing and stimulating the other" (McGrath 1987: 164), although there is still some disagreement about the exact nature of his hermeneutical development.

It has long been recognized that when Luther began his first series of lectures on the Psalms in 1513, he operated entirely within the parameters of the Scholastic exegetical tradition. This is most obvious in his employment of the Quadriga, a scheme for identifying and distinguishing the four senses of a text — the literal and three spiritual senses — which can be traced back at least to Augustine and John Cassian (Bornkamm 1948: 74-75). It originally emerged as an attempt to deal with the historical and eschatological distance between the people and events of the OT and believers on the other side of the resurrection and ascension of Christ. It was originally justified on the basis of the Pauline antithesis of letter and spirit (2 Cor. 3:6). As earlier essays in this volume attest, there was considerable reflection on and refinement of this scheme throughout the later medieval period, notably Nicholas of Lyra's suggestion (1472; see Nicholas of Lyra 1492) that the literal sense itself could be subdivided into the literal-historical sense and the literal-prophetic sense. This gave a higher profile to the original historical situation of OT texts while it preserved a prophetic reference to Christ. Luther's own suggestion that each element of the traditional fourfold approach could itself be either killing letter or life-giving spirit was a variation on Lyra's approach. Luther, in contrast to Lyra, gave an essentially negative appraisal of the literal-historical sense, equating it with the letter that kills (Ebeling 1951: 217-19; Preus 1969: 227-48). Lyra's literal-prophetic sense was the life-giving spirit, pointing the reader to the intersection of this text with Christian realities. The end result of this way of looking at the text of the Psalms was that Luther could concede eight meanings of the term "Mount Zion" (WA 55/1/1.4.3-19 = LW 10.4).

As Luther progressed through the Psalter, his use of the Quadriga was subjected to great strain by his rigorous application of the christological principle. Not very far into the series, as he expounded Psalm 4, he was able to say that "all four senses of Scripture flow into one very large stream" with Christ at its head.

> So, for example, the present psalm is understood first of all concerning
> Christ, who calls and is heard; then allegorically, concerning the church,
> His body; and finally, in a tropological sense, concerning any holy soul. It
> can also be understood thus with reference to the person of David and
> anyone at all. The reason for all is that God makes all His saints to be
> "conformed to the image of His Son"; for that reason the same words are
> suitable for all of them. (WA 55/2/1.63.11-16 = LW 10.52)

The important thing to notice here is that the starting point is not the reference to David but the reference to Christ, which Luther elsewhere labels
principali sensu, "the principal sense." The Quadriga is not yet gone (although
the anagogical sense is strangely absent), but significantly the reference to
Christ is explained not as the allegorical sense of the passage but as its literal
sense. While Luther does mention the historical figure of David in passing, in
practice he never really ties the psalms to their historical situation as a word
of God for Israel before the advent of Christ (Chau 1995: 188). Even his later
identification of "the faithful synagogue" as a significant factor in understanding the Psalms (again something that is anticipated in the medieval
exegetical tradition [Hendrix 1974: 264-79]) is not a clear lineal departure
from his earlier approach (Pilch 1970: 447). Even as late as his treatment of
Psalm 119 he could insist that the prophetic sense is the literal sense (WA
4.305.3-8 = LW 11.414).

While Luther's commitment to a christological reference remained constant, his disquiet about Quadriga and allegorical interpretation in general
intensified over the next few years. There is evidence of further movement
away from spiritual interpretations in his exposition of the seven penitential
psalms in 1517. The classical terminology continues to be used even in the
Romans lectures of 1515-16, but a shift is clearly taking shape. By the time Luther returned to the Psalms in 1518, he had not only abandoned the Quadriga
but had also given up the traditional expository framework of *glossae,* "[mar-
ginal and interlinear] glosses," and *scholia,* "exposition." He outlined his new
approach at the very outset of these lectures: "Our first concern will be for the
grammatical meaning, for this is the truly theological meaning" (WA 5.27.8).
Here he sought to do justice both to the literal meaning of the text in its OT
context and to its focus on Christ, which he remained convinced was the intention of the Holy Spirit in the text. A year later, in his early Galatians commentary, Luther would be insisting that although he did not entirely disap-
prove of the Quadriga ("that four-horse team"), it "is not sufficiently
supported by the authority of Scripture, the custom of the fathers or grammatical principles" (WA 2.550.34-35 = LW 27.311).

The significant shift, which underlies all else over these years, is Luther's redefinition of the letter-spirit antithesis. As we have seen, this antithesis was used to justify the move from the literal sense to the more fruitful spiritual senses. The basic conviction of most medieval exegetes was that each text of Scripture has a twofold meaning, and the most appropriate and edifying (the spiritual meaning) lies hidden within that which is less so. However, as Luther became less enamored of allegory and the spiritual senses it allowed (though he never entirely abandoned its use), he also came to see the letter and the spirit differently. Letter and spirit were not so much two levels of meaning as two elements in a dynamic, which can be traced throughout the OT and the NT. Both are at work in the single literal sense of the text.

Luther's new insight was not a sudden one; it developed gradually (Chau 1995: 181-84). Nevertheless, even in the early Psalms lectures Luther had begun to associate the letter-spirit antithesis with what would soon become his single most characteristic hermeneutical concern, the distinction between the law and the gospel (WA 4.9.28–10.12 = LW 11.160-61). This can be seen as early as his exposition of Ps. 45:1:

> Again, "to utter" can also signify by another mystery that it declares the spirit from the letter. The spirit is concealed in the letter, which is a word that is not good, because it is the law of wrath. But the spirit is a good word, because it is a word of grace. Therefore to draw this out of the letter is to utter the spirit itself. (WA 3.256.27-30 = LW 10.212-13)

As Luther came to appreciate the way the law-gospel dynamic productively explains Scripture and maintains its clear christological focus, the letter-spirit distinction became less significant in his approach to biblical texts (although it never disappeared entirely). No doubt this shift in thinking was reinforced by his realization that the appeal to spiritual meanings on the basis of the letter-spirit antithesis could easily become a way of evading the teaching of the Scriptures. Luther's responses to the attacks upon him by Jerome Emser of Leipzig in 1521 are full of precisely this charge. In exasperation Luther would be led to say: "Scripture does not tolerate the division of letter and spirit, as Emser so outrageously [divides them]" (WA 7.651.22-23 = LW 39.179).

Instead of looking behind the law for its deeper meaning, Luther repeatedly encouraged his readers to look forward to its fulfillment and resolution in the gospel of Jesus Christ. The law reveals human sinfulness and so drives us to Christ; the gospel is the answer to that sinfulness and offers us the forgiveness and life that can only be found in Christ (Forde 1983). "The entire Holy Scripture is divided into two words," he wrote in 1520, "the commandments or Law of God and his promise or pledge" (WA 7.23.29-30 = LW 31.348). A year later he was even more direct: "virtually every Scripture and an understanding of the whole of theology depends upon a right understanding of Law and Gospel" (WA 7.502.34-35). Luther would not at all have been content with a simple labeling of the OT as law and the NT as gospel. The dynamic he had uncovered was much more profound than that. As he wrote in the *Kirchenpostille*:

> There is no book in the Bible which does not contain both. Everywhere God has placed law and promise side by side. Through the law he teaches us what must be done; through the promise, how we can do it. That we refer to the New Testament as Gospel, more than we do the remainder of the Bible, is because it was written after Christ's coming and therefore after the divine promise had been fulfilled and publicly proclaimed through preaching, which before that time had been hidden in Scripture. Pay careful attention to this distinction no matter which book you may be reading, whether in the Old Testament or in the New Testament. Whatever contains promises is a book of the Gospel; where commandments are found, we have a book of law. Since, however, in the New Testament, promises form the principal content, as commandments do in the Old, the one may be designated as Gospel and the other as Law. (WA 10/1/2.159.7-19)

Recognition of this law-gospel dynamic gave Luther's interpretive endeavors a distinctive shape. The salvation-historical movement from law to gospel (ignoring the terminological anachronism) — a trajectory and momentum throughout the OT, attested to by the Lord Jesus himself (Luke 16:16), as well as the apostle Paul (Galatians 3–4) — is echoed, Luther believed, in the life of each Christian: brought to nothing by the law, but given life and health and freedom in the gospel. The law continues to perform this function in the life of the believer. The reality of sin in the Christian life (Luther's famous *simul iustus et peccator*, "at the same time a righteous person and a sinner") must be confronted by the law again and again. Only then will believers genuinely despair of their good works and flee from god to God. Rightly dividing law and gospel is thus a hermeneutical necessity with immense pastoral implications.

READING IN THE SPIRIT

For all that has been said, it would be a misreading of Luther to consider the study of Scripture an entirely academic activity, an application of the intellect to niceties of the law-gospel distinction and the like. For Luther, the reading and hearing of Scripture could never be entirely or even primarily an academic activity; it was always a religious activity, a microcosm as it were of the life of faith. As Luther famously remarked in the second series of Psalms lectures in 1519, "not understanding, reading, or speculation, but living, no, dying and being damned, make a theologian" (WA 5.163.28-29). Yet it was always a living, dying, and being damned in the presence of the word of God. This becomes clear in Luther's preface to the 1539 edition of his German works, where he sought to provide guidelines for "a correct way of studying theology" based on three rules presented in Psalm 119: *oratio, meditatio,* and *tentatio* — prayer, meditation, and spiritual struggle, an experiential reality also signified by *Anfechtung,* one of Luther's enduring contributions to the theological vocabulary of many languages. It is this third rule, this dimension of intense struggle — anguish in the light of God's revelation of himself — that Luther sees as critical. "This is the touchstone which teaches you not only to know and understand, but also to experience how right, how true, how sweet, how lovely, how mighty, how comforting God's word is, wisdom beyond all wisdom" (WA 50.660.1-4 = LW 34.286-87).

Hermeneutical effectiveness for Luther is always linked to hermeneutical integrity, and that integrity is not simply a matter of precision in handling the text but of recognizing your position before the God who addresses you by means of this text. As Luther remarked very early in his career, "Many speculate wisely but nobody is wise in Scripture and understands it if he does not fear the Lord. And he who fears more, understands more. For 'the fear of the Lord is the beginning of wisdom'" (WA 4.519.3-4). What we have here is not simply a theology of humility, but rather a recognition that there is a spiritual dimension to the interpretive task that cannot be reduced to human ingenuity. As Luther wrote to his friend Georg Spalatin in 1518:

> It is absolutely certain that one cannot enter into the Scripture by study or innate intelligence. Therefore your first task is to begin with prayer. You must ask that the Lord in his great mercy grant you a true understanding of his words, should it please him to accomplish anything through you for his glory and not for your glory or that of any other man. For there is no one who can teach the divine words except he who is their author, as he says, "They shall all be taught by God." You must therefore completely despair of your own diligence and intelligence and rely solely on the infusion of the Spirit. Believe me, for I have had experience in this matter. (WABr 1.133.31-39 = LW 48.53-54)

There is very obviously here a deep resonance with the theology of humility associated with Bernard of Clairvaux (see Stiegman 2001), as well as
certain elements of late medieval German mysticism. However, the roots of
this conviction are deeper than that and lie in a long tradition of *lectio divina*,
"sacred reading," which has been shown to have been joined to the academic
study of Scripture by the scholars of the Abbey of St. Victor in Paris (Evans
1984: 29; see also chapters 2 and 13 in the present volume). The study of Scripture was in fact part of one's devotion to Christ and could not be separated
from the broader contours of life lived in the presence of God. The interpreter
of Scripture is first and foremost a forgiven sinner standing in the presence of
his Creator, Redeemer, and Judge.

THE SPOKEN WORD WITH A SPECIFIC ADDRESS

One last feature of Luther's hermeneutical contribution is often overlooked.
Throughout his life Luther insisted that the word of God must be preached
and heard, not simply written and read (Graham 1987: 141-54). There is a peculiarly aural nature to the Scriptures, which is connected to the very nature
of the relationship between the living God and his people. This is especially
and essentially the case with the NT, which Luther held was not in the first instance a document, but rather a sermon (WA 10/1/1.17.4-14 = LW 35.123; WA
10/1/2.48.9-10; WADB 7.11.19-21 = LW 35.123). A lecture on Mal. 2:7 from 1526
boldly states Luther's concern:

> This is a passage against those who hold the spoken word in contempt.
> The lips are the public reservoirs of the church. In them alone is kept the
> word of God. You see, unless the word is preached publicly, it slips away.
> The more it is preached, the more firmly it is retained. Reading it is not as
> profitable as hearing it, for the live voice teaches, exhorts, defends, and re-
> sists the spirit of error. Satan does not care a hoot for the written word of
> God, but he flees at the speaking of the word. You see, this penetrates
> hearts and leads back those who stray. (WA 13.686.6-12 = LW 18.401)

In addition to this argument from the effectiveness of the spoken word,
an argument that is itself of a piece with the devotional approach we have already mentioned, there was a larger theological issue at stake as far as Luther
was concerned. He insisted that the shape of the Christian life was determined by the way God had chosen to relate himself to the human race. On
this side of the return of Christ, God has not given himself to be seen directly.

He reveals himself as the *Deus absconditus*, "the hidden God," by means of words rather than images. Christian discipleship, therefore, involves listening to the word of God and believing his promises, rather than seeing the form of God with our eyes. Indeed, he regularly suggests that "the ears alone are the organs of a Christian man" (WA 57/3.222.7 = LW 29.224).

In such a context, it is not hard to see why Luther privileges listening over reading, insisting that "it is the nature of the word to be heard" (WA 4.9.18-19 = LW 11.160). Critically, this also leads Luther to value preaching over writing, with his epigrammatic "the church is not a pen-house but a mouth-house" (WA 10-1/2.48.5). In his second series of lectures on the Psalms, Luther explained, "In the church it is not enough to write and read books, but it is essential to speak and hear. . . . For this reason we desire that there shall be more good preachers than good writers in the church" (WA 5.537.10-11).

Good preaching must, however, deal carefully with the text of Scripture and, in particular, care is needed to address the contemporary audience with the words meant for them. Luther's lectures and commentaries reveal the extent to which he was committed to the contemporaneity of the biblical text, and this commitment has been highlighted in more recent Luther scholarship (Brecht 1985-93: 1.289-90; Isaac 1996: 85; Maschke 2001). When dealing with the Scriptures, we are not dealing with merely ancient documents detailing God's activity in the past. As he wrote in the early commentary on Galatians:

> For if the divine Scriptures are treated in such a way as to be understood only with regard to the past and not to be applied also to our own manner of life, of what benefit will they be? Then they are cold, dead, and not even divine. For you see how fittingly and vividly, yes, how necessarily, this passage applies to our age. (WA 2.601.19-23 = LW 27.386)

Yet, uncontrolled application of the biblical text to contemporary issues and situations could be just as harmful as consigning the text to antiquity. In this connection, Luther sought to develop in his students and readers an ability to discern which words are properly addressed to them. This was the burden of his excursus in the midst of his sermons on Exodus, *How Christians Should Regard Moses* (1525):

> One must deal cleanly with the Scriptures. From the very beginning the word has come to us in various ways. It is not enough simply to look and see whether this is God's word, whether God has said it; rather we must look and see to whom it has been spoken, whether it fits us. That makes

all the difference between night and day. God said to David, "Out of you shall come the king," etc. But this does not pertain to me, nor has it been spoken to me. He can indeed speak to me if he chooses to do so. You must keep your eye on the word that applies to you, that is spoken to you. (WA 16.384.19–385.12 = LW 35.170)

All Scripture may well be organically and directly connected to Christ, but not all of Scripture is properly applied directly to the believer. Even those parts not directly addressed to us might be profitable, not least in the way they help unfold the person of Christ and his work on our behalf. Nevertheless, if we are to avoid following the fanatics into fanciful and dangerous distortion of the teaching of Scripture, care needs to be taken to examine the context for clues as to the intended addressee. By modern standards, Luther may well have regularly transgressed his own principle out of his concern to stress the contemporary, powerful, and effective word of God. Yet, in this principle of including context in search of meaning, as much as any other principle, Luther anticipated a key concern of modern hermeneutics.

LUTHER'S CONTRIBUTION

The last century and a half has witnessed a remarkable "Luther renaissance" with a torrent of studies of his life and work. In all of this, a constant focus of interest has been his attitude to Scripture and in particular his exegetical and hermeneutical principles. Luther's own insistence that he was simply a preacher of the word and that everything else flowed out of his engagement with the Scriptures is being taken very seriously. Careful investigation of his connection to the patristic and medieval exegetical tradition has opened up new perspectives on his work and has exposed the weaknesses in some earlier heroic presentations of him as one who created a Protestant approach to the Bible *ex nihilo*. It has also clarified the genuine innovations that came from his wrestling with that tradition. In more recent years, attempts have increasingly been made to explore and evaluate Luther's contribution on its own terms rather than imposing later canons of precision, consistency, and philosophical perspective. There may still be disagreement among Luther scholars on a number of these areas. Yet, few doubt the value of thinking through these issues "in conversation with" Luther. There is much that contemporary interpreters — often so quick to see how cultural factors distorted the hermeneutical endeavors of previous generations while slow to perceive their own cultural captivity — can yet learn from this Bible student of sixteenth-century Wittenberg.

We have been rightly warned of the danger of undue systematization when it comes to Luther's principles of biblical interpretation (Wood 1960: 11). The preoccupation with hermeneutics in general and biblical hermeneutics in particular, especially since the last quarter of the twentieth century, has led to a degree of precision, sophistication, and indeed abstraction that would be anachronistic to expect in the writings of this sixteenth-century exegete. Having said that, it is undoubtedly the case that Luther's influence on subsequent reflection about biblical interpretation has been immense. He played a major role in the eclipse of medieval exegetical methods. The search for spiritual meanings in biblical passages was replaced by an investigation of the theological import of the simple grammatical sense and the contexts of biblical passages. He gave classic expression to the principle of *claritas scripturae,* "the clarity of Scripture," and developed its implications in provocative directions. He reasserted and gave a more secure theological anchor to a christological approach to the entire Scripture in the law-gospel dynamic, which also laid bare the impact of biblical truth on the life of the Christian believer. His attention to the intended addressee of each biblical promise, exhortation, command, or warning sharpened this focus on Christ and provided a control on interpretation and application that could be derived from the text itself. Finally, these developments arose from, and in turn reinforced, Luther's own clear commitment to Scripture as the word of God, the final authority in matters of Christian faith and life.

BIBLIOGRAPHY

Allison, G. R.

1995   "The Protestant Doctrine of the Perspicuity of Scripture: A Reformulation of Biblical Teaching." Ph.D. dissertation, Trinity Evangelical Divinity School.

Barth, K.

1938   *Die Kirchliche Dogmatik. 1/2: Die Lehre vom Worte Gottes, Prolegomena zur Kirchliche Dogmatik.* Zurich: Theologische Verlag.

Beisser, F.

1966   *Claritas Scripturae bei Martin Luther.* Forschungen zur Kirchen- und Dogmengeschichte 18; Göttingen: Vandenhoeck & Ruprecht.

Bornkamm, H.

1948   *Luther und das Alte Testament.* Tübingen: Mohr.

Brecht, M.

1985-93   *Martin Luther.* Trans. J. L. Schaaf. 3 vols. Minneapolis: Fortress.

Callahan, J.

1996   "Claritas Scripturae: The Role of Perspicuity in Protestant Hermeneutics," *JETS*
        39: 353-72.

Chau, W. S.

1995   *The Letter and the Spirit: A History of Interpretation from Origen to Luther.* Ameri-
        can University Studies 7/167; New York: Lang.

Dockery, D. S.

1983   "Martin Luther's Christological Hermeneutics," *Grace Theological Journal* 4: 189-
        203.

Ebeling, G.

1942   *Evangelische Evangelienauslegung. Eine Untersuchung zu Luthers Hermeneutik.*
        Forschungen zur Geschichte und Lehre des Protestantismus 10/1; Munich:
        Lempp.

1951   "Die Anfänge von Luthers Hermeneutik." *ZTK* 48: 172-230.

Ellingsen, M.

1983   "Luther as Narrative Exegete." *JR* 63: 394-413.

Evans, G. R.

1984   *The Language and Logic of the Bible: The Earlier Middle Ages.* Cambridge: Cam-
        bridge University Press.

Forde, G. O.

1983   "Law and Gospel in Luther's Hermeneutic." *Int* 37: 240-52.

Graham, W. A.

1987   *Beyond the Written Word: Oral Aspects of Scripture in the History of Religion.*
        Cambridge: Cambridge University Press.

Hagen, K.

1993   *Luther's Approach to Scripture as Seen in His "Commentaries" on Galatians 1519-
        1538.* Tübingen: Mohr.

Hendrix, S. H.

1974   *Ecclesia in Via: Ecclesiological Developments in the Medieval Psalms Exegesis and
        the Dictata super Psalterium (1513-15) of Martin Luther.* Leiden: Brill.

Isaac, G. L.

1996   "In Public Defense of the Ministry of Moses: Luther's Enarratio on Psalm 90,
        1534-1535." Ph.D. dissertation, Marquette University.

Kooiman, W. J.

1961   *Luther and the Bible.* Trans. J. Schmidt. Philadelphia: Muhlenberg.

Luther, M.

1883   *D. Martin Luthers Werke: Kritische Gesamtausgabe.* Ed. J. K. F. Knaake and
        G. Kawerau. 127 vols. Weimar: Hermann Böhlaus Nachfolger.

1906-61 *Luthers Werke: Kritische Gesamtausgabe: Bibel.* 12 vols. Weimar: H. Böhlau.

1955-86 *Luther's Works.* Ed. J. Pelikan and H. T. Lehmann. 55 vols. St. Louis: Concordia; Philadelphia: Fortress.

McGrath, A. E.

1985 *Luther's Theology of the Cross: Martin Luther's Theological Breakthrough.* Oxford: Blackwell.

1987 *The Intellectual Origins of the Reformation.* Oxford: Blackwell.

1993 *Reformation Thought: An Introduction.* 2nd ed. Oxford: Blackwell.

Maschke, T.

2001 "Contemporaneity: A Hermeneutical Perspective in Martin Luther's Work." In T. Maschke, F. Posset, and J. Skocir, eds., *Ad Fontes Lutheri: Toward the Recovery of the Real Luther,* 165-82. Milwaukee: Marquette University Press.

Mostert, W.

1979 "Scriptura sacra sui ipsius interpres. Bemerkungen zum Verständnis der Heiligen Schrift durch Luther," *Lutherjahrbuch* 46: 60-96.

Nicholas of Lyra

1492 *Postilla Literalis super totam Bibliam.* 4 vols. Strasburg: Mentelin.

Pilch, J. J.

1970 "Luther's Hermeneutical 'Shift,'" *HTR* 63: 445-8.

Preus, J. S.

1967 "Old Testament *Promissio* and Luther's New Hermeneutic," *HTR* 60: 145-61.

1969 *From Shadow to Promise: Old Testament Interpretation from Augustine to the Young Luther.* Cambridge: Harvard University Press.

Reid, J. K. S.

1957 *The Authority of Scripture: A Study of the Reformation and Post-Reformation Understanding of the Bible.* London: Methuen.

Reinke, D. R.

1973 "From Allegory to Metaphor: More Notes on Luther's Hermeneutical Shift," *HTR* 66: 386-95.

Rothen, B.

1990 *Die Klarheit der Schrift* 1: Martin Luther, Die wiederentdeckten Grundlagen. Göttingen: Vandenhoeck & Ruprecht.

Ruokanen, M.

1987 "Does Luther Have a Theory of Biblical Inspiration?" *Modern Theology* 4: 1-16.

Stapulensis, Faber (= Jacques Lefèvre d'Étaples)

1979 *Quincuplex Psalterium. Fac-similé de l'édition de 1513.* Travaux d'Humanisme et Renaissance 170; Geneva: Droz.

Stiegman, E.

2001   "Bernard of Clairvaux, William of St. Thierry, and the Victorines." In G. R. Evans, ed., *The Medieval Theologians*, 129-55. Oxford: Blackwell.

Thompson, M. D.

1998   "*Claritas Scripturae* in the Eucharistic Writings of Martin Luther." *WTJ* 60: 23-41.

2003   *A Sure Ground on Which to Stand: The Relation of Authority and Interpretative Method in Luther's Approach to Scripture.* Carlisle: Paternoster.

Watson, P. S.

1947   *Let God Be God! An Interpretation of the Theology of Martin Luther.* London: Epworth.

Wood, A. S.

1960   *Luther's Principles of Biblical Interpretation.* London: Tyndale.

CHAPTER 11

Biblical Interpretation
in the Works of Philip Melanchthon

Timothy Wengert

Philip Melanchthon (1497-1560), Protestant reformer and professor at the University of Wittenberg from 1518 until his death, profoundly influenced both the method and the content of Christian biblical interpretation during the sixteenth century and beyond. Even his life story demonstrates how keenly committed he was to biblical exegesis. Concerning method, Melanchthon borrowed certain humanist techniques to develop a new rhetorical approach to the Bible, especially the Pauline corpus, and also employed commonplaces *(loci communes)* for biblical interpretation in far different ways from his contemporary Erasmus. Melanchthon managed to blend certain principles of dialectics with a Lutheran "law-gospel" hermeneutic.

Melanchthon's interpretations of biblical texts themselves had far-reaching effects. His published commentaries often set the framework for later exegetical debates, while preserving important aspects of medieval and patristic biblical interpretation. This is particularly true of his commentaries on Romans, Colossians, and the Gospel of John. He influenced not only a wide variety of students (many of whom became important commentators in their own rights), but also other readers, including Ulrich Zwingli and John Calvin.

LIFE STORY

Melanchthon was born in the southwest German town of Bretten, the son of Georg Schwartzerdt, the *Rüstmeister* (armaments minister) of the Electoral Palatinate (for this section, see Scheible 1997). After his father's death in 1508 he studied first at the Latin school in Pforzheim, where he resided in the home of a relative, the sister of the famous Hebraist and German humanist Johannes Reuchlin. Older scholarship assumed that Reuchlin was Melanchthon's great-uncle (see Scheible 1996: 41-50). In recognition of young Philip's blossoming skills in Greek, Reuchlin gave him a Greek grammar, inscribing it with the Hellenized form of his name, which quickly became his lifelong moniker: Melan (black) chthon (earth). After receiving a Bachelor of Arts degree from the University of Heidelberg in 1511, he journeyed to Tübingen, where he earned a Master of Arts degree in 1514. For the next several years he taught in the arts faculty and assisted at the printery of Thomas Anselm.

On Reuchlin's recommendation Melanchthon received a call in 1518 to teach Greek at the fledgling University of Wittenberg in Saxony. While teaching a variety of subjects in the arts faculty (Greek, Latin, rhetoric, and dialectics), he also began his theological studies there under Martin Luther and in 1519 received his first and only theological degree, the Bachelor of Bible. This gave him license to lecture not only on the Greek text of the Bible (which he could already do in the arts faculty), but also on the content of the Bible (using the Latin). There followed lectures on Matthew, Romans, 1-2 Corinthians, and John. After a brief hiatus (1523-24) during which Melanchthon served as rector of the University (the first married rector of a European university), he returned to lectures on the Bible by 1525. With the bestowal by the Elector of Saxony of a special professorship allowing him to lecture on any subject he desired, Melanchthon taught in both the arts and theology faculties for the rest of his life.

In work on rhetoric and dialectics he continued to hone his unique exegetical method. He applied that method to commentaries, especially on Proverbs, Romans, and Colossians, and wrestled with the meaning of the biblical text for his day and age. When the theological faculty of the University of Wittenberg began granting doctorates in the 1530s, several of his students, including Caspar Cruciger, Sr., and Georg Major, became members of the faculty and authors of their own biblical commentaries. These exegetes owed a great debt to their teacher's pioneering work and, in some cases, even read his manuscripts in their lectures.

MELANCHTHON'S METHOD OF BIBLICAL INTERPRETATION

Melanchthon grew up in a period of intense interest in and criticism of methods for interpreting texts, commonly called humanism. In connection with his thought, two opposing perspectives on humanism and its relation to the Reformation have arisen among scholars.

The one, typified by the work of Maurer (1967-69), views humanism and the Reformation as representing two opposing philosophies. Thus, Maurer argues, Melanchthon began his career as a humanist, but fell under the influence of Luther and became a Reformation theologian. Then, under the shadow of the debate over the free will between Luther and Erasmus, Melanchthon suffered a "crisis of vocation" (Maurer 1967-69: 2.419-28) and only reluctantly took up lectures on the Bible, now marked by certain humanistic tendencies. Humanism under this scheme denotes a philosophy that champions the human being and its powers and is tied to certain anthropological and theological presuppositions from classical antiquity.

Over against this view, some scholars (for example, Wengert 1987: 25-28), influenced especially by the work of Kristeller (1979) on Renaissance thought, have argued that humanism presented not a common philosophy but a common methodology and approach to texts marked by a concern for the sources *(ad fontes)*, for history, and for poetics, and by a proper use of the classical languages (Latin and, later, Greek and even Hebrew) and their literatures *(bonae litterae)*. Thus, humanism and the Reformation were not *ipso facto* incompatible, and many, if not all, of the Protestant Reformers were at the same time humanists, that is, committed to the study of the humanities. Despite more recent criticism of this approach by Frank (1995: 37-47), this second approach offers the best way to understand Melanchthon's method of biblical interpretation in its historical context. In short, Melanchthon used humanist methods without interruption throughout his career to present his Lutheran convictions about biblical texts.

Melanchthon and the Origins of Rhetorical Criticism

In 1522, Melanchthon burst on the European exegetical scene with the publication of his annotations on Romans and 1 and 2 Corinthians. Only the work on Corinthians has been published recently (MSA 4.15-132), with the work on 1 Corinthians translated into English by Donnelly (Melanchthon 1995). Using the common Renaissance ploy of authorial reluctance, Luther described in his preface to this work that he had managed to publish the annotations (actually lecture notes) against the will of their author. They in fact marked something of a revolution in the interpretation of Paul, and especially of Romans. Melanchthon was the first Christian exegete to organize and analyze Romans thoroughly on the basis of standard rules of rhetoric (for a detailed analysis, see Wengert 1996).

Ancient authors had occasionally noted Paul's use of rhetorical schemes and tropes in his letters, for example, his use of repetition in Phil. 4:4 or his reference to allegory in Gal. 4:24. This tradition passed into medieval scholastic commentaries, where, however, interpreters were far more interested in dividing the text (the so-called *divisio*), often employing Aristotelian philosophical categories (such as matter and form or causes) to that end (Wengert 1987: 107-9). The rise of humanism in the fifteenth century brought a renewed interest in proper speaking and the use of Cicero and Quintilian for constructing good speeches and analyzing ancient ones.

In 1519, Melanchthon contributed to the burgeoning number of rhetorical handbooks, publishing his *De rhetorica libri tres*. In 1520, he lectured on rhetoric and on Romans at the same time (see Schäfer 1997). Thus, in the 1521 edition of the lectures on rhetoric (the *Institutiones Rhetoricae*), one can observe how Romans has become, for Melanchthon, a model for good letter writing. This had not occurred to Erasmus, whose 1522 handbook on letter writing, *De conscribendis epistolis* (1968-80: 8.1-293), set the standard for style. Following the church fathers, Erasmus criticized Paul's style in several prefaces to his Greek NT.

More importantly, Melanchthon's various lectures on Romans, begun in the early 1520s, laid out in meticulous detail the rhetorical contours of Paul's letter. Melanchthon described, using standard language of classical rhetoric, the letter's *dispositio* (shape). Romans has, he said, an *epigraphē* (address), an *exordium* (a main body of arguments and answers to objections), and a conclusion. This shape was so important to Melanchthon that he devoted an entire work to this in 1529/30, the *Dispositio orationis in Epistolam Pauli ad Romanos* (The Shape of the Oration in Paul's Epistle to the Romans, 1834-60; CR 15.443-92, mistakenly labeled there as the first annotations). He also demonstrated how Paul used other kinds of rhetorical turns of phrase and figures of speech.

For Melanchthon, however, one of the most important aspects of analyzing a piece of literature was to recognize its *scopus* or *status,* that is, the author's central argument. On this basis, the exegete could interpret the entire document or at least important sections of it. Thus the *status* of Romans "is that we are justified by faith" (cited in Wengert 1996: 129). Melanchthon related all other arguments of the letter to this central theme or treated them as excursuses. In this regard, as Schäfer (1997) demonstrates, Melanchthon viewed the central portion of Romans (5:12–8:39) not in rhetorical categories but in dialectical categories, that is, as a *methodus,* a dialectical development of theological topics *(loci),* namely sin, law, and grace (see further below).

Melanchthon continued using rhetorical categories to interpret biblical texts throughout his career. Thus, in his lectures on John, again published by

Luther in 1523 "against the author's will," he viewed some of Jesus' speeches as orations and John himself as a historian (Wengert 1987: 170-82). Melanchthon's work on the OT, especially the Psalms, also employed rhetorical categories (Sick 1959). His scholia on Colossians, first published in 1527 (MSA 4.209-303; translated by Parker 1989) not only used such categories, but also subtly challenged Erasmus's interpretation for ignoring the main point of the Epistle (Wengert 1998). Schäfer (1963) edited Melanchthon's later work on Romans (1532) for publication in MSA 5 (a translation of the revised 1540 edition was made by Kramer 1992). Schäfer includes both a very helpful glossary of rhetorical terminology (based on definitions gleaned from Melanchthon's own works on rhetoric) and an outline of Melanchthon's *dispositio* of the Epistle (MSA 5.373-92; for an analysis of this work, see Schäfer 1963).

Dialectics and *Loci communes* in Melanchthon's Exegetical Method

A second hallmark of Melanchthon's exegetical method was his use of dialectical categories in the service of biblical interpretation. In the sixteenth century, dialectics, along with rhetoric and grammar, comprised the *trivium*, the basic parts of the standard introductory courses in the arts faculty. In 1520, Melanchthon published his first book on dialectics (CR 20.709-64). More importantly, in his 1521 published lectures on rhetoric, *Institutiones Rhetoricae* (Melanchthon 1521), he named, alongside the three classical genres of speeches (demonstrative, deliberative, and judicial), a fourth, the didactic, that which teachers employ in the classroom. Its basic rules for invention came, not from rhetoric at all, but from dialectics. Thus, this type of speech answered the questions first summarized by Aristotle, including: whether a thing exists, what it is, and what are its parts, its genus, its species, its causes, and its effects.

Melanchthon's concern for dialectics, especially as he combined it with rhetoric, profoundly affected his biblical interpretation in two very different arenas. In the first place, it allowed him, especially when interpreting Paul, to view the biblical text as combining rhetorical and dialectical arguments. As Schäfer (1997) has demonstrated, throughout his career Melanchthon viewed Rom. 5:12–8:39 as a *methodus* or dialectical argument on the theological topics *(loci)* of sin, law, and grace. Thus he could overcome one of the most frequent criticisms of Pauline rhetoric, that it inconsistently followed the rules of good letter writing. In the middle of a piece of good rhetoric, Melanchthon argued, Paul had inserted specific dialectical arguments proving with certainty that human beings are justified by faith. This move was crucial to

Melanchthon's theology, which based humanity's relation to God on God's sure and certain promises. Since, according to Melanchthon, rhetoric dealt with probabilities while dialectics dealt with certainties, it only made sense that at this point in Romans, Paul would treat the reader to arguments based upon dialectics (Schäfer 1997: 79-81).

In the second place, dialectics played a special role in the construction of *loci communes,* commonplaces. Scholarship is divided over the origin and function of *loci communes* in Melanchthon's thought. All agree (following the summary in Schneider 1990: 70-78) that *loci* represented Cicero's translation of the Aristotelian term *topoi.* Cicero defined it as *sedes argumentorum,* bases of arguments or proofs, and thus it is related to "definition" in dialectics. But as Wiedenhofer (1976: 1.373-76) has demonstrated, *loci* can also be "general headings" and thus relate very closely to rhetorical *inventio.* As a result, some viewed them primarily as headings or general topics into which the reader could distribute statements of an author. Thus, in his 1516 introduction to the Greek NT Erasmus could encourage the reader to develop what he called nestlets *(nidulae)* for sorting out the Scripture's themes (Erasmus 1968-80: 3.64-66). The examples Erasmus proposed overwhelmingly echoed his own moral philosophy. Finally, according to Wiedenhofer, *loci communes* also denote the principles and essence of a particular intellectual subject.

The other major figure besides Erasmus and before Melanchthon to champion the use of *loci communes* was Rudolf Agricola (see Joachimsen 1926; Maurer 1960; Wiedenhofer 1976; Schneider 1990; Hoffmann 1997). Melanchthon had received Agricola's *De inventione dialectica libri III* as a gift from his fellow worker in Anshelm's print shop, the future reformer of Basel, John Oecolampadius, and referred to it in his *De rhetorica libri tres* specifically in connection with *loci.* But scholarship is divided on Agricola's influence on Melanchthon. Joachimsen (1926) argues that Agricola's *De inventione* profoundly influenced Melanchthon's thought. Maurer (1960) replies that there was a development in Melanchthon's thought that began by using Erasmian rhetorical categories and that only after time did he come to view *loci communes* in dialectical terms — under the direct influence of Cicero and Aristotle. More recent researchers (Wiedenhofer 1976; Schneider 1990) have shown that Maurer's notions of Melanchthon's development understate the continuing importance of both dialectics and rhetoric in Melanchthon's method — something he learned from Agricola. As Hoffmann (1997) has shown in a comparison of Erasmus's and Melanchthon's interpretations of John's Gospel, Melanchthon's positive assessment and use of dialectics precisely mark the central divergence of his exegetical methods from those of

Erasmus. They both used humanist methods, but to different ends and in the service of very different theological perspectives.

In particular, Melanchthon used *loci communes* in his biblical interpretation, not simply as ethical topics for rhetorical use, but as axioms derived from the central principles and essence of theology. In Romans Paul himself, in Melanchthon's view, had in fact laid out these *loci communes* and developed a series of dialectic arguments concerning them. This insight into Pauline dialectics led Melanchthon to two important conclusions.

On the one hand, he viewed Romans itself as the key to the principal themes of the entire Scripture. Already in notes on the Greek text delivered in 1521, Melanchthon stated that "The Epistle of Romans is didactic, teaching what the gospel is and, indeed, the source of justification, and it is truly like a *methodus* of the entire Scripture and the whole letter consists in one *locus:* the source of justification" (cited in Wengert 1996: 128). In his later work on rhetoric, *Elementorum rhetorices libri duo* (Two Books on the Elements of Rhetoric, CR 13: 417-506; excerpted in MSA 5.388), Melanchthon defined *methodus* as "the right way or order for investigating and explaining either simple [dialectical] questions or propositions." In this case, Melanchthon spelled out the particular proposition involved: the gospel, namely, the source of justification.

Luther, most likely under the influence of Melanchthon, made much the same point in his 1522 preface to Romans for the new German translation of the NT (WADB 7.2-26; translated in LW 35.365-80). There he claimed that "This epistle is really the chief part of the New Testament, and is truly the purest gospel" (WADB 7.2; LW 35.365). He then included a discussion of the chief terms in Paul, what Melanchthon called the *loci communes,* followed by a *dispositio* of Paul's argument. It is no wonder that Luther could claim he had learned dialectics from Melanchthon! Connecting early Lutheran arguments for the centrality of Romans in interpreting Scripture to Melanchthon's own method and view of the Pauline corpus helps explain what many have called Lutheranism's "canon within a canon." For these reformers, at any rate, the choice of Paul's letter to the Romans arose out of their exegetical method, and not simply out of polemical interests in combating Roman Catholic theology.

On the other hand, Melanchthon excerpted precisely these Pauline *loci communes* to form the basis of Protestantism's first systematic theology. After receiving the Bachelor of Bible in 1519, Melanchthon, under the medieval theological curriculum still operative in Wittenberg, was to have begun work on becoming a *Sententiarius,* a lecturer on Peter Lombard's *Sentences,* that medieval collection of patristic and biblical expositions of Christian doctrine (Scheible 1997: 34). Instead, he lectured on the chief Pauline *loci* treated in Romans and now included a wide range of biblical and patristic passages in support of his arguments. In 1521, he published these lectures under the title *Loci communes rerum theologicarum seu hypotyposes theologicae,* that is, *Commonplaces of Theological Matters* or *Theological Standards* (MSA 2/1.15-185; translated by Satre 1969). This book represented a kind of biblical theology in which the categories of one author, Paul, who offered the *methodus* for Scripture, now provided the basic topics for theological conversation and debate. This indicated a second way Melanchthon employed his *loci* method. Not only could one inquire after the *scopus* or *status* of a particular document and thus discover its integrating *locus communis,* but one could also, having now discovered in Paul the basic topics of Scripture, reverse the process and organize Scripture passages into their overarching categories, thereby disintegrating their original contexts. In this way, even in biblical commentary itself, Melanchthon could interrupt his interpretation of a specific passage to handle the general *locus communis* to which it was connected. These two competing tasks, arising out of a single method, marked much of Melanchthon's biblical interpretation throughout his career (for an example of how this operated in his interpretation of Colossians, see Wengert 1998: 48-64).

Law and Gospel

Melanchthon's use of dialectics and rhetoric in his exegetical method resulted in an important combination of two dialectical categories with central Lutheran theological concerns. As three different scholars (Fraenkel 1961; Wiedenhofer 1976; Wengert 1987) have pointed out in their analyses of very different aspects of Melanchthon's thought, the two most important dialectical questions for Melanchthon were *"Quid sit?"* and *"Quid effectus?":* What is the thing? and What are its effects?

The exegete must not simply inquire after the definition of a thing (intimately related to its *locus communis*), but also after its effect or impact on the hearer. According to Schneider (1990: 73) such a combination paralleled concerns of Erasmus for the affective aspects of biblical interpretation. In fact, the deep concern for a thing's effect or purpose, especially as it "moved the heart," marked much of Renaissance humanism (Aune 1994). However, this concern also corresponded to the developing Lutheran hermeneutical principle of law and gospel, which not only defined a text as law (command) or gospel (promise) but also analyzed the text's effect on the hearer as Word of God (Bizer 1964). Thus, law terrifies sinners and gospel comforts them. This hermeneutical shift meant a concomitant change in the interpretation of the traditional prooftext for allegory, 2 Cor. 3:6 ("The letter kills, and the Spirit gives life"). The exegete's task was no longer to penetrate (or escape) the killing literal sense in order to discover the spiritual meaning of a text. Instead, the text itself, as God's destroying and creating Word, effected death and life (or terror and comfort) in the hearer.

The emphasis on meaning and effect marked Lutheran biblical interpretation from its inception (see Wengert 1987: 31-42). Almost all the NT commentaries published in 1522-24 by Wittenberg theologians and their allies contained opening discussions of the distinction. It also played an important role in Melanchthon's *Loci communes Theologicae* (1969), first published in 1521. This distinction became the major theme of all of his subsequent biblical interpretation. He concerned himself not only with the text's definition but also with its effect as it alternatively terrified or comforted the conscience. Twice in crucial articles (4 and 12) of the Apology of the Augsburg Confession of 1531, that defense of the Confession presented to Emperor Charles V in Augsburg the previous year, Melanchthon prefaced exegetical debates by appealing to the distinction between law and gospel. Thus, he wrote in article 12.53, "These are the two chief works of God in [human beings], to terrify and to justify and quicken the terrified. One or the other of these works is spoken of throughout Scripture. One part is the law, which reveals, denounces, and condemns sin. The other part is the Gospel, that is, the promise of grace granted in Christ" (Kolb and Wengert 2000: 500-503, 581-91). He went on to emphasize that both law and gospel may be found throughout Scripture. It was never the case for either Melanchthon or Luther that they equated law with the OT writings or Gospel with the NT.

Melanchthon also took great pains to pass this concern on to later generations of Lutheran pastors and exegetes. In 1552, he authored the *Examen ordinandorum* (Exam for Ordinands) for the duchy of Mecklenburg, though it was later used more widely in Germany to train clergy. Under the heading "The Distinction between the Law and the Gospel," he wrote, "This distinction is one of the chief doctrines in the churches. And where one allows it to be extinguished (as it has been eradicated among the Papists), there follows terrible blindness, in that one imagines human beings are righteous through their works and merit forgiveness of sins with their own works" (MSA 6.186). Thus, for Melanchthon as for Luther, this hermeneutical distinction had direct results for both biblical interpretation and the central Christian teaching of justification.

If the distinction between law and gospel formed the backbone of Lutheran biblical hermeneutics, then distinctions among various uses of the law constituted the sinews of such an approach. It also caused endless theological debate. In 1522, Luther first conceived two uses of the law in comments on

Gal. 3:23-29, written at the Wartburg for his *Weihnachtspostil* (commentary on the appointed pericopes for the Advent and Christmas seasons) and seen through Wittenberg's presses by Melanchthon himself. There, building on a suggestion by Nicholas of Lyra for uses of the law in Israel, Luther expanded it to God's two uses of the law among all people: a first, or civil, use to keep order in the world and restrain the wicked; a second, or theological, use that puts to death, or terrifies, the conscience by revealing its sin (for these two paragraphs, see Wengert 1997c: 177-210).

Melanchthon discussed these two uses (*officia legis,* offices or functions of the law) in his 1527 *Scholia on Colossians* (1989) and in his 1532 commentary on Romans (1992). In the third edition of the *Scholia,* published in 1534, he increased the number of uses to three. Melanchthon invented this third use, called the didactic use among later Lutheran theologians, for two reasons. On the one hand, he was trying to correct certain antinomian tendencies in the theology of John Agricola of Eisleben, another student of Luther, who all but denied that the law had any role to play in the life of the Christian. On the other, he was reacting against the stance of certain moderate defenders of the Roman Catholic position who argued that the gospel itself includes moral demands and not just promises. In this use, not so much God (as in the first two uses) but Christians themselves "used" the law to discover God's will and to conform their lives to it. In the later so-called antinomian controversies of the 1550s and 60s, Lutherans debated the relation of law and gospel and the third use of the law. As a result, two articles (5 and 6) of the *Formula of Concord,* published in 1580, dealt with this issue (Tappert 1959: 477-81, 558-68) and defined the third use of the law as a guide to the Christian life, but understood it as revealing those works God desired (as opposed to self-chosen human works). Practically speaking, it defined the third use as applying the first and second uses in the Christian's life to restrain the old creature in the believer and drive the person again to Christ. On the basis of Melanchthon's work, Calvin also defined three uses of the law in his *Institutes of the Christian Religion* of 1536 (1960).

THE SCOPE OF MELANCHTHON'S BIBLICAL INTERPRETATION

Compared to Calvin, who preached and produced commentaries on nearly every book of the Bible, Melanchthon's output of biblical commentaries was more limited. However, when one also examines the wide range of interpretive guides and the impact of specific exegetical insights, his importance becomes more obvious. At the same time, Melanchthon was also a significant conduit for passing on to the Protestant exegetical tradition a lasting respect for patristic and (to a lesser extent) medieval biblical interpretations (for this section, see Wengert 1997a, and for Melanchthon's earliest work, Barton 1963).

Aids for Biblical Interpretation

As described in the previous section, Melanchthon's exegetical method owed a great deal to his work in the humanities, especially the *trivium*, grammar, rhetoric, and dialectics. In 1518, Thomas Anshelm printed Melanchthon's Greek grammar (CR 20.1-180), which saw at least twenty-five reprints in one edition or another during its author's lifetime. As mentioned above, his first books on rhetoric and dialectics appeared in 1519 and 1521. He continued to produce other volumes on these subjects, crucial to his biblical method, throughout his life (see CR 13.413-752 and 20.709-64).

At the same time, he produced textbooks on theology, also intended to aid students in biblical interpretation. His various editions of the *Loci communes* (Latin, 1521-22, 1535, 1543; Melanchthon's German translation, 1555; MSA 2; CR 21-22) guided the reader in constructing appropriate theological commonplaces for biblical texts. This form of biblical theology paid tribute to Melanchthon's conviction that the various voices in the Scripture finally united around the basic themes of Christian theology. He expounded the Nicene Creed in a similar way, first to complete the lectures of Caspar Cruciger, Sr., in 1548 (*Enarratio Symboli Niceni* = "An Exposition of the Nicene Creed"; see Wengert 1989: 421-22; CR 23.193-346) and then as separate lectures in 1557 (*Explicatio Symboli Niceni* = "An Explanation of the Nicene Creed"; see Wengert 1989; CR 23.347-584). This interest in the Creed as a summary of Christian doctrine and a rule for biblical interpretation reflected the demands of Wittenberg's theological curriculum, which recommended lectures on the Creed.

Wittenberg's theological curriculum, written by Melanchthon in 1533 and revised in 1546, also shaped other aspects of Melanchthon's contributions to biblical interpretation. It required regular lectures on Romans, John, the Psalms, Genesis, and Isaiah, and on Augustine's treatment of Pauline theology, *On the Spirit and the Letter*. This helps explain why Melanchthon lectured on Romans, for example, at least nine times (lecture notes or published commentaries have survived for six of those occasions; Bizer 1966: 9-30, 39-85). He also produced works on John and some Psalms and a brief introduction to Isaiah.

Melanchthon also concerned himself with the geography of the Holy Land, helping to publish a new edition of Eusebius of Caesarea's *Hieronymi ecologa de locis Hebraicis* (A Selection from Jerome on Hebrew Places, *MBW* 252 [1977]) and a new map of Palestine (MBW 6352), preparing his own brief explanation of some place names (CR 20.439-52). He also took great pains to reconstruct biblical history, giving it pride of place in his history of the world. He based this all-encompassing work on the so-called *Chronicon Carionis,* a history of the world by Johann Carion published by Melanchthon in 1532. By Melanchthon's death in 1560, his lectures had reached Charlemagne. He was also deeply involved in Wittenberg's translation of the Bible into German and Latin. The German translations of 1 and 2 Maccabees were his own work. He also wrote many declamations on biblical themes (Wengert 1997a: 114-17).

Melanchthon's Commentaries on the Bible

At the end of the seventeenth century, Gottfried Arnold, author of a self-proclaimed non-sectarian church history, wrote that Melanchthon had led people away from the Bible (Wengert 1997a: 106). Despite work in the eighteenth century by the first Melanchthon scholar, Theodore Strobel, to refute that notion, in the twentieth century the well-known scholar Kurt Aland could still argue that Melanchthon held almost no lectures in Wittenberg's theological faculty (Wengert 1997a: 106). Among others, the report of John a Lasco, the Polish reformer, refuted this notion when he reported that 1500 people attended Melanchthon's lectures on the Bible at Wittenberg (CR 44.330). In fact, Melanchthon's frequent interpretations of the Bible had a profound effect on contemporaries.

Although not as well known for OT lectures as his more famous colleague, Luther, Melanchthon did not neglect the Hebrew Bible completely. Early works on selected passages in Genesis and Exodus were published in 1523 (CR 13.761-92; Melanchthon 1910-26 SM 5/1.3-19). They have received full treatment in Sick (1959), who also analyzes Melanchthon's work on the Psalms. Indeed, Melanchthon produced several works on the Psalms. In the 1540s and 50s he lectured on the *dispositio* of Psalms 1-60 and 110-132; the chief themes of these notes on the Psalms were published posthumously by his son-in-law Caspar Peucer (CR 13.1245-1472). Melanchthon also wrote brief introductions to some of the prophetic books (Isaiah, Jeremiah, Lamentations, Haggai, Zechariah, and Malachi, CR 13.793-822, 981-1016).

Next to Romans and Colossians, however, there was no book that received more attention from Melanchthon than Proverbs. Error-filled annotations from 1525, published without Melanchthon's approval, were replaced with new *scholia* in 1529 (*Nova scholia in Proverbia Salomonis,* MSA 4.305-464). A third commentary (*Explicatio Proverbiorum Salomonis,* third edition: CR 14.1-88) came out in 1550, some two years after Melanchthon's lectures on the book and merited revised editions in 1552 and 1555. He also produced a commentary on Ecclesiastes in late 1550, printed in CR 14.89-160. In his final work on Proverbs, as elsewhere, Melanchthon, who also lectured on Aristotle's *Ethics* (see Barnes 1984), stressed the difference between Solomon's proverbs and pagan writers. Their philosophy retains small parts of the law, especially pertaining to the second table of the Decalogue (although Phocylides mentions something about the wrath of God); they know nothing of the Mediator, forgiveness of sin, reconciliation, or faith (CR 14.4). Concern for the theological center of Proverbs runs throughout Melanchthon's interpretation of the book.

The final, at first glance surprising, contribution by Melanchthon to OT interpretation is his work on Daniel. The apocalyptic Luther, whose interest in the end of the world is well documented, was assisted by an equally apocalyptic Melanchthon. Volz (1955/56) suggests that Melanchthon even influenced Luther's lengthy preface to the German translation of Daniel, first published in 1530. More substantial than a preface to a commentary (which never appeared) and his assistance in the work of Justus Jonas on Daniel 7 (Wengert 1997a: 125-26) was his commentary on Daniel, published in 1543. It bore the title *A Commentary on the Prophet Daniel in Which the Most Corrupt Status of Our Age and the End of the Turkish Cruelty Is Described* (CR 13.823-980). Calvin requested a copy of it, and, twelve years later, a French translation with Calvin's own outline of Daniel appeared in Geneva. Melanchthon's commentary itself interpreted Daniel's visions (Daniel 7–12) as predictions of history from the prophet's time to 1542, where the last, savage monarchy is the Turks. According to Barnes (1988), this apocalyptic expectation marked much of sixteenth-century Lutheranism.

Melanchthon produced some of his most enduring work on the NT. On the Gospels themselves he penned a variety of commentaries. Two *postils,* commentaries on the Gospel texts appointed for the church year, appeared under his name (Buchwald 1924). Both reflected Melanchthon's ongoing duty to provide Latin sermons on early Sunday mornings, especially designed for the many foreign students in Wittenberg. Thus, although Melanchthon was not a pastor or preacher, he also provided sermon helps (Schnell 1968). The first *postil,* representing sermons delivered between 1541 and 1544, came out in 1544 with a preface written by Melanchthon (CR 14.161-528). The second appeared in 1594-95, compiled by Christopher Pezel from notes on sermons delivered in 1548 and beyond (CR 24). Among other things, these sermons demonstrate that Melanchthon continued to use allegory in his biblical interpretation (Wengert 1987: 194-98).

The two sets of annotations on Matthew had very different origins. The first, published in 1523, based upon lectures delivered between 1519 and 1520 immediately after he received his Bachelor of Bible, appeared without Melanchthon's (or Luther's) approval (MSA 4.133-208). The other, likewise published without Melanchthon's consent in 1558, consisted of sermon helps on difficult passages in Matthew written over a fifteen-year span, specifically for a Wittenberg preacher (CR 14.535-1042).

Perhaps more influential than Melanchthon's sermon helps were his commentaries on the Gospel of John. The first, published by Luther in 1523 without the author's permission, contained lecture notes from 1522 and 1523, and represented the first Protestant commentary on that important book (Wengert 1987; CR 14.1043-1220). On the basis of an interpretation of John 1:1-14 found in Martin Luther's 1522 Christmas Postil (WADB 10/1/1: 237-38; LW 52: 82), Melanchthon interpreted the entire Fourth Gospel as not simply opposing christological heresies, as medieval and patristic exegetes had done, but as aimed at the problem of salvation and faith, as reflected in John 1:12. In his introduction he reflected this shift: "Ebionites are those who deny Christ's divinity. Those are twice Ebionites who, although they attribute divinity to Christ, nevertheless do not put it to use [in remitting sins]" (CR 14.1047; translation in Wengert 1987: 149). By refocusing interpretation of John on faith and salvation, Melanchthon introduced an entirely new set of interpretive questions for Johannine exegesis and refocused many old ones. In the 1540s, Melanchthon's student, Caspar Cruciger, Sr., published his lectures on John (probably based on Melanchthon's own outline of the Gospel). He followed Melanchthon's soteriological perspective, and was the first interpreter of the Fourth Gospel ever to make John 20:30-31 the central theme of the book (for the incorrect attribution of this text, found in CR 15.1-440, to Melanchthon, see Wengert 1989 and 1992).

Melanchthon's interpretation of Romans played a crucial role in the development of Protestant biblical interpretation, as has already been demonstrated above. Whereas Luther's only lectures on Romans (1515-16) were not available (except for two manuscripts) until modern editors published them (WADB 57; LW 25), Melanchthon's comments were widely available beginning in 1522. The first set of annotations was reprinted no less than ten times by 1525. In 1529/30 Melanchthon published his *Dispositio*, or outline, of Romans (CR 15.441-92). In 1532, the first edition of his *Commentarii* on Romans appeared (MSA 5). It reflected his latest understanding of justification, hammered out in the *Apology of the Augsburg Confession* the previous year. It was also the first time that Melanchthon interpreted Romans 9–11 in connection with the locus on the church, and not the locus on justification and, hence, predestination. The revised 1540 edition (CR 15.493-796; translation: Kramer 1992) also included what might be termed a defense of his *Apology*. Finally, from 1552 to 1553, Melanchthon lectured on Romans a final time and produced his last commentary, the *Epistolae Pauli scriptae ad Romanos enarratio* = "An Exposition of the Epistle of Paul Written to the Romans" (CR 15.797-1052). Here he took on certain intra-Lutheran opponents, especially Andreas Osiander, who had attacked Melanchthon's forensic understanding of justification, and wished to replace it with an interpretation that stressed the "indwelling of Christ's divine nature in the heart of the believer" (Scheible 1997: 200-203).

Melanchthon did not neglect other parts of the Pauline corpus (for a somewhat limited examination of Melanchthon on Paul, see Schirmer 1967). His early annotations on 1-2 Corinthians (MSA 4.15-132) were published with Romans in 1522. These, too, argued for a soteriological center to these books. Thus, he could write about the opening chapters of 1 Corinthians that, although the book deals with a variety of topics, "Only this seems worth noting. In recounting at the beginning the loci of this epistle, the most distinguished one is hardly neglected. It concerns justification, or the power of the gospel, or the knowledge of Christ, or the distinction between the wisdom of the flesh and the wisdom of the spirit" (MSA 4.16, correcting Donnelly; see Melanchthon 1995: 29). An excursus on 2 Cor. 2:5 (MSA 4.95-98) contains some of Melanchthon's earliest comments on penance; one on 2 Cor. 3:6 (101-103) focuses on the Lutheran understanding of letter and spirit. In 1550, Melanchthon provided Paul Eber with lecture notes on 1 Corinthians (and some chapters of 2 Corinthians) for him to read publicly, which Eber then published in 1561, shortly after Melanchthon's death (CR 15.1053-1220). These notes contain some of Melanchthon's most detailed interpretations of passages on the Lord's Supper.

Melanchthon's work on Colossians deserves special mention. Not only was the *Scholia* of 1527 the first biblical commentary Melanchthon saw through the presses himself (MSA 4.209-303), but its subsequent edition in 1528 also contained important theological debates against Erasmus on free will, and John Agricola on the role of the law and repentance in the Christian life (Wengert 1997c and 1998). Whereas Erasmus viewed the early chapters of Colossians (especially Col. 2) in light of Paul's fight against Judaizers and thus regarded them as having very little practical application, Melanchthon viewed them as a summary of the entire gospel and, among other things, a refutation of justification by works or merit. The third edition of 1534 marked important changes in Melanchthon's understanding of law and the relation between faith and works. Most importantly, he developed for the first time the concept of a third use of the law, that is, the law functioning in the life of the believer. In the 1550s, Melanchthon returned to Colossians, and published in 1559 the final biblical commentary overseen by him. In its own day, it gained attention for what it said (and did not say) about Christ's ascension (Col. 3:1) in relation to the Lord's Supper controversies of the time and the presence of Christ in the Eucharist. It also attacked Osiander on justification.

Melanchthon's views on the letters to Timothy have survived in two forms. On the one hand, a commentary ascribed to Caspar Cruciger, Sr., and published in 1540 may in fact trace back to lectures or at least outlines prepared by Melanchthon (see Wengert, 1989). On the other hand, Melanchthon held his own lectures on 1 Timothy and 2 Timothy 1–2 between 1550 and 1551. These were published posthumously in 1561 (CR 15.1295-1396). In the 1522 preface for the German translation of the New Testament, Luther described 1 Timothy as a Pauline handbook for the Christian bishop. Cruciger and Melanchthon followed the same approach.

The Exegetical Tradition

Although Melanchthon set many of the themes for subsequent Protestant interpretation of the Bible, he did not operate in a vacuum. Not only did he use Luther's lectures on Romans to help in his own early lectures on that text, he also owed a profound debt to patristic exegesis and (to a lesser extent) to medieval interpretations. Sick (1959) has demonstrated this for the Old Testament (especially Psalms and, in particular, Augustine) and Wengert for John and Colossians (1987 and 1998). Although Melanchthon did not always cite the sources he used directly, certain patterns in his exegesis and certain traditional exegetical questions found their way into his work. For example, he used the *"quaestio"* central to medieval theological discussion of contradictions in the text, and mined medieval sources for patristic references. In later years, he even cited Peter Lombard directly.

On the question of Melanchthon's use of the tradition, an important debate involves the scope of his patristic knowledge and the consistency of its use. Meijering (1983) criticizes Melanchthon for using the fathers eclectically. Unlike Erasmus, who worked to create a *consensus patristicus*, Melanchthon picked and chose only those statements that supported his views. Meijering's view opposes that of Fraenkel (1961), whose thorough analysis of Melanchthon's use of the fathers uncovered what might be termed a historical herme-neutic. According to Fraenkel, Melanchthon was convinced that from the time of Cain and Abel the church has always been under attack by those who tried to import human reason and philosophy into its message of good news. Origen had introduced Plato into Christian theology, a fatal mistake that tainted even some of Augustine's work. In the Middle Ages, Aristotle replaced Plato, but the result was the same. Thus, Fraenkel argues that Melanchthon's supposed eclecticism actually arose out of a very sophisticated view of history that contradicted his Roman Catholic opponents, including Erasmus, whose patristic consensus excluded Lutheranism's justification by faith alone. More recently, Wengert (1998 and 1999) has shown that the same critical approach to the fathers was employed in Melanchthon's exegetical work. Moreover, the differences between Melanchthon and Erasmus, modern scholars have no-ticed, were also clear to the protagonists themselves. Thus, Erasmus criticized Melanchthon's exegesis in terms not unlike Meijering's own, and Melanch-thon returned the favor by railing against Erasmus's defense of Origen.

THE IMPACT OF MELANCHTHON'S BIBLICAL
INTERPRETATION ON HIS CONTEMPORARIES

Only since 1980 or so has the question of the ongoing influence of an exegete's biblical interpretation caught the attention of modern scholars. Even the scanty research to date bears witness to the deep impression Melanchthon made on contemporary exegetes. Looking at a single chapter from the Gospel of John (13), Wengert (1987: 215-31) demonstrates the effect of Melanchthon's annotations on Zwingli, John Brenz, and even the young Heinrich Bullinger, who read out portions of Melanchthon's text word-for-word to his own audi-ence. Kolb (1997) has shown in a study of Romans 9 the degree to which later Lutheran exegetes of all stripes depended on Melanchthon's earlier work. Muller (1997) has traced the complex contours of Melanchthon's effect on Calvin's interpretation of Romans. Here, the flattering reference to Melanch-thon in the preface of Calvin's work (CR 38.403-4), which masked a criticism of the older man's method, matched a critical appropriation of his exegetical insights and method.

Melanchthon's greatest influence, however, was on his own students. Here, two stand out. Caspar Cruciger, Sr., was Melanchthon's protégé and friend at the University of Wittenberg. Not only were Cruciger's lectures on 1 Timothy based on notes provided by Melanchthon, but his subsequent work on John, several Psalms, and the Nicene Creed was a direct result of Melanchthon's later theology and exegesis. His commentary on John (1546) reflected a growing interest among Wittenberg's theologians in ecclesiology, especially heightened by the collapse of talks with the Roman party in 1530 and again in 1541, by the call for a general council by Pope Paul III, and by the threat of war with Emperor Charles V.

Georg Major was perhaps Wittenberg's most prolific NT exegete (Wengert 1997b). On becoming a professor of theology in Wittenberg in 1544, he embarked on an ambitious campaign of preaching and lecturing that culminated in the publication of postils on the Gospels and Epistles for the church year and of commentaries on the entire Pauline corpus. He followed Melanchthon's method slavishly, providing a *dispositio* or outline of every book. He also published a life of Paul, one of the first of its kind. He turned his commentary on 1 Timothy into an exegetical version of Melanchthon's *Loci communes* by providing the reader with an outline of the theological commonplaces arranged in the order used in Melanchthon's now famous work. Although his own theological woes (he was caught up for most of his career in a dispute on the necessity of good works for salvation) besmirched his reputation among Lutherans, Major's monumental achievement in Pauline interpretation shows how one scholar applied Melanchthon's rhetorical approach to Romans to Paul's other Epistles. Major's commentaries bear fitting tribute to the lasting significance of Melanchthon's biblical interpretation for later generations.

Philip Melanchthon was one of the most influential biblical interpreters of the sixteenth century. He combined the latest literary techniques of Renaissance humanism with developments in Reformation theology to produce some of the most important commentaries of his age. His unique approach, especially to Paul's epistle to the Romans, combined rhetorical analysis of letters with a dialectical understanding of the main themes of Christian theology. This work and other commentaries on Colossians, Proverbs, and Daniel influenced Protestant exegesis of the Bible for generations.

BIBLIOGRAPHY

Agricola, R.

1992   *De Inventione dialectica libri.* Ed. L. Mundt. Tübingen: Niemeyer.

Aune, M.

1994   *"To Move the Heart": Rhetoric and Ritual in the Theology of Philip Melanchthon.* San Francisco: Christian Universities Press.

Barnes, J. (ed.)

1984   *The Complete Works of Aristotle. The Riverside Oxford Translation.* Princeton: Princeton University Press.

Barnes, R. B.

1988   *Prophecy and Gnosis: Apocalypticism in the Wake of the Lutheran Reformation.* Stanford: Stanford University Press.

Barton, P. F.

1963   "Die exegetische Arbeit des jungen Melanchthon 1518/19 bis 1528/29. Probleme und Ansätze." *ARG* 54: 52-89.

Bizer, E.

1964   *Theologie der Verheissung. Studien zur Theologie des jungen Melanchthon.* Neukirchen: Neukirchener.

Bizer, E. (ed.)

1966   *Texte aus der Anfangszeit Melanchthons.* Neukirchen-Vluyn: Neukirchener.

Buchwald, G.

1924   "Zur Postilla Melanchthoniana." *ARG* 21: 78-89.

Calvin, J.

1960   *Institutes of the Christian Religion.* Ed. J. T. McNeill. Trans. F. L. Battles. 2 vols. LCC 20, 21. Louisville: Westminster.

Carion, J.

1563   *Chronicon Carionis, expositvm et avctvm mvltis, et veteribus, et recentibus historiis . . . bearb. durch Ph. Melanchthon bzw. Kaspar Peucer.* Wittenberg: Peucer.

Cruciger, C.

1544   Letter to V. Dietrich. Manuscript 138. Richard C. Kessler Reformation Collection. Archives and Manuscripts Department. Pitts Theology Library, Emory University.

1546   *In Evangelium Johannis Apostoli Enarratio Caspari Crucigeri, recens editi.* Strassburg: Emmel.

Erasmus of Rotterdam

1968-80 *Ausgewählte Schriften.* Ed. W. Welzig. 8 vols. Darmstadt: Wissenschaftliche Buchgesellschaft.

Fraenkel, P.

1961   *Testimonia Patrum: The Function of the Patristic Argument in the Theology of Philip Melanchthon.* Geneva: Droz.

Frank, G.

1995   *Die theologische Philosophie Philipp Melanchthons (1497-1560).* Leipzig: Benno.

Hoffmann, M.

1997   "Rhetoric and Dialectic in Erasmus's and Melanchthon's Interpretation of John's Gospel." In Wengert and Graham (eds.) 1997: 48-78.

Joachimsen, P.

1926   "*Loci communes*. Eine Untersuchung zur Geistesgeschichte des Humanismus und der Reformation." *LJb* 8: 27-97.

Kolb, R.

1997   "Melanchthon's Influence on the Exegesis of His Students: The Case of Romans 9." In Wengert and Graham (eds.) 1997: 194-215.

Kolb, R., and T. J. Wengert (eds.)

2000   *The Book of Concord: The Confessions of the Evangelical Lutheran Church.* Minneapolis: Fortress.

Kristeller, P. O.

1979   *Renaissance Thought and Its Sources.* Ed. Michael Mooney. New York: Columbia University Press.

Maurer, W.

1960   "Melanchthons *Loci communes* von 1521 als wissenschaftliche Programmschrift." *LJb* 27: 1-50.

1967-69 *Der junge Melanchthon zwischen Humanismus und Reformation.* 2 vols. Göttingen: Vandenhoeck und Ruprecht.

Meijering, E. P.

1983   *Melanchthon and Patristic Thought: The Doctrines of Christ and Grace, the Trinity and Creation.* Leiden: Brill.

Melanchthon, P.

1519   *De rhetorica libri tres.* Basel: Froben.

1521   *Institutiones rhetoricae.* Basel: Petri.

1530   *Dispositio orationis, in Epistola Pauli ad Romanos.* Wittenberg: Clug.

1531   *Elementorum Rhetorices libri duo.* Wittenberg.

1834-60 *Philippi Melanthonis opera quae supersunt omnia.* Ed. K. Bretschneider and H. Bindseil. CR, 28 vols. Halle: Schwetschke.

1969   *Philipp Melanchthon: Loci communes theologici.* In *Melanchthon and Bucer,* ed. W. Pauck; trans. L. Satre, 3-152. LCC 19; Philadelphia: Westminster.

1989   *Paul's Letter to the Colossians.* Trans. D. C. Parker. Sheffield: Sheffield Academic Press.

1992   *Commentary on Romans by Philipp Melanchthon.* Trans. F. Kramer. St. Louis: Concordia.

1995   *Annotations on First Corinthians: Philipp Melanchthon.* Trans. J. P. Donnelly. Milwaukee: Marquette University Press.

Muller, R. A.

1997   " '*Scimus enim quod lex spiritualis est*': Melanchthon and Calvin on the Interpretation of Romans 7.14-23." In Wengert and Graham (eds.) 1997: 216-37.

Schäfer, R.

1963   "Melanchthons Hermeneutik im Römerbriefkommentar von 1532," *ZTK* 60: 216-35.

1997   "Melanchthon's Interpretation of Romans 5.15: His Departure from the Augustinian Concept of Grace Compared to Luther's," in Wengert and Graham (eds.) 1997: 79-104.

Scheible, H.

1996   *Melanchthon und die Reformation. Forschungsbeiträge.* Ed. G. May and R. Decot. Mainz: Zabern.

1997   *Melanchthon: Eine Biographie.* Munich: Beck.

Schirmer, A.

1967   *Das Paulus-Verständnis Melanchthon 1518-1522.* Wiesbaden: Steiner.

Schneider, J. R.

1990   *Philip Melanchthon's Rhetorical Construal of Biblical Authority: Oratio Sacra.* Lampeter: Mellen.

Schnell, U.

1968   *Die homiletische Theorie Philipp Melanchthons.* Berlin: Lutherisches Verlagshaus.

Sick, H.

1959   *Melanchthon als Ausleger des Alten Testaments.* Tübingen: Mohr.

Tappert, T. G.

1959   *The Book of Concord: The Confessions of the Evangelical Lutheran Church.* Philadelphia: Fortress.

Volz, H.

1955/56   "Beiträge zu Melanchthons und Calvins Auslegungen des Propheten Daniel." *ZTK* 67: 93-118.

Wengert, T. J.

1987   *Philip Melanchthon's Annotationes in Johannem in Relation to Its Predecessors and Contemporaries.* Geneva: Droz.

1989   "Caspar Cruciger (1504-1548): The Case of the Disappearing Reformer." *SCJ* 20: 417-41.

1992   "Caspar Cruciger Sr.'s 1546 'Enarratio' on John's Gospel: An Experiment in Ecclesiological Exegesis." *CH* 61: 60-74.

1996   "Philip Melanchthon's 1522 Annotations on Romans and the Lutheran Origins of Rhetorical Criticism." In R. A. Muller and J. L. Thompson, eds., *Biblical Interpretation in the Era of the Reformation,* 118-40. Grand Rapids: Eerdmans.

1997a   "The Biblical Commentaries of Philip Melanchthon," in Wengert and Graham (eds.) 1997: 106-48.

1997b   "Georg Major (1502-1574): Defender of Wittenberg's Faith and Melanchthonian Exegete." In H. Scheible, ed., *Melanchthon in seinen Schülern,* 129-56. Wolfenbütteler Forschungen 73; Wiesbaden: Harrassowitz.

1997c   *Law and Gospel: Philip Melanchthon's Debate with John Agricola of Eisleben over Poenitentia.* Grand Rapids: Baker.

1998   *Human Freedom, Christian Righteousness: Philip Melanchthon's Exegetical Dispute with Erasmus of Rotterdam.* New York and Oxford: Oxford University Press.

1999   " 'Qui vigilantissimis oculis veterum omnium commentarios excusserit': Philip
        Melanchthon's Patristic Exegesis." In D. C. Steinmetz, ed., *Die Patristik in der Bibel-
        exegese des 16. Jahrhunderts* I, 115-34. Wolfenbütteler Forschungen 85; Wiesbaden:
        Harrassowitz.

Wengert, T. J., and M. P. Graham (eds.)
1997   *Philip Melanchthon (1497-1560) and the Commentary.* Sheffield: Sheffield Aca-
        demic.

Wiedenhofer, S.
1976   *Formalstrukturen humanistischer und reformatorischer Theologie bei Philipp Me-
        lanchthon.* 2 vols. Frankfurt am Main: Lang.

CHAPTER 12

John Calvin and the Interpretation of the Bible

Barbara Pitkin

The contributions of John Calvin (1509-64), the French Protestant reformer in Geneva, to the history of Christian biblical interpretation have long been recognized, frequently extolled, and occasionally contested. In many respects, Calvin's achievements represent the fruit of developments in biblical scholarship and new attitudes toward scriptural authority that were planted and cultivated in the medieval era and took firm root in the sixteenth century. Of course, there were many noteworthy contemporary exegetes, both Roman Catholic and Protestant, who sought to combine humanist learning with renewed appreciation for the authority of Scripture and who decisively shaped the practice of interpretation. Few, however, attained the widespread recognition that was accorded to Calvin; even fewer found their exegetical virtues so enduringly lauded, or their shortcomings so heavily criticized, by later generations.

In part, Calvin's reputation is due to the sheer volume of his work and the number and dissemination of his publications. Though popularly remembered as the defender of double predestination and the author of an important theological summary, the *Institutes of the Christian Religion* (1960 [1559]), he was not a man of one doctrine or even of one book. He was a busy pastor, preacher, teacher, and exegete, not to mention correspondent and polemicist. He lectured and preached on the Bible throughout his career, published commentaries on nearly every book of the OT and NT, and agreed to have his sermons, which were delivered extemporaneously, preserved by a team of scribes. His academic training was in law, not theology, but he was knowledgeable about biblical teaching and had formed opinions about interpretation prior to embarking on his career as a minister. Before beginning his position as a lecturer in sacred Scripture in 1536, he had already tried his hand at the commentary genre in his first publication, a 1532 commentary on Seneca's *De clementia* (1969 [1532]), and had begun to express his ideas on how the Bible should be interpreted in his 1535 preface to Olivétan's French NT (1958 [1535]) and in the first edition of the *Institutes* (1975 [1536]). A comprehensive but concise overview of Calvin's work on the Bible can be found in de Greef (1993: 89-120).

Calvin's interest in proper interpretation of the Bible is not surprising, given that he shared with most other sixteenth-century "evangelicals" an insistence on "Scripture alone" as the ultimate authority in matters of faith as well as the conviction that the central meaning of Scripture was fundamentally clear and intelligible. Studies of Calvin and the Bible thus have often centered on his doctrine of Scripture and the issue of biblical authority or on his ideas about the methods and goals of interpretation (Reuss 1853; Farrar 1884, 1886; Fuhrman 1952; Haroutounian 1958; Forstman 1962; Kraus 1977; Gerrish 1982; Gamble 1985, 1987, 1988).

Important as these issues are, however, the picture these studies have yielded of Calvin as an expositor is partial and largely theoretical. They have treated his discussions of the authority of Scripture and considered the relationship in the *Institutes* between the OT and the NT. They have also derived general principles from Calvin's commentaries. Where commentaries and, to a lesser extent, sermons were cited or used as illustrations, there was rarely any detailed analysis. Apart from a few essays written to promote interest in newly-appearing editions of Calvin's exegetical works (e.g., Tholuck 1831), little attention was given to the actual content of Calvin's exposition in commentaries and sermons. Despite calls to recognize the diversity among Protestant interpretations and to appreciate Calvin's reliance on past exegetical tradition (e.g., Kraus 1977: 8, 11), until recently only a handful of studies have taken seriously the need to explore both the discontinuity *and* the continuity of Calvin's exegesis with previous and contemporary patterns of interpretation (see especially Steinmetz 1982, 1986, 1988, 1990a, 1990b, 1991).

Recent scholarship has expanded earlier understandings of Calvin as an exegete by supplementing ongoing discussions of his hermeneutical theory (Zachman 2002) and understanding of biblical authority with careful attention to the range of his exegetical activity and more detailed analysis of his actual exposition. In addition, studies of the history of biblical interpretation have filled out a rich picture of the exegesis of Calvin's contemporaries and predecessors. Together, these factors have revised earlier judgments that seemed to imply that his exegetical achievements were virtually without precedent and their quality beyond comparison (e.g., Schaff 1892: 462). These studies have also shed light on what is truly distinctive in his use of the Bible.

In what follows, I will draw together some of the most significant findings of this recent research in order to locate Calvin's interpretation of the Bible *within* the history of Christian exegesis. The discussion will reaffirm the importance of Calvin's contributions to this history, even as it underscores two points: that much of his exposition of Scripture was not unique and that some of the most distinctive aspects of his biblical interpretation were those that certain contemporaries and later generations judged most problematic.

First I will discuss two important developments in the past twenty-five years that, building on precedents in research up through the mid-1980s, have reshaped the image of Calvin as an expositor. Then I will detail three new points of focus that have emerged from this body of scholarship and that continue to guide investigations into Calvin and the Bible. Finally, I will outline distinctive features of Calvin's biblical interpretation. The fact that the focus remains specifically on Calvin's exegetical work should not imply that the Bible was not important for his theological, catechetical, and polemical writings, or that these have no bearing on the theme of biblical interpretation in his works. Indeed, as the discussion will show, the question of how best to formulate the relationship between Calvin's scriptural exposition and his *Institutes* has been a major issue in recent years. Nevertheless, since the most significant advances in our understanding of Calvin and the Bible have come through the study of his actual exposition of scriptural passages, and, given the focus of this series on the history of biblical interpretation per se, it seems prudent to focus here on Calvin's exegetical activity in particular.

NEW PERSPECTIVES ON CALVIN
AS AN INTERPRETER OF THE BIBLE

As already mentioned, the two most important developments in recent scholarship on Calvin's exegesis have been a more precise understanding of the context of his comments and a more detailed study of his exposition of biblical passages. Though these perspectives have dominated research only since the mid-1980s, they were not entirely unprecedented.

In the first place, the long-held assumption that there was something distinctive about Calvin's exegesis led naturally to comparisons between his method and those of his contemporaries (especially Luther) and the preceding tradition. However, important studies of medieval exegesis that underscored the variety of and development in interpretive methods (Spicq 1944; Smalley 1952; de Lubac 1954-64) and the range of attitudes toward scriptural authority (Oberman 1966) meant that all subsequent efforts to compare or contrast Calvin with others would have to become much more nuanced. In this vein, Walchenbach (1974) investigated explicit and implicit references in Calvin's commentaries to the exegesis of Chrysostom. He concluded that Calvin's use of Chrysostom intensified between 1539 and 1546, a period in which, as subsequent studies have shown, Calvin's earlier interest in patristic theology became even more pronounced (Zillenbiller 1993; van Oort 1997; see also Ganoczy and Müller 1981). Ganoczy (1976) investigated Calvin's theology and (with Scheld 1983) Calvin's hermeneutics, setting these in the context of late medieval and humanist debates over the relative authority of church and Scripture and a rebirth of interest in the apostle Paul. Torrance (1988) viewed Calvin's hermeneutics through a different medieval lens, namely, the philosophy and epistemology of Scotus, Occam, and Major. Gerrish (1982) revisited the question of the authority of Scripture and the guidelines for interpretation in Calvin and Luther, taking into account the need to view these against their medieval background.

Overlapping with the time period of these initial studies, Steinmetz began exploring Calvin's exegetical context in a slightly different and less theoretical way in the early 1980s (e.g., 1982, 1986, 1988). In this series of essays comparing Calvin's exegesis with that of his predecessors and contemporaries (many republished in his *Calvin in Context* [1995]), Steinmetz set a new standard for distinguishing Calvin's "original insights" from the exegetical commonplaces or "lore" that he received from others. His approach is noteworthy for its focus on comparing interpretations of biblical passages (rather than on general hermeneutics) and for its specific rather than generalized depiction of the contexts (traditional and contemporary) that shaped Calvin's interpretation. The impact of this pioneering work has been profound, both in terms of the contribution of Steinmetz's own writings and through the investigations of others who have shared a similar comparative method (McKee 1984, 1988; Backus 1984; Schreiner 1986, 1989, 1994, 1996; de Kroon 1988; Thompson 1991, 1992, 1994, 1997, 2001; Kok 1993, 1996; Lane 1997; Pitkin 1999a, 2006a, 2006b, 2007; Marcuse 2005; Pak 2006a, 2006b; Blacketer 2006).

All of these most recent studies analyzing Calvin's exegesis in the context of ancient, medieval, and contemporary interpreters also build on the second important development in Calvin scholarship, namely, an interest in his actual biblical exposition. Anticipated by a few French and German monographs earlier in the twentieth century (e.g., Goumaz 1917, 1948; Mülhaupt 1931; Schellong 1969; see also Kraus 1968), English-language treatments of Calvin's interpretation of scriptural passages owe their largest debt to Parker's numerous works (see bibliography). Parker provided the impulse to take seriously Calvin's biblical exposition itself, to identify more precisely Calvin's sources for his exegetical work, and to attend to the distinctive features of the different genres of Calvin's interpretation (commentaries, sermons, and lectures). Parker's scholarship reflected and furthered the long-standing interest in methodological issues. Subsequent research in this area has yielded much more precise understandings of the versions of the Bible and other sources Calvin used, of his knowledge of biblical languages, of what he meant by the simple literal meaning of the text, and how this commitment to the plain meaning — especially with respect to the OT — fit with his Christian theological commitments (de Greef 1984; Opitz 1994; Puckett 1995; Engammare 1995, 1996b; Lane 1996, 1997, 1999). Even more significantly, Parker combined his studies of Calvin's method with detailed analysis of Calvin's exposition.

A similar dual focus governs Paluku Rubinga's investigation of Calvin's commentary on Isaiah (1978) and Girardin's meticulous study of the commentary on Romans (1979). Such efforts provided further impetus to the trend represented in the major works by Steinmetz, McKee, Schreiner, and Thompson mentioned earlier. These studies, along with those of Wright (1986), Woudstra (1986), Pitkin (1993, 1999a, 1999b), Engammare (1994, 2000), Marcuse (2005), and the contributors to a recent volume devoted to Calvin's biblical interpretation (McKim 2006) add precision to the picture of Calvin's biblical interpretation and heighten appreciation for his work as an exegete. Some of the most interesting work underway in this area involves analysis of Calvin's sermons, to be discussed in the next section.

DIRECTIONS IN CURRENT RESEARCH ON CALVIN'S BIBLICAL INTERPRETATION

Emerging from this body of scholarship are three focal points that guide current research: continued interest in Calvin's "context," greater sensitivity to and appreciation of biblical exposition as a distinct genre, and heightened attention to Calvin's preaching. Undergirding these trends are several ongoing editorial projects, specifically, critical editions of previously unpublished sermonic material (the *Supplementa Calviniana*, 1936-), a new edition of Calvin's works (*Ioannis Calvini Opera Omnia*, 1992-), and an important multi-volume bibliography of the publication and dissemination of his writings (Peter and Gilmont, 1991, 1994, 2000). Also relevant for situating Calvin's expository activity are a number of historical studies that shed light especially on Calvin's preaching and pastoral activity in Geneva (e.g., Kingdon 1985; Naphy 1994; Lambert 1998; Spierling 2005).

Contexts for Calvin's Exegesis

By far the most complex issue is that of Calvin's intellectual context, and no study of his biblical interpretation can now safely ignore this. Years ago, Kraus cautioned against speaking monolithically about "*the* biblical exegesis of the Reformation" and urged scholars to remember the importance of exegetical tradition for Calvin, who "was unwilling to give up the consensus of interpretation" (1977: 8, 11). Subsequent studies have explored Calvin's "context" from various angles: his immediate intellectual context, the sources he probably used, and, less fully, the impact or reception of his exegetical work. Attention to context requires that Calvin not be read in isolation from prior and contemporary interpreters, both those whose commentary he may have consulted and those who reflect the dominant interpretive climate of his day.

Reassessments of the relationship between medieval and sixteenth-century exegesis have yielded a view of Calvin's place in an interpretive tradition that contrasts sharply with the image of him as the forerunner, "father," or even founder of the modern historical-critical method that can be seen in some of the older literature (e.g., Farrar 1886; Schaff 1892; but also Torrance 1988: 61, 72). Calvin embodied tendencies common to his age that also had deep roots in the exegetical tradition. For example, he shared with earlier and contemporary exegetes a concern for reconciling the "letter" of Scripture with its spiritual meaning, respect for the exegesis of the "fathers," and an interest in grammar and philology. Consequently, Calvin's insistence on the literal sense and his alleged repudiation of all allegory, his wide reading in patristic exegetes such as Chrysostom and Augustine, and his employment of philological tools such as the knowledge of biblical languages and classical rhetoric are no longer seen as constituting a "break" with the past. Rather, these elements are viewed in continuity with a medieval tradition that was itself not uniform (Spicq 1944; Oberman 1966; Schreiner 1994).

Like earlier exegetes such as Hugh and Andrew of St. Victor (Smalley 1952; see also chapter 2 above), Thomas Aquinas (Reyero 1971), Nicholas of Lyra (Krey and Smith 2000), and Lefèvre d'Étaples (Bedouelle 1976), Calvin and many of his contemporaries emphasized the dignity and even priority of the "literal" sense of Scripture. Nonetheless, their desire to find a *simple* literal sense distinguished their efforts from previous approaches. Earlier interpreters reconciled the letter with the spirit of Scripture through the idea that Scripture possesses both a literal and multiple spiritual senses (e.g., the *quadriga*, i.e., a literal sense and the three spiritual senses of allegory, tropology, and anagogy) or in some cases through the notion of a duplex literal sense. Calvin and those who adopted a similar program did not seek spiritual senses beyond the text but rather spiritual senses within the text (Muller 1996) and tended to overstuff this single, literal sense with spiritual meanings (Steinmetz 1997; see also Burnett 2004). Though Calvin eschewed "bad" allegories, he embraced "good" allegories such as Paul's in Galatians 4, preferring, however, to call these typologies, similitudes, or anagogies (Thompson 2000: 35).

Also in continuity with the exegetical past, Calvin and other sixteenth-century Reformers did not practice interpretation in isolation, but sought guidance, especially from the great interpreters of the ancient church. Granted, sixteenth-century interpreters, Calvin among them, were arguably better read in the fathers than most of their predecessors, thanks to the availability of new comprehensive editions of the fathers' works produced by scholars such as Beatus Rhenanus (see D'Amico 1988) and Erasmus (see Den Boeft 1997; see also chapter 9 above). Moreover, Calvin was part of the Reformation's overall reevaluation of the authority of the previous tradition. However, this did not mean that he rejected tradition entirely; indeed, his respect for patristic exegesis has long been recognized (e.g., Tholuck 1831; Schaff 1892: 465). Recently, Steinmetz has shown more precisely how earlier interpretive patterns "conditioned" Calvin's reading of Scripture, both in raising key questions and suggesting answers based on the texts, as well as by providing a fund of "exegetical lore," such as the customary practice of comparing Abraham's laughter to the astonishment of the Virgin Mary (1995: 73).

Finally, Calvin and many contemporaries shared with the exegetical tradition an interest in grammar and philology. To be sure, their skill in these matters had been heightened by developments in humanistic textual scholarship, and their exegesis took into account more diversity in the transmitted biblical texts. But knowledge of biblical languages and concern with textual matters, including establishing the best text, did not constitute a reversal of medieval practice but rather a shift in emphasis (Muller 1996: 12-13). Taken together, these reassessments underscore how much of Calvin's method and commentary were not unprecedented.

Much of the work on the historical precedents underlying Calvin's interpretation of Scripture has relied on a broad, representative portrayal of ancient, medieval, and contemporary patterns of interpretation to determine where Calvin is making an original point or is repeating a traditional insight.

Complementing these efforts to locate Calvin in relation to the dominant traditions that shaped the exegetical world of his day are a few studies that seek to determine exactly which sources he actually used in the course of his commentary and preaching, and how he used them (Parker 1971, 1992; Walchenbach 1974; Engammare 1995, 1996b, 2000; Lane 1996, 1997, 1999; see also Ganoczy and Müller 1981; van Oort 1997; Thompson 2000: 32-39; Backus 2000). Seeking to add precision to studies that suggested what works Calvin *might* have used (Verhoef 1968; see also Ganoczy 1969), these more specific investigations focus on his actual citations of or clear references to Bible versions or traditional interpretations. In general they conclude that Calvin, though widely read in a number of the fathers, had a relatively modest collection of writings ready to hand when preparing his commentaries and lectures. Moreover, he may have relied on medieval compendia or works of contemporaries for traditional insights and often "cited" both the fathers and biblical passages from memory. Indeed, in his biblical commentaries, and even more so in his sermons, Calvin refrains from citing others' views, mentioning them (usually anonymously) only when he has reason to disagree with them (van Oort 1997: 675, 677-78; see also Steinmetz 1995: 98; Lane 1999: 3-4; see Pitkin 2007: 328, 335, 339).

Of course, simply identifying explicit references cannot explain Calvin's relationship to traditional and contemporary exegetes. The most complete image of Calvin's context emerges from the combination of the "extensive" approach of those who study Calvin against the rich texture of Christian (and sometimes Jewish) exegesis, with the "intensive" approach of those who focus on which aspects of this tradition Calvin actually cites (see Thompson 2000: 33). Taking both into account, we find an interpreter who is well acquainted with the major features of patristic theology and exegesis, acquired through his own study of newly available sources or through a passing familiarity with the major medieval textbooks of Gratian (Winroth 2000) and Peter Lombard (Rosemann 2004). He is also familiar with the exegetical works of such contemporaries as Luther (see chapter 10 above), Melanchthon (see chapter 11), Bucer (see Roussel 1988), and others. Comparison with the works of others is therefore fruitful and demonstrates that Calvin truly did learn from other commentators, especially the ancient ones, as he himself claimed in the dedicatory epistle to his Romans commentary (1981 [1540]). At the same time, as an exegete Calvin was always pressed for time. When writing a commentary, preparing a lecture, or thinking about one of the eight sermons he might preach in a given week, he had little time to consult his sources but instead relied chiefly on his memory, theological instincts, and rhetorical skill in crafting his comments. Sometimes Calvin's alleged "independence" may have stemmed simply from the fact that he worked in haste (Thompson 2000: 50). In addition, as will be discussed more fully below, Calvin's understanding of the aim of scriptural exposition led him to eschew detailed engagement with others' ideas in his commentaries, sermons, and lectures.

The final piece in the complex issue of Calvin's context is the vastly under-researched area of the impact or reception of his exegesis. Most of the work in this area has focused once again on Calvin's exegetical method, in which has been glimpsed an affinity with a post-liberal biblical hermeneutics (Frei 1974; Greene-McCreight 1998) or, in contrast, with a fruitful homiletical strategy (DeVries 1996) that may exist compatibly with modern historical criticism. Despite concerns that such comparisons may tend toward anachronism, I am convinced that they constitute an important chapter in the "reception" of Calvin's biblical work. Whether or not the developments they pursue are in genuine continuity with Calvin's use of the Bible is a complex matter. What is clear is that these largely thematic comparisons must be complemented by more historical studies of how Calvin's exegetical works were actually used by subsequent interpreters. For example, Thompson (2000: 41-49) has determined that excerpts from Calvin's commentary on Genesis were unwittingly incorporated by the editors of two seventeenth-century compilations, mistaken for glosses of the sixteenth-century hebraist Vatable. Further work in this area will need to attend to the general dissemination of Calvin's exegetical writings (Pettegree 1997) and to the specific citation of his interpretation by other exegetes, and will need to weigh all of this against Calvin's reputation among subsequent generations.

The Relationship between Exegesis and Theology

A second characteristic of current scholarship has been greater sensitivity to and appreciation of Calvin's exegetical work as a distinct genre and, with this, an interest in understanding how best to view the place of the exegetical works within the broader corpus of his writings. Calvin himself indicated his view of the relationship between the *Institutes* and his biblical commentaries in prefaces written in 1539-41 for the *Institutes* and for his first biblical commentary (see Muller 2000: 27-31). Here he distinguished the *Institutes* as a topically organized "summary of religion," which serves as a guide for reading Scripture, from the commentaries, which follow a course of continuous textual exposition and do not digress into long doctrinal summaries (Calvin 1863-1900: 2.1-2; 1960: 4-5). Of course, this division followed a traditional medieval pattern (and patristic, if one includes the sole instance of Origen), which also distin-

guished between biblical commentary and doctrinal summaries such as
Lombard's *Sentences* or Aquinas's *Summa Theologiae*.

In the first place, then, recent scholarship has sought to counter the relative neglect of the exegetical works in much of the earlier literature on Calvin.
Building on a more intimate knowledge of the substance of Calvin's exposition, some scholars are now beginning to probe ways of understanding the
complex relationship between the exegetical and the dogmatic literature. This
relationship has been characterized as a "hermeneutical circle" (Ganoczy 1976:
43-47), as "symbiotic" (McKee 1989: 168), as "stereoscopic" (McKee 1991: 224),
and as "reciprocal" (Steinmetz 1995: 14; cf. 130). Examinations of how discussions raised in the commentaries have been incorporated into the revisions of
the *Institutes* are shedding light on Calvin's theological method (McKee 1989,
1991; Pitkin 1999b). Investigations of the treatment in his commentaries and
sermons of such themes as faith, providence, divine justice, and the noetic effects of sin have demonstrated the complex interplay between his theological
and exegetical work (Schreiner 1994; Steinmetz 1995: 23-39; Pitkin 1999b).
Sometimes the biblical text challenges Calvin's theological presuppositions, as,
for example, in the portrayal of the relationship between faith and signs in
passages such as John 2:11, 23-25; 3:2; and 6:14 (Pitkin 1999a; cf. John 4:48; 7:31;
11:45). To resolve these conflicts, Calvin often views such passages through the
lens of other passages, which sheds light on how he prioritizes certain scriptural perspectives and uses these to resolve apparent discrepancies in biblical
views. At other times (as in the case of Rom. 1:18-23 or Ps. 8:2), he pursues an
idiosyncratic reading of the text in order to confirm a distinctive theological
conviction (Steinmetz 1995: 31; Pitkin 2001; cf. Pak 2006b). Sometimes the text
allows him to explore themes from a different angle than the one taken in the
Institutes. All these elements add precision to our understanding of how Calvin understood the Bible's unity, of which passages functioned as norms for
his theology and exegesis, and of how theology shaped exegesis and vice versa.

Calvin's Preaching

Related to this heightened valuation of the exegetical works in general is a new
emphasis on Calvin's preaching, including an interest in discerning its distinctive features vis-à-vis the commentaries and lectures. Building on Stauffer's
groundbreaking study of Calvin's sermons on Genesis (1978; see also Mülhaupt
1931), monographs treating Calvin's preaching on Job (Schreiner 1994), the Synoptic Gospels (DeVries 1996), Deuteronomy (Blacketer 2005), Acts (Moehn
2001), and Ezekiel (de Boer 2004a) have appeared in recent years. In 1992,

Parker published a thorough revision of his initial study (1947) of the general character of Calvin's preaching activity. Complementing these investigations are, on the one hand, shorter studies of Calvin's preaching on particular passages and examinations of general themes in his preaching (Barrois 1965; Stauffer 1980; Peter 1984; Fischer 1984; Schreiner 1986, 1989; Millet 1988; Engammare 1994; Armstrong 1997; DeVries 2004) and, on the other hand, fresh analyses of his preaching activity and the dissemination of his sermons (Peter 1972, 1975; Stauffer 1977; Gilmont 1995; Engammare 1995, 1996a; de Boer 1999, 2000). What Armstrong has characterized as "renaissance of interest in Calvin the Preacher" has been "stimulated and enriched" by the recent editions of sermons that existed previously only in manuscript (1997: 192-93). According to Peter's estimate, Calvin preached over four thousand sermons in Geneva (1984: 23), a clear indication of the importance of preaching for his work.

As in the commentaries and lectures, Calvin preached extemporaneously through a biblical book verse-by-verse, from the OT in his weekday sermons. Beginning in 1549, he preached on six weekdays every other week. He preached from the NT on Sunday mornings, always picking up where he left off the previous Sunday. Sunday afternoons he preached again on the NT or occasionally on a psalm. In 1549 a stenographer began transcribing his sermons, and some were published in his lifetime, but most remained in manuscript and were in fact sold off as scrap paper in 1805. Initial study of the surviving and recovered sermons (some 1400) has suggested that the doctrine proclaimed from the pulpit does not differ substantially from that found in the commentaries or the *Institutes*. Nonetheless, there are significant differences in emphasis and delivery, and sometimes in interpretation and application (Armstrong 1997: 196). Engammare has shown, for example, that Calvin's sermons on Genesis 3 and 6 emphasize different dogmatic principles and suggest distinct contemporary applications from those explored in the commentary (1994; 2000: xlvi-l). Thompson has come to a similar conclusion regarding the treatment of Hagar in commentary and sermon (2001: 86-87). Finally, Marcuse has analyzed Calvin's treatment of other biblical saints in the Genesis commentary and sermons (2005). De Greef has observed that in contrast to the commentary on Deuteronomy, the sermons on Deuteronomy are more interested in applying the text to the present situation, do not refer as often to other biblical texts or the exegesis of others, frequently utilize the first-person plural, and exhibit a stronger pastoral concern (1988; see also Blacketer 2005). Nicole and Rapin (1984) have undertaken a preliminary comparison for the sermons and commentaries on Isaiah, while De Boer (2000) has examined the possible relationship between the sermons on Isaiah and the biblical studies or *congrégations* on the same book.

DISTINCTIVE FEATURES OF CALVIN'S
EXPOSITION OF THE BIBLE

In light of these new perspectives and directions, I turn now to the most distinctive aspects of the form, content, and purpose of Calvin's exegesis. By "distinctive," of course, I do not mean to imply that these features are necessarily unique to Calvin, but rather that they are essential characteristics of his approach. At times, however, some of these strategies and goals led him in directions not often pursued by his predecessors and contemporaries. At the conclusion of this inquiry, then, I will discuss in fuller detail three features that might be considered peculiar to Calvin's interpretation of the Bible.

Continuous Exposition and Lucid Brevity

With respect to the formal elements of scriptural exposition, Calvin drew on traditional and more recent patterns in order to develop a program for interpreting the Bible in a variety of settings and in two languages. He explained Scripture in four related but distinct venues: in academic lectures *(praelectiones)* held in Latin for students and other interested auditors, in sermons in French for the general populace, in formal commentaries for clergy and literate laity published in both Latin and French, and in weekly Bible study discussions *(congrégations)* conducted in French for ministers and interested laity (cf. de Greef 1993). Common to all of these is Calvin's exposition book-by-book and verse-by-verse rather than in a thematic fashion. The only deviations from this strict adherence to the order of the text were some of Calvin's treatments of Exodus through Deuteronomy and of the three Synoptic Gospels. In his commentaries on these he "harmonized" the material into a single narrative and then commented according to his regular pattern of continuous exposition. Also common to all forms of exposition was the general pattern of the comments. All the oral presentations were delivered extemporaneously. Calvin gave the section of text to be discussed, made a few philological, historical, or theological observations to explain its meaning, and then applied the text to the situation of his readers or audience. As one would expect, the explanatory comments, including references to the exegesis of others, were more prominent in the commentaries and lectures than in the sermons, although even there they do not figure largely. The sermons, in turn, dwelt more on the application of the text to the present situation, though this concern was not at all absent in the commentaries. Calvin clearly had a sense of the differences in genre and tailored his comments accordingly.

Of course, the practice of continuous exposition was not new to Calvin; neither was the use of philological tools or theological insights or the interest in applying the text to the present. What gives Calvin's combination of all of these its distinctive stamp is his self-professed commitment to what he calls "lucid brevity" *(perspicua brevitas)* in exposition (Calvin 1981 [1540]: 1). He transformed a Renaissance love of brevity that itself drew on Quintilian (Millet 1992; Parker 1992: 87) into a method that Steinmetz has said constitutes one of his principal contributions to the intellectual heritage of the Reformation (1995: 14). In the dedicatory letter accompanying his very first biblical commentary in 1540, Calvin claimed that "the chief virtue of an interpreter consists in clear brevity" (1981 [1540]: 1) and indicated his wish to conform his exposition to this ideal. This meant that his comments would be kept relatively brief and would not digress into related subjects, especially avoiding dogmatic excursus and philological intricacy. This form, Calvin thought, was best suited to the purpose of biblical interpretation. Though detailed philological examination, rhetorical analysis, and consideration of historical background, theological import, and the exegesis of others all provided tools for understanding, in the actual exposition they were kept to a minimum.

This ideal of lucid brevity manifests itself differently in the various forms of exposition. In the commentaries, Calvin is most concise and balances his brief philological observations with explanations of what the text means and occasionally with succinct suggestions about how to apply the message. In the lectures Calvin discusses the text in somewhat more detail (de Greef 1993: 107). In the sermons he spends little time on the technical aspects and speaks at much greater length about the implications for contemporary belief and behavior. In fact, according to the sixteenth-century editors who published some of his sermons, Calvin was reluctant to have them appear in print precisely because he felt they did not adhere to his ideal. He is said to have found them too prolix and too concerned with the situation of his particular congregation (Gilmont 1995; Moehn 2001: 191-92). Perhaps, however, one might suggest simply that Calvin accommodated his method of "lucid brevity" to the specific needs and capacities of those for whom he was expositing. Parker has stressed that *perspicua brevitas* is best understood not as a style of writing but as "the rhetorical method by which the expositor achieves his task of revealing the mind of the writer" (1992: 91). While the sermons are undoubtedly more wordy and repetitive, this strategy was best suited to render the biblical writer's message clear to those listening.

The Mind of the Author and the Literal Sense

Calvin's biblical exposition took the form it did because he felt this was the form best suited to convey the content most appropriate to a work of scriptural interpretation. In his dedicatory letter to his 1540 Romans commentary (1981: 1), Calvin claimed that the aim of interpretation was to determine and make intelligible the "mind of the author" (*mens scriptoris,* p. 1). This concern for authorial intention reflects his humanistic interests, but the idea also has roots in the ancient and medieval church. Traditionally, interpreters recognized a multiplicity of meanings, all of which were intended by the divine author of Scripture. Calvin, however, prioritized the mind of the *human* biblical writer writing under the guidance of the Holy Spirit. Presupposing a firm knowledge of biblical languages and history, he attended to the historical situation and the stylistic peculiarities of the various biblical authors, even within a single book.

In his commentary on the Psalms, for example, Calvin sought whenever possible to refer each psalm to a particular event in Israel's history or in the life of the psalmist (not always assumed to be David), often distinguishing between the psalmist's meaning and the use of a passage by a NT writer. For instance, in Ps. 8:5 ("For you have made him a little lower than the angels") David is speaking of human nature before the Fall. Heb. 2:7 refers this verse to Christ, but, for Calvin, the author is not explaining the original meaning of the text of the psalm. He is rather enriching his own subject by accommodating this verse to a different meaning (Calvin 1863-1900: 39.93). Similarly, Calvin resolved the apparent conflict presented in the statements about faith and works by Paul and James (Rom. 3:28 and Jas. 2:26) by arguing that, out of concession to their respective opponents, Paul and James use "faith" and "justify" in different ways (1981 [1540]: 77). Even in his sermons Calvin always attended to the intention of the author, even while he related this to his local audience. Having explained the author's meaning, Calvin then applied this to his readers or auditors by drawing analogies between the original situation described in the text and contemporary circumstances. The lessons derived from the text were both doctrinal and moral, depending on the content of the pericope and the circumstances in which Calvin interpreted.

Thus, the ideal of interpretation, to explain the mind of the author, is also aimed at a larger goal, namely, the edification of the faithful. The different genres of biblical exposition were all part of a broader program to proclaim the gospel and nurture faith. In his preface to Olivétan's French NT, Calvin stressed the christological focus of all of Scripture and of all scriptural interpretation: "This is what we should in short seek in the whole of Scripture: truly to know Jesus Christ and the infinite riches that are comprised in him and are offered to us by him from God the Father" (1958: 70). What is distinctive here is not the goal — Christ as the *scopus* (focal point or center) of Scripture is a commonplace among many pre-critical commentators — but the range of approaches Calvin advocated in pursuing it. For the general populace, Christ was proclaimed and faith in Christ nurtured through the exposition of Scripture in the sermon, the singing of psalms, and the recitation of the Lord's Prayer in the liturgy. Calvin wrote catechisms and established a program of parish catechetical services to guide the laity in their understanding of Scripture; he also intended that instruction in the basic prayers and tenets of evangelical faith take place in the schools and at home (Kingdon 2004). At a more advanced level, public lectures on Scripture and the weekly Bible studies afforded interested and educated persons the opportunity to learn more (de Boer 2004b). Such persons could also read Calvin's commentaries and sermons, as well as his *Institutes*. For ministers and theology students, Calvin intended his commentaries and *Institutes* to support their efforts to teach the faith: the *Institutes* by providing a topically ordered and detailed summary of biblical teaching, and the commentaries by providing a "compendium" and guide to interpretation. Ministers, too, participated in the *congrégations* and took turns leading these communal studies, which were modeled on the practice of the Zurich church. It is important to underscore the communal dimension of interpretation for Calvin. Again, this was not unique to his program, but the idea that the meaning of Scripture is not puzzled out on one's own, but discerned in the context of worship and study with others, is an important feature of his approach to interpretation (see the discussion of congregational interpretation in chapter 14 below and of *lectio divina* in chapter 2 above).

Calvin drew the various elements of his interpretation from the practices of different contemporaries and predecessors and combined them into a program that, for all the eclecticism of its origins, was remarkable in its breadth and coherence. What is most impressive, perhaps, about his interpretation of the Bible is his orderly and comprehensive combination of strategies: an interest in a single "literal" sense packed with spiritual significance, a focus on the mind of the human author, a commitment to verse-by-verse exposition, explanations that aimed to be as clear and brief as possible given the circumstances in which he was interpreting, and a concern to apply the lessons of Scripture to the present situation. Yet it is not merely the combination of strategies that is striking, for in the course of pursuing his program, Calvin at times draws unprecedented or at least uncommon exegetical conclusions. When it comes to specifying what truly distinguishes Calvin's exposition of the Bible from the readings of others, one is drawn to three peculiarities: his deep appreciation of the integrity and unity of the biblical past, the role of Paul in his interpretation, and his harsh criticism of many biblical personages.

In order to best unfold the mind of the biblical writer, Calvin focused on the "historical," "literal," or "genuine" sense of the text — that is, the meaning conveyed by the words, or the meaning that the author intended. As discussed earlier, his emphasis on the literal sense followed certain medieval trends and drew also on Renaissance humanist interest in the original setting of the text and the author's style (see chapter 9 above). For Calvin, the literal-historical sense was not the bare, grammatical sense; nor did it refer to the history behind the text in the way it often does in modern historical criticism. Rather, it included both the "history" or the events that the author narrated and the spiritual or moral lessons that the writer sought to inculcate — lessons, moreover, applicable both to those in the author's original setting and to later generations of the faithful. Calvin's exegesis thus evidenced a deep appreciation of the actual history of Israel and the early church, an appreciation he shared with the Antiochene exegetes of the early church, Nicholas of Lyra, and contemporaries such as Bucer, Oecolampadius (see Roussel 1988), and Melanchthon (see chapter 11 above). Yet, he related this *historia* to his sixteenth-century present in a way that sought to preserve the integrity of the past to a greater degree than did most of his like-minded contemporaries (with the probable exception of Bucer).

The most pronounced examples of this are in Calvin's treatment of OT prophecies and the Psalms. For example, Calvin usually connected OT passages referring to the "day of the Lord" to a time of judgment within the history of ancient Israel and understood the prophecies in Daniel as referring to events fulfilled around the time of Christ's first coming (Muller 1990: 70-71; Pitkin 2007). Moreover, in his explanation of Isa. 7:14 ("Behold, a virgin shall conceive and bear a son"), he understands the verse to be a prediction of Christ but at the same time criticizes "all writers, both Greek and Latin," for moving too quickly to assert this. Instead, Calvin labors to show how the promise of Christ has everything to do with assuring Ahaz that Jerusalem will be delivered by reminding him of the foundation of the divine covenant. While he maintains the traditional Christian reference to Christ, he also tries to demonstrate how precisely this meaning is both relevant and appropriate to Ahaz's situation (1863-1900: 36.155).

In his interpretation of NT passages citing from the OT, Calvin noted, often critically, where the NT writer had applied the passages in a way that deviated from the original sense, as, for example, in the citation of Ps. 8:5-6 in Hebrews 2 (Calvin 1863-1900: 55.23-25; cf. Pak 2006b). He was not the only sixteenth-century exegete to follow these paths. Bucer, for example, also focused on the psalms in Israel's history (Hobbs 1978), and most good hebraists also raised questions about the citation of the OT in the NT. Nevertheless, in the case of Ps. 19:4, cited in Rom. 10:18, Calvin is the first to resolve an apparent discrepancy by arguing that Paul, like the psalmist, is also talking about the glory of God revealed to the Gentiles in nature (Calvin 1981: 235-36; Hobbs 1990: 94-97). Such reversals of traditional exegesis were controversial and led to a famous dispute at the end of the sixteenth century over Calvin's "judaizing" exegesis. Steinmetz (1999a: 145) suggests that Calvin's rejections of traditional exegesis are best viewed as an attempt to ground the church's dogmatic claims on the best possible scriptural foundation. For Calvin, this meant a reading of Scripture where the present did not eclipse the past and where dogmatic concerns emerged only when the human author might reasonably be assumed to be giving voice to them.

The Authority of Paul and the Exegetical Tradition

Calvin's commitment to the literal or genuine sense and the mind of the author did not mean that he believed that an interpreter could arrive at the meaning of a biblical text simply by contemplating the words on the page without any additional guidance. Fundamentally, one needed the guidance of the Holy Spirit. One profited also from reading in community, whether literal or literary. Moreover, one needed a prior theological orientation in order to approach Scripture armed with an understanding of what one ought to seek there. Calvin thus prepared the *Institutes* and his catechisms as such guides. This raises the question of which theological presuppositions played the most important role in shaping Calvin's hermeneutic and exegetical practice. Not surprisingly, he was fundamentally a "Pauline theologian": both his biblical theology and his hermeneutic reflected emphases found principally in the Pauline and deutero-Pauline writings (Ganoczy 1976), even if the biblical figure with whom he most identified himself was not Paul but David. Moreover, he began his exegetical lectures with and wrote his first commentaries on the Pauline Epistles. But this leads to a further question: what *kind* of a "Pauline theologian" was Calvin?

Recognizing the priority of Paul for Calvin's theology and the preeminent place of Paul's writings in Calvin's interpretive program, scholars have begun investigating how Calvin characteristically read Paul and in what ways his use of Paul might be distinctive (Walchenbach 1974; Girardin 1979; Ganoczy and Scheld 1983; Parker 1980, 1992: 31-35; Steinmetz 1995: 23-39, 110-

41; Holder 2006). I have examined the understanding of faith that emerges in Calvin's commentaries on Paul and have suggested how this fundamentally Pauline understanding of the nature and function of faith accords with the idea of faith set forth in the *Institutes*. Moreover, I have argued that this "Pauline" view functions as a lens through which he views other NT images of faith (1999b: 9-97). Steinmetz has undertaken several comparative investigations of Calvin's commentary on Romans and found that, consistent with his ideals of interpretation, Calvin focused his exposition of Paul on the mind of the writer. He only occasionally engages the interpretations of others, usually only to disagree with them. This can give the impression that Calvin's reading of Paul was remarkably original or independent, as it appears, for example, in his reading of Rom. 8:1-11 (Steinmetz 1995: 122-41). In fact, however, his exegesis frequently shares questions, concerns, and even the substance of others' interpretations of the same passage, as can be seen, for example, in his interpretation of Abraham in Romans 4 (1981: 79-102; Steinmetz 1995: 64-78). It is clear that he used the exegesis of others not as "authorities" in the medieval sense but as "partners in conversation" (Steinmetz 1995: 136). Backus (2000: 274) and Lane (1999: 3-4) suggest that this way of using patristic literature is different from the way Calvin uses the fathers in the *Institutes* and in his polemical writings.

One should not underestimate the importance of these "partners," even when they go unnamed. Often Calvin would have agreed with their readings of Paul, as in the case of Rom. 7:14-25, where he, along with the majority of his Protestant and Roman Catholic contemporaries, followed the reading of the older Augustine and applied Paul's description of an inner conflict to believers rather than to those outside grace (Steinmetz 1995: 110-21). Thus, in his reading of Paul he often swims with the broad stream of Pauline interpretation, which makes his occasional struggles against the current all the more impressive. One such instance is Calvin's "singular" interpretation of Rom. 1:18-32 (Steinmetz 1995: 23-39). Most Western interpreters of this passage held, along with Paul himself, that humans perceive God in the created order and then proceed to suppress this knowledge because of sin. Calvin, however, argued that because of sin, fallen human beings misperceive God's self-revelation in nature, and this culpable misperception in turn leads them to further suppression of the knowledge of God. Here Calvin's explanation of the "mind of Paul" was decisively shaped by his own assumptions about the character of human fallenness. Although his dismal assessment of fallen human nature had its basis in his particular reading of other parts of the Pauline corpus, it led to an idiosyncratic and unprecedented interpretation of Paul's meaning in Romans 1.

Harsh Depictions of Biblical Figures

Calvin's low estimate of fallen human nature manifested itself throughout his exegetical work and often distinguished his interpretations from prior and contemporary tradition. For example, in his treatment of the so-called immoralities of the patriarchs, Calvin's criticisms were much more severe than those of his predecessors and contemporaries, and he rarely, if ever, drew on any of the traditional excuses offered for patriarchal misbehavior (Thompson 1991). Similarly, his characterizations of the behavior of Hagar and Ishmael (Thompson 1997; 2000: 33-39; 2001: 83-87), Judah and Tamar (Steinmetz 1995: 79-94), the Samaritan woman in John 4 (Farmer 1996), and Nicodemus (Pitkin 1999a) were all significantly more negative than the more favorable, or at least mixed, assessments offered by other interpreters. That Calvin took the depictions of the fallenness of the biblical characters to new lows will come as no surprise to those familiar with his theological anthropology. But this alone cannot account for his negativism, since even those who approached his dismal assessment of the effects of sin, such as Luther, mingled their criticisms with more favorable judgments. What is truly striking is the way that Calvin frequently went against traditional patterns of exegesis and even the literal details of the biblical text itself to underscore a more dismal view of fallen human nature and, indeed, of enduring sin in the lives of the regenerate. For example, while other interpreters were critical of Hagar and Ishmael and held that God was justified in sending them into the desert, they also judged Hagar's divine rescue and Ishmael's blessing favorably. Calvin alone treats them as completely reprobate (Thompson 2000: 35). Furthermore, while all interpreters criticized Nicodemus for not making an open defense of Jesus before the Pharisees (John 7:50-51), they excused him by saying that his faith was as yet imperfect, that he was being cautious, or that his question served a commendable aim. Calvin, however, while he admitted "some small spark of godliness" in Nicodemus's question, charged that he was not yet a true disciple, that the seed of the gospel was choked within him, and that his question itself showed no noteworthy sentiment about Christ (Pitkin 1999a: 879).

If Calvin's negativism is not simply a product of what Farrar judged was a "general abhorrence of mankind" that was allegedly endemic to Calvinism (1886: 352), what might account for it? Consideration of the several possibilities for explaining Calvin's harshness not only illuminates the issue at hand but points to some of the most important elements in his interpretation of the Bible as a whole. Thompson suggests two possible reasons for Calvin's severity toward the biblical faithful and three for his harshness toward the reprobate Hagar and Ishmael. With respect to the patriarchs, Calvin's concerns are practical and pastoral: because the patriarchs are held up as examples for imitation, he wants to be sure that his readers or auditors do not conclude that they can imitate their misconduct. Other interpreters also caution against using patriarchal misconduct as a precedent, but Calvin is "virtually alone . . . in his refusal even to cite traditional excuses, as if he fears his hearers will seize even a flimsy excuse as a warrant for foolish imitation" (Thompson 1991: 44). In addition, Calvin thinks that excusing patriarchal misbehavior impugns the authority of Scripture: "it dishonors Scripture to read its silence as excusing the very sins which it elsewhere so loudly condemns" (Thompson 1991: 44). Thus, underlying Calvin's distinctive interpretations are his goal of edification and his practice of resolving discrepancies by viewing difficult passages through the "lenses" of other Scriptures (usually, but not always, Pauline).

With respect to Hagar and Ishmael, Thompson suggests that Calvin's harshness may well have reflected the fact that he was busy; he did not have time to consult many sources in preparing his commentary on Genesis and thus could not avail himself of other arguments that might have served to mitigate this harshness. Second, he may well have been reacting against what he felt to be the excessively positive assessment of Hagar and Ishmael in one of the commentaries he did use, Luther's lectures on Genesis. Calvin used Luther as a sourcebook for the opinions of Nicholas of Lyra and others, but "slighted" Luther's own favorable interpretations of Hagar. Finally, Calvin was expressing his hostility toward the Roman Church, which he, following Paul's allegory in Galatians 4, identified with the Hagarites and Ishmaelites of his own day (Thompson 2000: 38-39; 2001: 86). Here again, the peculiar character of Calvin's interpretation reflects his understanding of the ideal of scriptural interpretation: lucid and brief explanation of the mind of the divinely-inspired author. Though Calvin used sources, he did not cite every opinion in his interpretation and in fact probably did not have time to read as broadly as he might have liked. And, despite his professed commitment to explaining the mind of the biblical writer, Calvin disregards what are clearly positive elements in Hagar's story, "correcting" these with an analogy drawn from his own day according to which, to his mind, Hagar's spiritual descendents had willfully forsaken the true church.

CONCLUSION

Calvin's exegetical strategies for dealing with the *historia* of the Bible, for determining the complex and challenging "mind" of his central biblical authority, Paul, and for explaining the all-too-human shortcomings of the biblical characters were controversial even in his own day. As unprecedented as these strategies might seem to have been, however, they too built on contemporary trends in Christian biblical exegesis. What distinguished them, and what distinguished Calvin's biblical interpretation as a whole, was often the consistency of his commitment to lucid brevity and the mind of the author, the comprehensiveness of his program, and the extremity of some of his conclusions. Nearly all Christian interpreters valued the letter of biblical history, but few if any were so consistent as Calvin in seeking to preserve the integrity and unity of that history — as Christian salvation history, to be sure, but as history nonetheless. Furthermore, while many Protestant interpreters read Paul similarly, Calvin arrives at a highly original reading of Pauline anthropology. Likewise, while all readers of Genesis were critical of Hagar and Ishmael, only Calvin consigns them to hell (Thompson 2000: 38). Thus, Calvin's peculiar brand of Paulinism and deep suspicion of human motivations sometimes skewed his reading of the literal details of the biblical text. This serves to underscore the fact that, for Calvin, neither the genuine sense of Scripture nor the mind of the author was simply to be read off the page. As he himself admitted, certainly with a degree of humanist etiquette, his preferred method for seeking the meaning of the text was not the only way, even though he believed that "lucid brevity" was the best strategy.

BIBLIOGRAPHY

Aquinas, Thomas

1964-75 *Summa Theologiae.* 59 vols. Cambridge: Blackfriars.

Armour, M. C.

1992 "Calvin's Hermeneutic and the History of Christian Exegesis." Ph.D. dissertation, University of California, Los Angeles.

Armstrong, B. G.

1997 "Exegetical and Theological Principles in Calvin's Preaching, with Special Attention to His Sermons on the Psalms." In W. H. Neuser and H. J. Selderhuis, eds., *Ordenlich und Fruchbar. Festschrift für Willem van't Spijker*, 191-209. Leiden: Groen.

Backus, I.

1984 "L'Exode 20,3-4 et l'interdiction des images. L'emploi de la tradition patristique par Zwingli et Calvin." *Nos Monuments d'art et d'histoire* 3:319-22.

1996 "Bible: Biblical Hermeneutics and Exegesis." In H. Hillerbrand, ed., *The Oxford Encyclopedia of the Reformation*, 1:152-58. New York: Oxford University Press.

2000   "Calvin and the Greek Fathers." In R. J. Bast and A. C. Gow, eds., *Continuity and Change: The Harvest of Late Medieval and Reformation History*, 253-76. Leiden: Brill.

Backus, I. (ed.)

1997   *The Reception of the Church Fathers in the West: From the Carolingians to the Maurists.* 2 vols. Leiden: Brill.

Barrois, G. A.

1965   "Calvin and the Genevans." *Theology Today* 21: 458-65.

Bedouelle, G.

1976   *Lefèvre d'Étaples et l'intelligence des écritures.* Geneva: Droz.

Blacketer, R. A.

2005   *The School of God. Pedagogy and Rhetoric in Calvin's Interpretation of Deuteronomy.* Studies in Early Modern Religious Reforms 3; Dordrecht: Springer.

2006   "The Moribund Moralist: Ethical Lessons in Calvin's Commentary on Joshua." In W. Janse and B. Pitkin, eds., *The Formation of Clerical and Confessional Identities in Early Modern Europe*, 169-86. Dutch Review of Church History 85. Leiden: Brill.

Burnett, R.

2004   "John Calvin and the *'Sensus Literalis.'*" *SJT* 57: 1-13.

Calvin, John

1844-56   *Calvin's Commentaries.* 45 vols. Edinburgh: Calvin Translation Society. Repr. in 22 vols. Grand Rapids: Baker, 1981.

1863-1900 *Ioannis Calvini opera quae supersunt omnia.* Ed. W. Baum, E. Cunitz, and E. Reuss. 59 vols. Brunswick: Schwetschke.

1936-   *Supplementa Calviniana: sermons inédits.* Neukirchen: Neukirchener.

1958   "Preface to Olivétan's New Testament." In J. Haroutounian, ed., *Calvin: Commentaries,* 58-72. LCC 23. Philadelphia: Westminster.

1959-72   *Calvin's New Testament Commentaries.* Ed. D. W. Torrance and T. F. Torrance. Grand Rapids: Eerdmans.

1960   *Calvin: Institutes of the Christian Religion* (1559). Ed. J. T. McNeill. Trans. F. L. Battles. 2 vols. LCC 20-21; Philadelphia: Westminster.

1969   *Calvin's Commentary on Seneca's* De Clementia. Introduction, trans., and notes by F. L. Battles and A. M. Hugo. Leiden: Brill.

1975   *Institutes of the Christian Religion: 1536 Edition.* Trans. and annotated by F. L. Battles. Grand Rapids: Eerdmans.

1981   *Iohannis Calvini commentarius in epistolam Pauli ad Romanos.* Ed. T. H. L. Parker. Studies in the History of Christian Thought 22; Leiden: Brill.

1992-   *Ioannis Calvini Opera Omnia.* Geneva: Droz.

D'Amico, J.

1988   *Theory and Practice in Renaissance Textual Criticism: Beatus Rhenanus Between Conjecture and History.* Berkeley: University of California Press.

de Boer, E. A.

1999   "Pagina Obscura in Geneva: A Fragment from a Sermon by John Calvin." *CTJ* 34: 162-79.

2000   "Jean Calvin et Ésaïe 1 (1564). Édition d'un texte inconnu, introduit par quelques observations sur la différence et les relations entre congrégation, cours, et sermons." *RHPR* 80: 371-95.

2004a   *John Calvin on the Visions of Ezekiel: Studies in John Calvin's "Sermons inédits," especially on Ezek. 36–48.* Leiden: Brill.

2004b   "The Presence and Participation of Laypeople in the Congregations of the Company of Pastors in Geneva." *SCJ* 35/3: 651-70.

De Lubac, H.

1954-64   *Exégèse médiéval. Les quatre sens de l'écriture.* 4 vols. Paris: Aubier.

1998   *Medieval Exegesis: The Four Senses of Scripture.* Vol. 1. Trans. M. Sebanc. Grand Rapids: Eerdmans.

2000   *Medieval Exegesis: The Four Senses of Scripture.* Vol. 2. Trans. E. M. Macierowski. Grand Rapids: Eerdmans.

Den Boeft, J.

1997   "Erasmus and the Church Fathers." In I. Backus, ed., 1997, 2:537-72.

DeVries, D.

1996   *Jesus Christ in the Preaching of Calvin and Schleiermacher.* Columbia Series in Reformed Theology. Louisville: Westminster John Knox.

2004   "Calvin's Preaching." In D. K. McKim, ed., 2004, 106-24.

Engammare, M.

1994   "Le Paradis à Genève. Comment Calvin prêchait-il la chute aux Genevois?" *ETR* 69: 329-47.

1995   "Calvin connaissait-il la Bible? Les citations de l'Écriture dans ses sermons sur la Genèse." *BSHPF* 141: 163-84.

1996a   "Calvin Incognito in London: The Rediscovery in London of Sermons on Isaiah." *Proceedings of the Huguenot Society* 26: 453-62.

1996b   "Joannes Calvinus trium liguarum peritus? La question de l'Hébreu." *Bibliothèque d'Humanisme et Renaissance* 58: 35-60.

2000   "Introduction." In Jean Calvin, *Sermons sur la Genèse.* Supplementa Calviniana: Sermons inédits 11: vii-lvii. Neukirchen: Neukirchener.

Farmer, C. S.

1996   "Changing Images of the Samaritan Woman in Early Reformed Commentaries on John." *CH* 65: 365-75.

Farrar, F. W.

1884   "Calvin as an Expositor." *Expositor* 7: 426-44.

1886   *History of Interpretation. Eight Lectures Preached Before the University of Oxford in the Year MDCCCLXXXV.* London: Macmillan.

Fischer, D.

1984   "L'élément historique dans la prédication de Calvin. Un aspect original de l'homilétique de Réformateur." *RHPR* 64: 365-86.

Forstman, H. J.

1962   *Word and Spirit: Calvin's Doctrine of Biblical Authority.* Stanford: Stanford University Press.

Frei, H. W.

1974   *The Eclipse of Biblical Narrative: A Study of Eighteenth and Nineteenth Century Hermeneutics.* New Haven: Yale University Press.

Fuhrman, P. T.

1952   "Calvin, the Expositor of Scripture." *Int* 6: 188-209.

Gamble, R.

1985   *"Brevitas et facilitas:* Toward an Understanding of Calvin's Hermeneutic." *WTJ* 47: 1-17.

1987   "Exposition and Method in Calvin." *WTJ* 49: 153-65.

1988   "Calvin as Theologian and Exegete: Is There Anything New?" *CTJ* 23: 178-94.

Ganoczy, A.

1969   *La Bibliothèque de l'Académie de Calvin.* Geneva: Droz.

1976   "Calvin als paulinischer Theologe. Ein Forschungsansatz zur Hermeneutik Calvins." In W. H. Neuser, ed., *Calvinus Theologus,* 39-69. Neukirchen-Vluyn: Neukirchener.

Ganoczy, A., and K. Müller

1981   *Calvins Handschriftliche Annotationen zu Chrysostomus. Ein Beitrag zur Hermeneutik Calvins.* Wiesbaden: Steiner.

Ganoczy, A. and S. Scheld

1983   *Die Hermeneutik Calvins. Geistesgeschichtliche Voraussetzung und Grundzüge.* Veröffentlichungen des Instituts für Europäische Geschichte Mainz 114. Wiesbaden: Steiner.

Gerrish, B. A.

1982   "The Word of God and the Words of Scripture: Luther and Calvin on Biblical Authority." In B. A. Gerrish, ed., *The Old Protestantism and the New: Essays on the Reformation Heritage,* 51-68. Edinburgh: Clark.

Gilmont, J. F.

1995   "Les sermons de Calvin. De l'oral à l'imprimé." *BSHPF* 141: 146-62.

Girardin, B.

1979   *Rhétorique et Théologique. Calvin, le Commentaire de l'Épître aux Romains.* ThH 54. Paris: Beauchesne.

Goumaz, L.

1917   *La Doctrine du Salut d'après les commentaires de Jean Calvin sur le Nouveau Testament.* Lausanne: Payot.

1948   *Timothée, ou le ministère évangelique d'après Calvin et ses commentaires sur le nouveau testament.* Lausanne: La Concorde.

Greef, W. de

1984   *Calvijn en het Oude Testament.* Amsterdam: Bolland.

1988   "Das Verhältnis von Predigt und Kommentar bei Calvin, dargestellt am Deuteronomium-Kommentar und den -Predigten." In W. H. Neuser, ed., 1988, 195-203.

1993   *The Writings of John Calvin: An Introductory Guide.* Trans. L. D. Bierma. Grand Rapids: Baker.

1995   *"De Ware Uitleg." Hervormers en hun verklaring van de Bijbel.* Leiden: Groen.

Greene-McCreight, K.

1998   " 'We Are Companions of the Patriarchs' or Scripture Absorbs Calvin's World," *Modern Theology* 14: 213-24. Repr. in L. G. Jones, ed., *Theology and Scriptural Imagination,* 51-62. Directions in Modern Theology; Oxford: Blackwell, 1999.

Haroutounian, J.

1958   "Introduction: Calvin as Biblical Commentator." In *Calvin: Commentaries,* 15-50. LCC 23; Philadelphia: Westminster.

Hobbs, R. G.

1978   "Martin Bucer on Psalm 22: A Study in the Application of Rabbinic Exegesis by a Christian Hebraist." In O. Fatio and P. Fraenkel, eds., *Historie de l'exégèse au XVIe siècle. Textes du colloque internationale tenu à Genève en 1976,* 144-63. Geneva: Droz.

1990   "*Hebraica Veritas* and *Traditio Apostolica:* Saint Paul and the Interpretation of the Psalms in the Sixteenth Century." In D. C. Steinmetz, ed., 1990: 83-99.

Holder, W.

2006   *John Calvin and the Grounding of Interpretation: Calvin's First Commentaries.* Studies in the History of Christian Traditions 127; Leiden: Brill.

Kingdon, R. M.

1985   *Church and Society in Reformation Europe.* London: Variorum.

2004   "Catechesis in Calvin's Geneva." In J. van Engen, ed., *Educating People of Faith,* 294-313. Grand Rapids: Eerdmans.

Klerk, P. de (ed.)

1995   *Calvin as Exegete: Ninth Colloquium on Calvin and Calvin Studies, May 20-22, 1993.* Grand Rapids: Calvin Studies Society.

Kok, J. E.

1993   "The Influence of Martin Bucer on John Calvin's Interpretation of Romans: A Comparative Case Study." Ph.D. diss., Duke University.

1996   "Heinrich Bullinger's Exegetical Method: The Model for Calvin?" In R. A. Muller and J. L. Thompson, eds., 1996: 241-54.

Kraus, H. J.

1968   "Vom Leben und Tod in den Psalmen. Eine Studie zu Calvins Psalmen-Kommentar." In M. L. Henry, ed., *Leben angesichts des Todes. Beiträge zum theo-*

logischen Problem des Todes. Helmut Thielicke zum 60. Geburtstag, 27-46. Tübingen: Mohr.

1977   "Calvin's Exegetical Principles." *Int* 31: 8-18.

Krey, P. D. W., and L. Smith (eds.)

2000   *Nicholas of Lyra: The Senses of Scripture.* Studies in the History of Christian Thought 90; Leiden: Brill.

Kroon, M. de

1998   "Bucer und Calvin: Das Obrigkeitsverständnis beider Reformatoren nach ihrer Auslegung von Römer 13." In W. H. Neuser, ed., 1998, 209-24.

Lambert, T.

1998   "Preaching, Praying and Policing the Reform in Sixteenth-Century Geneva." Ph.D. diss., University of Wisconsin-Madison.

Lane, A. N. S.

1996   "Did Calvin Use Lippoman's *Catena in Genesim?*" *CTJ* 31: 404-19.

1997   "The Sources of Calvin's Citation in His Genesis Commentary." In A. N. S. Lane, ed., *Interpreting the Bible: Historical and Theological Studies in Honour of David F. Wright,* 47-97. Leicester: Apollos.

1999   *John Calvin: Student of the Church Fathers.* Edinburgh: Clark/Grand Rapids: Baker.

Lombard, Peter

1971-81 *Sententiae in IV libris distinctae.* Ed. I. C. Brady. 2 vols. 3rd ed., rev. Grottaferrata: Collegii S. Bonaventurae ad Claras Aquas.

McKane, W.

1984   "Calvin as a Commentator on the Old Testament." *NGTT* 25: 250-59.

McKee, E. A.

1984   *John Calvin on the Diaconate and Liturgical Almsgiving.* Travaux d'Humanisme et Renaissance 197; Geneva: Droz.

1988   *Elders and the Plural Ministry: The Role of Exegetical History in Illuminating John Calvin's Theology.* Travaux d'Humanisme et Renaissance 223. Geneva: Droz.

1989   "Exegesis, Theology, and the Development in Calvin's *Institutio:* A Methodological Suggestion." In E. A. McKee and B. G. Armstrong, eds., *Probing the Reformed Tradition: Historical Studies in Honor of Edward A. Dowey, Jr.,* 154-72. Louisville: Westminster John Knox.

1991   "Some Reflections on Relating Calvin's Exegesis and Theology." In M. S. Burrows and P. Rorem, eds., *Biblical Hermeneutics in Historical Perspective,* 215-26. Grand Rapids: Eerdmans.

McKim, D. K.

2006   *Calvin and the Bible.* Cambridge: Cambridge University Press.

McKim, D. K. (ed.)

2004   *The Cambridge Companion to John Calvin.* Cambridge: Cambridge University Press.

Marcuse, D. K.

2005   "The Reformation of the Saints: Biblical Interpretation and Moral Regulation in John Calvin's Commentary and Sermons on Genesis." Ph.D. diss., Duke University.

Millet, O.

1988   "Sermons sur la Résurrection. Quelques remarques sur l'homilétique de Calvin." *Bulletin de la Société de l'Histoire de Protestantisme Français* 134: 683-92.

1992   *Calvin et la dynamique de la parole. Étude de rhétorique réformée.* Paris: Librairie Honoré Champion.

Moehn, W. H. T.

2001   *God Calls Us to His Service: The Relation Between God and His Audience in Calvin's Sermons on Acts.* Travaux d'Humanisme et Renaissance 345; Geneva: Droz.

Mülhaupt, E.

1931   *Die Predigt Calvins. Ihre Geschichte, ihre Form und ihre religiösen Grundgedanken.* Leipzig: De Gruyter.

Muller, R. A.

1990   "The Hermeneutic of Promise and Fulfillment in Calvin's Exegesis of the Old Testament Prophecies of the Kingdom." In D. C. Steinmetz, ed., 1990, 68-82.

1996   "Biblical Interpretation in the Era of the Reformation: The View from the Middle Ages." In R. A. Muller and J. L. Thompson, eds., 1996, 3-22.

2000   *The Unaccommodated Calvin: Studies in the Foundation of a Theological Tradition.* Oxford Studies in Historical Theology. New York: Oxford University Press.

Muller, R. A., and J. L. Thompson (eds.)

1996   *Biblical Interpretation in the Era of the Reformation: Essays Presented to David C. Steinmetz in Honor of His Sixtieth Birthday.* Grand Rapids: Eerdmans.

Naphy, W.

1994   *Calvin and the Consolidation of the Genevan Reformation.* Manchester: Manchester University Press.

Neuser, W. H. (ed.)

1980   *Calvinus Ecclesiae Doctor.* Kampen: Kok.

1984   *Calvinus Ecclesiae Genevensis Custos.* New York: Lang.

1998   *Calvinus Servus Christi.* Budapest: Ráday-Kollegiums.

Nicole, P.-D., and C. Rapin

1984   "De l'Exégèse à l'Homilétique. Evolution entre le Commentaire de 1551, les Sermons de 1558 et le Commentaire de 1559 sur le Prophète Esaïe." In W. H. Neuser, ed., 1984: 159-63.

Oberman, H. A.

1966   *Forerunners of the Reformation: The Shape of the Late Medieval Thought Illustrated by Key Documents.* New York: Holt, Rinehart and Winston.

Opitz, P.

1994   *Calvins Theologische Hermeneutik.* Neukirchen: Neukirchener.

Pak, G. S.

2006a "The Judaizing Calvin: Sixteenth-Century Debates over the Messianic Psalms." Ph.D. diss. Duke University.

2006b "Luther, Bucer, and Calvin on Psalms 8 and 16: Confessional Formation and the Question of Jewish Exegesis." In W. Janse and B. Pitkin, eds., *The Formation of Clerical and Confessional Identities in Early Modern Europe,* 149-68. Dutch Review of Church History 85; Leiden: Brill.

Paluku Rubinga, N. H.

1978 "Calvin commentateur du prophete Isaie. Le Commentaire sur Isaie, un traité de son hermeneutique." Ph.D. diss., Université des Sciences Humaines de Strasbourg.

Parker, T. H. L.

1947 *Oracles of God: An Introduction to the Preaching of John Calvin.* London: Lutterworth.

1966 "Calvin the Biblical Expositor." In G. E. Duffield, ed., *John Calvin,* 176-89. Courtenay Studies in Reformation Theology 1; Appledorn: Sutton Courtenay. Repr. Grand Rapids: Eerdmans, 1968.

1971 *Calvin's New Testament Commentaries.* Grand Rapids: Eerdmans. 2nd rev. ed. Louisville: Westminster John Knox, 1993.

1980 "Calvin the Exegete: Change and Development." In W. H. Neuser, ed., 1980: 33-46.

1986 *Calvin's Old Testament Commentaries.* Edinburgh: Clark. Repr. Louisville: Westminster John Knox, 1993.

1992 *Calvin's Preaching.* Louisville: Westminster John Knox.

Peter, R.

1972 "Jean Calvin, prédicateur." *RHPR* 52: 111-17.

1975 "Rhétorique et prédication selon Calvin." *RHPR* 55: 249-72.

1984 "Génève dans la predication de Calvin." In W. H. Neuser, ed., 1984, 23-48.

Peter, R., and J.-F. Gilmont

1991 *Bibliotheca Calviniana. Les oeuvres de Jean Calvin publiées au XVIe siècle.* 1: *Écrits théologiques, littéraires et juridiques 1532-1554.* Geneva: Droz.

1994 *Bibliotheca Calviniana. Les oeuvres de Jean Calvin publiées au XVIe siècle.* 2: *Écrits théologiques, littéraires et juridiques 1555-1564.* Geneva: Droz.

2000 *Bibliotheca Calviniana. Les oeuvres de Jean Calvin publiées au XVIe siècle.* 3: *Écrits théologiques, littéraires et juridiques 1565-1600.* Geneva: Droz.

Pettegree, A.

1997 "The Reception of Calvinism in Britain." In W. H. Neuser and B. A. Armstrong, eds., *Calvinus Sincerioris Religionis Vindex: Calvin as the Protector of Purer Religion,* 267-89. Kirksville: Sixteenth Century Essays and Studies.

Pitkin, B.

1993 "Imitation of David: David as a Paradigm for Faith in Calvin's Exegesis of the Psalms." *SCJ* 24: 843-63.

1999a "Seeing and Believing in the Commentaries of John by Martin Bucer and John Calvin." *CH* 68: 865-85.

1999b   *What Pure Eyes Could See: Calvin's Doctrine of Faith in Its Exegetical Context.* Oxford Studies in Historical Theology. New York: Oxford University Press.

2001   "Psalm 8:1-2." *Int* 55: 177-80.

2006a   "Calvin as a Commentator on the Gospel of John." In D. K. McKim, ed., 2006, 164-98.

2006b   "The Spiritual Gospel? Christ and Human Nature in Calvin's Commentary on John." In W. Janse and B. Pitkin, eds., *The Formation of Clerical and Confessional Identities in Early Modern Europe,* 187-204. Dutch Review of Church History 85; Leiden: Brill.

2007   "Prophecy and History in Calvin's Lectures on Daniel (1561)." In K. Bracht and D. du Toit, eds., *Die Geschichte der Daniel: Auslegung in Judentum, Christentum und Islam,* 323-47. BZAW 371; Berlin: de Gruyter.

Puckett, D. L.

1995   *John Calvin's Exegesis of the Old Testament.* Columbia Series in Reformed Theology; Louisville: Westminster John Knox.

Reuss, E.

1853   "Calvin considéré comme Exégète." *Revue de théologie et de philosophie chrétienne* 6: 223-48.

Reyero, M. A.

1971   *Thomas von Aquin als Exeget. Die Prinzipien seiner Schriftdeutung und seine Lehre von den Schriftsinnen.* Einsiedeln: Johannes.

Rosemann, P. W.

2004   *Peter Lombard.* New York: Oxford University Press.

Roussel, B.

1988   "De Strasbourg à Bâle et Zurich. Une 'École Rhéane' d'Exégèse (ca. 1525–ca. 1540)." *RHPR* 68: 19-39.

Schaff, P.

1892   "Calvin as a Commentator." *Presbyterian and Reformed Review* 3: 462-69.

Schellong, D.

1969   *Calvins Auslegung der synoptischen Evangelien.* Munich: Kaiser.

Schreiner, S. E.

1986   "'Through a Mirror Dimly': Calvin's Sermons on Job." *CTJ* 21: 175-93.

1989   "Exegesis and Double Justice in Calvin's Sermons on Job." *CH* 58: 322-38.

1994   *Where Shall Wisdom Be Found? Calvin's Exegesis of Job from Medieval and Modern Perspectives.* Chicago: University of Chicago Press.

1996   "'The Spiritual Man Judges All Things': Calvin and the Exegetical Debate about Certainty in the Reformation." In R. A. Muller and J. L. Thompson, eds., 1996: 189-215.

Smalley, B.

1952   *The Study of the Bible in the Middle Ages.* Oxford: Blackwell. Repr. Notre Dame: University of Notre Dame Press, 1964.

Spicq, C.

1944   *Esquisse d'une histoire de l'exégèse latine au moyen âge.* Paris: Vrin.

Spierling, K. E.

2005   *Infant Baptism in Reformation Geneva: The Shaping of a Community, 1536-1564.* St. Andrews Studies in Reformation History. Aldershot: Ashgate.

Stauffer, R.

1977   "Un Calvin méconnu. Le prédicateur de Genève." *BSHPF* 123: 184-203.

1978   *Dieu, la création et la providence dans le prédication de Calvin.* Basler and Berner Studien zur historischen und systematischen Theologie; Bern: Lang.

1980   "Quelques aspects insolites de la théologie du premier article dans la prédication de Calvin." In W. Neuser, ed., 1980, 267-89.

Steinmetz, D. C.

1982   "John Calvin on Isaiah 6: A Problem in the History of Exegesis." *Int* 36: 156-70.

1986   "Calvin and Melanchthon on Romans 13:1-7." *Ex Auditu* 2: 74-81.

1988   "Calvin and Abraham: The Interpretation of Romans 4 in the Sixteenth Century." *CH* 57: 443-55.

1990a   "Calvin and the Divided Self of Romans 7." In K. Hagen, ed., *Augustine, the Harvest, and Theology (1300-1650): Essays Dedicated to Heiko Augustinus Oberman in Honor of His Sixtieth Birthday,* 300-313. Leiden: Brill.

1990b   "Calvin and the Patristic Exegesis of Paul." In D. Steinmetz, ed., 1990, 100-118.

1991   "Calvin and the Natural Knowledge of God." In H. A. Oberman and F. A. James, eds., *Via Augustini: Augustine in the Later Middle Ages, Renaissance and Reformation: Essays in Honor of Damasus Trapp, OSA,* 142-56. Leiden: Brill.

1995   *Calvin in Context.* New York: Oxford University Press.

1997   "Divided by a Common Past: The Reshaping of the Christian Exegetical Tradition in the Sixteenth Century." *Journal of Medieval and Early Modern Studies* 27: 245-64.

1999a   "The Judaizing Calvin." In D. Steinmetz, ed., *Die Patristik in der Bibelexegese des 16. Jahrhunderts,* 135-46. Wolfenbütteler Forschungen 85; Wiesbaden: Harrassowitz.

1999b   "The Scholastic Calvin." In C. Trueman and R. S. Clark, eds., *Protestant Scholasticism: Essays in Reassessment,* 16-30. Carlisle: Paternoster.

Steinmetz, D. C. (ed.)

1990   *The Bible in the Sixteenth Century.* Durham: Duke University Press.

Tholuck, A.

1831   "Calvins Verdeinst als Ausleger der heiligen Schrift." *Litterarischer Anzeiger für christliche Theologie und Wissenschaft überhaupt* 41-43:321-44. Repr. in *Vermischte Schriften grösstentheils apologetischen Inhalts.* Hamburg: Perthes, 1839. ET "Calvin as an Interpreter of Holy Scriptures." In *John Calvin: Commentaries on the Book of Joshua,* 345-75. Edinburgh: The Calvin Translation Society, 1854.

Thompson, J. L.

1991   "The Immoralities of the Patriarchs in the History of Exegesis: A Reappraisal of Calvin's Position." *CTJ* 26: 9-46.

1992　*John Calvin and the Daughters of Sarah: Women in Regular and Exceptional Roles in the Exegesis of Calvin, His Predecessors, and His Contemporaries.* Geneva: Droz.

1994　"Patriarchs, Polygamy, and Private Resistance: John Calvin and Others on Breaking God's Rules." *SCJ* 25: 3-27.

1997　"Hagar: Victim or Villain? Three Sixteenth-Century Views." *CBQ* 59: 213-33.

2000　"Calvin's Exegetical Legacy: His Reception and Transmission of Text and Tradition." In D. L. Foxgrover, ed., *The Legacy of John Calvin.* 31-56. Calvin Studies Society Papers 1999; Grand Rapids: CRC Product Services.

2001　*Writing the Wrongs: Women of the Old Testament among Biblical Commentators from Philo through the Reformation.* Oxford Studies in Historical Theology. New York: Oxford University Press.

2004　"Calvin as Biblical Interpreter." In D. McKim, ed., 2004, 5:58-73.

Torrance, T.

1988　*The Hermeneutics of John Calvin.* Edinburgh: Scottish Academic.

Van Oort, J.

1997　"John Calvin and the Church Fathers." In I. Backus, ed., 1997, 2:661-700.

Verhoef, P. A.

1968　"Calvin's Exegetical Library." *CTJ* 3: 5-20.

Walchenbach, J.

1974　"John Calvin as Biblical Commentator: An Investigation in Calvin's Use of John Chrysostom as an Exegetical Tutor." Ph.D. diss., University of Pittsburgh.

Winroth, A.

2000　*The Making of Gratian's Decretum.* Cambridge: Cambridge University Press.

Woudstra, M. H.

1986　"Calvin Observes What 'Moses Reports': Observations on Calvin's Commentary on Exodus 1–19." *CTJ* 21: 151-74.

Wright, D. F.

1986　"Calvin's Pentateuchal Criticism: Equity, Hardness of Heart, and Divine Accommodation in the Mosaic Harmony Commentary." *CTJ* 21: 33-50.

Zachman, R. C.

2002　"Gathering Meaning from the Context: Calvin's Exegetical Method." *JR* 82: 1-26.

Zillenbiller, A.

1993　*Die Einheit der katholischen Kirche: Calvins Cyprianrezeption in seinen ekklesiologischen Schriften.* Veröffentlichungen des Instituts für Europäische Geschichte Mainz 151; Mainz: von Zabern.

CHAPTER 13

Biblical Interpretation in Medieval England and the English Reformation

Lee W. Gibbs

This brief survey begins with consideration of Bede (c. 672-735) and his time, continues by marking a few of the most significant guideposts on the course of biblical interpretation in England from the early and later Middle Ages through the English Renaissance and Reformation, and ends with the publication of the King James Version of the Bible in 1611.

Much of the past literature on the history of exegesis during this long period is now recognized as seriously defective. On the one side (for examples, see Farrar 1886: 245-46), there still remain traces of the scholarly distortion caused by previously overdrawn distinctions between the more cultured and normative age of the church fathers and the time of the barbaric "Dark Ages," which immediately followed the collapse of the Roman Empire in the West. At the other end of the spectrum, the widespread perception continues to flourish that the exegetical methods of the major Protestant Reformers of the sixteenth century anticipated modern critical exegesis (for examples, see Farrar 1886: 357-58) and that the hermeneutical assumptions of the Reformation were far more akin to those of biblical interpreters in the nineteenth and twentieth centuries than to those of the medieval exegetes.

Over against these distortions, contemporary scholarship is emphasizing that there are at both ends underlying continuities which are just as important as the discontinuities or major shifts in emphasis. On the one hand, biblical interpretation in the seventh and eighth centuries is now being recognized more and more as in large part an extension of the methods and meanings of the church fathers into the social context of a new and different medieval western Europe (Holder 1990). On the other hand, the sixteenth-century

Reformers are now regarded not only as emphasizing the theological or spiritual meaning embedded in the literal sense of the text but also as belonging to what has been called "the pre-critical model," which is more in continuity with trajectories of medieval biblical interpretation than with tendencies in modern so-called "critical" exegesis (Muller and Thompson 1996).

Such insights, when combined with other recent trends in biblical scholarship such as the new emphasis upon the Bible as literature and reader-oriented interpretation of texts (McKnight 1988; Carroll 1998) enable the contemporary reader to see that all the different hermeneutical methods employed by scholars during the era under review have enabled Christian interpreters of the past to allow the Bible to speak meaningfully and relevantly in the idiom of their own times. All these various methodologies may also now be recognized as having potential meaning and relevance for readers today.

The first part of this chapter deals with two of the most characteristic institutions of the Middle Ages, the monastic religious orders and the schools, with the latter concentrating themselves into universities during the twelfth century. Until the rise of Scholasticism in the twelfth and thirteenth centuries, the tradition of biblical exegesis in the West was principally monastic. Monasticism extended the tradition of the fathers and provided education for monks pursuing the spiritual life. In monasteries following the various rules of their respective traditions, the monks intensely pursued what was called the *lectio divina* ("divine reading") of Scripture. Here it was not so much the text itself that was considered most important as the experience of reading it and gaining personal benefit from it (Leclercq 1969).

By 1100, at least north of the Alps, leadership passed from the monastic schools to the urban cathedral schools under the direction of secular masters. Theological students were first trained in the liberal arts (the medieval *trivium* of grammar, rhetoric, and logic and the *quadrivium* of astronomy, arithmetic, geometry, and music) and then taught to study the Bible and approved authorities by use of the dialectical, or questioning, method. Some of the most famous of these early schools were located in northern Europe: Paris, Orléans, Chartres, Cologne. The triumph of the Scholastic curriculum and methodology associated with these schools on the continent occurred almost simultaneously in England (Gluntz 1933: x) at the Universities of Oxford and Cambridge (Moorman 1953: 131-35), thereby assuring the uninterrupted interpenetration of continental and English thought throughout the later Middle Ages.

In the schools, unlike the monasteries, Scripture was read mainly to elucidate intellectual and moral problems. The text was examined and *quaestiones* were propounded and answered by means of the *disputatio.*

Knowledge was the principal object of the search. The text itself was all-important: it was the subject of the *lectio* and was called *sacra pagina* ("sacred page"). These two ways of reading Scripture — the first, *lectio divina*, remaining in favor in the monasteries and the second, *sacra pagina*, becoming dominant in Scholasticism — were both widely practiced in the later Middle Ages.

THE MIDDLE AGES

The patristic era ended in the West by the turn of the seventh century. The invasions from the North and the subsequent missionary activities in areas occupied by pagan Germanic tribes brought patristic times to a close. Yet there was undoubted continuity between the patristic era and the early Middle Ages. One of those continuities was provided by the canon of Scripture. The Bible played a central part in English Christianity from its earliest days. The Bible known and used in the earliest English church from the fifth century on was the Latin Bible in the version prepared by Jerome between 383 and 405, commonly known as the Latin Vulgate. Loewe (1969) has written an excellent brief survey of the history of the Latin Vulgate during the Middle Ages (see also Brown 2003). In no part of the western world was this version of Scripture studied more diligently and copied more carefully than in Great Britain and Ireland. One of the most reliable extant mss. of the Vulgate was copied in England at one of the twin monastic foundations of Jarrow and Wearmouth under the direction of Abbot Ceolfrid and presented to Pope Gregory II in 716 (Boutflower 1912); it is now in the Laurentian Library at Florence. Such copying of the Bible and regular *lectio divina* were traditional parts of monastic life.

The Venerable Bede

A second continuity of the Middle Ages with the past was the ongoing authority of the church fathers. Standing at a major transitional time in history, the work of the Venerable Bede clearly reflects this continuity. Bede has rightly been regarded as both the last of the fathers and one of the foremost theologians of the early Middle Ages. His immediate heirs greatly treasured his writings. They did not hesitate to identify him as a father, including him with the other giants of the patristic age. Both Alcuin of York (735-804) and Roger Bacon (1214-92) recommended Bede's writings alongside those of Augustine, Ambrose, Jerome, and Gregory.

Although Bede is best known today for his *Ecclesiastical History of the English People* (completed in 731), he was better known in the Middle Ages for his biblical commentaries, which he himself regarded as primary (Bede 1990: 329-31; Muller 1996: 9). As a preliminary to his biblical exegesis, Bede made an analysis of rhetorical figures and tropes in both Testaments in his *De schematibus et tropis* (Bede 1973). Watson and Hauser (1994: 102), however, note that Bede did not discuss invention and arrangement and thus virtually equated rhetoric with style. He also studied some Greek and a little Hebrew, but his exegetical work remained almost completely confined to the Vulgate and the Latin exegetical tradition.

Bede's biblical commentaries (e.g., 1985; 1989) consist of long series of notes on various biblical books. His working methods show him to be the natural heir of late antiquity. He makes extensive excerpts from established authorities available to him — most notably the western fathers Ambrose (see Ramsay 1997), Augustine (H. Chadwick 1986), Jerome (Kelly 1968), and Gregory (Barmby 1908). While Bede patiently sought out tradition as conveyed by these fathers, he also exhibited a considerable independence of interpretation and regarded it as legitimate to express his own judgments.

In Bede's commentaries, exegesis for the purpose of spiritual edification is evident, and his continued use of allegory was often closely related to such devotional study. His commentaries also reveal another important fact about early medieval exegesis: it was intended almost exclusively for the clerical elite (McLure 1985). From the time of Gregory the Great on there were few educated laity in western Europe; lay people were regarded as little better than Jews, who could manage only the literal sense of Scripture. All learning was concentrated in the church, and most of it in the monasteries. Bede's exegetical works were intended not only to enhance private devotional study and the public reading of Scripture in church and monastic services but also to train English clergy to better carry out their missionary activity of making converts among the unlettered pagans (McLure 1985: 19). For example, he describes the aim of his notes on Genesis (Bede 1967) as the provision of a basic beginner's guide for the *rudis lector* ("the poorly educated reader") — a beginning which could also serve as a starting point for the more erudite.

Alcuin of York

If a biblical "commentary" was to Bede and his contemporaries primarily a selection of patristic writings coupled with a guide to explain their use, the same was also true of the Carolingians, whose main aim was to cull material from as many patristic sources as possible. Alcuin of York (c. 735-804), an English student of Bede who became Charlemagne's chief educational advisor and the central figure in the so-called Carolingian renaissance, introduced the Franks to knowledge that had been preserved in the British monasteries. He cited Bede as his authority for relying as exclusively as possible upon the authority of the fathers. In his *Commentary on the Gospel of St. John* (Alcuin 1863) he acknowledged that he had employed his own judgment in culling passages from the fathers, but he also exercised great caution to avoid setting down anything that was contrary to their interpretations. The program of the Carolingian revival of learning, as stated by Charlemagne himself, was that of Augustine's *De doctrina christiana* (Augustine 1962; see also Norris 2003): learning as a preparation for Bible study. Bible study meant study of the sacred text together with the fathers; the two kinds of authority were inseparable. Therefore study of the commentaries of Alcuin and his associates is mostly study of their sources.

Lanfranc of Bec

Like Alcuin and his followers, the Norman monk Lanfranc (d. 1089), founder of the Abbey of Bec in France and later Archbishop of Canterbury, relied on the patristic writings and resented any attempt to evade that authority. For Lanfranc, the introduction of any "new interpretations" of passages of Scripture was regarded as "pertinacious arrogance" (1880). Lanfranc also exhibited a great interest in improving the Vulgate texts, and the copying of the Scriptures flourished in the monasteries that fell under his influence.

John Scotus Eriugena

John Scotus Eriugena (c. 810-77), an Irishman and another Carolingian, was one of the most original of the ninth-century commentators. He possessed a sufficient knowledge of Greek to enable him to consult works written in that language, which enabled him to notice a number of discrepancies between what the Greek fathers had taught and what was generally accepted in his day. This led him to question the accepted authorities, and he even admitted that the fathers sometimes contradicted each other (Smalley 1983: 39). He therefore placed the works of the fathers on a lower plane than Scripture, which, as the inspired and authoritative Word of God, could not be self-contradictory. This is seen, for example, in his *Commentary on the Gospel of John* (1852a) and in the fragments that remain from a homily on John 1:1-4 (1852b). The metaphysical content of Scripture also interested him more than allegories and moralities.

In these exegetical works, Eriugena was not satisfied with the sharp distinction between the word and its spiritual meaning, as assumed by the school of Alcuin (McGinn 1996). What is needed, he countered, is a sound intellectual understanding of the text. The language itself has everything in it, if only the mind is taught to draw it forth. Eriugena's position encouraged the labor of interpretation and also the effort to obtain the best possible text. He examined textual variants, seeking a fuller understanding of Scripture (Otten 1996). A solitary and deeply original thinker, Eriugena and his works were later condemned at church councils at Paris in 1210 and again at Sens in 1225 (Lynch 1967).

The Gloss

With the rise of the medieval schools and universities, the Bible was prescribed as a "set book" for theologians. The student who wanted to become a master of theology had to attend lectures on the sacred page. With the centralization of studies at Oxford and Paris, one of the methods of exegesis that evolved was the gloss, or standard commentary. Anselm (d. 1117) and Ralph (d. 1134 or 1136) of Laon, borrowing from earlier masters, undertook the production of a gloss (a running commentary) on the entire text of Scripture. They did not complete their work, but their successors took it over and eventually published in c. 1135 the *Glossa Ordinaria* (the *Standard Gloss*), which became the standard work of its kind (see Froelich and Gibson 1992).

Other academic functions emerged that supplemented university lectures, including the *disputatio* (disputation) and the university sermon. These academic exercises determined the form, and so to a great extent the content, of medieval exegesis. *Sacra pagina* (the sacred page) marked the final stage of study; the scholar came to it fresh from completing the liberal arts. Developments in grammar, dialectic, and rhetoric always influenced Bible studies. So also did the prevalent philosophy, as may be seen in the contrast between the followers of the Neo-Platonism of St. Augustine (see Burnaby 1933) and those theologians influenced during the twelfth and thirteenth centuries by the newly recovered works of Aristotle.

The "Sense(s)" of Scripture

Spicq (1944: 173-78, 209-15) points to the two major directions taken in the history of later medieval exegesis. The first focused on fourfold exegesis (literal, allegorical, tropological, and anagogical), emphasizing allegory and trope. The second, while hardly hostile toward the spiritual meanings of the text, argued for a more "literal" or historical interpretation of the text.

Medieval authors, including those in England, had long recognized "the four senses of Scripture." Farrar (1886) refers to a Bishop Longland, who preached a sermon before the University of Oxford in 1525 on the text "she hath also furnished her table" (Prov. 9:2), taking it to mean that Wisdom had set forth in her spiritual banquet the four courses of history, tropology, anagogy, and allegory. Longland also defended the fourfold sense of Scripture in another sermon that he preached in Westminster Abbey on November 27, 1527. All medieval exegesis consisted in moving on from the literal to the spiritual sense(s) of the Bible. The three spiritual senses (allegorical, moral, and anagogical) were traditionally regarded as being inseparably related to the virtues of faith, love, and hope respectively.

The medieval four senses were rooted in the writings of Origen (c. 185–c. 254), whose biblical commentaries had been translated into Latin by Jerome. Origen had developed a threefold method of interpreting Scripture based on the trichotomy of *sōma* (body), *psychē* (soul), and *pneuma* (spirit) (Origen 1857). In the fifth century, John Cassian (360-435) added a fourth, the "mystagogical" or mystical sense (O. Chadwick 1968). Thomas Aquinas (1225-74) formulated an influential "synthesis" regarding the four senses (Aquinas 1953; see also Nichols 2003) when he said: "The spiritual sense contains nothing necessary to faith which is not plainly expressed somewhere in Scripture under the literal sense" (1953: I.1.a.10; 1: 9b-11a).

The medieval exposition of Scripture according to the allegorical, tropological or moral, and anagogical senses has been regarded by most modern scholars of the "critical" persuasion to be subjective, fanciful, and irrelevant, and therefore of interest only to historians. But new literary and reader-oriented approaches in recent biblical interpretation not only make accessible a new appreciation of past exegesis but also offer the possibility for contemporary readers to seek and find meaning and relevance in the medieval expositions of the spiritual senses of Scripture.

A growing appreciation of the medieval four senses can also be discerned in the later work of Smalley (3rd ed., 1983), a modern scholar deeply committed to the ideals of the literal or historical interpretation of Scripture. Her earlier almost exclusive concentration on the literal or historical interpretation of Scripture was criticized by de Lubac (1959-64), and Smalley came to acknowledge the validity of this critique, confessing that she had looked at the spiritual exposition from the outside, and thereby overlooked its central place in the medieval concept of Scripture and consequently of medieval faith:

> Medieval exegesis has more continuity with its remote biblical past than I realized. . . . There is also more continuity than I thought in ideas on the reader's as well as of the writer's responsibilities. The reader of a text, whether biblical or classical, was expected to be more active and less passive than his modern counterpart. He took less interest in the mind of the author and more in the author's product; he put his own meaning into it. The text was more alive than its author to him. This likeness in attitude underlines the continuity between ancient, patristic and medieval modes of thinking (Smalley 1983: viii).

Nevertheless, after further acknowledging her past and continued neglect of monastic commentaries based upon the *lectio divina* that were written after the rise of the secular schools, Smalley continues to argue her original thesis that the "secular" schools offered more scope for interest in and study of the literal, and it is on those individuals in those schools that she persists in focusing her attention (1983: xiii-xix).

The Victorines

In the age of the emergent universities, the greatest burden of biblical interpretation fell to the friars and the great scholastics (Smalley 1983: 85-263). The basis of Scholasticism was the course in liberal arts (the medieval *trivium* of grammar, rhetoric, and logic; and the *quadrivium* of mathematics, geometry, music, and astronomy). This course was followed, by those who so chose, with a postgraduate course in theology, law, or medicine. The course in theology included, besides attendance at lectures, participation in the disputations which formed a very important part of medieval academic life (Crewdson 1941). At Oxford and Paris, a sober and rational interpretation was carried on by Franciscan and Dominican professors. The School of St. Victor in France — which included the Englishmen Hugh (Smalley 1983: 85-106), Richard (Smalley 1983: 106-11), and Andrew (Smalley 1983: 112-95) — all supported a more literal/historical exegesis than, for example, the enormously popular and influential allegorical/spiritual exegesis of the Song of Solomon by Bernard of Clairvaux (1859).

Andrew of St. Victor (d. 1175) was an English monk who became a canon of St. Victor in Paris around 1125. Around 1145, he returned to England as prior of the newly founded Victorine community of Shobdon, and he later moved to Wigmore in Herefordshire. At St. Victor, he had been the pupil of Hugh of St. Victor (1096-1141). Hugh stimulated among his students two wholly distinct types of biblical study: on the one hand, an enlargement of symbolic interpretation and, on the other, serious study of the literal meaning. Andrew undertook the second. He somewhat facetiously professed to confine himself to the literal meaning of the text, claiming that he could not afford all the commentaries or glossed books necessary for elaborating the spiritual meaning. Andrew believed that the meaning of a text had to be sought in the text itself, and not in external authorities, however venerable they might be (Smalley 1983: 112-95). He had a strong preference for the literal sense of Scripture, and believed that Moses used earlier sources when writing the Pentateuch — as opposed to the general belief that he had been directly inspired to write.

Andrew's greatest originality, however, was his willingness to make use of contemporary Jewish exegesis. The Jewish exegesis to which he was attracted was the rational and literal method developed in the school of Rashi. Andrew believed that the Jews were closer to the atmosphere of biblical times than contemporary Christians were and therefore that their interpretation of the OT offered better insights into the original meaning. For example, he rendered a Jewish or literal interpretation of the messianic prophecies in Isaiah (Smalley 1983: 147-56). It is possible that Andrew made some study of the Hebrew language himself but more likely that he acquired most of his knowledge of the original text from Jewish scholars of his acquaintance. In any case, his commentaries on the OT (Smalley 1983: 186-95), of which fifteen different manuscripts have been discovered to date, reveal an awareness of Hebrew almost unique in the Middle Ages.

Herbert of Bosham (c. 1120-94), another Englishman, was Andrew's most distinguished pupil (Smalley 1983: 186-95). Like Andrew, Herbert went to the Jews for help on the literal meaning of the OT and accepted what they told him. But he went further than Andrew, studying Hebrew for himself. One of the thoughts that troubled him was: if the Jews turned out to be right in their interpretation of the OT, would the Christian faith still be valid (Smalley 1983: 164-65)? No other twelfth-century Christian writer is known to have expressed this doubt or discussed this question, and it gives Bosham an important place in the history of biblical scholarship. Herbert, along with Andrew, was ready to acknowledge that OT passages quoted in the NT as messianic may not have been so intended by the original authors. For example (Smalley 1983: 194-95), Herbert inclined toward the opinion that Ps. 68:18 refers to Moses rather than Christ, in spite of Paul's exegesis of this passage in Eph. 4:8; and Andrew accepted the Jewish interpretation of the man of sorrows in Isaiah 53 as referring collectively to the Jews of the Babylonian Captivity.

Stephen Langton (d. 1228), who later served as Archbishop of Canterbury, was of English extraction but migrated to Paris as a student and became one of the principal theologians of the University of Paris. A member of the School of St. Victor, he worked to spread Victorine ideas, and as a result of his efforts, the literal interpretation of Scripture gained ground in France and England as the proper foundation for the spiritual exposition of the text (for details on Langton's life, work, and commentaries see Smalley 1983: 196-263). Langton wrote a number of commentaries on Scripture, and continued the Victorine tradition of consulting Jewish rabbis on the literal or historical meaning of OT texts.

Biblical Languages and Translations

The decline of high Scholasticism during the fourteenth and fifteenth centuries was accompanied by the rise of nationalism (Moorman 1953: 150-51). The appearance of literatures in the vernacular was enhanced by the invention of printing. A vast new market for books opened up. With Greek scholars fleeing west from a dying Byzantium, scholars in western Europe were once more able to study the biblical languages. The text of the Latin Vulgate was discovered to be less than perfect. The need grew for new translations and a more critical interpretation of the Bible (Moorman 1953).

So far as we know, the first complete English Bible was produced as a result of the influence and activity of John Wycliffe (c. 1324-84; Daniell 2003: 66-95). In common with later Protestantism, Wycliffe emphasized the necessity of providing laypeople the opportunity of reading the Bible in the vernacular. He wrote commentary notes on the entire Bible and strongly advocated the authority of Scripture over against that of the church and its traditions. He became convinced of the absolute truth of the literal sense of the Bible, a position which he defended in his *De Veritate Sacrae Scripturae* (*On the Truth of Holy Scripture,* 1378; Wycliffe 2001).

The earliest English version of the Bible was published in 1380, with little if any of the work actually done by Wycliffe; it was a very literal translation of the current Latin Vulgate text. The later Wycliffe version of 1384, a revision undertaken by his secretary John Purvey (Bruce 1961: 16-20), demonstrated a much greater sensitivity to the English language. This revised version remained the only Bible in English until the sixteenth century.

RENAISSANCE AND REFORMATION

The way to the Reformation interpretation of Scripture was led not only by Wycliffe, but also by the work of the Christian Renaissance humanists (Grafton and Jardine 1986). By 1450, the new spirit of inquiry was clearly discernible in western Europe, and by 1500, the so-called Renaissance of learning and of culture was abroad almost everywhere. The growing desire for a return *ad fontes,* "to the sources," included a return to the original languages of Scripture. Scholars were demanding a more accurate Vulgate text, revised by study of the original Hebrew and Greek. As far back as Roger Bacon (c. 1214-92), there were attacks on corruptions in the Vulgate text (Bacon 1900: 66-81). Bacon argued that the text of Jerome had been corrupted by foreign readings taken over from the liturgical books of the church or from the biblical quotations of the fathers, and he pointed out examples of additions, subtractions, and false juxtapositions. He claimed that if the letter of the Vulgate text is false or doubtful, then the literal and spiritual senses will contain unspeakable error. He suggested that an older ms. should be preferred to a more recent and that a majority of ms. readings are to be preferred to a minority of mss. He also suggested that when any doubt remains, the reader should go back to the original Hebrew and Greek (Hackett 1997). Erasmus thought that there could be no true theological understanding of the Scriptures without a thorough understanding of Hebrew, Greek, and Latin (Aldridge 1966: 18-19, 98-128). The Hebrew and Greek studies of Erasmus and other Christian humanists, along with their attacks on corruptions of Latin texts, laid the foundation for a more philological interpretation that tended to give a new prominence to the literal and historical sense.

It was the desired goal of many humanists of the sixteenth century (Gilmore 1952) to be *trium linguarum gnarus,* "well acquainted with three languages," that is, Hebrew, Greek, and Latin. In England, Richard Foxe (c. 1448-1528; see Chisolm-Batten 1889; Thompson 1900; Fox 1929), Bishop of Winchester, founded Corpus Christi College, Oxford, as a trilingual college. However, it was difficult to obtain competent teachers in Hebrew and Greek, and England lagged behind academic centers on the Continent in this regard.

The effect of Renaissance humanists' focus on the Hebrew of the OT and the Greek of the NT led to a decline in the exclusive hold of the Latin version. The first printed Hebrew Bible was published by Soncino Press in 1488, and the first printed Greek NT, the *editio princeps* of Erasmus, in 1516 (Augustin 1991). Scholars like Erasmus and reformers like Luther spoke and worked for the right of all persons to read the sacred text. The vernacular languages, including English, had developed to the point where they could be used as literary media and, like Hebrew and Greek, were studied in the newly founded English schools and colleges (Evans 1985: 81-88). These and other factors combined to set the stage for the production of the first printed English Bible.

John Colet

John Colet (c. 1466-1519) was the most outstanding English humanist of his time (Gleason 1989). He studied at Oxford and later at Paris and Italy. Colet returned to England in 1496 after a prolonged visit to the Continent, where he had come into contact with the "new learning." The "new learning," as contrasted with "the old Scholasticism," refers to all the contributions and influence of Renaissance humanists who were changing both the direction of studies and the method of study in the universities (Moorman 1953: 150-53). During his time in Italy, he may well have encountered the Neoplatonism being taught at the Platonic Academy of Marsilio Ficino and Pico della Mirandola in Florence. In 1505, Colet became Dean of St. Paul's in London, and five years later he founded St. Paul's School where boys could learn Greek as well as Latin (McDonnell 1909).

In 1497, shortly after Colet's return from the Continent to Oxford, he delivered a course of lectures on Paul's Epistle to the Romans. These lectures have been partially reconstructed from his manuscript notes, which were discovered in the library of Corpus Christi College (Colet 1985b: v-viii). These lectures clearly demonstrate his humanist learning and sympathies. In his principles of biblical interpretation he broke away from the methods of the medieval Scholastics and expounded the text in accordance with the plain meaning of the words viewed in relation to their historical context. The lectures were not a series of dissertations on isolated texts. Rather, Colet began at the beginning of the Epistle and went through it to the end, treating the work as a whole. Nor were the lectures formed by linking together the recorded comments of church authorities. There are very few quotations from the fathers or from the schoolmen. Colet demonstrated a remarkable freedom from the prevailing method of the patristic interpreters and many of his contemporaries, namely, their love for allegorizing. He was primarily concerned with the meaning that the apostle intended to convey to the specific congregation to whom the Epistle was addressed. To Colet, the letters of Paul were the earnest words of a man speaking to particular human beings and their actual needs.

Colet's manuscript exposition of 1 Corinthians is also preserved at Cambridge. Apparently it is in his own handwriting, with his own corrections (see Colet 1985a). Throughout his exposition, he again strove to portray the letter as one written by an apostle concerned with the specific problems of a particular congregation. He presented it as an Epistle intended to correct the conduct of the Corinthians in some practical areas in which they had erred. He expressed admiration for the wisdom of Paul's method of first praising that part of the Corinthians' conduct which he could praise before proceeding to criticize them. Though Lorenzo Valla (c. 1406-57; see Schwahn 1896) had already begun to cast doubts upon the authenticity of the Pseudo-Dionysian writings, including the *Celestial Hierarchy* (Dionysius the Areopagite 1947), Colet accepted these writings as those of the Apostle Paul's first-century disciple. The influence of the Neoplatonism of these Pseudo-Dionysian writings can be discerned in some of the strange and fanciful analogies that Colet drew from Paul's distinction in 1 Corinthians between celestial and terrestrial bodies and their differing orders of glory (Colet 1985a). He illustrated his exposition of the Epistle with diagrams to give graphic expression to these fancied analogies (1869).

Erasmus of Rotterdam

Colet was a good friend of Desiderius Erasmus of Rotterdam (c. 1466-1536) and was largely responsible for bringing Erasmus to Oxford in 1499. Erasmus was the best known of the northern humanists and was widely recognized as the most learned man of his age. Erasmus owed to Colet much of his insight into a different method of biblical interpretation — one that contrasted with the disputational Scholastic way. In the dedicatory epistle to his *Paraphrases on Romans* (Erasmus 1984), Erasmus offered a sharp contrast to Scholastic interpretation of Scripture, stating that his purpose was to help the reader arrive at the original and genuine meaning of the text. This approach, like Colet's, was in direct contrast with the Scholastic method, which elaborated on every detail (Aldridge 1966). The primary aim was pedagogical rather than disputational, and the method used was based upon a form of textual criticism that was primarily rooted in philology.

Erasmus paid a second visit to England in 1506 and a third in 1511. His third visit was his longest. It was spent mainly at Cambridge, where he served both as Professor of Greek and as Lady Margaret Professor of Divinity. During his years at Cambridge, Erasmus gave himself especially to the study of Jerome and the NT (1992). Here also, he laid the foundations of his edition of the Greek NT (1967), which first appeared in 1516. Though based on insufficient ms. material, this edition exercised a profound influence on theological studies and was revised several times during Erasmus's lifetime.

Erasmus envisioned not only a rebirth of the classical literature of antiquity as such, but a Christian spiritual Renaissance that was to be the basis and the underlying principle behind this rebirth of antiquity. The means by which this renaissance was to be accomplished was through a return to the sources. His desire for Christian reform was based on the Scriptures as the primary source. In his *In Novum Testamentum Praefationes* (*New Testament Prefaces,* Erasmus 1967), Scripture is regarded not only as the highest source, but also as the basis for purifying the corruptions of the church. Erasmus wanted theologians to learn Greek and Hebrew so that they could draw from this primary source (Aldridge 1966: 18-19). However, even though Scripture is the highest and primary source, the sources remain plural. Erasmus spent a great deal of his scholarly life editing not only his Greek text of the NT but also select Greek and Roman classics (such as Plato and Seneca) and the church fathers (Rummel 1985).

Although Erasmus's philological method has been preferred by most modern interpreters and has been regarded as consonant with the exegesis of the magisterial Protestant Reformers, the medieval fourfold interpretation was not entirely discontinuous with the logic and intentions of Reformation-era biblical interpreters. Recent scholars of the Reformation have been pushing their researches on the Reformers' sources and precedents in exegesis back into the Middle Ages (Muller and Thompson 1996).

Beginning

The watchword of the Protestant Reformation was *sola scriptura* ("Scripture alone"). The tendency was to break with allegorical interpretation (which was included within the fourfold senses) and to concentrate on the literal and historical meaning. Luther appreciated and used the philological method that Erasmus developed from *ad fontes;* however, Luther and the first generation of Reformers remained deeply immersed in medieval categories of thought. For instance, they tended to interpret "Scripture alone" in a traditional christological or "typological" way that stressed the fulfillment of the OT in the NT. Previously, Calvin's exegetical methods were seen to presage the critical method of the nineteenth and twentieth centuries. Now, however, many contemporary scholars see his methods as a perpetuation of the legacy of his forebears (Muller 1996: 8).

The interpretation of Scripture by the English churchmen of the sixteenth century deserves special treatment, in keeping with the peculiar development of the English Reformation. The earliest apologists of the Church of England argued mainly with the English Catholics, who rejected the Royal Supremacy of Henry VIII and his successors over the English Church (Neill 1965: 52-132). The apologists who wrote toward the end of the century also had to contend with the opinions of more extreme proponents of the Reformation, as voiced by the nascent Puritans, that is, by the Elizabethan Presbyterians as represented by Walter Travers (c. 1548-1642; Knox 1962), and Thomas Cartwright (1535-1603; Pearson 1966). What was to become known by the end of the century as "the Elizabethan Settlement" in religion was largely the outcome of controversies that raged in the church of Henry VIII.

Thomas Cranmer

Thomas Cranmer (1489-1555), who became Archbishop of Canterbury in 1532 during the rule of Henry VIII, and was later burned at the stake for heresy under Mary Tudor, became the leader of the Protestant faction. Cranmer's sympathies were frankly with the Protestant side; yet, he had to placate the king, who hoped to establish a National Catholicism. Cranmer therefore did his best, as long as Henry lived, to avoid too sharp a conflict with the Catholic party. A treatise entitled *Confutation of Unwritten Verities* is attributed to him (1846), and though it may not be entirely of his own pen, it corresponds closely with his doctrine. In this treatise, Cranmer argues not only that the canon of the Bible contains "in itself fully all things needful for our salvation" but he takes issue with the authority of the church fathers: "without the written word of God [they] are not able to prove any doctrine in religion" (1846: 2.7). For Cranmer, neither unwritten oral traditions deriving from the Apostles nor church councils have more authority than the Word of God. Cranmer maintained the "real presence" of Christ in the celebration of the Eucharist, while explicitly rejecting the Catholic dogma of transubstantiation, and he removed traditional Catholic prayers for the dead from his draft of the *Book of Common Prayer* (Booty 1976). The church, although a register or treasury to keep the books of God's holy will and testament, has no authority or power of its own over the written Word; nor does it have any capacity to make new articles of the faith besides Scripture or contrary to Scripture (1846: 2.59).

In spite of these Protestant proclivities, however, Cranmer, whether purposely or not, gravitated toward a *via media,* mediating between Roman Catholicism and the Protestantism of some of the more radical Reformers. He acknowledged, for example, that even though the church has no authority of its own over against that of Scripture, it still bears witness to the authenticity of the canonical books as the Word of God: "We believe the holy canon of the Bible, because the primitive Church of the apostles and eldest writers next to their time, approved them in their register, that is to say, in their writings" (1846: 2.59). In this passage and elsewhere, Cranmer clearly expressed his view of the superiority of the primitive church, that is, "the authority of the best learned and most holy authors and martyrs that were in the beginning of the Church and many years before the antichrist of Rome [the Pope] rose up and corrupted it altogether" (1846: 2.7). Cranmer never renounced his commitment to this principle of the primary authority of Scripture, supported by the secondary authority of the first church fathers. Yet, even among the old fathers, Cranmer rejected some of the "traditions" that they espoused, such as prayers for the dead and the doctrine of transubstantiation, as not having support in the Bible.

William Tyndale

Meanwhile, in England and Scotland during the sixteenth century, translations of the Bible into the vernacular flourished, but few commentaries were written. The translation of William Tyndale (c. 1494-1536) was the first of these sixteenth-century efforts, even though it was never completed (Daniell 2003: 133-59; Bruce 1961: 28-52). Tyndale was educated at Oxford and Cambridge. He was attracted to Lutheran ideas around 1522, when he proposed an English translation of the Bible to the Bishop of London. The clergy in the English Church, however, with government support, disapproved Tyndale's developing proto-Protestant views and opposed his project. He therefore left England in 1525, and went to Hamburg to continue his work. As a scholar long indebted to Erasmus, Tyndale decided to translate directly from the original Hebrew and Greek. For the NT, he used Erasmus's Greek text, supplemented by his Latin text (especially the Greek-Latin parallel text editions of 1519 and 1522), Jerome's Vulgate, and Luther's 1522 German NT (see Todd 1964). Tyndale's NT was printed in Cologne in 1526, with revisions in 1534 and 1535 (1848b; see also 2000). The text was equipped with an apparatus of marginal notes, including references to parallel passages in the inner margin. Some of the notes were based on Luther's commentaries; others were written to make the sense of the text clearer.

Tyndale's NT of 1526 (see Bruce 1961: 30-31; Daniell 2003: 144-47) was accompanied by an important introduction, *A Pathway to Scripture* (Tyndale 1848a), which has been called "the oldest hermeneutical study in English" (Bray 1996: 175). Tyndale argued that the OT is the law and the NT is the gospel, but, he continued, they belong together in the Christian Bible. The novelty is that the gospel does not abolish the law but reaffirms it and declares its true purpose (Tyndale 1848a: 7-28). Tyndale's hermeneutic made the OT as well as the NT a guidebook for the Christian life: the great men of the OT were models of faith for Christians to emulate just as much as those of the NT.

Tyndale's knowledge of Hebrew was sufficient to enable him to understand the essentials of Hebrew vocabulary and syntax and to grasp the idiom of biblical Hebrew. He therefore undertook the translation of the OT and made a significant contribution to that end, although he was unable to complete the work before his death (Bruce 1961: 41-42; Daniell 2003: 147-49). For the Pentateuch and historical books he had the Hebrew text, the LXX, the Vulgate, and Luther's German versions. He published the Pentateuch in 1530 and Jonah in 1531. He spent ten years in Antwerp, where he was apprehended in 1535, and was imprisoned for a year and a half near Brussels (Bruce 1961; Daniell 2003). During his captivity, he probably completed the text through Chronicles, before being burned at the stake on October 6, 1536. He was officially condemned not only because of his association with Lutheran doctrine but also because the ecclesiastical authorities were provoked by his pejorative comments about popes and bishops and by the substitution in his translation of new terms for more approved ones such as "elder" for "priest," "repentance" for "penance," and "congregation" for "church."

Miles Coverdale

The completion and publication of the first complete English Bible was the work of Miles Coverdale (1488-1569). He had studied at Cambridge but like Tyndale was a convert to Lutheran ideas (Dallman 1925) and therefore also found it discreet to spend some years outside England. Tyndale's translation was the basis of Coverdale's work on the NT and the Pentateuch. For those sections of the OT in which he did not use Tyndale, Coverdale translated from the Latin and German. It is generally doubted that he knew much if any Hebrew, but his acquaintance with German was good. He used the Vulgate order of the books rather than the Hebrew order in his OT and included the Apocrypha, though he questioned its authority. In 1535, he published his translation of the entire Bible (Bruce 1961: 53-64; Daniell 2003: 173-89). He was later prominent in the production of the Great Bible of 1539 (Bruce 1961: 67-80; Daniell 2003: 198-220), also known as "Cranmer's Bible," with its preface added in 1540 (Bruce 1961: 71-72; Daniell 2003: 208-9).

Coverdale became Bishop of Exeter in 1551, but was exiled in 1554 and went to Geneva, where it seems likely that he worked on the Geneva Bible (1560; Bruce 1961: 86-92; Daniell 2003: 291-319). He returned to England in 1559, but took little part in public affairs.

The "Great Bible"

The first authorized Bible in England was the Great Bible of 1539 (Bruce 1961: 67-80; Daniell 2003: 198-220), so called because of its size. It was also called "Cranmer's Bible" (Bruce 1961: 71-72; Daniell 2003: 208-9) from a preface to the second edition (1540) written by the archbishop. Use was made of the Vulgate, Erasmus's Latin NT, and the *Complutensian Polyglot* (a Hebrew-Greek-Latin edition of the Bible published in six volumes at Complutum, Spain, in 1522-26 by Cardinal Ximénes [Bruce 1961: 24; Daniell 2003: 119]; see also chapters 9, 15, and 16 in this volume). It is Coverdale's version of the Psalms, revised by himself for the Great Bible of 1539, that still appears in the English *Book of Common Prayer* (Booty 1976).

In 1543, restrictions were placed on the reading of the Bible; the authorized Great Bible alone was allowed, and its reading was limited to the upper classes. Toward the end of the brief reign of Edward VI (b. 1537, reigned 1547-53), Protestant forces made some advance, and the restrictions on reading the Bible were removed. But during the reign of Mary Tudor (1553-58), the restrictions were again imposed. Some of the English refugees who fled to the Continent during Mary's reign settled in Geneva. Among these refugees the next important contribution to the promulgation of the Scriptures in English was made in the preparation and publication of the so-called "Geneva Bible."

The Geneva Bible

The Geneva Bible appeared in 1560, with a dedicatory epistle to Queen Elizabeth I. Its notes were pointedly Calvinistic in doctrine and therefore offended readers who objected to Calvinism. Calvin (Wendel 1997), Theodor Beza (Geisendorf 1967), John Knox (Marshall 2000), and for a time Miles Coverdale (see above) were all associated with the project. The NT, published in 1557, is mainly credited to William Whittingham, a brother-in-law of Cal-

vin and the successor of John Knox as minister to the English congregation at
Geneva. Tyndale's 1534 edition was the chief basis, along with Beza's Latin
translation and commentary (Beza 1565; see also Booty 1976). The OT consisted of a revision of the Great Bible by careful reference to the Hebrew, and
with the guidance of Latin editions. It was published together with a careful
revision of the NT in 1560. The Geneva Bible was the most scholarly and accurate translation so far produced in English and immediately received widespread reception and usage. For half a century, the people of England and
Scotland read the Geneva Bible in preference to any other version and learned
much of their biblical exegesis from the notes.

The Bishops' Bible

Once translated, the Geneva Bible was the version appointed to be read in
churches in Scotland; however, it was not as acceptable for this purpose in
England. Leaders in church and state, not to mention the queen herself, did
not appreciate the outspoken Calvinism of its annotations. An attempt was
therefore made by the authorities to produce a revision of the Great Bible to
supplant the Geneva and other competing editions. The archbishop of Canterbury, Matthew Parker, formed a committee of revisers in 1564. Since the
majority were bishops, the new version was called "The Bishops' Bible"
(Parker, et al. 1568). The first edition was published in 1568. Some sections are
close to the Great Bible, especially in the OT and Apocrypha, while others depart freely from it. In some of these departures, the influence of the Geneva
Bible is evident; even many of the Geneva Bible's marginalia were taken over.

In spite of its defects, the Bishops' Bible became the second "authorized" English version (Bruce 1961: 92-95; Daniell 2003: 338-47). Although
never officially so designated by the Queen, it was endorsed by a convocation
of bishops, who in 1571 ordered its possession and use by every bishop and
archbishop. This version eventually displaced the Great Bible as the one "appointed" to be read in the churches. Nevertheless, the Bishops' Bible, although ecclesiastically approved, failed to replace the Geneva Bible in popular esteem and usage.

The Douai-Rheims Bible

Meanwhile, another influential achievement occurred in the form of a Roman Catholic Bible in English. Supporting this venture were Catholic refu-

gees from England, led by William Cardinal Allen, president and founder of the English college at Douai (Douay), France, which had temporarily been removed to Rheims (MacCaffrey 1970). Defending the need for a Roman Catholic translation, Allen mentions the Protestant distortions of the meaning of the text and the fact that Catholic preachers were at a disadvantage in quoting the Bible in English without a version of their own (Allen 1882). Approval of lay reading of the Bible was definitely not intended. In fact, the undertaking was not at first officially sanctioned by the church at all but was essentially a part of the Jesuit program of recapturing England for Catholicism.

The translation was made chiefly by Gregory Martin and then revised by Allen, both Oxford graduates. Although completed by 1582, only the NT was published at Rheims; the publication of the OT was delayed until 1609 (MacCaffrey 1970). By this time, the college had moved back to Douai, and the version is therefore known as the "Douay," "Douay-Rheims," or "Rheims-Douay" Bible. The complete Bible was not published until 1633-35, at Rouen. The title page of this version proclaimed that it was translated out of the "authentical Latin," referring to the Vulgate. Annotations by Allen in the form of marginalia and notes at the ends of chapters rival the Geneva Bible in profuseness and match it in polemical nature. This version exerted a considerable influence upon the King James revision. Its chief significance, however, lay in Roman Catholic circles, where it was not only the first translation into English but also the first to eventually receive official recognition (MacCaffrey 1970).

John Jewel

Defenders of the Church of England during the late sixteenth century generally followed the middle way, which had earlier been forged by Thomas Cranmer. John Jewel (1522-71), a Fellow of Corpus Christi College, Oxford, and later bishop of Salisbury, wrote his *Apology of the Church of England* in 1562 (Jewel 1848a) against the English Catholics. He began his defense with a clear assertion of the primacy of Scripture above all other sources. Furthermore, he argued, since Holy Writ is the work of the Spirit of God, it must also be understood through the Spirit. Like Cranmer, Jewel appealed to the Spirit who guided the fathers of the early church. Jewel claimed that the Church of England had, as closely as possible, restored the ancient purity of apostolic times and the pattern of the primitive church. He regarded "the primitive church" to have existed "for the space of six hundred years after Christ" (1848a: 100). Even though Jewel called upon the authority of the Catholic fathers of this early period, he argued that their authority was not equal to Scripture. He cites them not "as ground, or principles, or foundations of the faith, but only as interpreters, or witnesses, or consenters unto the faith" (Jewel 1848b: 3.128).

Thomas Harding

The English Recusant Thomas Harding (1516-72) published his *A Confutation of a Booke Intituled an Apologie of the Church of England* in 1565 (facsimile edition 1976). Writing after the Council of Trent (1545-63), Harding argued against Jewel that, although Scripture should be acknowledged as the supreme source of faith and morals, its meaning is not always clear, as is demonstrated by the fact that heretics as well as orthodox teachers allege it. In Harding's view, the Holy Spirit in such obscure matters leads to the authority of the church, and the true meaning or interpretation of Scripture cannot be grasped apart from the church's tradition. Tradition he broadly defined as "the Catholic sense and understanding of the Holy Scriptures, which has been delivered unto us by the Holy Fathers of *all* ages and *all* countries where the faith has been received" (as cited by Jewel 1848b: 3.240; see also Collinson, Hunt, and Walsham 2002: 37-39; Southern 1950: 50-62).

Even the most moderate of the Elizabethan Puritans reaffirmed the magisterial Reformers' doctrine of the unique authority and sufficiency of the Scriptures. Some of the more radical Protestants, such as the Presbyterians Walter Travers (Knox 1962) and Thomas Cartwright (Pearson 1966), went farther by rejecting for church use any custom or tradition that was not specifically enjoined in Scripture. Hence, they rejected many aspects of the worship and polity of the Church of England as non-scriptural and "popish."

Richard Hooker

In response to this challenge, Richard Hooker (1554-1600) emerged as far and away the ablest and foremost sixteenth-century apologist and theologian of the Church of England. His sermons and the eight books of his monumental treatise *Of the Lawes of Ecclesiastical Politie* (published intermittently between 1593 and 1662, books VI-VIII posthumously; see Stanwood 1981; McGrade 1993) were directed not only against the Elizabethan Presbyterians but also against the Roman Catholics. He consciously strove to delineate the position of the established Church of England as neither Calvinist nor Roman (Gibbs 2002). Even though Hooker's basic position remains constant, his emphasis varies depending on whether he is addressing Geneva or Rome.

Hooker (1977: 1.124-30) clearly affirmed the central Protestant principle of *sola scriptura*. He qualified this affirmation, however, by immediately going on to restrict the perfection and sufficiency of the Scriptures *to the purpose for which they were given*, namely, the eternal salvation of human beings. Hooker further qualified this Protestant principle when he argued that belief in Holy Writ as the word of God has to be established both by reason and by the witness or authority of the church. Hooker accordingly rejected the dismissal by English Puritans of all those aspects of Christian worship and church polity that were not explicitly mandated in Scripture. He found no clearly formulated church polity prescribed in the Scriptures and therefore relegated this issue to the realm of human (not divine) law and consensus.

On the other side, Hooker challenged the Roman Catholics whenever they appealed to sources outside the Scriptures as necessary for salvation. This challenge included the appeal to church councils and to unwritten traditions, even if such traditions claimed to be of "apostolic" origin (Hooker 1981: 14-103; 1990; Gibbs 2002).

Hooker most clearly defined his preferred approach to the exegesis of Scripture when he said: "I holde it for a most infallible rule in expositions of sacred scripture, that where a literall construction will stand, the farthest from the letter is commonlie the worst" (Hooker 1977: 2.252). Yet, he always subordinated his preference for the more literal to an overarching christocentric principle. Like Luther, Hooker believed that in Scripture there is a central and Christ-centered core and that it is only within this essential sphere that literal interpretation and strict obedience are in order (Grislis 1972: 191, 197-98).

The King James Version

Shortly after Hooker's death, all the earlier efforts of translating the Bible into English reached their climax with the publication of the KJV in 1611 (Bruce 1961: 76; Daniell 2003: 431-33). When James came to the English throne in 1603, he brought with him pronounced Protestant views and a personal interest in biblical study and translation. The Bishops' Bible had failed to displace the Geneva Bible, and the Puritans were objecting, among other things, to the "authorized" versions. It was the Puritans who provided the immediate occasion for the new revision. In January 1604, at the Hampton Court Conference, John Rainolds, Puritan president of Corpus Christi College, Oxford, and Richard Hooker's former tutor and lifelong friend, asked James to order a new translation of the Bible that would be more accurate in terms of the original languages. Although there was no immediate action on this petition, the idea appealed to the king, who gave the order for the new translation. Annoyed by what he considered to be seditious comments in the marginalia of the Geneva Bible, the king restricted marginal notes exclusively to those necessary for explanation of the Hebrew or Greek (Bruce 1961: 97). The new translation was completed and ready for publication in 1611. Although the title page reads that this version was "Appointed to be read in Churches," and even though the KJV has come to be known as *the* Authorized Version, no official act of authorization is known to exist.

Although officially a revision of the Bishops' Bible, especially of the second edition of 1572, the KJV derived relatively little from that version. The Tyndale and Geneva versions contributed much more, and among the unnamed sources are contributions from the Rheims NT, Luther's German Bible, and various Latin translations, including that of Theodore Beza (Daniell 2003: 439-42, 447-50). In general, however, the final result was still basically the inherited Tyndale-Coverdale text. The Geneva Bible was the next greatest influence. Moreover, Hebrew scholarship had much improved in England since the mid-sixteenth century. Increasing familiarity with Jewish commentaries on the OT was an important factor in the translation. The result was a version generally superior to its predecessors in accuracy and refinement of literary style.

But the new version also had its weaknesses. The underlying text was far from satisfactory (Daniell 2003: 460; Bruce 1961: 109, 111-12, 127-28). The translators' knowledge of Hebrew was still defective, and there was no standard edition of the Hebrew Masoretic Text of the OT. In the NT, there were no papyri to help with the Greek *koine*. The late and corrupt text of Erasmus, as popularized and slightly modified by Stephanus and Beza, was necessarily used, since nothing better was available. Moreover, there were many archaisms, misspellings, and other errors that were corrected in later editions.

Nevertheless, whatever its weaknesses, and however slow its initial usage, the KJV remained for two and one half centuries *the* Bible of English-speaking Protestantism and exerted a wide and lasting influence, not only in religion, but also in literature and every other area of contemporary English-speaking culture. Many have held, and continue to hold, that it is the greatest monument of English prose.

CONCLUSION

As we reach the end of our rapid survey of biblical interpretation in England from the early Middle Ages through the Renaissance and Reformation, it is fitting to recall that there are striking continuities as well as discontinuities at all of the historical boundaries. It is also fitting to recall that we have encountered along the way several very different approaches to the reading of the Scriptures. Without dismissing or disparaging any of the valuable contributions made during recent centuries by innumerable scholars dedicated to the historical-critical paradigm of biblical studies who have valued the literal-historical sense (Barton 1998: 9-20), the contemporary reader is now free to also appreciate what some recent scholars have called "the superiority of pre-critical exegesis" (Muller and Thompson 1996), including not only the medieval four senses of Scripture but also different ways of interpreting the "spiritual" meaning which we have, if only briefly, encountered in this chapter. In every age, individuals and groups have approached the Scriptures with different presuppositions in mind and with various methods of reading, but always finding the living Word of God for themselves and others in their own particular time and place.

BIBLIOGRAPHY

Alcuin of York

1863   *Commentaria in Sancti Joannis Evangelium. PL* 100:733-1007.

Aldridge, J. W.

1966   *The Hermeneutic of Erasmus.* Richmond: John Knox.

Allen, W.

1882   *The Letters and Memorials of William, Cardinal Allen.* Ed. T. F. Knox; London: Nutt.

Aquinas, Thomas

1953   *Summa Theologiae.* Prima Pars, Quaestio 1, Articulus 10. 1.9b-11a. Ottawa: Comissio Piana.

Augustin, C.

1991   *Erasmus: His Life, Works and Influence.* Trans. J. C. Grayson; Toronto: University of Toronto Press.

Augustine of Hippo

1962   *De Doctrina Christiana de Vera Religione.* CCSL 32:76-77.

Bacon, R.

1900   *Linguarum Cognitio.* In J. H. Bridges, ed., 3:66-81. *Opus Maius.* Oxford: Clarendon.

Barmby, J.

1908   *Gregory the Great.* London: SPCK.

Barton, J. (ed.)

1998   *The Cambridge Companion to Biblical Interpretation.* Cambridge: Cambridge University Press.

Bede, the Venerable

1967   "Praefatio," in *Libri Quattuor in Principium Genesis.* CCSL 118A:1.

1973   *De Schematibus et Tropis: A Translation.* Ed. and trans. G. H. Tannenhaus. In J. M. Miller, et al. (eds.), *Readings in Medieval Rhetoric.* Bloomington: Indiana University Press.

1985   *The Commentary on the Seven Catholic Epistles.* Trans. D. Hurst; Kalamazoo: Cistercian.

1989   *The Commentary on the Acts of the Apostles.* Trans. L. T. Martin. Kalamazoo: Cistercian.

1990   *Ecclesiastical History of the English People.* Rev. ed. Trans. Leo Sherley-Price. London: Penguin.

Bernard of Clairvaux

1859   *Sermones in Cantica Canticorum.* PL 183:799-1198.

Beza, T.

1565   *Novum Testamentum, cum versione Latina veteri, et nova Theodori Bezae.* Geneva. 2nd folio edition 1582; 3rd folio edition 1589; 4th folio edition 1598.

Booty, J. E.

1976   "History of the 1559 *Book of Common Prayer.*" In J. E. Booty, ed., *The Book of Common Prayer 1559: The Elizabethan Prayer Book.* London: Associated University Presses.

Boutflower, D. S. (ed. and trans.)

1912   *The Life of Ceolfrid, Abbot of the Monastery at Wearmouth and Jarrow.* London: Sunderland, Hills. Repr. 1991: Lampeter: Llanerch. [written by an unknown 8th century monk]

Bray, G.

1996   *Biblical Interpretation: Past and Present.* Downers Grove: InterVarsity.

Brown, D.

2003   "Jerome and the Vulgate," *HBI*[1], 355-79.

Bruce, F. F.

1961   *The English Bible: A History of Translations.* London: Lutterworth.

Burnaby, J.

1933   *Amor Dei: A Study of the Religion of St. Augustine.* London: Hodder & Stoughton.

Carroll, R. P.

1998   "Poststructuralist Approaches: New Historicism and Postmodernism." In J. Barton, ed., 1998:50-66.

Chadwick, H.

1986   *Augustine.* Oxford: Oxford University Press.

Chadwick, O.

1968   *John Cassian.* 2nd ed.; London: Cambridge University Press.

Chisolm-Batten, E.

1889   *The Life of Bishop Richard Fox.* Privately published.

Colet, J.

1869   *Two Treatises on the Hierarchies of Dionysius.* London: Bell and Daldy.

1985a   *Commentary on First Corinthians.* Ed. and trans. B. O'Kelly and C. A. L. Jarrot. Binghamton: Medieval & Renaissance Texts & Studies.

1985b   *Commentary on Romans: A New Edition.* Trans. B. O'Kelly and C. A. L. Jarrot. Binghamton: Medieval & Renaissance Texts & Studies.

Collinson, P., A. Hunt, and A. Walsham

2002   "Religious Publishing in England, 1557-1640." In J. Barnard and D. F. McKenzie, eds., *The Cambridge History of the Book in Britain* 4: *1557-1695*, 29-66. Cambridge: Cambridge University Press.

Cranmer, T.

1846   *A Confutation of Unwritten Verities.* In *Works* 2. Cambridge: Cambridge University Press.

Crewdson, T. E.

1941   *History of the Schoolmen.* London: Williams and Norgate.

Croatto, J. C.

1987   *Biblical Hermeneutics: Towards a Theory of Reading as the Production of Meaning.* Maryknoll: Orbis.

Dallman, W.

1925   *Miles Coverdale, Bishop of Exeter.* St. Louis: Concordia.

Daniell, D.

2003   *The Bible in English: Its History and Influence.* New Haven: Yale University Press.

Dionysius the Areopagite

1947   *"The Mystical Theology" and "The Celestial Hierarchies."* Ed. and trans. The Editors of the Shrine of Wisdom; Godalming: Shrine of Wisdom.

Erasmus, D.

1522   *Novum Testamentum Omne.* Basel: Froben.

1956   *Das Neue Testament . . . nach der Deutschen Übersetzung D. Martin Luthers.* Stuttgart: Württembergesche Bibelanstalt.

1967   *In Novum Testamentum Praefationes.* Ed. and trans. G. B. Winkler. Darmstadt: Wissenschaftliche Buchgesellschaft.

1984   *Paraphrases on Romans and Galatians.* Ed. R. D. Sider. Trans. and annotated J. B. Payne, A. Rabil, and W. S. Smith, Jr. Toronto: University of Toronto Press.

1992   *The Edition of St. Jerome.* Ed. and trans. J. F. Brady. Toronto: University of Toronto
          Press.

Eriugena, John Scotus

1852a   *Commentarius in S. Evangelium secundum Joannem.* In H. J. Floss, ed., *Patrologiae
          Latinae.* Turnholt: Brepols.

1852b   *Homilia in Prologum S. Evangelium secundum Joannem.* In H. J. Floss, ed., *Patro-
          logiae Latinae.* 122:283-96. Turnholt: Brepols.

Evans, G. R.

1984   *The Language and Logic of the Bible: The Earlier Middle Ages.* Cambridge: Cam-
          bridge University Press.

1985   *The Language and Logic of the Bible: The Road to Reformation.* Cambridge: Cam-
          bridge University Press.

Farrar, F. W.

1886   *History of Interpretation.* New York: Dutton. Repr. 1961: Grand Rapids: Baker.

Fox, R.

1929   *Letters of Richard Fox, 1486-1527.* Ed. P. S. and H. M. Allen. Oxford: Clarendon.

Froelich, K., and M. T. Gibson (eds.)

1992   *Biblia Latina cum glossa ordinaria: Facsimile reprint of the* Editio Princeps *of
          Adolph Rusch of Strasbourg, 1480/81.* Turnhout: Brepols.

Geisendorf, P. F.

1967   *Theodore de Bèze.* Geneva: Jullien.

Gibbs, L. W.

2002   "Richard Hooker's 'Via Media' Doctrine of Scripture and Tradition." *HTR* 95:
          227-35.

Gilmore, G. P.

1952   *The World of Humanism, 1453-1517.* New York: Harper.

Gleason, J. B.

1989   *John Colet.* Berkeley: University of California Press.

Gluntz, H. H.

1933   *History of the Vulgate in England from Alcuin to Roger Bacon.* Cambridge: Cam-
          bridge University Press.

Grafton, A., and L. Jardine

1986   *From Humanism to the Liberal Arts in Fifteenth-Century Humanities: Education
          and Europe.* Cambridge: Cambridge University Press.

Grant, R., and D. Tracy

1984   *A Short History of the Interpretation of the Bible.* 2nd ed. Philadelphia: Fortress.

Grislis, E.

1972   "The Hermeneutical Problem in Richard Hooker." In W. Speed Hill, ed., *Studies in Richard Hooker: Essays Preliminary to an Edition of His Works,* 159-206. Cleveland: Case Western Reserve University Press.

Hackett, J.

1997   "Roger Bacon: His Life, Career and Works." In J. Hackett, ed., *Roger Bacon and the Sciences: Commemorative Essays,* 8-23. Leiden: Brill.

Harding, T.

1976   *A Confutation of a Booke Intituled An Apologie of the Church of England.* Ilkley: Scolar (facsimile reprint of 1565 original).

Holder, A. G.

1990   "Bede and the Tradition of Patristic Exegesis." *ATR* 72: 230-32, 393-406.

Hooker, Richard

1977a   *Of the Laws of Ecclesiastical Polity, Preface, Books 1-4.* Ed. G. Edelen. FLEWRH 1; Cambridge: Belknap.

1977b   *Of the Laws of Ecclesiastical Polity, Preface, Book 5.* Ed. W. S. Hill. FLEWRH 2; Cambridge: Belknap.

1981   *Of the Laws of Ecclesiastical Polity, Preface, Books 6, 7, 8.* Ed. P. G. Stanwood. FLEWRH 3; Cambridge: Belknap.

Jewel, J.

1848a   *Apology of the Church of England.* In *The Works of John Jewel.* The Parker Society, eds. 3:49-112. Cambridge: Cambridge University Press.

1848b   *Defence of the Apology,* in *The Works of John Jewel* 3:113-626. Parker Society, eds. Cambridge: Cambridge University Press.

Kelly, J. N. D.

1968   *Jerome: His Life, Writings, and Controversies.* London: Duckworth. Repr. 2000. Peabody: Hendrickson.

Knox, S. J.

1962   *Walter Travers: Paragon of Elizabethan Puritanism.* London: Methuen.

G. W. H. Lampe (ed.)

1969   *The Cambridge History of the Bible 2: The West from the Fathers to the Reformation.* Cambridge: Cambridge University Press.

Lanfranc of Bec

1880   "*Incipit Praefatio in Omnes Epistolas Sancti Pauli.*" *PL* 150:101-6.

Leclercq, J.

1969   "From Gregory the Great to Bernard." In G. W. H. Lampe, ed., 1969: 183-97.

Loewe, R.

1969   "The Medieval History of the Latin Vulgate." In G. W. H. Lampe, ed., 1969: 102-54.

Lubac, H. de

1959-64   *Exégèse Médiévale. Les Quatre Sens de l'Écriture.* Paris: Aubier.

Lynch, L. E.
1967   "John Scotus Erigena." In *New Catholic Encyclopaedia* 7:1073. New York: McGraw-
        Hill.

MacCaffrey, J.
1970   *History of the Catholic Church from the Renaissance to the French Revolution.* Phila-
        delphia: Ayer.

Marshall, R. K.
2000   *John Knox.* Edinburgh: Birlinn.

Marx, A.
1973   "Rashi." In *Essays in Jewish Biography,* 61-86. New York: Arno.

McDonnell, M. F.
1909   *The History for St. Paul's School for Boys.* London: Chapman and Hall.

McGinn, B.
1996   "The Originality of Eriugena's Spiritual Exegesis." In G. van Riel, C. Steel, and J. J.
        McEvoy, eds., 1996: 55-80.

McGrade, A. S.
1993   "The Three Last Books and Hooker's Autograph Notes." In *Of The Laws of Ecclesi-
        astical Polity: Introductions, Commentary, Preface and Books I-IV.* FLEWRH 6:233-
        47. Binghamton: Medieval & Renaissance Texts and Studies.

McKim, D. K. (ed.)
1986   *A Guide to Contemporary Hermeneutics: Major Trends in Biblical Interpretation.*
        Grand Rapids: Eerdmans.

McKnight, E. V.
1988   *Post-Modern Use of the Bible: The Emergence of Reader-Oriented Criticism.* Nash-
        ville: Abingdon.

McLure, J.
1985   "Bede's 'Notes on Genesis' and Training of the Anglo-Saxon Clergy." In K. Walsh
        and D. Woods, eds., *The Bible in the Medieval World: Essays in Memory of Beryl
        Smalley,* 17-30. 3rd ed.; Oxford: Blackwell.

Moorman, J. R. H.
1953   *A History of the Church in England.* London: Black.

Morgan, R., with J. Barton
1988   *Biblical Interpretation.* Oxford: Oxford University Press.

Muller, R. A.
1996   "Biblical Interpretation in the Era of the Reformation: The View from the Middle
        Ages." In R. A. Muller and J. L. Thompson, eds., *Biblical Interpretation in the Era of
        the Reformation,* 3-22. Grand Rapids: Eerdmans.

Muller, R. A., and J. L. Thompson

1996 "The Significance of Precritical Exegesis: Retrospect and Prospect." In R. A. Muller and J. L. Thompson, eds., *Biblical Interpretation in the Age of the Reformation,* 335-45. Grand Rapids: Eerdmans.

Neill, S.

1965 *Anglicanism.* Harmondsworth: Penguin.

Nichols, A.

2003 *Discovering Aquinas: An Introduction to His Life, Work, and Influence.* Grand Rapids: Eerdmans.

Norris, R. A., Jr.

2003 "Augustine and the Close of the Ancient Period." *HBI*[1], 380-409.

Olszowy-Schlanger, J.

2001 "The Knowledge and Practice of Hebrew among Christian Scholars in Pre-Expulsion England: The Evidence of 'Bilingual' Hebrew-Latin Manuscripts." In N. de Lange, ed., *Hebrew Scholarship and the Medieval World,* 107-28. Cambridge: Cambridge University Press.

Origen of Alexandria

1857 ΠΕΡΙ ΑΡΧΩΝ/De Principiis, Book 4. *PG* 11:363-66.

Otten, W.

1996 "The Parallelism of Nature and Scripture: Reflections on Eriugena's Incarnational Exegesis." In G. van Riel, C. Steel, and J. J. McEvoy, eds., 1996: 80-90, 97-100.

Parker, M., Archbishop of Canterbury

1568 *The. holie. Bible. conteynyng the olde Testament and the newe.* London: Iugge.

Pearson, A. F. S.

1966 *Thomas Cartwright and Elizabethan Puritanism.* Gloucester: Smith.

Ramsay, B.

1997 *Ambrose.* London: Routledge.

Riel, G. van, C. Steel, and J. J. McEvoy (eds.)

1996 *Iohannes Scottus Eriugena: The Bible and Hermeneutics.* Leuven: Leuven University Press.

Rummel, E.

1985 *Erasmus as a Translator of the Classics.* Toronto: University of Toronto Press.

Schwahn, W.

1896 *Lorenzo Valla.* Berlin: Mayer and Muller.

Smalley, B.

1941 *The Study of the Bible in the Middle Ages.* 1st ed.; Oxford: Clarendon.

1952 *The Study of the Bible in the Middle Ages.* 2nd ed.; Oxford: Blackwell.

1983 *The Study of the Bible in the Middle Ages.* 3rd ed.; Oxford: Blackwell.

Southern, A. C.

1950   *Elizabethan Recusant Prose, 1559-1582: A Historical and Critical Account of the Books of the Catholic Refugees Printed and Published Abroad and at Secret Presses in England Together with an Annotated Bibliography of the Same.* London: Sands.

Spicq, C.

1944   *Esquisse d'une Histoire de l'Exégèse Latine au Moyen Âge.* Paris: Vrin.

Stanwood, P. G.

1981   "Textual Introduction: The Last Three Books." In Hooker 1981: xiii-lxxv.

Steinmetz, D. C. (ed.)

1990   *The Bible in the Sixteenth Century.* Durham: Duke University Press.

Thompson, H. L.

1900   *Christ Church.* London: Robinson.

Tiffany, F. C., and S. H. Ringe

1996   *Biblical Interpretation: A Roadmap.* Nashville: Abingdon.

Todd, J. M.

1964   *Martin Luther.* London: Burns and Oates; New York: Newman (subsequently Paulist).

Tyndale, W.

1848a   "A Pathway into the Scripture." In *Doctrinal Treatises and Introductions to Different Portions of the Holy Scriptures.* Ed. H. Walter, for the Parker Society; Cambridge: Cambridge University Press.

1848b   *Works.* Ed. The Parker Society. Cambridge: Cambridge University Press.

2000   *The New Testament: The Text of the Worms Edition of 1526 in Original Spelling, Translated by William Tyndale, Edited for The Tyndale Society by W. R. Cooper, with a Preface by David Daniell.* Ed. W. R. Cooper; London: British Library.

Ward, B.

2003   "Douay Bible." In *Catholic Encyclopaedia* 5:140-41. New York: Appleton.

Watson, D. F., and A. J. Hauser

1994   *Rhetorical Criticism of the Bible: A Comprehensive Bibliography with Notes on History and Method.* Leiden: Brill.

Wendel, F.

1997   *Calvin: Origins and Development of His Religious Thought.* Trans. P. Mairet. Grand Rapids: Baker.

Wycliffe, J.

2001   *On the Truth of Holy Scripture.* Ed. and trans. I. C. Levy; Kalamazoo: Western Michigan University Press.

CHAPTER 14

Biblical Interpretation
among the Anabaptist Reformers

Stuart Murray

"Radical Reformation" refers both to sixteenth-century Anabaptism and, more broadly, to the multi-faceted radicalism that accompanied the magisterial Reformation that impacted Europe during that century. Here we will focus on Anabaptism, within which the more significant hermeneutical developments are apparent, although this movement must be set in the context of sixteenth-century radicalism and the recurrent radical tradition of which it was the latest expression (Snyder 1995: 11-49).

Anabaptism operated mainly in territories now comprising Switzerland, Austria, the Czech Republic, Germany, Alsace, and the Netherlands. Its distinguishing features included christocentrism, new birth, discipleship in the power of the Spirit, believers' churches free from state control, economic sharing, and a vision of restoring NT Christianity. It drew adherents primarily from poorer sections of society, though early leaders included university graduates, monks, and priests. Persecuted by Catholics and Protestants, its leaders traveled widely, ignoring parish and national boundaries, evangelizing, baptizing, and forming congregations. Assessing the numerical strength of an underground movement is difficult; Anabaptism influenced many more people than those baptized as members (Clasen 1972: passim).

The traditional view of Anabaptism as a radicalizing of Luther and Zwingli has been challenged by recognition of the influence of Thomas Müntzer and the Zwickau prophets, other radical reformers, and spiritualists. Monastic reform movements, the *devotio moderna*, Franciscan Tertiaries, pre-Reformation radicals, humanism, Erasmus, German mysticism, peasant unrest, millenarian hopes, anticlericalism, and popular pamphleteers all con-

---

Early Anabaptist Writers

Balthasar Hubmaier (1485-1528; *A Brief Apologia*)
Thomas Müntzer (1489-1525; *Prague Manifesto*, 1521-22)
Hans Denck (1495-1527)
Melchior Hoffman (1495-1543)
Pilgram Marpeck (1495-1556; *Testamentserleutterung*, c. 1544)
Menno Simons (1496-1561; *Treatise on Christian Baptism*, 1539)
Dirk Philips (1504-68)

---

tributed to the radical reformation context within which Anabaptism developed (Williams 1992: 73-174).

Historians identify four main branches — Swiss Brethren, South German/Austrian Anabaptists, Dutch Mennonites, and communitarian Hutterites — comprised of numerous groups gathered around charismatic leaders. These do not coincide precisely with different (though not mutually exclusive) hermeneutical approaches practiced by early Anabaptists, such as literalists, spiritualists, and apocalypticists. Mennonite scholars formerly identified Swiss Brethren and Dutch Mennonites as normative, evangelical Anabaptists, in contradistinction to spiritualistic or revolutionary groups. This perception, however, unduly homogenizes the Swiss and Dutch groups and excludes significant Anabaptist themes and personalities (Goertz 1996: 6-35).

Anabaptism was a diverse, complex, and fluid but coherent movement; various stimuli provoked its development, resulting in significant regional variations. Even though Anabaptists shared several central convictions, there were divergent views on various wings of the movement, and some sharp disagreements. Anabaptism achieved greater uniformity of belief and practice by mid-century (Pearse 1998: 29-116).

ANABAPTIST HERMENEUTICS

Significance

There are several reasons for investigating long-ignored Anabaptist hermeneutical principles. First, Anabaptist hermeneutics developed contemporaneously with the mainstream Reformers' hermeneutics, the approach from which the beleaguered historical-critical method derived. Anabaptists, though indebted to the Reformers' methodology, recognized its limitations and advocated different approaches. Reappraisal of this sixteenth-century alternative provides historical support for attempts to address limitations of the historical-critical method, revealing weaknesses in its Reformation roots, and offering perspectives similar to those advocated by recent critics (Fiorenza 1984; Rowland and Corner 1990).

Second, key hermeneutical issues emerged from debates between Anabaptists and Reformers, Spiritualists, and other Anabaptist leaders: the relationship between the Testaments, the Spirit's role in interpretation, the hermeneutical significance of the congregation, the epistemological significance of obedience, and the extent to which Scripture is perspicuous. The Reformers' triumph and the suppression of Anabaptism ensured that the Reformers' hermeneutical views were embraced by subsequent generations. However, these issues continue to be contentious. Therefore, it is worthwhile to reexamine the Anabaptist tradition, especially since the tradition that developed from the Reformers' hermeneutics has failed to provide adequate resolution (Swartley 1984: 11-28).

Third, many recent ecclesial developments resonate with ways Anabaptists dealt with similar issues. Examples include the challenge of liberation theologies to the traditional relationship between understanding and application and the challenge of charismatic movements to persistent marginalization of the Spirit in hermeneutics. Anabaptists rejected many prevailing ideological commitments and developed a hermeneutic appropriate for a movement of the poor, powerless, and oppressed. This provides a sixteenth-century vantage point from which to assess liberationist developments. As a movement within which the relationship between Word and Spirit was extensively explored, Anabaptism offers resources for developing a hermeneutic for charismatic churches, and insights into strained relationships between such churches and those whose emphasis is on the Word (Murray 2000: 220-35).

Fourth, Anabaptist practices were developed in congregations, rather than in seminaries. They represent an alternative historical paradigm and a heritage as long as that of the scholarly approach. Studying this approach and appreciating its value can contribute toward closing the widely acknowledged gap between scholars and churches.

Fifth, Anabaptists, unlike Reformers and most scholarly interpreters, were mainly poor, uneducated, and persecuted. This gave them insights into Scripture that were less accessible to their more comfortable contemporaries, but analogous to the experience of the early churches and of many Christian communities today. At the start of the third millennium — for the first time since early in the first millennium — most Christians are poor. Furthermore, persecution is the experience of a surprisingly high number of them. Anabaptist perspectives are thus pertinent in many parts of the church today.

Sixth, Anabaptist hermeneutics is significant as one expression of an interpretative approach that has characterized numerous fringe groups throughout church history. Studying these groups reveals not only diversity, but also areas of fundamental agreement that distinguish them from their mainstream contemporaries. The persistence of this alternative approach suggests it may contain valuable elements neglected by others.

Finally, the Anabaptists' rejection of the Constantinian synthesis of church and state affected their biblical interpretation, just as its acceptance by Catholics and Protestants influenced their hermeneutics. This rejection is clearly reflected in Anabaptist presuppositions, methods, and conclusions. Thus, Anabaptist hermeneutics today offers an approach, with historical roots as deep as the Reformers', that is more appropriate for interpreting Scripture in post-Constantinian contexts (Murray 2000: 7-13; 2003).

Discerning Anabaptist Hermeneutics

To understand Anabaptist hermeneutics, merely examining significant leaders' writings is inadequate. The contribution of leaders, especially those who were educated, was substantial, and provided foundational teaching for Anabaptist congregations. They did not, however, provide authoritative answers to every doctrinal question or authoritative interpretations of every biblical text. Ordinary Anabaptists were more involved than their Reformed counterparts in interpreting Scripture. Though most relied on hearing and memorizing Scripture, they also reflected on it and participated in the congregational process of discerning its meaning and application. This every-member approach had profound implications for Anabaptist hermeneutics (Snyder 1991).

Nevertheless, the frequency with which key texts and arguments appear in records of Anabaptists under interrogation indicates that their leaders provided tools for their brothers and sisters to explore Scripture. Often these comprised topical concordances — systematic collections of biblical quotations. More than biblical indices, they provided hermeneutical assistance to help readers interpret an otherwise bewildering array of texts and guided congregations toward doctrines, practices, stories, and ethical stances regarded as having the greatest significance for discipleship (Fast and Peters 2001: passim).

Anabaptism did not produce systematic theologians. Its focus was pragmatic rather than intellectual, concerned with obeying rather than analyzing and categorizing Scripture. Its confessions concentrated on ecclesiological and ethical rather than theological matters. Nor were there opportunities to produce many theological treatises. Most of its leading thinkers died young, before they had developed systematic presentations or had time and freedom to write at length. There is, therefore, no definitive Anabaptist statement on hermeneutics. But this does not mean a coherent hermeneutic cannot be discovered from their writings (Yoder 1977: passim).

There are substantial discussions of hermeneutical issues, particularly in the writings of leaders who lived into the second generation. Menno Simons and Dirk Philips contributed thoughtful statements on methodology, with copious applications. Pilgram Marpeck's *Testamentserleutterung* is an extensive treatment of the relationship between the Testaments, in which he explains his hermeneutical principles. There are, in various Anabaptist writings, sections on hermeneutical issues — the use of allegory, the Spirit's interpretative role, and the relationship between the Testaments. These sources must be augmented by considering how Anabaptist congregations functioned and how Scripture was used in practice (Klassen and Klaassen 1978: 555-66).

Anabaptists were divided into geographically separated groups gathered around influential leaders who infrequently met other regional leaders. Anabaptist writings reveal hermeneutical variation, criticisms of each other, and instances of mutual dependence and recognition of shared insights. Although this may appear to undermine the possibility of discovering a coherent Anabaptist hermeneutic, variants may, in fact, enrich the hermeneutic, explicate certain features, and confirm that certain aspects were typical of the whole movement rather than local expressions.

Anabaptist hermeneutics developed in debate with opponents, as well as through internal conversations. Anabaptist leaders were opposed not only by Reformers and Catholics, but also by other radical groups, such as Spiritualists. On some issues their stance differs, depending on which opponents they were confronting. This must be recognized in attempting to discern hermeneutical norms (Klassen and Klaassen 1978: 107-58, 369-75).

Nevertheless, despite variations and difficulties in discovering an authoritative view, a coherent and distinctive Anabaptist hermeneutic emerges from their writings and practice. Contemporary opponents certainly assumed Anabaptist groups agreed on hermeneutical principles. And the fact that uneducated Anabaptists operated according to common principles of biblical interpretation indicates a shared outlook across the movement (Goertz 1996: 114).

SIX CORE CONVICTIONS

Six central Anabaptist hermeneutical principles can be identified, albeit expressed and nuanced in different ways across the movement (Swartley 1984: 5-10).

Scripture Is Self-Interpreting

A crucial component was the conviction that Scripture is self-interpreting. Statements from Anabaptist leaders demonstrate widespread confidence about the clarity of Scripture and its sufficiency without external additions. Repeatedly, Anabaptists on trial declared that their views were derived from no source other than Scripture and that Scripture was sufficiently clear to justify these (Murray 2000: 36-42).

The Schleitheim Confession (1527; see Yoder 1977) emphasized the importance to the Swiss Brethren of taking biblical teaching at face value. Balthasar Hubmaier, the leader with the most extensive theological training, strongly affirmed the right of private interpretation, and insisted Scripture was straightforward enough to be understood and obeyed (Klaassen 1966; see also Pipkin and Yoder 1990).

Marpeck advocated a similar approach in German congregations. Like Hubmaier, he resisted introducing complications, preferring to accept biblical texts as they stood. He believed that discussing complications produced theological wrangling, led to Scripture being downgraded, and confused ordinary Christians. Marpeck rejected the imposition of an interpretative grid on Scripture to force passages into consistency with preconceived theological positions. He defended private interpretation, and insisted Scripture was sufficient without external additions. Among the Hutterites, Peter Riedeman expressed the same conviction (Riedeman 1970: 198).

Dutch Anabaptists shared Marpeck's perspective, but only after they recognized the dangers of concentrating interpretative authority in the hands of dominant leaders, and the dangers of allowing unnecessarily complex and speculative systems to influence interpretation. Apocalyptic Anabaptists, such as Melchior Hoffman, accepted the conviction that all could interpret Scripture, but this did not mean all were equally skilled, or that all passages were susceptible to interpretation by every believer. Menno, reacting against speculative systems, expressed confidence in Scripture's clarity and simplicity (Simons 1956: 452, 519).

Statements from Anabaptists on trial demonstrate that their leaders' attitudes had enfranchised the membership and produced tremendous faith and confidence, even in the face of clever questioning and severe pressure (van Braght 1950: 559, 597).

Multiple references in Anabaptist writings and testimonies to the clarity and sufficiency of Scripture indicate a significant hermeneutical claim. Anabaptists were concerned that the Reformers were paying lip service to the plain sense of Scripture and the right of private interpretation, but hedging these convictions with many qualifications. Their repeated insistence that Scripture is simple, clear, and plain urged a more radical approach. They challenged the Reformers' reliance on reason, increasing restriction of interpretation to pastors and scholars, bondage to doctrinal considerations and traditional interpretations, and the use of external means to evade rather than explain Scripture. Anabaptists protested the Reformers' claim that uneducated people were unable to interpret Scripture, believing that scholarship did more harm than good and obscured rather than clarified Scripture. Anabaptists argued that predetermined doctrinal emphases were stifling biblical studies and precluding openness to fresh revelation. They opposed the Reformers' tendency to regard Scripture as frequently ambiguous, seeing this as another device to evade its challenge. The Reformers agreed that Scripture was clear on doctrinal issues, but were not as decisive about ecclesiology or ethics; Anabaptists refused to separate these issues (Murray 2000: 42-50).

Criticisms of the principle that Scripture is self-interpreting include that it is necessary because the interpreters in the movement are uneducated and that it indicates a naive overconfidence rather than a substantive methodology. The Reformers argued that, concerned about undue sophistication, Anabaptists failed to appreciate textual difficulties that cannot be resolved without research into linguistics, history, culture, and other issues where scholarship is helpful. What many readers assume to be the plain sense of Scripture may bear little resemblance to the meaning intended by the author in a different cultural setting. Anabaptists' commitment to interpretative enfranchisement came perilously close to the indefensible position that all believers can interpret Scripture equally well. Another criticism is that, if Reformers interpreted Scripture in accordance with preconceived *doctrinal* convictions, Anabaptists interpreted Scripture in accordance with preconceived convictions of *their own*. For those claiming Scripture is clear, a serious problem (increasingly apparent as the movement spread) was the difficulty of resolving disputes about the meaning of Scripture. Some Anabaptists recognized these inadequacies, welcomed contributions from scholars, and insisted that other hermeneutical principles could also be used to ensure proper interpretation (Murray 2000: 50-64).

The hermeneutical principle of Scripture as self-interpreting resembled the approaches of radical reformers such as Karlstadt and Müntzer and challenged prevailing assumptions (Snyder 1995: 25-31). For thousands of Christians, during the formative years of the movement, this approach was genuinely liberating. Whatever its shortcomings and imbalances, and despite the inherent danger of anarchy, this approach enfranchised people in ways the Reformation promised but failed to deliver.

Christocentrism

Confidence that Scripture was clear and that all Christians could interpret it applied preeminently to passages containing the words and actions of Jesus. The belief that Jesus clarified what was previously obscure appears frequently in Anabaptist writings (Klaassen 1981a: 147-49).

Among the Swiss, this conviction appears repeatedly. Christocentrism, for Hans Pfistermeyer, meant that Jesus' words took precedence over all other words in Scripture, and that Christ was the interpreter of the OT. It was by the words of Christ that Michael Sattler asked to be judged as to his faithfulness to the whole of Scripture. Similarly, Felix Mantz instinctively drew on the example and teaching of Jesus when arguing ethical or ecclesiological points (Baylor 1991: 96).

Riedeman's writings demonstrate that Hutterites shared this christocentric approach. Comparing the Testaments, he concluded that what God really wants from his people could only be found by listening to Jesus, rather than hunting through OT "shadows" (Riedeman 1970: 195-96).

Among South German Anabaptists, Jesus' example and the overall thrust of his teaching, rather than his explicit commands, were accorded primary significance. Hans Denck regarded Jesus' example as determinative, disallowing Christians from treating OT teachings and examples as normative (Furcha 1988: 105).

It is arguable that a different approach was evident among apocalyptic Anabaptists like Melchior Hoffman, Hans Hut, Bernhard Rothmann, and David Joris, who concentrated on prophetic and apocalyptic passages, and interpreted Scripture in light of their interpretation of these. They adopted a dispensationalist approach, whereby different ethical requirements and spiritual responses were appropriate in different eras of history. Christocentrism was not absent, but it was harder to maintain as apocalyptic passages took center stage (Waite 1994: 239).

In Münster christocentrism was abandoned and OT practices became normative — with disastrous consequences for the Münsterites, whom the besieging armies massacred, and for the whole Anabaptist movement, which came to be regarded as equally dangerous. This incident explains the determination of Menno and other Dutch leaders to resist the still-popular apocalyptic approach and to be thoroughly christocentric. Menno, like Hubmaier, was confident that Jesus' words and example were clear and straightforward by comparison with other parts of Scripture. By the 1540s, as eschatological prophecies remained unfulfilled, apocalyptic interpretation waned and christocentrism became normative (Simons 1956: 186, 312, 749).

Christocentrism meant that the Bible was not flat: some passages had greater authority for doctrine and practice than others. The NT took precedence over the OT, and Gospel accounts of Jesus' life and teachings were the pinnacle of God's revelation and primary in all questions of interpretation. Christocentrism meant that the whole Bible pointed to Jesus. The OT prepared the way, pointing forward to him as the fulfilment of all God's promises. The NT pointed back to him as founder and head of the church, its source of life and power, and the example it followed (Philips 1992: 102, 305).

For Marpeck especially, christocentrism was a deliberate policy to ensure Jesus was honored as the unique Son of God and authoritative interpreter. Anabaptists were deeply concerned to honor Christ, to give him first place in all aspects of life. They feared that the Reformers' emphasis on learning and reason enthroned Christ dogmatically but dethroned him in relation to discipleship. For Marpeck, this had implications for biblical interpretation: Jesus was the preeminent revelation of God, who unlocked the secrets of Scripture (Klassen and Klaassen 1978: 438-40).

Christocentrism, at its best, was not a literalistic and legalistic application of Jesus' teaching. Although some Anabaptists called Jesus the new lawgiver and treated his sayings as prooftexts, others regarded his example, lifestyle, spirit, relationships, and intention as crucial for interpreting the rest of Scripture. Christocentrism also meant that a living experience of Jesus was a prerequisite for hermeneutics. The historical Jesus was central to the text, and the Christ of faith was central to the life-experience of interpreters. Anabaptists based their hermeneutics on a combination of the objective basis of Christ's human life and the subjective basis of their experience of him (Klassen and Klaassen 1978: 450-51).

Reformed interpretations were *christological:* Jesus was the supreme revelation of God to humankind, and his death, resurrection, and ascension were God's central acts in history, through which salvation was available to believers. With this, Anabaptists heartily agreed. However, the Reformers' emphasis was less on Jesus himself and more on his salvific acts and the doctrine of justification by faith. Thus, Reformers' hermeneutics can be termed *soteriological:* their understanding of salvation provided the hermeneutical key to Scripture. Anabaptist hermeneutics were *christocentric,* focusing on Jesus himself, rather than primarily on doctrines describing his redeeming work: Jesus was not only redeemer, but also the example to imitate and the teacher to obey. Christocentrism was tied more firmly to the human Jesus and, consequently, Anabaptists' interpretations differed significantly from the Reformers' (Murray 2000: 70-87).

Anabaptists were charged with literalism and legalism, naively trying to copy Jesus and turning him into a new law-giver, rather than viewing him as the unique Savior whose sacrifice freed them from bondage to law-keeping. Although some Anabaptists slipped into literalism and legalism in their determination to obey Jesus' teachings, their hermeneutic was often more sophisticated. Most refused to settle for the Reformers' generalities, but many heeded the spirit and intention of Jesus as well as his specific words and actions (Swartley 1984: 77-90).

The Reformers suspected that the emphasis on Jesus as example threatened *sola gratia* and smacked of works-righteousness. Anabaptists argued repeatedly that they were not reverting to works-righteousness and that the Reformers were unbalanced in teaching "faith alone." Anabaptists were accused of overemphasizing the human Jesus and underemphasizing the risen Lord. By emphasising an aspect of christology they felt was being neglected, Anabaptists have given an unwarranted impression that they were less committed to other aspects of christology. They have also been criticized for selectivity, listening to sayings of Jesus that fit most naturally into their presuppositions and that endorsed their own convictions.

Christocentrism acted as a corrective to the Reformers' doctrinal approach. It was more radical in that it called for a life of costly discipleship based on the example of Jesus and less radical in that it mediated between the Reformers' emphasis on faith alone and traditional Catholic teaching. Constant reference to Jesus' words and actions challenged the Reformers, questioning the development of theology detached from the historical Jesus. And on ethical issues, the Anabaptist practice of starting with Jesus produced different conclusions from those reached by the Reformers, who struggled to relate Jesus to their ethical convictions (Murray 2000: 87-93).

The Two Testaments

In the sixteenth century, the relationship between the Testaments was much debated. Within Christendom, many issues were decided by reference to the

OT, but those with new access to Scripture were questioning the legitimacy of this in light of NT principles.

Views about the relationship between the Testaments can be plotted between opposite poles of continuity and discontinuity. Anabaptists were generally located considerably closer to the discontinuity pole than Reformers. For Anabaptists, this undergirded many disagreements with Reformers, and they wrote extensively to explain and defend their practice (Murray 2000: 97-106).

Swiss Anabaptists assumed that true interpretations could be found by carefully comparing the Testaments and treating the NT as primary. They preferred this to imposing uniformity on Scripture, which would leave OT practices unaffected. Participants in the Bern Debate (1538), though acknowledging the value of the OT, curtailed its scope by granting it validity wherever Christ had not suspended it and wherever it agreed with the NT. Hubmaier expressed the same concern that using the OT as if it were of equal authority should not compromise the NT (Harder 1985: 289).

Dutch Anabaptists were convinced that the NT represented a radical change from the Old; thus, the Testaments could not be regarded as equivalent. Dirk Philips complained about his contemporaries' illegitimate use of the OT. However strongly they emphasized discontinuity between the Testaments, most Dutch Anabaptists did not regard this as challenging Scripture's essential unity as the Word of God — but the primary focus was on discontinuity (Philips 1992: 273, 317).

Marpeck was the most radical Anabaptist leader on this issue, convinced that the OT functioned as the foundation of a house and the NT as the house itself: while the foundation was important, foundation and house must be distinguished (Klassen and Klaassen 1978: 222-23).

There were, however, important and influential exceptions to this approach. Hut, Hoffman, and others interested in eschatology, used apocalyptic and prophetic passages regardless of which Testament they were in. As noted above, the Münsterites treated the OT as normative. Sabbatarian Anabaptists Oswald Glait and Andreas Fischer attempted to apply OT laws in the contemporary context (Liechty 1989: passim).

Anabaptists taught both continuity and discontinuity. They argued not for rejection of the OT or for divorce of the Testaments but that the NT was radically new and could not be interpreted in unbroken continuity with the OT. The New did not revoke the Old or make it worthless, but the Old was subsumed in the New and could not function in isolation from it.

Treating the Testaments thus had significant implications and led to major differences between Anabaptists and Reformers. Many ecclesiological and ethical practices, including persecution, were justified from OT passages.

Anabaptists believed this discounted the newness of the NT, subordinating it to the OT. They argued with Reformers not about how to interpret OT passages but about whether the OT was the place to seek ethical and ecclesiological guidance (Murray 2000: 106-11).

Anabaptists have been criticized for their deprecation of the OT, their failure to appreciate the essential unity of Scripture, their use of allegory to harmonize OT texts with the NT, and their inadequate recognition of the importance of the OT as the necessary framework for reading the New — a framework Jesus and the apostles used freely. Neither Reformers nor Anabaptists succeeded in handling the OT well. The Reformers' insistence on the unity of Scripture and on treating the OT seriously was compromised by their tendency to justify practices from OT texts in ways that marginalized Jesus. Anabaptists challenged this, but in the process some came close to jettisoning the OT (Murray 2000: 111-21).

A major influence on the development of this Anabaptist perspective toward the OT was their experience of being assaulted by Reformers with a battery of OT texts to destroy the Anabaptists' position on ethical and ecclesiological topics. Two responses were possible: to argue that the OT was not authoritative or to show how the Reformers were misinterpreting it. Anabaptists, unable or unwilling to adopt the latter course, opted for the former. As a strategy to defend their convictions and provide a coherent approach to Scripture in the face of persistent challenges, this succeeded. But this position should not be defended uncritically by advocates of Anabaptist hermeneutics or preclude the development of a more satisfactory treatment of the relationship between the Testaments (Swartley 1984: 91-105).

Spirit and Word

The relationship between Spirit and Word was a major hermeneutical issue of the Reformation. Anabaptists were not alone in struggling to give sufficient room for the Spirit, while safeguarding the normative authority of Scripture. Not surprisingly, they were charged with erring in both directions, accused of both literalism and spiritualism.

There were significant differences among Anabaptist groups and between first-generation and second-generation practices. Accusations of literalism generally focus on Swiss Brethren and Hutterites; accusations of spiritualism on South German Anabaptists and some followers of Hoffman. Spiritualism, more characteristic of the first generation, was gradually replaced by reliance on accepted interpretations.

However, labeling Anabaptism as literalistic or spiritualistic fails to reflect its diversity. Some groups inclined toward literalism to be faithful to Christ's commands; others relied on the Spirit to communicate the essential truth of God's revelation. In certain groups, both tendencies were held in tension or were used without attempting to harmonize them, regarding reliance on the Spirit and adherence to the letter as complementary (Murray 2000: 125-31).

Among Swiss Anabaptists, Mantz and Grebel were on the literalist wing; Hubmaier and Sattler were more moderate, although Sattler is often characterized as a literalist by comparison with others. Hutterites, too, were generally on the literalist wing. The suggestion that the written word was necessary but secondary, rejection of simple literalism, and the terminology of "inner" and "outer" are associated with South German Anabaptists. Among these, Hut, Denck, Jakob Kautz, and Hans Bünderlin were nearer the spiritualist wing, whereas Melchior Rinck was closer to the Swiss approach. Dutch Anabaptism was divided between spiritualists (like Hoffman, Obbe Philips, Joris, and Nicolaas van Blesdijk) and more literalist interpreters (like Menno Simons and Dirk Philips). The center ground was held by Marpeck, who, in debates with Schwenckfeld, the Reformers, and the Swiss Brethren, sought a balanced position (Swartley 1984: 91-105; Snyder 1995: 51-100).

Anabaptists' emphasis on the Spirit in hermeneutics owed much to the influence of Karlstadt, Müntzer (Snyder 1995: 25-31), and Schwenckfeld (Snyder 1995: 35-38) on different sections of the movement. Another significant factor, anticlericalism, was evident in both Anabaptism and the peasants' movement. Hermeneutical reliance on the Spirit enfranchised uneducated believers, challenging the clergy's interpretative monopoly. Anabaptists believed that relying on the Spirit would result in more faithful application of Scripture than relying on tradition, learning, or human reason (Goertz 1996: 36-67).

The emphasis on the Spirit in the Anabaptists' hermeneutics is reflected in numerous references in their writings. Reliance on the Spirit was expected to check naive and legalistic interpretations: believers who, left to their own resources, would misinterpret or simply not comprehend Scripture could rely on the Spirit for insight. Openness to the Spirit was preferred to reliance on education and scholarship: the Spirit was the true teacher and guide, on whom educated and illiterate believers alike should depend. There was generally no opposition between reliance on the Spirit and common sense; approaches that polarized Spirit and reason were unwelcome. The Spirit's work included not only explanation of Scripture but also conviction and persuasion, so that interpreters acted on it. Furthermore, an important consequence of reliance on the Spirit was openness to correction and fresh revelation (Murray 2000: 131-38).

Safeguards were built into this principle and guidelines were issued to protect the unwary from error. Marpeck warned interpreters not to force the Spirit or allow personal desires to masquerade as the Spirit's leading. Menno urged that reason be used to check against wild interpretations. Locating primary interpretative authority in the congregation was another safeguard; as it pondered Scripture, the congregation could anticipate the Spirit's direction in both individual contributions and emerging consensus (Swartley 1984: 73).

Anabaptists shared in contemporary discussions about the relationship between Word and Spirit. These discussions were given urgency by the recovery of the Bible, the experience of spiritual phenomena, and challenges to traditional ecclesiastical authority. They offered alternatives to the Reformers, who seemed to give inadequate room to the Spirit, and to the Spiritualists, who seemed to give inadequate room to the Word. Sometimes the Anabaptists erred in the direction of spiritualism or literalism; sometimes they were naïve or over-confident. But many Anabaptists demonstrated a firm commitment to both Word and Spirit, and challenged anyone who was tempted to denigrate either (Murray 2000: 139-54).

Congregational Hermeneutics

What Anabaptists believed about ecclesiology, the Spirit, and the interpretative competence of all required a communal approach to biblical interpretation. Anticlerical and egalitarian impulses in the movement and its social context militated against tendencies to restrict the teaching office to recognized leaders. Anabaptist congregational hermeneutics represented a refusal to endorse the Spiritualists' autonomous individualism, a rejection of the Catholics' drastic curtailing of private interpretation by the authority of ecclesiastical traditions, and a qualification of the Reformers' application of *sola scriptura*, which disenfranchised most Christians and replaced priestly tyranny with a tyranny of the preacher (Snyder 1995: 299-364).

Some Reformers initially held similar views advocating the congregation's interpretative role and minimizing the rights of secular authorities. But as the Reformers abandoned these positions, the Anabaptists moved in the opposite direction, denying secular rulers jurisdiction over biblical interpretation. The concomitant divergence over ecclesiology ensured that only Anabaptists would explore congregational hermeneutics. For Anabaptists, a hermeneutical community must comprise committed believers eager to obey Scripture and open to the Spirit. Anabaptists assumed such congregations existed. The Reformers, adopting a gradualist approach to reform and territorial rather than believers' churches, lacked congregations capable of functioning as hermeneutical communities.

Commitment to congregational hermeneutics was not uniform throughout the movement. Some, especially South Germans, emphasized the Spirit's role in the individual; others, including Hoffman, Joris, other Melchiorite leaders, and the Hutterites, restricted interpretation to designated leaders. But *some* interpretative role for the congregation was recognized widely throughout the sixteenth century (Packull 1977: passim).

The Swiss explored this extensively. Their congregations developed in opposition to the experiences of churches that disallowed multiple participation, discussion, and communal judgment. This was regarded as contrary to Scripture, a form of robbery or bondage. Anabaptist congregations expected many to participate, using gifts they had received and being sensitive to the Spirit's prompting. Their earliest "congregational order" assumes a communal process of interpreting Scripture (Peachey 1971: 5-22).

Some German groups adopted similar practices. Marpeck insisted that congregations rather than Spirit-filled individuals were responsible for establishing and expounding the truth. Comparing the Swiss order with the orders used by the Hutterites and Marpeck's congregations indicates the foundational influence of the Swiss order. Similar phrases are found in all three orders, encouraging various people to teach and congregations to weigh contributions carefully, although most Hutterite communities depended heavily on chosen leaders. That congregational interpretation was practiced among some Dutch Anabaptists is clear from critical comments in Obbe Philips's *Confession:* whereas the Swiss regarded multiple participation as evidence of a "spiritual congregation," a disillusioned Obbe regarded multiple participation as evidence of the opposite (Baylor 1991: 224-25).

Sensitive congregational leadership was crucial for congregations operating as hermeneutical communities: the leaders' task was to guide rather than to dominate and to be facilitators rather than sole participants. Their primary concern was to ensure that Scripture was being read and, through the contributions of all members, understood and applied. This leadership style differed greatly from that of mainstream Reformation pastors. Itinerant leaders, such as Conrad Grebel (Ruth 1975), Hans Hut, and Hans Denck, and theologically trained pastors, like Balthasar Hubmaier, were respected teachers. Their contributions carried great weight and might discourage contributions from others who thought differently. However, the readiness of such leaders to submit to corporate discernment ensured that their prominence did not entirely undercut the congregational principle (Murray 2000: 157-65).

Menno agreed that congregations needed teachers, but he did not ex-

pect teachers to dominate proceedings. Hubmaier wanted scholars to help
with technical details, such as how to translate passages, and to explain how
others had interpreted passages, but not to override other members of the
congregation. In groups relating to Marpeck, leadership was regarded as a gift
and was allowed to operate freely, but leaders remained subject to the authority of the community. Congregational hermeneutics does not require that every contribution carry equal weight but that every contribution be weighed
(Klassen and Klaassen 1978: 56).

It is unclear how widespread communal hermeneutics was, how firmly
it was rooted in Anabaptist congregations, or how long it survived. In South
German and Melchiorite congregations, with strong spiritualist and prophetic influences, congregational impulses flourished only briefly. However,
the loss of leaders through persecution may have led to a greater practice of
communal hermeneutics. In many Swiss, German, and Dutch congregations
where communal hermeneutics was practiced in the early years, it was gradually replaced by reliance on congregational leaders and received understandings of Scripture. Nevertheless, in later sixteenth-century accounts of Anabaptist worship services, there are glimpses of congregations still operating as
hermeneutical communities (Oyer 1998).

Another indication that some Anabaptist leaders encouraged dialogue
and interaction is their frequent exhortation that readers search Scripture
themselves to see if what their leaders were teaching them was correct. This
openness to correction is especially evident in Marpeck's writings, but similar
statements appear in Swiss and Austrian branches of the movement. Menno
professed openness to correction and further revelation. While he fell short of
this ideal, his writings indicate that openness to correction was influential in
Dutch Anabaptism. Such statements are conspicuous by their absence in the
writings of Reformers, who saw their task as providing authoritative interpretations (Klassen and Klaassen 1978: 177, 204, 260-61).

Criticisms of communal hermeneutics focus on the definition of the
congregation and tendencies towards fragmentation, disagreement, and inco-
herence within Anabaptism. Anabaptist ecclesiology guaranteed substantial
local autonomy: each congregation was responsible for decisions about doctrine, conduct, and biblical interpretation. But if each was hermeneutically
autonomous and if each claimed the Spirit's anointing, who was to judge
matters? Divisions — some bitter — over issues of interpretation troubled
Anabaptists. The mistakes, disagreements, and poor interpretations that
sometimes occurred suggest Anabaptist leaders underestimated potential
problems. Differences in emphasis, strong and impatient leaders, cultural
variations, and the pressure of persecution threatened to tear Anabaptism

apart. But it survived, albeit battered and bloodied, and left a coherent legacy: there was, despite serious problems, remarkable unity across the movement (Klaassen 1981a: 198).

Another criticism argues that congregational hermeneutics simply pools ignorance. However, Anabaptists, who were very biblically literate, believed that interpretation involved listening to the Spirit and that Scripture was simple enough for all to understand, at least in part. Studying together enabled each to share insights provided by the Spirit. Seeking consensus helped them discard unreliable interpretations, and confirm those that were helpful. Furthermore, the Spirit's presence was promised in a special way in the congregation. Congregations were undoubtedly prone to domination by vocal characters and those with more experience or education. But the strength of communal hermeneutics was its refusal to exclude its weakest members, since the Spirit was available to all. The ploughboy might sometimes understand Scripture better than the theologian (Pipkin and Yoder 1990: 51).

A limitation on Anabaptist practice was the virtual exclusion of Christian wisdom from prior centuries. The focus was on present consensus, and little attention was given to past consensus. Seeking freedom from binding traditions and believing the church was fallen, Anabaptists drew sparingly on the wisdom of earlier Christians. This released them from dependence on past authorities and freed them to make fresh discoveries, but it also impoverished their interpretation and deprived them of scholarly and spiritual counsel.

Thus, there were weaknesses in this communal approach. Anabaptists had few precedents as they pioneered it, but those who persevered gradually refined it. It also had significant strengths, especially their conviction that every member of the congregation could contribute to the interpretative task and their openness to correction. Their concern for truth, readiness to listen to anyone under the authority of Scripture, and willingness to consider fresh interpretations rather than squeezing texts into conformity with set creeds present a continuing challenge to biblical interpreters in succeeding generations (Murray 2000: 171-83).

Hermeneutics of Obedience

Anabaptists often complained that biblical interpretation was divorced from application: emphasis was placed on attaining a theoretical understanding of Scripture rather than putting the teaching of Scripture into practice. They were unimpressed by the quality of discipleship in state churches and by the Reformers' ethical teaching; they concluded that these factors indicated deficiencies in the way Scripture was interpreted. Reformers argued that sound doctrine was the basis for Christian lifestyle; Anabaptists were unconvinced that the Reformers' teachings resulted in true discipleship (Murray 2000: 186-94).

This concern led Anabaptists to emphasize the clarity of Scripture. They understood that there were difficulties in interpreting Scripture, but highlighting interpretative problems was a disincentive to obeying Scripture. Uncertainties about the meanings of certain texts encouraged hesitation rather than bold and radical action. Emphasizing that much of Scripture was easy to understand and needed simply to be obeyed, not endlessly debated, removed excuses for compromise, delay, and inaction. Scripture, they insisted, was difficult to apply, because of its costly challenge, but was generally not difficult to understand. Anabaptists were frustrated by the Reformers' apparent evasion of biblical challenges under cover of discussions about precise meanings of texts (van Braght 1950: 469).

The decision to locate interpretative authority in congregations should be similarly understood. Academics were poorly placed to test the validity of their conclusions: although experts in linguistics, theology, and church history, their interpretative context was theoretical rather than practical. Congregations were better placed to test the adequacy of interpretations in their communal life, worship, and witness. The emphasis within communal hermeneutics was on application, rather than on interpretation.

Marpeck rejected any division between interpretation and application. Interpreters should not explain Scripture and abdicate responsibility for applying it. Not only was deference to secular authorities unbiblical and detrimental to reformation, but it also drove an unacceptable wedge between interpretation and application (Klassen and Klaassen 1978: 179, 299).

This is why the Swiss Brethren deserted Zwingli. On the interpretation of Scripture, Zwingli and the Brethren essentially agreed, but they profoundly disagreed about its application. Zwingli left application to the Zurich City Council, but the Brethren regarded this as compromise that undermined the hermeneutical process by stopping short of obedient action. Zwingli was concerned about implementing Scripture, but accepted a distinction between explaining its meaning and applying its implications. This the Brethren rejected: interpretation and application were both vital aspects of a single process (Estep 1976: 15-22).

The contrast between the Reformers' theological approach and the more pragmatic Anabaptist approach reappears in the writings of Menno Simons and Dirk Philips. Their interpretation was interrelated with their involvement in congregations. Tentative understandings of Scripture were tested and refined as Menno and Philips explored practical implications in congregational settings, and the congregations' needs and concerns posed questions and perspectives with which to approach Scripture.

Anabaptists also regarded obedience as a crucial prerequisite of hermeneutics: ethical qualifications took precedence over intellectual abilities or official appointments. Living in obedience to Christ and submission to Scripture were more important than education, linguistics, or doctrinal correctness. Hut argued that discovering the truth was achieved not by studying in universities but by following and obeying Christ. Menno argued that teachers should be judged by their obedience to Scripture: only those whose lives showed they were regenerate should be trusted as interpreters. Dirk Philips insisted on two qualifications: an experience of the Spirit, and an upright life (Klaassen 1981a: 87).

One aspect of this ethical qualification, which by definition excluded state church preachers, was that interpreters must be free from the influence of secular power and vested interests. Those wary of offending the authorities or disturbing the status quo were not free to interpret faithfully. Issues of finance and safeguarding a comfortable lifestyle were sometimes seen as determinative. These issues were raised throughout the Anabaptist movement (Klassen and Klaassen 1978: 299). This emphasis on obedience constituted an attempt to protect congregations from the falsehood that would creep in if ethical criteria were absent. Only those actively committed to discipleship could be trusted to interpret Scripture. They might be less equipped academically, but their ignorance was not as perilous as the falsehood taught by scholars who were not truly following Christ.

Readiness to obey texts being studied was vital for effective interpretation. Without such obedience, one could expect no help from the Spirit and consequently no real understanding of Scripture. Contrary to accusations, Anabaptists did not suggest that interpreters must be perfect before they could understand Scripture. They differentiated between occasional sins, which did not disqualify interpreters, and a sinful lifestyle, which did. Menno taught that blindness resulted from sinful living, since interpreters wanted to justify their sinfulness, not to understand and obey God's will. Anabaptists regarded obedience to one's present understanding of Scripture and openness to obeying new understandings (appropriated by faith, eager desire, and diligent study) as hermeneutical prerequisites. They were confident such obedience would find a response from God, from whom true interpretation came (Swartley 1984: 65).

Obedience played another crucial role in Anabaptist hermeneutics: interpretations were subject to ethical testing before they could be accepted.

Menno and Dirk Philips placed great weight on the ethical consequences of interpretations and discounted any that led to unacceptable results. This principle was connected with Anabaptist christocentrism: interpretations were judged by how they related to the life and teachings of Jesus. Conformity to Christ, rather than to abstract ethical norms, was the plumbline Anabaptists used to measure proffered interpretations (Murray 2000: 194-97).

Although both the Reformers and the Anabaptists examined the ethical consequences of interpretations, they disagreed about what norms to apply. For the Reformers, social stability was crucial. For Anabaptists, obedience to Christ's specific teachings and imitation of his lifestyle outweighed social stability, as the congregations committed themselves to establishing a new social order (in their churches, at least), rather than preserving the existing one. They can be criticized for failing to apply Scripture to social and political issues beyond their own communities, but freedom from concern about maintaining social and ecclesiastical givens enabled them to consider interpretations others excluded as dangerous and destabilizing.

Various criticisms can be leveled against this approach. First, although interminable discussion about understanding to the detriment of application is problematic, a balance between these is possible. Until some understanding of Scripture is attained, activism and superficial applications are unfruitful. A hermeneutical spiral, whereby action and reflection mutually increase understanding and obedience, is better than the virtual opposition of these elements.

Second, Anabaptists seem insufficiently aware of the subtlety of sin and weakness of the human will. Their ethical expectations were inevitably selective, so they judged interpreters and interpretations by selective criteria.

Third, their identification of falsehood, not ignorance, as the enemy failed to consider the possibility of would-be disciples honestly believing untruth or interpreting Scripture wrongly.

Fourth, evaluating interpretations by their ethical results presupposes prior commitments and risks subjecting Scripture to human opinions about its meaning. Focusing on Jesus as the norm provided some protection, in that these presuppositions were christocentric; however, if Jesus is interpreted in light of the same presuppositions, a vicious circle results. If, prior to coming to the biblical text, we have settled ethical commitments that preclude any possible interpretation that contradicts or challenges these commitments, we fail to engage openly with the text itself. If we base such ethical commitments on presuppositions about the example and teaching of Jesus but do not allow these presuppositions to be open to challenge by texts about the example and teaching of Jesus, christocentrism is no protection against eisegesis.

Finally, focusing on ethics can hinder encountering the Christ to whom

Scripture points. The Anabaptists' experience of the Spirit provided some protection against this, but the danger remains that even Christ-centered principles might obscure Christ himself (Murray 2000: 201-202).

Nevertheless, this emphasis on obedience was a significant feature of Anabaptist hermeneutics, which challenged traditional approaches to biblical interpretation by teaching that application was integral to interpretation; emphasizing ethical, rather than academic, qualifications for interpreting; and insisting that Christians operate with an epistemology of obedience. Anabaptist hermeneutics also provide a historical basis for considering contemporary movements that emphasize reflection on action rather than the traditional movement from theory to practical application (Swartley 1984: 45-61).

THE CONTINUING CONTRIBUTION
OF ANABAPTIST HERMENEUTICS

The six principles described above were all operative within the Anabaptist movement in its early years, but the continuing hermeneutical tradition derived from this period has been selective. The congregational testing of these hermeneutical principles led to some of them being abandoned or recast. The disappearance of apocalyptic and spiritualist groups resulted in their hermeneutical approaches being discredited and discarded; the balance between Word and Spirit shifted toward the former. The charismatic phase developed into a settled tradition, in which widespread interpretative enfranchisement and experience of communal hermeneutics were largely replaced by the authority of leaders and accepted interpretations. But the legacy of the early years continues to inspire some interpreters today (Murray 2000: 206-18).

Anabaptist hermeneutics can be understood as comprising not six principles, but rather six areas where competing tendencies were held in creative tension. Thus, the tension between adherence to the letter and reliance on the Spirit characterized the whole movement. Some groups emphasized one more than the other, but throughout the movement this tension was maintained in a way that differentiated Anabaptist hermeneutics from competing alternatives. Similarly, the tension between enfranchising all to interpret and relying on trusted teachers was resolved differently in various times and places. But agreement that enfranchisement was vital and attempts to explore its communal dimension differentiated Anabaptism from the Reformers' preacher/scholar domination and the Spiritualists' individualism.

For Anabaptist hermeneutics to be a useful contemporary resource, we must ask whether these principles can be combined into an integrated hermeneutical approach. Surveys of Anabaptist hermeneutics face two temptations, both of which result in artificiality. One is to imagine that Anabaptists developed a fully integrated hermeneutic in which the six principles were carefully synthesized. The other is to imagine that Anabaptists operated with distinct and unconnected principles and to treat them in isolation.

Anabaptist hermeneutics was not a unified or fully integrated system. It developed in piecemeal fashion under pressurized circumstances and among diverse groups. Common convictions, however, produced an approach to biblical interpretation in which various principles acted as checks and balances. Not all were operative in every Anabaptist group, nor was the balance between them uniform, nor was their integration often explicit. But from the movement as a whole emerges a paradigm offering a more sophisticated and nuanced framework than any sixteenth-century congregation would have recognized, but which is nevertheless true to the spirit and direction of Anabaptist hermeneutics (Snyder 1995: 365-96). The synthetic model that can be extracted from Anabaptist hermeneutical principles and practices is that of a Spirit-filled disciple, confidently interpreting Scripture within a community of such disciples, aware that Jesus Christ is the center from which the rest of Scripture must be interpreted (Augsburger 1967: passim).

This approach had weaknesses:

- marginalization of scholarship, depriving Anabaptist communities of helpful tools for interpreting Scripture,
- inadequate handling of the OT and lack of interest in applying Scripture to society, and
- tendencies toward literalism and legalism that hindered a more sophisticated approach, not necessarily to be equated with dilution and evasion.

However, even these inadequacies contain important warnings. First, the development of more sophisticated methodologies has demonstrated the relevance of the Anabaptists' suspicions about dilution and evasion. Second, the history of the interpretation of the OT and its use to justify many practices that cannot be supported on NT grounds underscores the Anabaptists' concern about its misuse. Third, a mutually helpful relationship between scholars and congregations has still not been satisfactorily established.

Anabaptism was one of several movements between the fourth and sixteenth centuries that rejected the Constantinian synthesis. Although detailed analysis of earlier radical movements is rarely possible because of the paucity of surviving records, there are indications that these movements employed similar hermeneutical principles (see Murray 2003). Anabaptist hermeneutics represents the suppressed but persistent testimony of many other marginalized groups, a non-Constantinian hermeneutical tradition broader and longer than that embodied in sixteenth-century Anabaptism alone.

The primary contribution of Anabaptism to contemporary hermeneutics is as a conversation-partner, offering fresh historical perspectives on issues debated in the sixteenth century but unresolved centuries later and providing surprisingly relevant insights on issues that have emerged in recent decades. And because Anabaptist insights are appreciated across an unusually wide range of traditions, Anabaptist hermeneutics can be a catalyst for interaction between those who would not normally be conversation-partners, encouraging them to learn from each other (Murray 2000: 220-53).

BIBLIOGRAPHY

Augsburger, M. S.
1967   *Principles of Biblical Interpretation.* Scottdale: Herald.

Baylor, M. G. (ed. and trans.)
1991   *The Radical Reformation.* Cambridge: Cambridge University Press.

Clasen, C.-P.
1972   *Anabaptism: A Social History, 1525-1618.* Ithaca: Cornell University Press.

Davis, K. R.
1973   *Anabaptism and Asceticism.* Scottdale: Herald.

Deppermann, K.
1987   *Melchior Hoffman.* Trans. M. Wren; Edinburgh: Clark.

Estep, W. R. (ed.)
1976   *Anabaptist Beginnings (1523-1533).* Nieuwkoop: De Graaf.

Fast, G., and G. A. Peters (trans.)
2001   *Biblical Concordance of the Swiss Brethren, 1540.* Ed. C. A. Snyder. Kitchener: Pandora.

Fiorenza, E. S.
1984   *Bread Not Stone.* Boston: Beacon.

Friesen, A.
1998   *Erasmus, the Anabaptists, and the Great Commission.* Grand Rapids: Eerdmans.

Furcha, E. J. (ed. and trans.)
1988   *Selected Writings of Hans Denck, 1500-1527.* Lewiston: Mellen.

Goertz, H.-J.
1996   *The Anabaptists.* Trans. T. Roberts. London: Routledge.

Harder, L. (ed.)
1985   *The Sources of Swiss Anabaptism.* Scottdale: Herald.

Klaassen, W.
1966   "Speaking in Simplicity: Balthasar Hubmaier." *MQR* 40: 139-47.

Klaassen, W. (ed.)
1981a   *Anabaptism in Outline.* Scottdale: Herald.
1981b   *Sixteenth Century Anabaptism: Defences, Confessions and Refutations.* Trans.
        F. Friesen. Waterloo: Institute of Anabaptist and Mennonite Studies.

Klaassen, W., W. Packull, and J. Rempel (trans.)
1999   *Later Writings by Pilgram Marpeck and his Circle* 1. Kitchener: Pandora.

Klassen, W., and W. Klaassen (eds. and trans.)
1978   *The Writings of Pilgram Marpeck.* Scottdale: Herald.

Krahn, C.
1981   *Dutch Anabaptism.* Scottdale: Herald.

Liechty, D.
1989   *Andreas Fischer and the Sabbatarian Anabaptists.* Scottdale: Herald.

Murray, S. W.
2000   *Biblical Interpretation in the Anabaptist Tradition.* Waterloo: Pandora.
2003   "Faith, Church and Nation: An Anabaptist Perspective." Presented to the Commis-
        sion on Faith, Church and Nation, September 2003. London: Anabaptist Network.
        = http://www.anabaptistnetwork.com/node/view/93].

Oyer, J. S.
1998   "Early Forms of Anabaptist *Zeugnis* after Sermons." *MQR* 72: 449-54.

Packull, W. O.
1977   *Mysticism and the Early South German-Austrian Anabaptist Movement, 1525-1531.*
        Scottdale: Herald.
1995   *Hutterite Beginnings.* Baltimore: Johns Hopkins University Press.

Peachey, P.
1971   "Answer of Some Who Are Called (Ana)baptists: Why They Do Not Attend the
        Churches: A Swiss Brethren Tract." *MQR* 45: 5-32.

Pearse, M.
1998   *The Great Restoration.* Carlisle: Paternoster.

Philips, D.
1992   *The Writings of Dirk Philips, 1504-1568.* Ed. and trans. C. J. Dyck, W. E. Keeney, and
        A. J. Beachy. Scottdale: Herald.

Pipkin, H. W., and J. H. Yoder (eds. and trans.)

1990 *Balthasar Hubmaier, Theologian of Anabaptism*. Scottdale: Herald.

Riedeman, P.

1970 *Account of Our Religion, Doctrine, and Faith*. Rifton: Plough.

Rowland, C., and M. Corner

1990 *Liberating Exegesis*. London: SPCK.

Ruth, J. L.

1975 *Conrad Grebel, Son of Zurich*. Scottdale: Herald.

Simons, M.

1956 *The Complete Writings of Menno Simons, c. 1496-1561*. Ed. J. C. Wenger; trans. L. Verduin. Scottdale: Herald.

Snyder, C. A.

1991 "Orality, Literacy and the Study of Anabaptism." *MQR* 65: 371-92.

1995 *Anabaptist History and Theology: An Introduction*. Kitchener: Pandora.

Snyder, C. A. (ed.)

2001 *Sources of South German/Austrian Anabaptism*. Trans. W. Klaassen, F. Friesen, and W. O. Packull. Kitchener: Pandora.

Swartley, W. M. (ed.)

1984 *Essays on Biblical Interpretation: Anabaptist-Mennonite Perspectives*. Elkhart: Institute of Mennonite Studies.

Van Braght, T. J.

1950 *Martyrs' Mirror*. Trans. Joseph F. Sohm. Scottdale: Mennonite.

Waite, G. K. (ed. and trans.)

1994 *The Anabaptist Writings of David Joris, 1535-1543*. Waterloo: Herald.

Wenger, J. C.

1973 "An Early Anabaptist Tract on Hermeneutics." *MQR* 42: 26-44.

Williams, G. H.

1992 *The Radical Reformation*. Kirksville: Sixteenth Century Journal Publishers.

Yoder, J. H. (ed. and trans.)

1977 *The Schleitheim Confession*. Scottdale: Herald.

CHAPTER 15

Biblical Interpretation
in the Catholic Reformation

Guy Bedouelle

The term "Counter-Reformation" designates Catholicism's reaction to the political, theological, and cultural shock of the Protestant Reformation. This reaction, until recently almost unanimously accepted as coming after the years 1520-40, has become the object of much reflection. Religious history of the fifteenth and sixteenth centuries has shown how, at the heart of the Roman Church, its renewal after the Council of Trent was grafted onto far older movements, such as the religious orders, ancient and more recent, the spirituality of the laity, and the return to the ancient languages and the classical authors, pagan and Christian. Thus, a "*Catholic* Reformation" had been gathering momentum for a long time. Nevertheless, we must focus on the results of the Council of Trent to see how this impetus was implemented by the papacy and by the bishops, once they had become aware of it.

But one cannot deny that along with this movement, attitudes arose from reaction against, aversion to, or fear of Protestant intuitions and convictions that justify the name "*Counter*-Reformation." In applying this distinction to the domain of the Bible, we could say, on the one hand, that the exegesis of the Bible for the purposes of teaching and preaching stemmed rather from the *Catholic* Reformation. On the other hand, interdiction or at least warnings against translations into national languages and their use in the liturgy arose from Protestant claims, and subsequently became part of the *Counter*-Reformation. It will be important in these pages to specify, when we

---

Translated by Schuyler Kaufman.

can, whether the uses being described belong to the *Catholic* or the *Counter-Reformation*.

This Reformation was laboriously developed in the second half of the sixteenth century, became established in the first third of the seventeenth century, around 1630-40, and waned around the turn of the seventeenth and eighteenth centuries. Here we will consider the interpretation of the Catholic Bible from the Council of Trent, which began in 1545 and came to an end in 1563, up to what is conventionally called "the crisis of the European Conscience," which the French historian Paul Hazard (1990) places between 1680 and 1715. To make it more concrete, we shall focus on the period that extends, globally, between the sums of biblical knowledge that were the *Bibliotheca Sancta* of Sixtus of Sienna, dating from 1566, and *L'Histoire critique du Vieux Testament* (*Critical History of the Old Testament;* 1st ed. 1678), or *L'Histoire critique des principaux commentateurs du Nouveau Testament* (*Critical History of the Principal Commentators of the New Testament,* 1693), written by Richard Simon.

The parts of Europe in which the Catholic Reformation was implemented were determined by the principle of *cuius regio, eius religio* (the religion of each country is the religion of its prince). They included the Latin nations Italy and Spain (to which Portugal was annexed 1580-1688) and the latter's possessions in America from Mexico to the southern part of the Americas. Catholic France contained a Calvinist minority protected by the Edict of Nantes (which was revoked at the end of our period in 1685), to which Canada, France's colony in North America, must be added. Some of the lands administered by the Hapsburgs in central Europe were once part of the Protestant Reformation but became "recatholicized." In the same period, Poland, which absorbed Lithuania in 1569, also attempted a penetration into Orthodox lands. More specific cases included the Catholic cantons of Switzerland and Ireland under English rule.

If there is a Catholic interpretation of the Bible, there is also a "Catholic Bible," the contents of which were defined by the Council of Florence in 1442 (Gill 1959). The Council of Trent's approval in 1546 simply repeated that (Jedin 1965: 2.81). This scriptural canon includes the texts known to Protestants as the Apocrypha. The notion of "deuterocanonical" books (those entered later into the Christian canon of Scripture) did not have the official stamp of the time, although this notion was common among Catholic exegetes. This Catholic Bible was usually the Latin Vulgate, which was declared "authentic" by the Council of Trent and which, in the version promulgated in 1592, was, in contrast to translations into the vernacular, accessible to the laity without restriction. The commentators were evidently attentive to the Hebrew and the Greek texts.

Having thus determined the boundaries of our study, we shall examine the bases of interpretation that the Council of Trent allowed. We shall then seek to clarify that interpretation, beginning with those who formulated it, and the mission that they assigned to the knowledge and transmission of the Bible. What forms of interpretation were proposed or utilized by pastors, theologians, mystics, missionaries, and, finally, scholars?

THE BASES OF SCRIPTURAL INTERPRETATION

The handful of Catholic bishops who met at Trent, in the north of Italy, on the borders between the Latin and Germanic territories, in mid-December 1545, faced a double quandary: How to proceed? And where to begin? These questions not only addressed the method but also implied a choice of priority for the council: should they reemphasize doctrine or denounce abuse? For strategic reasons, political authorities advocated beginning by repressing abuses, but the papacy maintained that the first duty of the council was to clarify dogma. Finally, a mixed solution was found and ratified on January 22, 1546: the council would take the line of reestablishing doctrine and denouncing abuses concerning relevant matters while maintaining an order that would keep the dogmatic priorities. One could think that this double approach would provide Tridentine texts with their operative force where preceding councils had run aground. Even if the circumstances prevented an exact parallel between theology and discipline from functioning completely in line with the council, we nevertheless see it fully applied to matters that concerned Scripture.

In effect, the council fathers found themselves in agreement quickly enough to begin the work of studying Scripture and finding the "abuse" concerning its application. Thus, on April 8, 1546, they voted on two questions, one on Scripture and the apostolic traditions and the other on the issues pertaining to reform within the church. On June 17, the fathers voted a primary text on original sin, whose understanding is grounds for differences among theologians, especially between Protestants and Catholics. In addition, the council adopted a text of "discipline" on teaching and preaching of Scripture. By then, the bases of scriptural interpretation of the Catholic Reformation were set, for the council did not return explicitly to these problems. Let us now examine principal features of this interpretation.

The Ecclesiastical Interpretation of the Bible

The first great debate hinged on the authority of the Bible as the foundation of revelation. Behind this, evidently, was the need to specify the position of the church in relation to the *sola scriptura* of the Protestant reformers. The council proclaimed that divine revelation reaches us "in the written books and in the unwritten traditions which have come down to us, having been received by the apostles from the mouth of Christ Himself, or from the apostles by the dictation of the Holy Spirit, and have been transmitted as it were from hand to hand" (Neuner and Dupuis 1976: 70). Thus, the council considered the holy books one part of revelation and the apostolic traditions as the other, partially in reference to John 20:30: "Jesus did in the sight of his disciples many other signs, which are not written in this book."

Certain points should be mentioned here. The council took care to reunite Scripture and apostolic traditions under the encompassing term "the gospel." It likewise refused to say that the truth of this gospel is found in line with one or the other, but, on the contrary, declared that they all be received "with the same feeling of piety and of respect" — which invalidates, or at least attenuates, the idea of the "two sources" that Catholic theology proposed later on. This gospel "is the source of all salvific truth and all moral law."

However, the council never intended to exclude the ecclesiastical traditions and the teaching of the church. Furthermore, these teachings added to the Bible and the apostolic traditions, grounding the Catholic faith on "the received councils, the constitutions and decrees of the popes and the holy Fathers, and the consensus of the Catholic Church."

The question remains: precisely who is in charge of the authentic interpretation of this corpus, and, in particular, of Holy Scripture? The answer is given by the decree *De reformatione,* voted on the same date as the preceding, on April 8, 1546 (Neuner and Dupuis 1976: 71), in which the council fathers decreed that

> no one, relying on his own prudence, twist Holy Scripture in matters of faith and morals that pertain to the edifice of Christian doctrine, according to his own mind, contrary to the meaning that holy mother the Church has held and holds — since it belongs to her to judge the true meaning and interpretation of Holy Scripture — and that no one dare to interpret the Scripture in a way contrary to the unanimous consensus of the Fathers. . . .

This text is the foundation on which the activity of the "Magisterium ordinarium" of the church is reaffirmed, essentially by the teaching of the

pope and the bishops, but also through the supervision of publications
through the Congregation of the Index. We see also the role assigned to the
tradition drawn from the teaching of the fathers of the church. But their
"unanimous consent" was rare, and in fact, when declared by the Magisterium, had to be taken for granted as the same as the "consensus of the Catholic Church" of which the previous texts speak. Behind this monopoly of the
right interpretation, there is, of course, the affirmation that this Magisterium
is assisted by the Holy Spirit. In a way, tradition is the manifestation of the
church receiving Scripture.

The Ecclesiastical Determination of the Bible

The Council of Trent was well aware that the actual determination of the biblical corpus, the canon, was the work of the church. That is what the discussion
on the canonicity of Scripture is about. There were numerous discussions at
Trent to decide whether the council should take into account differences in the
genre or the reception of the biblical books, of which the theologians had
warned. Some of the fathers proposed to distinguish the books that serve to
ground the faith from those intended to edify the faithful, differentiating a
"canon of faith" from a "canon of morals," those whose authors are known and
those that remain anonymous, those that the church first accepted and those
that followed. In the end, one argument dominated: to imply that distinctions
in the canon of Scripture are necessary would go against the intention of the
council, which was to strengthen and reassure believers. It would introduce an
element of doubt regarding certain books, whereas all are inspired by the Holy
Spirit. That is why the fathers revisited the list of the Council of Florence, adding discreetly the adjective "Davidic" to the Psalter and attributing fourteen
epistles to the Apostle Paul, including Hebrews. The council asked that they be
received as holy and canonical with all their parts "as one has customarily read
them in the Catholic Church," and as one finds them in the Vulgate.

The text on discipline also specifies the status of the Vulgate. The council showed itself prudent, proclaiming neither that this translation was above
reproach, nor that one must consider Jerome its author, nor that it could be
said in any manner to be inspired. The Vulgate was declared "authentic,"
which simply meant that it is a sufficiently faithful translation in the sense
that it contains no heresy and thus that it is fit to serve for argumentation,
catechism, and preaching. The council decided to establish a more accurate
version, not one corrected from the Hebrew and Greek, as called for by the
great humanists, following Valla, but one established according to the best

mss. The result, after much work and long delays, was the Sixto-Clementine edition, so named because it was overseen by the popes Sixtus V (in a rather maladroit fashion, it should be said) and Clement VIII, and published on November 9, 1592. Sixtus V had more success with the edition of the Septuagint, based essentially on the Codex Vaticanus Graecus 1209, which appeared in 1587, was well received, and proved to be lasting.

Thus, the church, having consolidated the biblical corpus in attesting its canonicity, supervised and determined the bases of biblical interpretation. There is nothing new there, but the insistence of the council on these points from the beginning of its work, clearly in opposition to the Protestant Reformers, accusing them of cutting off the integrity of the Bible and especially of twisting its orthodox sense. In other words, Scripture, according to the Tridentine spirit, should play a role in the frontlines of the Catholic rejuvenation through preaching, the task entrusted to pastors.

THE BIBLE OF THE PASTORS

On June 16, 1546, the Council of Trent mandated a program of biblical formation to ensure that "the celestial treasure of the holy books not be delivered to negligence." Each bishop was required to arrange for a chair in Holy Scripture to be conferred on a person dignified by his morals as well as by his learning.

But the preaching of the "Holy Gospel of Jesus Christ" is "no less necessary than the teaching of Scripture." This devolved squarely on the bishops, who had to assure it in person, but it was also entrusted to parish curates, who were held to it at least on Sundays and feast days. Here we see, in a more concrete way, the mandate to avoid deriving an interpretation in preaching that comes of one's own personal sense. This was avoided as carefully as clothing the sermon in subtleties so that the obvious and traditional meaning might be lost, because there is a sense of the biblical texts "that is held by and that holds the Holy Mother Church, to whom it appertains to judge of the true news of the Holy Scriptures." Catholic preaching was thus obligated to be biblical, clear, orthodox, and not driven by a desire to charm, self-glorify, or, worse, flatter and cheat, but to edify.

The Bible of the Catechism

Envisioned as early as 1546 and somewhat prepared at Trent, the writing of a catechism was ordered by the council just as it was concluding in 1563. The

Roman Catechism was made public in October 1566, and its purchase was then rendered obligatory by the diocesan synods. It was directed to the parish curates to be the base of their Sunday preaching and of their catechism of the sacraments during the centuries of the Catholic Reformation. Unlike a treatise of theology, it does not treat Scripture as such, but rather is permeated with Scripture, and quotes the fathers of the church.

The catechism is organized in four parts: the Apostles' Creed, the Seven Sacraments, the Decalogue, and the Lord's Prayer. It is inaccurate to claim that the catechism is a kind of biblical commentary, for it is rather a condensation of church teaching that mixes scriptural and patristic citations, theological considerations, and pastoral recommendations. At the same time, its authors affirm strongly at the end of their preface that "These four principal points, according to us, enclose all the pith of the Holy Scriptures and even all of Christianity."

The Languages of the Bible

How were biblical truths to be communicated to various Christian peoples who did not know the biblical languages — Hebrew, Greek, and Latin — used on the placard hung on the cross (John 19:20), according to an argument dear to enemies of translations into the common languages? The debate over translating the Bible is inseparable from that on the language in which the liturgy is celebrated (see Bedouelle 1990).

At the Council of Trent itself, the question of translation remained open and disputed. The Council showed great prudence, striving to avoid inflexible rules, even for the liturgy. Latin was chosen, according to the circumstances that prevailed at the time. This was not, however, because Latin was considered a sacred language. Rather, this was a "Counter-Reformation" attitude, since Protestant theologians, opposing traditional practice, held that the use of Latin must be abolished. The council itself did not pronounce on vernacular translations of the Bible.

Bishops and theologians were convinced that all translation is interpretation and that it was therefore necessary to be able to control it. At the same time, it was difficult not to admit that the propagation of Christianity was originally done in languages understood by those who were addressed with the biblical message. The enemies of translation in the sixteenth century invoked the lack of dignity, sacredness, and precision in national languages; what prevailed was the fear that, in the process, heresies would slip in. That is why all translations made by Protestants were forbidden to Catholics.

The Roman Church adopted an uncomfortable position. From the point of view of its own legitimation, it pronounced great praise of Holy Scripture, but its doctrinal prudence, the result of its confronting Protestant propaganda, or at least of being confronted by it, obliged the Roman Church to refuse to disseminate Scripture without rigorous control. At the same time, it fully realized the pastoral necessity for the laity to have access to the Bible. In effect, it was squaring the circle.

There are thus several levels. Evidently there was no general prohibition on reading Scripture. Clerics and scholars could have access to it through the Vulgate, or even the Hebrew and Greek texts; thus, it was the literate laity who were at stake. The first solution, judicial and always revocable, was given by the rules contained in the preface to the Roman Index of 1564. Rule IV declares: "If Bibles in vernacular languages are permitted to all without discrimination, there will result, due to human imprudence, more damage than profit." It thus anticipated the possibility of a bishop, on the favorable advice from a curate or confessor, authorizing some to read Bibles translated "by Catholic authors" if the readers judged capable of "strengthening [their] faith" by such reading. But the rule was hardened in 1590, and again in 1595, reserving authorization to the Holy See itself. The clumsiness of the procedure became overtly dissuasive and in fact acted to accentuate the separation of clerics and laity, or, more exactly, of scholars and ordinary people. The rule was applied unevenly, strictly in Spain, more flexibly in France.

It is true that there were generalized exceptions. Thus, English Catholics, often taking refuge in foreign lands, had access, for the purpose of preparing for all eventualities in argumentation and preaching, to a Catholic Bible, called the Rheims-Douai, after the seminaries in exile where it was composed. The NT was published in 1582 and the OT in 1600. Translated from the Vulgate, but with knowledge of the original texts, and accompanied by notes defending Catholic doctrine, this version is a text of combat as well as of edification. The moment the French Edict of Nantes was revoked in 1685, thousands of New Testaments and Psalters were distributed to new converts who renounced Protestantism. In 1757, Benedict XIV gave permission for all to read the Bible in the vernacular, so long as the text was accompanied by notes orienting any interpretation toward the Catholic tradition.

Even if personal reading of the Bible characterized the Protestant identity of the time, Catholics had, contrary to the generally held idea, excellent knowledge of the Bible by indirect means, and this is what the church advocated. Normally, in effect, the solution lay in vernacular preaching that included commentary on the Epistle and Gospel portions, which had been read in Latin. Many of the faithful could have global access to the Bible through the perspective of the paraphrased text, which is the method recommended by the Catholic Reformers, with the teaching of sacred history, which gave the majority what we call a truly biblical culture. Then there were hymns adapted from the Psalms, sacred theater, and especially images, not so much paintings as engravings, which were widespread. The Catholic Reformation was moreover attentive to their accuracy. While it did not create a centralized organ to control religious images, it gave bishops the mission to oversee their decency and orthodoxy. Indeed, devotions and legends surrounding the saints were not lacking in Catholicism of the sixteenth and seventeenth centuries, but they were not spread without supervision and did not contradict the interpretation of the Bible that the theologians enacted for the most limited circles.

THE BIBLE OF THE THEOLOGIANS

Near the end of the period we are considering, at the beginning of the eighteenth century, the commentators of the Bible could be defined as exegetes in the sense that we now understand it. They were first of all theologians who commented on the Bible and consulted the original languages. A unity of theological learning was retained, which made them accept Holy Scripture as the ultimate explanation of the world. It is true that verses of the Bible, often isolated from their context, served as an arsenal for controversy. However, it is more by overall interpretation — of nature, of civil government, and of salvation as it is believed in the Roman Church — that the Bible played a premier role in the development of the Catholic mentality in the sixteenth and seventeenth centuries, claiming that there exists an order, willed by God, created in the beginning, and then reestablished by the redemption.

The Cosmological Order

The Bible gives us access to knowledge of the world and of history. The commentators see in it the unfolding of knowledge from Adam, received by Moses, and amplified by divine revelation. The Italian Jesuit and papal legate to Poland and Muscovy, Antonio Possevino, published *Bibliotheca selecta de ratione studiorum (Selected Library of the Order of Studies)* in 1583. It was well known in Jesuit colleges, which educated the elite young men of the Counter-Reformation. This tract describes how Moses gave us access to the true knowledge of theology, certainly, but also of natural history, cosmology, geography, world history, law, poetry, medicine, and mathematics. Had Moses himself not been instructed in the science of the Egyptians, as the NT itself attests (Acts 7:22)? This is why those defending this idea find it so important to keep Moses as the authentic author of the Pentateuch. While the character of Solomon also takes up science and universal wisdom, he is seen above all as the model of governing according to God.

Of course, it is also by the Bible that other religions are judged. Catholic biblical scholars incorporated such religions in some form into the core of revelation. Thus, Daniel Huet, in the famous *Demonstratio evangelica* of 1679, opines that it is to Moses that one should refer the myths believed and celebrated in the different parts of the world. However distorted or badly transmitted, they have one common origin coming, one and all, from him. The Bible is thus at the same time the means and the evidence of a unity of the cosmos, of an order at the very heart of the diversity of cultures, and of a universality of Christian truth.

The Political Order

The autonomy of politics, its independence from the church, and also, according to Machiavelli, from current morality, was strongly contradicted by the Catholic theologians, who found their examples and their arguments in Holy Scripture. For these theologians, politics should be subsumed within the general government of the world by divine providence. In 1613, *De providentia Numinis et animi immortalitate libri duo adversus Atheos et Politicos,* a treatise by the Jesuit Leonard Lessius, sought to prove this role of Providence "against atheists and politicians."

After the assassination of Henri IV of France in 1610 and the trial and execution of Charles I in England in 1649, Catholic theologians turned their attention to teaching regarding tyrannicide, appealing more to history than to the Bible. However, they returned to Scripture in the great debate over the divine right of kings, which questions the indirect power of the papacy over temporal government. Cardinal Bellarmine, who also played a great role in the establishment of the text of the Vulgate, intervened vigorously in the debate to defend the ultimate arbitration of the papacy in Christian society. Bellarmine used numerous arguments from Scripture, although the framework of his reasoning was borrowed from Aristotle. The institution by God himself of leaders for Israel in the desert, then of judges and of kings in the promised land, shows the supernatural origin of authority. But in these passages of the OT, which, according to Bellarmine, the NT does not nullify, we see how holders of political power have the duty to protect the true religion. Should they not do this, they will be abandoned by God. The use of Romans 13, on obedience to civil authorities, combined with Matt. 18:17-18 on the power of the apostles to bind and loose, ends with the justification of the state as an instrument for the good of the church, or, more exactly, of Christianity.

All the treatises on the instruction of princes are based on Scripture, centered on the figure of Solomon, without forgetting the prophets who denounce alliances with pagans and recourse to false gods. The moment when the French monarchy attained its height of absolutism, Bossuet drafted the seminal work of the genre, *Politique tirée des propres paroles de l'Écriture sainte (Politics Drawn from the Actual Words of the Holy Scripture)*, published posthumously in 1709. Whereas his *Discours sur l'Histoire universelle (Discourse on Universal History)* of 1681 was based entirely on accounts from the Old Testament, the *Politics* (also addressed to the Dauphin, son of Louis XIV, whose tutor he was) was a selection of maxims and biblical episodes organized to perpetuate the idea of royalty, absolute but wise and benevolent, in the image of the divine government. The Bible is used to support absolutism, to be sure, but it primarily furnishes the prince with a mirror of duties and of virtues.

In his *Discours sur l'Histoire* and overall in his preaching and his controversy with Protestants, Bossuet considered civil and religious dissension, the breaking up into "sects," as largely due to individual interpretation of Holy Scripture. Without the teaching of the church and tradition based on the revealed texts, the Christian cannot but err on the way to salvation, which is the aim pursued by Holy Scripture.

The Doctrinal Order

The heirs of the Council of Trent, that is, Catholic theologians of the modern period, wanted to indicate to Christians the one way to salvation through the "true meaning of Scripture." The best known Jesuit biblical commentator, Juan Maldonado (Maldonatus) taught at Paris, at the Collège de Clermont. In his inaugural lecture of 1565 he opined that Protestants read Scripture without true qualification, for not only did their professors interpret Scripture, but also "their soldiers, merchants, tailors, carpenters, locksmiths," refuting the consequences that certain Reformers drew from the priesthood of all believers. He dedicated himself "to conserve our ancient religion, bequeathed from the beginning by the voice of Christ, next by writings of the Apostles, and the very Holy Fathers as by so many testaments." In addition, in his treatise *De constitutione theologiae (On the Constitution of Theology)*, Maldonado posed the problem of the "clarity of Scripture" *(claritas Scripturae)*, dear to

Reformers who believed, wrongly according to him, that they could thus affirm the simplicity of understanding Scripture. He then approached the ultimate question: How can we prove that it is through the Holy Spirit that we understand the Scriptures?" The response, of course, is the church, assisted by that very Holy Spirit.

However, Maldonado certainly guided the Catholic Reformation toward a serious and equally learned reading of the Bible by clerics in the course of their study and in their ministry. His own commentaries on the Prophets and above all on the Gospels provided the example of this work, strongly marked by refutation of the commentaries of the Protestant Reformers, especially of Calvin, whom he considered as "the noblest interpreter of the heretics."

In the first third of the seventeenth century, another Jesuit, a Flemish professor at Louvain and at the Roman College in Rome, Cornelius van den Steen, whose humanist name, *"à Lapide,"* means "from the stone," provided a commentary on practically the whole Bible, except for the book of Job and the Psalms. His work began with the 1614 edition of his commentary on the Pauline Epistles and came to an end with the publication of the last volume by his disciples after his death in 1637. The complete edition, continually republished throughout the eighteenth century, comprises eleven huge folio volumes (1908).

Following Bellarmine, who had been criticized for this same idea, Cornelius introduced an important distinction. He said that while the Law and the Prophets were the object of immediate and direct inspiration for the historical accounts and moral exhortations, it would be better to speak of the "assistance of the Holy Spirit." Nevertheless, for him, all science and knowledge are contained in the literal sense of Holy Scripture. He himself gave priority to the historical sense but did not refuse to serve the other traditional senses where they shed light on the text and on doctrine. But he disapproved of the allegorical sense, considering it closer to fantasy than to reality.

The Jesuits, as we have seen, distinguished themselves by making a certain specialty — indeed, almost a monopoly — of biblical study. They sought to demonstrate by Scripture, for the purpose of teaching it, the order of the doctrine of salvation as presented by the Catholic Church. At the end of the Catholic Reformation period, however, it was a French Benedictine, Augustin Calmet, who published his *Commentaire litteral sur tous les livres de l'Ancien et du Nouveau Testament (Literal Commentary on All the Books of the Old and the New Testament).* This French work appeared between 1707 and 1716 to great success. It is a work of extraordinary scholarship, aided and sustained by Calmet's confreres in the Benedictine abbeys, and includes Jewish and Protestant viewpoints on the texts he treated. This work, scientific, non-polemical, and intelligent, marked the entry of encyclopedic erudition into biblical interpretation. It also coincided with the decline of the Catholic Reformation.

THE BIBLE OF THE MYSTICS

The mystics provided one of the most powerful forces of the Catholic Reformation. These men and women were most often, but not exclusively, to be found in cloistered monasteries and convents. The phenomenon developed particularly in sixteenth-century Spain, especially among the Carmelites, and in seventeenth-century France, advanced by Francis de Sales (1567-1622) and Pierre de Bérulle (1575-1629) — as well as in Italy and Flanders.

In their approach to the Bible, there is a certain contrast between the men, often professors of theology and preachers familiar with Holy Scripture, and the women, who were restricted in their reading of the Bible to the vernacular. For example, the first biography of Teresa of Avila (1515-82) recounts that she dismissed a novice who wanted to keep her Bible. As a result, the question arose regarding the level of biblical knowledge that the Carmelites in sixteenth-century Spain could have had, for in their accounts and in their writings, they demonstrated a biblical knowledge that could hardly be called sparse.

Theirs was a profound grasp of the Bible, not merely book-based knowledge. Scripture reached these feminine cloisters primarily through the liturgy — the mass, the chanting of the liturgical hours, marked day after day by the recitation of certain texts — although they were in Latin — and through preaching and spiritual conferences. Normally letters of spiritual counsel cited the Bible. Yet John of the Cross (1542-91), for example, cited the Bible more often in his mystical works than in his letters of spiritual counsel. We also know that "biblical maxims" adorned the walls of the Carmelite convents and were thus incessantly read and memorized in the confined space of the cloister.

However, it is not so much the text of Scripture itself that is found at the origin of the spiritual experience of mystics as it is a particular biblical image. We find this in the method exemplified by the *Spiritual Exercises* of Ignatius Loyola (1491-1556), undoubtedly the most widely known work of the Catholic Reformation. Rather than a text, it is a landscape, a biblical episode, a parable, or even a religious setting which forms the basis for silent prayer. Yet, as described by those who have experienced it, at the onset of the mystical experience one finds Scripture. Verses come to mystics' minds with a new, fulfilling, existential meaning, most often, in Carmelite mysticism, culminating in a theology of Christ's cross, giving them the full vision of God's design for the world and providing the true key to interpretation.

When these mystics of the sixteenth century speak of Scripture, they give it a central role. When read in the tradition, it is "loving wisdom" for Teresa of Avila and a synonym of divine authority for John of the Cross. Indeed, the hermeneutical rule for mystics of that time is contained in one of the precepts that makes *The Imitation of Christ* of Thomas à Kempis (1380-1471) perennially read (1.5): "All Scripture must be read in the same Spirit as that which dictated it."

Thus, mystics do not propose one particular interpretation of Scripture; rather, they willingly accept the plurality and even the multiplicity of meanings. Their experience of God leads them to an intimate, personal understanding that has no real need of contact with the actual text of the Bible. Indeed, this insight into the divine mystery, springing from mystical experience, is spontaneously directed to the contents of Holy Scripture, which are rediscovered in some way.

The same character of internalization and experience may be found among French female mystics in the seventeenth century. But the attitude of the founders of the French mystical school is different, because a love of Scripture and a remarkable biblical culture could be found among them at that time. Reading the works of Francis de Sales (see Mackey 1892-1904; de Sales 1989), we notice the omnipresence of the Bible, with a particular affection for the Psalms and for the Song of Songs, which he had studied with the Benedictine scholar Gilbert Genébrard (1537-97) in 1584. Song of Songs, which is the preferred text of all the Catholic mystics, is very present in his *Treatise on the Love of God* (1616), which contains 1200 biblical citations.

Francis de Sales was only willing to enter into controversy with Protestants by using arguments taken from the Bible. In his preaching he declared he would give a "simple and clear" interpretation, and his outlines for sermons show how he conceived it under the three medieval forms of spiritual sense (allegorical, tropological, anagogical). His most important work for the dissemination of his spirituality is *L'Introduction à la vie dévote (The Introduction to the Devout Life)* (1609, ET 1989), which includes 250 citations from the Bible. Yet we find there the paradox of the Catholic attitude at this time. In this book there is only one short paragraph on Scripture, recommending to the devout, among all the counsels on moral life, liturgical practice, and a life of prayer: "Be devout to the Word of God, whether you hear it in easy conversation with your spiritual friends or you hear it in a sermon." In short, when one is a Catholic layperson in the seventeenth century, one speaks of the Scripture, one listens to it, one lives it intensely, but one does not read it.

The spirituality of the French school of the seventeenth century was learned from and permeated by the Bible. The early-eighteenth-century Jansenist current of Port-Royal (see Arnauld 1683) was fond of mystical and supernatural phenomena and was very committed to reading the Bible, for which it furnished the beautiful French translation of Lemaistre de Sacy between 1672 and 1684 (see chapter 16 below). The figure of Blaise Pascal (1623-62), whose scientific genius and power of thought illumined his time, demonstrated the importance of the Bible for a lay mystic who showed exceptional abilities. Self-taught in matters of Holy Scripture, Pascal drew from the Vulgate, from a polyglot Bible of the sixteenth century, and from the French translation of Louvain. His *Mémorial,* written in a night of ecstasy on November 23, 1654, is formed of some verses of the OT and the Gospel of John. His *Pensées,* which are fragments of an unfinished apology for Christianity, are the product of a hermeneutic inspired by Augustine at an innovative and traditional time. Sometimes literal, its force comes of what it retains of the essential: "Jesus Christ, on whom the two Testaments focus, the Old Testament as its expectation, the New as its model, both as their center."

THE BIBLE OF THE MISSIONARIES

The centuries of the Catholic Reformation saw a remarkable missionary expansion in America and in Asia. As to the New World, which opened to Europeans at the end of the fifteenth century, the question that first arose for the theologians was the absence of any reference to this continent in the Bible. The existence of the New World nullified the unity of the human race, which the Bible affirmed in the list of Noah's descendants (Gen. 10:32). Indeed, we find ingenious solutions, as there were enough mysterious names in the OT for those who sought to discover the Americas there. In any case, the principal position is clear: reality could not contradict Scripture, since it is the Bible itself which enlightens reality. Such is the position of the Jesuit José de Acosta in his *Historia Natural y moral de las Indias* (1590, reprinted 1892).

An even more difficult theological question was posed by the story of salvation: why has God apparently forgotten a whole continent while announcing redemption? The curate of the Beguinage of Anvers, John Frederick Lumnius, published (1567) a work on the last judgment and the "vocation" of the Indies. He read Matt. 20:1-16, the parable of the laborers invited to work in the vineyard, as the basis for his argument for an interpretation of the new circumstances of the times. According to the indirect sense that he drew:

The eternal and infallible wisdom foresaw that the unknown peoples stayed hidden in the very distant isles as if they stayed idle on a vacant lot all day. When evening came, although they only did the last of the work, they were the first to receive their wages. These workers — these are the peoples of the Indies.

What role did the Bible play in evangelization and the mission of the Catholic Reformation? In opposition to the excessively demanding *Requirimiento* (see Frohock 2004: 31) of the earlier times that recounted world history (somewhat abridged) from Adam to the pope in languages that were unintelligible to the natives, Bartolomé de Las Casas argued for a peaceful evangelization, proposing to follow to the letter the instructions in Matthew 10. This became the model for resistance to the Christian conquest and enslavement of the Indians and to colonization (see Frohock 2004: 33, 126-28). It also inspired the Jesuit missionaries and the establishment of "reductions" in Paraguay and in Brazil. In America, by reason of an evangelization opposed to the idolatrous paganism of the Indians, the doctrine was proposed in a direct fashion, but the Bible did not occupy a central place. When the Inca Garcilaso de la Vega drafted his *Commentarios reales,* published at the beginning of 1609, he did not use the Bible to find his analogies between Christianity and the native religions of Peru.

For various reasons, when missionaries wanted to announce the message of salvation in Asia, they again did not resort directly to Scripture. Scripture was inserted into the summaries of Christian doctrine, which gave it a place among the diverse points recommended for belief. This procedure of a *Compendium* of Christian verities was put into use throughout the missionary world. Thus the Jesuit Matteo Ricci, traveling to China in 1583, managed the following year to draft a small work in Chinese, *The True Meaning of the Lord of Heaven.* In it, certain Christian doctrines were proposed, even customs that were strange to the Chinese, such as ecclesiastical celibacy. Of course, doctrine presupposes Scripture, and Ricci made use of the Ten Commandments, yet there are only fifteen or so explicit biblical citations in his manual. The teaching of Christ's resurrection was delayed to a later stage, just as the Bible did not figure in the primary missionary catechism, while parallels with the doctrine of Confucius, as the Latins called him, are frequent.

Such "inculturation," for a progressive implantation in civilizations totally alien from the biblical world, prevented a direct transmission through the words and accounts of the Bible, save, perhaps, that of the creation. This was applied in Japan and in India. However, when Jerome Xavier was summoned to the court of the Great Mogul Akbar for the philosophical jousts that the royal syncretist was fond of, Xavier had his own treatise *Fuente de Vida (Source of Life)* translated. In this book, the Bible of the Christians is presented to a far greater extent, doubtless because it is compared with other sacred writings such as the Koran. Xavier then composed a *Mirror of the Sanctity of the Life of the Lord Jesus* (1602), which he also had translated into Persian, as he did for the Psalms and the Gospels.

THE BIBLE OF THE SCIENTISTS

At the beginning of the sixteenth century, Nicholas Copernicus issued his hypothesis of heliocentrism, which opposed the doctrine received from Ptolemy and Aristotle of a fixed earth at the center of the universe. The contradiction with Holy Scripture caused an immediate upheaval: do not Pss. 19:5-7 and 104:19 (in the Hebrew numeration) affirm that the earth is immobile and that the sun and the other stars move, and Josh. 10:12-13 that the sun halted temporarily?

Nevertheless, heliocentrism received scientific confirmation by observation of the sky through the telescope focused by Galileo Galilei, who presented the Copernican doctrine in several works. In his writings Galileo proposes a new hermeneutic, aspiring to be faithful, as he said on the day he abjured heliocentrism, "to all that the Holy Church holds, and preaches, and teaches." As early as December 1613, in a letter addressed to the Benedictine Benedetto Castelli, Galileo affirmed the constraining character of the laws of nature (which is also a book that God has given us; see Pedersen 1983). In case of apparent conflict, it was the literal interpretation of the Bible that must take precedence. He refined his hermeneutic in his letter to Christine of Lorraine, Grand Duchess of Tuscany, in 1615. In questions of natural order, what is said in Scripture is explicated by conformity to the opinions of the time when it was drafted, and on the level of comprehension of those to whom it was directed. The Scriptures have a finality that is religious and not scientific. This is what is meant by the famous expression of Cardinal Baronius, who cited Galileo: "The intention of the Holy Spirit is to teach us how we are to go to heaven, not how the heavens go."

Literal exegesis does not apply to certain texts of the Bible, which reflect too closely the mentality of their authors. Galileo could moreover rely on the decree of the Council of Trent on Scripture, because, as we have seen, it affirms, apparently in a restrictive fashion, that "The Gospel is the source of all salvific truth and of all moral law," and that the personal interpretation of the Bible is forbidden "in matters of faith and of morals."

Those censoring Galileo did not rally to this position. Numerous external factors were raised or assumed by historians of "the Galileo affair." At least for their censors, Galileo's opinions were not so different from those professed by Giordano Bruno, Tommaso Campanella, or Giulio Cesare Vanini, in a sometimes ingenious mélange of philosophy, hermetism, and scientific hypotheses, which had been condemned. In addition, the fact that Galileo was not a theologian himself seemed to challenge the clerical monopoly on Holy Scripture, which had been established in the Catholicism of the Counter-Reformation.

One need not assume that Galileo's argument led scholars toward a double truth, that of science and that of the Bible. The seventeenth-century Catholic remained convinced of the unity of the truth. Marin Mersenne, an eminent scholar and a member of the Minim order who corresponded with Descartes, Pascal, Torricelli, and others, altered this perspective: It is right, he wrote in the preface of his commentary on Genesis (1623; see also Yates 2001: 201), to abandon the teachings of Aristotle and to accept new discoveries, "if it all seems more conformed to the truth of Holy Scripture, insofar as it refers to God himself as the Father of all truth." He was aware of the literary devices that use Scripture and retain the possibility of a plurality of meanings.

As for Descartes, he clearly differentiated the two spheres of science and Scripture, but ultimately he thought that philosophical and scientific reason, properly directed, could only confirm the truth of Scripture, the truth of "the religion in which God has done me the grace to be instructed from my childhood" as he says in his *Discours de la méthode (Discourse on Method)*.

CONCLUSION

Even in the spirit of the Counter-Reformation, the Bible was an instrument of Christian instruction for many, in spite of its limited access. During the sixteenth and seventeenth centuries, Scripture never ceased being interpreted and questioned by those who preached, taught, or spread Catholic doctrine, or who rediscovered it in their mystical experiences. It remained important, in spite of periods of absences, in a civilization more orally centered, secure in the unity of human knowledge.

Richard Simon's arduous work (1678, 1689, 1693) marked the birth of "critical" exegesis, particularly since he wanted to renew the classic concept of scriptural inspiration. This initiated exegetical science, widening the gap between the reader and the text. The importance of this turning point was realized only later. The vigor with which Bossuet attacked Simon's positions, even after the death of his opponent, showed how profound the shift toward criti-

cal biblical exegesis was. This gave occasion to reread the biblical scholars
who from Erasmus to Galileo and their successors had anticipated this more
critical approach.

Persuaded that Scripture would only be read according to the interpreter of the tradition, that is, the church, Catholicism gives it a central place,
if at times implicit, but always within the framework of this tradition: the fathers, the liturgy, the doctrine of the theologians, the determinations of the
magisterium. The Bible thereby favored the flowering of a culture and of a piety that was original and established up to the end of the eighteenth century.
Owing to its theoretical and practical rejection of *Scriptura sola,* Catholicism
avoided the confrontation with dominating criticism and science until the
crisis of modernism at the beginning of the twentieth century.

BIBLIOGRAPHY

Acosta, J. de
1894   *Historia Natural y moral de las Indias.* Madrid: Anglés. Repr.; orig. Seville, 1590.

Armogathe, J.-R. (ed.)
1989   *Bible de tous les temps* 6: *Le Grand Siècle et la Bible.* Paris: Beauchesne.

Arnauld, A.
1683   *La logique ou l'art de penser. Contenant outre les regles communes, plusieurs observa-
          tions nouvelles, propres à former le jugement.* Paris: Desprez.

Backus, I., and F. Higman (eds.)
1990   *Théorie et pratique de l'exégèse. Actes du colloque sur l'exégèse biblique au XVIe siècle
          (1988).* Geneva: Droz.

Bedouelle, G.
1990   "Le débat catholique sur la traduction de la Bible en langue vulgaire." In Backus
          and Higman (eds.), 1990: 39-76.
2002   *La réforme du catholicisme, 1480-1620.* Paris: Cerf.

Bedouelle, G., and B. Roussel (eds.)
1989   *Bible de tous les temps.* 5: *Le temps des Réformes et la Bible.* Paris: Beauchesne.

Bireley, R.
1999   *The Refashioning of Catholicism, 1450-1700.* London: Macmillan.

Bossuet, J. B.
1681   *Discours sur l'histoire universelle.* Paris: Mabre-Cramoisy.
1709   *Politique tirée des propres paroles de l'Ecriture sainte.* Paris: Mabre-Cramoisy.

Calmet, A.

1707-16 *Commentaire litteral sur tous les livres de l'Ancien et du Nouveau Testament.* 23 vols. Paris: Emery.

Congar, Y.

1960-63 *La Tradition et les traditions.* 2 vols. Paris: Fayard.

Delville, J.-P.

2004 *L'Europe de l'exégèse au XVI siècle. Interprétations de la parabole des ouvriers à la vigne (Matthieu 20, 1-16).* BETL 174; Leuven: University Press/Peeters.

Dumeige, G.

1975 *La foi catholique.* Paris: L'Orante.

Fantoli, A. (ed.)

1999 *Sciences et religions de Copernic à Galilée, 1540-1610. Actes du colloque international organisé par l'Ecole française de Rome, en collaboration avec l'École nationale des chartes et l'Istituto italiano per gli studi filosofici, avec la participation de l'Universita di Napoli "Federico II," Ronze, 12-14 décembre 1996.* Ecole française de Rome; Paris: Boccard.

Fragnito, G.

2001 *Church, Censorship and Culture in Early Modern Italy.* Cambridge: Cambridge University Press.

Frohock, R.

2004 *Heroes of Empire: The British Colonial Protagonist in America, 1596-1764.* Newark: University of Delaware Press.

Gill, J.

1959 *The Council of Florence.* Cambridge: Cambridge University Press.

Greenslade, S. L. (ed.)

1963 *The Cambridge History of the Bible 3: The West from the Reformation to the Present Day.* Cambridge: Cambridge University Press.

Hazard, P.

1990 *The European Mind: The Critical Years, 1680-1715.* New York: Fordham University Press.

Jedin, H.

1957-58 *A History of the Council of Trent.* 2 vols. Edinburgh: Nelson.
1965 *Histoire du concile de Trent.* 2 vols. Paris: Desclée.

Lapide, C. à (Cornelius van den Steen)

1908 *The Great Commentary of Cornelius à Lapide.* 8 vols. Edinburgh: Grant.

Laplanche, F.

1994 *La Bible en France entre mythe et critique, XVIe-XIXe siècle.* Paris: Michel.

Lessius, L.

1613   *De providentia Numinis et animi immortalitate libri duo adversus Atheos et Politicos.* Antwerp: Officina Plantiniana.

1631   *Ravvleigh His Ghost. Or, a feigned apparition of Syr VValter Ravvleigh: To a Friend of His, for the Translating into English, the Booke of Leonard Lessius (That Most Learned Man) Entituled, De prouidentia numinis, & animi immortalitate: Written against Atheists, and Polititians of These Dayes, Translated by A. B.* Saint Omer: G. Seutin.

Lumnius, L.

1567   *De extremo Dei judicio et Indorum vocatione libri duo Antuerpii.* Anvers: Antonium Tilenium Brechtanum.

Machiavelli, N.

1916   *The Prince.* Trans. W. K. Marriott. New York: Macmillan.

Mackey, H.B.

1892-1904   *Oeuvres de St François de Sales.* Annecy: Archives de la Visitation d'Annecy.

Mersenne, M.

1623   *Quaestiones in Genesim.* Paris.

Neuner, J., and J. Dupuis (eds.)

1976   *The Christian Faith in the Doctrinal Documents of the Catholic Church.* 2nd ed.; Dublin: Mercier.

O'Malley, J.

2000   *Trent and All That: Renaming Catholicism in the Early Modern Era.* Cambridge: Harvard University Press.

Pedersen, O.

1983   *Galileo and the Council of Trent.* Studi Galileiani 1; Rome: Specola vaticana.

Po-Chia Hsia, R.

1998   *The World of Catholic Renewal, 1540-1770.* Cambridge: Cambridge University Press.

Prat, J. M.

1856   *Maldonat et l'université de Paris au XVIe siècle.* Paris: J. Lanier.

Sales, F. de

1989   *Introduction to the Devout Life.* Ed. and trans. J. K. Ryan. New York: Doubleday.

Schmitt, P.

1985   *La Réforme catholique. Le combat de Maldonat (1534-1583).* Paris: Beauchesne.

1999   *Sciences et réligions de Copernic à Galilée (1540-1610).* Rome: École française de Rome.

Simon, R.

1678   *A Critical History of the Old Testament.* London: Davis.

1689   *A Critical History of the Text of the New Testament.* London: Taylor.

1693   *L'Histoire critique des principaux commentateurs du Nouveau Testament.* Rotterdam: Leers.

Yates, F. A.
2001   *Occult Philosophy in the Elizabethan Age.* Routledge Classics; London: Routledge.

CHAPTER 16

Scriptures in the Vernacular Up to 1800

Lynne Long

TRANSLATION AND INTERPRETATION

Scriptures in the vernacular not only require the twin processes of interpretation and translation for their making, but also provide the source for the interpretative practice of their readers. It is hardly surprising, then, that the subject of Scripture translation inspires passion and controversy: it was a serious challenge to be addressed and defended in the age of Jerome (347-420), provoked debate and dissent throughout the medieval and Reformation eras, and remains a source of contention today.

The process of translation requires interpretation on the part of the translators, since in order to translate properly the translators have to understand thoroughly the meaning of the source text (Evans 2001: 189). Translating the Bible also demands a considerable level of scholarship as well as linguistic expertise. As Augustine (354-430) says, "Translators frequently deviate from the author's meaning if they are not particularly learned" (2004: 436). The translators' understanding of the text is transferred to the target language, but only within the limits of the translation tools currently available, such as source texts, critical editions of sources, commentaries, and linguistic scholarship. The tools at the translators' disposal have varied with the time and circumstances of the translation. Then, the second part of the procedure, reading the translated text, demands a similar interpretive process, but this time on the part of the reader, especially if the translation is from an earlier age. "Any thorough reading of a text out of the past of one's own language and literature," says Steiner, "is a

---

Non-English/German Vernacular Versions

Niccolò Malermi/Malerbi (Italian, 1490)
Jacques Lefèvre d'Étaples (French, 1528)
Pierre Robert Olivétan (French, 1535)
Hans Tausen (Danish, Pentateuch 1535)
Olaus and Lars Petersson (Swedish, NT 1526; whole Bible 1541)
Michael Agricola (Finnish, early 1540s)
Theological Faculty of Louvain (French, 1550)
Casiodoro de Reina (Spanish, OT 1567; NT 1569)
Giovanni Diodati (Italian, 1604; rev. 1640)
Isaac le Maistre de Sacy (French, from the Vulgate, 1666-70)

---

manifold act of interpretation" (1992: 18). There is danger inherent in both processes.

It is generally accepted that the act of translation involves negotiation on several levels — linguistic, cultural, and semantic. Languages have different characteristics, and they evolve over time. Consequently, each reinterpretation in the form of translation runs the risk of distancing the reader from the source text(s). Of course, the longer Christianity continues, the more interpretations are available. Some of these translations have functioned as source texts, so long is the tradition of their authority. As a result, the dynamics of Bible translation constantly refer back to what are considered to be the original sources in an attempt to reconstruct the original message. The multiplicity of sources both facilitates and complicates translation.

"Reading" the Bible, in the sense of interpreting its meaning, was historically considered to be the province of scholars and theologians. The pre-Reformation Bible was written in Latin or Greek, and this provided a natural barrier that prevented misreading or misinterpretation, since access to Scripture was through sermons, or priests' explanations. Even when the vernacular Bible was first available in print, there genuinely remained what Kastan calls "the abiding fear of common access to the Scriptures" (1997: 57). This fear was partly due to a perceived loss of power and authority on the part of the mediators of the text, but it was also due to the idea that reading without a mediator might lead to heretical interpretation. Heresy meant damnation, and was to be avoided at all costs, including, if necessary, restricting access to the text.

Issues relating to vernacular Bible translation are many; but one of the main concerns has always been the part played by human agents. The prophets, the Gospel writers, the composers of the Psalms were divinely inspired. Does the translator share the same inspiration, or does the translator provide one further layer of language between the original text and the reader? There were many writers involved in the making of the Scriptures. The canon of the Bible includes a range of genres and styles: from genealogy, narrative, history, and parables to proverbs, poetry, prophecy, and theology. Some of the prophetic and poetic sections have always been challenging, like Isaiah 53 or the Song of Solomon. There is always the risk that a translation by one person or by a committee will impose a unified style upon a collection of texts that were originally inherently distinctive. Even the NT is "not all of a piece: St. Paul in his epistles is, at times and for the most part, a decent prose stylist; the Greek of the Gospels by contrast is distinctly odd Greek, even, not to put too fine a point on it, rather bad Greek" (Lawton 1990: 67). Should the translator correct the source text or improve the style? In the more obscure sections, should the translator make clear in the target text what remains obscure in the source? It is easy to see how, given the status and function of the text, this kind of intervention could be justified. It has always been the perception that the Scriptures, as the word of God, are a direct communication between God and humankind. Since the very procedures used in transfer from one language to another necessarily involve both a linguistic shift and a human and fallible agent — the translator — translation may represent a difficult, unsatisfactory, and even undesirable process. The main concern is whether God's message might be changed or manipulated through translation.

The earliest vernacular translations of Scripture had no such difficulties, as long as they took the form of interlinear glosses on the source text, and functioned as a memory aid. In this mode they remained a support to interpretation, rather than an interpretation in their own right, and consequently presented no problem. However, a word-for-word, or literal translation, while preserving the integrity of the source text when written as a gloss or presented interlinearly, changes function and form when it stands alone. Detaching the translation from the source text transfers the authority of the source text to the translation. It conceals the linguistic relationship between the two texts and is the historical point at which the word-for-word gloss, now inadequate, is necessarily converted into more of a sense-for-sense translation. Once the gloss becomes detached from the source and stands alone, even in a fairly close word-for-word translation between source and target language, some linguistic change is inevitable, as has been observed by twentieth-century linguistic theorists (Catford 1965; Vinay and Darbelnet 1995). Jerome, writing nearly sixteen hundred years earlier, was fully aware of the same linguistic problem, the change that necessarily proceeds from the act of translation. He was also conscious of the particular impact of Bible translation and the enormity of possibly changing the word of God. He wrote in his famous letter to Pammachius in 395 that, when translating from Greek, he was happy to use a sense-for-sense strategy rather than word-for-word translation, except in the case of Scripture where "even the syntax contains a mystery" (Robinson 2002: 25). It seems that the episode of Babel in Gen. 11:1-9 made translation "an impossible necessity" (Jasper 2005: 105).

If the motive for translating is to reveal or promote understanding of Christian truths, how then is the reader to understand the meaning of the text if the translation retains the syntactic strangeness of the foreign source, as it does in a word-for-word translation? However, the danger of a sense-for-sense strategy, or the use of functional or dynamic equivalence, as Nida describes it (1964: 159), is that the translator, in attempting to re-create the impact made by the original, moves away from the original words, makes a particular interpretation, and fixes it in the target text, glosses and alternative readings notwithstanding.

Translators must always make impossible choices. There are occasions, for example, when the nature of the target language requires the definition of what is ambiguous in the source text. The Latin word *anima,* for example, could be equally well translated as "life," "soul," "spirit," "breath," or "wind," according to the interpretation of the context. Sometimes the target language makes ambiguous what is well-defined in the source text. The contemporary English "you" covers singular or plural, familiar or formal. Most modern and classical European languages define number and sometimes formality vs. familiarity in the expression of second person pronouns. English retains that ability only by the use of the archaic "thou." Luke 22:32 requires differentiation of singular and plural in the second person: using "thee" to achieve it raises issues of archaisms and consistency throughout, while using a different strategy raises issues of relevance (Gutt 2000).

A step further toward clarifying the content is tempting, particularly if the message is paramount. Paraphrasing, however, explains the meaning in a way that encompasses knowledge other than that to be found in the text, and may become more like a commentary on the original than a translation of it. An examination of facsimiles of early vernacular translations of the Bible will show that they (see, e.g., Tyndale 1998; Whittingham 1998) regularly had more commentary than translated text. A further complication in an already unstable situation is the fact that "language is in perpetual change" (Steiner 1992: 18). Each translation requires negotiation with the language of its time. What is more, each translator comes to the task with cultural, contextual, and

sometimes doctrinal bias. Then there are those readers who require a degree
of archaism in the text as a marker of the special nature of the content and of
the status of the text. By contrast, some readers are attracted by the modernity
of the target text language and the direct relevance of the Gospels to modern-
day situations. The idea of a permanently fixed translation in English or in
any other living language is not merely elusive, but flawed as a concept, a legacy precluded by Babel.

In looking at individual vernacular Scriptures, then, it is important to
know the context and function of each particular translation, what tools the
translators had at their disposal in terms of source texts and commentaries,
and the general strategies of translation. It could be argued that the first attempt at scriptural interpretation or translation of the Gospels was the transfer from oral tradition to written text: the writing down in not very good
Greek of events that took place in dialect Aramaic. Jerome edited the subsequent Latin translations of these codices into the Vulgate NT which, together
with his Latin version of the OT, took on the status of original and remains
the preferred source text of the Roman Catholic Church. Having the same
text both for exegetical purposes and as the source text for translations provides advantages in consistency of doctrine and in unity for the authorizing
body. Living target languages in constant flux, new perspectives in biblical
scholarship and linguistic studies, new audiences — all these eventually require revised and updated target texts. Many of the vernacular translations of
the Bible were indeed revisions or editings of previous translations. The first
complete English Bible, however, was separate from its source text, and had
no earlier written examples or traditions to follow, apart from some tenth-
century Anglo-Saxon Gospels and versions of the Psalms.

THE WYCLIFFITE VERSIONS

The Lollard English Bible of the 1380s and 90s (Craigie 1954) set the pattern
associating translation with heresy. The Lollard group was known for its use
of the vernacular at a time when vernacular languages were considered inferior and unsuitable vehicles for literary and religious texts. Dante Alighieri's
De Vulgari Eloquentia of 1304-1305 (Dante 1996) argues (in Latin) for the use
of the Italian vulgar tongue as a literary vehicle; but many of his European
contemporaries had yet to be convinced that the various vernaculars were
worthy media. Common people spoke the vernacular; they were expected to
leave the interpretation of Scripture to their betters, and be content with
what was mediated to them through the priests. In the debate on vernacular

scriptural translation at Oxford in 1401, William Butler and Thomas Palmer argued on social, linguistic, and literary grounds that the Bible in English should not be sanctioned (Ellis 2001: 20-24). They maintained not only that English Bibles would be incorrect, since translation is impossible, but also that simple lay people should not read the Bible, because it is too difficult for them and it is not their place to read it (Deanesly 1966: 399-436). Vernacular texts were considered subversive and dangerous because they challenged the canonical status of the classical languages and laid texts open to the general reader. The Wycliffite versions challenged contemporary ideas of the status of scriptural language and showed that it was possible to translate into the vernacular. At the same time, these versions demonstrated the vast demands of a project to translate the complete Bible and highlighted the need for revision, both during the process of translation, and following its completion. Viewed from a modern standpoint, these translations demonstrate the limitations of using Jerome's Vulgate as the single source text and show the close relationship in holy texts between interpretation and translation.

In late-fourteenth-century Europe, literacy was becoming more widespread, while printing remained an unknown technology. Manuscript production, painstakingly copying texts by hand, was both time-consuming and expensive, and the end product was vulnerable to copyists' errors, fire, and humidity. Use of the vernacular languages, as opposed to Latin, had been on the increase throughout Europe since the 1360s (Long 2001: 99), and the oral tradition of the Bible in the vernacular languages was also strong. In England, for instance, the Bible was conveyed publicly to the common people in the vernacular mainly through sermons and preaching (see Owst 1926), but also through private family readings of vernacular texts based on, or referring to, biblical sources. Popular contemporary texts in the vernacular, such as *The Vision of Piers Plowman* by William Langland, the anonymous poems known as *The Pearl, Cleanness,* and *Patience* (Anderson 1996), and the works of Geoffrey Chaucer (Benson 1987) all include references to biblical material that were well known to their intended audience.

The established church in this period was in a state of disarray — there were two popes for a time — and was in need of reorganization and reform of its corrupt polity and practices. John Wyclif (d. 1384), an Oxford theologian and preacher, used the Bible as a basis both for his criticism of the church and for his reformed doctrines, some of which were seen as heretical. Support for his ideas and the authority for his thinking could be demonstrated to the laity only by means of a vernacular Bible (Deanesly 1966: 225). As a result, some of Wyclif's followers, working under difficult and pressured conditions, produced a complete English translation of the Bible as an alternative authority to the church.

The practical problems were considerable, not least because the text had to be handwritten. The haste with which the work was done, the limited tools available to the translators, the restrictions imposed by the Latin Vulgate as the only source text of that time, and the unsophisticated scholarship of the translators, resulted in a rough and literal first version that required immediate revision. There was no precedent to follow, no well-tried method or strategy to assist the group, no other English translations to consult. The early version kept closely to the Latin source and syntax to the extent that it was at times difficult to understand (see Daniell 2003: 76-85). In this first attempt, there were many errors, and the difficulties of translating in sections, rather than with a concept of the whole text, produced some disjointed passages. The revision, which followed almost immediately, was far more coherent, and appears to have been at least overseen, if not actually completed, by a single translator. The prologue to the revision contains a chapter defending the translation strategies employed and describes the difficulties of establishing an accurate source text (Long 2001: 85-87).

Nevertheless, even with a reliable text, using a Latin source alone meant that some linguistic issues were left to the translator to interpret. For example, Latin, in contrast to Greek, rarely provides an article before a noun, whereas translation into English requires both the insertion of the article and a decision whether to translate it as definite or indefinite. There is considerable difference in scriptural terms between "*a* son of God" and "*the* son of God," between "*a* good shepherd" and "*the* good shepherd." A Greek codex would have helped with this and other issues.

The 250 or so surviving complete and partial manuscripts of the Wycliffite Bible witness how much support there was in the fourteenth century for vernacular Scripture (Rex 2002: 75). Politically, though, the appearance of an English translation alarmed the church. This was as much for its association with the perceived heresies of Wyclif and the Lollard group he represented (although the translation itself contained nothing untoward) as for the devaluation of the church's role in the interpretation of Holy Writ. One of the most contentious issues of the times was open access to the Scriptures as opposed to access through the mediatory priest. The strictly hierarchical nature of society in those times conflicted with the idea of equal opportunity: vernacular translation gave access to the Bible to lay people who, it was genuinely believed, had neither the capacity nor the sophistication to read the Bible. The unlearned, unwary, and unworthy reader might well misinterpret or misunderstand and be brought to heresy, whereas simply listening to the Bible was not so dangerous: *lectio est inductiva in errorem potius quam auditus* — "reading is more conducive to error than listening"

(Deanesly 1966: 403). The result was a series of constitutions against Wyclif and the Lollards, forbidding anyone to translate Holy Scripture into English "on his own authority" and forbidding the reading of English Scriptures unless they had been "approved by the diocesan of the place" (Hargreaves 1969: 393). This meant that both activities remained very firmly under the jurisdiction of the church, and any scriptural interpretation was limited to more easily controlled sources. Lollard activity continued sporadically until well into the fifteenth century, and connections have been made between Lollardy and the Protestant Reformation (see Marshall 2003: 33-34).

Modern laws place no such strictures on translating the Bible and reading it in the vernacular. However, even today there remain issues over the use of certain translations, conflicts over the method of translating, and discussions as to which translations are most faithful. The words "Bible translation" or similar phrase, introduced into an Internet search engine, will produce numerous sites with wide ranges of information and opinion. The word "heretic" has been applied to modern translators and their methods just as it was applied to Wyclif and his followers for their ideas. Because of the interpretive processes involved in translation and the reluctance of medieval church authorities to allow translation into the vernacular, Bible translation has long been associated with sedition and heresy. Throughout history, vernacular translation has often been the consequence of and support for new interpretive perspectives. Martin Luther, for example, supported his own reforming ideas with a new German translation of the Bible in the sixteenth century.

ERASMUS AND LUTHER

Desiderius Erasmus (d. 1536), humanist reformer and European scholar (see chapter 9 above), rather naively hoping that a less corrupt Latin Vulgate source text might contribute to a wider program of reform in the rest of the church, produced an emended text of the NT in 1516. He supported his corrections by publishing the new Latin translation side-by-side with the Greek original he had consulted (Daniell 2003: 116). The Greek text he used was "an imperfect instrument" (Wright 2001: 199) and needed some patching, but nevertheless provided Europe with an accessible comparison to Jerome's Vulgate for the first time in centuries. The Greek text he printed was intended as justification for his corrections to the Vulgate, but became a source in its own right for would-be translators who had not previously had access to a Greek source text.

The first to take advantage of the newly available Greek source text was the German Reformer Martin Luther (1483-1546). He had already made clear his objections to contemporary church practices and required a vernacular German Bible that would speak to the ordinary people in a language to which they could relate and that would be meaningful to them (see Smith 1911: 263-70). His NT was first published in 1522, followed in 1534 by the complete Bible (see Smith 1972). In the *Sendbrief vom Dolmetschen* (Open Letter on Translation) of 1530, Luther sets out his theories of translation (Robinson 2002: 84; Lindberg 2000: 48). Luther's constant use of the verb *verdeutschen,* which means "to translate" in the sense of "to make German," "to germanize," reveals his domestication strategy. "I have constantly tried in translating," he says, "to produce a pure and clear German *(rein und klar Deutsch)*" (Lindberg 2000: 49). He argues that the insertion of the Latin word *sola* ("alone"), or in German *allein,* in Rom. 3:28, much criticized at the time, is needed because German syntax and style require it: *Das ist aber die Art unsrer deutsche Sprache* ("for that is the nature of our German language") (1530: 20).

Luther's aim was to make the Bible into a German text rather than to produce a translation into a German that still reflected the syntax, forms, and idiosyncrasies of Latin or Greek. This process involved, among other tasks, making sense of the more obscure passages. Later on, in paragraph 12 of the *Sendbrief vom Dolmetschen,* he gives the example of the Latin phrase *ex abundantia cordis os loquitur* in Matt. 12:34. Translated literally, this phrase would read "out of the abundance of the heart the mouth speaks," but Luther challenges the advocates of this literal translation: *Sage mir, ist das deutsch geredet? Welcher Deutsche verstehet solches?* ("Tell me, is that how a German speaks? What German person would understand such a thing?"). He goes on to advocate the choice of a German idiom that would be recognized by people such as the mother in her house or the ordinary man, leaving the reader in no doubt as to his intended audience (Luther 1530: 21).

The significant effect of this domestication strategy was to detach the text from the Latin-literate church hierarchy and to transform it into something readable and understandable for the ordinary German person. Schleiermacher, writing in the nineteenth century, describes this kind of translation process as naturalization — leaving the reader alone as much as possible and moving the text toward the reader (Biguenet and Schulte 1992: 37-54; see also Schleiermacher 1977; Munday 2001: 27-28). Modern translation theorists (Berman 1985; Venuti 1995) have related this kind of domestication to appropriation: taking over the text and removing markers that would announce it as foreign to its readers. Luther's strategy would be described today as functional or dynamic equivalence as outlined by Nida (1964: 159-66). The strategy he chose allowed him to make changes to doctrine (by introducing *sola,* for example) through the process of translation. This was as shocking to the authorities as Luther's ideas on the sacraments. His translation of the Bible into German was not the first (see Panzer 1778), but it was certainly the most influential translation, and it had a significant effect on the German language in the following centuries.

Luther's teachings and influence were well known throughout Europe and quickly reached those sympathetic to reform in England. This alarmed both the church and the orthodox Henry VIII (1498-1547), who had received the accolade of Defender of the Faith from the pope for his treatise against Luther (Henry VIII 1966).

ENGLISH VERSIONS OF THE FIRST HALF
OF THE SIXTEENTH CENTURY

Tyndale's Translation and Luther's Influence

One of the most important names in the development of the English Bible is that of the sixteenth-century translator William Tyndale (c. 1494-1536; see Williams 1969). Often overlooked in the face of the popularity and huge impact of the KJV (1611) is the fact that many of the phrases appreciated and taken up by subsequent translators had their origins in Tyndale's pioneering translation of the NT. Tyndale's translation was done in response to calls for reform in the church as well as the needs of an increasingly literate lay population. His work was timely in one sense, as there was a general movement toward vernacular Bibles in Europe, but it was mistimed in another, as the political situation in England was difficult and dangerous, with a very orthodox-minded Henry VIII competing with the pope for control of the English church.

By the time Tyndale began his 1525 English translation of the NT, both the practical and scholarly tools for translating the Bible had increased considerably. Printing had improved the speed and lowered the cost of production and distribution. After the fall of Constantinople in 1453 and the resulting dispersal of scholars throughout Europe, access to the source texts and reference texts had increased (Runciman 1965: 8-9). Greek language teachers and resources for translating from Greek were more easily obtainable. Biblical scholarship and public literacy had improved. Humanist scholarship, with its interest in preserving ancient mss., had revived interest in both the linguistic roots and the literal meaning of the Scriptures and became "an important element in the widespread movement of reform" (Carleton 2001: 100).

In 1524, having tried unsuccessfully to find support in London for his own project to translate the Bible, William Tyndale settled in Germany and two years later produced the first edition of his English NT (Tyndale 2000). The timing of the publication and the German connection, plus the fact that he made use of some of Luther's prologues and notes, connected him strongly with the German Reformer. As a consequence and also because nothing happened in England without Henry's approval, the king ordered his archbishop Wolsey to intercept and destroy the Bibles. This was done with varying success, as many copies still found their way into English homes, and the money paid as an inducement to surrender the illegal Bibles was used to finance printing more Bibles. In 1534, however, Tyndale was betrayed to the church authorities and, after a period of imprisonment, was burned at the stake in Antwerp for heresy in 1536 (Williams 1969: 60).

Tyndale had not only the Greek and Latin source texts to work from, but also Luther's new translation into German. According to a contemporary account, he was "so skilful in seven tongues, Hebrew, Greek, Latin, Italian, Spanish, English, French, that whichever he speaks, you would think it his native tongue" (Isaacs 1954b: 146). Such linguistic competence would have given him access to whatever other vernacular resources were available. The main objections to Tyndale's English translation of the NT, according to Thomas More (1478-1535), who wrote a dialogue against him in 1529 (More 1981), rested on the interpretation of three words: "priest," "church," and "charity" (Pollard 1911: 126). Tyndale translated "priest" as "senior," "church" as "congregation," and "charity" as "love." As More points out (Pollard 1911: 128), "he [Tyndale] had a mischievous mind in the change." The choice of vocabulary was designed to reinterpret the words and shift them away from their accepted current meanings. In the same way that having the Bible in English diminished the mediatory role of the Church, using the word "senior" and later "elder" for "priest" removed the connotations of anointed authority from the position and challenged the idea of special powers and privileges. Similarly, using the word "congregation" for "church" reminded everyone, including the authorities, that the laity was as much a part of the church as its hierarchy was. The use of "love" for "charity" had a similar effect. *Caritas* in Latin expressed the higher, virtuous love people had for God or for each other, while *amor* denoted the lower physical love between a man and woman, with all its negative connotations of sin. Using one word, "love," for both gives each concept the same status. The idea was, through the reinterpretation of specific vocabulary, to lessen the absolute power of those in high authority in the church and increase the profile of its ordinary members.

Tyndale's legacy was a linguistic basis on which to build future complete Bible translations and a precedent to support the challenge to the church authorities, who refused to allow a Bible in English. After his death, there was immediate and unprecedented activity in the field of Bible translation in England. Much of Tyndale's work is retained in the translations that followed, but without his name attached, showing that it was more the taint of heresy than the quality of his translation that marred the progress of his translation career. The many editings of the NT that came after him kept the greater part of his phrasing: "Nine-tenths of the Authorised [KJV] NT is still Tyndale, and the best is still his" (Isaacs 1954b: 160).

Post-Tyndale Editing

William Tyndale may have been a lone pioneer of the English Reformation Bible when he began, but after his death others were more than ready to take up the work. His legacy consisted of the NT, the Pentateuch (1530), and Jonah (1531), so that it was left to Miles Coverdale (d. 1569) to produce, in 1535, the first complete printed Bible in English. Politically, events had moved very quickly in England. King Henry's marriage in 1533 with the pregnant Anne Boleyn finally brought about the break with Rome. For a while, his new wife's Lutheran leanings made the king more favorable toward the idea of a vernacular Bible for general distribution. The new Archbishop, Thomas Cranmer (1489-1556), took the opportunity to petition for an English translation. The king, although wary, was not opposed to the idea. Meanwhile, Thomas Cromwell (1485-1540), Henry's reformist chancellor, lost no time in engaging Coverdale to work on a complete English translation.

Coverdale used the English NT and the parts of the OT that Tyndale had managed to complete before his death, but he dared not refer to Tyndale's input except obliquely: if he had used Tyndale's name the translation would not have been approved. Coverdale had no knowledge of Hebrew, and so used Luther's German version to bridge the gaps in his knowledge. His version of Psalms was his own and was included in the *Book of Common Prayer*.

In 1537, a certain Thomas Matthew — probably a pseudonym for John Rogers (c. 1500-1555), an associate of Tyndale — put together another complete English Bible, composed from various sources. It included Tyndale's NT and Pentateuch, and Coverdale's Apocrypha. Some use was made of contemporary European versions, including Olivétan's (c. 1506-1538) French version (see below). The notes included comments from Luther, Tyndale, Erasmus, Bucer (1491-1551), and others. Neither Coverdale's nor Matthew's Bible was satisfactory (see Isaacs 1954b: 175). "The former could not satisfy scholars, not being made from the originals; the latter would offend the conservatives by its notes and origin" (Greenslade 1963: 141).

The answer seemed to lie in a revision of Matthew's version by Coverdale. This was done under Thomas Cromwell's auspices, and all contentious comments were removed. Letters from Paris (Pollard 1911: 234-46) record the difficulties experienced in the printing process, since it was becoming increasingly difficult to find printers prepared to take on the work. Coverdale's revision of Matthew's Bible was not published until 1539, owing to diplomatic problems with France (Greenslade 1963: 151). The revision was called the Great Bible, and eventually became a great success. Also, in 1539, the layman Richard Taverner (c. 1505-75) completed his own revision of Matthew's Bible. Taverner's expertise lay in his excellent command of Greek, but it is difficult to determine exactly his contribution to the mainstream trends since scholars are divided as to whether he produced a further revision or was "effectively starting again" (Daniell 2003: 219).

The second edition of Coverdale's revision of Matthew's Bible, further revised, appeared in 1540 after the downfall and execution of Thomas Cromwell. Following the tradition of making no reference to those who had fallen out of favor with the king, Cromwell's preface was replaced by one from Archbishop Cranmer, and the enterprise consequently became known as Cranmer's Great Bible. This edition was still a "patchwork of revision" and "far from being a direct translation from the Hebrew and Greek" (Isaacs 1954b: 178). In response to pressure from the more conservative bishops, in 1542 Henry VIII ordered another revision of the Great Bible according to the Vulgate. This rather surprising and retrograde step seemed to reflect the king's increasing anxiety about the whole question of a vernacular Bible. This was confirmed in 1546, when the king's decree strictly limited Bible reading to the upper levels of society.

Each Bible produced in this period was the product of a collating, editing, and revising process that reflected the pressures of the age and of the task. Translating the complete Bible is a huge undertaking for any one person, which was why each translation relied on help from other contemporary European versions, from commentaries, or from philological notes. This period of history, both in Britain and continental Europe, was one of uncertainty and change — a time in England when opportunities had to be seized while they were available, before the king changed his mind. Politics, society, the monarchy, law, and religion were linked in a way difficult to appreciate in modern times.

Once the Bible was available in English, it was difficult to suppress except by law, but this is exactly what Henry VIII did in 1543, when a royal decree declared "no woman, except noblewomen and gentlewomen . . . no artificers, apprentices, journeymen, serving men of the degrees of yeomen, husbandmen or labourers were to read the New Testament to themselves or to any other, privately or openly, on pain of one month's imprisonment" (Isaacs 1954b: 179-80). Henry's dilemma over the introduction of a vernacular Bible seems difficult to understand today, but in the context of his time it was understandable. On the one hand, a Bible in English had seemed the ideal way to provide an authority other than the church to refer to and to build up an idea of nationhood and Englishness. It gave status to the growing canon of English literature and encouraged literacy. It helped to reinforce Henry's authority over the English church. On the other hand, the king remained conservative in his religious views, and was genuinely worried that open access by the common people to the word of God might demean the Bible's status (Daniell 2003: 164-65; see also Long 2001: 153-56). Individual reading might lead to individual interpretation, questioning, or, even worse, heresy and sedition. Challenge to the status quo was something every monarch feared.

Just as the function and use of an English translation of the Bible had become more complex, so the availability of source texts had increased. Jerome's Vulgate had occupied the central position as official "original" for centuries, and considerable shift in mindset was required to make room for alternative source texts. Contemporary European language versions, however good their provenance, were seen as unsatisfactory substitutes for codices in the original language. The problem was that the translator needed expertise not just in Latin, which was all the Vulgate demanded, but also Greek and Hebrew, if original language sources were employed. The process of translation could not avoid setting another layer between the source and target text: the more translations of translations there were, the more layers separated the reader from the source. Meanwhile, ordinary people, unaware of the interpretive complications, listened to and read their Bibles when they were permitted, and made what sense they could of the situation.

Henry's heir Edward VI (1537-53) was ten when he came to the throne. During his reign, the production of English Bibles and prayer books flourished. When Queen Mary (1516-58) succeeded him six years later, the situation was reversed, and she attempted to reinstate Catholicism. The English Bible of her reign, destined to be popular throughout the Elizabethan age (1558-1603), and to be the Bible of Shakespeare and his contemporaries, was in fact produced abroad by religious exiles in Geneva.

EUROPEAN VERNACULAR BIBLES

The Reformation in Europe has most usefully been described as a "series of parallel movements" (Cameron 1991: 1). It is at this point in the narrative that the various language groups of exiled Reformers gather in self-governing towns that were sympathetic to reform, notably Strasbourg, Zurich, and Geneva. Prior to the Reformation and to the development of printing, each area of Christian Europe had its own translation history as far as the vernacular Bible was concerned. Most countries had partial translations, especially of the Gospels and the Psalms; most had restrictions or prohibitions of translations by the clergy; and most had traditions of the use or non-use of the vernacular.

Luther's activities had a profound and polarizing effect on Europe, not only in strictly religious terms, but also in breaking ties to the central church authorities in Rome and in achieving political autonomy for governments. Lutheranism spread northward to Denmark, where Hans Tausen (1494-1561) produced the Pentateuch in Danish in 1535, and to Sweden, where the Petersson brothers, Olaus (1493-1552) and Lars (1499-1573), were instrumental in producing the Swedish NT in 1526 and eventually the complete Bible of 1541. The Swedish king, Gustav Vasa (Gustavus Adolphus, 1496-1550), took over the wealth and organization of the church in much the same way as Henry VIII did in England (see Andersson 1956: 126; Oakley 1966: 72; Scott 1977: 126-29). The Finnish reformer Michael Agricola (1510-57) went to Wittenberg to study under Luther in 1536 and produced the NT in Finnish in the early 1540s (Heininen 1999: 57-61). The same decade saw Polish and Hungarian vernacular Bibles (Elton 1999: 206).

In France, Jacques Lefèvre d'Étaples (1455-1536), a Catholic priest who hoped for reform from within the church, was the first to translate the whole Bible in 1528. He used the official Catholic source text, the Vulgate, but made use of the Greek NT and Erasmus's emended Latin text. In 1535, Pierre Robert Olivétan produced an improved French translation. Thomas Matthew used Olivétan's annotations in making his English translation. Calvin later revised the Olivétan Bible, and it ran to many editions. Although Lefèvre's version was put on the index of forbidden books by the church, an official Catholic translation was considered necessary to counter Protestant teaching, and in 1550, the Theology Faculty at Louvain University produced a French Bible. As in England, these various translations were interdependent to a greater or lesser degree: Olivétan was largely influenced by Lefèvre, and the Louvain version was influenced by Olivétan (Lortsch 1910; Bogaert 1991). A century later, Isaac le Maistre de Sacy spent three years in the Bastille (1666-70) for his Jansenist views and passed the time translating the Bible from the Vulgate (Delassaut 1957).

In Spain, the situation was far more complex (Olin 1990). The famous translation project at the University of Alcalá, the making of the *Complutensian Polyglot*, was "a philological attempt to establish authoritative texts" (Pym 2000: 165) in Latin, Greek, Hebrew, and Aramaic. The publication of the first volume in 1516 coincided with Erasmus's emended Latin Vulgate NT with Greek, used by Luther for his translation into the German vernacular, which was perceived to be heretical. The works of both Luther and Erasmus circulated in Spain. The connection between translation and heresy was clear to the Roman church (see above). The Polyglot Bible, commissioned by the open-minded Cardinal Ximénez de Cisneros (1436-1517), could be viewed as a translation. Although the pope lent manuscripts to encourage the (academic, not popular) study of the Scriptures, and Cisneros's translation received the papal imprimatur, the Inquisition and the papacy were two different bodies. The Spanish Inquisition was quick to make life difficult for potential Bible translators. As a result, Juan de Valdes, Francisco de Enzinas, and Juan Pérez de Pineda, all of whom had worked on the project, were forced to flee Spain. Most of these scholars spent some time in Geneva and produced translations of parts of the Bible in Spanish. The complete Bible in Spanish (OT 1567, NT 1569) was the work of Casiodoro de Reina, a monk with reformist sympathies who was influenced by the work of Erasmus and the project at Alcalá (Pym 2000: 170-71). He left his monastery in Seville in 1556 for Geneva, and later London, where he served a community of Spanish refugees and began work on his translation (Kinder 1975: 36). In 1569, the Spanish Bible was printed in Basel. Casiodoro's version, later revised by Cipriano de Valera in 1602, was used until the twentieth century (Pym 2000: 171).

Italian translations appear not to have been numerous, perhaps owing to the connection of classical Latin to medieval Italian coupled with the physical presence of the Vatican. There were two main Italian vernacular versions. Niccolò Malermi or Malerbi produced the earliest in 1490, of which there is a copy in the Metropolitan Museum of New York. The second was completed in 1604 in Geneva by Giovanni Diodati (see Betts 1905; McComish 1989) and revised in 1641.

Given the European context of Reformation activity and Bible translation and the change to a pro-Catholic monarch in England, it comes as no surprise that the next English vernacular version of the Scriptures should come from the continent.

ENGLISH VERSIONS AFTER 1550

The Geneva Bible

Mary, Edward's half-sister and Henry's elder daughter, intended to return England to Catholicism in the shortest possible time. English Protestants, who could no longer safely practice their reformed faith at home, found refuge in international communities already established on the continent. The exiled communities became "an experiment . . . in religious colonization: the first to be undertaken by Tudor Englishmen, and the training school for all their later undertakings" (Garrett 1966: 15). Geneva was already one of the centers renowned for learning and included such notable figures as John Calvin and John Knox. Many Protestant clergy found refuge there, including Miles Coverdale, who may have been involved, given his previous experience, in the Geneva project to translate the Bible into English (Danner 1999: 61). Much of the academic activity in the European Protestant communities focused on study and translation of the Bible since the theology of the exiles centered on the principle of *sola scriptura*. The preface to the completed Geneva Bible, dated 1560, sets the "knollage and practising of the worde of God" unequivocally as central to Protestantism (Pollard 1911: 279). Although English translations already exist, maintained the preface writers, they "require greatly to be perused and reformed" in the light of new scholarship.

Genevan scholars also provided French, Italian, and Spanish vernacular translations as well as editions of the Vulgate as a source text (Daniell 2003: 292). Consequently, when William Whittingham (1524-79), scholar, humanist, and leader of the English Church in Geneva, translated the NT in 1557, he had many tools at his disposal. His text was "diligently revised by the most approved Greke examples and conferences of translations in other tonges" (Pollard 1911: 276) and had contributions from Calvin and Theodore Beza (1519-1605) (Isaacs 1954b: 182-83). The text was divided into verses and sections and printed in Roman type in quarto size: everything was done to make the work accessible, convenient, and easy to use. The complete Bible, printed in Geneva at the beginning of Elizabeth's reign, was destined to become the most popular version in England at that time. It was never officially recognized by English church authorities, but it was certainly the Bible in most general use among both ordinary people and scholars (Daniell 2003: 129). Shakespeare's extensive use of the Bible is based on the Geneva version, and the biblical quotations used in Miles Smith's preface (see Rhodes and Lupas 1997) to the KJV are also from the Geneva Bible. Many sermons took their texts from the Geneva Bible rather than from the Bishops' Bible.

The annotations of the Geneva version were more notorious for their association with Calvin than they were for their actual content, in the same way that Tyndale's work was suspect for its association with Luther rather than for the wording of the translation itself. But the monarchs Mary, Elizabeth, and James all had reason to be wary of some Genevan theology. John Knox (1513-72) had written *The First Blast of the Trumpet against the Mon-*

strous Regiment of Women in 1558 (1995) against the rule of women in general and of Mary in particular, since she was a Catholic. Christopher Goodman's tract *How Superior Powers Ought to Be Obeyed*, of the same year, with a preface by Whittingham, advocated the removal of monarchs who refused to follow the true religion. Elizabeth, although of the "right" religion when she came to the throne in 1558 on Mary's death, remained the wrong sex and continued to be unsympathetic toward the Geneva community. She was not even placated by Theodore Beza's gift of some of his work (Danner 1999: 42). John Knox's association with the Geneva community ensured the acceptance of the Geneva Bible as the Bible of Scotland (Wright 2001: 208), but guaranteed that James would dislike both the religious group and the Geneva Bible because of the implication that the monarch could be overruled or even deposed in matters of religion.

The 1560 Geneva Bible was successful because it was the product of good scholarship and had the reader very much in mind. The presentation of the text and the accompanying comments were all intended to be helpful. While some of the annotations defined a particular point of view or the doctrine of predestination, most were simply scholarly notes on the content. A comparison of Tyndale's and the Geneva's NTs shows that much of Tyndale's translation remains; the Bishops' Bible provides the basis for the OT. The Elizabethan reader found much that was already familiar because the successive translations were based on much that had gone before. The translation process of the text itself had become generally one of fine-tuning rather than of radical reinterpretation.

In 1576, however, the Geneva NT was revised by Laurence Tomson (1842; McGrath 2001: 114, 128), who added some more contentious and particularly Calvinist notes. In 1595, these were combined with the comments of Junius the Elder on Revelation (Daniell 2003: 352; Greenslade 1963: 158; Gribben 2000). The added notes altered the context of the translation and gave it the framework of a specific interpretation, even though the text itself had only minor changes. Polarization of religious opinion toward the end of the sixteenth century and the proliferation of Protestant versions required a response from the Catholic faction in the form of an official Catholic English Bible.

The Rheims-Douai Version

Just as the Protestant communities had set up centers abroad in Mary's reign, so the accession of Elizabeth (1558) created a new set of exiles. The Catholic college in Douai became the focus for the training of missionary priests to be sent to England to minister to the covert Catholic community. The need for a Catholic English Bible to counter the Protestant versions was considered so critical to the survival of the Catholic Church in England that the traditional arguments against translating were put aside (Long 2002: 16). The preface to the 1582 NT, published at Rheims, where the college was temporarily based, states very clearly that the translation was done only "upon special consideration of the present time, state and condition of our countrie, unto which divers thinges are either necessarie, or profitable and medecinable now, that otherwise in the peace of the Church were neither much requisite, nor perchance wholly tolerable" (Pollard 1911: 302).

The main translator, Gregory Martin (d. 1582), used the Vulgate as the basis of the translation (as he was obliged to do by the 1546 ruling of the Council of Trent), but referred to the Greek where necessary for clarification of definite articles. There was great controversy at the time about the corruption of the Vulgate text and about changes made in the various Latin editions (Creehan 1963: 208). Some of the Greek codices had also proved to be unreliable. A Bible translation is only as reliable as its sources; interpretation proceeds as much from the source text used as from the notes or commentary attached to the text. The publication of Martin's NT met with bitter polemics because of both his use of the Vulgate as source text and the interpretative notes that accompanied his translation.

William Fulke (1538-89), seeking to refute Martin's work, produced a dual text consisting of the Rheims version with its annotations alongside the Bishops' Bible (1589). Ironically, by doing this, he gave the Rheims-Douay version more publicity and circulation than it would otherwise have had in Elizabethan England. The translation has a strong Latinate flavor and uses ecclesiastical terminology wherever possible. Martin made some improvements to the rendering of the definite article and was not afraid to make unacknowledged use of the best phrasing of the Geneva and Bishops' Bibles. In this oblique way Tyndale made contributions to the Catholic English version. Similarly, in some places where the Rheims NT improved on the Bishops' and Geneva Bibles, the phrasing was woven, again unacknowledged, into the KJV.

The King James Version

James VI of Scotland (1566-1625) became James I of England in 1603 on the death of Elizabeth. He inherited not only a diverse and potentially dangerous religious climate but also a period of outstanding literary scholarship and culture. The new king was a good scholar, open-minded, and very well read.

He wrote several treatises on such subjects as monarchy, the evils of tobacco, and witchcraft. He also paraphrased the book of Revelation and made a metrical version of the Psalms, so he had some idea of the processes of translation. His opening address at the Hampton Court Conference (James I and VI 1918) demonstrated his appreciation of his political position with regard to religion. "Particularly in this land," he said, "King Henry VIII towards the end of his reign altered much, King Edward VI more, Queen Mary reversed all, and lastly Queen Elizabeth (of famous memory) settled religion as it now standeth. . . . I see yet no such cause to change as confirm what I find settled already" (McGrath 2001: 157).

A request made toward the end of the conference by John Rainolds (or Reynolds; 1549-1607) on behalf of the Puritan delegation that there should be a new translation of the Bible came as a welcome suggestion to James (Isaacs 1954a: 197; Long 2001: 191; Daniell 2003: 435). The king's natural inclination was toward tolerance of differing religious views, and he recognized the advantages both for himself and for the country in having a new translation unconnected with any specific group. The existing available vernacular Bibles — the Geneva version, the Bishops' Bible, and the Rheims NT — were the product of particular factions and particular times. The Geneva Bible retained associations with a group ready to justify challenging, even deposing, a monarch over religious issues. In addition, biblical scholarship had progressed since the vernacular versions were made, and they were already in need of revision. The English language had developed and flourished almost beyond recognition in the Elizabethan age and was more able than ever to take on the challenge of a new translation.

The story of the making of the KJV has been recounted in detail elsewhere (Isaacs 1954a; Bois 1970; Opfell, 1982; Daniell 2003: 427-50; for a more general audience McGrath 2001; Nicolson 2003). The most obvious difference in the strategy for translation lay in the emphasis on scholarship rather than on the views of any particular religious persuasion. The six companies of translators, two each at Oxford, Cambridge, and Westminster, contained experts who were scholars and linguists. Biblical scholarship, grammatical knowledge of Hebrew, Aramaic, and Syriac, and the availability of Jewish commentaries like David Kimhi's (see Talmage 1975; see also chapter 4 above), had all greatly improved since Tyndale's time (Greenslade 1963: 3.164), although the Geneva Bible had taken account of Kimhi (Opfell 1982: 23). In addition, James required any other scholars who had worked in Hebrew or Greek and had noticed any mistakes or difficulties in the previous translations to inform the companies of their findings (Isaacs 1954a: 198). Contemporary European vernacular translations were also used for comparative analysis. Finally, in the rules for translating (Opfell 1982: 139-40), number eleven allowed for "any learned man in the land" to be applied to in case of difficulty. By including as many people as possible in the venture James perhaps hoped to achieve the "middle course between the rigour of literal translation and the liberty of the paraphrasts," an approach advocated by Richard Hooker in Book Five of his *Treatise of the Laws of Ecclesiastical Polity of 1593* (1977: 68). The system certainly had built-in safeguards to prevent polarized factions from dominating. And there were to be no contentious theological notes, only linguistic clarifications.

Interestingly, the translation was not to be a completely new venture. The Bishops' Bible was to be the basis, with Tyndale's, Matthew's, Coverdale's, Whitchurch's, and the Geneva versions to be used when they agreed better with the source texts (Isaacs 1954a: 200). Very few translations of the Bible have been done without any reference to other translations or commentaries. The Wycliffite group had no English precedent to follow except the Anglo-Saxon Gospels, but they made extensive use of Nicholas of Lyra's commentary. Tyndale had Luther's German version and Erasmus's Greek and Latin NT as reference texts. The English vernacular translations that followed Tyndale all refer back to him in some measure.

At the point in history when the KJV translators began their work, it would have been difficult for them to produce a completely new translation, since there is a limit to the number of ways in which even a rich language like English can express certain concepts. Using the Bishops' Bible as the basis reinforced the authority of the state-appointed church hierarchy of Elizabeth's reign while acknowledging that revision and correction might come through use of competing versions. The Bishops' Bible also provided common ground for both translators and receivers. A new translation using the familiar wording and rhythms of the Bishops' Bible would be most acceptable to the target audience. The people were accustomed to the sound of the Bishops' Bible being read aloud in church. They knew its chapter and verse divisions and were used to the names of places and people in it. In this sense, the translators looked backward to an older version and in doing so retained the authority and sense of tradition perceived as being required by the status of the text. They translated into the kind of language that was used at the time for literature and sermons, and they fed into the text recognizable, slightly archaic biblical vocabulary already familiar through private reading of the Geneva Bible and public reading of the Bishops' Bible. Their translation strategy was to avoid too much unnecessary change to the central text of the nation while restoring its credibility as a vernacular version in light of new scholarship and at the same time uniting the country in the use of one official translation. As

Opfell comments, "Uneven though the translation was in places, overall it was magnificent" (1982: 119).

The KJV was not an overnight success with its intended audience. Many people, including Miles Smith, writer of the new Bible's preface to the reader, were accustomed to and preferred the Geneva version and continued to quote from it. Some years passed before King James's project took over the central ground from the Geneva Bible, which continued to be printed until 1644, was the Bible the Pilgrims brought to America, and the source for Oliver Cromwell's 1643 pocket Soldiers' Bible. Eventually, as time went on, the KJV took over as the mainstream Christian text in English and began to feed back into the language and literature of the culture from which it was formed (McGrath 2001: 286-87, 293).

After the King James Version: New Scholarship and Revisions

Although nothing seriously threatened the dominance of the KJV until the beginning of the eighteenth century, this is not to say that there was no translation activity in what remained of the seventeenth. The original KJV, produced and first printed in 1611, was itself subsequently corrected and altered in minor respects with each new edition. The OT part of the Rheims-Douay version appeared in 1610, and in 1639 there was a literal version from Henry Ainsworth, presenting parts of the OT (Isaacs 1954a: 225), but neither of these challenged the mainstream official text appointed to be read in churches.

Increased trade led to greater availability of mss. and the interchange of biblical scholarship. Cyril Lucar (1570-1638), Patriarch of Alexandria, sent a fifth-century Greek codex of the complete Bible to James I as a gift (see Metzger and Ehrman 2005: 153, 667). By the time it arrived in 1627, James had died and his heir Charles I (1600-49) received it (Parker 2001: 118). Then, between 1654 and 1657, Brian Walton (c. 1600-61; Todd 1821) published a polyglot Bible in Greek, Latin, Syriac, Ethiopic, and Arabic, with the Gospels in Persian, for the express purpose of making available points of comparison (Hall 1963: 93). He gave all the texts not in Latin a Latin translation for access by scholars. An Anglican scholar and curate, Walton was aided by some of the best scholars of the age.

The latter part of the seventeenth century also saw the beginning of the discipline of paleography, or dating of manuscripts by the study of handwriting. Categorizing manuscripts in a coherent way made the study of source texts more productive, but also raised criticism of this methodology, which was considered by some to be an attack on the "original" *textus receptus*

(Erasmus's 1516 Greek text) because it questioned the integrity of the received text. Arguments raged as to which ms. provided the most reliable source text and therefore the most reliable translation. It is interesting to see that similar issues form the basis of critique for modern translations, with one particular faction prioritizing the legitimacy of the KJV because it was based on the *textus receptus* and not on the Alexandrian codices presented to the English king in 1627 (White 1995; Carson 1978; Ankerberg and Weldon 2003).

The controversies that were raised, the improved scholarship, and the continuing development of literary styles in English literature during the eighteenth century, inspired both professional and amateur translations. Oxford scholar John Mills (c. 1645-1707) published a lifetime's work of collating and recording different biblical mss. shortly before his death (Mills 1707; see also Metzger and Ehrman 2005: 154-59, 164). Daniel Mace (d. c. 1753) produced a Greek and English parallel text of the NT in 1729 (Metzger and Ehrman 2005: 157-58, 330). A contemporary of his, Richard Bentley (1662-1742), began work on a critical edition of the Greek and Latin NT in an attempt to restore the elusive original fourth-century text (Metzger and Ehrman 2005: 156-60, 227). Bentley's work was never published, but his work illustrates the great interest of the age in the source texts of the vernacular Bible and the improving availability of resources for the translators (for details on Mills's and Bentley's works, see Fox 1954).

Richard Challoner (1691-1781) produced a revision of the Rheims-Douay Bible that provided one of the most interesting contributions to vernacular translations of his time. Between 1749 and 1772, he produced several revisions of both the OT and NT (e.g., 1914 [1763-64]), as well as a book treating the lives of the saints (1745), and an English prayer book that includes parts of the mass in English (1795). Comparison of the revised Rheims-Douay with the KJV shows that the latter heavily influenced the changes (Newman 1859). Challoner was obliged to use the Vulgate as his source because it was the preferred Catholic original, but he worked within those constraints to bring the Rheims-Douay closer to the official English text.

John Wesley's (1703-91) NT (1755) amounted to a revision of the KJV in the light of Bengel's 1734 critical edition of the Greek text, which included variations from previously unavailable Greek mss. Many of Wesley's revisions appear to have been accepted by the 1870 revisers of the authorized version (Weigle 1963: 368). In 1764 the Quaker Anthony Purver produced a "New and Literal" translation of the complete Bible which was "on the whole a good and much underrated specimen of the middle style" (Isaacs 1954a: 230). This was followed in 1768 by Edward Harwood's *A Liberal Translation of the NT; Being an Attempt to Translate the Sacred writings with the same Freedom,*

Spirit, and Elegance, with which other English Translations from the Greek Classics have lately been executed. Harwood's free translation reflects the style of eighteenth-century prose and has been much criticized for its paraphrasing. "Our Father," for example, becomes "O Thou great governour and parent of universal nature." Harwood's idea was to encourage the young people of the day to read the Gospel by translating into a modern idiom and making the text clear (Isaacs 1954a: 231). His "evasive glosses," "false translations," and "blundering criticisms" were refuted in the same year by an open letter from William Julius Mickle (Mickle 1768).

The later part of the eighteenth century was a time of considerable translation activity when many individuals, such as Philip Doddridge, George Campbell, and James Macknight produced complete or partial translations (Weigle 1963: 368). Such translations, although privately done, had a long and unexpected afterlife, as they were edited, revised, and even combined into a subsequent edition which combined Campbell's Gospels, Doddridge's Acts and Revelation, and Macknight's Epistles (Campbell, Doddridge, Macknight, 1818).

The KJV eventually became even more in need of revision, particularly in the light of improvements in biblical scholarship. The continuing distance between the official translation and the language of the day inspired scholars to try their hands at translation. The distinction between private and public devotions perhaps encouraged the publication of books such as Philip Doddridge's reflections on the NT called *The Family Expositor* (1761). The Bible was very much the central literary as well as religious text of the age, and its interpretation was featured in the literature of Milton, Defoe, Bunyan, and Dryden. With the development of literature, both the language and the subject matter of the Bible became firmly embedded in the English canon.

CONCLUSION

Translation of the Bible is much more complex than the translation of other literary or narrative texts because the Bible is frequently used to support doctrinal positions and its nuances of meaning have been debated for many centuries. Any process of translation can be political and manipulative; thus, the history of European Bible translations and their interpretation makes little sense outside the historical context of each translation. What has often obscured the translation narrative has been the insistence of some commentators on prioritizing Reformation and Counter-Reformation issues. By emphasizing differences in ways of thinking, they focus on differences in the translations rather than similarities.

The idea of each person's having a fixed status and position in society, so prevalent in medieval times but so alien to modern thinking, meant that, for many centuries, there was serious concern over the layperson's worthiness to read the Bible. Literacy was restricted not by intelligence but by opportunity; orality was the main vehicle for transmission and exposition of the Scriptures. The written text therefore became particularly venerated for its mystery and, in pre-printing days, for its rarity.

Translation issues were well known and understood from Jerome onward. The early history of translation into the vernacular was colored almost entirely by fear of heresy, even to the extent that anything more than a gloss of the Latin text was considered a dangerous exercise. A vernacular translation separate from its source text could so easily be heretical that in pre-Reformation times it was automatically considered so unless sanctioned by the official church. These elements make the story of Bible translation into the vernacular a very lively one, but they also tend to obscure the issues of sources and function, which, in a long history of translating, should not be overlooked. Add to this the evangelical dimension of taking God's word to every people in their own language, and we can see that there remains a good deal of research still to be done in the area of Bible translation history.

BIBLIOGRAPHY

Anderson, J. J. (ed.)
1996   *Sir Gawain and the Green Knight, Pearl, Cleanness, Patience.* London: Dent.

Andersson, C. I.
1956   *A History of Sweden.* Trans. C. Hannay; New York: Praeger.

Ankerberg, J., and J. Weldon
2003   *The Facts on the King James Only Debate.* Eugene: Harvest House.

Augustine of Hippo
2004   "On Christian Doctrine." In B. D. Ehrman and A. S. Jacobs, eds., *Christianity in Late Antiquity: 300-450 CE,* 433-38. Oxford: Oxford University Press.

Benson, L. (ed.)
1987   *The Riverside Chaucer.* Oxford: Oxford University Press.

Berman, A.
1985   "Translation and the Trials of the Foreign." In L. Venuti, ed., 1985: 285-97.

Betts, M.
1905   *Life of Giovanni Diodati, Genevese Theologian, Translator of the Italian Bible.* London: Thynne.

Biguenet, J., and R. Schulte (eds.)

1992   *Theories of Translation: An Anthology of Essays from Dryden to Derrida.* Chicago: University of Chicago Press.

Bogaert, P.-M.

1991   *Les Bibles en Français. Histoire illustrée du Moyen Age à nos jours.* Turnhout: Brepols.

Bois, J.

1970   *Translating for King James.* London: Lane.

Cameron, E.

1991   *The European Reformation.* Oxford: Oxford University Press.

Campbell, G., P. Doddridge, and J. Macknight

1818   *The New Testament, translated from the Original Greek, etc.* (Gospels by Campbell, Acts and Revelation by Doddridge, Epistles by Macknight). London: Lepard.

Carleton, K.

2001   *Bishops and Reform in the English Church, 1520-1559.* London: Boydell.

Carson, D. A.

1978   *The King James Version Debate: A Plea for Realism.* Grand Rapids: Baker.

Catford, J. C.

1965   *A Linguistic Theory of Translation.* London: Oxford University Press.

Challoner, R.

1745   *Britannia sancta: or, the lives of the most celebrated, British, English, Scottish and Irish saints who have flourished in these islands from the earliest times of Christianity down to the change of religion in the sixteenth century.* London: Meighan.

1795   *A Manual of Prayers and Other Christian Devotions: to which are added the ordinary of the Mass in Latin and English, with an explanation of the festivals and the calendar corrected according to the late regulations.* London: Coghlan.

Challoner, R. (ed.)

1914   *The Holy Bible, Translated from the Latin Vulgate, Diligently Compared with the Hebrew, Greek, and Other Editions in Divers Languages . . . with Annotations, References, and an Historical and Chronological Table, published with the Approbation of His Eminence James Cardinal Gibbons, Archbishop of Baltimore.* New York: Kenedy (orig. Dublin 1763-64).

Craigie, W. A.

1954   "The English Versions (to Wyclif)." In H. W. Robinson, ed. 1954: 139-40.

Creehan, F. J.

1963   "The Bible in the Roman Catholic Church from Trent to the Present Day." In S. L. Greenslade, ed. 1963: 3.199-237.

Daniell, D.

2003   *The Bible in English.* New Haven and London: Yale University Press.

Danner, D. G.

1999   *Pilgrimage to Puritanism.* New York: Lang.

Dante Aligheri

1996   *De Vulgari Eloquentia.* Ed. and trans. S. Bottrill. Cambridge: Cambridge University Press.

Deanesly, M.

1966   *The Lollard Bible.* Cambridge: Cambridge University Press (1st ed. 1920).

Delassaut, G.

1957   *Le Maistre de Sacy et son temps.* Paris: Nizet.

Doddridge, P.

1761   *The Family Expositor.* 6 vols. London: Hitch.

Ellis, R.

2001   "Figures of English Translation." In R. Ellis and L. Oakley-Brown, eds., *Translation and Nation: Towards a Cultural Politics of Englishness,* 7-47. Clevedon: Mutilingual Matters.

Elton, G. R.

1999   *Reformation Europe 1517-1559.* Oxford: Blackwell.

Erasmus, D.

1516   *Desiderius Erasmus, Novum Instrumentu omne, diligenter ad Erasmo Roterodamo recognitum et emendatum, non solum ad graecam veritatem, verum etiam ad multorum utriusque linguae codicum, eorumque veterem simul et emendatorum fidem, postremo adprobatissimorum autorum citationem, emendationem, et interpretationem, praecipue, Origenis, Chrysostomi, Cyrilli, Vulgarii, Hieronymi, Cypriani, Ambrosii, Hilarii, Augustini, una cum Annotationibus, quae lectorem doceant, quid qua ratione mutatum sit. Quisquis igitur amas veram theologiam, lege, cognosce, ac diende judica. Neque statim offendere, si quid mutatum offenderis, sed expende, num in melius mutatum sit. Apud inclytam Germaniae Basilaeam* [*The entire NT, diligently researched and corrected by Erasmus of Rotterdam, &c*]. Basle: Johann Froben (2nd ed. 1519; 3rd ed. 1522; 4th ed. 1527; 5th ed. 1535).

Evans, G. R.

2001   "The Middle Ages to the Reformation." In J. Rogerson, ed., 2001: 180-91.

Fox, A.

1954   *J. Mill and Richard Bentley: A Study of the Textual Criticism of the NT, 1675-1729.* Oxford: Blackwell.

Fulke, W.

1589   *The Text of the New Testament of Iesus Christ translated out of the Vulgar Latin by the Papists of the Traiterous seminary at Rhemes, etc.* London: Deputies of Christopher Barker (available in the British Museum).

Garrett, C. H.

1966   *The Marian Exiles*. Cambridge: Cambridge University Press.

Goodman, C.

1558   *How Superior Powers Ought to Be Obeyed*. Ed. P. S. Pole. Whitefish: Kessinger.

Greenslade, S. L.

1963   "English Versions of the Bible AD 1525-1611." In S. L. Greenslade, ed., 1963: 3.141-74.

Greenslade, S. L. (ed.)

1963   *The Cambridge History of the Bible*. Vol. 3: *The West from the Reformation to the Present Day*. 3 vols. Cambridge: Cambridge University Press.

Gribben, C.

2000   "Deconstructing the Geneva Bible: The Search for a Puritan Poetic." *Literature and Theology* 14:1-16.

Gutt, E.-A.

2000   *Translation and Relevance: Cognition and Context*. Oxford: Blackwell/ Manchester: St. Jerome (1st ed. 1991).

Hall, B.

1963   "Biblical Scholarship: Editions and Commentaries." In S. L. Greenslade, ed., 1963: 3.38-93.

Hargreaves, H.

1969   "The Wycliffite Versions." In G. W. H. Lampe, ed., 1969: 2.387-415.

Heininen, S.

1999   "Mikael Agricola und die Entstehung der finnischen Schriftsprache." In P. Lehtimäki, ed., *Sprachen in Finnland und Estland*, 57-61. Wiesbaden: Harrassowitz.

Henry VIII

1966   *Assertio Septem Sacramentorum adversus Martin Luther*. Ridgewood: Gregg.

Hooker, R.

1977   *Of the Laws of Ecclesiastical Polity, Book 5*. Ed. W. S. Hill. FLEWRH 2; Cambridge: Belknap (orig. 1593).

Isaacs, J.

1954a   "The Authorised Version and After." In H. W. Robinson, ed., 1954: 196-234.
1954b   "The Sixteenth Century English Versions." In H. W. Robinson, ed., 1954: 146-95.

James I and VI

1918   *The Political Works of James*. Ed. I. C. H. McIlwain. Cambridge: Harvard University Press.

Jasper, D.

2005   "Settling Hoti's Business." In L. Long, ed., 2005: 105-14.

Kastan, D. S.

1997   "'The noyse of the new Bible': Reform and Reaction." In C. McEachern and D. Shuger, eds., *Henrician England in Religion and Culture in Renaissance England*, 46-68. Cambridge: Cambridge University Press.

Kinder, A. G.

1975   *Casiodoro de Reina: Spanish Reformer of the Sixteenth Century.* London: Tamesis.

Knox, J.

1995   *The First Blast of the Trumpet against the Monstrous Regiment of Women.* In *Selected Writings of John Knox: Public Epistles, Treatises, and Expositions to the Year 1559*, 360-436. Ed. K. Reed. Dallas: Presbyterian Heritage.

Lampe, G. W. H.

1969   *The Cambridge History of the Bible*, Vol. 2: *The West from the Fathers to the Reformation.* Cambridge: Cambridge University Press.

Langland, W.

1995   *The Vision of Piers Plowman.* Ed. A. V. Schmidt. London: Dent.

Lawton, D.

1990   *Faith, Text and History: The Bible In English.* Hemel Hempstead: Harvester Wheatsheaf.

Lindberg, C. (ed.)

2000   *The European Reformation Sourcebook.* Oxford: Blackwell.

Long, L.

2001   *Translating the Bible: From the Seventh to the Seventeenth Century.* Aldershot: Ashgate.

2002   "Spiritual Exile: Translating the Bible from Geneva and Rheims." In S. O. Ouditt, ed., *Displaced Persons: Conditions of Exile in European Culture*, 11-20. Aldershot: Ashgate.

Long, L. (ed.)

2005   *Translation and Religion.* Clevedon: Multilingual Matters.

Lortsch, D.

1910   *Histoire de la Bible France.* Librairie-éditions Emmaüs; St. Légier: P.E.R.L.E. (re-edited and modernized 1984).

Luther, M.

1530   *Ein Sendbrief von Dolmetschen und Fürbitte der Heiligen.* Ed. H. S. M. Amburger-Stuart. London: Duckworth (repr. 1940).

Luther, M. (trans.)

1972   *Die Bibel, oder, Die ganze Heilige Schrift des Alten und Neuen Testaments nach der Übersetzung Martin Luthers.* Stuttgart: Deutsche Bibelstiftung.

Luzzi, G.

1942   *La Bibbia in Italia — L'eco della riforma nella repubblica lucchese — Giovanni Diodati, e la sua versione italiana della Bibbia.* Torre Pellice: Claudiana.

Malermi, N.

1490   *Biblica Italica.* Venice: Giovanni Ragazzi, for Lucantonio Giunta.

Marshall, P.

2003   *Reformation England: 1480-1642.* London and New York: Arnold.

McComish, W. A.

1989   *The Epigones (A Study of the Theology of the Genevan Academy at the Time of the Synod of Dort, with Special Reference to Giovanni Diodati).* Allison Park: Pickwick.

McGrath, A.

2001   *In The Beginning: The Story of the King James Bible.* New York: Doubleday.

Metzger, B. M., and B. D. Ehrman

2005   *The Text of the New Testament: Its Transmission, Corruption, and Restoration.* 4th ed. New York and Oxford: Oxford University Press.

Mickle, W. J.

1768   *A Letter to Mr. Harwood, wherein some of his evasive glosses, false translations, and blundering criticisms in support of the Arian heresy, contained in his liberal translation of the New Testament are pointed out and confuted.* London: Rivington.

Mills, J.

1707   *Novum Testamentum.* Privately published.

More, T.

1981   *The Complete Works of St. Thomas More,* Vol. 6: *A Dialogue Concerning Heresies.* Ed. T. M. C. Lawler, G. Marc'hadour and R. C. Marius; New Haven: Yale University Press.

Munday, J.

2001   *Introducing Translation Studies: Theories and Applications.* London: Routledge.

Newman, H.

1859   "The History of the Text of the Rheims and Douay Version of the Holy Scripture." *The Rambler* (July): 145-69.

Nicolson, A.

2003   *God's Secretaries: The Making of the King James Bible.* New York: HarperCollins.

Nida, E. A.

1964   *Towards a Science of Translating.* Leiden: Brill.

Nida, E. A., and Taber, C. R.

1969   *The Theory and Practice of Translating.* Leiden: Brill.

Oakley, S.

1966 *The Story of Sweden.* London: Faber and Faber.

Olin, J.

1990 *Catholic Reform from Cardinal Ximenes to the Council of Trent.* New York: Fordham University Press.

Opfell, O.

1982 *The King James Bible Translators.* Jefferson and London: McFarland.

Owst, G. R.

1926 *Preaching in Medieval England.* Cambridge: Cambridge University Press.

Panzer, G. W.

1778 *Geschichte der nürnbergischen Ausgaben der Bibel von Erfindung der Buchdrucker-kunst an bis auf unsere Zeiten.* Nürnberg: Raspe.

Parker, D.

2001 "The New Testament." In J. Rogerson, ed., 2001: 110-33.

Pollard, A.

1911 *Records of the English Bible.* London: Frowde for Oxford University Press.

Pym, A.

2000 *Negotiating the Frontier.* Manchester: St. Jerome.

Rex, R.

2002 *The Lollards.* Basingstoke: Palgrave.

Rhodes, E. F., and D. Lupas (eds.)

1997 *The Translators to the Reader.* New York: American Bible Society.

Robinson, D. (ed.)

2002 *Western Translation Theory.* 2nd ed. Manchester: St. Jerome [1st ed. 1997].

Robinson, H. W. (ed.)

1954 *The Bible in Its Ancient and English Versions.* London: Oxford University Press (1st ed. 1940).

Rogerson, J.

2001 *The Oxford Illustrated History of the Bible.* Oxford: Oxford University Press.

Runciman, S.

1965 *The Fall of Constantinople 1453.* Cambridge: Cambridge University Press.

Schleiermacher, F.

1977 "On the Different Methods of Translating." In A. Lefevere, *Translating Literature: The German Tradition from Luther to Rosenzweig,* 66-89. Assen: Van Gorcum.

Scott, F. D.

1977 *Sweden — The Nation's History.* Minneapolis: University of Minnesota Press.

Smith, P. (ed., trans.)

1911   *The Life and Letters of Martin Luther.* London: John Murray.

1972   *Die Bibel, oder, Die ganze Heilige Schrift des Alten und Neuen Testaments nach der Übersetzung Martin Luthers.* Stuttgart: Deutsche Bibelstiftung.

Steiner, G.

1992   *After Babel.* 2nd ed. Oxford: Oxford University Press (1st ed. 1975).

Talmage, F.

1975   *David Kimhi: The Man and His Commentaries.* Cambridge: Harvard University Press.

Todd, H. J. (ed.)

1821   *Memoirs of the Life and Writings of the Right Rev. Brian Walton.* London.

Tomson, L. (ed.)

1842   *Genevan New Testament MDLVII.* London: Bagster.

Tyndale, W. (trans.)

1998   *1536 Tyndale New Testament Facsimile.* Vintage Archives; Greenwood: Capstone (repr. Antwerp: Marten Emperowr 1536).

2000   *The New Testament 1526 translated by William Tyndale.* Ed. W. R. Cooper; London: The British Library/The Tyndale Society.

Venuti, L.

1995   *The Translator's Invisibility: A History of Translation.* London and New York: Routledge.

Venuti, L. (ed.)

2000   *The Translation Studies Reader.* London and New York: Routledge.

Vinay, J.-P., and P. Darbelnet

1995   *Comparative Stylistics of French and English: A Methodology for Translation.* Trans. J. C. Sager and M.-J. Hamel. Amsterdam: Benjamins.

Weigle, L.

1963   "English Versions since 1611." In S. L. Greenslade, ed., 1963: 3.361-82.

White, J. R.

1995   *The King James Only Controversy: Can You Trust the Modern Translations?* Minneapolis: Bethany House.

Whittingham, W., A. Gilby, T. Sampson *et al.* (trans.)

1998   *1560 Geneva Bible Facsimile.* Vintage Archives; Greenwood: Capstone (repr. Geneva: Rowland Hall, 1560).

Williams, C. H.

1969   *William Tyndale.* London: Nelson.

Wright, D.

2001   "The Reformation to 1700." In J. Rogerson, ed., 2001: 192-241.

Contributors

Carol Bakhos, University of California at Los Angeles

Guy Bedouelle, Université de Fribourg, Switzerland

Paul M. Blowers, Emmanuel School of Religion

J. Keith Elliott, University of Leeds

Russell Fuller, University of San Diego

Lee W. Gibbs, Cleveland State University

Robert A. Harris, The Jewish Theological Seminary

Alan J. Hauser, Appalachian State University

Lynne Long, The University of Warwick

Mary A. Mayeski, Loyola Marymount University

Stuart Murray, Associated Mennonite Biblical Seminary

Christopher Ocker, San Francisco Theological Seminary

Barbara Pitkin, Stanford University

Erika Rummel, Wilfrid Laurier University

Mark D. Thompson, Moore Theological College

Duane F. Watson, Malone University

Timothy Wengert, The Lutheran Theological Seminary at Philadelphia

Index of Ancient, Medieval and Pre-Modern, and Modern Authors

MEDIEVAL AND PRE-MODERN AUTHORS

MODERN AUTHORS

Index of Subjects

Index of Primary Sources